IRISH CATHOLIC
CATECHISM
FOR ADULTS

IRISH CATHOLIC
CATECHISM
FOR ADULTS

IRISH EPISCOPAL CONFERENCE

VERITAS

Published 2014 by
Veritas Publications
7–8 Lower Abbey Street
Dublin 1
Ireland
publications@veritas.ie

ISBN 978 1 84730 409 4

The *Irish Catholic Catechism for Adults* has taken as its source text the *United States Catechism for Adults*, which was developed by the Ad Hoc Committee to Oversee the Use of the *Catechism of the Catholic Church* of the United States Conference of Catholic Bishops (USCCB). This edition for the Irish Church was developed by the Council for Catechetics of the Irish Episcopal Conference. It was approved by the plenary meeting of the Irish Episcopal Conference in December 2012 and subsequently received the *recognitio* of the Holy See in April 2014.

United States Catechism for Adults © 2006 United States Conference of Catholic Bishops, Washington, DC 20017. All rights reserved.

A catalogue record for this book is available from the British Library.

Designed by Veritas Publications
The cover shows a crucifixion plaque from the seventh or eighth century found at St John's, near Athlone; it possibly originates from an early Christian cemetery in Rinnagan, Co. Roscommon. The plaque is made from hammered bronze, and would originally have been attached to a book cover or a shrine.
Photo © National Museum of Ireland
Indexer: Eileen O'Neill
Printed in Ireland by WG Baird, Antrim

CONTENTS

Part III. Christian Morality: The Faith Lived

Part IV. Prayer: The Faith Prayed

Conclusion and Appendices

PONTIFICIUM CONSILIUM
DE NOVA EVANGEUZATIONE PROMOVENDA
DECREE

Prot. N. Cat/64/2014/P

Christ, revealer and revelation of the Father, commanded the Apostles to preach the Gospel which He promulgated in His own person in order that, through their preaching, they might communicate the gifts of God to mankind until His return in glory. The Church, faithful to the command of her Lord and in accordance with the tradition of the Apostles, has always held in high esteem catechetical formation as a means of keeping alive the proclamation and transmission of the Word of God. Accordingly, the Pontifical Council for the Promotion of the New Evangelization, which is charged with the granting of the necessary approval of the Apostolic See for catechisms and other writings pertaining to catechetical instruction, has examined the *Catholic Catechism for Adults*, submitted by the Irish Episcopal Conference as required by Canon 775 § 2 of the *Code of Canon Law* and Article 3 § 4 of the Apostolic Letter *Fides per doctrinam*, hereby

APPROVES

and confirms the aforementioned Catechism in the version submitted to this Dicastery by His Eminence Seán Cardinal Brady, Archbishop of Armagh, President of the same Episcopal Conference, on March 24, 2014.

Notwithstanding any provision to the contrary.

Given from the Seat of the Pontifical Council for the Promotion of the New Evangelization on April 25, 2014, Feast of St Mark the Evangelist.

✠ Salvatore Fisichella
PRESIDENT

✠ Octavio Ruiz Arenas
SECRETARY

PREFACE

If you are an older reader, 'catechism' will possibly mean a slim, soft green-covered schoolbook containing questions and answers about Christian doctrine, such as 'Who made the world?' If you are a middle-aged or younger reader, you might have heard from your parents and grandparents of the 'penny catechism' and associated it with a past age of childhood education. So it may be a surprise to find that this book is a catechism, and that it announces itself as being 'for adults'.

A catechism is an authoritative statement of the teachings of the Catholic faith. It is the 'go-to' resource for any serious query about what Catholics believe, how Catholics pray and the different details of Catholic life. For the believer or sincere seeker, this Catechism will provide easily understood information, with clear explanations and apt examples. For both Catholics and others, we hope that this Catechism might inspire and console, stimulate and encourage, nourish and satisfy the heart and soul as well as the mind. It is our deepest wish that these chapters will support prayer and practice as much as discussion and enquiry.

This Catechism is intended for the spiritual formation of adult Catholics and for the religious information of other interested readers.

What's the background to this Catechism?

On 11 October 1992, the thirtieth anniversary of the opening of the Second Vatican Ecumenical Council, St John Paul II offered the entire Church the *Catechism of the Catholic Church* as a 'reference text' for a catechesis renewed at the living sources of the faith. In the Apostolic Constitution, *Fidei Depositum,* at the beginning of this Catechism, it states that such a universal catechism 'might be, as it were, a point of reference for the catechisms or compendiums that are prepared in various regions'.

Accordingly, the Irish Episcopal Conference decided that an *Irish Catholic Catechism for Adults* should be produced, and to this end in 2008 the Irish Conference wrote to the United States Conference of Bishops seeking permission to adapt the *United States Catholic Catechism for Adults* for use in Ireland. Approval for such an adaptation was received both from the United States Conference and from the Pontifical Council for the New

Evangelisation. Under the guidance of the Catechetics Commission/Council of the Irish Episcopal Conference, with practical help and guidance from the Office of the Catechism in the United States, this work of adaptation is now completed.

The publication of the Adult Catechism is taking place in the pontificate of Pope Francis, with his emphasis on evangelisation and sharing the Good News of Jesus Christ with others. In *Lumen Fidei*, we are reminded that 'it is impossible to believe on our own. Faith is not simply an individual decision which takes place in the depths of the believer's heart, nor a completely private relationship between the "I" of the believer and the divine "Thou", between an autonomous subject and God. By its very nature, faith is open to the "We" of the Church; it always takes place within her communion' (no. 39).

For adults?

The Adult Catechism responds to the proposal made by the Irish National Directory for Catechesis, *Share the Good News,* that adult faith development should be given priority in Ireland.

All of us need to rediscover the Good News, recognise how it shapes our lives, and see how each of us can effectively live our faith as a witness to Jesus Christ in the Ireland of today. Our study of the *Irish Catholic Catechism for Adults* will help us reflect on our lives, give an account of our hope, savour the truths of faith and experience the joy of faith. Then, in love, we can begin to share our precious faith with our neighbours.

The *Irish Catholic Catechism for Adults*, therefore, is not primarily for schools. It may, of course, be used by teachers, but in the first instance it is not the present-day equivalent of the 'Green Catechism'. It is for adults, and that fact is very important. It may also serve as a resource for those involved in the Rite of Christian Initiation of Adults.

What does 'for adults' mean? It might suggest that its language is difficult and complicated, and that the content is advanced and technical. However, effort has been made to keep the writing as accessible as possible, and to present the material simply and straightforwardly.

'For adults' means that the readers of this book will be, for the most part, Catholics who are baptised Church members, who have received some religious education, who know the story of Jesus Christ and his life, death,

Resurrection and Ascension, who have a basic understanding of the Scriptures, God's revelation and its meaning, who are familiar up to a point with sacramental and religious life, and who want to deepen and strengthen their faith in order to recover an enthusiasm for their spiritual life.

There will be readers, of course, who are not sure about their religious beliefs, who are Christian in upbringing, though not necessarily by conviction. Nevertheless, such readers are curious, searching, questioning and open to what Christianity and Catholicism have to say. In a word, readers are expected to 'come as they are', and so this Catechism is written in such a way that it can be easily delved into.

The *Irish Catholic Catechism for Adults* tries to meet you where you are. It uses an adult methodology for personal learning, learning that reaches to our spirit, our individuality, our history, our particular situations and private aspirations. It tries to engage with our everyday life and personal existence.

Each chapter commences with a biography or short account of one of the saints or holy persons (many of whom are Irish) who tried to follow the Christian path in their own time and circumstance, a life story which may parallel aspects of our personal stories today. In many ways, even in the twenty-first century, we have much in common with those who went before us.

Each chapter then presents a section of God's revelation through Jesus Christ in the Holy Spirit that relates to that story. It places the teaching alongside questions and doubts that arise from our daily life and our country's culture and tries to resolve them.

Each chapter also includes short sections on particular points of doctrine, useful quotations from popes, bishops and Christian writers, prayers and Scripture passages that are relevant to the topic of the chapter, as well as summaries of the important points in the teaching, and questions for further discussion.

The *Irish Catholic Catechism for Adults* presents life and faith together, sets the teachings of Jesus in an encounter with daily life, invites us to judge what we ought to do about our faith, and gives us the encouragement and information we need to return to daily life in a more Christian way.

Thanks

We congratulate all the members of the Council for Catechetics for overseeing this project with enthusiasm. We offer our gratitude also to the

Episcopal Commissions/Councils for Doctrine, Education, Theology and Liturgy for their professional contributions. Special thanks to Veritas for the preparation and production of this text.

We pray that the Triune God, Father, Son and Holy Spirit, who inspired the saints, doctors and martyrs of the Church in Ireland in the past, may guide us in a new evangelisation. May we teach the faith in such a way that the members of the Church today will truly be Christ's disciples of this new millennium.

✠ Seán Brady
Archbishop of Armagh
Primate of All Ireland

✠ Diarmuid Martin
Archbishop of Dublin
Primate of Ireland

✠ Dermot Clifford
Archbishop of Cashel & Emly

✠ Michael Neary
Archbishop of Tuam

ABBREVIATIONS

Church Documents

AG   Second Vatican Council, *Decree on the Church's Missionary Activity (Ad Gentes Divinitus)*

CCC   *Catechism of the Catholic Church*

CCEO   *Code of Canons of the Eastern Churches (Codex Canonum Ecclesiarum Orientalium)*

CIC   *Code of Canon Law (Codex Iuris Canonici)*

DD   Saint John Paul II, *Day of the Lord (Dies Domini)*

DS   H. Denzinger and A. Schonmetzer, *Enchiridion Symbolorum*

DV   Second Vatican Council, *Dogmatic Constitution on Divine Revelation (Dei Verbum)*

EE   Saint John Paul II, *On the Eucharist (Ecclesia de Eucharistia)*

EN   Pope Paul VI, *On Evangelization in the Modern World (Evangelii Nuntiandi)*

EV   Saint John Paul II, *The Gospel of Life (Evangelium Vitae)*

FC   Saint John Paul II, *On the Role of the Christian Family in the Modern World (Familiaris Consortio)*

GS   Second Vatican Council, *Pastoral Constitution on the Church in the Modern World (Gaudium et Spes)*

HV   Pope Paul VI, *On the Regulation of Birth (Humanae Vitae)*

LG   Second Vatican Council, *Dogmatic Constitution on the Church (Lumen Gentium)*

NA   Second Vatican Council, *Declaration on the Relation of the Church to Non-Christian Religions (Nostra Aetate)*

NMI   Saint John Paul II, *At the Close of the Great Jubilee of the Year 2000 (Novo Millennio Ineunte)*

PO   Second Vatican Council, *Decree on Priestly Life and Ministry (Presbyterorum Ordinis)*

RCIA   Rite of Christian Initiation of Adults

RVM   Saint John Paul II, *On the Most Holy Rosary (Rosarium Virginis Mariae)*

SC   Second Vatican Council, *Constitution on the Sacred Liturgy (Sacrosanctum Concilium)*

SGN   Irish Episcopal Conference, *Share the Good News: National Directory for Catechesis in Ireland*

UR   Second Vatican Council, *Decree on Ecumenism (Unitatis Redintegratio)*

UUS   Saint John Paul II, *On Commitment to Ecumenism (Ut Unum Sint)*

Books of the Bible

Old Testament

Gn	Genesis
Ex	Exodus
Lev	Leviticus
Num	Numbers
Deut	Deuteronomy
Jos	Joshua
Jg	Judges
Ruth	Ruth
1 Sm	1 Samuel
2 Sm	2 Samuel
1 Kgs	1 Kings
2 Kgs	2 Kings
1 Chr	1 Chronicles
2 Chr	2 Chronicles
Ezra	Ezra
Neh	Nehemiah
Tob	Tobit
Jdt	Judith
Est	Esther
1 Mac	1 Maccabees
2 Mac	2 Maccabees
Job	Job
Ps	Psalms
Prov	Proverbs
Eccl (Qo)	Ecclesiastes
Song	Song of Songs
Wis	Wisdom
Eccles (Sir)	Sirach
Is	Isaiah
Jer	Jeremiah
Lam	Lamentations
Bar	Baruch
Ez	Ezekiel
Dn	Daniel
Hos	Hosea
Jl	Joel
Am	Amos
Ob	Obadiah

Jon	Jonah
Mic	Micah
Nah	Nahum
Hab	Habakkuk
Zeph	Zephaniah
Hg	Haggai
Zec	Zechariah
Mal	Malachi

New Testament

Mt	Matthew
Mk	Mark
Lk	Luke
Jn	John
Acts	Acts of the Apostles
Rm	Romans
1 Cor	1 Corinthians
2 Cor	2 Corinthians
Gal	Galatians
Eph	Ephesians
Phil	Philippians
Col	Colossians
1 Th	1 Thessalonians
2 Th	2 Thessalonians
1 Tm	1 Timothy
2 Tm	2 Timothy
Ti	Titus
Phm	Philemon
Heb	Hebrews
Jas	James
1 Pt	1 Peter
2 Pt	2 Peter
1 Jn	1 John
2 Jn	2 John
3 Jn	3 John
Jude	Jude
Rv	Revelation

INTRODUCTION

[The Catechism of the Catholic Church*] is meant to
encourage and assist in the writing of new local catechisms,
which must take into account various situations and cultures,
while carefully preserving the unity of faith and fidelity to
Catholic doctrine.*

– Saint John Paul II, *The Deposit of Faith*
(*Fidei Depositum*), IV, no. 4

On 11 October 1992, St John Paul II published his apostolic constitution *The Deposit of Faith*, promulgating the *Catechism of the Catholic Church* (CCC). He chose the publication date to mark the thirtieth anniversary of the opening of the Second Vatican Council.

Saint John Paul II envisioned the *Catechism* as a sure and authentic reference text for teaching Catholic doctrine and particularly for preparing local catechisms. The bishops of the United States subsequently discussed in depth what they might do to follow the pope's call to prepare a local catechism. It would need to take into account the local situation and culture, while at the same time preserving the unity of faith and fidelity to Catholic teaching found in the *Catechism of the Catholic Church*. In June 2000, the bishops determined that a national adult catechism would be an effective way to achieve this goal.

The Irish Bishops examined the *United States Catholic Catechism for Adults* when it was published in 2006. They decided that a similar catechism would be suitable for Ireland and asked permission from the United States Conference of Catholic Bishops to produce a version for the Irish Church. The United States Conference of Catholic Bishops graciously granted permission, and this publication is the result.

Before describing the content and approach of this adult catechism, several preliminary matters need to be presented. First, it should be noted that historically the term *catechism* has acquired a variety of meanings. It comes from a Greek word that means 'to echo'. Before the invention of the printing press in 1450, in the Church and elsewhere, learning was mainly an oral experience. A Church teaching would be recited, and the listener would be instructed to 'echo' it, or repeat it, until it was learned. This way of learning has been around since before the Church. Jewish teachers from both before and after the time of Jesus taught the Scriptures by again and again asking the learner to repeat verses.

The invention of the printing press made it possible to adapt the 'speak and echo' method of catechesis into a question-and-answer approach that could be fixed in print. The Church adopted this approach. It is especially evident in the influential catechisms of St Peter Canisius (1521–97) and St Robert Bellarmine (1542–1621).

THE *ROMAN CATECHISM*, 1566

A third development in catechisms occurred when the bishops at the Council of Trent in 1563 undertook the production of a printed catechism that would be a comprehensive, systematic presentation of Catholic teachings. Saint Pius V completed this work and published it as the *Roman Catechism* in 1566. It sought to present Catholic truths from the viewpoint of their inherent coherence and value for instructing the faithful. It became the enduring sourcebook for local catechisms up to its last edition in 1978.

Until the second half of the twentieth century, for Irish Catholics the word 'catechism' meant the *Maynooth Catechism*. It was inspired largely by an earlier catechism published by Archbishop James Butler of Cashel in 1775 called the *Butler Catechism*. The *Maynooth Catechism* in the Butler tradition, fruit of the 1875 plenary synod of the Irish Bishops, was the first Irish joint effort to provide a national catechism acceptable to all. This Maynooth–Butler catechism of 1882 was an influential text supplying 42 per cent of the questions and answers in the *Baltimore Catechism* (1885) and adopted in its entirety in Australia. The *Maynooth Catechism*, or 'Green Catechism' as it came to be popularly known, gave unity to the teaching and understanding of the faith of Irish Catholics right up to the dawn of the Second Vatican Council in 1962.

At that time, St John XXIII articulated a vision for the Fathers of the Second Vatican Council that charged them to guard and present more effectively the deposit of Christian doctrine in order to make it more accessible to the Christian faithful and all people of goodwill in the contemporary world.

THE *CATECHISM OF THE CATHOLIC CHURCH*, 1992

Eventually, it became clear that the development of a new universal catechism would be beneficial, especially since there had been significant growth in issues and insights in the Church and in society since 1566. In 1985, a synod of bishops was convened in Rome to celebrate the twentieth anniversary of the conclusion of the Second Vatican Council. Many of the synod fathers expressed the desire for a universal catechism that would be a reference book for the catechisms that would be prepared in various regions. The proposal was accepted, and the outcome was the *Catechism of the Catholic Church*, published in 1992. A new edition, which contained some modifications, was released in 1997.

This *Catechism of the Catholic Church* is arranged in four parts: 'The Profession of Faith'; 'The Celebration of the Christian Mystery'; 'Life in Christ'; and 'Christian Prayer'. Its content is faithful to Apostolic Tradition, Scripture and the Magisterium. It incorporates the heritage of the Doctors, Fathers and saints of the Church. At the same time, it illuminates, with the light of faith, contemporary situations, problems and questions.

The *Catechism* begins with God's Revelation, to which we are called to respond in faith, worship, moral witness and a life of prayer. The entire text is guided by the fact that Christian life is rooted in the creative and providential outpouring of the Holy Trinity. The *Catechism* centres itself on the saving life, teachings, death, Resurrection and Ascension of Jesus Christ, the Son of God and Son of Mary. This text is a work by and of the Church.

The goal of the *Catechism of the Catholic Church* is to help facilitate the lifelong conversion of the whole person to the Father's call to holiness and eternal life. At its heart is the celebration of the Christian mysteries, especially the Eucharist and the life of prayer. Users of the *Catechism* are called to witness Christ, the Church and God's Kingdom of salvation, love, justice, mercy and peace in the world.

While the *Catechism* is addressed to a number of audiences – bishops, priests, teachers, writers – it is meant for all the faithful who wish to deepen their knowledge of the Catholic faith. Further, it is offered to every person who wants to know what the Catholic Church teaches.

THE *IRISH CATHOLIC CATECHISM FOR ADULTS*

The *Irish Catholic Catechism for Adults* is a reworking of the *United States Catholic Catechism for Adults*, including much of its doctrinal and devotional material, while inserting it in the Irish local, cultural, social and religious context. The United States text is itself an adaptation of the *Catechism of the Catholic Church*, providing an appropriate text for adult faith formation, religious education and private study. So it is fitting that, as the Irish Church in the nineteenth century gave the *Maynooth Catechism* as a model for the *Baltimore Catechism*, the American Church, in our time, returns the favour.

This text follows the *Catechism*'s arrangement of content: 'The Creed'; 'The Sacraments'; 'Moral Life'; and 'Prayer'. It emphasises the Trinity, Jesus Christ, the Sacraments, moral principles and the heritage of the Doctors and saints of the Church. It is an organic and systematic expression of the Apostolic Tradition, expressed in an inspired way in Sacred Scripture and authoritatively interpreted by the Magisterium of the Church.

The Structure of Each Chapter of This Book

1. Story or Lesson of Faith
2. Teaching: Its Foundation and Application
3. Sidebars
4. Relationship of Catholic Teaching to the Culture
5. Questions for Discussion
6. Doctrinal Statements
7. Meditation and Prayer

CANONISATION

A canonisation today is the Church's official declaration, through the decision of the pope, that a person is a saint, truly in heaven and worthy of public veneration and imitation. The process begins by naming the person 'Venerable', a 'Servant of God' who has demonstrated a life of heroic virtue. The next stage is beatification, by which a person is named 'Blessed'. This step requires one miracle attributed to the intercession of the Servant of God. For canonisation, a second miracle is needed, attributed to the intercession of the Blessed and having occurred after the individual's beatification. Miracles are not required for martyrs. The pope may dispense with some of the formalities or steps in the process.

1. Stories or Lessons of Faith

One of the deeply held beliefs of the Irish people through the ages has been the connection with our dear departed. This human value reflects the revealed truth in the article of the Creed: the 'Communion of Saints'. The Church is an assembly throughout space and time of all the people of God, living and dead. (cf. CCC, no. 946)

The communion of saints means that 'none of us lives for himself and none of us dies for himself' (Rm 14:7). This is true of the living and those who have died. The life and death of Jesus Christ is for our salvation and sanctification. Similarly, the lives and deaths of the holy ones who preceded us work to our benefit as well. The saints intercede for us with Christ, to the Father, in the Spirit, by their eternal concern for those whom they love. They provide an example and a headline for us, surely, but more than that, their actions and merits, through Christ and the sacraments, links both the living and risen people, earth

and heaven, time and eternity, indeed, the past, the present
and the future, in a holy and beneficially effective exchange
of grace, so that '… what each one does or suffers in and
for Christ bears fruit for all'. (CCC, no. 961)

The preface and most of the chapters start with stories of Catholics, many
from Ireland. As far as possible, this *Irish Catholic Catechism for Adults* relates
the Church's teachings to the culture of Ireland, both to affirm positive
elements in our culture and to challenge the negative. One way of doing
this is found in the stories that begin each chapter. Most of these narratives
are biographical sketches of Irish saints or other outstanding Catholics who
represent the variety of witnesses to the Catholic way of life. These stories
give us glimpses of how Catholics participated in Ireland's history and
culture. Those chosen for these examples are Catholics whose lives or actions
illustrate a particular Church teaching. From the earliest days of the Church,
when St Athanasius wrote the life of St Anthony of the Desert, it was clear
that telling stories about saints and holy people encourages others to want
to be like them and is an effective way of teaching Catholic doctrine.

2. Teaching: Its Foundation and Application

In each chapter, the introductory story is followed by a presentation of a
particular teaching. This foundational teaching provides expositions on
aspects of the Creed, the Sacraments, the Commandments and prayer. A
few comments about each of these sections are now given.

A. Creed: The Faith Professed

When we pray or recite the Creed, we can be reminded that Catholicism is
a revealed religion. God is the author of our faith. All that we are expected
to believe is summed up in the revelation of Jesus Christ. God has spoken
all that is necessary for our Salvation in Jesus, the Word made flesh. God
also gives us the gift of faith that enables us to respond, accept and live out
the implications of Divine Revelation. In this first section of the book, the
roles of Apostolic Tradition, Scripture and Magisterium are clearly outlined.

FATHERS AND DOCTORS OF THE CHURCH

The title 'Father of the Church' has been given to those whose sanctity and teaching served to help others understand, defend and pass on the Faith. Those who have achieved this distinction lived from the earliest days of the Church up to the last Father in the West (present-day Western Europe), St Isidore of Seville (sixth century), and the last Father in the East (present-day southeastern Europe and Asia Minor), St John Damascene (seventh century).

The golden age of the Fathers in the fourth and fifth centuries included such figures as St Basil, St John Chrysostom, St Athanasius and St Gregory Nazianzen in the Eastern Church, and St Jerome, St Ambrose and St Augustine in the Western Church.

The title 'Doctor of the Church' has been applied to persons from any era in the Church's history whose sanctity and writings have had a profound influence on theological and spiritual thought. Doctors of the Church include such figures as St Thomas Aquinas, St Catherine of Siena, St Anthony of Padua, St Teresa of Ávila, St John of the Cross, St Robert Bellarmine and St Thérèse of Lisieux.

B. Sacraments: The Faith Celebrated

The second section of this text deals with the celebration of the Christian mystery in the liturgy and the Sacraments. Through the Sacraments the Holy Spirit makes available to us the mysteries of God's revelation in Christ. The saving gifts of Christ's ministry are encountered in the liturgy and are available to us. This is evident in the Sacraments of Initiation (Baptism, Confirmation, the Eucharist), the Sacraments of Healing (Penance and the Anointing of the Sick) and the Sacraments at the Service of Communion (Marriage and Holy Orders). Through the Sacraments, God shares his holiness with us so that we, in turn, can make the world holier.

C. Christian Morality: The Faith Lived

The third section of this text offers an extensive exposition of the foundations of the Christian moral life. Themes of covenant, grace, happiness, sin, forgiveness, virtues, the action of the Holy Spirit, the call to love God and neighbour, the dignity of the person and the Church's social teachings are part of the foundational elements for morality. Subsequently, when the Ten Commandments are presented, it is easier to see how the Covenant with God comes first and how the Commandments are ways in which we live out this Covenant. In the Sermon on the Mount, Jesus presents to us a summary of the New Covenant in the Beatitudes. Hence, the Commandments are more than moral laws; our commitment to living them flows from our response to the Covenant we have with God, as members of the Church strengthened by the Holy Spirit.

D. Prayer: The Faith Prayed

The last section of this text bears an essential relationship to the second section on the liturgy, which is the prayer life of the Church herself. This section deals with vocal prayer, meditation and contemplation, and the types of prayer – adoration, petition, intercession, thanksgiving and praise. A special chapter is devoted to a commentary on the Our Father, which is the Lord's Prayer. It seemed suitable here to acknowledge the special link between doctrine and prayer so that a Church teaching is not seen as an abstract idea, and so that prayer not be without a solid doctrinal foundation.

3. Sidebars

The doctrinal section in each chapter is followed by a sidebar composed of three questions with answers taken from the *Catechism of the Catholic Church*. This is one of several ways in which the reader is drawn to explore the extensive resources of the universal *Catechism*. Throughout the text, other sidebars on various topics appear where appropriate.

4. Relationship of Catholic Teaching to the Culture

The next section in each chapter returns to the theme of relating Church teaching for an Irish society. There are many issues to address, such as human dignity, fairness, respect, solidarity and justice. Each chapter contains a reflection on how its teaching can apply to our culture. Sometimes there are positive elements; at other times, challenges are to be met. Issues such as disbelief, relativism, subjectivism and differences about morality highlight conflicts between Church teachings and the present culture. The purpose of this section in each chapter is to point to the way in which the Church proclaims salvation to the culture, based on confidence in the validity and relevance of Catholic teaching.

It might also be helpful to note that in keeping with cultural practice, the text uses horizontally inclusive language, that is, describing human persons according to both male and female genders. The only exceptions to this practice are when the *Catechism* or some other source is quoted directly. References to God in this text maintain traditional usage.

5. Questions for Discussion

Following the section of each chapter that addresses aspects of faith as applied to Irish culture are questions that allow the readers to explore personal and communal ways of internalising the teaching of the Church.

6. Doctrinal Statements

Following both a story of faith and a concise review of the Church's teaching and its relation to the culture, each chapter contains a review of points of doctrine covered in the chapter.

7. Meditation and Prayer

As far as possible, this book is meant to draw the reader into a prayerful attitude before God. Every chapter concludes with a meditation drawn from a saint or spiritual writer. A catechism needs to be more than a summary of teachings. God has called all of us to prayer and holiness. Doctrines are distillations of prayer and thought made possible by the Holy Spirit's guidance of the Church. Prayer is the gate that leads us to a deeper understanding of the Word of God and to the hidden treasures of doctrinal teachings. A formal prayer is presented at this point in each chapter. It is usually drawn from the Church's liturgy or from traditional prayers of the Church so that the reader may become more familiar with the prayer life of the universal Church. There is also a collection of some traditional Catholic prayers in the appendix.

Glossary

Finally, an alphabetised glossary of many terms appears at the end of this book. The definitions are brief. It is recommended that readers also consult the *Catechism of the Catholic Church*, which has an extensive glossary. While studying the *Irish Catholic Catechism for Adults*, readers can consult these glossaries for definitions of words that are not familiar to them.

CONCLUSION

It is our hope that this *Irish Catholic Catechism for Adults* will be an aid and a guide for deepening faith. It may serve as a resource for the Rite of Christian Initiation of Adults (RCIA) and for the ongoing catechesis of adults. It will also be of interest to those who wish to become acquainted with Catholicism. Finally, it can serve as an invitation for all the faithful to continue growing in the understanding of Jesus Christ and his saving love for all people.

PART I

THE CREED:
THE FAITH PROFESSED

1 MY SOUL IS YEARNING FOR YOU, MY GOD (Ps 42:2)

THE HUMAN QUEST FOR GOD
– CCC, NOS. 27–43

IRISH MISSIONARY MONKS

Our ancestors, the Celts, were a wandering people. They originated in central Europe, and through the centuries migrated east, to Galatia in Turkey, and west, to France (ancient Gaul) and Spain (Galicia). Eventually they arrived on these islands around the second century before Christ and settled in England, Scotland, Wales and Ireland. Though they spread over a vast expanse of territory, the Celts never formed a strong and united political state. The Angles and Saxons (Germanic tribes) conquered England in the sixth century AD but, while the rulers changed, the native population remained Celtic. Celts survive to this day in the six most western parts of Europe: Britanny in France, Galicia in Spain, Cornwall in England, Ireland, Scotland and Wales.

The Celtic people of Ireland, Scotland and Wales welcomed the coming of Christianity. The ancient Celtic religion had much in common with Christianity, including a familiarity with the spirit world, an appreciation for creation and nature, and an awareness of the after-life and immortality. The Celts placed a high value on learning and literature, on personal sacrifice and asceticism (spiritual training) and on humble heroism. It is no accident, then, that the early Irish and British Celtic Christian monks, following the example of the Apostles and the history of their ancestors, took to the sea and the road to spread the Christian Gospel back to a Europe in disarray after the collapse of the Roman Empire.

From Sedulius in the fifth century to Malachy of Armagh, friend of St Bernard of Clairvaux, and the Franciscan Duns Scotus in the twelfth, Irish and Celtic monks and priests criss-crossed Europe and beyond, bringing with them their missionary zeal, their apostolic fervour and their scholarly reputation. As they fanned out throughout the continent, Ireland became known as the 'land of saints and scholars'. Historians since agree that the influence of Ireland on Europe's Christian Middle Ages was important and impressive.

What is particularly noteworthy about many of these men and women is their intense humanity and their sheer energy. Probably the most energetic was St Columbanus. He first travelled to the continent from Ireland in 575 when England and Germany were still pagan, and France and Italy were in chaos. He and his disciples and followers were responsible for the foundation of over one hundred European monasteries during the next century. He himself established the great monasteries of Luxeuil in France and Bobbio in Italy, where his name and memory is still green.

Another was St Brendan the Sailor who lived in the sixth century. His travels quickly became legendary, as his attempts to preach the Gospel to the mysterious islands of the Atlantic brought him to the edge of the known world and beyond. The story of his travels thrilled Europe for many centuries, and provided evidence that Irish monks did land on Iceland and could indeed have reached the coast of North America years before the Norsemen and Christopher Columbus.

One who never left the island of Ireland, but whose name was carried afar, was Brigid of Kildare. Irish missionaries brought her devotion with them. Though little is known of her life, it is clear that her influence on the early Celtic Church was immense. She was called 'Mary of the Gael', and it has even been claimed that the English word 'bride' is derived from her name.

The Celtic saints' stories of endeavour, zeal, enthusiasm and energy are stimulating and encouraging. They were inspirational leaders and extraordinary teachers. They tapped into the depths of human desire, pursued it to heroic lengths, but directed it to the preaching of the Kingdom of Heaven and spreading the Word of God. In so doing, they just might have laid one of the foundations for modern European civilisation.

But nothing could have been further from their minds. They were seeking God himself. One monk wrote:

> To go to Rome, much labour, little profit!
> The King you seek there,
> unless you bring him with you,
> you will not find.

And they knew, unlike tourists and travellers today, that they would probably never return home. They accepted the sacrifice of exile for Christ. As the greatest of them all, St Columcille of Iona, said:

> There is a grey eye
> That will look back upon Erin.
> It shall never see again
> The men of Erin nor her women.

THE UNIVERSAL DESIRE FOR GOD

The desire for God is written in the human heart, because man is created by God and for God.

– CCC, no. 27

People have always asked fundamental questions: Who am I? Where did I come from? Where am I going? Why do I need to struggle to achieve my goals? Why is it so hard to love and be loved? What is the meaning of sickness, death and evil? What will happen after death?

These questions relate to human existence. They also move one to ask questions about the divine because they pertain to God's existence. When asked with ever-deeper reflection, they uncover an inner sense of longing for God. They challenge our minds, but the mind's answers are not always sufficient. We must also become aware of the mysterious yearning of the human heart.

God has planted in every human heart the hunger and longing for the infinite, for nothing less than God. Saint Augustine, a theologian from the fifth century, said it best: 'Our heart is restless until it rests in you' (St Augustine, *The Confessions*, bk. 1, chap. 1, 1; cf. CCC, no. 30).

How is our quest for God awakened? God first pursues us; this spurs us to search for him for whom we were made. The *Catechism* presents three paths through which every person can come to God: creation, the human person and Revelation. In the next chapter, Revelation will be presented as the greatest and most essential path to God. He is discovered also through creation and through the mystery of our inner life.

THROUGH CREATION

The heavens declare the glory of God.

– Ps 19:2

Ever since the creation of the world, the invisible existence of God and his everlasting power have been clearly seen by the mind's understanding of created things.

– Rm 1:20

Saint Augustine asks us to look at the beauty of the world and let it open us to God. 'Question the beauty of the earth, question the beauty of the sea … question the beauty of the sky … All respond, "See, we are beautiful". Their beauty is a profession. These beauties are subject to change. Who made them if not the Beautiful One who is not subject to change?' (St Augustine, Sermon 241, no. 2; cf. CCC, no. 32).

Throughout the history of the Church, Christians have seen the universe as evidence of God's existence. The order, harmony and beauty of the world point to an intelligent Creator. The purposefulness of creation from the inanimate to human life similarly points to a wise Creator. The fact that all visible things come to be and eventually pass out of earthly existence points to an eternal Creator who has no beginning and no end and who sustains all that he has created (cf. CCC, no. 32).

THROUGH THE HUMAN PERSON

I thank you who wonderfully made me.

— Ps 139:14

Every human person seeks to know the truth and to experience goodness. Moral goodness appeals to us. We treasure our freedom and strive to maintain it. We hear the voice of our conscience and want to live by it. We long for absolute happiness.

These experiences make us aware of our souls and our spiritual nature. The more we become aware of these truths, the more we are drawn to the reality of God who is the Supreme Good. These are the seeds of eternity within us that have their origins only in God. Saint Augustine confirmed this insight when he prayed, 'That I may know myself, that I may know you.'

Since this is true, why have so many not found God?

Many reasons account for the lack of familiarity with God. The presence of so much suffering and pain in the world disheartens some and moves them to rebel against the idea of a God who would let this happen. Some do not know who God is because no one has shared the Good News of his self-revelation with them. Ignorance of religion or indifference to it is another cause.

The scandalous behaviour of some believers frequently drives honest seekers away from religion. Sinful conduct weakens the ability of many to assume responsibility for their actions and causes them to hide from God (cf. Gn 3:8; Jn 3:19ff.). Others may resist acknowledging God because they do not wish to follow and obey God. Still others may allow their lives to become so cluttered, hectic, or busy that there is little room for God.

Throughout history, people have yearned for God. Despite obstacles and occasions of violent opposition to belief in God, millions of people have continued to search for God. The spiritual dynamism of the human heart, having its origin in God, endures in countless and inspiring ways. Often, just when the shadows of doubt and scepticism appear to have laid the great search to rest, our yearning for God surges again to witness to the light of God's inherent attractiveness in human life.

FROM THE CATECHISM

1. How have people expressed their quest for God throughout history?
In many ways, throughout history down to the present day, men have given their expression to their quest for God in their religious beliefs and behaviour: in their prayers, sacrifices, rituals, meditations and so forth. These forms of religious expression, despite the ambiguities they often bring with them, are so universal that one may well call man a *religious being* (cf. Acts 17:26-28). (CCC, no. 28)

2. What do we mean by 'proofs' for God's existence?
Created in God's image and called to know and love him, the person who seeks God discovers certain ways of coming to know him. These are also called proofs for the existence of God, not in the sense of proofs in the natural sciences, but rather in the sense of 'converging and convincing arguments', which allow us to attain certainty about the truth. These 'ways' of approaching God from creation have a twofold point of departure: the physical world and the human person. (CCC, no. 31)

3. Can we know God?
The Church teaches that the one true God, our Creator and Lord, can be known with certainty from his works, by the natural light of human reason (cf. First Vatican Council, can. 2 §1: H. Denzinger and A. Schonmetzer, *Enchiridion Symbolorum* [DS] 3026). (CCC, no. 47)

SEEKERS IN THE DESERT

Religious culture in Ireland used to be one of 'dwelling'. Irish people in the past seemed content and satisfied with their religious home. Now, some Irish people feel quite lost. The familiar landmarks no longer comfort and direct them. They describe themselves as 'spiritual' but not 'religious', and confess to be 'seekers' for a religious home. They travel in a cultural landscape that in some important ways provides support for belief in God, while at the same time discourages and corrodes the faith in practice. In common with the rest of European culture, the religious and human landscape of Ireland seems like a desert. As Pope Benedict XVI said on the occasion of his inauguration:

> And there are so many kinds of desert. There is the desert of poverty, the desert of hunger and thirst, the desert of abandonment, of loneliness, of destroyed love. There is the desert of God's darkness, the emptiness of souls no longer aware of their dignity or the goal of human life. The external deserts in the world are growing, because the internal deserts have become so vast.

Nevertheless, there are shoots of green and signs of new life. Some younger people who had once drifted away from faith, today are seeking a connection with a Catholic Church community. Among the many causes of this, two stand out: the experience of having children who need a proper upbringing, and the experience of one's own longing for direction, meaning and hope.

Catholicism in Ireland continues to attract members each year. The new intercultural society, the return of Irish emigrants, the change in family situations, urbanisation and the flux that Irish society is in, has meant that more adults are seeking the sacraments and to join the Catholic Church. Through the RCIA, the pastoral process for initiating new members, the Church leads them to knowledge of the truths of faith, to the celebration of the Seven Sacraments, to commitment to the moral life – including the forming of a social conscience – and to the practice of prayer.

The Church does more than welcome new members; she forms disciples. Seekers can begin to find in the Church fulfilment of their heart's desires. They are invited to undertake a spiritual journey that is focused on Jesus Christ and his Kingdom of salvation, love, justice and mercy. Jesus reminds us that this Kingdom is already in our midst, and as his disciples we are called to assist him in bringing it to its fullness.

This is the Church's invitation to seekers who want to discover a satisfying answer to their spiritual hungers. Her invitation is rich: to seekers, old and new, and to those who might label themselves as alienated or indifferent, the Church offers Jesus Christ and his love, the fulfilment of hope. The Church offers a way of belonging that teaches truths that free one from sin and its power. The Church initiates members into an intimate relationship with God – indeed, into a participation in the divine life – where one will find genuine joy and fulfilment. This is all possible because of Jesus Christ and his love.

FOR DISCUSSION

1. What are you looking for in life? What are your goals and ideals? How does God and the Church play a part in what you are seeking? How is your life a journey toward God?
2. As a seeker, how do you look for truth? When you hear of truth or behold beauty or experience goodness, what do you think? If you seek for God, what has made this possible? What have you found in your search thus far?
3. As a Catholic, how are you searching for God? Why does seeking God keep your relationship with him dynamic? How does the Church help you in your search for God? How does your family affect your faith?

DOCTRINAL STATEMENTS

- God has planted in every human heart the hunger and longing for the infinite – for nothing less than himself.
- Only in God will we find the truth, peace and happiness for which we never stop searching. Created in God's image, we are called to know and love the Lord.
- God can be known with certainty from his works in creation and from the spiritual nature of the human person by the light of natural reason, although there are many difficulties in coming to this knowledge because of humanity's historical and sinful condition.
- By our openness to goodness and truth, our experience, our sense of moral goodness, our listening to the voice of conscience and our desire for happiness, we can discern our spiritual soul and can come to see that this could only have its origin in God.

- We can speak of God even if our limited language cannot exhaust the mystery of who he is.
- While we can come to know something about God by our natural power of reason, there is a deeper knowledge of God that comes to us through Divine Revelation.

MEDITATION

Where did I find you, that I came to know you? You were not within my memory before I learned of you. Where, then, did I find you before I came to know you, if not within yourself, far above me? …

Late have I loved you, O Beauty ever ancient, ever new, late have I loved you! … Created things kept me from you; yet if they had not been in you they would not have been at all. [O eternal truth, true love and beloved eternity. You are my God. To you I sigh day and night.] … You were with me but I was not with you. Created things kept me from you; yet if they had not been in you they would not have been at all. You called, you shouted and you broke through my deafness. You flashed, you shone and you dispelled my blindness. You breathed your fragrance on me; I drew in breath and now I pant for you. I have tasted you; now I hunger and thirst for more. You touched me and I burn for your peace.

– St Augustine, *The Confessions*, bk. 10, chap. 26, 27, 37

PRAYER

Like the deer that yearns
    for running streams,
so my soul is yearning
    for you, my God.

My soul is thirsting for God,
    the living God;
when can I enter and appear
    before the face of God?

My tears have become my bread,
    by day, by night,
as they say to me all the day long:
    'Where is your God?'

These things will I remember
    as I pour out my soul:
For I would go to the place
    of your wondrous tent,
    all the way to the house of God,
    amid cries of gladness and thanksgiving,
    the throng keeping joyful festival.

Why are you cast down, my soul;
    why groan within me?
Hope in God; I will praise him yet again,
    my saving presence and my God.

                                          – Ps 42:2-6

God loves each one of us as if there were only one of us to love.
                                        – St Augustine

2 GOD COMES TO MEET US

GOD REVEALS A PLAN OF LOVING GOODNESS – CCC, NOS. 50–67

GOD REVEALS HIS HOLY NAME

Moses was tending the flock of his father-in-law Jethro, the priest of Midian. Leading the flock across the desert, he came to Horeb, the mountain of God. There an angel of the Lord appeared to him in fire flaming out of a bush. As Moses looked on, he was surprised to see that the bush, though on fire, was not consumed. So he decided, 'I must go over to look at this remarkable sight to see why the bush is not burned'.

When the Lord saw him coming over to look at the sight more closely, God called out to him from the bush, 'Moses! Moses!'

Moses answered, 'Here I am.'

God said, 'Come no nearer! Remove the sandals from your feet, for the place where you stand is holy ground. I am the God of your father, the God of Abraham, the God of Isaac, the God of Jacob. The cry of the Israelites has reached me and I have truly noted that the Egyptians are oppressing them. Come now! I will send you to Pharaoh to lead my people the Israelites out of Egypt.'

But Moses said, 'Who am I that I should go to Pharaoh and lead the Israelites out of Egypt?'

God answered, 'I will be with you; and this shall be your proof that it is I who have sent you: when you bring my people out of Egypt, you will worship God on this very mountain.'

'But,' Moses said to God, 'when I go to the Israelites and say to them, "The God of your fathers has sent me to you", if they ask me "What is his name?" what am I to tell them?'

God replied, 'I am who am.' Then he added, 'This is what you shall tell the Israelites: I am sent me to you … This is my name forever; this is my title for all generations.'

But Moses said to the Lord, 'If you please, Lord, I have never been eloquent, neither in the past, nor recently, nor now that you have spoken to your servant; but I am slow of speech and tongue.'

The Lord said to him, 'Who gives one man the gift of speech and no such gift to another? Is it not I, the Lord? Go then! It is I who will assist you in speaking and will teach you what you are to say.'

Yet Moses persisted, 'If you please, Lord, send someone else.'

Then the Lord relented, 'Have you not your brother, Aaron the Levite? I know that he is an eloquent speaker. He shall speak to the people for you. He shall be your spokesman. I will assist both you and him and teach the two of you both what you are to do.' (Adapted from Exodus 3:1-15; 4:10-16)

The Old Testament is filled with numerous occasions where God reveals himself, such as he does to Moses in this passage from Exodus. The event of God's self-disclosure to Moses at the burning bush is an excellent introduction to the mystery of God's revelatory acts, a truth of our faith that is the focus of this chapter.

GOD REVEALS HIS LOVING PLAN TO SAVE US

By natural reason man can know God with certainty, on the basis of his works. But there is another order of knowledge, which man cannot possibly arrive at by his own powers: the order of divine revelation.

— First Vatican Council, *Dogmatic Constitution on the Catholic Faith* (*Dei Filius*), no. 1870

Through the use of reason, we can learn much about God from both creation and conscience, but Revelation enables us to learn about God's

FROM THE CATECHISM

1. How does God freely reveal himself?

This he does by revealing the mystery, his plan of loving goodness, formed from all eternity in Christ, for the benefit of all men. God has fully revealed this plan by sending us his beloved Son, our Lord Jesus Christ, and the Holy Spirit. (CCC, no. 50)

2. What response to Revelation did God plan for men and women?

By revealing himself, God wishes to make them capable of responding to him, and of knowing him and of loving him far beyond their own natural capacity. (CCC, no. 52)

3. If Revelation is complete, what is the next step?

Even if Revelation is already complete, it has not been made completely explicit; it remains for Christian faith gradually to grasp its full significance over the course of the centuries. (CCC, no. 66)

inner life and his loving plan to save us from sin and share in his divine life. No amount of unaided thinking could penetrate such a mystery. God freely chose to share this hidden mystery with us. God's sharing was an act of friendship for us, revealing himself as one reveals his or her heart to a friend. Love does such things.

God's Revelation unfolded gradually throughout history. 'Wishing to open up the way to heavenly salvation, he manifested himself to our first parents from the very beginning. After the fall, he buoyed them up with the hope of salvation, by promising redemption' (Second Vatican Council, *Dogmatic Constitution on Divine Revelation* [*Dei Verbum*; DV], no. 3; cf. Gn 3:15).

God continued over the succeeding centuries to provide providential care for those he created in his image and likeness. He called Abraham to make of him a great nation, a chosen people through whom salvation would come to the world. In the encounter of God with Moses, God reveals himself as

'I am who am'. These words reveal something about God, who, nevertheless, still remains mysterious. God is revealed as the source of all that is, but who he is will be revealed still further as he continues his loving work for his people. The prophets, in reflecting on God's actions, will make clearer the nature of God. But the clearest Revelation will come in Jesus Christ.

'At many moments in the past and by many means, God spoke to our ancestors through the prophets; but in our time, the final days, he has spoken to us in the person of his Son' (Heb 1:1-2). This Son was Jesus Christ, the fullness of Revelation. Wonderful indeed is this mystery of our faith in Jesus Christ, as we say in professing it, 'He was made visible in the flesh, / justified in the Spirit, / seen by angels, / proclaimed to the gentiles, / believed in throughout the world, / taken up in glory' (1 Tm 3:16).

Revelation is the self-disclosure of the living God. God shows himself by both great deeds, as narrated for us in Scripture, and by the words that illumine the meaning of these deeds (see DV, no. 2). In Revelation, the tremendous gulf between God and the human race is bridged. More profoundly, God desires to have an intimate relationship with all people. The process of Revelation, which took centuries to unfold, reached its magnificent fulfilment in the life, death and Resurrection of Jesus Christ.

Revelation is the act by which God speaks to and forms a covenant people.[1] The covenant between God and humanity was first established with Noah after the great Flood, when God in his mercy promised that never again would there be a catastrophe that threatens the existence of all of humanity. God entered into a covenant later with Abraham and then with the people of Israel at the time of their exodus from slavery in Egypt under the leadership of Moses. He affirmed that they will always be his people.

This is the grand drama of the dialogue between God and his people that takes place in the lived history of the people encompassed by his love. It includes the people's inspired interpretation of historical events that reflects an ever-greater understanding of God's will and presence as they advanced on their pilgrimage through the centuries.

It requires faith to respond to God's revealing word and to perceive the divine action in history. There are those who do not have faith or who

---

[1] A covenant was originally a treaty in which an overlord and a vassal accepted certain responsibilities toward each other. In the Old Testament, this idea of covenant became the primary analogy for the relationship between God and his people.

consciously reject living in faith. They cannot or will not perceive God's presence or action in the world and sometimes scoff at or ridicule those who do. But for many people, God makes faith possible and, with the guidance of the Holy Spirit, faith helps those people to grow in an appreciation of how God has worked in history to love and save us.

God's Revelation disturbed and changed the patriarchs, prophets, Apostles and others. When Moses encountered God in the burning bush, Moses trembled and took off his shoes, for he stood on holy ground (cf. Ex 3:1-6). Isaiah beheld the glory of God, and when the vision disappeared he saw himself in a brand-new light, 'Woe is me! I am lost, for I am a man of unclean lips' (Is 6:5). Faced with the revelation of divine power in Jesus, Peter begged, 'Leave me, Lord; I am a sinful man' (Lk 5:8). Revelation calls for a response of faith and conversion, not just in times past, but today as well.

Because the Christian covenant is definitive, there will be no new public Revelation until the final glorious manifestation of Jesus Christ at the end days (DV, no. 4). All that is needed for salvation has already been revealed. What are called *private revelations*, that is, messages such as those given by the Blessed Virgin Mary at Lourdes and Fatima, add nothing to what was publicly revealed up and through Christ but can help inspire a more profound commitment to what has been revealed through public Revelation.

THE GOSPEL AND CULTURE

The split between the Gospel and culture is without a doubt the drama of our time.

– Pope Paul VI, *On Evangelisation in the Modern World*
(*Evangelii Nuntiandi*), no. 20

Religion does not exist in a vacuum. It operates in a given culture at a particular moment in time. The understanding of a living God who has revealed a loving plan to save us takes place in real time. There is much in our culture that is good and favourable to faith and morality. The freedom to practise our faith is a treasured principle in our society.

But there are troubling developments. Most history today is taught from a secular viewpoint. Such a prevailing attitude often makes it hard for believers to realise there is a starting point in God's Revelation for understanding human history. The culture in which we live is, in many ways, individualistic, secular and materialistic. This poses a challenge to Christians and other believers who are asked to respond in faith to God who has revealed himself. It often requires great patience and much virtue to live a faith-filled life, to hand on Gospel values to children and others, and to interact with people – often the young – whose lives are affected by counter-Christian cultural currents.

In many ways, attitudes and actions in Europe are fostering a 'culture of disbelief'. The principle of complete separation of State and Church is being more and more widely espoused. The actual separation of Church and State represents political and civic maturity but society has reached the stage in which people of faith are under pressure to act publicly as though religion does not matter. This has caused many believers to think their faith is strictly a private matter and that it should have no influence on society and politics. This is an exaggerated deference to pluralism and tolerance. The truth should be shared or given witness to, but of course with respect and love.

The Church's response is to bring the Gospel into our culture in order to build on what is positive in it and to change what is not. This is one aspect of evangelisation, the proclamation of the Gospel to all peoples. It assumes that we first must be evangelised ourselves, calling each other to an intimate relationship with Jesus Christ. It means embracing truth, beauty and goodness wherever it can be found in our society, while at the same time removing falsehood and injustice from our land.

We must remember that all is not darkness. There are rays of light in our culture shed by Jesus, the Light of the World. There are seeds of the Word in our society sown by Jesus, the tireless Sower of love and truth. We do not work alone. The Holy Spirit is our teacher and guide.

Cultural change is slow, but it can take place through perseverance and God's grace. Evangelisers need a broad vision as well as wisdom, courage, fortitude and perseverance. Evangelising a culture relies on deep insight into the mysteries of our faith and a keen vision for understanding the basis of our culture.

Culture is not just an abstraction; it is the sum of the beliefs, attitudes and practices of individuals and communities. Evangelising a culture means dealing with people. It involves more than persuading people of the truth of Christ and the Church. Sharing the Gospel with others means offering them its transforming power, not just for their minds, but also for their hearts. In our daily prayer, we need to lift up our fellow citizens and their needs to God's loving concern for them.

The Catholic Church provides us with numerous ways to witness and teach the truth and love of Jesus Christ. Church history shows that the renewal of faith is frequently accompanied by a return to the truths of the faith and witnessing to those truths. Such a renewal of faith will gradually influence our culture.

FOR DISCUSSION

1. When friends and family members converse with one another, what do they reveal about themselves? What does God reveal of himself to us in treating us as friends and family members? How does God's Revelation give meaning to our lives?
2. What is meant when we say that we have a 'revealed' religion? What are positive features in our culture? How can culture be converted and transformed by the Gospel?
3. What would help you to spend more time reading and praying over God's revealed word in Scripture? Why can we say that growth in our faith will strengthen us to affect public policy with our beliefs?

DOCTRINAL STATEMENTS

- Revelation is the self-disclosure of the living God and his plan to save us. Revelation shows us that God desires to have an intimate and loving relationship with everyone.
- The process of Revelation took centuries to unfold. God gradually communicated the divine mystery by words and deeds.
- From the beginning, God established a personal relationship with our first parents. After the Fall, he encouraged them with the hope of Salvation by promising them Redemption.

- God's Revelation resulted in a relationship with people that is called a *covenant* in Scripture. Scripture tells us that God entered into a covenant with Noah and all living beings (cf. Gn 9:16).
- Revelation is an act by which God speaks to and forms a covenant people beginning with Abraham. He then chose Moses through whom the divine law was given to the covenant people.
- Through the prophets God prepared the covenant people to look forward to the coming of the Messiah who would bring the salvation destined for all people.
- Revelation reached its fullness in God's Son, Jesus Christ. The Son is the Father's definitive Word. No new public revelation will occur before the final, glorious manifestation of Jesus Christ.
- God's Revelation is transmitted to us by Apostolic Tradition and Scripture. This is the topic of our next chapter.

MEDITATION

Jesus Christ is the definitive revelation of God:

> Christ, the Son of God made man, is the Father's one, perfect, and unsurpassable Word. In him he has said everything; there will be no other word than this one. Saint John of the Cross, among others, commented strikingly on Hebrews 1:1-2: 'In giving us his Son, his only Word (for he possesses no other), he spoke everything to us at once in this sole Word – and he has no more to say ... because what he spoke before to the prophets in parts, he has now spoken all at once by giving us the All Who is His Son. Any person questioning God or desiring some vision or revelation would be guilty not only of foolish behaviour but also of offending him, by not fixing his eyes entirely upon Christ and by living with the desire for some other novelty.'
>
> – CCC, no. 65, citing St John of the Cross,
> *The Ascent of Mount Carmel*, 2, 22, 3-5

PRAYER

Forever is your word, O Lord,
    standing firm in the heavens.
From age to age is your truth;
    like the earth, it stands firm.
Your word is a lamp for my feet,
    and a light for my path.

– Ps 119:89-90; 105

Do your utmost to support your faith with goodness.

– 2 Pt 1:5

Religion, for Christians, is not a 'blind search for God'. It is a relationship, a response of faith to God revealed to us in human history and in our times too. God reaches out to us in all our ups and downs, calling each person into ongoing and deepening conversion.

– SGN, 26

3 PROCLAIM THE GOSPEL TO ALL CREATION (Mk 16:15)

THE TRANSMISSION OF DIVINE REVELATION – CCC, NOS. 74–133

HANDING ON THE FAITH

Saint John XXIII (pope from 1958 to 1963 and declared Saint by Pope Francis on 27 April 2014) believed that the Church needed a pastoral renewal that would enable the Church to minister more effectively to contemporary society. In his time he sensed that new ways were needed to communicate Christian doctrine to reveal the inherent attractiveness of the Gospel, while protecting its integrity. He said in his address to the bishops at the opening of the Second Vatican Council in 1962, 'Christian doctrine should be guarded and taught more efficaciously'. When he spoke about the Church as being the source of unity for all peoples, he based his teaching on Jesus Christ, the one and only Saviour who prayed at the Last Supper, 'you are in me and I am in you, so that they also may be in us' (Jn 17:21). In his opening address to the bishops on 11 October 1962, St John XXIII explained his vision for the Second Vatican Council, the twenty-first Ecumenical Council.[2] He proposed five points for achieving this goal:

1. *Be filled with hope and faith. Do not be prophets of gloom.* 'Divine Providence is leading us to a new order of human relations, which by men's own efforts and even beyond their very expectations, are directed toward God's superior and inscrutable design.'

---

[2] An Ecumenical Council is a gathering of bishops from around the world called together by the pope or approved by him. The Second Vatican Council was held from 1962 to 1965.

2. *Discover ways of teaching the faith more effectively.* 'The greatest concern of the ecumenical council is this: that the sacred deposit of Christian doctrine should be guarded and taught more efficaciously.'

3. *Deepen the understanding of doctrine.* Authentic doctrine 'should be studied and expounded through the methods of research and the literary forms of modern thought. The substance of the ancient doctrine and deposit of the faith is one thing, and the way in which it is presented is another.'

4. *Use the medicine of mercy.* 'Errors vanish as quickly as they arise, like fog before the sun. The Church has always opposed these errors. Frequently she has condemned them with the greatest severity. Nowadays, the Spouse of Christ prefers to make use of the medicine of mercy rather than that of severity. She considers that she meets the needs of the present day by demonstrating the validity of her teaching rather than by condemnation.'

5. *Seek unity within the Church, with Christians separated from Catholicism, with those of non-Christian religions and with all men and women of goodwill.* 'Such is the aim of the Second Vatican Ecumenical Council which ... prepares, as it were, and consolidates the path toward that unity of mankind where truth reigns, charity is the law and whose extent is eternity.' (St John XXIII, *Rejoice, O Mother Church [Gaudet Mater Ecclesia]*, opening address at the Second Vatican Council [11 October 1962])

Saint John Paul II noted that the Second Vatican Council owes much to the immediate past. He wrote the following:

The Second Vatican Council was a providential event. It is often considered as a new era in the life of the Church. This is true, but at the same time it is difficult to overlook the fact that the Council drew much from the experience of the immediate past, especially from the intellectual legacy left by Pius XII. In the history of the Church the 'old' and the 'new' are always closely interwoven. Thus it was for the Second Vatican Council and for the activity of the popes connected with the Council, starting with John XXIII, continuing with Paul VI and John Paul I, up to the present pope. (St John Paul II, *On the Coming of the Third Millennium [Tertio Millennio Adveniente]*, no. 18)

TRANSMITTING GOD'S REVELATION

Sacred Tradition and Sacred Scripture, then, are bound closely together and communicate one with the other. For both of them, flowing out from the same divine well-spring, come together in some fashion to form one thing and move towards the same goal.

— CCC, no. 80, citing DV, no. 9

Saint John XXIII and the Second Vatican Council itself illustrate how the Church constantly draws upon Tradition and Sacred Scripture. This chapter examines these foundations of Church teaching because it is through Tradition and Scripture that the Church knows God's Revelation and transmits it from one generation to another.

SACRED TRADITION

Jesus Christ, the divine Son of God become man, is the fullness of Revelation by his teaching, witness, death and Resurrection. On the road to Emmaus, the risen Jesus showed the two disciples how the teachings of the prophets were fulfilled in him and proclaimed by his own lips. Just before his Ascension, Christ commissioned the Apostles to preach the Gospel to all whose hearts would be open to receive them. The revealed Word of God in the Gospel would be for everyone a source of saving truth and moral discipline.

He commanded the Apostles to proclaim and witness his Kingdom of love, justice, mercy and healing, foretold by the prophets and fulfilled in his

THE BIBLE

The Church accepts and venerates the Bible as inspired. The Bible is composed of the forty-six books of the Old Testament and the twenty-seven books of the New Testament. Together these books make up the Scriptures. The unity of the Old and New Testaments flows from the revealed unity of God's loving plan to save us. The books of the Old Testament include the Pentateuch, historical books, the books of the Prophets, and the Wisdom books. The New Testament contains the four Gospels, the Acts of the Apostles, letters from St Paul and other Apostles, and concludes with the Book of Revelation.

The *canon* of the Bible, which is a term that refers to the books the Bible contains, was fixed within the first centuries of the Church. These books that make up both the Old and New Testaments were identified by the Church as having been divinely inspired. At times, people challenged the divinely inspired character of some of the books in the Bible. In 1546, the Council of Trent declared that all the books in both the Old and New Testament were inspired in their entirety. This declaration was subsequently confirmed by both the First Vatican Council (1869–70) and the Second Vatican Council (1962–65). Those books whose divinely inspired character was challenged appear in non-Catholic Bibles identified as either the 'Deuterocanonical Books' or the 'Apocrypha'.

Paschal Mystery. Jesus sent them the Holy Spirit to enable them to fulfil this great commission, to give them needed courage and to help them in their evangelising work.

Graced by the Holy Spirit, the Apostles did what Jesus commanded them. They did this orally, in writing, by the heroic sanctity of their lives, and by ensuring that there would be successors for this mission. The first communication of the Gospel was by preaching and witness. The Apostles proclaimed Jesus, his Kingdom and the graces of salvation. They called for the obedience of faith (hearing and obeying God's Word), the reception of Baptism, the formation of a community of believers, gathering for the Eucharist and generosity to the poor.

The Apostles chose men to be bishops to succeed them and handed on to them 'what they received from Jesus' teaching and example and what they learned from the Holy Spirit' (CCC, no. 83). The pope and bishops in union with him are successors of the Apostles and inherit the responsibility of authoritative teaching from them. We call this teaching office the *Magisterium*. 'The task of giving an authentic interpretation of the Word of God, whether in its written form or in the form of Tradition, has been entrusted to the living, teaching office of the Church alone' (CCC, no. 85, citing DV, no. 10).

All the faithful share in understanding and handing on revealed truth. 'The whole body of the faithful ... cannot err in matters of belief. This characteristic is shown in the supernatural appreciation of faith (*sensus fidei*) on the part of the whole people, when, "from the bishops to the last of the faithful", they manifest a universal consent in matters of faith and morals' (CCC, no. 92, citing Second Vatican Council, *Dogmatic Constitution on the Church* [*Lumen Gentium*; LG], no. 12). Another way of understanding this truth is the principle that the Holy Spirit, dwelling in the Church, draws the whole body of the faithful to believe what truly belongs to the faith. 'By this appreciation of the faith, aroused and sustained by the Spirit of truth, the People of God, guided by the sacred teaching authority (*magisterium*), and obeying it, receives not the mere word of men, but truly the word of God (cf. 1 Th 2:13), the faith once for all delivered to the saints (cf. Jude 3)' (LG, no. 12).

Tradition is the living transmission of the message of the Gospel in the Church. The oral preaching of the Apostles and the written message of salvation under the inspiration of the Holy Spirit (Bible) are conserved and handed on as the Deposit of Faith through the Apostolic Succession in the Church. Both the living Tradition and the written Scriptures have their common source in the revelation of God in Jesus Christ. This is particularly important to understand and believe when one is faced with the postmodern attitude that Tradition cannot be trusted, and that what the Church teaches as Tradition is really just a reflection of particular judgements and biases.

THE GOSPELS

The four Gospels and the rest of the New Testament were written down over time by those Apostles and others associated with them who worked under the inspiration of the Holy Spirit (cf. CCC, no. 76, citing DV, no. 7). Among all the books of Scripture, the Gospels hold a special place of honour because they tell us about Jesus Christ, his person and message. The Gospels were formed in three stages:

1. *The life and teachings of Jesus:* The Church affirms that the Gospels faithfully hand on what Jesus did and taught for our salvation (cf. CCC, no. 126, citing DV, no. 19).

2. *The oral tradition:* What Jesus said and did, the Apostles preached to others. They brought to their preaching a deeper understanding of what they had experienced, having been instructed by the events of Christ's life and enlightened by the Holy Spirit (cf. CCC, no. 126, citing DV, no. 19).

3. *The written Gospels:* 'The sacred authors, in writing the four Gospels, selected certain of the many elements which had been handed on, either orally or already in written form; others they synthesised or explained with an eye to the situation of the churches, while sustaining the form of preaching, but always in such a fashion that they have told us the truth about Jesus' (CCC, no. 126, citing DV, no. 19).

Knowing that what Tradition teaches has its ultimate foundation in Jesus Christ helps a person of faith to respond to Tradition with trust. The theological, liturgical, disciplinary and devotional traditions of the local churches both contain and can be distinguished from this Apostolic Tradition (cf. CCC, Glossary, 'Tradition').

SACRED SCRIPTURE

Sacred Scripture is inspired by God and is the Word of God. Therefore, God is the author of Sacred Scripture, which means he inspired the human authors, acting in and through them. Thus, God ensured that the authors taught, without error, those truths necessary for our salvation. *Inspiration* is the word used for the divine assistance given to the human authors of the books of Sacred Scripture. This means that guided by the Holy Spirit, the human authors made full use of their talents and abilities while, at the same time, writing what God intended. There are many in modern society who find incredible the belief that Scripture contains the inspired Word of God and so reject the Bible as a collection of stories and myths. There are others who profess belief in the Triune God and are even identified as 'Scripture scholars' who work to 'demythologise' the Scriptures, that is, they remove or explain away the miraculous as well as references to God's revealing words and actions. It is important to understand in the face of such challenges to Scripture that it is not simply the work of human authors as some critics allege, but truly the Word and work of God.

INTERPRETATION OF SCRIPTURE

When interpreting Scripture, we should be attentive to what God wanted to reveal through the authors for our salvation. We need to see Scripture as a unified whole with Jesus Christ at the centre. We must also read Scripture within the living Tradition of the whole Church, so that we may come to grasp a true interpretation of the Scriptures. The task of giving an authoritative interpretation of the Word of God has been entrusted to the Magisterium. Last, we need to remember and recognise that there is a coherence of the truths of faith within Scripture (cf. CCC, nos. 112–114).

The Church recognises two senses of Scripture, the literal and the spiritual. In probing the literal meaning of the texts, it is necessary to determine their literary form, such as history, hymns, wisdom sayings, poetry, parable or other forms of figurative language. 'The *literal sense* is the meaning conveyed by the words of Scripture and discovered by exegesis [the process scholars use to determine the meaning of the text], following the rules of sound interpretation: "All other senses of Sacred Scripture are based on the literal'" (CCC, no. 116, citing St Thomas Aquinas, *Summa Theologiae* I, 1, 10).

The spiritual senses of Sacred Scripture derive from the unity of God's plan of salvation. The text of Scripture discloses God's plan. The realities and events of which it speaks can also be signs of the divine plan. There are three spiritual senses of Scripture:

1. The *allegorical sense*. We can acquire a more profound understanding of events by recognising their significance in Christ; thus the crossing of the Red Sea is a sign or type of Christ's victory over sin and also of Christian Baptism;
2. The *moral sense*. The events reported in Scripture ought to lead us to act justly. As St Paul says, they were written 'to be a lesson for us' (1 Cor 10:11);
3. The *anagogical sense* ... We can view realities and events in terms of their eternal significance, leading us toward our true homeland: thus the Church on earth is a sign of the heavenly Jerusalem. (CCC, no. 117)

The Church's Scripture scholars are expected to work according to these principles to develop a better understanding of Scripture for God's people. Interpretation of Scripture is ultimately subject to the judgement of the Magisterium, which exercises the divine commission to hold fast to and to interpret authoritatively God's Word.

OTHER BIBLICAL INTERPRETATIONS

Our response to God's call to holiness involves regular, prayerful study of Scripture. 'Such is the force and power of the Word of God that it can serve ... the children of the Church as strength for their faith, food for the soul and a pure and lasting font of spiritual life' (CCC, no. 131, citing DV, no. 21).

Catholic biblical scholars have made distinguished contributions to scriptural studies. Their outstanding service to the Church has assisted believers to grow in their faith by an authentic understanding of Scripture. Two of the various challenges they face come from interpretations posed,

FROM THE CATECHISM

1. Why must Revelation be transmitted?
God '[wills everyone] to be saved and to come to the knowledge of the truth': that is, of Christ Jesus. Christ must be proclaimed to all nations and individuals, so that this revelation may reach to the ends of the earth. (CCC, no. 74, citing 1 Tm 2:4; cf. Jn 14:6)

2. How is Apostolic Tradition linked to Apostolic Succession?
Christ the Lord ... commanded the apostles to preach the Gospel (CCC, no. 75, citing DV, no. 7; cf. Mt 28:19-20; Mk 16:15). In order that the full and living Gospel might always be preserved in the Church the apostles left bishops as their successors. They gave them 'their own position of teaching authority'. (CCC, no. 77, citing DV, no. 7; St Irenaeus, Adv. Haeres)

3. Why does the Church venerate Scripture?
The Church has always venerated the Scriptures as she venerates the Lord's Body. She never ceases to present to the faithful the bread of life, taken from the one table of God's Word and Christ's Body. In Sacred Scripture, the Church constantly finds her nourishment and her strength. (CCC, nos. 103–104; cf. DV, no. 21)

on the one hand, by those who interpret the Bible only in a literal fashion, and, on the other hand, by those who deny the supernatural aspects of the Gospels.

BIBLICAL LITERALISM

Some Christians of many denominations – often called Fundamentalists – have adopted the supremacy of Scripture as their sole foundation. They also approach Scripture from a viewpoint of private interpretation. This they do in the strictest literal sense without appreciation of the various literary forms that the biblical authors used within the specific cultural circumstances in which they were writing.

The Church's response to Fundamentalism is that Revelation is transmitted by Apostolic Tradition and Scripture together. The Church and Apostolic Tradition existed before the written New Testament. Her Apostles preached the Gospel orally before writing it down. The Apostles appointed bishops to succeed them with the authority to continue their teaching. Scripture alone is insufficient. Authoritative teaching is also needed. That is given to us by the Church's teaching office. Catholics, then, accept Scripture and Tradition as one 'sacred deposit of the Word of God' (CCC, no. 97, citing DV, no. 10). Although this sets us apart from those who believe only in the Bible as their source of revelation, Catholics accept and honour both Scripture and Tradition 'with equal sentiments of devotion and reverence' (CCC, no. 82, citing DV, no. 9).

In response to biblical literalism, the Church holds that 'the books of Scripture firmly, faithfully and without error, teach that truth which God, for the sake of our salvation, wished to see confided to the sacred Scriptures' (DV, no. 11). At the same time, the Church recognises that the interpreter of Scripture needs to attend to the literary forms – such as poetry, symbol, parable, history, song or prayer – in which the Bible is written. The interpreter 'must look for that meaning which the sacred writer ... given the circumstance of his time and culture, intended to express and did in fact express, through the medium of a contemporary literary form' (DV, no. 12).

HISTORICAL REDUCTIONISM

Another challenge comes from scholars and others who deny the supernatural aspects of the Gospels, such as the Incarnation, Virgin Birth, miracles and the Resurrection. We call this *reductionism* because it reduces all Scripture to the natural order and eliminates the reality of divine intervention.

The Church's Pontifical Biblical Commission has dealt with approaches of this kind in its publications *Instruction on the Historical Truth of the Gospels* and *The Interpretation of the Bible in the Church*. The Pontifical Biblical Commission lists five unacceptable assumptions found in forms of scriptural interpretation:

1. the denial of a supernatural order
2. the denial of God's intervention in the world through revelation
3. the denial of the possibility and existence of miracles
4. the incompatibility of faith with historical truth
5. an almost *a priori* denial of the historical value of the nature of the documents of revelation. (Pontifical Biblical Commission, *Historical Truth of the Gospels* [1964], no. 5)

The Church approaches Scripture as God's revealed Word. Its authors wrote under the guidance and inspiration of the Holy Spirit. The Bible is more than a human work; it is God's words put into human words. It will always be a fountain of faith for those who read it in a spirit of prayer.

FOR DISCUSSION

1. Read again St John XXIII's thoughts about sharing and spreading the faith in a more effective way. How would they help you share your faith with others? What is both consoling and challenging about the way God has chosen to transmit his Revelation?
2. Why might you say it makes perfect sense for Jesus to commission followers to carry on his saving vision? How do leaders of the Catholic Church continue the vision of Jesus in our times?
3. How does the Church help you to understand the Bible? How do the bishops in communion with the pope ensure that the full and living Gospel will always be preserved in the Church?

DOCTRINAL STATEMENTS

- Jesus Christ, the fullness of Revelation, entrusted his mission to the Apostles. They transmitted Christ's Gospel through their witness, preaching and writing – under the guidance of the Holy Spirit – meant for all peoples until Christ comes in glory.
- Divine Revelation is transmitted through Apostolic Tradition and Sacred Scripture, which flow from the same divine wellspring and work together in unity toward the same goal.

- 'The Church, in her doctrine, life and worship, perpetuates and transmits to every generation all that she herself is, all that she believes' (DV, no. 8, §1). This is what is meant by the term *Tradition*.
- Because of the divine gift of faith, God's People as a whole never ceases to receive and reflect on the gift of Divine Revelation.
- The teaching office of the Church, the Magisterium – that is, the pope and the bishops in communion with him – has the task of authoritatively interpreting the Word of God, contained in Sacred Scripture and transmitted by Sacred Tradition.
- Sacred Scripture is inspired by God and truly contains the Word of God. This action of God is referred to as *Inspiration*.
- God is the author of Sacred Scripture, inspiring the human authors, acting in and through them. Thus God ensured that the authors taught divine and saving truth without error.
- The Catholic Church accepts and venerates as inspired the forty-six books of the Old Testament and the twenty-seven books of the New Testament. The unity of the Old and New Testaments flows from the revealed unity of God's loving plan to save us.
- Our response to God's Revelation is faith, by which we surrender our whole selves to him.

MEDITATION

Go Gladly to the Sacred Text Itself: From the Second Vatican Council on the Bible

[We] forcefully and specifically exhort all the Christian faithful … to learn the 'surpassing knowledge of Jesus Christ' (Phil 3:8) by frequent reading of the divine scriptures. 'Ignorance of the Scriptures is ignorance of Christ' (St Jerome). Therefore, let them go gladly to the sacred text itself, whether in the sacred liturgy, which is full of the divine words, or in devout reading, or in such suitable exercises and various other helps which, with the approval and guidance of the pastors of the Church, are happily spreading everywhere in our day. Let them remember, however, that prayer should accompany the reading of sacred Scripture, so that a dialogue takes place between God and man …

Just as from constant attendance at the Eucharistic mystery the life of the Church draws increase, so a new impulse of spiritual life may be expected from increased veneration of the Word of God.

– DV, no. 25–26

PRAYER

Let your scriptures be my chaste delight ...
O Lord, perfect me and reveal those pages to me!
See, your voice is my joy. Give me what I love ...
May the inner secrets of your words be
laid open to me when I knock.
This I beg by our Lord Jesus Christ in whom are hidden all the
treasures of wisdom and knowledge (Col 2:3). These are the
treasures I seek in your books.

– St Augustine, *The Confessions*, bk. 11, chap. 2, nos. 2–4

Stand firm, then, brothers, and keep the traditions that we taught you, whether by word of mouth or by letter.

– 2 Th 2:15

Scripture and Tradition are central to the life of the Church and to catechesis. The apostles entrusted to the whole Church the message of salvation, the 'sacred deposit' of faith which is contained in Scripture and Tradition.

– SGN, 47

4 BRING ABOUT THE OBEDIENCE OF FAITH

FAITH AS THE HUMAN RESPONSE TO GOD'S REVELATION – CCC, NOS. 142–196

JOHN HENRY NEWMAN: THEOLOGIAN OF FAITH AND CHURCH

John Henry Newman was born in London on 21 February 1801. He was educated in Oxford and there he began a career as teacher and preacher. After his conversion to Catholicism, except for an interlude in Rome and visits to Italy, his home was Birmingham. Between 1851 and 1858, however, he commuted, lived and worked between Birmingham and Dublin.

John Henry Newman was raised a Protestant, but at the age of fifteen he underwent a religious conversion. He tells us that he became intensely aware of two self-evident beings: himself and the Creator. This convinced him that spiritual awareness begins with the heart, that God opens himself in a close relationship with the individual person.

Newman attended Oxford University, but at first did not do well in his examinations. Later he won a teaching fellowship at Oriel College. He decided to study for ordination as an Anglican priest. He proved to be a gifted college educator, a devoted tutor to students, and a popular preacher. His fame grew as a religious writer, a creative thinker, an attractive but retiring personality, a man of energy and deep spirituality, and a poet.

His convictions about Church history and theological development propelled him to an influential position among a group of clergy and laymen called the 'Oxford Movement' or 'the Tractarians'. They were concerned about the state of the Church of England, a subject they dealt with in a series of tracts or pamphlets, many of them Newman's. His studies and research led him to the conclusion that faith is both personal and communal. This was his second spiritual insight. God's revelation calls not just for rational thought, but also for simple assent given by a believing people, the Church. The Church teaches with the experience of the ages, remains open to the promptings of the Spirit and is faithful to the revealing Word.

Newman's thinking gradually led him to the conclusion that the Catholic Church had preserved the tradition and passed on the teaching of the Apostles more faithfully than the Anglican Church of his upbringing, education and vocation. Along with the group of young men who had formed a small community with him in Littlemore, near Oxford, he became a Catholic in 1845. Two years later, he was ordained a Catholic priest in Rome. At the suggestion of the pope and the invitation of the Catholic Bishop of Birmingham, he set up a branch of St Philip Neri's Oratory in that city. He was to live there for the rest of his life.

England of the nineteenth century was in the throes of the Industrial Revolution, suffering from widespread individual and social dislocation, shaken by scepticism and doubt in religious and political authority and enjoying rising confidence in the power of science and technology. Newman did not turn his back on these realities. He believed that the revelation of God must be applied and interpreted for the particular time and for individuals. Christian teaching is unchanging, but explanations develop. Another context can display a different aspect of the truth, by making more obvious things implicit in the original statement. These ideas Newman clarified in his book *On the Development of Christian Doctrine*, a source for the theology of the Second Vatican Council.

The rest of Newman's life was marked by a number of challenges. One challenge was the commission given to him by the Irish Bishops to set up a Catholic University in Dublin and to serve as its first rector. This necessitated his travelling back and forth between England and Ireland for seven years. It also involved him trying to reconcile his own educational hopes and the more modest expectations of the Irish Bishops. Though his efforts were frustrated, there was one lasting result:

Newman's lectures, published as *The Idea of a University*, delivered in the Rotunda Hospital Assembly Room, today still define a Catholic approach to university education. The physical legacy of Newman's stay in Dublin is Newman House on St Stephen's Green and the exquisite University Church beside it, which he commissioned his friend, the architect John Hungerford Pollen, to design.

He continued to write and preach at the Oratorian house in Birmingham for the next forty years. A series of books exploring the topics of faith, the Church and the spirituality of the individual, such as *The Grammar of Assent, On Consulting the Faithful in Matters of Doctrine, Apologia Pro Vita Sua* and a huge correspondence running to many volumes, show him to be at the heart of English Catholic thought for four decades. In relation to the lay faithful he said, 'I want a laity, not arrogant, not rash in speech, not disputatious, but men who know their religion, who enter into it, who know just where they stand, who know what they hold and what they do not, who know their Creed so well that they can give an account of it, who know so much of history that they can defend it' (*Present Position of Catholics in England*, Chapter 9).

Newman's influence at university level drew many others to follow him into the Catholic Church. Because of his university work and the success of his efforts to teach the faith, centres of Catholic faith and worship at secular colleges and universities are often called Newman Centres.

In 1879, Pope Leo XIII elevated Newman to the rank of cardinal. John Henry Cardinal Newman died on 11 August 1890 at the age of eighty-nine.

Newman and his companions experienced their departure from the Church of England as painful and lonely. They left behind many close friends, inspiring teachers and holy pastors. As 'bridge people', Newman and his colleagues braved the darkness of doubt, the cold of isolation, the pain of misunderstanding. They witnessed to the personal dimension of faith as well as to Church teaching and community. Though he was a theologian of faith and Church for the nineteenth and twentieth centuries, John Henry Newman is just as much an ecumenical saint for the twenty-first century. It was fitting that Pope Benedict XVI beatified him in Birmingham during the papal visit to England of 2010.

IN THE ACT OF FAITH WE RESPOND TO GOD'S LOVING REVELATION

By his Revelation, 'the invisible God, from the fullness of his love, addresses men as his friends and moves among them, in order to invite and receive them into his own company.' The adequate response to this invitation is faith.

— CCC, no. 142, citing DV, no. 2

God makes himself known to us through Revelation in order both to give us something and to draw a response from us. Both this gift of God and our response to his Revelation are called *faith*. By faith, we are able to give our minds and hearts to God, to trust in his will and to follow the direction he gives us. Saint Paul describes this response as the obedience of faith (cf. Rm 16:26). We have many examples of faith. For instance, in Scripture we read of Abraham, who trusted in God's promise to make of him a great nation, and of Moses who, in faith, responded to God's call to lead his people out of slavery in Egypt to the Promised Land. The Virgin Mary is the perfect model of faith. From her 'yes' to God at the Annunciation to her silent assent at the Cross, Mary's faith remained firm. No wonder we hear Mary's faith acclaimed in the Gospels, 'Blessed is she who believed that the promise made her by the Lord would be fulfilled' (Lk 1:45).

Our response to God in faith is an act so rich in meaning that the *Catechism* explores its complexity in a number of ways.

BECOME A BELIEVER IN THE LORD JESUS (ACTS 16:31)

Our faith life is a grace or a gift that brings us into a personal, loving union with the Father, Son and Holy Spirit. This grace enables us both to hear the Word of God and to keep it. The qualities of faith listed here remind us of the basic ways in which we express our belief in God and that challenge us to apply our faith in our daily lives:

1. *Faith is a personal and communal relationship.* 'Faith is first of all a personal adherence ... to God. At the same time ... it is a free assent to

the whole truth that God has revealed' (CCC, no. 150). A personal faith says, 'I believe in God.' This is an act of belief in the one, true and living God. It is as though we gather all that we are, and gratefully give our hearts and minds to God. We have a personal relationship with the Triune God, Father, Son and Holy Spirit. But faith is also communal. It is not just a private act. In the assembly of believers at Mass, we profess our faith together and join our hearts as we experience ourselves as the Body of Christ. Our personal faith brings us into a relationship with God's people and the faith of the entire people strengthens us in our relationship with God.

2. *Faith seeks understanding and is a friend of reason.* Faith as a grace or gift from God makes it possible to gain some understanding of all that he has revealed to us, including the totality of his plan as well as the many mysteries of faith. Growth in understanding God's Revelation is a lifelong process. Theology and catechesis help us. We never completely understand these divine mysteries, but we often gain insight into them. In this context, faith and reason work together to discover truth. To ever suppose that human thought or scientific research can or should be in conflict with faith is a mistaken approach because this position denies the basic truth that everything has been created by God. Scholarly and scientific research that is carried out in a manner faithful to reason and to moral law will not conflict with truth as revealed by God (see CCC, no. 159).

3. *Faith is necessary for salvation.* 'Believing in Jesus Christ and in the One who sent him for our salvation is necessary for obtaining that salvation' (CCC, no. 161). 'Faith is necessary for salvation. The Lord himself [teaches]: "He who believes and is baptised will be saved, but he who does not believe will be condemned"' (CCC, no. 183, citing Mk 16:16).[3]

4. *Faith is a gift of grace.* God not only speaks to us, he also gives us the grace to respond. To believe in Revelation we need the gift of faith. Peter was able to see that Jesus was the Messiah, not from 'flesh and blood', that is, not by means of reason or common sense, but by the grace of the Father (cf. Mt 16:16-18). When by faith and Baptism we enter the

---

[3] For the Church's teaching about the salvation of those who have not known Christ or the Gospel, see CCC, no. 1260, and Chapter 11 of this book.

Church, we already share in eternal life. Faith perceives this in ever deepening ways, as through a glass darkly (cf. 1 Cor 13:12).

5. *Faith is a free, human act.* Faith is a gift of God which enables us to know and love him. Faith is a way of knowing, just as reason is. But living in faith is not possible unless there is action on our part. Through the help of the Holy Spirit, we are able to make a decision to respond to Divine Revelation, and to follow through in living out our response. God never forces his truth and love upon us. He reveals himself to us as free human beings, and our faith response to him is made within the context of our freedom. At Capernaum, Jesus asked the Apostles, 'Do you want to go away too?' Peter answers for them, 'Lord, to whom shall we go?' (Jn 6:67-68). Peter's response is freely sought and freely given. The same is true with each of us.

6. *Faith believes with conviction in a message.* We have seen that faith is a relationship with God. Now we note that it is also belief in a message. This message is found in Scripture and Tradition and is transmitted to us through many means such as liturgical prayers and the Creeds. Faith fills us with conviction because God guarantees the truthfulness of what he revealed. 'Our gospel came to you not only in words, but also in power and in the Holy Spirit and with great effect' (1 Th 1:5). The Spirit assists us to be believers. 'Only faith can guarantee the blessings that we hope for, or prove the existence of realities that are unseen' (Heb 11:1).

THE FAITH PILGRIMAGE

Faith is therefore both a relationship with God as well as an engagement with the truths that he reveals. In other words, faith refers to both the act by which we accept God's word and the content of what he has revealed to us.

Abraham, whom the Church calls our 'father in faith', and Mary, the first among all disciples, show by their acts of trust in God that faith is a process of growth, day by day. Like any other relationship, our faith communion with God develops in stages. It is a journey, a pilgrimage. On this journey, there will be periods of temptation, worry, shadows and darkness. Many saints experienced such tests. But Jesus has sent us the Holy Spirit to enlighten and guide us on the way.

FAITH REQUIRES SUBMISSION

JOHN HENRY NEWMAN
ON FAITH FROM THE APOSTLES

In 1849, Fr Newman (as he then was) published one of his first sermons as a Catholic, but delivered to a congregation of Catholics and Anglicans, in which he wrote of the necessity of trusting in God's Word and submitting in faith to the teaching authority of the Church. Newman's words can be read and reflected upon in light of contemporary trends towards deciding for oneself what to believe:

> [In the time of the Apostles] ... A Christian was bound to take without doubting all that the Apostles declared to be revealed; if the Apostles spoke, he had to yield an internal assent of his mind ... Immediate, implicit submission of the mind was, in the lifetime of the Apostles, the only, the necessary token of faith ... No one could say: 'I will choose my religion for myself, I will believe this, I will not believe that; I will pledge myself to nothing; I will believe just as long as I please, and no longer; what I believe today I will reject tomorrow, if I choose. I will believe what the Apostles have as yet said, but I will not believe what they shall say in time to come.' No; either the Apostles were from God, or they were not; if they were, everything that they preached was to be believed by their hearers; if they were not, there was nothing for their hearers to believe. To believe a little, to believe more or less, was impossible; it contradicted the very notion of believing. (John Henry Newman, 'Faith and Private Judgement', *Discourses to Mixed Congregations* [1849])

Our faith encounter with God's revealed message takes time and maturity to probe its meaning and gain some hint of the awe and majesty to which divine truths point. There is brilliant light as well as shadows. We are pilgrims of love and truth ever seeking and longing for closer union with God.

The ultimate goal of a life of faith is eternal union with God in heaven. Through the gift and experience of faith, we are able not only to look ahead to what awaits us, but also to experience here some of God's divine life, 'a taste in advance' of our sharing life with him forever (see CCC, no. 163). While living a life of growing in faith might seem like a waste of time and energy to sceptics and non-believers, both because the objects of faith cannot always be proven and because faith often 'produces' little of measurable value, believers know the strength, the wisdom, the confidence and hope that a life of faith gives.

CATHOLIC IRELAND IN THE NINETEENTH CENTURY

The Scientific Revolution of the seventeenth century, the Enlightenment of the eighteenth, and the Industrial Revolution of the nineteenth century transformed religious, intellectual, social and political life in Europe and America. Most of those three revolutions, however, passed Ireland by.

The most important of the revolutions was the Enlightenment, also known as the Age of Reason. Educated people across Europe came to believe that they knew things that their forefathers did not know: that they were uniquely 'enlightened'. Therefore, they put all authority in doubt – religious, political, intellectual and social. Each person could be completely autonomous, a law unto oneself, and could figure everything out individually. Scepticism ruled philosophical thought. Republicanism and popular democracy deposed monarchy and nobility. A clockwork universe and random human events replaced God's providence for creation and purpose for history. Only republicanism had a deep effect on Irish history at the time.

The situation of the Catholic Irish was quite different from that of other European peoples. Catholic Irish people were a majority population, colonially and religiously oppressed, economically backward, educationally deprived and culturally impoverished. Because of oppression, the Catholic Church was demoralised, its popular support weak, its organisation patchy,

FROM THE CATECHISM

1. Why do we say faith is both personal and communal?
Faith is a personal act – the free response of the human person to the initiative of God who reveals himself. But faith is not an isolated act. No one can believe alone, just as no one can live alone. You have not given yourself the faith as you have not given yourself life. The believer has received faith from others and should hand it on to others. (CCC, no. 166)

2. What should we recall about the *formulas* of faith such as those found in the creeds?
We do not believe in formulae, but in those realities they express, which faith allows us to touch ... All the same, we do approach these realities with the help of formulations of the faith which permit us to express the faith and hand it on, to celebrate it in community, to assimilate and live on it more and more. (CCC, no. 170)

3. What role does the Church play in handing on the faith?
The Church, 'the pillar and [foundation] of truth', faithfully guards 'the faith which was once for all delivered to the saints'. She guards the memory of Christ's words; it is she who from generation to generation hands on the apostles' confession of faith. (CCC, no. 171, citing 1 Tm 3:15; Jude 3)

church services irregular and religious education non-existent. So the philosophical and theological consequences of Enlightenment thinking had no audience among Irish Catholics or their religious leaders. The advances of science and the growth of industry in the early nineteenth century were also mostly irrelevant for Ireland.

The Irish Bishops and religious leaders devoted their energies to re-founding the Church, providing places of worship, hospitals and a Catholic education system from primary school to university. When John Henry

Newman arrived as the rector of the new Dublin Catholic University, he came with concerns about matching Oxford or Cambridge in a Catholic mode, that is, through exploring intellectual and educational questions. The Bishops, by contrast, were concerned with political questions, like the relationship with the British government and its education policy, the amount of control and influence to allow state agencies and lay academics in Catholic education, the ever-present threat of violent republican revolution, and the chronic scarcity of resources in a poor country. It is no wonder, therefore, that bishop and rector were sometimes at cross-purposes.

During the rest of the century, bishops and religious, such as Paul Cardinal Cullen of Dublin, Archbishop Mac Hale of Tuam, Edmund Rice, Catherine McAuley, and many others, succeeded in building a strong social and religious infrastructure of diocese, parish, school, hospital and foreign mission. The Irish Catholic Church was linked closely to Rome and the Papacy, its worship was based on sacramental service and popular devotion, and by the end of the century and the 1916 Rising, commanded the loyalty of most of the population.

CATHOLICS IN IRELAND TODAY

Some of the questions that faced nineteenth-century Irish Catholic leaders are still current. For example, the role of the state and its relationship to religion in general, and Catholicism in particular, is a point of discussion today. Due to the popular support for the Church, the newly independent Irish state incorporated much of Catholic social and family teaching into its legal framework, and was happy that Christian churches in general, and the Catholic Church in particular, bore the burden of managing national schools, establishing secondary schools, providing a high proportion of hospital beds and founding social and pastoral services. Naturally, the Catholic Church and other churches asserted a Christian ethos for these institutions.

There are two approaches to this discussion: one approach is that any agency funded by public money should be completely religion-neutral. This is the tradition of Enlightenment thinking, whereby religious convictions are regarded as private opinion only, with no rights in the public square.

The other approach may be described as that of 'Pluralism', and it is the compromise reached in practice in the United Kingdom and in many of its dominions. This approach recognises that religious bodies do discharge public duties, such as healthcare and education, and can legitimately be publicly funded for the provision of these services, on the condition that they are appropriately regulated and financially accountable. This is the tradition that the Irish state inherited, and has operated to the present time.

CHALLENGES TO FAITH

Difficulties for faith and religious communities arise in areas where religious values conflict with those of the secular state or the prevailing culture. Christianity and Catholicism are counter-cultural: that is, they oppose the culture if and when Gospel values are in conflict with it. Issues such as the teaching of religion in schools, the refusal to promote materialism and consumerism, the advocacy of human rights and social justice, the protection of human life from the first moment of conception to natural death, respect for the human person, and the defence of the family and local community can and do excite disagreement, argument and conflict between religious and state agencies.

Another development has been the arrival in Ireland of Enlightenment thinking. Late to the scene, and somewhat changed from its eighteenth-century ancestor, a new freedom of thought and liberal cast of mind became evident throughout Irish life since the latter part of the 1960s. It has been described as 'an ideological secularism, a belief that we are self-sufficient and self-explanatory and do not need religious faith'. (Secularism means a belief that this life and this world and age are all that matters.)

A proportion of Irish 'cradle' Catholics have also adopted this worldview, and, with agnostics, atheists and humanists, have begun to insist on state-provided, lay-controlled and religion-free educational and health services, along with a totally secular public policy.

The Church, however, continues to apply principles flowing from her faith to public policy, most notably in her teaching on the dignity of the human person and the culture of life. The Church's advocacy for the poor, the elderly, children and immigrants are further examples of the Church's commitment to advance social justice. The Church's unflagging pro-life stand is an outstanding example of calling our society and government to protect life from the first moment of conception to natural death.

The Catholic Church and other religious bodies are expected to contribute to the public welfare, the stability of society and the moral order. This presumes that Catholic bishops and other religious leaders are encouraged to act as opinion formers, develop policy positions and influence public discourse. That should not mean, of course, that the state is under obligation to adopt Catholic ideas or Christian proposals in all aspects of public life. That would entail that religious leaders usurp the responsibilities proper to politicians and public servants. To restrict religious leaders, however, from making public pronouncements and expressing political opinions on matters of public interest, is a denial of civic and religious liberty.

The Church is rightly concerned that Church assets and contributions of religious people will be devoted to purposes in which they believe. At a more fundamental level, Catholics, with other religious bodies, are concerned that parents are able to exercise their human and civic right to educate their children in religion, receive pastoral and spiritual care when they are sick or dying, and be suitably assisted or supported by the state to do this. This may mean entering into dialogue and partnership with public bodies to determine an appropriate governance and division of responsibilities for schools, hospitals and other institutions in a variety of situations.

On a more general level, the Church's dialogue with secularism is helped by joining with thoughtful people who are raising basic questions: Who are we? What is the meaning of suffering, evil and death? Why has modern progress not eliminated them? What is the value of our country's achievements in light of their cost to human dignity and life? These questions point us to the transcendent origins of humanity. The resulting discussion can awaken the seeds of eternity planted by God in each soul.

Finally, we need to affirm again our faith that Jesus Christ can show all of us the way – believers to stronger faith and others to be brought to faith. When we are newly aware of the Holy Spirit's power to transform us and others, we will have both the energy and imagination to find paths to faith for those in need. We always need to rediscover the truth that the key to our history is to be found in Jesus, the Lord of history. Beneath all the rapid changes in our culture, there are still many people who possess and live enduring values rooted in Christ, who 'is the same today as he was yesterday and as he will be for ever' (Heb 13:8). We need to rely on our faith in Christ when we reflect on the mystery and dignity of man and woman, and as we address challenges to faith and its relationship to culture.

FOR DISCUSSION

1. In what ways do you find it difficult to be open about your faith in public situations? How have you been able to apply your faith to family issues, community development and political decisions?
2. What steps might you take to make your faith more effective in our culture? What help in this regard do you expect from the Church?
3. Who are outstanding models of faith that inspire you to deeper faith and practice? How is your faith bringing you closer to God and to a deeper understanding of his message?

DOCTRINAL STATEMENTS

- Faith is a gift from God. He not only enters a relationship with us but also gives us the grace or help to respond in faith.
- In faith we surrender our whole being to God who has revealed himself to us. This involves the assent of the intellect and will to the Revelation that God has made in words and deeds.
- By faith, we enter a relationship of trust in God as well as belief in the message of truth that he has revealed.
- Faith is a free, conscious, human act. Faith is a way of knowing, just as reason is, though it is different from reason. Faith involves the whole of the human being. Aided by the Holy Spirit we exercise faith in a manner that corresponds to our human dignity.
- Faith is a supremely personal act: 'I believe.' It is also communal, occurring within the life and worship of the Church. In the assembly of believers at Mass, as we join together in the Profession of Faith (or Creed), we experience ourselves as the Body of Christ.

- By faith we believe with conviction in all that is contained in the Word of God, written or handed down, which the Church proposes for belief as divinely revealed.
- Faith is necessary for salvation. 'Believing in Jesus Christ and in the One who sent him for our salvation is necessary for obtaining that salvation' (CCC, no. 161).
- We have two forms of the Creed that we use for prayer and worship: the Apostles' Creed, the ancient baptismal Creed of the Church of Rome; the Nicene Creed, from the first two Ecumenical Councils – Nicea in 325 and Constantinople in 381.
- A Creed is a brief, normative summary statement or profession of Christian faith. Creeds are also called Symbols of Faith.

MEDITATION

'The obedience of faith' (Rm 13:26; cf. 1:5; 2 Cor 10:5-6) 'is to be given to God who reveals, an obedience by which man commits his whole self freely to God, offering the full submission of intellect and will to God who reveals', and freely assenting to the truth revealed by Him. To make this act of faith, the grace of God and the interior help of the Holy Spirit must precede and assist, moving the heart and turning it to God, opening the eyes of the mind and giving 'joy and ease to everyone in assenting to the truth and believing it'. To bring about an ever-deeper understanding of revelation the same Holy Spirit constantly brings faith to completion by His gifts.

– DV, no. 5

PRAYER

'I believe' (Apostles' Creed) is the faith of the Church professed personally by each believer, principally during Baptism. 'We believe' (Niceno-Constantinopolitan Creed) is the faith of the Church confessed by the bishops assembled in council or more generally by the liturgical assembly of believers. 'I believe' is also the Church, our mother, responding to God by faith as she teaches us to say both 'I believe' and 'We believe'.

– CCC, no. 167

The Apostles' Creed is so called because it is rightly considered to be a faithful summary of the Apostles' faith. It is the ancient baptismal symbol of the Church of Rome. Its great authority arises from this fact: it is 'the Creed of the Roman Church, the See of Peter, the first of the Apostles, to which he brought the common faith'.

– CCC, no. 194

The *Niceno-Constantinopolitan* or *Nicene Creed* draws its great authority from the fact that it stems from the first two ecumenical Councils (in 325 and 381). It remains common to all the great Churches of both East and West to this day.

– CCC, no. 195

The Apostles' Creed

I believe in God,
the Father almighty,
Creator of heaven and earth,
and in Jesus Christ, his only Son, our Lord,
who was conceived by the Holy Spirit,
born of the Virgin Mary,
suffered under Pontius Pilate,
was crucified, died and was buried;
he descended into hell;
on the third day he rose again from the dead;
he ascended into heaven,
and is seated at the right hand of God the Father almighty;
from there he will come to judge the living and the dead.

I believe in the Holy Spirit,
the holy catholic Church,
the communion of saints,
the forgiveness of sins,
the resurrection of the body,
and life everlasting. Amen.

Nicene Creed

I believe in one God,
the Father almighty,
maker of heaven and earth,
of all things visible and invisible.

I believe in one Lord Jesus Christ,
the Only Begotten Son of God,
born of the Father before all ages.
God from God, Light from Light,
true God from true God,
begotten, not made, consubstantial with the Father;
through him all things were made.
For us men and for our salvation
he came down from heaven,
and by the Holy Spirit was incarnate of the Virgin Mary,
and became man.

For our sake he was crucified under Pontius Pilate,
he suffered death and was buried,
and rose again on the third day
in accordance with the Scriptures.
He ascended into heaven
and is seated at the right hand of the Father.

He will come again in glory
to judge the living and the dead
and his kingdom will have no end.

I believe in the Holy Spirit, the Lord, the giver of life,
who proceeds from the Father and the Son,
who with the Father and the Son is adored and glorified,
who has spoken through the prophets.

I believe in one, holy, catholic and apostolic Church.
I confess one Baptism for the forgiveness of sins
and I look forward to the resurrection of the dead
and the life of the world to come. Amen.

The Chief Spiritual Works of Mercy
- To admonish sinners
- To instruct the ignorant
- To counsel the doubtful
- To comfort the sorrowful
- To bear wrong patiently
- To forgive all injuries
- To pray for the living and the dead

(from *A Catechism of Catholic Doctrine*, Dublin: M. H. Gill and Son Ltd, 1951)

Faith is the assurance of things hoped for,
the conviction of things not seen.

— CCC, no. 146, citing Heb 11:1

We tend to think of faith first of all, perhaps, as an assent to doctrines; in other words, our mind's acceptance of statements of the Church's teaching. But faith, hope and love are 'theological virtues', meaning that they concern primarily our relationship with God and affect our relationships with one another. We believe first of all not in statements, however important and central, but in God, and we believe not only with our minds but with our whole selves.

— SGN, 44

5 I BELIEVE IN GOD

FAITH IN GOD AS MYSTERY AND TRINITY; BELIEF IN GOD,
THE FATHER ALMIGHTY, CREATOR OF HEAVEN AND EARTH
– CCC, NOS. 199–349

NICHOLAS CALLAN: PRIEST AND SCIENTIST

At the beginning of the nineteenth century, the word 'science' did not mean the systematic exploration of nature and the study of the properties of material things. Scholars who followed these pursuits were called 'natural philosophers'. It was only decades later that scientists claimed status as a distinct profession. It was nearer the end of the nineteenth century before it was seriously argued that science and religion could be diametrically opposed. So the religion and science debate was not an issue in the early 1800s.

Thus it was no surprise that a priest like Nicholas Callan from Co. Louth was appointed as Professor of Natural Philosophy in the National Seminary of St Patrick at Maynooth in 1826 and spent the next thirty-eight years there teaching mathematics, mechanics, electricity, astronomy and experimental methods to the student priests of Ireland. It may, however, be a surprise, or at least worthy of note, that during his academic career he made major discoveries and inventions, some of which, like the ignition systems in our cars, are still commonly in use. He contributed enough to be regarded justly as one of Ireland's scientific pioneers.

Nicholas Joseph Callan was born between Drogheda and Dundalk in the last days of the eighteenth century. He came from a prominent farming family and attended the Dundalk Academy where he was taught by William Nielson, a Presbyterian minister. He entered the National Seminary at Maynooth in 1816, where he studied the usual subjects, the Classics and English, for two years before beginning

Natural Philosophy, taught by Cornelius Denvir, later the Bishop of Down and Connor. This, as we have seen, was what we would today call 'science', and involved experimentation and observation of physical phenomena.

Callan advanced to theology classes for the last three years of his studies and was ordained to the priesthood in 1823. A fine scholar, he was duly sent to Rome's Sapienza University for further study. There he was awarded a Doctorate in Divinity in 1826. While in Rome, he came across the scientific discoveries of Volta and Galvani, who gave their names to the electric volt and the process of galvanisation.

The new doctor returned to Maynooth, and replaced his teacher in the Chair of Natural Philosophy when Dr Denvir resigned in the same year. He was to stay in that post for the rest of his life. He developed the course that was taught to the seminarians first by himself, and then by his successors, for the rest of the nineteenth century.

Callan was an inveterate experimenter, designer and engineer. In those heady early inventive days, scientists fashioned their own apparatus to test their ideas by adapting machinery, improvising gadgets and constructing the equipment they required. Callan left behind him a bewildering selection of batteries, coils, cells, motors, plates, wires and a wide variety of scientific instruments. Many of these can be seen today in Maynooth's museum.

His first love was electricity. Within ten years, he had produced the breakthrough that made his reputation: the induction coil. He combined previous ideas to build a coil which could produce a current of an estimated sixty thousand volts with fifteen inch sparks. He progressed to improving battery design for storing electricity, and constructed electrical motors to convert electrical energy into physical work. He saw that electricity was an energy source of great potential, and predicted its use for light and locomotion. He even anticipated the electric car, long before the petrol automobile was invented. With his vision of sustainable energy, he was well ahead of his time.

How did Nicholas Callan come across to his students and colleagues? His teaching set high standards and he could be sharp in class. He was a small man, 'a quaint old scholar and savant'. He generated more memories and stories among the priests of Ireland than many of his colleagues in the seminary, and was universally held in amused affection. His classes were on occasion memorable, as he opened up the minds of his students to the new world of currents and coils, power and resistance, magnets and batteries. There are stories of shocked scholars (literally) – one losing consciousness with a charge of electricity. Legend has it that the poor boy was none other than William Walsh, the future Archbishop of Dublin. The college authorities, naturally enough, asked Fr Callan to take more precautions, particularly with students, and subsequent experiments were carried out on several unfortunate turkeys instead.

Nicholas Callan personally was a modest man, not trumpeting his own inventions or discoveries. He named his pioneering electrical battery after the college rather than himself. He reported his discovery of the induction coil in a journal at the time of the discovery, but it was only some decades later that he spoke about it to the British Association of the Advancement of Science.

Nicholas Callan was a Catholic priest and a serious scientific pioneer. The Catholic Church has often been accused of being the enemy of science. Nicholas Callan, and other believers, who embrace both science and religion fervently, put the lie to this. The list of notable Catholics in the history of science is long and glorious. Among the names are those of Galileo, Descartes, Pascal, Pasteur, Ampere, Volta, Galvani, Lavoisier and Fermi. The accusation of the Church's opposition invariably cites the Galileo controversy, but that is more the exception than the rule.

Indeed, like Nicholas Callan, some famous inventors and scientific pioneers were Catholic priests, clerics or monks, including Nicholas Copernicus, Gregor Mendel and John Philip Holland among others. Probably the most illustrious priest-scientist of the modern era is Georges Lemaître (1894–1966), a Belgian professor at Louvain. He is the one credited with proposing the theory of the expanding universe from a primeval atom. Lemaître's idea was at first ridiculed by many scientists, but is now the accepted account of what has happened. We know it now by the title hung on it by his early scientific critics: the Big Bang Theory.

Father Callan saw no contradiction between the priest and the scientist. He thought of science as discovering the design of God in things. He was personally a saintly and holy man. His students regarded him as 'a holy priest', even though they pretended to fear he might blow the college up with his experiments! He was also generous, both with his money and his time. During the years of the Famine, in the 1840s, he donated his salary from Maynooth to famine relief. Less well-known is his publishing project. He translated about twenty books by St Alphonsus Ligouri, the founder of the Redemptorist Order, from Italian for the Irish Catholic faithful, anonymously. Saint Alphonsus was a famous confessor, and Nicholas Callan himself spent much time hearing confessions.

In latter years, Nicholas Callan suffered a stroke, and he died on 10 January 1864. His memory is preserved to this day in the Callan Lecture Hall at Maynooth, built on the site of his laboratory and classroom. This great pioneer of science, and an Irishman of faith, can be called to mind every time we turn the ignition key in our cars and Callan's induction coil comes into use.

GOD IS HOLY MYSTERY

It is right and just to sing of You, to bless You, to praise You, to thank You, to worship You – for You are God ineffable, inconceivable, invisible, incomprehensible, always existing and ever the same, You and Your only begotten Son and Your Holy Spirit.

— Anaphora of the Liturgy of St John Chrysostom

God's home is in inaccessible light, and no human being has seen him or is able to see him (cf. 1 Tm 6:16). Revelation tells us that he is living and personal, profoundly close to us in creating and sustaining us. Though he is totally other, hidden, glorious and wondrous, he communicates himself to us through creation and reveals himself through the prophets and above all in Jesus Christ, whom we meet in the Church, especially in Scripture and the Sacraments. In these many ways, God speaks to our hearts where we may welcome his loving presence.

We do not confuse the word *mystery* with the term as it applies to a detective story or a scientific puzzle. The mystery of God is not a puzzle to be solved. It is a truth to be reverenced. It is a reality too rich to be fully grasped by our minds, so that while it continues to unfold, it always remains mostly beyond our comprehension. The mystery of God is present in our lives and yet remains hidden, beyond the full grasp of our minds.

God, who always remains beyond our comprehension, has shown himself to us throughout the history of salvation. His relationship with Israel is marked by all kinds of loving deeds. He, ever faithful and forgiving, is ultimately experienced by human beings through his Son, Jesus Christ and the Holy Spirit. His love is stronger than a mother's love for her child or a bridegroom's for his beloved. Saint John proclaims, 'God is love' (1 Jn 4:8). Jesus has revealed that God's very being is love.

GOD IS THE TRINITY

The mystery of the Most Holy Trinity is the central mystery of the Christian faith and of Christian life.

– CCC, no. 261

The Old Testament shows God as one, unique, without equal. 'Listen, Israel, the Lord our God is the one, only Lord' (Deut 6:4; Mk 12:29). He created the world, made a covenant with his people and is the Father of the poor, the orphan and the widow.

In the Creeds, we profess our faith in God as 'Father almighty'. His fatherhood and power illumine each other by his care for us, by adopting us as sons and daughters in Baptism and by being rich in mercy to forgive our sins. Scripture constantly praises the universal power of God as the 'Mighty One of Jacob' and the 'Lord of hosts' (Gn 49:24; Is 1:24ff.). God's power is loving, for he is our Father.

God's parental tenderness can also be expressed by the image of motherhood, which emphasises God's immanence, the intimacy between Creator and creature. The language of faith thus draws on the human experience of parents, who are in a way the first representatives of God for man. But this experience also tells us that human parents are fallible and can disfigure the face of fatherhood and motherhood. We ought therefore to recall that God transcends the human distinction between the sexes. He is neither man nor woman: he is God. He also transcends human fatherhood and motherhood, although he is their origin and standard: no one is father as God is Father. (CCC, no. 239)

Jesus revealed God as *Father* in a new sense. God is Father in his relation to Jesus, his only begotten Son. At the Last Supper, Jesus calls God 'Father' forty-five times (cf. Jn 13–17). The Son is divine, as is the Father (cf. Mt 11:27). In a later chapter, Jesus as the Second Person of the Trinity will be discussed further.

Before the Passion, Jesus promised to send the Holy Spirit as teacher, guide and consoler. The Spirit's appearance at Pentecost and at other events in the New Testament gives ample evidence of the Holy Spirit as the third Person of the Trinity. This, too, will be discussed in a later chapter.

The mystery of the Holy Trinity is the central mystery of the Christian faith and life. God reveals himself as Father, Son and Holy Spirit. The doctrine of the Trinity includes three truths of faith.

First, the Trinity is One. We do not speak of three gods but of one God. Each of the Persons is fully God. They are a unity of Persons in one divine nature.

Second, the Divine Persons are distinct from each other. Father, Son and Spirit are not three appearances or modes of God, but three identifiable persons, each fully God in a way distinct from the others.

Third, the Divine Persons are in relation to each other. The distinction of each is understood only in reference to the others. The Father cannot be the Father without the Son, nor can the Son be the Son without the Father. The Holy Spirit is related to the Father and the Son who both send him forth.

All Christians are baptised in the name of the Father and of the Son and of the Holy Spirit. The Trinity illumines all the other mysteries of faith.

GOD IS CREATOR OF HEAVEN AND EARTH

The first line of the Bible says, 'In the beginning God created heaven and earth' (Gn 1:1). The first three chapters of the Book of Genesis have shaped the religious thought of Jews and Christians; indeed they have shaped the literature of the Western world – about God as 'Creator of heaven and earth' (Apostles' Creed), 'of all things visible and invisible' (Nicene Creed), and about the creation of the human race, of the Fall and of the promise of salvation through the story of Adam and Eve. These three chapters must be read by anyone who wants to understand the meaning of the world and humanity.

Catechesis on creation is of major importance. Where do we come from? Where are we going? These two questions about our origin and our end are the underlying issues of the human search for meaning. These are the questions that the Bible helps us to answer.

Beginning with Genesis, all Scripture states the following truths in relation to God's work of creation:

- *God created the world out of his wisdom and love.* Creation is not the result of blind fate or complete chance;
- *God made the universe 'out of nothing'.* This means that the world is not a 'part' of God or made from some pre-existing substance. The world depends on God for its existence; God is independent of his creation and distinct from it, even though creation is sustained in existence by his Providence: 'It is in him that we live, and move, and exist,' as St Paul preached to the people of Athens (Acts 17:28);
- *Creation reflects God's goodness and wisdom.* The creation story in Genesis affirms the goodness of creation: 'God saw all he had made, and indeed it was very good' (Gn 1:31). Because the universe is destined for the human family, whom he calls to a personal relationship with himself, it is ordered in a way that allows the human intellect to perceive God's hand working in and through it. As the *Dogmatic Constitution on Divine Revelation (Dei Verbum)* of the Second Vatican Council teaches, 'God who creates and conserves all things by his Word (cf. Jn 1:3), provides men with constant evidence of himself in created realities' (DV, no. 3; cf. Rm 1:19-20).

The answers to questions about the origins of the world and humanity provided by God's own Revelation are intimately linked with the meaning and purpose of the world and humanity. This provides a distinctive worldview that differs dramatically from those shaped by other philosophies and points of view. In Pantheism, the development of the world is identified with the development of God. In Dualism, our origins are explained by the perpetual conflict of good and evil. According to Deism, God abandons the world, once made, to itself. There is also materialism, in which the world is understood to have come from preexisting matter that developed naturally and not as a result of any type of divine action or plan.

THE ANGELS

It is a truth of faith that God, the 'maker ... of all that is seen and unseen', created a realm of spiritual beings who do not share the limitations of a physical body and yet exist as the result of his all-powerful, loving act of creation. We call these spiritual beings *angels*. 'As purely spiritual creatures angels have intelligence and will: they are personal and immortal creatures, surpassing in perfection all visible creatures, as the splendour of their glory bears witness' (CCC, no. 330). Angels glorify God and work for our salvation. The Church celebrates the memory of certain angels (St Michael, St Gabriel and St Raphael) who were God's messengers.

Some of the angels turned against God and were driven out of heaven and into hell. Their leader is called Satan, and they are referred to as devils or demons in Scripture. They tempt us to evil (cf. CCC, nos. 391, 1707). But their power is limited and is never greater than God's.

THE VISIBLE WORLD

In the first of two creation stories (cf. Gn 1–2:4), Scripture describes the creation of the visible world as a succession of six days of divine 'work', after which God 'rested' on the seventh day, the Sabbath. From the earliest times, Christian writers and biblical scholars have been aware that the language in the story is symbolic, for the six 'days' of creation could hardly be solar days, since Genesis says that the sun was not made until the fourth day. The sequence of creation reported in Chapter 1 of the Book of Genesis is not literal or scientific, but poetic and theological. It describes a hierarchy of creatures in which human beings are the summit of visible creation. By ending the sequence of creation with the Sabbath, the story points to the adoration of God the Creator as the focal point of all the works of creation. 'The heavens declare the glory of God, / and the firmament proclaims the work of his hands' (Ps 19:2).

The *Dogmatic Constitution on Divine Revelation* of the Second Vatican Council reminds us that 'in Sacred Scripture, God speaks through human beings in human fashion', and that if we are 'to ascertain what God has wished to communicate to us, [we] should carefully search out the meaning which the sacred writers really had in mind' (DV, no. 12). It goes on to say, 'In determining the intention of the sacred writers, attention must be paid, *inter alia* [among other things], to literary forms'. Chapters 1 and 2 of Genesis use symbolic language to convey fundamental truths about God and ourselves.

It may be helpful to recall how important symbols are in everyday human life. Being a unity of body and spirit, we express and perceive spiritual realities through material symbols. God also speaks to us through visible creation: light and darkness, wind and fire, water and earth, trees and their fruit. Scripture uses all these to speak of God and to symbolise his greatness and his nearness.

In language, symbols are often used to communicate a truth. Symbolic language in Scripture, as in literature in general, may use poetry, parable, story comparisons or metaphors, or other literary forms. In today's world, we often use novels, films, plays, songs and other creative works to communicate reality in a manner that simple factual presentations cannot do as effectively.

Through the stories of creation in Chapters 1 and 2 of Genesis, God reveals himself as the Creator of all that exists, showing particularly a tender love for the high point of his creation: man and woman. The majesty and wisdom of God's creation are celebrated in the eloquence of the prophets, the lyricism of the Psalms and the Wisdom writings of the Old Testament. Through his Incarnation, death and Resurrection, Jesus Christ renews all creation, making it his own and filling it with the Holy Spirit.

DIVINE PROVIDENCE

God guides his creation toward its completion or perfection through what we call his *Divine Providence*. This means that God has absolute sovereignty over all that he has made and guides his creation according to the divine plan of his will. At the same time, both the evidence of the world that we discover by our human endeavours and the testimony of Sacred Scripture show that for the unfolding of his plan, God uses secondary causes, including the laws of physics, chemistry and biology, as well as the cooperation of our own human intellect and will. The Father of all continues to work with his Son, who is eternal Wisdom, and with the Holy Spirit, who is the inexhaustible source of life, to guide creation and humanity to the fullness of God's truth, goodness and beauty.

THE REALITY OF EVIL

If God has created all things to be good and cares providentially for his creation, why does evil exist? There is no quick answer to this challenging question. Christian faith, after centuries of reflecting on the answers revealed in the Bible, provides the only comprehensive answer. This answer includes the drama of sin, the love of God who sent his only Son to be our Redeemer and Saviour, and the call of God to sinful humanity to repent and to love him in return.

We may ask why God did not create a world so perfect that no evil could exist in it. God freely willed to create a world that is not immediately at its state of ultimate perfection, but one that must journey toward that perfection through time. 'In God's plan this process of becoming involves the appearance of certain beings and the disappearance of others, the existence of the more perfect alongside the less perfect, both constructive and destructive forces of nature' (CCC, no. 310). Physical evil can thus exist alongside physical good because creation has not reached its ultimate perfection. On this journey, created realities remain limited and thus subject to decay and death.

As intelligent and free creatures, both angels and human beings must make their way to their ultimate destinies by using their intellect and will to make free choices. They can and must choose between loving God – who has shown his love for them in creation and Revelation – and loving something else. Thus moral evil – the evil of sin – can also exist in this state of journeying (cf. CCC, nos. 309–313). God permits such moral evil in part out of respect for the gift of freedom with which he endowed created beings. But his response to moral evil is an even greater act of love through the sending of his Son who offers his life to bring us back to God. 'Who for our sake paid Adam's debt to the eternal Father, and, pouring out his own dear Blood, wiped clean the record of our ancient sinfulness ... O truly necessary sin of Adam ... O happy fault that earned so great, so glorious a Redeemer!' (Easter Proclamation [*Exsultet*] at the Easter Vigil).

Saint Catherine of Siena said, to 'those who are scandalised and rebel against what happens to them': 'Everything comes from love, all is ordained for the salvation of man, God does nothing without this goal in mind' (*Dialogue on Providence*, chap. IV, 138).

ISSUES OF FAITH AND SCIENCE

Catholic philosophy and theology have traditionally held that the human intellect comes to know the truth through scientific discovery and philosophical reasoning and can even come to a knowledge of God and many of his purposes through an understanding of created realities.

The *Pastoral Constitution on the Church in the Modern World* (*Gaudium et Spes*; GS) of the Second Vatican Council teaches that 'methodical research in all branches of knowledge, provided it is carried out in a truly scientific manner and does not override moral laws, can never conflict with the faith, because the things of the world and the things of faith derive from the same God. The humble and persevering investigator of the secrets of nature is being led, as it were, by the hand of God in spite of himself, for it is God, the conserver of all things, who made them what they are' (CCC, no. 159, citing GS, no. 36).

Enlightenment thinking deeply affected educated opinion in Europe and the English-speaking world in the eighteenth and nineteenth century. Its religious counterpart was Deism, which claimed that while God exists, he simply created the world and left us to our own devices. Irish Catholic thinking was not greatly influenced by Deism in the past, but with more

FROM THE CATECHISM

1. What does faith in God mean?

It means coming to know God's greatness and majesty. It means living in thanksgiving. It means knowing the unity and true dignity of all men. It means making good use of created things. It means trusting in God, even in adversity. (CCC, nos. 223–227)

2. Why does the Creed begin with God?

Our profession of faith begins with *God*, for God is the First and the Last, the beginning and the end of everything. The [Creed] begins with God the *Father*, for the Father is the first divine person of the Most Holy Trinity; our Creed begins with the creation of heaven and earth, for creation is the beginning and foundation of all God's works. (CCC, no. 198)

3. What is the importance of God's Revelation about creation?

Creation is the foundation of 'all God's saving plans', the 'beginning of the history of salvation' that culminates in Christ. Conversely, the mystery of Christ casts conclusive light on the mystery of creation and reveals the end for which 'in the beginning God created the heavens and the earth': from the beginning, God envisioned the glory of the new creation in Christ. (CCC, no. 280, citing the *General Catechetical Directory*, no. 51, and Gn 1:1)

education in recent decades, the average Irish person now could well be an unacknowledged Deist. Irish people may not be as aware of God being present or his power exercised or his will being done at all times in the world around us as, for example, our grandparents were, who said 'God willing', or 'Please God' at every eventuality. But even for today's Irish Catholic, an unconscious Deism is often combined with a deep faith in God's providence for the individual human being, for instance in the areas of sickness, welfare, vocation and family.

The Catechism highlights the importance of the teaching on Creation. The doctrine of Creation means that the world is not God, but is not independent of God, and, crucially, that God is not the world. We may not be always conscious of the power of God during our everyday lives but it is the case that our individual origin and continued existence depends totally upon the will of God, whether or not we are aware of it. This is the bottom line in belief for the Catholic, for the Christian, and indeed for many religious people. But holding to the truth that God created the world by no means impedes Catholic and Christian scientists from engaging in scientific research.

This does not mean that there have not been conflicts between science and religion. For example, in the seventeenth century, Galileo, building on previous discoveries, held firmly to the conviction that the earth moves around the sun. This was not acceptable to many of his contemporaries, including Church authorities. As a result, he was subjected to a Church investigation and placed under house arrest for the rest of his life. Saint John Paul II ordered a study of Galileo's case, which resulted in his exoneration in 1992.

In modern times, the scientific teaching on evolution has also led to difficulty for Christians. In America and in the United Kingdom (including Northern Ireland), the debate about evolution has become polarised between biblical literalism and Darwinism, when, in fact, there are many who accept physical and biological evolution as the work of the divine Creator. Catholics in general, and Irish Catholics in particular, while maybe tending towards Deism theologically and philosophically, have less difficulty with the Bible being interpreted spiritually or analogically or symbolically or in narrative terms. Hence in Ireland, the evolution debate has never been so sharp nor so divisive in educational terms as in other English-speaking lands.

The Catholic Church, however, has continued to uphold the principle that there is no intrinsic conflict between science and religion. In his 1950 encyclical *Concerning Some False Opinions Threatening to Undermine the Foundations of Catholic Doctrine (Humani Generis),* Pope Pius XII applied this principle to the controversial theories of evolution, which have often been used in a materialistic or agnostic sense to argue against any divine intervention in the work of creation: 'The [Magisterium] of the Church does not forbid that, in conformity with the present state of human sciences

FROM SAINT JOHN PAUL II

The Bible itself speaks to us of the origin of the universe and its makeup, not in order to provide us with a scientific treatise but in order to state the correct relationship of humanity with God and the universe. Sacred Scripture wishes simply to declare that the world was created by God. (St John Paul II, Address to the Pontifical Academy of Sciences [3 October 1981])

and sacred theology, research and discussions, on the part of [people] experienced in both fields, take place with regard to the doctrine of evolution, in as far as it inquires into the origin of the human body as coming from pre-existent and living matter' (no. 36). At the same time, Pope Pius XII reiterated the doctrine that each human soul is immortal and individually created by God.

Saint John Paul II made a further commentary on this question in his 1996 Message to the Pontifical Academy of Sciences. While acknowledging the scientific evidence in favour of evolution, he cautioned that the theories of evolution that consider the human soul the seat of the intellect and will by which the human person comes to know and love God 'as emerging from forces of living matter' would not be compatible with the truth about the dignity of the human person as taught in Revelation. This position does not conflict with the nature of scientific methodology in the various fields, since their method is one of observation and correlation. The spiritual dimension of the human person is of a different order that is related to, yet transcends, the material world, and that is not reducible simply to the physical aspects of our being, which can be more readily studied by the scientific method.

Among scientists, a lively debate about aspects of Darwin's theory of natural selection as the key to evolutionary hypothesis continues. Christian faith does not require the acceptance of any particular theory of evolution, nor does it forbid it, provided that the particular theory is not strictly materialistic and does not deny what is essential to the spiritual essence of the human person, namely that God creates each human soul directly to share immortal life with him. At a popular level, the Bible itself speaks to us of the origin of the universe and its make-up, not in order to provide us with a scientific treatise but in order to state the correct relationship of humanity with God and the universe. Sacred Scripture wishes simply to declare that the world was created by God (St John Paul II, Address to the Pontifical Academy of Sciences [3 October 1981]). The Bible is not a scientific textbook and should never be read as such; rather it reveals what God wants us to know for the sake of our salvation.

FOR DISCUSSION

1. Knowing that God is rich in mercy and that he is love, how does this affect your attitude toward him? Toward your neighbour?
2. How did God progressively reveal his mystery as a unity of three Persons? How would you teach the doctrine about God to others?
3. What are some practical ways you would reply to creationists and atheistic evolutionists? Why is the dialogue between religion and science necessary and valuable?
4. What is your personal position about the presence of God in your life? Does God affect every aspect of your life? Of the lives of others? Of the course of history? Of the movements of the visible universe? Of your personal destiny? Of your ultimate happiness?

DOCTRINAL STATEMENTS

- God is a holy mystery. As the Byzantine Church sings, 'You are God, ineffable, inconceivable, incomprehensible, always existing and ever the same, You and Your only begotten Son and Your Holy Spirit' (Anaphora of the Liturgy of St John Chrysostom).
- The Old Testament reveals God as One, unique and without equal. 'Listen, Israel, the Lord our God is the one, only Lord' (Deut 6:4; Mk 12:29).
- Our faith in God, the only One, leads us to adore him as our origin and destiny and to love him with all our hearts.
- God is truth. 'Yes, Lord ... you are God indeed, your words are true' (2 Sm 7:28). His words cannot deceive. This is why we can trust his truth

and fidelity. Saint John goes further when he writes, 'God is love' (1 Jn 4:8).

- The mystery of the Holy Trinity is the central mystery of the Christian faith and life. God alone reveals himself as Father, Son and Holy Spirit.
- Jesus revealed God as *Father* in a new sense. God is Father in relation to his only Son. The Son is divine, as is the Father. The Father testified to the unique relationship of Jesus to him as his Son at the baptism in the Jordan and at the Transfiguration: 'This is my Son, the Beloved' (Mt 3:17, 17:5).
- Before the Passion, Jesus promised to send the Holy Spirit as teacher, guide and consoler. The revelation of the Holy Spirit at Pentecost and in the rest of the New Testament testify to his divinity.
- We do not speak of three gods in the Trinity, but of one God. Father, Son and Spirit are not three modes of God, but three distinct Persons who are the same divine being. They are also in relation to each other, for all three Persons work together in the works of creation, Redemption and sanctification.
- God is almighty. The Church often addresses God as almighty, believing that nothing is impossible with him. He shows almighty power by converting us from our sins and by restoring us to grace.
- For some, the presence of evil in the world raises questions. However, God sheds some light of understanding on the mystery of evil through the death and Resurrection of his Son. Faith in the Resurrection gives us hope. Full understanding will come only in eternal life.
- God alone created the universe freely and without any help. No creature can create or call into being something or someone 'out of nothing', as he did.
- God created the world to show forth and share divine glory. We are called to share in his truth, goodness and beauty.
- God keeps the world in existence by the power of the Son and by the Holy Spirit as giver of life. Through Divine Providence, God guides all creatures with wisdom and love to their final goal.
- Angels are spiritual creatures who glorify God and work for our salvation. The Church venerates angels who help her on the pilgrimage to God and protect every human being.
- Some angels turned against God and were driven from his presence. Led by Satan and followers, called devils, they tempt us to evil.

MEDITATION

God's Providential Care

God has a special love for every human person and a special plan for each of us. Often enough, God's plan is not what we would expect. Look at the lives of great people like St John Paul II or Blessed Teresa of Calcutta. During World War II, Karol Wojtyła (St John Paul II) was a labourer and an actor, but led by God, he entered an underground seminary. Born in Albania, Blessed Teresa found herself seeking out the dying in the gutters of Calcutta. Have the lives of these two unfolded according to their original plans? Surely not. If and when we accept God's love in our lives, he can ask surprising and sometimes challenging things of us.

Why do so many of us tend to brush aside God's plan for us in our lives? It seems to be because we find it hard to imagine how he can be so loving to us, especially in awkward surroundings. Yet if the divine Word of God could become one of us by taking on our human nature with the cooperation of a young woman in Nazareth, God can surely touch our lives.

PRAYER

Act of Faith

O my God, I firmly believe that you are one God
in three divine Persons, Father, Son and Holy Spirit;
I believe that your divine Son became man and died for our sins,
and that he will come to judge the living and the dead.
I believe these and all the truths which the Holy Catholic
Church teaches,
because you have revealed them,
who can neither deceive nor be deceived.

My Lord and my God, give me everything
that brings me closer to you.

– St Nicholas of Flüe

6 MAN AND WOMAN IN THE BEGINNING

THE CREATION OF MAN AND WOMAN, THE FALL AND THE PROMISE – CCC, NOS. 355–421

SAINT VINCENT DE PAUL: SAINT OF GOD'S LOVE

Thousands of people around the world are members of the Society of St Vincent de Paul. But Vincent de Paul was not the founder of the society that bears his name. That was done by Blessed Frederic Ozanam, two hundred years later, and you can read that story in Chapter 31.

Vincent de Paul was born in 1581 in a small village called Pouy (but now called Vincent de Paul) in the south of France. A family friend who was a lawyer saw to it that Vincent was sent to school and eventually to college, encouraging his father to contribute what he could. Vincent himself started a small school to help with his expenses. He was ordained a priest at the early age of twenty.

Then Vincent disappears for a few years. Later he explained that he had been kidnapped by pirates and sold as a slave in North Africa. He wrote letters that tell the tale graphically. He had worked, in turn, for a fisherman, an alchemist, and then for a lapsed Catholic who had converted to Islam, marrying three wives. Vincent eventually persuaded the man to escape with him by boat to Italy and return to the Church.

Some historians think that it could not have happened that way. Others judge that Vincent should be taken at his word. No one, however, doubts that Vincent originated the story himself. In any case, whatever happened, it was a big interruption to his career plans. Ever the networker, he arrived in Paris, making contacts with sponsors and influential people who could help him find a parish or chaplaincy with

73

a good living attached. But a couple of upsets awaited, which placed even his priestly vocation itself in jeopardy.

First, he was falsely accused of theft, a charge which hung over him for six years. Vincent resolved to react patiently, despite his normal assertive manner, until he was eventually cleared. Then Vincent was tempted to abandon the faith. He was so afflicted that he prayed to God to be relieved. His prayer was answered, but the bout of unbelief lasted for years. The despair lifted only when he decided to dedicate his life to the service of the poor and the spread of the Gospel.

Conversions are seldom abrupt and sudden. Vincent had been in touch during this period with a number of reforming priests and bishops who were intent upon renewing the French Church. Vincent was deeply influenced by them. In particular, he was coming to realise that the will of God was at work in his own life, sweeping him on like a leaf on a river.

Vincent tried to decide exactly what God wanted for him. His lay contacts – especially Madame De Gondi who gave him opportunities to work as a priest – inspired him by introducing him to the country people on the family's large estates. Her husband, a naval commander, took the young priest to meet the prisoners condemned to the French convict galleys. Vincent arrived at the conclusion that God was calling him to preach the Good News of Jesus to the poor.

One tip Vincent learned during his 'dark night of the soul' was that a gesture or action could indicate a sincere belief or deep conviction. He had advised others to point at a church building as a sign of belief in God. He himself wrote out a copy of the Creed, placed it in his breast pocket, and put his hand on it as a prayer of faith. It was a small step to conclude that one's personal contact with poor people is necessary if a Christian is to spread the Good News of the Gospel and fulfil the command to love the neighbour as oneself for the love of God. The work is the prayer.

In 1617, at the age of thirty-six, Vincent turned to the task of evangelising the poor. He began to organise independent lay groups in each parish he visited, called Confraternities of Charity, to provide help and material assistance to the poor of the district. A unique feature of these groups was Vincent's insistence on lay leadership. In 1625, the De Gondis funded a group of priests under his direction, the Congregation of the Mission (CM), to conduct retreats and missions in the country districts. Today they are known in Ireland as the Vincentian Fathers.

The well-off people of the Confraternities sometimes needed help themselves to provide care for poor sick people. Vincent proposed others to supplement their efforts. A co-worker from his early efforts in parish renewal, Louise de Marillac (Mademoiselle Le Gras), masterminded the new foundation. The result is the Company of Daughters of Charity, the largest Catholic order in the world today. Louise was often considered to be in Vincent's shadow, but recently her true stature has been revealed as a founder in her own right, an effective manager and a true original mind.

Vincent never lost his interest in raising money, nor his flair for making connections. Throughout his life, he cultivated friends in high places. The difference was, however, that now both were for the love of God, the preaching of the Gospel and charity for the poor. All the resources he acquired were for the poor and their care.

Vincent was a natural team-player, able to collaborate with anybody, high up or low down, provided that the Kingdom of God was being advanced. He moved easily through the salons of the famous to the hovels of the poor. He was a driven man, urged on by the love of God for us and the love we should extend to our fellow men and women. 'The poor are our masters,' he said, in the words of St Philip Neri. 'We leave God to go to God,' he would encourage the Daughters of Charity, indicating that Christ was to be found in every poor person we encounter.

Both Vincent and Louise died in the same year, 1660. It was indeed appropriate that two people who collaborated so closely in charity went to their reward together.

CREATED IN GOD'S IMAGE

God willed the diversity of his creatures and their own particular goodness, their interdependence and their order. He destined all material creatures for the good of the human race. Man, and through him all creation, is destined for the glory of God.

– CCC, no. 353

'God created man in the image of himself … male and female he created them' (Gn 1:27). In figurative and symbolic language, Scripture describes God's creating the first man and woman, Adam and Eve, and placing them in Paradise. They were created in friendship with God and in harmony with creation. The Church teaches that theirs was a state of original holiness and justice, with no suffering or death (cf. CCC, no. 376; GS, no. 18).

The first man and woman were qualitatively different from and superior to all other living creatures on earth. They were uniquely made in the image of God, as are all human beings, their descendants. What does this mean? God's image is not a static picture stamped on our souls. God's image is a dynamic source of inner spiritual energy drawing our minds and hearts toward truth and love, and to God himself, the source of all truth and love.

To be made in the image of God includes specific qualities. Each of us is capable of self-knowledge and of entering into communion with other persons through self-giving. These qualities – and the shared heritage of our first parents – also form a basis for a bond of unity among all human beings. To be made in God's image also unites human beings as God's stewards in the care of the earth and of all God's other creatures.

Another important aspect of our creation is that God has made us a unity of body and soul. The human soul is not only the source of physical life for our bodies but is also the core of our spiritual powers of knowing and loving. While our bodies come into being through physical processes, our souls are all created directly by God.

God created man and woman, equal to each other as persons and in dignity. Each is completely human and is meant to complement the other in a communion of persons, seen most evidently in marriage.

Finally, we need to recognise that God created the first humans in a state of original holiness and justice, so that we are able to live in harmony with his plan. By his gracious will, he enabled us to know and love him, thus calling us to share his life. Our first parents also had free will and thus could be tempted by created things to turn away from the Creator.

THE FALL

The doctrine of original sin is, so to speak, the 'reverse side' of the Good News that Jesus is the Saviour of all men, that all need salvation, and that salvation is offered to all through Christ.

– CCC, no. 389

Why is it that, with the best of intentions, we find it so difficult to do what is right? We can look for an explanation in the opening chapters of the Book of Genesis. Here the seemingly endless struggle between good and evil is described in the imagery of the serpent tempting Adam and Eve with the forbidden fruit.

God said to them, 'You are free to eat of all the trees in the garden. But of the tree of the knowledge of good and evil you are not to eat; for, the day you eat of that, you are doomed to die' (Gn 2:16-17). The tempter, however, said, 'No! You will not die! God knows in fact that the day you eat it your eyes will be opened and you will be like gods, knowing good from evil' (Gn 3:4-5). Adam and Eve chose their own desires, based on a lie, over God's will and plan. Sin entered the world through this decision to choose themselves over God and his plan.

Through the Fall of Adam and Eve, the harmony of creation was also destroyed. If we continue to read the Book of Genesis, we see how Adam and Eve became aware of their sinful condition, were driven out of the garden, and were forced to live by the sweat of their brow. The beauty and harmony of God's creative plan was disrupted. This was not the way it was meant to be. Once sin entered into life and into our world, all harmony with God, with self, with each other and with the world around us was shattered. We call the Fall and its results 'Original Sin'.

Each one of us is heir to Adam and Eve. Their sin shattered God's created harmony, not only for them but also for us. We experience the effects of Original Sin in our daily life. This explains why it is so difficult to do good or to do what we should.

UNDERSTANDING THE IMPACT OF ORIGINAL SIN

Scripture uses figurative language in describing the account of the Fall in Genesis 3 but affirms an event that took place at the beginning of human history. The language is figurative, but the reality is not a fantasy. The gift of freedom, given to the first man and woman, was meant to draw them closer to God, to each other and to their destiny. God asked them – as he asks us – to recognise their human limits and to trust in him. In the temptation, they were lured into trying to surpass their being human. 'You will be like gods' (Gn 3:5). They abused their freedom, failed to trust God and disobeyed his command. They lost paradise and its gifts. And death became part of the human experience. For the people of ancient Israel, sin was a spiritual death that leads to separation from God, the source of life, and consequently, to the death of the body.

The sin of Adam and Eve has been called Original Sin since the time of St Augustine (AD 354–430). But the Church's belief in an ancient alienation from God was part of Revelation from the start.

What is Original Sin? It is a deprivation, a loss of the original holiness and righteousness with which our first parents were created. When God made them, he filled Adam and Eve with all the grace and virtue they would ever need, and they experienced a close relationship with God beyond our ability to know. Because of the unity of the human race, everyone is affected by the sin of our first parents, just as, in turn, humanity is restored to a right relationship with God by Jesus Christ. 'It was through one man that sin *came into the world*, and through sin death, and ... Just as by one man's disobedience many were made sinners, so by one man's obedience are many to be made upright ... however much sin increased, grace was always greater' (Rm 5:12, 19, 20b). Though Original Sin has had far-reaching consequences, of greater consequence has been God's mercy to us through the death and Resurrection of Jesus Christ.

Do we commit Original Sin? Original sin 'is a sin "contracted" and not "committed" – a state and not an act' (CCC, no. 404). Each of us inherits Original Sin, but it is not a personal fault of ours. It is a deprivation for each of us of original holiness and justice. This inheritance leaves us in a world that is subject to suffering and death, as well as in an environment in which the accumulated sins and failings of others disturb peace and order.

FROM THE CATECHISM

1. What are some implications of being made in the image of God?
Of all visible creatures only man is 'able to know and love his creator' (GS, no. 12). He is 'the only creature on earth that God has willed for its own sake' (GS, no. 24), and he alone is called to share, by knowledge and love, in God's own life. (CCC, no. 356)

2. What is the main result of Original Sin?
By his sin, Adam, as the first man, lost the original holiness and justice he had received from God, not only for himself but for all human beings. (CCC, no. 416)

3. Why didn't God prevent the first man from sinning?
God gave us free will and would not interfere with the use of our free will:

> Christ's inexpressible grace gave us blessings better than those the demon's envy had taken away. (CCC, no. 412, citing St Leo the Great, *Sermo* 73, no. 4)

What is the effect of Original Sin upon us? Original Sin underlies all other sins and causes our natural powers of knowing and loving to be wounded. We are subject to ignorance, which makes it difficult for us to know the truth, and for some, even to believe that truth exists. We also endure suffering and death and have a disorder in our appetites and an inclination to sin. This inclination is called *concupiscence*. Because sin alienates us from each other, it weakens our ability to live fully Christ's commandment of love for one another.

It is Jesus Christ who frees us from Original Sin and our own actual sins. By Baptism, we share in the redemptive act of Jesus' death and Resurrection, are freed from Original Sin and are strengthened against the power of sin and death. We are reconciled to God and made members of his holy people, the Church.

UNDERSTANDING SIN

In recent times the comment frequently arises, What's happened to sin? Where has sin gone? There is a perceptible discomfort in our culture with the notion of sin as an evil for which we must give an account to God, our Creator, Redeemer and Judge. This tendency applies not just to everyday evil acts, but even more so to Original Sin, something that seems to have little to do with us. The origin of this attitude may be found in an underdeveloped sense of Revelation: 'Without the knowledge Revelation gives of God we cannot recognise sin clearly and are tempted to explain it as merely a developmental flaw, a psychological weakness, a mistake ... Only in the knowledge of God's plan ... can we grasp that sin is an abuse of the freedom that God gives to created persons' (CCC, no. 387).

Connected with this is the popular notion or attitude of self-help. According to this attitude, all we need to do is fill the mind with lots of inspirational knowledge and reach out for insights. In this viewpoint, we are able to resolve all our shortfalls by ourselves. But sin is not a weakness we can overcome by our own effort. It is a condition from which we need to be saved. Jesus is our Saviour.

Central to our journey of faith is the awareness of forces within us that oppose each other and cause us conflict. One drive flows from our being created in the image of God, with all the gifts and abilities that brings. The other force results from the effects of Original Sin, which can cause us to act with selfishness and malice. In his Letter to the Romans, St Paul describes his own experience of this conflict: 'I do not understand my own behaviour; I do not act as I mean to, but I do things that I hate ... the good thing I want to do, I never do; the evil thing which I do not want' (Rm 7:15, 19). He had actually met the Risen Lord Jesus in an extraordinary vision on the Damascus Road and later saw eternal glory itself (cf. 2 Cor 12:2). But he still experienced the inner war within his soul caused by the after-effects of Original Sin. In maddening frustration, he cried out, 'What a wretched man I am! Who will rescue me from this body doomed to death?' (Rm 7:24). It was his faith that 'however much sin increased, grace was always greater' (Rm 5:20).

No matter how sinful we human beings become, the desire for God never dies while we are on earth. No matter how holy we grow, the sting of evil always gnaws at us from the effects of Original Sin. Saint Paul shared with us his spiritual struggle on the journey to holiness. He gives us courage. In Jesus Christ, we can overcome the power of sin, for it is the Lord's desire that all come to salvation.

FOR DISCUSSION

1. When you hear yourself described as being created in the image of God, what comes to your mind? What would help you perceive that being made in God's image encourages you to do good things? How should a person created in God's image live?
2. Why do you think some people are not comfortable with the teachings about Original Sin and their personal sins? Saint Paul writes, 'the good thing I want to do, I never do; the evil thing which I do not want' (Rm 7:19). He discovered an inner war between evil and good. In what ways could you identify with his analysis?
3. Why do some people think they can win salvation on their own? Why is that approach mistaken? Why is Jesus the answer to the need for salvation?

DOCTRINAL STATEMENTS

- God created man and woman in his image as his creatures called to love and to serve him and to care for creation.
- Each person is a unity of body and soul. God directly creates the immortal soul of each human being.
- God created human beings as male and female, equal to each other as persons and in dignity. Man and woman complement each other in a communion of persons.
- 'Because of its common origin *the human race forms a unity* for "from one ancestor [God] made all nations to inhabit the whole earth" … "This law of human solidarity and charity", without excluding the rich variety of persons, cultures and peoples, assures us that all men are truly brethren' (CCC, nos. 360–361, citing Acts 17:26 and Pope Pius XII, *Summi Pontificatus*, no. 3).

- Revelation teaches about the state of original holiness and justice of man and woman before sin. Their happiness flowed from their friendship with God.
- The account of the Fall in Genesis 3 uses figurative language, but it affirms a primeval event, a sin that took place at the beginning of history (cf. CCC, no. 390).
- Tempted by the Evil One, man and woman abused their freedom. They opposed God and separated themselves from him.
- 'By his sin Adam, as the first man, lost the original holiness and justice he had received from God, not only for himself, but for all human beings' (CCC, no. 416).
- Adam and Eve transmitted to all future generations a human nature wounded by their sin and deprived of original holiness and justice. This deprivation is called Original Sin.
- Because of Original Sin, human nature is subject to ignorance, suffering, death, disorder in our appetites and an inclination to sin – an inclination called concupiscence.
- But the victory over sin that Jesus accomplished has provided greater blessings than those taken away. 'However much sin increased, grace was always greater' (Rm 5:20). Baptism delivers us from Original Sin.
- Because every human being is made in the image of God, each one has a desire for union with God. Humanity has been reconciled to God by the redemptive death and Resurrection of Jesus Christ.

MEDITATION

Although set by God in a state of rectitude, man, enticed by the evil one, abused his freedom at the very start of history. He lifted himself up against God, and sought to attain his goal apart from him. Although they had known God, they did not glorify him as God, but their senseless minds were darkened and they served the creature rather than the creator (cf. Rm 1:21-25). What Revelation makes known to us is confirmed by our own experience. For when man looks into his own heart he finds that he is drawn towards what is wrong and sunk in many evils which cannot come from his good creator. Often refusing to acknowledge God as his beginning, man has also upset the relationship which should link him to his last end; and at the same time he has broken the right order that should reign within himself as well as between himself and other men and all creatures.

Man therefore is divided in himself. As a result, the whole life of men, both individual and social, shows itself to be a struggle, and a dramatic one, between good and evil, between light and darkness. Man finds that he is unable of himself to overcome the assaults of evil successfully, so that everyone feels as though he is bound by chains. But the Lord himself came to free and strengthen man, renewing him inwardly and casting out that 'prince of this world' (Jn 12:31), who held him in the bondage of sin (cf. Jn 8:34). For sin brought man to a lower state, forcing him away from the completeness that is his to attain.

Both the high calling and the deep misery which men experience find their final explanation in the light of this Revelation.

– GS, no. 13

PRAYER

We adore you, O Christ, and we praise you,
Because by your holy Cross you have redeemed the world.

Where is the heart that loves? In the thing that it loves. Consequently, where our love is, there our heart is captive. It cannot escape, it cannot reach higher or go to right or left: there it is fixed. Where the miser's treasure is, there is his heart: where our heart is, there is our treasure. And it is a sad thing that the things that hold us captive are for the most part quite unworthy things. It is self-love that attaches and binds us to the very sorts of things that most disturb us and upset us. Our passions enslave us.

– St Vincent de Paul

7 THE GOOD NEWS: GOD HAS SENT HIS SON

SON OF GOD, SON OF MARY,
MYSTERIES OF CHRIST'S LIFE
– CCC, NOS. 422–570

THE BISHOP AND THE MEDICAL MISSIONARY: JOSEPH SHANAHAN AND MARY MARTIN

Pioneers are seldom well-prepared. Their ships are unseaworthy by the standards of subsequent times. They underestimate dangers, rely too much on luck and good fortune, and hope that favourable conditions always attend their travels. They do not thoroughly research their destination. They have no adequate map of the land. They fail to prepare the expedition properly. All this, of course, is strictly in hindsight. Pioneers are those who first see unexplored territory, and lured by the unknown, set off in high and enthusiastic expectation. No one has been there before or returned to tell them anything before they depart. We cannot blame them for their ignorance.

Early Christian missionaries to West Africa were like that. West Africa was known as 'the White Man's Grave', and with good reason. The climate was hot and humid. Living conditions were unhealthy and the foreign missionaries were open to infection. Food was plentiful but unfamiliar to northern digestion. The missionaries were very isolated. It took time to realise what was needed and to organise a systematic and ultimately very successful mission. Two of the key people who accomplished that were Bishop Joseph Shanahan and Mother Mary Martin.

Joseph Shanahan was born in Glankeen, Co. Tipperary on 6 June 1871. He attended Rockwell College, a Holy Ghost school, because a relative was in the order and he had inspired the young lad to become a missionary in Africa. Shanahan was ordained in 1900 and sent to Onitsha, Nigeria in 1902.

Father Shanahan was a strong young man, tall and robust, striking in appearance, resolute and determined in character. He made an immediate impression. Within three years, Shanahan had been appointed Prefect-Apostolic for the territory of southern Nigeria. He decided to concentrate on what is now called infrastructure. He built churches and priests' houses to provide a healthy and supportive environment for the missionaries. He discerned that education was the lever of progress for the people and undertook to found schools, source teachers and provide books and materials. Due to lack of priests and nuns, he proceeded to train and employ lay catechists for the villages. He decided to travel to the tribes in the interior, negotiating with chiefs, baptising children and setting up parishes and schools.

Priests were needed for the mission and Shanahan returned to Europe in 1913 to recruit students. He met with failure in Ireland, France and Rome, and returned to Africa disappointed. By the end of his next tour of duty in 1920, he was exhausted and ill from his exertions and needed a rest at home. But again he failed to recruit any missionaries to help him.

Joseph Shanahan was consecrated bishop, when the Prefecture became the new Vicariate of southern Nigeria, in Maynooth on his forty-ninth birthday, 6 June 1920. He addressed the students at the seminary and put to them a proposition: would some of them volunteer for a few years to go on the African mission, after which time they could return to their dioceses? Ten students volunteered. 'The moving appeal of the tall, apostolic man with long white beard and flashing eyes produced a profound impression,' one of the volunteers recalled later. From this appeal, the St Patrick's Missionary Society (the Kiltegan Fathers) was born.

The bishop then tried to attract women volunteers to the mission lands, and for that purpose founded the Missionary Sisters of Our Lady of the Holy Rosary (the Killeshandra Sisters) who devoted themselves to the work of education in Nigeria. His efforts were also instrumental in the foundational work of Mother Mary Martin of the Medical Missionaries of Mary.

During the 1920s, Bishop Shanahan's health deteriorated so badly that eventually he was forced to resign and leave Nigeria in 1932. In retirement he served the Carmelites in Nairobi, Kenya, as chaplain for five years until his death on Christmas Day, 1943. In 1956, his remains were transported to be interred in Onitsha Cathedral in the Southern Nigeria he served so well.

When Fr Shanahan arrived in Nigeria in 1906, the number of Catholics in the Prefecture was 1,488 in twenty-four parishes and schools. When Bishop Shanahan retired in 1932, the Catholics of the Vicariate numbered 110,049 and there were 1,386 churches and schools.

Mary Martin was born in Glenageary, County Dublin, on 25 April 1892, the daughter of a well-known commercial family. Her father was killed in a shooting accident when she was fifteen, and she herself suffered from health problems in childhood. Mary trained as a nurse just before the outbreak of the First World War, and served in the military hospitals of Malta during the Gallipoli campaign. After peace was declared in 1918, she decided to devote herself to the care of the sick. Father Joseph Shanahan was visiting Ireland in 1920, and a meeting with him changed her life. He invited her to come as a lay volunteer to his Prefecture.

In 1921, the young nurse arrived in Nigeria. When she saw the health and sanitary conditions of the people of the countryside, she resolved to found a congregation of nuns to care for the sick, especially the mothers and children. At that time, however, the Church forbade religious to engage in any surgical or maternity work. In the meantime, Bishop Shanahan advised her to prepare for the foundation by completing a novitiate herself. She spent the next decade volunteering, disappointed that her plans for the new congregation of religious could not be realised, and receiving some encouragement, but no support.

Then in 1936, the ban was lifted by the Vatican. Mary Martin moved quickly to seek approval for her proposal, sailed for Nigeria and professed her vows in Port Harcourt Hospital. Unfortunately upon her arrival she contracted malaria and suffered a very serious heart attack. She returned to Ireland to recover and to begin recruiting novices for the newly instituted Medical Missionaries of Mary. With the permission of Cardinal MacRory, she opened a novitiate in Drogheda, which became the maternity hospital of Our Lady of Lourdes.

In the intervening decades, the Medical Missionaries spread rapidly in the mission countries, and Mother Mary, as she was now familiarly known, was the organising genius for the rapidly expanding congregation. She received recognition from the International Red Cross, the Royal College of Surgeons in Ireland, and Nigeria for her contributions to world health. Drogheda honoured her as the first woman to receive the Freedom of the Borough. Mother Mary Martin died in 1975.

Both Bishop Shanahan and Mother Mary were ahead of their times in leading the Irish missionary movement in a systemic approach to poverty and oppression. Their work in education and healthcare in Nigeria continued the teaching and healing apostolate of Jesus Christ in the modern world. Their mission preceded the work of the multitude of young Irish lay people from organisations like Trócaire, Concern, Viatores Christi and so many other non-governmental agencies who bring support and hope to the developing world in our times.

GOSPEL PORTRAITS OF JESUS

If we want to know Jesus, we should know the Scripture. This is certainly true about the Gospels of Matthew, Mark, Luke and John, which were written 'that you may [come to] believe that Jesus is the Christ, the Son of God, and that believing this you may have life through his name' (Jn 20:31).

We ponder Christ's person and his earthly words and deeds in terms of *mystery*. His earthly life reveals his hidden divine Sonship and plan for our salvation. His parables, miracles, sermons and wisdom sayings help us 'so that, as we recognise in him God made visible, we may be caught up through him in love of things invisible' (Preface I of the Nativity of the Lord).

The Gospels tell us a lot of what we know about Jesus. In two of the Gospels, we hear of his birth in the town of Bethlehem, to a young virgin named Mary. None of the Gospels tell much of the first thirty years of his life. We know he lived in the town of Nazareth with his mother and foster father, St Joseph, and that he learned to be a carpenter like his foster father. The Gospels concentrate mostly on the events of his public life or ministry, which began when he was around the age of thirty. Jesus spent the last three years of his life travelling around the lands of ancient Israel, teaching the people of the Kingdom of God and confirming his identity as the Son of God through the miracles and wonders he performed. He gathered around him many disciples from whom he selected twelve who became the Apostles.

In the Gospels, we see and hear Jesus summon others to accept, live and share the Kingdom of God. The proclamation of the Kingdom of God was fundamental to Jesus' preaching. The Kingdom of God is his presence among human beings calling them to a new way of life as individuals and as a community. This is a Kingdom of salvation from sin and a sharing in divine life. It is the Good News that results in love, justice and mercy for the whole world. The Kingdom is realised partially on earth and permanently in heaven. We enter this Kingdom through faith in Christ, baptismal initiation into the Church, and life in communion with all her members.

The words of Jesus, expressed in his parables, the Sermon on the Mount, his dialogues and the Last Supper discourse are calls to holiness through accepting his Kingdom and salvation. Jesus did not abolish the Law of Sinai, but rather fulfilled it (cf. Mt 5:17-19) with such perfection (cf. Jn 8:46) that he revealed its ultimate meaning (cf. Mt 5:23) and redeemed the transgressions against it (cf. Heb 9:15). The miracles and other deeds of Jesus are acts of compassion and signs of the Kingdom and salvation.

In the mystery of the Transfiguration, we gain a foretaste of the Kingdom. A hymn of the Byzantine liturgy spells it out for us:

> You were transfigured on a mountain. Your disciples contemplated your glory, Christ God, so that when they saw you crucified, they would understand that your passion was freely willed. They would announce to the world that you are truly the splendour of the Father. (*Kontakion* for the Feast of the Transfiguration, Byzantine tradition)

Above all it is in the Paschal Mystery, which is the saving Passion, death and Resurrection of Jesus, that we participate most profoundly in the mystery of Christ. Here is the heart of the Kingdom and salvation to which we are called. In Christ, we die to self and sin. We rise to participate in his divine life through the Resurrection. This is made possible for us through the Sacraments.

Our access to the Gospels is made possible by doing faith-filled reading of the sacred texts, by listening to them in the Church's liturgy and by witnessing their meaning in our lives and in the lives of others. We can benefit greatly from the number of available Scripture commentaries and Bible study groups that are sponsored by local parishes.

TRUE GOD AND TRUE MAN

Who is Jesus Christ? He is the Second Person of the Blessed Trinity, conceived by the Holy Spirit and born of the Virgin Mary. He is true God and true man.

> The unique and altogether singular event of the Incarnation of the Son of God does not mean that Jesus Christ is part God and part man, nor does it imply that he is the result of a confused mixture of the divine and the human. He became truly man while remaining truly God ... During the first centuries the Church had to defend and clarify this truth of faith against the heresies that falsified it. (CCC, no. 464)

Because of various heresies that departed from the Apostolic Tradition, the Church needed to defend and clarify the true being of Christ. The first major heretical movement, Gnosticism, denied the humanity of Christ. Its advocates taught that the body was an unworthy dwelling place for God. They thought that the Incarnation could not have happened. The Church asserted Christ's true coming in the flesh, born of the Virgin Mary. Moreover, in a real body, he truly suffered and died on the Cross.

> The son of God ... worked with human hands; he thought with a human mind. He acted with a human will, and with a human heart he loved. Born of the Virgin Mary, he has truly been made one of us, like us in all things except sin. (GS, no. 22)

CHRISTOLOGICAL TEACHINGS OF EARLY COUNCILS
(CF. CCC, NOS. 465–468)

Nicea (AD 325): Jesus Christ is the Son of God by nature and not by adoption. He is 'begotten', not made, of the same substance as the Father.

Ephesus (AD 431): Since the one who was born of Mary is divine, Mary is rightly called 'Mother of God'.

Chalcedon (AD 451): Jesus Christ, Son of God, is true God and true man. His divine and human natures remain together without confusion, change, division, or separation.

Second Constantinople (AD 553): There is only one person – a divine person – in Jesus Christ. The human acts of Jesus are also attributed to his divine person.

It is important to understand that Jesus had a human soul. He was also endowed with true human knowledge, which always worked in harmony with the divine wisdom to which Jesus' knowledge was united. Jesus also possessed a true human will, which always cooperated with his divine will.

A second major heresy, called Arianism because it was taught by a man named Arius, claimed that Jesus was not God. This Alexandrian priest argued that the 'Word' which became flesh in Jesus was not God, but a created being, marvellous but created nonetheless. Arius and his disciples believed it was unfitting to even think that a human being could be God. To counter Arius, the Council of Nicea (AD 325) reaffirmed the faith of the Church that Jesus was really God, 'begotten, not made, of one substance with the Father'.

A third heresy, Nestorianism, denied the unity of Jesus Christ as God and man. The Nestorians argued that the divine Son of God dwelled inside the human Jesus of Nazareth, but that they were not really one as one person. They insisted that Mary could be called 'Mother of Jesus' but not 'Mother of God', as if the man Jesus and the divine Son were two separate persons. The Council of Ephesus (AD 431) rejected this heresy and professed that Mary is the Mother of God, the *Theotokos* (Birth-giver of

FROM THE CATECHISM

1. What does the name Jesus mean?
Jesus means in Hebrew: 'God saves' … Since God alone can forgive sins, it is God who, in Jesus his eternal Son made man, 'will save his people from their sins'. (CCC, no. 430, citing Mt 1:21)

2. Why is Jesus called Christ?
The word 'Christ' [*Christos*] comes from the Greek translation of the Hebrew *Messiah*, which means 'anointed'. It became the name proper to Jesus … because he accomplished perfectly the divine mission that 'Christ' signifies. (CCC, no. 436)

3. How does Jesus model discipleship for us?
In all of his life, Jesus presents himself as *our model*. He is 'the perfect man', who invites us to become his disciples and follow him. In humbling himself, he has given us an example to imitate, through his prayer he draws us to pray and by his poverty he calls us to accept freely the privation and persecution that may come our way. (CCC, no. 520, citing GS, no. 38)

God; sometimes translated as 'God-bearer'). Jesus Christ is the divine Son of God who became man in the womb of Mary. The one who was born of Mary is the same one – the same person – who has existed with the Father and the Holy Spirit from all eternity.

Understanding that Jesus is both fully human and fully divine is very important. The Church has consistently defended this teaching against attempts to present one or the other as somehow less. If the Crucifixion and Resurrection were events that involved God only, then we are not saved. If Jesus was not divine, he would have been just another good man whose death and Resurrection would not have saved us. It is necessary to believe that the mystery of the Incarnation means that Jesus was both fully God and fully man.

JESUS IS THE SAVIOUR OF ALL

Only in him is there salvation; for of all the names in the world given to men, this is the only one by which we can be saved.

– Acts 4:11-12

At the beginning of the third millennium, the world celebrated global awareness and the diversity of cultures. The revolution in communications, transportation and computer technologies is making us all aware of peoples and diversity in ways seldom experienced so directly in times past. Irish people are uniquely aware of global diversity, as emigration and the missionary movement brought Irish men and women to every corner of the world.

Amid the excitement generated by global awareness, it is helpful to point out that God's plan to save the world has been global from the very start. Christ's final words to his Apostles precisely present a global scale to their mission: 'Go, therefore, make disciples of all the nations' (Mt 28:19).

The energetic missionaries of the Church have brought the Good News of Jesus Christ to every part of the world. Time after time the Church has incarnated the Gospel in yet another new and fascinating culture. If anyone is an expert in cultural pluralism, it is the Church, whose Gospel outreach has evangelised ancient Judea, Greece and Rome, Egypt and North Africa, the tribal communities that flowed into northern Europe, the Medieval and Renaissance worlds, the far-flung lands of Asia and the new fields opened up by the discovery of America. In recent times, the Church's revitalised mission to Africa and Asia is yet another chapter in her proclamation of Christ to the world.

While we correctly celebrate the rich variety of cultures, we also are reminded that unity and harmony in Christ constitute the greatest value and hope for the human community. There should be no clash of cultures or civilisations, but rather the growth of universal respect for everyone's human dignity. We search for unity as we honour ethnic and cultural diversity. This is a unity that reflects the unity of the Holy Trinity itself. The mission of the Catholic Church is the Lord's plan to unite all people in the love of Jesus Christ, the Saviour of all. This unity can never detract from the uniqueness of cultures that pluralism recognises and respects.

FOR DISCUSSION

1. Why is it important for you to appreciate the truth that the person, words and deeds of Jesus as seen in the Gospel accounts are mysteries revealing to us the hidden plan of God for our salvation? Conversely, what happens when this is forgotten?
2. The New Testament and the early Church Councils affirm in faith that Jesus is true God and true man. What is the value for our faith life in appreciating this truth of Revelation? What happens if we forget any aspect of Christ's identity?
3. What is your experience of cultural diversity? How has such diversity influenced your sensitivity to others? Why is God's plan for the unity of all peoples through the love of Christ an even greater value?

DOCTRINAL STATEMENTS

- 'The whole of Christ's life was a continual teaching: his silences, his miracles, his gestures, his prayer, his love for people, his special affection for the lowly and the poor, his acceptance of the total sacrifice of the Cross for the redemption of the world and his Resurrection are the actualisation of his word and the fulfilment of Revelation' (CCC, no. 561).
- The name *Jesus* means 'God saves'. 'For of all the names in the world given to men, this is the only one by which we can be saved' (Acts 4:12). The title *Christ* means 'anointed one' (*Messiah*).
- The title *Son of God* refers to the truth that Jesus Christ is the unique and eternal Son of the Father. At Christ's Baptism and Transfiguration, the Father says of Jesus, 'This is my Son, the Beloved' (Mt 3:17; 17:5). To profess Jesus as *Lord* is to believe in his divinity.
- The only Son of the Father, the eternal Word, became man at the appointed time, without ceasing to be God. He was conceived by the Holy Spirit and born of the Virgin Mary.
- Jesus Christ is true God and true man united in one divine Person.
- 'The son of God ... worked with human hands; he thought with a human mind. He acted with a human will, and with a human heart he loved. Born of the Virgin Mary ... he is like us in all things except sin' (GS, no. 22).

- In the Incarnation, we behold the mystery of the union of the divine and human natures in the one person of God's Son. Somehow, in a way we cannot completely grasp, Jesus had both human knowledge and a human will and divine knowledge and a divine will.
- As disciples of Christ, we are called to conform ourselves to him until he is formed in us.
- The mysteries of Christ's infancy and hidden life invite us to identify with Christ's obedience to Mary and Joseph as well as the example of his holiness in the daily work of family and work in the long years at Nazareth.
- The mysteries of Christ's public life draw us to learn discipleship from the teachings of his baptism, his temptation in the desert, his preaching and witness of the Kingdom of Heaven, his Transfiguration, his voluntary journey to Jerusalem to face his Passion and his entry into Jerusalem, where he completed the work of our salvation through his death and Resurrection.

MEDITATION

Why Did the Word Become Flesh?

The Word became flesh to save us from sin and reconcile us to God. 'For God sent his Son into the world not to judge the world, but so that through him the world might be saved' (Jn 3:17).

By the Incarnation we are made aware of the depth of God's love for us. 'This is the revelation of God's love for us, that God sent his only Son into the world that we might have life through him' (1 Jn 4:9).

When the Son of God became man he became a model of holiness for us. 'This is my commandment: love one another, as I have loved you' (Jn 15:12).

God became man that we may partake in the divine nature. 'The greatest and priceless promises have been lavished on us, that through them you should share the divine nature' (2 Pt 1:4).

PRAYER

Lord Jesus Christ, Son of the living God,
have mercy on me, a sinner.

I can never cease to speak of Christ for he is our truth and
our light.

— Pope Paul VI

When we have understood God's love for us in Jesus Christ, a
lifelong journey begins, in which we seek to let the *euaggelion* – the
'Good News' of Christ's loving life, ministry, passion, death and
resurrection – speak in our hearts.

— SGN, 30

8 THE SAVING DEATH AND RESURRECTION OF CHRIST

PASCHAL MYSTERY, UNITY OF THE SAVING DEEDS – CCC, NOS. 571–664

MATT TALBOT: HOPE FOR THE LOST

 'An elderly man collapsed in Granby Lane yesterday, and on being taken to Jervis Street Hospital, he was found to be dead. He was wearing a tweed suit, but there was nothing to identify who he was.' So reported the *Irish Independent* on Monday, 8 June 1925. The previous day was Trinity Sunday. The man was wearing a tweed suit, his Sunday best, because he was going to 10 o'clock Mass in the Dominican Church, his second Mass that day. The dead man was eventually identified as Matthew Talbot, a pious and humble worker in the north inner city, who during the week wore clean but shabby overalls. As the Mercy Sisters prepared the body for burial, they found chains around his body, and holy medals, which indicated that the chains had a religious significance. The discovery was precisely described, recorded and witnessed. The story spread quickly and a small crowd attended the funeral on 11 June 1925. Matt Talbot was sixty-nine years old.

That looked like the end of the story, but it was only the beginning. An obscure and secret life would soon be revealed. Matt Talbot's story was destined to intrigue everyone and encourage many. Others, however, would see Matt Talbot as a peculiar person. The quiet little man in his tweed suit going to Mass excited a controversy in death that he never would have dreamed of while alive.

Matthew Talbot was born in Aldborough Court on the North Circular Road, Dublin, on 2 May 1856, and was baptised in the Pro-Cathedral a few days later. His father was a foreman on the docks and a heavy drinker. Matthew was rebellious at school. His Christian Brother teacher described him as 'a mitcher' which suggests that he spent as little time as he could at his desk. According to his parents' nature as disciplinarians, his father put him to work at the age of twelve with a wine merchant. Matt began to help himself to the leftovers, and arrived home on occasion somewhat inebriated.

He graduated to serious drinking in young adulthood. At that time, employers would pay their workers in the public house, and this was the downfall of Matthew Talbot. Much of his wages each week would go on drink. On one occasion, having run out of money, he sneakily appropriated the violin from the fiddler at the pub, and sold it so that he and his friends could continue to drink. Then a piece of bad luck changed his fortunes, like the Prodigal Son in the Gospel of Luke. He was sick for a week and missed his wages. That weekend, he waited for his pals to buy him a drink – but they ignored him. The shock brought Matt to his senses. He went home and announced to his long-suffering mother, 'I am going to take the pledge'. This was the promise of total abstinence from alcoholic drink, usually taken for a month or so. One would have expected, given his past history, that the young man would 'fall off the wagon' (break his pledge) a few times. But so far as is known, Matt Talbot kept his first promise for three months, and then renewed it for longer, and finally for life. The year was 1884. Matt was twenty-eight years old. He had been drinking steadily for fifteen years. Upon taking the pledge, he never drank again.

Matt Talbot reformed his life completely. He adopted a strict regimen of sleeping, eating, praying and working. He lived his life as obedient as a monk, rising at 2.30 a.m. to pray, attending early Mass at 5 a.m. or 6 a.m., eating frugally, working diligently, visiting the church for private prayer when he could, visiting the Jesuits at Gardiner Street or Clonliffe College for advice and direction, reading spiritual books and mortifying his body for penance. After work each day, he would visit the church again and then head home to 18 Upper Rutland Street for supper, prayers and bed.

The penitential practices he adopted have attracted most attention, favourable and unfavourable. He would kneel bolt upright at Mass. He ate his meals kneeling. He ate sparingly, dry bread and cocoa being a staple. He slept on a board bed. He wore a chain around his body as a reminder of his service to Mary. He fasted regularly during Lent – the 'Black Fast' of toast and black tea. He refused to pamper himself in any way. If he arrived early for Mass, and the church was still locked, he would kneel on the steps outside until the door was opened.

But Matt Talbot did not neglect his duties, his friends or his family. His mother lived with him for many years in Rutland Street. He was in touch with his sisters who lived nearby. He had several close friends who understood him and appreciated his values and ideals. As a worker on the docks and then with T&C Martin (Mother Mary Martin's building family), he had a reputation for being strong and reliable, good-natured and quiet. He attracted no attention to himself. Matt tried to trace the unfortunate fiddler whose violin he pawned for alcohol, but was unsuccessful. So he donated money to charity and had Masses offered for the musician in reparation for his deed.

But all of this emerged after his death. As more and more details about his life became known, Matt Talbot became an example for those trying to fight alcohol or any addiction. The Archdiocese of Dublin investigated the life story of this humble son of the north city and found that it was coherent, credible and inspiring. The Archbishop then initiated the process of canonisation and the first stage was completed when Pope Paul VI declared Matt Talbot 'Venerable' in 1975. This means that Matt Talbot practised heroic virtue. Beatification, if it comes with time, means that Matt Talbot could be prayed to, and celebrated liturgically, in Ireland. Canonisation extends the permission to pray to and celebrate a liturgy to the universal Church.

There is no doubt, however, that today some are uneasy with the idea of Matt Talbot as an example of virtue or character. They suspect that he was mentally unstable, especially because of his severe mortifications. This shows an unfortunate misunderstanding of the place of penitential practice and, indeed, mystical awareness in the spiritual life. Matt Talbot specifically adopted the way of life of the early Irish monks under the direction of a spiritual advisor. This was not an unbalanced and isolated individual indulging in unhealthy fantasies. Our contemporary culture commends those who commit to incredible exertion and hardship for the sake of sport or physical achievement. Why do we not accord the same respect for the demands of the spiritual life?

Matt Talbot seems a most unlikely mystic, but it is unmistakable that he is one. He enjoyed such a close intimacy with his loving Father and the Blessed Virgin, with the Holy Spirit and with Jesus, that it sustained his recovery from serious addiction and his remarkable religious life through forty-one years of sobriety.

LIFT HIGH THE CROSS

In suffering and death his humanity became the free and perfect instrument of his divine love which desires the salvation of men.

– CCC, no. 609

In a number of ways, Jesus warned his followers that pain and death would be an essential part of his mission. Right after he made Peter the rock on which the Church would be built, he predicted his Passion. 'Jesus began to make it clear to his disciples that he was destined to go to Jerusalem and suffer grievously at the hands of the elders and chief priests and scribes and to be put to death and to be raised up on the third day' (Mt 16:21). When Peter protested this possibility, Jesus rebuked him, 'You are thinking not as God thinks but as human beings do' (Mt 16:23). Jesus predicted his Passion again after the Transfiguration (cf. Mt 17:22-23).

Not only would Jesus accept the Cross, he expected the same willingness from his disciples. 'If anyone wants to be a follower of mine, let him renounce himself and take up his cross every day and follow me' (Lk 9:23). Jesus explained this truth further by means of an agricultural image. 'Unless a wheat grain falls into the earth and dies, it remains only a single grain; but if it dies it yields a rich harvest' (Jn 12:24). Jesus noted that the greatest expression of love is to die for the beloved. 'No one can have greater love than to lay down his life for his friends' (Jn 15:13).

Because Christ's suffering and death was the instrument of salvation, from what did he save us? We needed to be saved from sin and its damaging effects. God's plan to save us involved having the Son of God enter into this world to be like us in all things except sin. Divine love made this possible.

Jesus, Son of God, was sent by the Father to restore the harmony between himself and humanity that had been disrupted by sin. He came to teach and show us love. Jesus was without sin, but in his human nature, he was subject to all that human beings suffer, including hatred from others, torture and death itself. He proclaimed the coming of God's Kingdom by his words and deeds in obedience to the will of his Father. He showed the full meaning of all that had been revealed in the Old Testament. But some did not want to hear his message. They opposed him and turned him over to the administration of the Roman Empire in Palestine to be put to death.

On the Cross, Jesus freely gave his life as a sacrifice. His sacrifice was an act of atonement, that is, it makes us one again with God by the power of divine mercy extending to us the Father's forgiveness of our sins. His sacrifice is also called an *act of satisfaction* or *reparation*[4] because he lives out fully the Father's call to human beings to be faithful to his plan for them, thus overcoming the power of sin. It is also an *expiation*[5] for our sins, which in the understanding of Scripture means that God takes the initiative in bringing about reconciliation to himself. In the words of Christian Tradition, Jesus' sacrifice merits salvation for us because it retains forever the power to draw us to him and to the Father.

Who is responsible for the death of Jesus? Every one of us from the dawn of history to the end of time who in pride and disobedience has sinned is in some way responsible. Historically, some Jewish leaders handed Jesus over to Pontius Pilate, the Roman governor who condemned Jesus to death on the Cross.

It is wrong to blame the Jewish people for the death of Christ in the manner that often has been done in history. 'The Church does not hesitate to impute to Christians the gravest responsibility for the torments inflicted upon Jesus, a responsibility with which they have all too often burdened the

---

[4] *Reparation* means 'making amends for a wrong done or for an offence, especially for sin, which is an offence against God. By his death on the cross, the Son of God offered his life out of love for the Father to make reparation for our sinful disobedience' (CCC, Glossary).
[5] *Expiation* is 'the act of redemption and atonement for sin which Christ won for us by the pouring out of his blood on the cross, by his obedient love "to the end" (Jn 13:1)' (CCC, Glossary).

Jews alone' (CCC, no. 598). At the Second Vatican Council, the Church made the following declaration regarding the Jewish people:

> Neither all Jews indiscriminately at that time, nor Jews today, can be charged with the crimes committed during his Passion ... [T]he Jews should not be spoken of as rejected or accursed as if this followed from holy Scripture. (CCC, no. 597; citing Second Vatican Council, *Declaration on the Relation of the Church to Non-Christian Religions* [*Nostra Aetate*; NA], no. 4)

The Apostles' Creed professes that after his death and burial, Jesus descended into hell. In the language of the early Church, this meant that Jesus went into the realm of the dead, from which he called out all the just people who had lived before him to enter with him into the glory of the Kingdom of Heaven. A popular icon of the Eastern Churches pictures the risen Jesus with his hands reaching into the realm of the dead to draw out Adam and Eve.

> In his human soul united to his divine person, the dead Christ went down into the realm of the dead. He opened Heaven's gates for the just who had gone before him. (CCC, no. 637)

CHRIST IS RISEN! ALLELUIA!

Christ's Resurrection is an object of faith in that it is a transcendent intervention of God himself in creation and history.

– CCC, no. 648

When we speak of the Paschal Mystery, we refer to Christ's death and Resurrection as one inseparable event. It is a mystery because it is a visible sign of an invisible act of God. It is paschal because it is Christ's passing through death into new life. For us it means that we can now die to sin and its domination of our lives, and we pass over into divine life already here on earth and more completely in heaven. Death is conquered in the sense that not only do our souls survive physical death, but even our bodies will rise again at the end of time at the Last Judgement and resurrection of the dead.

The Resurrection narratives in all four Gospels – though differing in details because of varying viewpoints of the different authors – maintain a similar structure in the narration of the events. At dawn on the Sunday after Christ's death, Mary Magdalene and a companion go to the tomb to anoint the dead body of Jesus. They find the tomb is empty. They meet an angel who proclaims the Resurrection of Jesus: 'He is not here, for he has risen' (Mt 28:6). They are told to bring the Good News to the Apostles. Mary Magdalene leads the way and is celebrated in the liturgy of the Church as the first witness to the Resurrection.

Next come the appearance narratives when Jesus appears to the Apostles and disciples in a number of instances. Saint Paul summarises these appearances in his first Letter to the Corinthians (cf. 1 Cor 15:3-8). Finally, the disciples are commissioned to bring the Gospel to the world.

While the empty tomb of itself does not prove the Resurrection, since the absence of Christ's body could have other explanations, it is an essential part of the proclamation of the Resurrection because it demonstrates the fact of what God has done in raising his Son from the dead in his own body. When St John entered the empty tomb, 'He saw and he believed' (Jn 20:8).

HISTORICAL EVENT

The Resurrection is historical in that it actually took place at a specific time and place, and therefore there were witnesses to its impact. Mary Magdalene met the Risen Christ and embraced his feet. Thomas the Apostle saw Jesus and the wounds and said, 'My Lord and my God' (Jn 20:28). Two disciples walked with Jesus on the road to Emmaus and recognised him in the Breaking of the Bread (cf. Lk 24:13-35). All the Apostles saw him (cf. Jn 20:19-23). Saint Paul tells us he met the Risen Lord on the Road to Damascus (cf. Acts 9:3-6). He also writes that five hundred people saw Jesus on a single occasion (cf. 1 Cor 15:3-8).

None of the witnesses to Jesus' Resurrection expected it. In fact, they were demoralised by the execution of Jesus. Even when they did see him, some had lingering doubts. 'When they saw him they fell down before him, though some hesitated' (Mt 28:17). In other words, they were not easily convinced, nor were they caught up in some kind of mystical self-delusion or hysteria. Some of them even died as martyrs rather than deny what they had witnessed. In this light, their testimony that the Resurrection was a historical event is more convincing (cf. CCC, nos. 643–644).

A TRANSCENDENT EVENT

The reality of Christ's Resurrection is also something beyond the realm of history. No one saw the actual Resurrection. No evangelist describes it. No one can tell us how it physically happened. No one perceived how the earthly body of Christ passed over into a glorified form. Despite the fact that the risen Jesus could be seen, touched, heard and dined with, the Resurrection remains a mystery of faith that transcends history.

Its transcendent quality can also be inferred from the state of Christ's risen body. He was not a ghost; Jesus invited them to touch him. He asked for a piece of fish to show them that he could eat. He spent time with them, often repeating teachings from the days before the Passion but now in the light of the Resurrection. Nor was it a body like that of Lazarus, which would die again. His risen body would never die. Christ's body was glorified; it is not confined by space or time. He could appear and disappear before the Apostles' eyes. Closed doors did not bar his entry. It is a real body, but glorified, not belonging to earth but to the Father's realm. It is a body transformed by the Holy Spirit (cf. 1 Cor 15:42-44). The Holy Spirit 'gave life to Jesus' dead humanity and called it to the glorious state of Lordship' (CCC, no. 648).

What do we learn from Christ's Resurrection? If Jesus had not risen, our faith would mean nothing. Saint Paul makes this clear in his first Letter to the Corinthians: 'Now if Christ is proclaimed as raised from the dead, how can some of you be saying that there is no resurrection of the dead? If there is no resurrection of the dead, then Christ cannot have been raised either, and if Christ has not been raised, then our preaching is without substance, and so is your faith' (1 Cor 15:12-14). We also learn that, by raising him from the dead, the Father has placed his seal upon the work accomplished by his only begotten Son through his Passion and death. We see now the fullness of Jesus' glory as Son of God and Saviour.

FROM THE CATECHISM

1. How was Jesus able to save all of us?

No man, not even the holiest, was ever able to take on himself the sins of all men and offer himself as a sacrifice for all. The existence in Christ of the divine person of the Son, who at once surpasses and embraces all human persons and constitutes himself as Head of all mankind, makes possible his redemptive sacrifice for all. (CCC, no. 616)

2. Why did Jesus die on the Cross?

Jesus came 'to give his life as a ransom for many' (Mt 20:28). By his loving obedience to the Father, he fulfilled the atoning mission of the suffering Servant, 'he was pierced for our offences, crushed for our sins ... by his stripes we were healed' (Is 53:5) (cf. CCC, nos. 599–618).

3. How is Christ's Resurrection a work of the Trinity?

The three divine persons act together as one ... The Father's power 'raised up' Christ his Son ... Jesus is conclusively revealed as 'Son of God in power according to the Spirit of holiness by his Resurrection from the dead'. (CCC, no. 648, citing Rm 1:3-4)

> As for the Son, he effects his own Resurrection by virtue of his divine power ... he affirms explicitly: 'I lay down my life, that I may take it again.' (CCC, no. 649, citing Jn 10:17-18)

THE ASCENSION INTO HEAVEN

The Paschal Mystery culminates in the Ascension of Jesus. After his appearance here on earth in his risen body, and 'he gave his instructions to the apostles he had chosen through the Holy Spirit' (Acts 1:2), Jesus 'was lifted up while they looked on, and a cloud took him from their sight' (Acts 1:9):

Christ's ascension marks the definitive entrance of Jesus' humanity into God's heavenly domain, whence he will come again (cf. Acts 1:11) ... Jesus Christ, the head of the Church, precedes us into the Father's glorious kingdom so that we, the members of his Body, may live in the hope of one day being with him for ever. Jesus Christ, having entered the sanctuary of heaven once and for all, intercedes constantly for us as the mediator who assures us of the permanent outpouring of the Holy Spirit. (CCC, nos. 665–667)

FROM DOUBT TO FAITH

When the women reported the Resurrection to the Apostles, 'this story of theirs seemed pure nonsense, and they did not believe them' (Lk 24:11). The Apostles thought they were seeing a ghost when Jesus first appeared to them. Thomas refused to believe unless he could touch the nail marks.

Within a few decades, there arose heretics who denied the Resurrection because they did not think Jesus had a body at all. Greeks believed in the immortality only of the soul. Bodies did not endure beyond death. Resurrection was impossible. Nonetheless, the Apostles and other witnesses who came to faith in the Resurrection preached its reality and centrality to faith. Unless it happened, there would be no Church and no Eucharist. Early Christian believers died by the thousands for their faith in the Risen Christ and his salvation.

In our present culture, there are some who present new denials of the Resurrection. They distort the language of the New Testament to support their disbelief. Arbitrarily they 'reinterpret away' what the authors of the text said and meant. In their view, the Resurrection 'appearances' were either warm memories of Jesus, projections of their inner needs, or inward spiritual experiences – not real appearances, despite the concrete descriptions in the New Testament documents. Such sceptics seem to mean, 'It was impossible, so it did not happen'.

The Resurrection makes credible everything Jesus did and taught. It discloses how Jesus accomplished God's eternal plan for our salvation. Through it we taste heavenly gifts and the glory of the age to come. The power of the Resurrection reminds our culture that grace is always more powerful and effective than sin and evil.

FOR DISCUSSION

1. When Jesus says our discipleship involves the Cross, what does this mean for you? In what ways do you find yourself resisting this part of Christ's call? What is your 'way of the Cross'?
2. How would you help people come to faith in the Resurrection of Christ? Why is it so central to your faith?
3. How could you come to understand or experience the need for a Saviour? Why are the Cross and the Resurrection bound together in the Paschal Mystery?

DOCTRINAL STATEMENTS

- To many in Israel, Jesus seemed to be acting against the Law, the Temple and their faith in the One God.
- Christ suffered because he was 'rejected by the elders and the chief priests and the scribes' who handed 'him over to the gentiles to be mocked and scourged and crucified' (Mk 8:31; Mt 20:19).
- Jesus did not abolish the Law of Sinai. He fulfilled it and revealed its ultimate meaning (cf. Mt 5:17-19; 6:43-48).
- Jesus honoured the Temple, to which he journeyed for the major feasts and which he loved as God's dwelling on earth.
- By forgiving sins, Jesus manifested himself to be the Saviour (cf. Jn 5:16-18). Those who did not accept him as the Saviour saw him only as a man who claimed to be God, a blasphemer (cf. Jn 10:33).
- Our salvation flows from God's love for us because 'God loved us and sent his Son to expiate our sins' (1 Jn 4:10). 'Christ died for our sins, in accordance with the scriptures' (1 Cor 15:3).
- Jesus came 'to give his life as a ransom for many' (Mt 20:28). By his loving obedience to the Father, he fulfilled the atoning mission of the suffering Servant, 'he was being wounded for our rebellions, / crushed because of our guilt; / ... we have been healed by his bruises' (Is 53:5).
- The Son of God who became man truly died and was buried, but his body underwent no corruption. In his human soul united to his divine person, the dead Christ went to the realm of the dead and opened heaven for the just who came before him (cf. CCC, no. 637).

- Christ's Resurrection is an event that is historically attested to by the Apostles who really met the Risen One. The Resurrection is also a transcendent mystery because God the Father raises his Son from the dead by the power of the Holy Spirit.
- The empty tomb helped the disciples accept the fact of the Resurrection. When St John entered the tomb, 'he saw and he believed' (Jn 20:8).
- Christ is the 'first-born from the dead' (Col 1:18) and so is the principle of our own resurrection, now by the salvation of our souls and at the end of time, when new life will be given to our bodies.
- Christ's Ascension marks the definitive entrance of his humanity into heaven. Christ precedes us there so that we, the members of his Body, may live in the hope of being with him forever. Jesus intercedes constantly for us as our mediator and assures the permanent outpouring of the Holy Spirit.
- At the end of time, Jesus Christ will come in glory to judge the living and the dead.

MEDITATION

Saint John XXIII taught in *Paenitentiam Agere*, an encyclical he wrote on 1 July 1962:

> But the faithful must also be encouraged to do outward acts of penance, both to keep their bodies under the strict control of reason and faith, and to make amends for their own and other people's sins ... Saint Augustine issued the same insistent warning: 'It is not enough for a man to change his ways for the better and to give up the practice of evil, unless by painful penance, sorrowing humility, the sacrifice of a contrite heart and the giving of alms he makes amends to God for all that he has done wrong'. ... But besides bearing in a Christian spirit the inescapable annoyances and sufferings of this life, the faithful ought also take the initiative in doing voluntary acts of penance and offering them to God ... Since, therefore, Christ has suffered in the flesh, it is only fitting that we be 'armed with the same intent'. It is right, too, to seek example and

inspiration from the great saints of the Church. Pure as they were, they inflicted such mortifications upon themselves as to leave us almost aghast with admiration. And as we contemplate their saintly heroism, shall not we be moved by God's grace to impose on ourselves some voluntary sufferings and deprivations, we whose consciences are perhaps weighed down by so heavy a burden of guilt?

PRAYER

Now that we have seen the resurrection of Christ,
let us adore the all-holy Lord Jesus, the only Sinless One.
We bow in worship before your cross, O Christ,
and we praise and glorify your resurrection,
for You are God, and we have no other,
and we magnify your name.
All you faithful, come: let us adore the holy resurrection of Christ,
for behold, through the cross joy has come to the world!
Let us always bless the Lord, let us sing his resurrection,
for by enduring for us the pain of the cross, He has crushed
    death by his death.
    – Hymn from Easter Sunday, Byzantine Daily Worship

'O Virgin, I ask only three things:
the grace of God,
the presence of God,
and the benediction of God.'

    – Prayer of Matt Talbot

In the Creed … the Paschal Mystery of Christ's passion, death and resurrection, as the ultimate response to the human need for salvation, is affirmed, revealing the full extent of God's love for us and the possibility of our living, with all our sins forgiven, a new life in loving service of God and of one another.

– SGN, 52

9 RECEIVE THE HOLY SPIRIT (Jn 20:22)

THE REVELATION OF THE SPIRIT, JOINT MISSION OF SON AND SPIRIT – CCC, NOS. 683–747

NANO NAGLE: MOTHER OF IRISH CATHOLIC EDUCATION

During the period of the Penal Laws, Ireland was in the grip of relentless colonial exploitation and religious persecution. The distress and poverty of the rural population was harsh. Rebellion only invited more repression. When we hear the story of those heroes and heroines who tried to alleviate the hardship and lift the spirits of the poor, with little encouragement and less support, then we can appreciate the dire straits that afflicted Ireland at that time. One such heroine was Honora Nagle of Cork, known as 'Nano' Nagle, who later became Mother Mary of St John of God, and is now recognised as the Mother of Irish Catholic schools.

Nano Nagle was born in 1718 near Mallow in Co. Cork. Her family was reasonably well-off, given the miserable state of the country and the economic repression of Catholics at the time. Nano and her sister Anne were sent to school in Paris. Little detail is known about her youth, but a few stories have been passed on.

The two Irish girls enjoyed themselves in Parisian society, attending balls and parties as well as classes and lectures. One night – or rather early morning – coming home after a dance, Nano spotted a small group of worshippers outside a local church waiting quietly for the first Mass. The contrast between her life of pleasure and their daily round of devotion caused her to ponder on what really mattered in life.

On the death of their father, the sisters returned home to Ireland, Nano with a roll of fine silk to make dresses. When she looked for it to begin dressmaking, she found that her sister Anne had given the silk cloth away to raise money for the poor. Anne's charitable nature and her untimely death soon afterwards made a profound impression upon Nano. Her life underwent a complete conversion.

The surprising thing about Nano's conversion and subsequent commitment to the apostolic life was that she was so uncertain of her own ideas. This was not a woman of fixed determination and dogged resolve. She genuinely did not know precisely what to do, though she was very clear about the general direction.

At first she thought that she should return to France and join a religious order of nuns there. But a Jesuit confessor in the convent that she joined advised her to take up the care of the poor children and their Christian formation in Ireland instead, for that was the greater need. Then she attempted to found (and fund) schools for poor children in Cork city (she did have some independent means from her uncle's estate). She discovered, however, that to make any headway, a permanent institute, preferably of religious women, was required. This required that she find suitable women to train with the Ursulines in Paris who would then return and run her seven schools. Her next plan was to bring the Ursuline Sisters themselves to Ireland to establish their schools, and this she managed to do. The Ursulines arrived in 1771 and set up in Cork. But that was not the solution either, because as an enclosed order, the nuns could not adequately serve the schools of the poor.

Nano's supporters and advisers were equally confused. Her brother Joseph and her family were quite upset when she set up a school herself. They were afraid of a hostile reaction from the civil authorities. Equally, the parish priest, Fr Moylan, was at first opposed to her building a school for the same reason, but with time came around to her way of thinking. This was just as well, because later he was consecrated the Bishop of Cork and became the staunchest promoter of her achievements.

Finally, Nano Nagle decided that there was nothing for it but to found her own institute, with special concern for teaching poor children in Catholic schools. This she accomplished at Christmastime

1775, in a building close to the Ursulines, now part of the South Presentation Convent in Cork city. She called her society the Sisters of Charitable Instruction of the Sacred Heart of Jesus.

Nano Nagle's schools were certainly intended to form the children in the Catholic faith, giving instruction in the sacraments, inculcating a Christian way of life and preparing those who emigrated to keep the faith in new lands. But ever the practical woman, she ensured that secular subjects and vocationally useful crafts were taught as well. She knew that education was a grace and a gift in its own right, and that knowledge of God was to be gained through study of his creation. Her setbacks became the subject of a kind of discernment: 'It's a good sign of our future success that we should meet with crosses in the beginning … The best works meet with the greatest crosses.'

Nano spared herself no amount of work. She taught during the day in several locations, then visited the poor in the evening. Her first biographer described her thus: 'How often have we seen her after a well-spent day, returning thro' the darkness of the night, dripping with rain, mingled in the bustling crowd, moving thoughtfully along by the faint glimmering of a wretched lantern …' The lantern is the symbol of her sisters to this day. The hardships undertaken and energy expended in the care of the poor took their toll. Nano Nagle died on 26 April 1784 at the age of sixty-five. Her final words to the sisters were: 'Love one another as you have hitherto done.'

At Nano Nagle's death, much remained to be done. The sisters ran seven schools in three parishes in Cork. The canonical approval of the institute had not been secured. Bishop Moylan undertook to gain papal approval for the new religious order. In the final revision of the rule, the society was renamed the Sisters of the Presentation of the Blessed Virgin Mary. The rapid expansion of the Presentation Sisters proceeded apace, first in Ireland, and continues to this day around the world. Presentation foundations are to be found on every continent.

The work of Nano Nagle and her followers made it possible for other founders to enter the field of Irish Catholic education. Among them was Blessed Edmund Rice of the Irish Christian Brothers who adapted the Presentation rule for his own Christian Brothers, and Catherine McAuley, who did her novitiate with the Presentation Sisters. Pope Francis declared Nano Nagle 'Venerable' in October 2013.

JESUS GIVES US THE TRANSFORMING SPIRIT

Just before his Ascension, Jesus said these words to the Apostles: 'You will receive the power of the Holy Spirit which will come on you, and then you will be my witnesses not only in Jerusalem but throughout Judaea and Samaria, and indeed to earth's remotest end' (Acts 1:8).

These words of Christ to the Apostles are also addressed to each believer. The Holy Spirit comes to us as a teacher of the meaning and depth of Revelation. He also fills us with power, the grace to understand the Church's teachings and the wisdom to see how they apply to our lives. Finally, the Spirit puts courage into our hearts so that we can witness what we believe to believer and unbeliever alike.

The Acts of the Apostles shows how the Holy Spirit transformed the Apostles from being fearful disciples, huddling behind closed doors, into courageous witnesses for Christ.

> When Pentecost day came round, they had all met together, when suddenly there came from heaven a sound as of a violent wind which filled the entire house in which they were sitting; and there appeared to them tongues as of fire; these separated and came to rest on the head of each of them. They were all filled with the Holy Spirit and began to speak different languages as the Spirit gave them power to express themselves. (Acts 2:1-4)

Beginning with the gift of the Spirit at Pentecost, the disciples became dynamic missionaries. He filled those disciples with the gift of courage so that nothing stopped them from proclaiming the love of Christ for all people.

When we learn how to be open to the Holy Spirit, he shares with us the gift of understanding that contains the power to know Jesus and to give witness to him. At our Baptism, the Spirit works through the waters which take away Original Sin and actual sins and give us new life with the Triune

God. At Confirmation, the Holy Spirit is conferred by the anointing with the Chrism, by which the bishop seals us so that the Holy Spirit can strengthen us to pursue the mission of Christ to transform the world. At every Mass, the Holy Spirit changes the bread and wine into the Body and Blood of Christ by the ministry of the priest.

The Holy Spirit is dynamic, transforming our bodies into temples of God and our souls into dwelling places for Christ. Sometimes called the *Paraclete*, a term that describes him as advocate and consoler, the Holy Spirit wants to fill us with inspiration and encouragement.

We may not have to do great things, but we are called to do everyday duties with great love. The Holy Spirit is essentially Love. Love can change those we meet and change ourselves in each encounter. Because of the Holy Spirit our whole being, mind, heart, soul and body can be permeated with Love.

> 'God is Love' and love is his first gift, containing all others. 'God's love has been poured into our hearts through the Holy Spirit who has been given to us.' (CCC, no. 733, citing 1 Jn 4:8, 16 and Rm 5:5)

A rich example of the Holy Spirit's transforming power can be seen in the life of the Blessed Virgin Mary, the mother of Jesus. She is God's masterpiece, transformed by him into a luminous witness of grace from the moment of her conception. The angel Gabriel rightly addressed her as 'full of grace'. It is also by the power of the Holy Spirit that Mary conceived Jesus, the Son of God.

> Finally, through Mary, the Holy Spirit begins to bring men, the objects of God's merciful love, *into communion* with Christ. And the humble are always the first to accept him: shepherds, magi, Simeon and Anna, the bride and groom at Cana, and the first disciples. (CCC, no. 725)

THE HOLY SPIRIT IS REVEALED GRADUALLY

The Holy Spirit is the last of the Persons of the Trinity to be revealed. Saint Gregory Nazianzus (AD 329–89) gives us an excellent picture of God's teaching method, slowly unfolding the truth about the Trinity. Scripture reveals the truth about the Trinity in three stages:

> The Old Testament proclaimed the Father clearly, but the Son more obscurely. The New Testament revealed the Son and gave us a glimpse of the divinity of the Spirit. Now the Spirit dwells among us and grants us a clearer vision of himself. (CCC, no. 684, citing St Gregory Nazianzus, *Theological Orations*, 5, 26)

The fact that the Holy Spirit is God – equal in being with the Father and the Son, of the same divine nature as they are (*consubstantial* with them), the Third Person of the Holy Trinity – took time to be recognised and proclaimed. In the Old Testament, the Holy Spirit is hidden but is at work. 'When the Church reads the Old Testament, she searches there for what the Spirit, "who has spoken through the prophets", wants to tell us about Christ' (CCC, no. 702). Both the Hebrew word and the Greek word for the *Spirit* originally meant a 'breath', or 'air', or 'wind'. The Spirit was thus understood to be the source of inspiration, life and movement within God's people.

Among these holy writings, the Church honours the promise that the Spirit of the Lord shall rest upon the Messiah and endow him with spiritual gifts (cf. Is 11:1-2), and the prophecy that the Messiah will be moved by him to 'bring the news to the afflicted, / to soothe the broken-hearted, / ... to proclaim a year of favour from [the Lord]' (Is 61:1-2).

The Gospels show us the dynamic action of the Holy Spirit. It is by the Spirit that Jesus is conceived in the womb of Mary. The Holy Spirit appears in the form of a dove over Jesus at his baptism in the Jordan. He leads Jesus into the desert before he starts his public mission. In the Last Supper discourse in John's Gospel, Chapter 16, Jesus speaks at length about the promised revelation and the sending of the Holy Spirit.

The Holy Spirit is again revealed at Pentecost, when the seven weeks after Easter have concluded. 'Christ's Passover is fulfilled in the outpouring of the Holy Spirit, manifested, given and communicated as a divine person:

of his fullness, Christ, the Lord, pours out the Spirit in abundance' (CCC, no. 731).

The Acts of the Apostles and the various epistles of the New Testament give us further evidence of the presence and action of the Holy Spirit in the first-century Church. Later, in response to a denial of the divinity of the Spirit, the First Council of Constantinople (AD 381) declared as the constant faith of the Church the divinity of the Holy Spirit.

Even though the Holy Spirit is the last Person of the Trinity to be revealed, we must understand that, from the beginning, he is a part of the loving plan of our salvation from sin and of the offer of divine life. He has the same mission as the Son in the cause of our salvation. When the Father sends the Son, he also sends the Holy Spirit:

> When the Father sends his Word, he always sends his Breath. In their joint mission, the Son and the Holy Spirit are distinct but inseparable. (CCC, no. 689)

The Holy Spirit continues to give us knowledge of God, living and active in the Church. The *Catechism* sets out eight ways in which the Holy Spirit provides us with an experience of God's presence (cf. CCC, no. 688):

- When we pray and study the Scripture which the Holy Spirit inspired, we can sense his presence in the biblical words
- When we read the lives of the saints, their teachings and witness, we can be motivated to holiness by their example which was shaped by the Holy Spirit
- When we assent with obedience to the teachings of the Magisterium, we are guided by the Holy Spirit. His presence is uniquely experienced at Ecumenical Councils
- When we actively participate in the liturgies and Sacraments of the Church, we enter into a sacred moment when the Holy Spirit opens us to experience God, especially in the Eucharist
- When we give ourselves to prayer, whether that be the Rosary or the Liturgy of the Hours or meditation or other prayers, the Holy Spirit prays within us and intercedes for us

FROM THE CATECHISM

1. What is our faith regarding the Holy Spirit?
To believe in the Holy Spirit is to profess that the Holy Spirit is one of the persons of the Holy Trinity, consubstantial with the Father and the Son: 'with the Father and the Son he is worshipped and glorified.' (CCC, no. 685, citing the Nicene Creed)

2. What are images of the Holy Spirit in Scripture?
In Scripture, some of the images of the Holy Spirit are fire, cloud and light, seal, hand, finger of God and dove (cf. CCC, nos. 696–701).

3. How are water and anointing, symbols of the Holy Spirit?
Water: ... signifies the Holy Spirit's action in Baptism, since after the invocation of the Holy Spirit it becomes the efficacious sacramental sign of new birth. (CCC, no. 694)

Anointing: The ... anointing with oil also signifies the Holy Spirit ... In Christian initiation, anointing is the sacramental sign of Confirmation, called 'chrismation' in the Churches of the East. (CCC, no. 695)

- When we offer ourselves to the various missionary or apostolic efforts of the Church or see signs of those efforts, we can sense the Holy Spirit at work in the world
- When we recognise the charisms and ministries which help build the Church, we also understand that it is the Holy Spirit providing us with the leadership we need
- When we dwell on the great Tradition of the Church, its marvellous history and its host of saintly witnesses, we sense the Holy Spirit's sustaining power through it all.

GIFTS AND FRUITS OF THE HOLY SPIRIT

Gifts of the Holy Spirit: Wisdom, Understanding, Right Judgement, Courage, Knowledge, Reverence and Wonder and Awe in God's Presence. (cf. Is 11:1-2)

Fruits of the Holy Spirit: Love, Joy, Peace, Patience, Kindness, Goodness, Generosity, Gentleness, Faithfulness, Modesty, Self-Control and Chastity. (cf. Gal 5:22-23)

THE SPIRIT IS THE IMMEDIACY OF GOD

Our Irish society is undergoing an obvious process of secularisation. Despite a general turning away from organised religion, many of our countrymen and women, and those who have recently settled among us, still respect things of the spirit. And it is true that people are still capable of being moved, and even deeply affected, by a sign of the transcendent, or a revelation of wonder and awe in the depths of human experience. In the Catholic Church, a devotion to the Holy Spirit is evident in movements such as Charismatic Renewal, Marriage Encounter, Cursillo and similar outpourings of faith.

Catholic parishes regularly witness and celebrate the transformative power of the Holy Spirit at the conferral of the Sacrament of Confirmation and in the parishes' support for the journey of candidates in the Rite of Christian Initiation of Adults. In a special way, the immediacy of the Holy Spirit in the life of the Church is remembered on Pentecost Sunday as we hear of the Apostles and disciples gathered in the Upper Room and receiving the Holy Spirit.

FOR DISCUSSION

1. When in your life would you say you experienced God's presence? What were the occasions and the value of these experiences?
2. The Holy Spirit is the Sanctifier who calls us to holiness. When you hear about being called to be holy, what thoughts arise in your mind? What would you need to do to be more holy?
3. How do you see the gifts and fruits of the Holy Spirit at work in people you know?

DOCTRINAL STATEMENTS

- Before his Ascension, Jesus said to the Apostles, 'You will receive the power of the Holy Spirit which will come on you, and then you will be my witnesses not only in Jerusalem but throughout Judaea and Samaria, and indeed to earth's remotest end' (Acts 1:8).
- Whenever the Father sends his Son, he always sends his Spirit: their mission is inseparable.
- The life of the Blessed Virgin Mary shows us the power of the Holy Spirit. She was made by the Holy Spirit into a witness of grace from the moment of her conception. It is also by the power of the Holy Spirit that Mary conceived Jesus, the Son of God.
- By the anointing of the Holy Spirit at his Incarnation, the Son of God was consecrated as Christ (*Messiah*).
- At Pentecost, Peter said of Jesus that 'the Lord and Christ whom God has made is this Jesus whom you crucified' (Acts 2:36). From this fullness of his glory, Jesus poured out the Holy Spirit on the Apostles and the Church.
- The Holy Spirit builds up, animates and sanctifies the Church. He prepares us to go out and bring others to Christ. He opens our minds to understand Christ's death and Resurrection. He makes present for us the mystery of Christ, especially in the Eucharist and brings us to communion with God that we may bear much fruit (cf. CCC, no. 737).

▬▬▬ MEDITATION ▬▬▬

In the life of faith there are always two movements: God in search of us and we in search of God. The poet Francis Thompson described God's attempts to reach us in terms of his being the 'Hound of Heaven'. Thompson said he felt God coming after him and yearning to give him love. But the poet was not ready:

> I fled Him, down the labyrinthine ways
> of my own mind ... I hid from him.

At the same time, God has stamped in our souls a longing for himself. We are born with a longing for the divine that cannot be satisfied by anyone or anything short of God. We are created to be seekers for the absolute love, which is God. Thompson not only experienced God as the hound pursuing him; he also felt his own hunger and thirst for God. One day he stopped running, turned and rushed toward God:

> Naked, I wait Thy love's uplifted stroke!
>   My harness, piece by piece, Thou hast hewn from me ...
> I am defenseless, utterly.

And God, the other seeker, in this spiritual drama says:

> Rise, clasp my hand, and come!

The Holy Spirit presided over this spiritual adventure. It is the mission of the Spirit to help us draw near to God. When the Holy Spirit is present and active in our lives, we can have an experience of his presence.

PRAYER

Come, Holy Spirit, fill the hearts of your faithful.
And kindle in them the fire of your love.
Send forth your Spirit and they shall be created.
And you shall renew the face of the earth.
Let us pray.
Lord, by the light of the Holy Spirit you have taught the hearts
of your faithful.
In the same Spirit, help us to know what is truly right
and always to rejoice in your consolation.
We ask this through Christ, Our Lord. Amen.

When the Spirit of truth comes he will lead you to
the complete truth.

— Jn 16:13

10 THE CHURCH: REFLECTING THE LIGHT OF CHRIST

THE IMAGES AND MISSION OF THE CHURCH
– CCC, NOS. 748–810

PETER IS A ROCK AND A LOVING PASTOR

The account in Chapter 16 of Matthew begins with Jesus and the Apostles' arrival at Caesarea Philippi, a city that was twenty-five miles north of the Sea of Galilee. In this setting, Jesus asks the Apostles who people thought he was. They replied that some thought Jesus was John the Baptist, others that he was Elijah, or Jeremiah, or one of the prophets. They wondered if Jesus was one of the great prophets come back from the dead.

Jesus asked them, 'Who do you say I am?' Simon Peter alone replied, 'You are the Christ, the Son of the living God' (v. 16). Jesus praised Peter's reply, noting that he had not arrived at such an insight through his own human abilities. Peter had received a revelation from God and had spoken from his faith. 'Simon son of Jonah, you are a blessed man! Because it was no human agency that revealed this to you but my Father in heaven' (v. 17).

Jesus then proceeded to make Peter the rock on which he would build the Church. Beneath the backdrop of a temple built on a rock and devoted to the idolatrous worship of an emperor, Peter, whose name means 'rock', is chosen to lead God's Church. 'You are Peter and on this rock I will build my community' (v. 18). Jesus went further and promised to give Peter the 'keys to the Kingdom of Heaven', that is, authority to shepherd the Church. Jesus also promised that the gates of hell will not prevail against the Church. These words are a reminder that, while disorder and chaos might threaten the Church, they will never prevail over the Church because of Christ's protection. This scene ends with Christ's prediction of his suffering and death.

John 21:15-17 recounts a Resurrection scene. The risen Jesus spoke to a repentant Peter, who is filled with sorrow because of his triple denial of Christ, 'Simon son of John, do you love me more than these others do?' Peter replied, 'Yes, Lord, you know I love you.' Jesus said to him, 'Feed my lambs.' Jesus repeated the question two more times, and Peter strongly professed his love. Each time Jesus commissioned him to feed his lambs and sheep, that is, the members of the Church.

This scene complements the one in Matthew. There, Jesus called Peter to be the rock of the Church. Here, Christ summoned Peter to be a shepherd who loves Jesus and the Church's people.

Peter was one of the Twelve Apostles, all chosen by Jesus to be the foundation of his Church. At the head of the Twelve, Jesus placed Peter. From Jesus, the Twelve received the mandate to preach the Gospel to all nations. Peter ultimately made his way to Rome, where he died as a martyr. In establishing the Twelve Apostles with Peter at their head, Jesus gave the Church the basic structure of its leadership.

THE CHURCH AS MYSTERY

The Church is essentially both human and divine, visible but endowed with invisible realities, zealous in action and dedicated to contemplation.

> – CCC, no. 771, citing Second Vatican Council,
> *Constitution on the Sacred Liturgy*
> (*Sacrosanctum Concilium*; SC), no. 2

The Church is a holy mystery because of her origin in the Holy Trinity and her mission to be the Sacrament of Salvation (the sign and instrument of God's plan to unite all under Christ).

The Holy Trinity brought the Church into being. The Father called the Church into existence. The Son established the Church. The Holy Spirit filled the Church with power and wisdom at Pentecost. The Holy Trinity abides with the Church always, creatively and providentially. The Church, empowered by the Holy Spirit, brings Christ's salvation to the world. She is the instrument of God's universal call to holiness. At the same time, the Church is made up of a sinful people. Yet despite the personal sinfulness of her members, the Church remains holy by the presence of Jesus and the Holy Spirit who permeates her.

MEANINGS OF THE WORD *CHURCH*

The word *Church* is a translation of biblical words: the Hebrew word *qahal*, and the Greek word *ekklesia*, both of which mean 'gathering of people or community' for worship. It was first applied to the people of Israel whom God called into existence. The Church is also called into existence by God. Responding to the proclamation of the Gospel begun by the Apostles, men and women embrace God's gift of faith and through Baptism become members of the community of the Church.

The word *Church* means the people gathered by God into one community, guided today by the bishops, who are the successors of the Apostles and whose head is the Bishop of Rome, the Pope. The term *Church* also applies to specific geographical communities called dioceses. It also applies to the buildings where the faithful gather for the Sacraments, especially the Eucharist, and to families who are called domestic churches.

PLANNED BY THE FATHER

How did the Church come to be?

From the beginning, the Church was part of God's plan for sharing his divine life with all people. There was a gradual formation of God's family through a series of events described in the Old Testament: God's covenant with Abraham as the father of a great people, the liberation of ancient Israel from slavery in Egypt and their establishment in the Promised Land, and their solidification as a nation through the kingship of David.

FOUNDED BY JESUS CHRIST

Jesus brought about the fulfilment of the Father's plan for the Church first by his preaching and witnessing the Good News of the Kingdom, with its gifts of salvation from sin and participation in divine life. The seed and beginning of the Kingdom was the little flock whom Jesus shepherded as his family. Jesus established the beginnings of a visible structure of the Church that will remain until the Kingdom is fully achieved, through his choice of the Twelve Apostles, with Peter as the head.

By his Cross, Jesus gave birth to the Church:

> The Church is born primarily of Christ's total self-giving for our salvation, anticipated in the institution of the Eucharist and fulfilled on the cross. 'The origin and growth of the Church are symbolised by the blood and water which flowed from the open side of the crucified Jesus.' 'For it was from the side of Christ as he slept the sleep of death upon the cross that there came forth the "wondrous sacrament of the whole Church".' As Eve was formed from the sleeping Adam's side, so the Church was born from the pierced heart of Christ hanging dead on the cross. (CCC, no. 766, citing LG, no. 3, and SC, no. 5)

REVEALED BY THE SPIRIT

The Holy Spirit revealed the Church at Pentecost, coming upon the Apostles and the disciples with a transforming fire, forming them into a visible community and empowering them to proclaim the Gospel of Jesus Christ.

The early Church Fathers taught that there was an inseparable link between the Holy Spirit and the Church: 'Where the Church is, there also is God's Spirit; where God's Spirit is, there is the Church' (St Irenaeus, *Against Heresies*, III, 24.1). So forceful is the presence of the Spirit in the life of the early Church that the New Testament narrative of the Church's early growth, the Acts of the Apostles, is often called the 'Gospel of the Holy Spirit'.

The Acts of the Apostles and early Church history show how the Holy Spirit bestowed gifts on the community of believers for their roles and responsibilities in serving the Church. This was a dynamic process that illustrated the abiding presence and action of the Spirit along with the increased understanding of the Faith. From Pentecost onward, the Church began her earthly pilgrimage that will be fulfilled one day in glory. The Holy Spirit maintains the stability, durability and continuity of the Church both in favourable and unfavourable historical circumstances.

THE CHURCH MANIFESTS THE HOLY TRINITY

The Church is the continuing manifestation of the Father, Son and Holy Spirit. The Church exists by the will of God the Father and his plan to gather all people under the Lordship of his Son. As Head of the Church, Jesus Christ continues to fill her with his life and saving grace, pouring into her the Holy Spirit with his gifts of unity, peace and love.

CHURCH AS THE SACRAMENT OF SALVATION

To say that the Church is a sacrament is to say that she is a mystery, being both visible and spiritual.

The visible Church is a public institution, with a hierarchical government, laws and customs. She is visible in her worldwide membership of millions of believers who gather in Christian homes, parishes, dioceses, monasteries, convents and shrines to praise God and then to go forth to witness Christ and serve the world in love, justice and mercy.

This Church is also a spiritual reality, with interior bonds of faith and love forged by the Holy Spirit. The Church as both visible and spiritual is traditionally described as the Mystical Body of Christ. It is a living body, sustained by the hidden work of the Holy Spirit.

The complexity that characterises the Church as a visible institution and, at the same time, a spiritual reality causes some to miss the basic unity of the

Church. The Holy Spirit is the source of unity of all the aspects of the Church. The Holy Spirit integrates the visible aspects of the Church with the invisible aspects in such a way that the Church is always a unity of both aspects.

> In the unity of this Body [of which Christ is the head], there is a diversity of members and functions. All members are linked to one another, especially to those who are suffering, to the poor and persecuted. (CCC, no. 806)

The Church is the sacrament of salvation. 'The Church is like a sacrament – a sign and instrument, that is, of communion with God and of unity among all men' (CCC, no. 775). The Church is a sacrament of the union of all people with God and a sacrament of the unity of all peoples – for the Church gathers people 'from every nation, race, tribe and language' (Rv 7:9).

The Spirit communicates to us the salvation gained for us by Jesus Christ through the Church and her Seven Sacraments. 'The Church "is the visible plan of God's love for humanity", because God desires "that the whole human race may become one People of God, form one Body of Christ, and be built up into one temple of the Holy Spirit"' (CCC, no. 776, citing Pope Paul VI [June, 22, 1973]).

THE CHURCH IS THE PEOPLE OF GOD

[God] has ... willed to make men holy and save them,
not as individuals without any bond between them, but
rather to make them into a people who might acknowledge
him and serve him in holiness.

– CCC, no. 781

Chapter two of the *Dogmatic Constitution on the Church* (*Lumen Gentium*) gives prominence to a scriptural and patristic image of the Church as the People of God. The Father began this formation process with the Israelites and brought it to fulfilment in the Church. A person is initiated into God's people not by physical birth, but by a spiritual birth through faith in Christ and Baptism. God's people include the popes, patriarchs, bishops, priests, deacons, the laity, religious men and women – each group with its special mission and responsibility.

Jesus Christ is the head of this people whose law is love of God and neighbour. Its mission is to be the salt of the earth and the light of the world and a seed of the possibility of unity, hope, salvation and holiness for humanity. Its destiny is the Kingdom of God, already partially experienced on earth and fully known in heaven. All God's people, through their Baptism, participate in Christ's offices of priest, prophet and king.

A PRIESTLY PEOPLE

All of the baptised share in Christ's priesthood. This participation is called the 'common priesthood of all the faithful'. Their works, prayers, activities of family and married life, apostolic endeavours, relaxation and even the sufferings and setbacks of life can become spiritual offerings pleasing to God when united to the sacrifice of Christ. Such acts of God's people become forms of divine worship that by his design sanctify the world.

Based on the common priesthood of all the faithful and ordered to its service is the ordained, ministerial priesthood. This priesthood is conferred by the Sacrament of Holy Orders.

> The ministerial priesthood differs in essence from the common priesthood of the faithful because it confers a sacred power for the service of the faithful. (CCC, no. 1592)

In a later chapter, we will reflect on the unique role of those in Holy Orders and on the special service they provide the whole Body of Christ.

A PROPHETIC PEOPLE

God's people also share in Christ's role as prophet. This means both teaching and witnessing God's Word in the world. A real prophet, by teaching and good example, leads others to faith. Saint Francis of Assisi once said, 'Preach always. Sometimes use words'. Priests, laity and religious can all collaborate in the Church's missionary and evangelisation activity, catechetical ministry, the teaching of theology and the use of all forms of contemporary media. While witness is essential, we should be always aware of opportunities to share our faith verbally with each other and with all those who do not yet profess it. This prophetic role is exercised with the guidance of the bishops, who have a special teaching responsibility entrusted to them by Christ.

A ROYAL PEOPLE

God's people share in Christ's kingly mission, which is to lead others through loving service to them. Jesus came not 'to be served but to serve, and to give his life as a ransom for many' (Mt 20:28). We are called, in imitation of the Lord Jesus, to be people who offer ourselves willingly in service to others. Actions of such service can point to Christ's Kingdom of love, justice, mercy and salvation to all persons, cultures, governments and other structures of society. We are also called to a life of service to the Church herself. Servant leadership is a responsibility of all God's people within their differing roles and responsibilities. Bishops have a particular responsibility of leadership and governance in the Church.

> 'Lay members of the Christian faithful can cooperate in the exercise of this power [of governance].' ... The Church provides for their presence at particular councils, diocesan synods, pastoral councils; the exercise *in solidum* of the pastoral care of a parish, collaboration in finance committees and participation in ecclesiastical tribunals, etc. (CCC, no. 911, citing *Code of Canon Law*, can. 129 §2)

THE CHURCH AS COMMUNION

The image of the Church as Communion has the value of connecting truths about the Church in a fruitful and harmonious manner. We begin with a definition of the Church as Communion.

> The Church as Communion is our loving fellowship and union with Jesus and other baptised Christians in the Church, the Body of Christ, which has its source and summit in the celebration of the

Eucharist by which we are joined in divine love to the communion of the Father, Son and Holy Spirit. (cf. CCC, Glossary)

The Church, the Body of Christ, is the assembly of people gathered into her by Baptism and their participation in the Sacraments, especially the Eucharist, which open their minds and hearts to the Trinity, a loving communion of divine persons. In this communion of the Church, the members are called to love God, others and self, and so to be a communal witness of the love by which Christ saved the world. By divine love, we are joined to the communion of the Father, Son and Holy Spirit.

At the centre of the Gospel message is God's desire to share the communion of Trinitarian life with us. Jesus came to invite everyone to participate in the loving communion that Father, Son and Spirit have with each other. All creation is meant to show us the Trinity's plan of love for us. Everything Jesus did pointed to this goal.

In the Church, the Holy Spirit works in us to achieve the same purpose. When we say God is love, we are doing more than applying an abstract quality to the Lord. We testify in faith that God as Trinity wants to relate to us and to be engaged in our world.

This truth in no way diminishes the mystery of God as totally other, unique, awesome, majestic and pure holiness. But love within the Trinity makes possible a divine closeness to us. Love preserves the mystery and yet overcomes what might have been a gulf between us and God. Unity and communion with God in the Church also calls us to become a source of unity for all people.

UPON THIS ROCK – A COMMUNITY OF LOVE

Often, the freedom of a community is placed in opposition to the loyalty required by an institution. Even in the Irish tradition of the *meitheal,* in which neighbours extend cooperative help to one of their number at a time of heavy work such as the harvest season, the obligation for friendly assistance has to be paid back. The support of the community is founded on a reciprocal and communal duty of mutual aid for all in the work-team. But the sense of endless freedom is sometimes in tension with belonging to the Church as a community of believers.

FROM THE CATECHISM

1. How did the Second Vatican Council relate Christ as the light of humanity to the Church?

'Christ is the light of humanity ... By proclaiming his Gospel to every creature, it may bring to all ... that light of Christ which shines out visibly from the Church.' ... By choosing this starting point the Council demonstrates that the article of faith about the Church depends entirely upon the articles concerning Jesus Christ. (CCC, no. 748, citing LG, no. 1)

2. What do we learn from the scriptural images of the Church, such as Body of Christ, sheepfold, cultivated field and temple?

The images taken from the Old Testament are variations of a profound theme: the People of God. In the New Testament, all these images find a new centre because Christ has become the head of his people, which henceforth is his Body. Around this centre are grouped images taken 'from the life of the shepherd or from cultivation of the land, from the art of building or from family life and marriage'. (CCC, no. 753, citing LG, no. 6)

3. How is the Church the Temple of the Holy Spirit?

'What the soul is to the human body, the Holy Spirit is to the Body of Christ, which is the Church' (St Augustine, Sermon 267, 4) ... The Holy Spirit is 'the principle of every vital and truly saving action in each part of the Body' (Pope Pius XII, *The Mystical Body* [*Mystici Corporis*]: DS 3808). (CCC, nos. 797–798)

When it comes to the Church, some claim that its institutional needs take a toll on the values of community and relationships. Institutions require time, money and effort for their maintenance. Since the Second Vatican Council highlighted the Church as the People of God, does this not mean that our energies should be focused on people, not buildings, committees, laws and rules? Should we not recapture the simplicity of Christ's relationship with his disciples and the intimacy of the early Church as described in the Acts of the Apostles?

In response, we would say this is not an 'either/or' situation. There is no doubt that the Church is called to be a community of love in the Father, the Son and the Holy Spirit. The risen Jesus himself presented a model of Church leadership based in love when he solicited three affirmations of love from Peter (cf. Jn 21:15-17). At the same time, though, the Church has many structures that are needed to build up the bond of love.

Jesus himself established one of those structures of the Church when he named Peter as the rock of the Church, the head of the Apostles (cf. Mt 16:18). While St Paul taught us that love is the greatest gift of the Holy Spirit (cf. 1 Cor 13:1-13), he also listed administration as a gift of the Spirit (cf. 1 Cor 12:28).

The Church needs an institutional framework for its stability, continuity and mission for serving the cause of the Gospel and opening people to God's call to holiness. Problems with the institution are not arguments for its removal, but for its renewal. Just as the Son of God took on our human flesh and just as a soul needs a body, so a community needs to be organised to serve and be served. The Church is a community that is served by a multiplicity of structures.

■ FOR DISCUSSION ■

1. How is the Church viewed as a mystery? What would you see as the link between the Church as mystery and your faith?
2. Why is the image of the Church as People of God important? What is meant by the description of the Church as a Sacrament of Salvation?
3. How does the understanding of the Church as Body of Christ shape your faith? Why is the link between the Holy Spirit and the Church so vital?

▬▬ DOCTRINAL STATEMENTS ▬▬

- The word *Church* is based on both the Greek word *ekklesia* and the Hebrew word *qahal*, which mean the gathering of the community. It was first applied to the people of Israel, whom God called into existence. The Church was planned and formed by God, who called together into one those who accepted the Gospel.
- The Father prepared for the Church through a series of covenant events described in the Old Testament. Jesus fulfilled the divine plan for the Church through his saving death and Resurrection. The Holy Spirit manifested the Church as a mystery of salvation.
- The Church is a visible society and a spiritual community; she is a hierarchical institution and the Body of Christ; she is an earthly Church and one filled with heavenly treasures. Hence the Church is a complex reality that has human and divine elements.

The reality of the mystery of the Church is expressed in a variety of ways as follows:

- The Church is the sacrament of salvation, the sign and instrument of our communion with God (cf. CCC, nos. 774–776);
- The Church is the People of God. 'You are a *chosen race, a kingdom of priests, a holy nation* ... Once you were a *non-people* and now you are the People of God' (1 Pt 2:9-10). We become members of God's People through faith and Baptism (cf. CCC, nos. 781–786);
- The Church is the Body of Christ. Christ is the head, and we are the members. In the unity of this Body, there is a diversity of members and roles, yet everyone is linked together by Christ's love and grace, especially the poor, the suffering and the persecuted (cf. CCC, nos. 787–795);
- The Church is the Bride of Christ. 'Christ loved the Church and handed himself over [to death] for her that he might sanctify her' (cf. Eph 5:25-26; cf. CCC, no. 796);
- The Church is the Temple of the Holy Spirit. 'We are – the temple of the living God' (2 Cor 6:16; cf. 1 Cor 3:16-17, Eph 2:21; cf. CCC, nos. 797–801);

- The Church is a communion. The starting point of this communion is our union with Jesus Christ. This gives us a share in the communion of the Persons of the Trinity and also leads to a communion among men and women (cf. CCC, nos. 813, 948, 959);
- These truths about unity and communion in the Church call us to become a source of unity for all peoples.

MEDITATION

Christians do not make a house of God until they are one in charity. The timber and stone must fit together in an orderly plan, must be joined in perfect harmony, must give each other the support as if it were of love, or no one would enter the building. When you see the stones and beams of a building holding together securely, you enter the building with an easy mind ...

The work we see complete in this building is physical; it should find its spiritual counterpart in your hearts.

– St Augustine, Sermon 336, 1, 6

PRAYER

Father, you called your people to be your Church.
As we gather together in your name, may we love,
honour and follow you to eternal life in the kingdom
you promise.

– Prayer for the Dedication of a Church,
Liturgy of the Hours, vol. III, 1596

You are a *chosen race, a kingdom of priests, a holy nation.*

– 1 Pt 2:9

11 THE FOUR MARKS OF THE CHURCH

THE CHURCH IS ONE, HOLY, CATHOLIC AND APOSTOLIC
– CCC, NOS. 811–962

EDEL QUINN:
A THOROUGHLY MODERN MISSIONARY

Edel Quinn was born in Kanturk, Co. Cork in September 1907. Her father was a bank official, and the family moved around from town to town. School was often interrupted. Every couple of years, Edel would be uprooted from familiar friends and have to begin with new teachers and classmates in another town. Her reaction to such a broken-up education could have been to grow up a shy, quiet, reserved child. Edel turned out to be the opposite, however – a bright, easy-going, charming and accomplished youngster, who learned at an early age how to make friends easily, to influence others, and sell herself well. Behind the dancing eyes and ready smile, though, she cultivated a reflective and thoughtful nature.

In the course of her secondary schooling, Edel attended a convent boarding school in England. While there, she excelled in sport and cultural activities, being captain of the cricket team and accomplished in tennis and music. This early adjustment to another country and culture was to be providential for her later success.

Family difficulties meant that Edel was obliged to get a job on leaving school. As a young office worker, she was a typical girl of her time. But she was never one to go with the flow, just be one of the crowd. Edel was always her own person. She made an individual impression in whatever circle she moved, having superb social skills and demonstrating accomplished talent. Her colleagues and companions remarked that Edel Quinn was a serious woman of purpose and determination, conviction and values. She had character and wisdom beyond her years. This added to her attractiveness.

One of the first to fall under her charm was Pierre, a manager in the office. He proposed marriage to her, and Edel astonished him by confessing that she intended shortly to enter a contemplative convent as a Poor Clare nun. She continued, though, to keep in touch with Pierre for a number of years, and he remained a good friend.

In the event, Edel's religious vocation was frustrated when she fell ill with tuberculosis in February 1932, just before she was going to apply. The illness confined her for eighteen months in the Newcastle Sanatorium, Co. Wicklow. Tuberculosis treatment at that time involved fresh air and isolation, rather than the drug therapy which has now greatly reduced incidences of the dreaded lung disease. Edel never really managed to shake off the effects of the disease, and she suffered from an intermittent racking cough for the rest of her life.

Disappointed in her religious vocation, Edel returned to office work and, in her spare time, devoted herself to the Legion of Mary apostolate. During one summer holiday, she went on extension work for the Legion in Wales, and found that her disposition and talents were well suited to that kind of work. She proposed devoting her life to spreading the Legion of Mary in England, and this plan was being discussed when a request was received at Legion headquarters for help in extending the Legion in South Africa. This looked like a heaven-sent opportunity, because the climate was suitable for a tubercular patient like Edel. It would not have been the first time that someone with her complaint, transferred to the southern hemisphere, had thrived in the drier, warmer weather. But God had other plans, and when Edel finally got the Legion's permission and sailed to Africa, her destination was Mombasa in East Africa, a new territory and an altogether sterner test.

Frank Duff, the founder of the Legion of Mary, whom we will meet in Chapter 24, was the one who promoted Edel's candidacy for envoy, but the proposition had to be passed by the Central Council of the Legion. The idea of sending a sickly young girl on such a daunting task did not have an easy passage through the meeting, but Frank's support of the project was persuasive in the end. On her sea journey to Mombasa, Edel wrote to Frank Duff:

> I could not say thanks for fear of breaking down, perhaps; but it is good to feel one is trusted, and it will be a help in the days to come. I would like you to remember always, whatever happens, that I am glad you gave me the opportunity of going. I realise that it is a privilege and also only that you persisted I, personally, would never have been sent.

As an envoy of the Legion of Mary, Edel Quinn was, in effect, an ambassador, a missionary and a saleswoman all in one. She was an ambassador because she represented the Legion Concilium, the headquarters group in Dublin. She communicated their decisions, provided them with reports, and made official contact for them with bishops, religious and other representatives of Church and State. She was a missionary because she had the task of propagating the Legion in new territories, responding to requests for information, visiting dioceses, making presentations and answering questions. Finally, she was a down-to-earth saleswoman because when she entered a parish hall, or met a group of hesitant lay people, or contacted a bishop for the first time, it all came down to her winning ways, her gentle smile, her welcoming tone of voice and her vibrant personality.

Edel's territory was East Africa, that is, the countries of Kenya, Uganda, Mauritius, Nyasaland (in modern South Africa), Tanganyika and Zanzibar (both in modern Tanzania). She undertook many of the trips in an ancient Ford car. Her courage, persistence and good humour were much in evidence, particularly when there were breakdowns! During eight years of her tour of duty, she covered a vast area, founding praesidia, setting up national organisations and introducing the Legion to new dioceses and countries. It was clear, from the enthusiastic approval of bishops, that the Legion method was a fruitful formula for organising lay apostolic work in mission territories.

Eventually, however, the rigours of her work and her bad health wore her down. She fell ill with malaria and pleurisy. After a lengthy convalescence in South Africa, she came back to Nairobi, her headquarters, where she died on 12 May 1944, and was buried in the same cemetery as Bishop Joseph Shanahan.

Youth has its charm and energy, and Edel Quinn portrayed to Irish Catholics of the mid-twentieth century and to Legionaries of Mary worldwide a model of the lay missionary working in the apostolate. Twenty years before the Second Vatican Council proclaimed the vocation of all Christians in baptism to holiness and evangelisation, Edel Quinn provided a practical example of what a thoroughly modern lay missionary should look like. During the Vatican Council, the cause of her canonisation was introduced and in 1994 St John Paul II declared Edel Quinn 'Venerable'.

THE FOUR MARKS OF THE CHURCH

It is Christ who, through the Holy Spirit, makes his Church one, holy, catholic and apostolic, and it is he who calls her to realise each of these qualities.

– CCC, no. 811

In the earliest professions of faith, the Catholic Church identified herself as 'one, holy, catholic and apostolic'. We find these words in the Nicene Creed professed at Sunday Mass. Traditionally, they refer to what are known as the four marks of the Church, traits that identify the Church before the world.

Inseparably linked with one another, these four marks indicate the essential features of the Church and her mission on earth. Each mark is so joined with the others that they form one coherent and interrelated idea of what Christ's Church must be. They strengthen the faith of the believer and at the same time can attract non-Catholics to investigate the Church more fully. Because of the sinfulness of the Church's members, these marks are not always lived out fully, so we need to view them as both a reality and yet a challenge.

THE CHURCH IS ONE

The mark of oneness reflects the unity of the Trinity. The Holy Spirit, the bond of love between the Father and the Son, unites all the members of the Church as the one People of God. The Church professes one Lord, one faith and one Baptism and forms one body (cf. CCC, no. 866) under the leadership of the Holy Father, successor to Peter the Apostle. Within the Church there is a diversity of races, nations, cultures, languages and traditions, which are held together in one communion by the gift of love from the Holy Spirit. The unity that Christ bestowed on his Church is something she can never lose (cf. Second Vatican Council, *Decree on Ecumenism* [*Unitatis Redintegratio*; UR], no. 4; CCC, nos. 813, 815).

Tragically, members of the Church have offended against her unity, and throughout the centuries, there have developed divisions among Christians. Already in the fifth century, doctrinal disagreements led to the separation of some Christians in the eastern region of the Roman rupture between Rome and Constantinople in AD 1054. And in the sixteenth century, Western Europe experienced the divisions that followed the Protestant Reformation.

The Catholic Church has always been committed to the restoration of unity among all Christians. This commitment was intensified by the Second Vatican Council and led the Church to participate in what is called the ecumenical movement. The word *ecumenical* means 'worldwide' and, in a Catholic understanding, describes efforts 'for the reconciliation of all Christians in the unity of the one and only Church of Christ' (UR, no. 24; CCC, no. 822). This is to be a visible communion. 'Full unity will come about when all share in the means of salvation entrusted by Christ to his Church' (St John Paul II, *On Commitment to Ecumenism* [*Ut Unum Sint*; UUS], no. 86). 'Communion of the particular Churches with the Church of Rome, and of their Bishops with the Bishop of Rome, is – in God's plan – an essential requisite of full and visible communion' (UUS, no. 97). Ecumenism includes efforts to pray together, joint study of the Scripture and of one another's traditions, common action for social justice, and dialogue in which the leaders and theologians of the different churches and communities discuss in depth their doctrinal and theological positions for greater mutual understanding and 'to work for unity in truth' (UUS, nos.

18, 29). In dialogue the obligation to respect the truth is absolute. 'The unity willed by God can be attained only by the adherence of all to the content of revealed faith in its entirety' (UUS, no. 18). On the worldwide level, these dialogues are sponsored on the Catholic side by the Pontifical Council for the Promotion of Christian Unity, a Vatican office directly accountable to the pope.

The Catholic Church retains the structures of episcopal leadership and sacramental life that are the gift of Christ to his Church (cf. CCC, nos. 765, 766) and that date back to apostolic times. At the same time, the Catholic Church recognises that the Holy Spirit uses other churches and ecclesial communities 'as means of salvation, whose power derives from the fullness of grace and truth that Christ has entrusted to the Catholic Church' (CCC, no. 819; LG, no. 8). Depending on what and how much of the elements of sanctification and truth (UR, no. 3) these communities have retained, they have a certain though imperfect communion with the Catholic Church. There are also real differences. In some cases 'there are very weighty differences not only of a historical, sociological, psychological and cultural character, but especially in the interpretation of revealed truth' (UR, no. 19). (The word *church* applies to those bodies of Christians who have a valid episcopal leadership or hierarchy, while the phrase *ecclesial communities* refers to those bodies of Christians that do not have an apostolic hierarchy.)

THE CHURCH IS HOLY

The Church has her origin in the Holy Trinity, and that is the source of her holiness. In his plan for the salvation of humanity, God the Father willed the existence of the Church. Jesus Christ, the Son of God, established a community of disciples and died on the Cross for the forgiveness of sins. The Holy Spirit, sent by the Father and the Son, works within the Church to keep her members faithful to the Gospel. The Church is holy in her Founder, in her saints and in her means of salvation.

Through Baptism and Confirmation, Catholics have become a people consecrated by the Holy Spirit to the praise of God through Jesus Christ. Christians grow in holiness by working to live in conformity to the Gospel of Jesus and thus to become more like him, especially in the totality of his love for others shown by his sacrifice of himself on the Cross. But Christians also remain subject to temptation and sin, thus needing God's mercy and forgiveness. In teaching his disciples how to pray, Jesus included the following petition to the Father: 'Forgive us our trespasses as we forgive those who trespass against us.'

In the following parts of this catechism, the Sacraments, the Ten Commandments, the virtue of charity and prayer will be presented as sources of holiness for the Church.

THE CHURCH IS CATHOLIC

The word *catholic* means 'universal'. The Catholic Church has lived and continues to live in a diversity of cultures and languages because she is led by the Spirit of Christ to bring the Gospel to all peoples. She has known how to accept what is true and good in all cultures and, at the same time, to infuse the truth and goodness of her tradition and life into them. The process of inculturation includes this dynamic.

The Church is also catholic because of her universal extension and her presence in local communities that are known as dioceses, or eparchies in the case of Eastern Churches, and are called 'particular Churches'.

> The Church of Christ is really present in all legitimately organised local groups of the faithful, which, in so far as they are united to their pastors, are also quite appropriately called Churches in the New Testament ... In them the faithful are gathered together through the preaching of the Gospel of Christ, and the mystery of the Lord's Supper is celebrated ... In these communities, though they may often be small and poor, or existing in the diaspora, Christ is present, through whose power and influence the One, Holy, Catholic and Apostolic Church is constituted.
>
> (CCC, no. 832)

These local communities are linked together through their communion with the Church of Rome and her bishop, the pope.

In the Catholic Church, the word *Church* is also used to refer to those communities which have their own 'ecclesiastical disciplines, liturgical rites and theological and spiritual heritages' (cf. CCC, no. 835). Thus we speak of the Latin Church and the Eastern Churches.

The Church is catholic also because of her relationship to all people. First of all, 'the Church knows that she is joined in many ways to the baptised who are honoured by the name of Christian, but do not profess the Catholic faith in its entirety or have not preserved unity or communion under the successor of Peter' (CCC, no. 838, citing LG, no. 15). Thus there exists an imperfect communion between the Catholic Church and other Christian churches and faith communions.

The Catholic Church also acknowledges her special relationship to the Jewish people. The Second Vatican Council declared that 'this people remains most dear to God, for God does not repent of the gifts he makes nor of the calls he issues' (LG, no. 16). When God called Abraham out of Ur, he promised to make of him a 'great nation'. To the Jewish people, whom God first chose to hear his Word, 'belong the sonship, the glory, the covenants, the giving of the law, the worship and the promise; to them belong the patriarchs, and of their race, according to the flesh, is the Christ' (Rm 9:4-5; cf. CCC, no. 839). At the same time, 'remembering, then, her common heritage with the Jews and moved not by any political consideration, but solely by the religious motivation of Christian charity, she [the Church] deplores all hatreds, persecutions, displays of antisemitism levelled at any time or from any source against the Jews' (Second Vatican Council, *Declaration on the Relation of the Church to Non-Christian Religions* [*Nostra Aetate*; NA], no. 4).

The Church also recognises that she has a unique relationship to Muslims. 'The plan of salvation also includes those who acknowledge the Creator, in the first place amongst whom are the Muslims; these profess to hold the faith of Abraham, and together with us they adore the one, merciful God, mankind's judge on the last day' (CCC, no. 841, citing LG, no. 16). The Church engages in dialogue not only with Muslims but also with Hindus and Buddhists. 'She has a high regard for the manner of life and conduct, the precepts and doctrines which, although differing in many ways from her own teaching, nevertheless often reflect a ray of that truth which enlightens all men' (NA, no. 2). These dialogues are conducted on the local level and also on the international level through the Pontifical Council for Interreligious Dialogue.

Dialogue is a form of evangelisation. It is a way of making Christ and his Gospel known to others, while at the same time respecting their freedom of conscience and adherence to their own religious tradition. The Church has received from Christ the mandate to make him known to all people. She does this in many ways. Dialogue is one way, but another way is the missionary activity of the Church. Through the work of missionaries (priests, consecrated men and women and lay people) the Church makes Christ known as they teach the Gospel to others by word and deed, inviting them to respond to this proclamation by the commitment of faith.

THE CHURCH IS APOSTOLIC

The Church is built upon the foundation of the Apostles, who were chosen by Christ himself, and at whose head he placed Peter. The entire community of Christians received the Apostles' proclamation of the Gospel, and so the Church in her entirety is called 'apostolic'. Under the guidance of the Holy Spirit, the Church as a whole remains and will always remain faithful to the teaching of the Apostles. This is called the indefectibility of the Church, because she will never fall away from the Gospel.

To further ensure the Church's fidelity to the Gospel, Christ has willed that the Apostles be succeeded by the bishops. The Apostles acted together as a body, with Peter at their head, in their leadership of the Church. Thus they are called by the Church a 'college'. The college of bishops has succeeded the college of the Apostles, and it is the Bishop of Rome, the pope, who has succeeded the role of Peter as head of the college. Thus they are called by the Church a 'college', and their essential unity as one body is understood as the principle of collegiality.

Each bishop works in his particular diocese in a priestly shepherding and teaching role. He possesses the fullness of the priesthood and so is the principal celebrant of the Sacraments, especially the Eucharist, by which the Church grows in holiness and union with Christ. He is also the chief shepherd of the diocese and so is responsible for compassionate and loving governance of the people entrusted to him. And he is the chief teacher of his diocese, responsible for authentic proclamation of the Gospel.

'OUTSIDE THE CHURCH THERE IS NO SALVATION'

From the *Catechism*, nos. 846–847:

How are we to understand this affirmation, often repeated by the Church Fathers? Re-formulated positively, it means that all salvation comes from Christ the Head through the Church which is his Body: 'Basing itself on Scripture and Tradition, the Council teaches that the Church, a pilgrim now on earth, is necessary for salvation: the one Christ is the mediator and the way of salvation; he is present to us in his body which is the Church. He himself explicitly asserted the necessity of faith and Baptism, and thereby affirmed at the same time the necessity of the Church which men enter through Baptism as through a door. Hence they could not be saved who, knowing that the Catholic Church was founded as necessary by God through Christ, would refuse either to enter it or to remain in it' (LG, no. 14; cf. Mk 16:16; Jn 3:5).

This affirmation is not aimed at those who, through no fault of their own, do not know Christ and his Church: 'Those who, through no fault of their own, do not know the Gospel of Christ or his Church, but who nevertheless seek God with a sincere heart, and, moved by grace, try in their actions to do his will as they know it through the dictates of their conscience – those too may achieve eternal salvation' (LG, no. 16; cf. DS 3866–3872).

The teaching office of the college of bishops is called 'the Magisterium'. When all the bishops throughout the world, together with the pope, in the fulfilment of their teaching office proclaim a doctrine that has been divinely revealed, it must be accepted with the obedience of faith by the whole People of God. 'Bishops, as successors of the Apostles, receive from the Lord, to whom was given all power in heaven and on earth, the mission to teach all nations and to preach the Gospel to every creature … For bishops are preachers of the faith, who lead new disciples to Christ, and they are authentic teachers, that is, teachers endowed with the authority of Christ, who preach to the people committed to them the faith they must believe and put into practice, and by the light of the Holy Spirit illustrate that faith.' (Second Vatican Council Document: The Dogmatic Constitution on the Church – *Lumen Gentium*, ch. 3, pars. 24–5.)

However, at certain times, the bishops gather in an Ecumenical Council with the Pope, and they teach and proclaim a doctrine that must be accepted with faith because it is divinely revealed. The bishops of the world defined and proclaimed a divinely revealed doctrine at the First Vatican Council (1869–70). This was when they taught that under certain conditions the pope himself can proclaim a doctrine that is divinely revealed and must be believed by all. This is known as the dogma of papal infallibility.

The entire Church as a body is infallible because the Holy Spirit ensures that she will not err in matters of faith and morals. But this infallibility is exercised in a special way by the pope and the bishops when together they teach what has been divinely revealed either in the ordinary way of their day-to-day teaching or the extraordinary way of an Ecumenical Council or the pope himself.

The pope and bishops also together teach truths that flow from Divine Revelation or that are closely related to it. Sometimes they teach these truths as being definitive, which means they must be firmly accepted and held. Sometimes they teach in a less than definitive way, which requires a religious submission of will and mind.

LAITY

By Baptism, every member of the Church participates in Christ's role as priest, prophet and king (which is understood in terms of being the shepherd of his people). The laity do this in the context of their lives within families, parish communities, civic communities and the workplace. The everyday gift of themselves in love and care for others, often done at great personal cost, is a priestly offering that is joined to the sacrifice of Christ in the Eucharist. By words and deeds faithful to the Gospel, they evangelise others, thus fulfilling their prophetic role. By seeking to build the common good of society on the basis of moral principles, they strengthen civic communities and thus fulfil their kingly or shepherding role.

The laity are in the unique position of being able directly to infuse culture and society with the Gospel. But they also contribute to the vitality of the life of the Church through ministry as catechists and many other ministries. Most are volunteers, but some have been called to serve as salaried ministers. Working with their pastors, they enable the Church to witness to Christian faith and love before the world.

Edel Quinn is an example of a lay woman exercising her baptismal role of lay ministry. She did this in her work with the Legion of Mary at home in Ireland, but also, most especially, in her official position as an envoy of the Legion in East Africa. Her eight years of ministry were attended by many signs of grace. The Church has officially recognised her life of heroic virtue in declaring her 'Venerable'. 'All members of the Church should, therefore, be prepared to participate occasionally in ongoing education and training to further their own faith development and in order to minister more effectively, one to the other' (*SGN* 68).

CONSECRATED LIFE

From the beginning of the Church, there have been men and women who have chosen to live in a radical witness to Christ by imitating him as closely as possible in his poverty, chastity and obedience. In the course of the centuries, this commitment became more and more visible through the establishment of monasteries, religious orders and congregations and other types of institutes. Men and women professed publicly evangelical 'counsels' (vows) of poverty, chastity and obedience and committed themselves to stability of life within communities.

Among these traditions of consecrated life are the Augustinian, Carthusian, Benedictine, Dominican, Franciscan and Carmelite – all ancient orders – as well as more recent Congregations and Institutes of Religious Life. Edel Quinn was a member of the Legion of Mary and a lay missionary. Other members of the Church have consecrated and dedicated their lives down through the centuries. They enrich the Church not only by the

FROM THE CATECHISM

1. Are non-Catholic Christians guilty of separation from the Church?

One cannot charge with the sin of the separation those who at present are born into these communities [that resulted from such separation] and in them are brought up in the faith of Christ, and the Catholic Church accepts them with respect and affection as brothers ... All who have been justified by faith in Baptism are incorporated into Christ; they therefore have a right to be called Christians, and with good reason are accepted as brothers in the Lord by the children of the Catholic Church. (CCC, no. 818, citing UR, no. 3)

2. What does *particular Church* mean for Latin Catholics?

The phrase 'particular Church', which is [first of all] the diocese ... refers to a community of the Christian faithful in communion of faith and sacraments with their bishop ordained in apostolic succession. These particular Churches 'are constituted after the model of the universal Church; it is in these and formed out of them that the one and unique Catholic Church exists'. (CCC, no. 833, citing LG, no. 23)

3. What is the principal vocation of the laity in the Church?

By reason of their special vocation it belongs to the laity to seek the kingdom of God by engaging in temporal affairs and directing them according to God's will. (CCC, no. 898, citing LG, no. 31)

radicalness of their embrace of the evangelical counsels, but also by the many apostolates (e.g. education and healthcare) by which they follow Christ in his compassion and care for others.

MAKE DISCIPLES

This chapter has uncovered the richness of the Catholic Church, as she comes from her source in God himself. Catholics today are encouraged to share this life of the Church with others, thus enabling them to know Christ. This is evangelisation. Edel Quinn wanted to become a contemplative nun with the Poor Clares. Her bad health frustrated her desires. Instead, through God's grace, she was called to the most energetic and missionary of apostolates in East Africa. Father Daniel Eclid OFM collected some of Edel Quinn's short sayings with which she formed her mind and will, and passed on spiritual advice to others. He called them Edel Quinn's *Words of Life*. Here are some of them:

- Beg the grace to make the Divine Life a continuous reality in us, our union with God
- Of ourselves we know not what we desire, but the Paraclete will teach us
- Do all you can when things are easier, but do not feel tied down when work presses or when you do not feel well
- I could assist at Mass the whole day long. Resolve to be in chapel at least ten to fifteen minutes before Mass
- Our Lady, dwelling-place of the Trinity
- The Immaculate Heart of Mary is a symbol of God's love
- Our Mother's most precious gift to her children is the Cross
- We should realise that those things which run counter to our own plans and likings are graces one and all. The Will of God permits them for us
- Sufferings are precious
- An idealist who does not try to put his ideals into practice, is not worth much
- Let us try to give utterly, in every possible way, without counting the cost, to be spent for Christ
- We can never love too much; let us give utterly, and not count the cost
- Let us clothe ourselves with Christ. Ask Mary Mediatrix to pour his Divine Life into our souls
- It is no part of our duty to judge others, so let us not torment ourselves about their doings

- We will love our neighbour – and we will be unable to speak ill or criticise – if in each one we see Christ
- Act as Jesus and Mary would act towards other people. Remember that these others are the temples of God, and that we cannot know the motives of their acts
- One must be prepared for the difficulties which arise on the way. Even for the average person, to keep a good disposition under the daily preoccupations requires a constant battle
- Work for the day. The saints never lost time. Live for the day. Life is made up of days
- It is the will, the will, the will that matters
- Ask to be equally faithful when all is black
- What is impossible for us is possible for him; take him at his word.

FOR DISCUSSION

1. How do the Church's four marks strengthen your Catholic identity? How can we lessen mistrust and the misunderstandings that exist among the various Christian denominations in our community? What can we do to eliminate anti-Semitism?
2. How is the hierarchy – pope, bishops, priests and deacons – valuable for your growth in faith? What sources of spiritual strength do you receive from the Church's structures: parish, diocese, universal Church?
3. Identify practical ways to evangelise others. What are some benefits the Church receives from those who have embraced consecrated life? What are ways that the laity can help spread the faith?

DOCTRINAL STATEMENTS

- The four Marks of the Church – that she is one, holy, catholic and apostolic – are inseparably linked to each other, and all are essential to the Church's mission and pursuit of holiness.
- The Church is one. She professes 'one Lord, one faith, one baptism' (Eph 4:5). This unity, sustained by the Holy Spirit, includes a diversity of gifts, talents, cultures and rites.

- The Church is holy. Jesus, the founder, is holy and makes his holiness available through his death and Resurrection. The Holy Spirit imparts holiness to us, especially through the Sacraments. The Church's holiness shines in the saints, and most especially in the Blessed Virgin Mary.
- The Church is catholic. The word *catholic* means universal. All the means of salvation are found in the Church. The Church has the fullness of the faith, the Sacraments and apostolic succession. Jesus commissions us to bring the Gospel to all peoples at all times; hence the Church is 'by its very nature missionary' (Second Vatican Council, *Decree on the Church's Missionary Activity* [*Ad Gentes Divinitus*; AG], no. 2).
- The Church is apostolic. Jesus willed to build the Church on the foundation of the Apostles. The Church hands on the teaching of the Apostles through all generations. Christ shepherds the Church through Peter and the other Apostles, whose successors are the pope and the college of bishops.
- Under the guidance of the Holy Spirit, the Apostles chose bishops to succeed them. Helped by the priests and deacons, the bishops teach the faith; celebrate the Sacraments, especially the Eucharist; and guide the Church. Their responsibility includes concern for all the Churches in union with the pope.
- God calls lay people to witness and share their faith in the midst of the world. By their Baptism they share in Christ's priesthood and are sealed by the Spirit. They are thus called to holiness, to a prophetic witness in the world and to a kingly resolve to sanctify the world by their words and deeds.
- Those who live a life consecrated to God profess the evangelical counsels of poverty, chastity and obedience in a stable state of life recognised by the Church. They solemnly promise to surrender themselves to God with an undivided heart, thus liberating themselves to serve God, the Church and the needs of others.

MEDITATION

God first called the Israelites to holiness: 'You must therefore be holy because I am holy' (Lev 11:45). Saint Peter repeated this command of the Lord for the Christian people. 'As he who called you is holy, be holy yourselves in every aspect of your conduct, for it is written, *"Be holy, for I am holy"*' (1 Pt 1:15-16). God addresses this call to every member of the Church. He begins the life of holiness in us at our Baptism when we are made partakers of divine life through the gift of sanctifying grace. Holiness is a gift, which the Holy Spirit continually offers us. It should bear fruit in us as we live out our love of God, our neighbour and ourselves; grow in virtue; and work for justice and mercy for all, especially the poor and defenseless.

PRAYER

Praised be to you, Lord, for your holy Church founded on
    the apostles,
where we are gathered together into your community.
Praise be to you, Lord, for the cleansing power of Baptism
    and Penance
that you have entrusted to your apostles,
through which we are cleansed of our sins.

– Intercessions from Common of the Apostles,
Liturgy of the Hours, vol. III, 1668

The Church is the Bride of Christ.
Come let us worship Christ, the Bridegroom of his Church.

12 MARY: THE CHURCH'S FIRST AND MOST PERFECT MEMBER

MARY, MOTHER OF JESUS, MOTHER OF GOD, MOTHER OF THE CHURCH
– CCC, NOS. 484–507, 963–972, 2673–2677

OUR LADY APPEARS AT KNOCK

When the Blessed Virgin Mary appeared at Knock in 1879, some features distinguished this apparition from others. First of all, Mary did not say anything. This is quite unusual. Our Lady gave no verbal message, and made no formal request. Indeed, the Knock apparition came to be referred to as 'Our Lady of Silence'. Second, she appeared with other figures. The visionaries recognised Mary, St Joseph and St John, along with an altar with a lamb and a cross on it. Third, the apparition was seen outside the small church building, against the gable end, not inside the chapel as in other instances, nor in the open countryside as with others. Last, the apparition occurred once only, for a number of hours, to a group of fifteen people.

The most enigmatic and striking figure in the apparition is that of the lamb standing beneath the Cross. This is the symbol of the sacrificial lamb of the Old Testament and of the sacrifice of Jesus on the Cross in the Gospels, the Lamb of God who takes away the sins of the world. The lamb is a powerful sign, especially to those who are oppressed, and it speaks with particular power to a rural pastoral people.

A number of Marian apparitions had taken place in Europe in the previous decades so knowledge of the Virgin Mary and her possible apparitions was very familiar to the people of Ireland in the nineteenth century, and it is no surprise that the parish priest, Archdeacon

Bartholomew Cavanagh, and the people of the area were devoted to Our Lady of the Immaculate Conception. As a result, Fr Cavanagh, a holy and zealous man, decided to celebrate a series of one hundred Masses for the poor souls in Purgatory whom the Blessed Virgin would wish released from punishment.

The hundredth day of the series – 21 August 1879 – was raining and misty. That evening, the priest's housekeeper, Mary McLoughlin, went by foot to visit a friend, Mary Byrne, who lived some distance away. On the way, she passed the church, a small structure which could hold only about thirty people.

Outside, against the back wall, she spotted a number of white figures, which she took to be some new statues that the priest had acquired, and was going to move into the church later. Without investigating further, she continued on to visit her friend.

After an hour or so, she returned home, accompanied on the way by Mary Byrne. She had not told her companion about the new statues, but as they drew near, Mary Byrne saw the same shapes. The women then ascertained that they were not statues, but white gleaming apparitions, who seemed to them to be Our Lady and Saint Joseph, and a third form whom Mary Byrne identified as Saint John the Evangelist. The three figures were standing apparently above the grass, surrounded by a golden light, as if they were praying or worshipping. Six angels gently hovered around them. An altar, a lamb and a cross were behind them. The figures in the vision did not move.

Our Lady wore a full white cloak and a gold crown with sparkling points. She was praying with elevated hands and eyes looking up. Saint Joseph stood on Mary's right hand side, wore white and stood with head bowed. Saint John was on the left, turned slightly away, with right hand and index finger raised as though teaching, holding a book in his left hand and wearing on his head a short bishop's mitre. Mary Byrne later said that the entire vision was 'made of light' but that the brightest light came from the lamb.

The two women summoned their friends and neighbours, and soon fifteen people assembled at the church. They all saw the vision exactly the same way. The spectators ranged in age from five to seventy-five, and included men and women. The little group remained for two hours, reciting the Rosary, until the vision vanished.

Naturally enough, their account of the apparition excited great interest in the village and locality. Crowds of interested neighbours began to visit the church to view the gable wall and pray at the site of the wonder. Soon, cures and healings were being reported, the first occurring within ten days. The Archdeacon began to take reports and keep records of the stories of favours granted by prayer at the church. The total soon reached three hundred cures.

The diocesan authorities held a Commission of Inquiry within six weeks, which interviewed all the witnesses and took formal depositions from them about their experience. The conclusion of the Church investigation was that the witnesses' accounts were coherent and credible. In 1936, a second Church Commission again examined the three witnesses still living, Mary Byrne (Mrs O'Connell) and two others. Mary Byrne testified from her deathbed. The Commission concluded that the testimony of all three visionaries was trustworthy.

Through the next hundred years, Knock grew into a popular pilgrimage for Irish people and pilgrims travelling from abroad. It received papal support from Pius XII and John XXIII. The story of Knock's first century ends with another extraordinary parish priest. In the 1960s, Monsignor James Horan began the project of building a much larger church to accommodate the increasing crowds of pilgrims. This was completed in 1976. Three years later, on the centenary of the apparition, St John Paul II made a papal visit to Ireland, came on a personal pilgrimage to Knock, which he described as 'the goal of my journey to Ireland', and raised the status of the new church to that of basilica.

Today, Knock is Ireland's national Marian shrine and a major centre for international pilgrimage, welcoming over a million and a half visitors a year. As a footnote, Monsignor Horan generated sufficient political and financial support to build Knock Airport, now officially designated Ireland West Airport Knock, to cater for the pilgrims and travellers coming to the national shrine and to the province of Connacht.

GOD'S PLAN FOR MARY

The Second Vatican Council reminds us that Mary is a member of the Church who 'occupies a place in the Church which is the highest after Christ and also closest to us' (LG, no. 54). She is the first and the greatest of all the disciples of Christ.

When the Gospel of St Luke (cf. 1:26-38) narrates God's call to Mary, the Virgin of Nazareth, to be the Mother of the Saviour, his Son, from all eternity, she consents to this call with profound faith and trust. Thus, she 'gave to the world the Life that renews all things, and who was enriched by God with gifts appropriate to such a role' (LG, no. 56).

'BLESSED ARE YOU AMONG WOMEN'

An essential part of God's plan for the mother of his Son was that she be conceived free from Original Sin. 'Through the centuries the Church became ever more aware that Mary, "full of grace" through God, was redeemed from the moment of her conception' (CCC, no. 491).

In anticipation that she was to bear the Son of God, Mary was preserved from the time of her conception from Original Sin. We call this the Immaculate Conception. No sin would touch her, so that she would be a fitting and worthy vessel of the Son of God. The Immaculate Conception does not refer to the virginal conception and birth of Christ, but rather to Mary's being conceived without inheriting Original Sin.

In the course of time, the doctrine of the Immaculate Conception became more precisely enunciated, as its truth – long supported by the universal popular devotion of the faithful – was better understood by deepening theological inquiry. In 1854, Pope Pius IX proclaimed this dogma infallibly: that is, in his role as supreme teacher of the Church, he declared that this doctrine is divinely revealed and must be accepted with faith by the entire Church.

It is also the faith of the Church that Mary is to be called the 'Mother of God'. 'The One whom she conceived as man by [the power of] the Holy Spirit, who truly became her Son according to the flesh, was none other than the Father's eternal Son, the second person of the Holy Trinity. Hence the Church confesses that Mary is truly *Mother of God*" (CCC, no.

FROM THE CATECHISM

1. What is the role of Mary's faith in the plan of salvation?
The Virgin Mary 'freely cooperat[ed] in the work of man's salvation through faith and obedience' (LG, no. 56). She uttered her yes 'in the name of all human nature' (St Thomas Aquinas, *Summa Theologiae*, III, 30, 1). By her obedience she became the new Eve, the mother of all the living. (CCC, no. 511)

2. Does Mary intercede on our behalf?
This motherhood of Mary in the order of grace continues uninterruptedly ... Taken up into heaven she did not lay aside this saving office, but by her manifold intercession continues to bring us the gifts of eternal salvation. (CCC, no. 969, citing LG, no. 62)

3. How does the Church honour Mary?
The Church rightly honours the Blessed Virgin with special devotion. 'From the earliest times the Blessed Virgin is honoured under the title Mother of God, whose protection the faithful take refuge together in all their perils and needs ... This cult ... differs essentially from the cult of adoration, which is offered equally to the Incarnate Word and to the Father and the Holy Spirit, and it is most favourable to it' (LG, no. 66). The liturgical feasts dedicated to the Mother of God and Marian prayer, such as the rosary, an 'epitome of the whole Gospel', express this devotion to the Virgin Mary. (CCC, no. 971)

495, citing Council of Ephesus: DS 251). In the Eastern Churches Mary is honoured by use of the Greek expression *Theotokos* or 'Birth-giver of God' (sometimes translated as 'God-Bearer').

The Holy Spirit's power made possible the conception of Jesus in Mary's womb. There was no human father. The Gospels clearly present the virginal conception of Jesus as a divine work (cf. Mt 1:18-25; Lk 1:26-38).

Mary was always a virgin, both in conceiving Jesus, giving birth to him and remaining virgin ever after. God granted her this privilege to emphasise that this was a unique moment in history – the birth of Jesus who is the Son of God and the Son of Mary. The liturgy of the Church speaks of Mary as 'ever virgin'. In the early Church some denied this, arguing that the Gospels speak of the brothers and sisters of Jesus, and thus maintained that Mary did not remain a virgin after the birth of Jesus. But already in the fourth century, theologians pointed out that the Greek word for brother used in the New Testament can refer also to cousin. A second explanation was that these brothers and sisters were children of Joseph by a previous marriage. However, it is the constant teaching of the Church that Mary remained a virgin even after the birth of Jesus. In her virginity, Mary lived a life dedicated exclusively to her Son and his mission. Her example has been followed by some of Christ's disciples who have lived lives of consecrated virginity and celibacy from apostolic times to the present.

In the mystery of her Assumption, Mary experiences immediately what we all will experience eventually – a bodily resurrection like Christ's own. 'The Immaculate Virgin … when the course of her earthly life was finished, was taken up body and soul into heavenly glory and exalted by the Lord as Queen over all things, so that she might be more fully conformed to her Son, the Lord of lords and conqueror of death' (CCC, no. 966, citing LG, no. 59).

Finally, in Mary we behold what the Church is already like during her pilgrimage of faith – and what the Church will become at the end of the journey. 'Mary figured profoundly in the history of salvation and in a certain way unites and mirrors within herself the central truths of the faith' (LG, no. 65).

MARY AS MOTHER OF THE CHURCH

At the beginning of the third session of the Second Vatican Council, Pope Paul VI announced that Mary would be honoured under the title 'Mother of the Church'.

From Christ's conception until his death, Mary was united to her Son in his work of salvation. From the Cross, Jesus entrusted his beloved disciple to Mary, telling him to see her as his own mother (Jn 19:27). When the Apostles and disciples gathered to pray after the Ascension of Jesus, Mary was with them praying for the coming of the Holy Spirit. Mary continues to pray before God for the Church and all humanity.

Like Mary, the Church has a maternal role, giving birth to people in Christ. The Church can never cease to look at Mary, who gave birth to Jesus Christ. The Church contemplates Mary's motherhood in order to fulfil her own calling to be mother of the members of Christ's Mystical Body, the Church. Also like Mary, the Church is virginal. The description of the Church as virginal is used here in the spiritual sense of the undivided heart and of fidelity in its most luminous form. God calls all the members of the Church to fidelity to the union with him begun at Baptism and continued in the other Sacraments.

MARY'S MATERNAL INTERCESSION

In our culture, there can be a discomfort with praying for Mary's intercession on our behalf. This seems to be a mediating role that crosses a line set out in the First Letter to Timothy: 'For there is only one God, and there is only one mediator between God and humanity, himself a human being, Christ Jesus, who offered himself as a ransom for all' (1 Tm 2:5-6). So Jesus Christ is the one and only mediator. Jesus alone is the Saviour.

But this does not deny the possibility that Christ would permit others to share in his mediating role. Here on earth we routinely ask others for prayers. Instinctively, we turn to holy people for their prayers because they seem nearer to God. Why would we stop asking saints for their prayers after they die? If we believe they are in heaven, would not their prayers be even more effective?

From the earliest times, Christians have sought Mary's prayers and help. There has been the basic sense on the part of the Church that Mary continues in heaven to be concerned for the growth of all members of the Church into holiness and an intimate relationship with her Son.

━━━━━━━━━━━━━ FOR DISCUSSION ━━━━━━━━━━━━━

1. How would you explain to others the connection between Mary as the Mother of God and all her special gifts: the Immaculate Conception, perpetual virginity and the Assumption? Why is it important to understand that Mary, too, needed to be redeemed?
2. In what ways can you identify with Mary's 'yes' to God at the Annunciation? If Mary's life serves as an example for us of an undivided heart in response to the love of God, how are you able to daily demonstrate your love for God?
3. Mary was the greatest disciple of her Son. How are you growing in your call to discipleship?

━━━━━━━━━━ DOCTRINAL STATEMENTS ━━━━━━━━━━

• 'What the Catholic faith believes about Mary is based on what it believes about Christ, and what it teaches about Mary illumines in turn its faith in Christ' (CCC, no. 487).
• 'When the completion of the time came, God sent his Son, born of a woman' (Gal 4:4).
• An essential part of God's saving plan for the mother of his Son was that she be conceived free of Original Sin. 'Through the centuries the Church became ever more aware that Mary, "full of grace" through God, was redeemed from the moment of her conception' (CCC, no. 491). This is the doctrine of her Immaculate Conception.
• At the Annunciation, Mary responded to the angel Gabriel with these words: 'You see before you the Lord's servant, let it happen to me as you have said' (Lk 1:38). This was her consent to the Incarnation. From that moment onwards the Virgin Mary cooperated freely and in the obedience of faith with the plan of salvation. She uttered her yes to God 'in the name of all human nature' (St Thomas Aquinas, *Summa Theologiae*, III, 30, 1).
• The Gospels call Mary the 'Mother of Jesus'. Mary is truly the Mother of God since she is the mother of the Son of God made man. In the Eastern Churches Mary is honoured as the *Theotokos*, or 'Birth-giver of God'.

- Mary was always a virgin, in conceiving Jesus, in giving birth to him and for the rest of her life.
- 'The Most Blessed Virgin Mary, when the course of her earthly life was completed, was taken up body and soul into the glory of heaven, where she already shares in the glory of her Son's Resurrection, anticipating the resurrection of all members of his Body' (CCC, no. 974). This is the doctrine of her Assumption into heaven.
- 'We believe that the Holy Mother of God, the New Eve, Mother of the Church, continues in heaven to exercise her maternal role on behalf of the members of Christ' (Pope Paul VI, *Credo of the People of God*, no. 15).

MEDITATION

Magnificat (Lk 1:46-55)

After the Annunciation, the Virgin Mary went to stay with her cousin Elizabeth to assist Elizabeth in the forthcoming birth of her child. When Elizabeth saw Mary, she praised Mary's faith by saying, 'Blessed is she who believed that the promise made her by the Lord would be fulfilled' (Lk 1:45). Mary responded with a canticle in which she praised God. We reflect here on her words, known to us today as the *Magnificat*, which is the first word of this canticle in Latin:

> My soul proclaims the greatness of the Lord,
>   my spirit rejoices in God my Saviour;
> For he has looked with favour on his lowly servant,
>   and from this day all generations will call me blessed.
> The Almighty has done great things for me:
>   holy is his name.
> He has mercy on those who fear him
>   in every generation.
> He has shown the strength of his arm,
>   he has scattered the proud in their conceit.
> He has cast down the mighty from their thrones,
>   and has lifted up the lowly.

He has filled the hungry with good things,
    and has sent the rich away empty.
He has come to the help of his servant Israel
    for he has remembered his promise of mercy,
the promise he made to our fathers,
    to Abraham and his children for ever.

– Liturgy of the Hours; cf. Lk 1:46-55

PRAYER

Memorare

Remember, O most gracious Virgin Mary,
that never was it known that anyone
who fled to thy protection,
implored thy help or sought thy
intercession was left unaided.
Inspired with this confidence, I fly unto thee,
O Virgin of Virgins, my Mother.
To thee do I come. Before thee I stand, sinful and sorrowful.
O Mother of the Word Incarnate, despise not my petitions,
but in thy mercy hear and answer me. Amen.

– St Bernard of Clairvaux

Hail Mary, full of grace!

The Mother of Jesus, the Mother of the Son of God, having accepted a new mission from Jesus on the Cross, is embraced, too, as our mother, the mother of all believers, the Mother of the Church.

– SGN, 27

13 OUR ETERNAL DESTINY

LAST THINGS: RESURRECTION OF THE BODY, DEATH,
PARTICULAR JUDGEMENT, HEAVEN, PURGATORY, HELL,
LAST JUDGEMENT, NEW HEAVENS, AND NEW EARTH
– CCC, NOS. 988–1065

THE CHRISTIAN HOSPICE STORY

'Hospice', from the Latin *hospitium*, means guesthouse, and suggests welcome and hospitality towards the stranger. Related words are 'hospital', 'hotel' and 'host'. Early hospitals are found all over the pagan world, in India, Persia, Greece and Rome. Indeed, one of the first hospitals in written history was founded at Armagh in Ireland before 300 BC for the famous Red Branch Knights.

Jesus worked miracles of healing in addition to his ministry of prophecy and teaching, and he handed on the healing vocation to his disciples (cf. Lk 10:9; Mk 16:18). The early missionaries of the Christian Church practised healing as a sacred duty along with hospitality to fellow Christians who were travelling, and to all strangers who needed a place to stay. Among those most in need of hospitality were the sick and injured, particularly those away from home on pilgrimage. The innkeeper, in Jesus' parable of the Good Samaritan, was a role model for the true Christian host.

After the persecutions, official Christian institutions could be established to care openly for the sick. Fabiola founded the first hospital in Rome, and St Basil built a large hospital in Caesarea which housed doctors, nurses and patients. Such institutions were established everywhere, often located near the bishop's house or associated with a monastery.

In these hospitals, care was given according to current medical knowledge and Christian religious faith. Those suffering from the plague or various infectious diseases such as leprosy were isolated to

165

prevent contagion. Paramount was the spiritual welfare of the patient, especially because death was welcomed as the will of God and the entry to heaven. The dying person was treated with respect, surrounded by the rites of Anointing and Holy Communion (Extreme Unction and Viaticum) and attended by priest, family, friends and spiritual companions to keep the final vigil.

Modern times brought big changes in the care of the sick and dying. Health was viewed as a physical and social value, with costs and benefits for individual and society. Medicine became progressive and optimistic. Treatment always expected a cure. Diseases were conquered and illness healed. Attitudes to death and dying changed as a result. Death was regarded as an unmitigated evil, to be postponed indefinitely and even denied, rather than as – what it can be – a happy release and a blessed end.

Catholic hospitals and clinics had always preserved the religious perspective towards dying, even against the prevailing medical culture. A good example of this was Our Lady's Hospice in Harold's Cross, Dublin, established by the Irish Sisters of Charity, a congregation founded by the convert to Catholicism from Anglicanism, Mary Aikenhead. Two of the sisters, Mother Charles and Mother Philip, were convinced of the need for a house to care for the dying, the destitute poor and those who had no hope of recovery. Such patients were refused admission by the regular hospitals of the time because the doctors believed that they could not help them. Often their diseases had no remedy, and the fear of infection was high. Harold's Cross opened in 1879 with just nine beds, but it had grown to forty a year later. The hospice accepted everyone who needed its services.

A new 110-bed building was opened in 1886. The generosity of the people of Dublin from all sectors of society supported the work of the hospice through the years. The workers at Clery's department store, for example, once collected two thousand pounds in pennies. The work of Harold's Cross continues as it pioneers the best practice for the care of the dying.

In the 1960s, an English nurse who had worked in a Catholic home for the dying in London transformed contemporary medical thinking on death, and introduced the modern discipline of palliative care, especially for the terminally ill. 'Palliative' comes from the Latin word for 'cloak' and it means reducing suffering, and eliminating pain, even if the illness itself cannot be cured. In hospice work, palliative care aims at improving the quality of life for the dying patient.

Cecily Saunders was an Anglican nurse and doctor. She had an insight into the plight of the dying patient. Early on, she formed the opinion that 'many patients feel deserted by their doctors at the end. Ideally the doctor should remain the centre of a team who work together to relieve where they cannot heal, to keep the patient's own struggle within his compass and to bring hope and consolation to the end'.

She decided to found a hospice for the dying, at first intended to be an Anglican foundation, but she later agreed to establish it as a 'religious foundation of an open character'. She named it after St Christopher, the patron saint of travellers, reflecting the nature of dying patients being at the end of their life's journey.

From St Christopher's in London in 1967, the modern hospice movement began, establishing institutions for compassionate care for the dying in many countries. For Cecily Saunders, this was a religious vocation. 'I prayed to know how best to serve God' and God's response had come as she sat at the bedside of David Tasma, a Polish Jewish man dying of cancer. There she discovered the importance of managing pain, not just bodily suffering but spiritual, psychological and social pain as well. 'I didn't set out to change the world; I set out to do something about pain.'

The hospice movement reached Ireland in the 1980s, and since then a number of in-patient hospice units have been established by voluntary efforts around the country. These, in turn, serve as hubs for the provision of home hospice care, organised along the same principles. Hospice care in Ireland is heavily dependent upon voluntary support, both for funding and service. Like Our Lady's Hospice in Harold's Cross, the modern hospice movement depends largely on volunteer help and donations.

Cecily Saunders died in St Christopher's, her own hospice, on 14 July 2005 at the age of eighty-seven.

THE MEANING OF CHRISTIAN DEATH

Indeed for your faithful, Lord,
life is changed, not ended,
and, when this earthly dwelling turns to dust,
an eternal dwelling is made ready for them in heaven.

– Preface I for the Dead,
Roman Missal (3rd Typical Edition, 2011)

The final article of the Creed proclaims our belief in everlasting life. At the Catholic Rite of Commendation of the Dying we sometimes hear this prayer: 'Go forth, Christian soul, from this world ... May you live in peace this day, may your home be with God in Zion, may you see your redeemer face to face' (Prayer of Commendation of the Dying, no. 220). Death is the natural and inevitable end of life on earth. '[There is] a time for giving birth, a time for dying' (Eccl (Qo) 3:2). We change, we grow old and even death seems appropriate after a full life. 'The dust returns to the earth from which it came, and the spirit returns to God who gave it' (Eccl (Qo) 12:7).

But the reality of death and its finality give an urgency to our lives. 'Death puts an end to human life as the time open to either accepting or rejecting the divine grace manifested in Christ' (CCC, no. 1021). This teaching recognises that the death of a person marks an end to our earthly journey with its sorrows and joys, its sinful failures and the triumphs of Christ's saving grace and help.

The Church teaches that 'each man receives his eternal retribution in his immortal soul at the very moment of his death, in a particular judgement' (CCC, no. 1022). Saint John of the Cross (1542–91) wrote, 'At the evening of life, we shall be judged on our love' (*Dichos*, no. 64). Perfect love will make possible entrance into heaven, imperfect love will require purification and a total lack of love will mean eternal separation from God.

'Heaven is the ultimate end and fulfilment of the deepest human longings, the state of supreme, definitive happiness' (CCC, no. 1024). This will be brought about by a perfect communion with the Holy Trinity, the Blessed Mother, the angels and saints. Jesus Christ opened heaven to us by his death and Resurrection.

What is heaven like? Scripture uses a variety of pictures to help us understand heaven, such as a wedding party, a banquet, the Father's house, a state of unending happiness. But the real heaven is beyond any picture we can paint of it. 'What no eye has seen and no ear has heard, what the mind of man cannot visualise; all that God has prepared for those who love him' (1 Cor 2:9). Seeing God face to face in all his glory is the essential aspect of heaven. This is called the *beatific vision*. To make this possible God must reveal himself and give us the capacity to behold him.

> How great will your glory and happiness be, to be allowed to see God, to be honoured with sharing the joy of salvation and eternal light with Christ your Lord and God … to delight in the joy of immortality in the Kingdom of Heaven with the righteous and God's friends. (St Cyprian, Letter 58, 10, 1)

'The Church gives the name *Purgatory* to [the] final purification of the elect, which is entirely different from the punishment of the damned' (CCC, no. 1031). Those who die in the state of friendship with God but who are not fully purified and perfected are assured of their eternal salvation. However, they must undergo a purification to obtain the perfection of love and holiness needed to enter heaven, where they have a heart that is totally open to him. This process is called Purgatory. It is impossible for us to imagine what Purgatory is. Traditionally, it has been described as a purifying fire. Since the human soul cannot be touched by earthly flames, the image serves to recall that perfect love is achieved by a gradual and painful spiritual detachment from selfishness and self-centredness. The Church assists those in Purgatory through prayer and especially the Eucharist in their final process of purification. Offering Masses for the deceased is a most powerful way of aiding them. On 2 November of each year, the Commemoration of All the Faithful Departed (All Souls' Day) takes place. This is a day for special remembrance and prayer for the dead.

'The chief punishment of hell is eternal separation from God' (CCC, no. 1035). It is impossible for us to be united with God if we refuse to love him. When we sin seriously against God, neighbour, or self, we have failed to love God. Persistence in a state of serious sin reflects a choice to reject God's love and an intention to separate ourselves from him. Freely chosen eternal separation from communion with God is called hell. While images of fire have been used traditionally to picture *hell*, for example in the Scriptures, the reality exceeds our ability to describe the pain of isolation that comes from rejecting God's love.

Scripture and the teaching of the Church regarding heaven and hell emphasise a call to personal responsibility by which we use our freedom, aided by divine grace, to respond completely to God's love. There is always an urgent call to conversion and repentance. 'God predestines no one to go to hell' (CCC, no. 1037).

THE RESURRECTION OF THE BODY

The profession of our faith in God, the Father, the Son, and the Holy Spirit ... culminates in the proclamation of the resurrection of the dead on the last day and in life everlasting.

– CCC, no. 988

Faith in the resurrection of our bodies is inseparable from our faith in the Resurrection of Christ's body from the dead. He rose as our head, as the pattern of our rising and as the life-giving source of our new life. 'If the Spirit of him who raised Jesus from the dead has made his home in you, then he who raised Christ Jesus from the dead will give life to your own mortal bodies through his Spirit living in you' (Rm 8:11).

Belief in the resurrection of the body already existed in Christ's time among the Pharisees. Jesus performed miracles of raising the dead to life as symbols of his future Resurrection, and he associated these events with himself: 'I am the resurrection' (Jn 11:25).

> Christ, 'the first-born from the dead' (Col 1:18), is the principle of our own resurrection, even now by the justification of our souls (cf. Rm 6:4), and one day by the new life he will impart to our bodies (cf. Rm 8:11). (CCC, no. 658)

All the dead will rise when Jesus comes again to judge the living and the dead. In the final resurrection, our bodies will be transformed, though we do not know precisely how. The manner of our resurrection exceeds our understanding and imagination and is accessible only to our faith.

> Someone may ask: How are dead people raised, and what sort of body do they have when they come? How foolish! What you sow must die before it is given new life; and what you sow is not the body that is to be, but only a bare grain, of wheat I dare say, or some other kind … It is the same too with the resurrection of the dead: what is sown is perishable, but what is raised is imperishable … The dead will be raised imperishable … because this perishable nature of ours must put on imperishability, this mortal nature must put on immortality. (1 Cor 15:35-37, 42, 52, 53)

Every time we attend a funeral vigil or Mass, view a deceased body at a wake, or pass by a cemetery, we are reminded of this simple and profound article of the Creed, the belief in the resurrection of the body. It is a sobering belief, because it reminds us of the judgement yet to come, and at the same time it is a joyful belief that heralds life everlasting with God.

THE LAST JUDGEMENT

The Last Judgement will come when Christ returns in glory.

– CCC, no. 1040

Immediately after death, each person comes before God and is judged individually (the particular judgement) and enters heaven, Purgatory, or hell. Yet at the end of time when Christ returns in glory, a final judgement will occur when all are raised from the dead and assembled before God; then their relationship to him is made public (the general judgement).

The judgement scene in the Gospel of Matthew is perhaps the most accessible way to appreciate the Last Judgement. 'When the Son of man comes in his glory, escorted by all the angels, then he will take his seat on his throne of glory. All nations will be assembled before him and he will separate people one from another as the shepherd separates sheep from goats' (Mt 25:31-32). The sheep will inherit the Kingdom of God. The goats will be sent to the eternal fire prepared for the devil and his angels. In this parable, the criteria for being saved are described as whether one fed the hungry, gave water to the thirsty, welcomed the stranger, clothed the naked, cared for the sick and visited the prisoners. In each of these cases, it is Jesus himself who is thus treated. 'In so far as you did this to one of the least of these brothers of mine, you did it to me' (Mt 25:40). If we care for Jesus in these ways, we will receive the Kingdom. If we do not, we will be separated from him forever.

> The Last Judgement will come when Christ returns in glory. Only the Father knows the day and the hour … Christ … will pronounce the final word on all history [making clear] the ultimate meaning of the whole work of creation and of the entire economy of salvation … The Last Judgement will reveal that God's justice triumphs over all the injustices committed by his creatures and that God's love is stronger than death. (CCC, no. 1040)

THE NEW HEAVEN AND THE NEW EARTH

God is preparing a new dwelling and a new earth in
which righteousness dwells.

– CCC, no. 1048, citing GS, no. 39

Once the Kingdom of God arrives in its fullness at the end of time there will be a renewal of the universe in Christ. Scripture uses many images to describe this mysterious reality. There will be a new heaven and a new earth:

> 'Creation itself will be set free from its bondage to decay' (cf. Rm 8:19-23). The holy city of Jerusalem will descend from heaven to earth (cf. Rv 21:10). We do not know when or how this will happen. But we do know that God will make this happen. At the end of time, 'The universe itself, which is so closely related to man and which attains its destiny through him, will be perfectly re-established in Christ.' (LG, no. 48)

FROM THE CATECHISM

1. What happens when we die?

By death the soul is separated from the body, but in the resurrection God will give incorruptible life to our body, transformed by reunion with our soul. Just as Christ is risen and lives for ever, so all of us will rise at the last day. (CCC, no. 1016)

2. What is the beatific vision?

Because of his transcendence, God cannot be seen as he is, unless he himself opens up his mystery to man's immediate contemplation and gives him the capacity for it. The Church calls this contemplation of God in heavenly glory 'the beatific vision'. (CCC, no. 1028)

3. What does the Last Judgement call people to do?

The message of the Last Judgement calls men to conversion while God is still giving them the 'acceptable time … the day of salvation'. (CCC, no. 1041, citing 2 Cor 6:2)

CHRISTIAN DEATH

We do not like to think about death. There is much in our culture that distracts us from reflection about our final destiny. We are encouraged to think only about the present moment and to fulfil today's needs. But the Christian embraces the total reality of life and God's call to the fullness of life after death. Thus, for example, Christians assist those whose earthly journey is coming to an end. 'The dying should be given attention and care to help them live their last moments in dignity and peace. They will be helped by the prayer of their relatives, who must see to it that the sick receive at the proper time the sacraments that prepare them to meet the living God' (CCC, no. 2299).

Not only do we care for the dying to help them pass their final moments in dignity and peace, but we also maintain reverence for their bodies once they are deceased. 'The bodies of the dead must be treated with respect and charity, in faith and in the hope of the Resurrection. The burial of the dead is a corporal work of mercy [cf. Tob 1:16-18]; it honours the children of God, who are temples of the Holy Spirit' (CCC, no. 2300). The rituals accompanying respect for the dead include the funeral vigil (wake), the funeral itself, and the burial of the body or the cremated remains of the deceased at the cemetery. Participation in these rites enables friends and others to demonstrate reverence for the deceased, to pray together for the eternal repose of the deceased and to give the family of the deceased prayerful support.

CHRISTIAN FUNERALS

The Christian funeral liturgy tells us that life is changed, not ended. Funerals are acts of faith. In the dialogue between Martha and Jesus just before the raising of Lazarus, Jesus tells her, 'Your brother will rise again'. She replies, 'I know that he will rise in the resurrection on the last day.' Jesus then identifies himself as the Resurrection and the Life, and asks her, 'Do you believe this?' She responds, 'Yes, Lord, I have come to believe that you are the Messiah, the Son of God' (cf. Jn 11:17-27). We express this same belief at Christian funerals. Jesus, who walks with us through all our other events in life, is present at our funerals, the liturgy of the passage from death to eternal life. Arrangements for a funeral need to include a Mass and burial in a Catholic cemetery whenever possible.

It is preferable that the body be buried in a Catholic cemetery or columbarium (repository for cremated remains) consecrated for this purpose. We bury the body or the cremated remains of a person once washed with baptismal water, anointed with the oils of Confirmation and the Sacrament of the Sick and nourished by the Eucharist.

The Church prefers the burial of the body but does allow cremation. 'The Church permits cremation, provided that it does not demonstrate a denial of faith in the resurrection of the body' (CCC, no. 2301). Where cremation is chosen, the Church urges that if at all possible, the body be present for the funeral Mass with cremation taking place afterwards. The cremated remains should always be treated with the same respect given to the human body from which they came. After the funeral liturgy the cremated remains are buried in a grave or placed in a mausoleum or columbarium, not scattered.

END OF LIFE CARE –
ETHICAL AND PASTORAL ISSUES:
A SUMMARY OF THE STATEMENT FROM THE IRISH BISHOPS' COMMITTEE FOR BIOETHICS 2002

Palliative Care avoids two extremes. Advances in medicine and in technology mean that the taking of decisions about appropriate care for people who have advanced and progressive illness have become more complex. In caring for people who are dying, there are two extremes to be avoided: trying to keep people alive at all costs, even when it is clear that death is imminent, and deciding to end the life of a person on the basis that his or her life is no longer worth living.

Palliative care avoids both of these extremes in that it upholds absolute respect for human life, and acknowledges human mortality and the dominion we have over life. It is about maximising the quality of life remaining, while enabling patients to 'live until they die'.

Euthanasia is not acceptable. Euthanasia is any action or omission which is deliberately calculated to end the life of another human being, with or without that person's consent, on so-called health grounds. Euthanasia is morally unacceptable, not only because it would mean the introduction of a qualitative judgement on what is determined to be a worthwhile life or existence, but also because it would have an enormous effect on the ethos of healthcare provision.

The Catholic Church absolutely rejects euthanasia as a response to chronic or serious illness. This rejection is rooted in an understanding of the human person as someone who is called into life by God, and the ultimate meaning of whose life is to be found in relationship with God.

The Rights and Responsibilities of Healthcare Professionals. Healthcare professionals, although they act on behalf of the patient, are not just functionaries who are required to do whatever they are asked to do. They have a right and a duty to choose what is good, and to reject any course of action which conflicts with a conscience informed by true moral principles, even if this is requested by the patient or by the family.

Appropriate Pain Relief is not Euthanasia. The traditional Principle of Double Effect helps to explain why necessary pain relief, even if it sometimes results in an unintended and unavoidable reduction in the length of life, is not euthanasia. Given certain conditions, an action (including an omission) that results in death is not an action the nature of which is to cause death. For an action to be such, it must not issue from an intention to end life; moreover, the external act must not, according to its intelligible structure, result in the death of a human person, as when a poison is administered that will kill, even though the 'intention' is to provide relief rather than to end life.

The *Catechism of the Catholic Church* states that, 'Even if death is thought imminent, the ordinary care owed to a sick person cannot be legitimately interrupted (no. 2279).' In 2004, John Paul II taught that such ordinary care includes nutrition and hydration of the patient. This teaching was reiterated in 2007 by the Congregation for the Doctrine of the Faith in a document approved by Benedict XVI (cf. St John Paul II, *Address to the Participants in the International Congress on 'Life-Sustaining Treatments and Vegetative State: Scientific Advances and Ethical Dilemmas'*, 20 March 2004, *AAS* XCVI [2004], pp. 485–489; 2. Congregation for the Doctrine of the Faith, *Responses to Certain Questions of the United States Conference of Catholic Bishops Concerning Artificial Nutrition and Hydration* [1 August 2007], *AAS* XCIX (2007), pp. 820–821).

Euthanasia is Not Necessary. Requests for euthanasia frequently coincide with a bad period of symptom control, even a clinically treatable depression. The solution, in part, is to improve pain control. In the vast majority of cases unbearable pain can be avoided.

Some distress is not directly related to physical pain, but has its roots in issues such as fear, anxiety, loss of control and loss of independence. Good counselling, which is an integral part of palliative care, allows the patient, the family, and others who are closely involved to discuss these fears. Sedation may sometimes be required to deal with high levels of anxiety, but it should not be a first resort. While it can certainly help to reduce the experience of emotional stress, it also reduces the capacity of the patient to respond freely and deliberately to what is happening in his/her life. (Sedation is not the same as physical pain-relief; sedation deals with emotional distress.)

The Provision of Resources. There is need for provision of adequate resources for palliative care, not only in hospices, but in general hospitals and in the community. The inadequacy of such resources impinges directly on the quality of care that can be provided to those who are dying, and may be a contributory factor in the level of demand for euthanasia.

Spiritual and Sacramental Ministry. A comprehensive approach to healthcare must take account of the spiritual needs of the patient. All the key moments of life, including sickness and death, have the capacity to bring our relationship with God into sharper focus. Poor communication is an obstacle to spiritual care, because patients are often discouraged from even mentioning the possibility of death. By contrast, the ethos of sensitive but honest communication that is part of palliative care greatly facilitates the spiritual and sacramental care of those who are dying; the patient's questions are welcomed and answered appropriately. Talk of death and dying is not taboo. This means that if people pray with the patient, they can pray more honestly too.

▬▬▬▬ FOR DISCUSSION ▬▬▬▬

1. What experiences have you had that bring you to think about death? How does the Church's teachings about eternal life help shape your thinking about death?
2. When you read the New Testament teachings about the Last Judgement, such as in the parable of the sheep and goats (cf. Mt 25:31-46), what impact does this have on you? What does the Church teach about Purgatory? Why do we pray for the dead?
3. Why is the resurrection of our bodies important? In speaking of heaven or hell, why do we explain them in terms of our relationship with God?

DOCTRINAL STATEMENTS

- The Communion of Saints includes the faithful on earth, the souls in Purgatory and the blessed in heaven. In this Communion, the merciful love of God and his saints is always attentive to our prayers for one another here and for the souls of the faithful departed. The Communion of Saints also refers to 'holy things', above all the Eucharist, by which the believers are formed into one Body of Christ.

- 'The dying should be given attention and care to help them live their last moments in dignity and peace. They will be helped by the prayer of their relatives, who must see to it that the sick receive at the proper time the Sacraments that prepare them to meet the living God' (CCC, no. 2299).

- 'The bodies of the dead must be treated with respect and charity, in faith and in the hope of the Resurrection. The burial of the dead is a corporal work of mercy [cf. Tob 1:16-18]; it honours the children of God, who are temples of the Holy Spirit' (CCC, no. 2300).

- Immediately after death, each person comes before God and is judged individually (the particular judgement) and enters heaven, Purgatory or hell. Yet at the end of time, a final judgement will occur when all are assembled before God and their relationship to God is made public (the general judgement).

- The traditional designation of the four 'Last Things' refers to death, judgement, heaven and hell.

- The soul is immortal; it does not perish when it separates from the body at death. At the final resurrection, it will be reunited with the body.

- Those who die in the state of grace and friendship with God but who are not fully purified are assured of their eternal salvation. They must undergo a purification to attain the holiness needed to enter heaven. This process is called *Purgatory*. We pray for those in Purgatory, that they may soon be with God in heaven.

- Following the example of Christ, the Church warns the faithful of the sad reality of eternal death, also called hell, which is brought about by a person's free and permanent rejection of God and his love.

- 'The Last Judgement will come when Christ returns in glory … The Last Judgement will reveal that God's justice triumphs over all the injustices committed by his creatures and that God's love is stronger than death' (CCC, no. 1040).

MEDITATION

It is in regard to death that man's condition is most shrouded in doubt. Man is tormented not only by pain and by the gradual breaking-up of his body but also, and even more, by the dread of forever ceasing to be. But a deep instinct leads him rightly to shrink from and to reject the utter ruin and total loss of his personality. Because he bears in himself the seed of eternity, which cannot be reduced to mere matter, he rebels against death. All the aids made available by technology, however useful they may be, cannot set his anguished mind at rest. They may prolong his life-span; but this does not satisfy his heartfelt longing, one that can never be stifled, for a life to come ...

The Church, taught by divine revelation, declares that God has created man in view of a blessed destiny that lies beyond the limits of his sad state on earth.

– GS, no. 18

PRAYER

May you live in peace this day, may your home be with God in Zion,

with Mary, the Virgin Mother of God, with Joseph and all the angels and saints ...

May you return to [your Creator], who formed you from the dust of the earth ...

May you see your Redeemer face to face.

– Prayer of Commendation,
Rite of Commendation of the Dying, no. 220

I am not dying. I am entering eternal life.

– St Thérèse of Lisieux

PART II

THE SACRAMENTS:
THE FAITH CELEBRATED

14 THE CELEBRATION OF THE PASCHAL MYSTERY OF CHRIST

INTRODUCTION TO THE CELEBRATION OF THE LITURGY IN THE SACRAMENTS – CCC, NOS. 1076–1209

SAINT PATRICK: APOSTLE OF IRELAND

Some of the best known personages of Irish history came from abroad. The most famous Irishman of them all, of course, whose feast day is celebrated everywhere, was himself not born on the Emerald Isle.

Saint Patrick himself tells us, in the *Confession of St Patrick*, that his father owned a villa in a town called Bannavem Taberniae. It would probably have been in Roman Britain, somewhere on the coast of Wales or Scotland perhaps, or possibly in France. Local traditions are preserved in a number of sites in these places. Patrick was brought up a Christian on the edge of the Roman Empire. He was however not a committed Christian, as he admits to being a careless young man, religiously speaking, as he was growing up.

The Roman Empire at this time was in decline, and could not defend its borders effectively. Irish marauders attacked Patrick's home town and swept Patrick away to slavery to the hills of Ireland. As with Bannavem Taberniae, we are today not sure of the location for most of the events that Patrick tells us about in his record of captivity and escape. The *Confession of St Patrick* is very detailed, however, about his state of mind, heart and soul. He tells us that he spent long hours in reflection, and this turned to meditation on the truths he had been taught as a child, about God, about grace and divine providence. He tells us that loneliness and hardship led him to prayer and contemplation. He even experienced some mystical visions. When he finally managed to escape back home to safety, he was a changed person indeed. But he was not destined to stay home for long.

Patrick tells us that one vision gave him direction for the rest of his life. He heard the people of the western shore inviting him back to Ireland. He resolved to devote himself to the service of God, spent years in study and formation, was ordained deacon and priest, and eventually was made bishop with the mission of returning to Ireland to spread the Gospel. A setback involving an unnamed scandal, either before he left or after he had embarked on his mission, threatened to damage his reputation fatally. He assures us that this malicious report was about something that he had left entirely in the past, and did not affect his ministry at all. In the event, he was completely cleared and he moved on in the grace of God. It seems to have been a 'happy fault' because he probably wrote the *Confession* in response to this event.

Patrick does not give us historical details about his missionary years. He tells us of the many Irish baptisms and ordinations, the numbers of young people who became monks and nuns, and of the various difficulties and serious hostility, both from within the ranks of his fellow clergy and among the pagan opponents of his evangelisation. What is without doubt is that his missionary efforts were highly successful, but he attributes that entirely to God, who made use of the ill-educated, poor, sinful instrument to bring an entire people to the faith.

The first extensive biography of Patrick was written by Mirchiu two hundred years later. Historians generally regard it as unreliable because it clearly embroiders Patrick's ministry with miracles and legends connected with places and people. Nevertheless, two themes can be detected throughout the traditions about Patrick that may throw some light on his actual missionary methods.

Patrick seems, as a rule, to have contacted the chiefs of a district before approaching anyone else. This ensured that there was no concerted official opposition to the Christian message, as he had already acquired the sponsorship, or at least the license, of the secular power. In fact, he relates that he managed to convert many of the noble families, their daughters and sons, to the faith. His second emphasis was on Christian liturgy: Baptism, Eucharist, Confirmation and Ordination, and the monastic life that sustained it.

Patrick appears to have aligned Christianity, where he could, with native spiritual sensibilities. Flowing water, bonfires of celebration, pilgrimages and processions, the cycle through darkness and light of the different seasons, bleak hills and dark lakes, green fields and ancient woodlands were all evoked in the Church's life and worship. No doubt, Patrick's empathy for the deep significance of these cultural and emotional realities stemmed from the six years of his youthful captivity and slavery among the Irish people. The early Irish Christianity, which evolved from the Church left behind by St Patrick, evinces a unique and thoroughly Celtic love of nature. For example, many of the churches, monasteries and shrines of early Irish Christianity are places of stunning spiritual and natural beauty.

One story told by Mirchiu is so symbolic that we would want it to be true. Early on in his mission, Patrick approached Tara to meet the High King of Ireland at his stronghold. He stopped on the Hill of Slane, a day's journey away, as it was time for the Holy Saturday celebration. There, at sundown, he lit the Paschal Fire, even though there was an edict which forbade any fire in the realm until the king had ignited his. The Paschal Fire of the Christian missionaries was visible through the darkness at the citadel of the High King himself, King Laoire. The Druids warned the king that the fire on Slane should be put out that night, or else it would never be extinguished in Ireland. Neither magic nor other machinations could douse the fire, and Patrick went on to win the support of the king and the conversion of many of his subjects.

Patrick is said to have died on 17 March, either in 461 AD or 493 AD. Some historians favour the later date because they think Patrick was the second great missionary of Ireland, following in the footsteps of Palladius, and indeed believe that many of the events attributed to Patrick belong to the earlier apostle of Ireland.

Whether or not he was, strictly speaking, the first apostle historically, Patrick certainly made the greater impact. It is surely ironic that the Irish through the centuries have brought the celebration of St Patrick to every country under heaven, given that he was not himself Irish, and even more ironic that they commemorate him so enthusiastically and exuberantly, given that he was himself truly humble and self-effacing.

LITURGY CELEBRATES THE PASCHAL MYSTERY

The Church celebrates in the liturgy above all the Paschal
mystery by which Christ accomplished the work of our salvation.

– CCC, no. 1067

Part Two of the *Catechism*, containing two sections, deals with the liturgy of the Church. Section One presents the basic teachings about liturgy. Section Two presents the Seven Sacraments. The word *liturgy* comes from a Greek term meaning 'public work or work done on behalf of the people'. Liturgy always referred to an organised community. A work, then, done by an individual or a group was a liturgy on behalf of the larger community. All the worshippers are expected to participate actively in each liturgy, for this is holy 'work', not entertainment or a spectator event. Every liturgical celebration is an action of Christ the High Priest and of his Mystical Body, which is the Church. It therefore requires the participation of the People of God in the work of God.

Liturgy is centred on the Holy Trinity. At every liturgy the action of worship is directed to the Father, from whom all blessings come, through the Son in the unity of the Holy Spirit. We praise the Father who first called us to be his people by sending us his Son as our Redeemer and giving us the Holy Spirit so that we can continue to gather, to remember what God has done for us and to share in the blessings of salvation.

Through the liturgical celebrations of the Church, we participate in the Paschal Mystery of Christ, that is, his passing through death from this life into eternal glory, just as God enabled the people of ancient Israel to pass from slavery to freedom through the events narrated in the Book of Exodus (cf. Ex 11–13). The liturgies of the Church also help to teach us about Jesus Christ and the meaning of the mysteries we are celebrating.

A mystery is a reality that is both visible and hidden. Jesus Christ's death and Resurrection become present to us and effective for us in the liturgical life of the Church. His death and Resurrection are hidden now in the eternity of God, but as Risen Lord and Head of the Church, Jesus Christ calls us to share in them through the liturgy of the Church, that is, by the visible gathering of the community for worship and remembrance of what God has done for us. It is the Holy Spirit, the source of the Church's life, who draws us together through liturgical actions, the chief of which are the Sacraments. The term *liturgy* itself has a broader application than that of Sacrament, for it embraces all the official public prayer life of the Church, while the term *Sacrament* refers to a particular celebration of Christ's salvific work.

THE SACRAMENTS

The whole liturgical life of the Church revolves around the Eucharistic sacrifice and the sacraments.

– CCC, no. 1113

As we come to understand the Sacraments, it is important to recognise that the Sacraments have a visible and invisible reality, a reality open to all the human senses but grasped in its God-given depths with the eyes of faith. When parents hug their children, for example, the visible reality we see is the hug. The invisible reality the hug conveys is love. We cannot 'see' the love the hug expresses, though sometimes we can see its nurturing effect in the child.

The visible reality we see in the Sacraments is their outward expression, the form they take, and the way in which they are administered and received. The invisible reality we cannot 'see' is God's grace, his gracious initiative in redeeming us through the death and Resurrection of his Son. His initiative is called *grace* because it is the free and loving gift by which he offers people a share in his life, and shows us his favour and will for our salvation. Our response to the grace of God's initiative is itself a grace or gift from God by which we can imitate Christ in our daily lives.

The saving words and deeds of Jesus Christ are the foundation of what he would communicate in the Sacraments through the ministers of the Church. Guided by the Holy Spirit, the Church recognises the existence of

Seven Sacraments instituted by the Lord. They are grouped together in the following way:

- Sacraments of Initiation: Baptism, Confirmation (or Chrismation, as it is called in the Eastern Churches) and Eucharist
- Sacraments of Healing: Penance and Reconciliation and Anointing of the Sick
- Sacraments at the Service of Communion: Holy Orders and Matrimony.

What are the Sacraments? 'The sacraments are efficacious signs of grace, instituted by Christ and entrusted to the Church, by which divine life is dispensed to us' through the work of the Holy Spirit (CCC, nos. 1131; cf. no. 774).

First of all, Sacraments are efficacious signs: that is, they are effective. In human life, signs and symbols are found everywhere. Because we are both body and spirit, we express our inner selves through visible signs and symbols. We use them to communicate with each other in speech, gestures and deeds. Sacramental signs are different in the sense that Christ uses them to confer his life and grace. When these sacramental signs are celebrated, they reveal and make present the reality they signify. They are efficacious, that is, effective, because Jesus Christ is at work in them. 'It is he who baptises, he who acts in the sacraments in order to communicate the grace that each sacrament signifies' (CCC, no. 1127). As we reflect on the individual Sacraments in later chapters of this *Catechism*, we will see that each Sacrament brings with it some particular grace.

Second, Christ instituted the Sacraments. 'Adhering to the teaching of the Holy Scriptures, to the apostolic traditions, and to the consensus ... of the Fathers', we profess that 'the sacraments of the new law were ... all instituted by Jesus Christ our Lord' (CCC, no. 1114, citing the Council of Trent: DS 1600–1601).

Third, Jesus entrusted the Sacraments to the Church. By Christ's will, the Church oversees and celebrates the Sacraments. Throughout his earthly life, Christ's words and deeds anticipated the power of his Paschal Mystery. Sacraments confer the grace that comes forth from Jesus Christ and that appears in the life of the Church by the power of the Holy Spirit.

Fourth, the Sacraments transmit divine life. Our share in this life is God's grace, his gift to us. In the Sacraments, we encounter Jesus Christ. The Spirit heals us and draws us closer to Christ and makes us partakers in the life of the Holy Trinity. Depending on our responsiveness to the grace of each Sacrament, our loving union with Jesus can increase throughout our journey of faith. Fruitful reception of the Sacraments presupposes the faith of the one who receives them. This faith is preceded by the faith of the Church (cf. CCC, no. 1124). We grow in holiness, which is both personal and communal – a matter of personal sanctity and of unity with the mission and holiness of the Church.

Jesus gave us the Sacraments to call us to worship God, to build up the Church, to deepen our faith, to show us how to pray, to connect us with the living Tradition of the Church and to sanctify us. While God works primarily through the Sacraments, he also touches us through the community of the Church, through the lives of holy people, through prayer, spirituality and acts of love. But 'for believers, the sacraments of the New Covenant are *necessary for salvation* ... The fruit of the sacramental life is that the Spirit of adoption makes the faithful partakers of the divine nature' (CCC, no. 1129).

LITURGY IS THE BODY OF CHRIST AT PRAYER

> *Liturgy is an action of the whole Christ ... Liturgical services are not private functions but are celebrations of the Church.*
>
> – CCC, nos. 1136, 1140

When it comes to celebrating the Sacraments, there are four questions that need our attention: Who celebrates the liturgy? How is the liturgy celebrated? When is the liturgy celebrated? Where is the liturgy celebrated?

WHO CELEBRATES?

The entire Body of Christ, animated by the Holy Spirit, celebrates the liturgy. The celebrating assembly is the community of the baptised. Liturgy is not a matter of private prayer, but a public act of worship by the faithful gathered together by the power of the Spirit under the authority of the bishop, their teacher and shepherd. 'Mother Church earnestly desires that all the faithful should be led to that full, conscious and active participation in liturgical celebrations which is demanded by the very nature of the liturgy, and to which the Christian people ... have a right and an obligation by reason of their Baptism' (CCC, no. 1141). The faithful are called to come to the liturgy consciously prepared to make their thoughts agree with what they say and hear and to cooperate with divine grace.

Within the assembly, the ordained have a unique function of service. 'These servants are chosen and consecrated by the sacrament of Holy Orders, by which the Holy Spirit enables them to act in the person of Christ the head, for the service of all the members of the Church' (CCC, no. 1142). Thus, for example, priests preside at the Eucharist, in which the elements of bread and wine are changed into the Body and Blood of Christ. Priests act in the person of Christ, the Head of the Church, and in the name of the Church when presenting to God the prayers and self-offering of the people and when offering the Eucharistic sacrifice, above all as they proclaim the Eucharistic Prayer.

HOW DO WE CELEBRATE?

The Church celebrates the liturgy using an abundance of signs, symbols and rituals. We celebrate the Sacraments with scriptural readings, homilies, music, processions, blessings, bread, wine, oil, arms outstretched in prayer, gestures of peace, bowed heads, kneeling, standing, sitting, incense, holy water, flowers, candles, colours, ritual vestments, choirs and musical instruments.

We do this in a holy environment in which architecture, sculpture, paintings, icons and stained glass lend an ambience that speaks of the mystery of God and divine transcendence on the one hand, and the unity of God with the worshipping community on the other. Since the Son of

God honoured us by becoming incarnate – the true visible image of the invisible God – we use these signs and symbols to help us experience God's invisible presence.

The Liturgy of the Word is part of all sacramental celebrations. The reading of Sacred Scripture is meant to awaken a response of faith in the listeners. When the word is proclaimed, Christ himself speaks. Having encountered Christ in the word, the people enter with a deeper appreciation into the heart of the celebration. The signs that accompany this reading emphasise its dignity: the use of a beautiful book, a procession with the Book of the Gospels including incense and candles, an effective reading of the Scripture, a homily that breaks open the word, silent reflection and a prayerful response from the assembly. The combination of word and action helps make visible the invisible action of Christ and the Holy Spirit to open the hearts of the assembly to the grace of the particular sacramental celebration.

Liturgical Traditions and the Catholicity of the Church

The liturgical traditions or rites presently in use in the Church are the Latin (principally the Roman rite, but also the rites of certain local churches such as the Ambrosian rite, centred in Milan, Italy or those of certain religious orders) and the Byzantine, Alexandrian or Coptic, Syrian, Armenian, Maronite and Chaldean rites. In 'faithful obedience to tradition the sacred Council declares that Holy Mother Church holds all lawfully recognised rites to be of equal right and dignity, and that she wishes to preserve them in the future and to foster them in every way'. (CCC, no. 1203, citing SC, no. 4)

The rich variety of ecclesiastical disciplines, liturgical rites and theological and spiritual heritages proper to the local churches, 'unified in a common effort, shows all the more resplendently the catholicity of the undivided Church'. (CCC, no. 835, citing LG, no. 23)

WHEN DO WE CELEBRATE?

The Lord's Day

Central to the Church's liturgical life is Sunday, the day of Christ's Resurrection. The observance begins with the evening of the preceding day. It is a day when all Catholics are obliged to take part in the Mass. 'The Lord's Supper is its centre, for there the whole community of the faithful encounters the risen Lord who invites them to his banquet' (CCC, no. 1166). The Church encourages that Sunday, the 'Lord's Day', also be a day for rest and recreation. It is also a day when the faithful can devote themselves to works of mercy and to the apostolate. This is discussed again in the chapter on the Third Commandment.

The Liturgical Year

In the Liturgical Year, the Church celebrates the whole mystery of Christ from the Incarnation until the day of Pentecost and the expectation of Christ's second coming. The summit of the Liturgical Year is the Easter Triduum – from the evening of Holy Thursday to the evening of Easter Sunday. Though chronologically three days, they are liturgically one day unfolding for us the unity of Christ's Paschal Mystery. The presence of the Risen Lord and his saving work permeates the entire Liturgical Year: Advent, the Christmas Season, Lent, the Easter Season and Ordinary Time.

The Cycle of Saints

Besides the liturgical times just cited, the Church, with a special love, venerates Mary, the Mother of God, and also offers for the devotion of the faithful the memory of the martyrs and other saints. The veneration of Mary is evident in the number of feasts of the Blessed Virgin Mary. Mary is intimately linked to the saving work of her Son. Her feasts call us to admire and praise her as the outstanding fruit of Christ's redeeming work. Mary is the pure image of the kind of discipleship we hope to attain. She prays for us, loves us and always brings us to Jesus. The feasts and memorials of the martyrs and other saints are occasions to praise God for their identification with Christ's Paschal Mystery. They are examples to us of love for God and others, of heroic courage in practising faith and of concern for the needs of others. We also rely on their intercession when we present our needs to God in prayer.

The Liturgy of the Hours

Closely tied to the Eucharist in the daily liturgical life of the Church is the Liturgy of the Hours, especially Morning and Evening Prayer. The Liturgy of the Hours, in which the whole Church pours out her praise to God, prolongs the Eucharistic celebration and leads us back to it. Besides offering praise to God, the Church in the Liturgy of the Hours expresses the prayers and desires of the Christian faithful. This is evident especially in the Intercessions at Morning and Evening Prayer, the praying of the Our Father and the concluding prayer.

This public prayer of the Church is intended for the whole People of God. In this prayer Christ continues his priestly work and consecrates time. All God's people can participate in it according to their calling and circumstances. In this prayer, we harmonise our voices with praying hearts, and we come to a more profound understanding of the Psalms and other parts of Scripture that make up the largest part of the Liturgy of the Hours.

Even though the Liturgy of the Hours is celebrated in various ways in the Eastern and Latin Churches, the hymns, canticles and readings from Church Fathers, other saints and other Church writers offer us a rich meditation on God's Word. This public prayer prepares us for private prayer.

WHERE DO WE CELEBRATE?

In one sense, worship is not confined to any one place, for the whole earth is entrusted to God's people. But practically, when religious freedom is not suppressed, it is customary to build churches for divine worship. A church is 'a house of prayer in which the Eucharist is celebrated and reserved, where the faithful assemble, and where is worshipped the presence of the Son of God our Saviour' (CCC, no. 1181, citing Second Vatican Council, *Decree on Priestly Life and Ministry* [*Presbyterorum Ordinis*; PO], no. 5). While the church building is important, the worshipping community, 'living stones making a spiritual house' (1 Pt 2:5), is of greater importance. Nevertheless, church buildings should be dignified enough to reflect the importance of what takes place there. They should be beautiful places that foster prayer and a sense of the sacred.

FROM THE CATECHISM

1. What does Sunday and its vigil mean for Catholics?
Sunday, the 'Lord's Day', is the principal day for the celebration of the Eucharist because it is the day of the Resurrection. It is the pre-eminent day of the liturgical assembly, the day of the Christian family and the day of joy and rest from work. Sunday is the 'foundation and kernel of the whole liturgical year'. (CCC, no. 1193, citing SC, no. 106)

2. What are the criteria for the use of songs and music in the Liturgy?
Songs and music fulfil their function as signs ... when they are closely connected ... with the liturgical action, according to three principal criteria: beauty expressive of prayer, the unanimous participation of the assembly at the designated moments and the solemn character of the celebration. In this way they participate in the purpose of the liturgical words and actions: the glory of God and the sanctification of the faithful. (CCC, no. 1157)

3. What is the purpose of the Liturgy of the Word?
The Liturgy of the Word is an integral part of the celebration. The meaning of the celebration is expressed by the Word of God which is proclaimed and by the response of faith to it. (CCC, no. 1190)

THE LINK BETWEEN LITURGY AND LIFE

Our society favours being practical and tends to evaluate people and institutions in this light. Practicality has led to numerous inventions that have made life more humane. It also asks people to draw a closer link between theory and everyday life, urging them to be more down-to-earth.

But for some practical-minded people, religion appears to put too much emphasis on the next world rather than this one. Further, they claim that the time and effort devoted to ceremonies and otherworldly endeavours seems to have little value. They would want religion to confine itself to humanitarian deeds.

The Church has a vital role to play in shaping responsible citizens with moral character and with a willingness to contribute to the well-being of society. The liturgy and worship of the Church have much to do with these admirable goals. At divine worship, people receive the grace to help them to be formed ever more closely to Christ. The saving grace of the dying and rising of Christ are communicated to us in the Sacraments so that we might live more perfectly Christ's truth and virtues such as love, justice, mercy and compassion.

Every Mass ends with the mission to go forth and serve the Lord. This sending means that the love of God and neighbour and the moral implications of the Beatitudes and the Ten Commandments should be witnessed by the participants in everyday life. People of faith know that their liturgical experience provides a unique spiritual vision and strength for making this a better world.

The lives of the saints provide ample evidence of this truth. Saints of every age have improved healthcare and education and fostered the human dignity of the poor, the oppressed and the society at large. Saints attribute their remarkable energies to the power that comes from prayer and above all from the Sacraments, especially the Eucharist.

FOR DISCUSSION

1. How might you participate more fully, more consciously and more actively in the Sunday Mass? In a culture that is centred on the 'weekend', what can people do to observe Sunday as a day dedicated to God?

2. Review the definition of the Sacraments. How would you explain its elements to others? What can you learn from the sacred times in which liturgy is celebrated, such as Sunday, the Liturgical Year and the feasts and memorials of the saints?

3. In what ways are you aware of the link between liturgy and your daily life? What are some stories about people you know or read about that illustrate the connection between liturgy and Christian witness?

■ DOCTRINAL STATEMENTS ■

- In liturgy, we praise and adore the Father as the source of all the blessings of creation, salvation and divine adoption.
- 'The liturgy is the work of the whole Christ, head and body' (CCC, no. 1187). In liturgy, Christ the Son of God made flesh acts in the Sacraments in which he communicates his saving power for his Body the Church.
- In liturgy, the Holy Spirit brings the assembly to meet Christ, to make Christ's saving work present and to sanctify the members that they may witness Christ.
- 'The Sacraments are efficacious signs of grace, instituted by Christ and entrusted to the Church, by which divine life is dispensed to us' (CCC, no. 1131).
- The Church celebrates the Sacraments as an assembly of all the baptised, led by the ordained, each having a special role to play in the sacramental celebrations.
- The Holy Spirit prepares the faithful for the Sacraments by helping them to welcome the Word of God in faith.
- The Sacraments communicate to each person a participation in God's life and a growth of love and witness in the Church. This is grace, the result of God's favour and initiative.
- A liturgical celebration uses signs and symbols drawn from creation, human life and the history of salvation. Integrated into faith, the signs become bearers of the sanctifying action of Christ.
- The Liturgy of the Word is an important part of every liturgy because the proclamation of the Word of God and the response of faith to it help give meaning to the celebration.
- Sacred song and music, closely linked to the celebration, should lead to prayer, invite the participation of all in the assembly and reflect the sacred character of the Sacrament.
- Sacred images nourish faith in the mystery of Christ. Through images of Christ we are moved to adore him and his saving works. In images of Mary and the saints we venerate the persons represented.
- Sunday and its vigil celebrate Christ's Resurrection, and it is the day that the faithful are obliged to attend Mass, rest from work and engage in charitable works.

- In the course of the Liturgical Year, the Church unfolds the mystery of Christ's Incarnation, public ministry, death and Resurrection, Ascension, sending of the Holy Spirit and the Church's expectation of his second coming.
- The feasts and memorials of the Mother of God and the saints call us to praise God for what he has accomplished in them and to imitate their virtues.
- The faithful who pray the Liturgy of the Hours are united with Christ in giving glory to the Father and imploring the gifts of the Holy Spirit for the world.
- Our parish churches are places where the faithful gather for public worship and personal prayer. These holy places are images of the heavenly Kingdom to which we journey.
- 'The diverse liturgical traditions or rites, legitimately recognised, manifest the catholicity of the Church, because they signify and communicate the same mystery of Christ' (CCC, no. 1208).

MEDITATION

For two thousand years, Christian time has been measured by the memory of that 'first day of the week' (Mk 16:2, 9; Lk 24:1; Jn 20:1), when the Risen Christ gave the Apostles the gift of peace and of the Spirit (cf. Jn 20:19-23). The truth of Christ's Resurrection is the original fact upon which Christian faith is based (cf. 1 Cor 15:14), an event set at the centre of the mystery of time, prefiguring the last day when Christ will return in glory. We do not know what the new millennium has in store for us, but we are certain that it is safe in the hands of Christ, the 'King of kings and Lord of lords' (Rv 19:16); and precisely by celebrating his Passover not just once a year but every Sunday, the Church will continue to show to every generation 'the true fulcrum of history, to which the mystery of the world's origin and its final destiny leads'.

– St John Paul II, *At the Close of the Great Jubilee of the Year 2000* (*Novo Millennio Ineunte*; NMI), no. 35

From the *Confession of St Patrick*

I am, then, first and foremost a rustic, an untaught refugee indeed who does not know how to provide for the future. But this much I know for sure. Before I was humbled I was like a stone lying in the deep mud. Then he who is mighty came and in his mercy he not only pulled me out but lifted me up and placed me at the very top of the wall. I must, therefore, speak publicly in order to repay the Lord for such wonderful gifts, gifts for the present and for eternity which human mind cannot measure. ... My decision to write must be made, then, in the light of our faith in the Trinity. The gift of God and his eternal consolation must be made known, regardless of danger. I must fearlessly and confidently spread the name of God everywhere in order to leave a legacy after my death to my brothers and children, the many thousands of them, whom I have baptised in the Lord.

--- PRAYER ---

Sing a new song to the Lord,
    his praise in the assembly of the faithful.
Let Israel rejoice in its Maker,
    let Sion's sons exult in their king.
Let the faithful exult in glory,
    and rejoice as they take their rest.
Let the praise of God be in their mouths.

— Ps 149:1-2, 5-6

How I wept when I heard your hymns and canticles, being deeply moved by the sweet singing of your Church.

— St Augustine, *The Confessions*, bk. 9, chap. 6;
Liturgy of the Hours, vol. IV, 1337

St Patrick's Breastplate

Christ be with me.
Christ be beside me.
Christ be before me.
Christ be behind me.
Christ at my right hand.
Christ at my left hand.
Christ be with me everywhere I go.
Christ be my friend, for ever and ever.
Amen.

Lúireach Phádraig

Críost liom.
Críost romham.
Críost i mo dhiaidh.
Críost ionam.
Críost ar mo dheis.
Críost ar mo chlé.
Críost i mo chuideachta is cuma cá dtéim.
Críost mar chara agam, anois is go buan.
Áiméan.

… the liturgy is, indeed, the summit toward which all the activity of the Church is directed, and fount from which all her power flows.

– SGN, 73

15 BAPTISM: BECOMING A CHRISTIAN

BAPTISM IS THE FIRST OF THE SACRAMENTS OF INITIATION – CCC, NOS. 1210–1284

A BAPTISMAL WITNESS TO JUSTICE FOR MINORITIES: JOHN BOYLE O'REILLY

 A young, newly arrived Irish immigrant to Boston joined the Catholic newspaper, *The Boston Pilot*, as a journalist in 1870. John Boyle O'Reilly was then twenty-six years old but he had already packed into his short life enough stories and adventures to fill a book.

O'Reilly was born near Drogheda to a headmaster father and a nationalist mother. As a young man, he enlisted in the British army, where he worked covertly to advance the cause of the Irish Republican Brotherhood, otherwise known as the Fenians. His actions were discovered, and he was arrested and sentenced to death. Because of his youth, the sentence was commuted to a twenty-year prison term, and he was transported to Fremantle, the penal settlement in Western Australia.

O'Reilly was a pleasant, sociable, attractive and persuasive young man. With the help of two priests and other colonists, he managed to escape from prison. The arrangement was made that O'Reilly would be picked up by an American whaling vessel at sea. After eluding recapture in Mauritius by faking his suicide, he was transferred to another ship and brought to Liverpool. From there, he made his way to Boston, where he became a reporter for *The Boston Pilot*. It had been established as a Catholic newspaper by the Bishop of Boston in 1829, but in 1836 it was placed under lay control.

His first reporting job was on the failed Fenian invasion of Canada in 1870. This unfortunate experience convinced him of the futility of physical force to achieve Irish freedom. From then on, he turned his considerable intelligence and persuasive power to achieve progress for the Irish people through constitutional and political means.

He did not forget the prisoners, his cellmates, in Fremantle. In 1876 he joined with other Irish émigrés to organise the escape of six Fenian prisoners from Fremantle. The daring plan involved buying an American vessel, the *Catalpa*, arranging flight from a working party, a small boat to row the prisoners outside territorial waters, a rendezvous on the high seas and a long sea journey to the United States. The plan succeeded dramatically, and the sextet arrived in Boston to great acclaim and rejoicing.

In the same year, O'Reilly was appointed editor-in-chief of the *Pilot*. He also became part-owner, helping to bail out the ailing newspaper at a time of difficulty. He then proceeded to build the *Pilot* up from a small Catholic newspaper to a respected journal with a national reputation.

For the next twenty years, O'Reilly was the foremost influence in directing Irish immigrants through the process of cultural assimilation. For a time his literary talents and friendly attitude toward the Protestant establishment earned him a favoured place in society.

But he never forgot his ethnic roots or his Catholic faith. He used his gifts as a public speaker, civil rights leader, poet and novelist to bridge the gap between Catholics and Protestants in nineteenth-century Boston, while enhancing Catholic identity in the process. He wrote four books of verse, *Songs from the Southern Seas; Songs, Legends, and Ballads; The Statues in the Block;* and *In Bohemia*. He also wrote articles for *The Atlantic Monthly* and *Scribner's Monthly*. In his novel *Moondyne*, he drew on his youthful experience and his mature political and social vision for an exciting narrative that moved from England to Australia to America, just like its author some years before.

As the editor of *The Boston Pilot*, John Boyle O'Reilly was soon one of the most influential Irishmen in the United States. He used the *Pilot* as a platform for defending an independent Ireland and addressing the rights of African Americans and Native Americans. He compared the oppression that these minorities were suffering to that which the Irish immigrants were experiencing. These oppressed groups had a friend in this man. He openly campaigned in the *Pilot* for political candidates who were for social reform. He joined several charitable organisations, and no doubt influenced by his teacher father, was an outstanding proponent of Catholic education. He received honorary doctorates from Georgetown University in Washington DC, and Notre Dame University in South Bend, Indiana.

O'Reilly married Mary Murphy and had four daughters. He kept in close touch, naturally enough, with the situation in Ireland. Irish politicians asked him whether they should procure a pardon so that he could safely visit his native land in the improving national situation, but O'Reilly refused the outreach, vowing not to return until Ireland was free.

John Boyle O'Reilly's unexpected death in 1890 was termed a 'public calamity' by Cardinal Gibbons of Baltimore. When the funeral Mass was held in St Mary's Church, in Charlestown, near Boston, thousands of mourners came to pray and pay their respects. Politicians, philosophers, poets, journalists and educators of many creeds and persuasions united to pronounce tribute to one who had blazed such a trail for justice, peace, reconciliation, education and humanity. For a convicted felon and a branded convict, it was an extraordinary display. As a loyal patriot and warm family man, he had accomplished much in forty-six short years.

The *Catechism* says that all who are reborn as children of God in Baptism 'must profess before men the faith they have received from God through the Church and participate in the apostolic and missionary activity of the People of God' (CCC, no. 1270). God gave John Boyle O'Reilly the grace to live out, in a vigorous and inspiring manner, his baptismal commitment to the cause of Christ, the Church and God's Kingdom. He showed how the laity can bring the Gospel to society and can make a difference.

SACRAMENTS OF INITIATION

The Sacraments of Initiation – Baptism, Confirmation and the Eucharist – are the foundations of the Christian life. 'Baptism, the Eucharist, and the sacrament of Confirmation together constitute the "sacraments of Christian initiation", whose unity must be safeguarded' (CCC, no. 1285). We begin with our study of Baptism in this chapter and will treat the other two Sacraments in the following ones.

DYING AND RISING WITH CHRIST

*You cannot have forgotten that all of us, when we were
baptised into Christ Jesus, were baptised into his death.
So by our baptism into his death we were buried with him,
so that as Christ was raised from the dead by the Father's
glorious power, we too should begin living a new life.*

– Rm 6:3-4

*Baptism is birth into the new life in Christ. In accordance
with the Lord's will, it is necessary for salvation, as is the
Church herself, which we enter by Baptism.*

– CCC, no. 1277

In his dialogue with Nicodemus, Jesus taught that Baptism was necessary for salvation. 'In all truth I tell you, no one can enter the kingdom of God without being born through water and the Spirit' (Jn 3:5). After his Resurrection, Jesus met with the eleven Apostles and gave them the commission to preach the Gospel and baptise, telling them, 'Whoever believes and is baptised will be saved' (Mk 16:16). The word *baptism* in its origins is Greek and means 'immersion' and 'bath'. Immersion in water is a sign of death, and emersion out of the water means new life. To bathe in water is also to undergo cleansing. Saint Paul sums up this truth when he says, 'You have been buried with him by your baptism; by which, too, you have been raised up with him through your belief in the power of God who raised him from the dead' (Col 2:12).

The origin and foundation of Christian Baptism is Jesus. Before starting his public ministry, Jesus submitted himself to the baptism given by John the Baptist. The waters did not purify him; he cleansed the waters. 'He comes to sanctify the Jordan for our sake ... to begin a new creation through the Spirit and water' (St Gregory Nazianzen, *Liturgy of the Hours*, I, 634). Jesus' immersion in the water is a sign for all human beings of the need to die to themselves to do God's will. Jesus did not need to be baptised because he was totally faithful to the will of his Father and free from sin. However, he wanted to show his solidarity with human beings in order to reconcile them to the Father. By commanding his disciples to baptise all nations, he established the means by which people would die to sin – Original and actual – and begin to live a new life with God.

THE LITURGY OF BAPTISM

The meaning and grace of the sacrament of Baptism are clearly seen in the rites of its celebration.

– CCC, no. 1234

The eight major elements in the baptismal ceremony teach us the meaning of this Sacrament of Initiation and help us appreciate our life in Christ. Signs and symbols have their own capacity to communicate their meaning. Of course, the Sacrament is more than an instructive symbol; it accomplishes what it signifies.

The Sign of the Cross

At the beginning of the celebration, the celebrant traces the Sign of the Cross on the forehead of the one being baptised. This recalls Christ's saving death and the redemption it brought. Baptism is a Sacrament of salvation.

Readings from Scripture

Proclaiming the Word of God in the midst of the community sheds divine light on the celebration and is meant to build the faith of all the participants. One of the traditional names for Baptism is 'Illumination'. The Holy Spirit fills the heart and mind with the light of revealed truth and enables the response of faith.

Exorcism and Anointing

Baptism liberates us from sin. An exorcism prayer is recited over the one being baptised, preparing the person to renounce sin and be released from evil. The celebrant anoints the person to be baptised with the Oil of Catechumens (an oil that has been blessed by the bishop for the candidates for Baptism) or imposes hands on the person. In this way, the person is being called to renounce sin and to leave behind the domination of the power of evil.

Blessing the Baptismal Water

Baptismal water is blessed at the Easter Vigil. Outside the Easter Season, the water used for Baptism can also be blessed at each celebration of the Sacrament. The blessing prayer asks the Father 'that through his Son the power of the Holy Spirit may be sent upon the water, so that those who will be baptised may be "born of water and the Spirit"' (CCC, no. 1238).

Renunciation of Sin and Profession of Faith

Those being baptised are asked to reject sin and Satan, and to profess their faith in the Triune God. In the case of infants, parents, godparents and the entire community present for the liturgy do this on behalf of those who cannot yet speak for themselves.

The Essential Rite of the Sacrament

The bishop, priest, or deacon either pours water three times on the person's head or immerses the candidate in water three times. In the Latin Church, he accompanies the act with the words, '[Name], I baptise you in the name of the Father, and of the Son, and of the Holy Spirit.' The celebrant matches each pouring or immersion with the invocation of each of the Divine Persons. The ritual of immersion or washing helps us understand that our sins are buried and washed away as we die with Jesus, and we are filled with divine light and life as we rise from immersion in the water or are cleansed by the pouring.

In the Eastern liturgies the catechumen turns toward the East and the priest says: 'The servant of God, [Name], is baptised in the name of the Father, and of the Son, and of the Holy Spirit.' At the invocation of each person of the Most Holy Trinity, the priest immerses the candidate in the water and raises him up again. (CCC, no. 1240)

'Today in all the rites, Latin and Eastern, the Christian initiation of adults begins with their entry into the catechumenate and reaches its culmination in a single celebration of the three Sacraments of Initiation: Baptism, Confirmation, and the Eucharist' (CCC, no. 1233). After the completion of initiation, the neophytes or new members begin the period of continued learning and formation in Christian life called *Mystagogy*.

With regard to infants, in the Latin Church, the Sacraments of Confirmation and Eucharist are received at a later time after Baptism. This is partly because of the emphasis on the bishop as the ordinary minister of Confirmation. Though the bishop cannot baptise everyone, he has a role in everyone's initiation into the Church by confirming them. In the Eastern Churches, the Baptism of infants is followed in the same ceremony by Confirmation (Chrismation) and Eucharist.

The Anointing with Sacred Chrism

The celebrant anoints the newly baptised with the sacred Chrism (a perfumed oil signifying the gift of the Holy Spirit), so that united with God's people the person may remain forever a member of Christ, who is Priest, Prophet and King. In the liturgy of the Eastern Churches, this anointing is the Chrismation, or the Sacrament of Confirmation, and is done immediately after Baptism. At the initiation of adults into the Church at the Easter Vigil, Confirmation follows Baptism.

Reception of the White Garment and the Candle

Following the Anointing with Chrism, the minister of Baptism presents the newly baptised with a white garment and a candle. The white garment shows that the newly baptised have put on Christ and have risen with him. To be clothed in the baptismal white garment is to be clothed in Christ's protective love. Included in this ceremony is the admonition to keep the garment unstained by sin. The Book of Revelation describes the significance of the white robe: 'They have washed their robes white again in the blood of the Lamb' (Rv 7:14).

The candle is lit from the Paschal Candle, which represents the Risen Christ. The lighted candle reminds the newly baptised of the light of Christ they have received. It also reminds us that all those baptised in Christ are to be lights for the world.

These two symbols used at Baptism appear again in the Latin Church's funeral liturgy in the forms of the white pall covering the casket and the lighted Paschal Candle, which ordinarily stands near the casket. This is to remind us that the salvation and new life promised at Baptism can now be experienced fully by the one who has gone to God.

THE NECESSITY OF BAPTISM

As mentioned earlier in this chapter, the Lord himself affirms that Baptism is necessary for salvation. 'No one can enter the kingdom of God without being born through water and the Spirit' (Jn 3:5). Christ commanded his disciples to preach the Gospel, draw people to faith in him and baptise those who come to conversion. The Church does not neglect the mission she has received from Christ to ensure that all be baptised and reborn of water and the Spirit.

Who Can Baptise?

'The ordinary ministers of Baptism are the bishop and priest and, in the Latin Church, also the deacon. In case of necessity, any person, even someone not baptised, can baptise, if he has the required intention. The intention required is to will to do what the Church does when she baptises, and to apply the Trinitarian baptismal formula. The Church finds the reason for this possibility in the universal saving will of God and the necessity of Baptism for salvation' (CCC, no. 1256).

SPONSORS FOR BAPTISM

Whenever a person is baptised, as an infant, as a child or as an adult, there should be at least one person present who will act as sponsor for the one being baptised. The sponsor, commonly referred to as one's godmother or godfather, accepts the responsibility of helping the person grow in the Catholic faith. One who acts as a sponsor for an infant or child agrees to help the parents teach their child about the faith and how to live as a practising Catholic. One who acts as sponsor for an adult agrees to encourage and support the person, pray with and for the person and offer whatever help, information or support is needed while the person is preparing to enter the Church and then is living out the rest of his or her life as a practising Catholic.

For a person to act as a sponsor for Baptism, he or she must be at least sixteen years old, must have already received all the Sacraments of Initiation (Baptism, Confirmation and Holy Eucharist), and must be living in a way that demonstrates that one's faith is strong enough to be able to fulfil the responsibilities involved with being a sponsor. A sponsor who is married must be married in accord with the laws of the Church (cf. CIC, can. 874).

WHO CAN RECEIVE BAPTISM?

The Baptism of Adults

For adults today, the Church, after the Second Vatican Council, has restored the order of the Catechumenate in the Rite of Christian Initiation of Adults (RCIA). It outlines the steps for the formation of catechumens, bringing their conversion to the faith to a greater maturity. It helps them respond more deeply to God's gracious initiative in their lives and prepares them for union with the Church community. This process is meant to form them into the fullness of the Christian life and to become disciples of Jesus, their teacher. This includes an initiation into the mystery of salvation, the practice of faith, hope and love and other virtues in a succession of liturgical rites.

Persons baptised into another Christian church and now seeking full communion with the Catholic Church are also welcomed to participate along with catechumens in the RCIA in the process of learning about the Catholic faith and being formed in that faith. They bring to the process of preparation their prior experience of Christian life and prayer. For a baptised Christian, reception into full communion with the Catholic Church involves reception of the Sacrament of Penance and Reconciliation and then a Profession of Faith followed by the celebration of Confirmation and the Eucharist.

The Baptism of Infants

Infant Baptism has been practised since apostolic times. Infants need to be baptised because through this Sacrament, they are freed from Original Sin and are welcomed into the community of the Church, where they have access to the fullness of the means of salvation. Their parents, godparents and the parish community commit themselves to their ongoing formation in faith and knowledge of the tradition of the Church. The best gift that parents can give their children is a life in the Church. 'The Church and the parents would deny a child the priceless grace of becoming a child of God were they not to confer Baptism shortly after birth' (CCC, no. 1250; cf. *Code of Canon Law* [*Codex Iuris Canonici*; CIC], can. 867). However, the Church also teaches that the Baptism of an infant may be postponed if there is not a 'founded hope' that the child will be brought up in the Catholic Faith (CIC, can. 868 §2).

There are the children – born and unborn – who die without Baptism. The Church entrusts them to the mercy of God, who wills that all people be saved. We recall Christ's tender welcome of children saying, 'Let the little children come to me; do not stop them' (Mk 10:14). Because of this the Church confidently hopes for the salvation of children who die without Baptism.

Baptism of Blood, Baptism of Desire

Often the question is raised about those who die without Baptism. The *Catechism* offers this principle: 'God has bound salvation to the sacrament of baptism, but he himself is not bound by the sacraments' (CCC, no. 1257). The Church holds that those who suffer and die for their faith in Christ before they could be baptised are saved by Baptism of Blood.

Candidates for Baptism who die before they receive the Sacrament but have repented their sins and have embraced Christ's love are saved by what is called Baptism of Desire. What about those people who have never had the Gospel presented to them, who do not know Jesus or the Church, yet seek the truth and try to do God's will as they understand it? 'It may be supposed that such persons would have desired baptism explicitly had they known its necessity' (CCC, no. 1260).

EFFECTS OF BAPTISM

Sins Forgiven

By Baptism all sins are forgiven, Original Sin and all personal sins, and temporal punishment due to sin is removed. After one has been reborn in Christ, there is nothing to prevent one's entry into God's Kingdom.

However, though all sins are removed, there remains, as an effect of Original Sin, the inclination to sin that is called *concupiscence*. This inclination to sin shows itself in what is sometimes referred to as a darkening of the mind and a weakening of the will, that is, the inability to know clearly the right or wrong of an action and/or the lack of strength to resist temptation and always to do the right thing no matter how hard this is. The effects of Original Sin need not harm us so long as we seek strength to resist them through the Sacrament of Penance, the Sacrament of the Eucharist, prayer, a deepening spirituality, growth in virtue and a wholehearted dependence on God.

Adopted Children of God

Baptism also gives us new life as adopted children of God. We become sharers of divine life and temples of the Holy Spirit. We are now made righteous by God and live in a state of grace, that is, we live in union with God because of his gracious and loving initiative. Our permanence in the state of grace is called *sanctifying grace* because God 'sanctifies' us, that is, makes us his holy people by giving us his life. God continues to assist us by many helps that are called *actual graces*. Thus, we have the ability to live and act under the guidance and light of the gifts of the Holy Spirit. This helps us mature in goodness through the practice of virtues, such as the Cardinal Virtues: prudence, justice, temperance and fortitude.

RCIA STEPS

For adults who have not yet been baptised, the RCIA has three major liturgical rites: Acceptance into the Order of Catechumens; Election or Enrolment of Names; and Celebration of the Sacraments of Initiation. The celebration of initiation is followed by a postbaptismal catechesis, or *Mystagogy*. (For those already baptised, there are rites appropriate for their journey into full communion in the Catholic Church. These are sometimes celebrated separately from the catechumens and sometimes in a combined rite with the catechumens.)

The process begins with the **Precatechumenate**, in which the person shows initial faith in Jesus Christ and the Church. This is a time for inquiry and the exploration of the beginnings of faith.

After the person has been given a fundamental understanding of the Gospel and has decided to take the first step to become a member of the Church, the person is brought into the Catechumenate at the Rite of Acceptance.

The period of the **Catechumenate** is a time for exploring the teachings of the faith in a deeper and more systematic manner within the context of worship and prayer. At Sunday Mass, the catechumens with their catechists are often dismissed after the homily for further, prayerful study of the Scripture readings for the day.

This period concludes with the **Rite of Election or Enrolment of Names**, which takes place on the First Sunday of Lent. This rite is celebrated by the bishop or his delegate, usually at the cathedral of the diocese. The catechumens' suitability and resolve to be initiated into the sacramental life of the Church is supported by the testimony of their sponsors and catechists. After this, the catechumens become known as the Elect.

The Elect enter the stage of **Purification and Enlightenment** that occurs during the season of Lent. They prepare themselves for the reception of the Sacraments of Initiation by prayerful reflection. On the third, fourth and fifth Sundays of Lent, the Scrutinies are celebrated. These rites, which take place during Mass, offer opportunities for the Elect to reflect on the full meaning of the step they are preparing to take. They are meant to bring God's illuminating Word to the Elect so that whatever is weak or sinful in their hearts can be healed and so that whatever is good in them can be strengthened. The parish community joins them by examining their own lives and interceding with God for the Elect. This period concludes at the Easter Vigil, when the Elect receive the Sacraments of Initiation and become full members of the Church and are called neophytes.

From Easter to Pentecost, there is a period of post-baptismal catechesis, or **Mystagogy.** This is a time for the neophytes, or newly initiated, along with the members of the parish to come closer together as a faith community to examine more deeply the Gospel, to share in the Eucharist and to do works of charity. During this joyful time, the neophytes' enthusiasm can inspire the faithful of the parish, who in turn can share their experiences of the faith with them.

Initiated into the Church

By Baptism we become members of the Church, the Body of Christ. We share in the priesthood of Christ as well as his prophetic and royal mission. 'You are a chosen race, a kingdom of priests, a holy nation, a people to be a personal possession to sing the praises of God who called you out of the darkness into his wonderful light' (1 Pt 2:9). We enjoy the community we find in the Church, share our talents and gifts with its members, respond willingly to its teachings and requirements and assume the responsibilities that our membership implies.

FROM THE CATECHISM

1. Why are the rites of Baptism so helpful for understanding this Sacrament?

The meaning and grace of the Sacrament of Baptism are clearly seen in the rites of its celebration. By following the gestures and words of this celebration with attentive participation, the faithful are initiated into the riches this sacrament signifies and actually brings about in each newly baptised person. (CCC, no. 1234)

2. Why is sin possible after Baptism?

Certain temporal consequences of sin remain in the baptised, such as suffering, illness, death and such frailties inherent in life as weaknesses of character ... as well as an inclination to sin that Tradition calls *concupiscence.* (CCC, no. 1264)

God also gave us free will. While he gives us Baptism and the other Sacraments to help us make the correct choices, these Sacraments do not force a person to do good and to avoid sin.

3. What helps the growth of faith after Baptism?

For all the baptised, children or adults, faith must grow *after* Baptism ... For the grace of Baptism to unfold, the parents' help is important. So too is the role of the *godfather* and *godmother*, who must be firm believers, and ready to help the newly baptised – child or adult – on the road of Christian life. (CCC, nos. 1254–1255)

Bonded to Other Christians

Baptism provides a common foundation among all Christians, including those not yet in full communion with the Catholic Church. The Church recognises the validity of Baptism in other Christian Churches as long as the rite involves the pouring of or immersion in water, a Trinitarian formula, and the intention to baptise. Those who have been baptised have been saved

ARE CATHOLICS BORN-AGAIN?

A number of non-Catholic Christians call themselves 'born-again'. Catholics, for the most part, do not use this term. A 'born-again' Christian is one who has experienced a particularly intense moment of conversion that leads him or her to want to dedicate his or her life to God. It is a one-time action that is not necessarily tied to any type of baptismal rite. While we Catholics are born again as children of God in the Sacrament of Baptism, our rebirth happens in and through the grace of the Sacrament. Our rebirth in Baptism is also not a one-time event but a lifelong process through which we continually strive to die to sin and rise to new life in Christ. Catholics are indeed born again.

by their faith in Christ and the grace of Baptism. 'They therefore have a right to be called Christians and with good reason are accepted as brothers [and sisters] by the children of the Catholic Church' (CCC, no. 1271, citing UR, no. 3).

Baptismal Character

'Incorporated into Christ by Baptism, the person baptised is configured to Christ. Baptism seals the Christian with the indelible spiritual mark (*character*) of his belonging to Christ. No sin can erase this mark, even if sin prevents Baptism from bearing the fruits of salvation. Given once for all Baptism cannot be repeated' (CCC, no. 1272). This spiritual mark is also called a character, which St Augustine likened to distinctive brandings impressed upon soldiers and slaves during Roman times to signify the commander or owner to whom they belonged. Baptism marks us permanently as belonging to Christ, whose image we bear.

BAPTISM IS A CALL TO HOLINESS

Reborn … [the baptised] … must participate in the
apostolic and missionary activity of the People of God.

– CCC, no. 1270

'Baptism is the door to life and to the Kingdom of God. Christ offered the first sacrament of the new law to all that they may have eternal life. Baptism is, above all, the sacrament of that faith by which men and women, enlightened by the Spirit's grace, respond to the Gospel of Christ' ('Christian Initiation, General Instruction', *The Rites of the Catholic Church* [1976], no. 3).

In Baptism, the Holy Spirit moves us to answer Christ's call to holiness. In Baptism, we are asked to walk by the light of Christ and to trust in his wisdom. We are invited to submit our hearts to Christ with ever-deeper love. What is this light, this wisdom, this holiness? Jesus is clear about the high ideals to which he invites us:

> Be perfect, just as your heavenly Father is perfect. (Mt 5:48)
> Be compassionate just as your Father is compassionate. (Lk 6:36)
> Love one another, as I have loved you. (Jn 15:12)

The Lord Jesus, our divine teacher and model of all virtue, preached holiness of life to everyone without exception. Through Baptism, we are cleansed of all sin, are made partakers of the divine nature, and are truly sanctified. Our goal now is to hold onto this gracious act of sanctification that we have received from Christ. Saint Paul lays out a practical plan for holiness:

> As the chosen of God, then, the holy people whom he loves, you are to be clothed in heartfelt compassion, in generosity and humility, gentleness and patience. Bear with one another; forgive each other if one of you has a complaint against another. The Lord has forgiven you; now you must do the same. Over all these clothes, put on love, the perfect bond. (Col 3:12-14)

This is a strong challenge that we cannot meet by human strength alone. 'Accordingly, all Christians in the conditions, duties and circumstances of their life and through all these, will sanctify themselves more and more if they receive all things with faith from the hand of the heavenly Father and cooperate with the divine will, thus showing forth in the temporal service the love with which God has loved the world' (LG, no. 41). The baptised are called to transform the world with the light and power of the Gospel.

Living out one's Baptism is a lifelong responsibility. Growing in holiness and discipleship involves a willingness to continue to learn throughout one's whole life about the faith and how to live it. It also involves a willingness to support and encourage others who share the faith and who have committed themselves to the ongoing process of conversion of heart and mind to God, which results in the holiness to which we are called.

FOR DISCUSSION

1. Saint Paul tells us that in Baptism we die and rise with Christ. Why is it necessary to remember the 'dying' part? If you were to do a survey of what Baptism means to people, what answers do you think you would hear?
2. What differences do you see between some 'cradle Catholics' and those who have entered the Church through the RCIA? What are the responsibilities of godparents in looking after the growth in faith of the baptised they sponsor?
3. What is an effective way of attracting others to Christ?

DOCTRINAL STATEMENTS

- The Sacraments of Initiation are Baptism, Confirmation and Eucharist.
- The Risen Jesus commissioned the Apostles to baptise when he said, 'Go, therefore, make disciples of all nations; baptise them in the name of the Father and of the Son and of the Holy Spirit' (Mt 28:19-20).
- Baptism gives a person birth into new life. It is necessary for salvation and for entry into the Church.
- The rite of Baptism consists in immersing the person in water three times or pouring water on his or her head three times while invoking the Holy Trinity: the Father, the Son and the Holy Spirit.

- The effects of Baptism are delivery from all sins (Original and personal), reception of the grace of divine adoption, being made a member of Christ and a temple of the Holy Spirit, initiation into the Church and being made a sharer in Christ's mission as priest, prophet and king.
- Baptism seals the person's soul with a permanent spiritual mark or character identifying one as belonging to Christ. Because of this character, Baptism cannot be repeated.
- People who die for the faith, catechumens who died before being baptised, and those who do not know Christ or the Church through no fault of their own but who, by the action of grace, seek God sincerely and do his will can be saved even without being baptised.
- Infants have been baptised since apostolic times, for this is a gift from God and does not presuppose human merit. Children are baptised in the faith of the Church.
- Trusting in God's mercy, we confidently hope for the salvation of children who die without Baptism.
- In time of necessity such as the danger of death, all persons can baptise. The person baptising must intend to do what the Church does, by pouring water three times on the candidate's head while saying, 'I baptise you in the name of the Father and of the Son and of the Holy Spirit.'

━━━━━ MEDITATION ━━━━━

By three immersions and as many invocations, the great mystery of Baptism is performed. So the appearance of death is conveyed, and through the handing over of divine knowledge the baptised are enlightened. Therefore, if there is any grace in the water, it is not because of any power the water may possess, but because it derives from the power of the Spirit … The Lord, to prepare us for the risen life, lays before us all the gospel precepts. We must avoid anger, endure evil, be free from the love of pleasure and the love of money. So by our own choice we shall achieve those things which are the natural endowments of the world to come.

– St Basil the Great, *On the Holy Spirit*, XV, nos. 35–36

PRAYER

God the Father of our Lord Jesus Christ has freed you from sin,
given you a new birth by water and the Holy Spirit,
and welcomed you into his holy people.

He now anoints you with the chrism of salvation.
As Christ was anointed Priest, Prophet and King,
so may you live always as members of his body,
sharing everlasting life. Amen.

– Prayer for Anointing with Chrism, *Rite of Baptism*

You have been buried with him [Christ] by your baptism;
by which, too, you have been raised up with him through
your belief in the power of God who raised him from the dead.

– Col 2:12

Baptism is the entrance to life in the Spirit and the basis of the whole
Christian way of life. It is 'the foundation of communion among all
Christians'.

– SGN, 54

16 CONFIRMATION: CONSECRATED FOR MISSION

CONFIRMATION IS THE SECOND SACRAMENT
OF INITIATION
– CCC, NOS. 1285–1321

MARGARET AYLWARD: A VALIANT WOMAN

HOLY FAITH SISTERS

Margaret Aylward was a determined and persistent lady. She was born in Waterford in 1810 of a family in which both the paternal and maternal sides were independently wealthy and used to administering property. Margaret never lost her native management skills. She was organised, capable, meticulous and prudent in her business affairs and in the administration of her various establishments.

Initially Margaret seems to have been somewhat uncertain about which direction she should take in life. Irish Catholics had been emancipated from their civic handicaps in 1829, thanks to the work of the Great Liberator, Daniel O'Connell. It may be supposed that the spiritual and temporal need in the population, with the options which had just opened up for Catholic service of the poor, contributed to her indecision. Margaret Aylward did not know what God wanted of her.

The Aylwards were well connected in Waterford business life, and noted for charitable works. Edmund Rice, the founder of the Irish Christian Brothers (whom we will meet in Chapter 34), was a frequent visitor to their home, and Margaret's maternal uncle, Patrick Joseph Murphy, became a Christian Brother and first superior of Mount Sion Monastery. Another relative was the first Presentation Sister in Waterford, and the Aylward girls were to the fore in volunteering for the Presentation School and other charities.

In any case, Margaret was to try out a religious vocation twice, the first time with the Sisters of Charity at Stanhope Street in Dublin, and some time later with the Ursulines in Waterford, on both occasions without success. She did not seem to fit in and concluded, for the moment, that she was unsuited to religious life.

Margaret moved to Dublin in 1846 when she was thirty-six years old, a woman of striking appearance, straightforward in manner and full of life and vigour. Very soon she was heavily involved in the Marlborough Street Parish with the Ladies of Charity of St Vincent de Paul, a charitable organisation comprising laywomen which worked directly with the poor.

This group gradually evolved into an established institution, or to be more exact, Margaret 'grew it' to meet the needs of the poor and obey God's will. She recruited helpers, ran appeals for funds and publicised the good work in reports and public meetings. Her pragmatic and systematic mind looked for the causes of the widespread misery and degradation of the city. Her business instincts meant that the reporting and accounting were careful and comprehensive. The distribution of relief was certainly efficient, and as effective as the ladies could ensure. Before long, she had 148 helpers, a considerable contribution to the work of the Church in the centre of the city.

Already her characteristic way of operating had been set. She used every means of influence that she could deploy, from public meeting to private interview, from political lobbying to personal letter, to establish, support, develop, consolidate and expand her work. Margaret Aylward listened well, and taught her co-workers to follow her example. She heard what people were saying, and tried to incorporate their insights into the joint venture. At times she complained of the frustrations in making this effort; at other times her advisers and confidants would caution her that she had done enough to try to please everyone. But one thing was certain: when she knew what God wanted, nothing could divert her from her mission.

Margaret's motivation, and that of the Ladies of Charity, was not simple philanthropy nor the alleviation of poverty. The primary objective was the will of God, the spreading of the Kingdom and the salvation of souls. Also in action in the city's poorer districts at that time were the proselytising societies, the 'soupers', who worked at attracting destitute Catholics to take religious instruction in non-Catholic denominations by providing food, clothing and money.

The children of impoverished and desperate parents, the first casualties of poverty, were the most urgent target. Acting on the inspiration of a Vincentian priest from Phibsboro, Fr John Gowan CM, Lady Aylward (as she came to be known generally) established an organisation to take care of them. Saint Brigid's Orphanage was born.

The orphanage quickly developed an ethos of care and service appropriate to its purpose. It installed a system of 'boarding out' children to suitable foster families. This was controversial because other child services at the time favoured institutionalising children in one location to ensure uniform provision and a proper standard of care. The 'boarding out' system required constant monitoring and supervision of the nurses and foster families, as well as the children, but Margaret's business abilities were up to the challenge. Saint Brigid's grew from fostering forty-eight to 250 children in under ten years.

Margaret won real respect and willing support from key people in the city, notably Archbishop Paul Cullen. These contacts opened many doors to her inside the diocese and beyond. They also supported her further endeavours and helped her through the crises that pioneers face as a price of leadership. One such crisis was the 1860 affair of Mary Matthews, the focus of a tug-of-war between a Catholic and a Protestant parent where the orphanage and its director were caught in the middle. The court sentenced Lady Aylward to six months in prison for contempt of court in this controversial custody case. The *cause célèbre* excited the newspapers and gossip columnists on both sides of the Irish Sea. A visit from the Archbishop to the jail and a message and gift from Pope Pius IX in Rome were small consolations for a humiliating and stressful incarceration.

Time in prison gave Lady Aylward time to think. She emerged from jail sure of her goal and the way to get there. She would found schools for the poor children with whom she was now very familiar and gather a new religious group to ensure their Catholic education. With Fr Gowan aiding her, she proceeded towards those two goals, and by the end of her life she had established the network of schools and founded a new congregation: the Sisters of the Holy Faith. Margaret Aylward died on 11 October 1889 and is buried in the

Holy Faith Convent, Glasnevin, Dublin. She was a woman confirmed in faith who, like St Peter, confirmed the faith of many others, then and since.

THE SACRAMENT OF THE HOLY SPIRIT

The reception of the sacrament of Confirmation is necessary for the completion of baptismal grace … 'By the sacrament of Confirmation [the baptised] are more perfectly bound to the Church and are enriched with a special strength of the Holy Spirit.'

— CCC, no. 1285, citing LG, no. 11

Confirmation, together with Baptism and Eucharist, form the Sacraments of Initiation that are all intimately connected. In the Sacrament of Confirmation, the baptised person is 'sealed with the gift of the Holy Spirit' and is strengthened for service to the Body of Christ.

The prophets of the Old Testament foretold that God's Spirit would rest upon the Messiah to sustain his mission. Their prophecy was fulfilled when Jesus the Messiah was conceived by the Spirit and born of the Virgin Mary. The Holy Spirit descended on Jesus on the occasion of his baptism by John. Jesus' entire mission occurred in communion with the Spirit. Before he died, Jesus promised that the Spirit would be given to the Apostles and to the entire Church. After his death, he was raised by the Father in the power of the Spirit.

The New Testament reports many manifestations of the Holy Spirit, two of which we note here. Saint John's Gospel describes an outpouring of the Spirit on Easter night when Jesus breathed on the Apostles and said, 'Receive the Holy Spirit' (Jn 20:22). Saint Luke's Acts of the Apostles gives another account of the sending of the Holy Spirit at Pentecost, fifty days after the Resurrection of Christ (cf. Acts 2). Filled with the Holy Spirit, the Apostles proclaimed God's mighty deeds. Peter preached that this coming of the

Spirit fulfilled the prophecy of Joel: 'In the last days … I shall pour out my Spirit on all humanity' (Acts 2:17; cf. Jl 3:1).

Those who believed in the Apostles' preaching were baptised and received the Holy Spirit through the laying on of hands. The Apostles baptised believers in water and the Spirit. Then they imparted the special gift of the Spirit through the laying on of hands. 'The imposition of hands is rightly recognised by the Catholic tradition as the origin of the sacrament of Confirmation, which in a certain way perpetuates the grace of Pentecost in the Church' (CCC, no. 1288, citing Pope Paul VI, *Divinae Consortium Naturae*, no. 659).

By the second century, Confirmation was also conferred by anointing with holy oil, which came to be called sacred Chrism. 'This anointing highlights the name "Christian", which means "anointed" and derives from that of Christ himself whom God "anointed with the Holy Spirit"' (CCC, no. 1289, citing Acts 10:38).

THE LITURGY OF CONFIRMATION

The signs, symbols, ritual acts and words of the liturgy speak to us of the meaning of a Sacrament and of what Christ enacts in the event through his ministers and the disposition of the candidate. With this in mind, we reflect on the following elements of Confirmation: the anointing with sacred Chrism, the recipient, the essential rite, the ministers and the effects of the Sacrament.

The Anointing with Sacred Chrism

> *The post-baptismal anointing with sacred chrism in Confirmation … is the sign of consecration … those who are anointed, share more completely in the mission of Jesus Christ.*

> – CCC, no. 1294

In or near Holy Week, the bishop consecrates the sacred Chrism during the course of the Chrism Mass. It is used to anoint the newly baptised, to confer the Sacrament of Confirmation and to anoint bishops and priests during the celebration of the Sacrament of Holy Orders.

Anointing with oil has many meanings such as cleansing as part of a bath, limbering up the muscles of athletes and healing the wounds of the sick. Two other sacramental celebrations make use of blessed oil: 'The pre-baptismal anointing with the oil of catechumens signifies cleansing and strengthening; the anointing of the sick expresses healing and comfort' (CCC, no. 1294). The Oil of Catechumens is used in Baptism. The Oil of the Sick is used for the Sacrament of the Anointing of the Sick.

The Recipient of Confirmation

Each baptised person not yet confirmed can and should receive the Sacrament of Confirmation. In the Latin Church, it is customary to confirm candidates between the age of discretion, also called the age of reason, and about sixteen years of age. It is not uncommon that Catholics not confirmed during this period of their lives for a variety of reasons are confirmed as adults, often on Pentecost Sunday. The candidate should be in the state of grace (that is, without serious sin), be well prepared by prayer and catechesis and be committed to the responsibilities entailed by the Sacrament.

The Essential Rite of Confirmation

In continuity with the New Testament custom of laying hands on those who would receive the gift of the Spirit, the bishop extends his two hands over all those to be confirmed. He recites a prayer that begs the Father of our Lord Jesus Christ for the outpouring of the Holy Spirit and for the seven gifts traditionally associated with the Spirit. These gifts are permanent dispositions that move us to respond to the guidance of the Spirit. The traditional list of the gifts is based on Isaiah 11:1-3: wisdom, understanding, right judgement, courage, knowledge, reverence and wonder and awe in God's presence.

The essential rite then follows. In the Latin Rite, 'the Sacrament of Confirmation is conferred through the anointing with Chrism on the forehead, which is done by the laying on of hands, and through the words, "Be sealed with the gift of the Holy Spirit"' (Introduction to the *Rite of Confirmation*, no. 9). In the Eastern Churches, after a prayer for the presence and action of the Holy Spirit, the priest anoints the forehead, eyes, nose, ears, lips, chest, back, hands and feet of the candidate with *Myron* (holy oil).

With each anointing he says, 'The seal of the gift of the Holy Spirit'. The Eastern Churches call Confirmation 'Chrismation'.

> When Confirmation is celebrated separately from Baptism, its connection with Baptism is expressed, among other ways, by the renewal of baptismal promises. The celebration of Confirmation during the Eucharist helps underline the unity of the sacraments of Christian initiation. (CCC, no. 1321)

The connection between Confirmation and Baptism is also reflected in the choosing of a name by which the candidate will be confirmed, especially when the chosen name is one of the names by which the candidate was baptised.

The Minister of Confirmation

In the early Church, sacramental initiation always involved the bishop; the bishop was the ordinary minister of both Baptism and Confirmation. However, pastoral practice changed as the Church expanded rapidly. When bishops could no longer be present at all celebrations of Baptism, they chose to retain a role in the process of initiation by continuing to be the ordinary minister of Confirmation.

In the Latin Church, with the bishop as the minister of Confirmation, it is evident how this Sacrament can serve to strengthen the person's bond with the Church and her apostolic origins. However, there are also times when the bishop entrusts the celebration of the rite of Confirmation to a priest, such as in the case of the Baptism of an adult or the reception of an adult from another Christian community into full communion with the Church. Bishops may also give this permission in other cases.

In the Eastern Churches, Confirmation is conferred by a priest at the time of Baptism, and in some of these Churches, it is followed by the reception of the Eucharist. This practice underlines the unity of the three Sacraments of Initiation. The priest confirms with the *Myron* or oil consecrated by the bishop. This expresses the apostolic unity of the Church.

The Effects of Confirmation

> *Confirmation brings an increase and deepening of*
> *baptismal grace:*
> *— it roots us more deeply in the divine filiation [becoming*
> *adopted sons and daughters of God] which makes*
> *us cry, 'Abba! Father!';*
> *— it unites us more firmly to Christ;*
> *— it increases the gifts of the Holy Spirit in us;*
> *— it renders our bond with the Church more perfect;*
> *— it gives us a special strength of the Holy Spirit to*
> *spread and defend the faith by word and action as true*
> *witnesses of Christ, to confess the name of Christ boldly,*
> *and never to be ashamed of the Cross.*
>
> — CCC, no. 1303

As the words of the liturgy indicate, the person being confirmed is sealed with the Holy Spirit. This seal is called a *character*, marking the person forever as called to fulfil the Church's mission in all the circumstances of life.

> It is God who gives us, with you, a sure place in Christ and has both anointed us and marked us with his seal, giving us as pledge the Spirit in our hearts. (2 Cor 1:21-22)

THE MISSION AND WITNESS OF THE CONFIRMED

Confirmation deepens our baptismal life that calls us to be missionary witnesses of Jesus Christ in our families, neighbourhoods, society and the world. Through Confirmation, our personal relationship with Christ is strengthened. We receive the message of faith in a deeper and more intensive manner with great emphasis given to the person of Jesus Christ, who asked the Father to give the Holy Spirit to the Church for building up the community in loving service.

The Holy Spirit bestows seven gifts — wisdom, understanding, right judgement, courage, knowledge, reverence and wonder and awe in God's

FROM THE CATECHISM

1. Who may receive Confirmation?

Every baptised person not yet confirmed can and should receive the Sacrament of Confirmation. Since Baptism, Confirmation and Eucharist form a unity, it follows that 'the faithful are obliged to receive this sacrament at the appropriate time'. (CCC, no. 1306, citing CIC, can. 890)

2. How should candidates for Confirmation be prepared?

Preparation for Confirmation should aim at leading the Christian toward a more intimate union with Christ and a more lively familiarity with the Holy Spirit – his actions, his gifts and his biddings – in order to be more capable of assuming the apostolic responsibilities of Christian life. To this end catechesis for Confirmation should strive to awaken a sense of belonging to the Church of Jesus Christ, the universal Church, as well as the parish community. The latter bears special responsibility for the preparation of confirmands. (CCC, no. 1309)

3. Why do we not receive Confirmation more than once?

Confirmation, like Baptism, imprints a spiritual mark, or indelible character on the Christian's soul; for this reason one can receive this Sacrament only once in one's life. (CCC, no. 1317)

presence – to assist us in our mission and witness. The impact of these gifts accompanies us in the various stages of our spiritual development.

As the confirmed, we walk with the seven gifts of the Holy Spirit. Wisdom enables us to see the world from God's viewpoint, which can help us come to grasp the purpose and plan of God. It grants us the long-range view of history, examining the present in the light of the past and the mystery of the future. It saves us from the illusion that the spirit of the times is our only guide. The Spirit's gift of knowledge directs us to a contemplation, or thoughtful reflection, of the mystery of God – Father,

Son and Holy Spirit – as well as of the mysteries of the Catholic faith. We are drawn to meditative prayer, where we allow God to lead us while we rest patiently in the divine presence.

The gift of understanding stimulates us to work on knowing ourselves as part of our growth in knowing God. It is what St Augustine meant when he prayed, 'That I may know You, may I know myself.' When the Spirit pours fortitude or courage into our hearts, we can trust that we will be prepared to stand up for Christ and the Gospel when challenged. As the gift of counsel or right judgement grows in us, we can sense the quiet teaching that the Spirit gives us about our moral lives and the training of our consciences.

The gift of piety or reverence is an act of respect for the Father who created us, for Jesus who saved us and for the Spirit who is sanctifying us. We learn reverence for God and people from our parents and others who train us in virtue. The Spirit fills us with this gift at liturgy, which is a masterful school of reverence, as well as through popular devotions and piety.

Finally, the gift of fear of the Lord or wonder and awe in God's presence can infuse honesty into our relationship with God, a frankness that places us in awe before the majesty of God. Yet the gift also imparts an attitude of grateful wonder that God loves us and that we can share in his life.

When we are responsive to the grace of Confirmation and the seven gifts of the Holy Spirit, we begin to bear the fruits of the Spirit. The tradition of the Church names twelve fruits of the Holy Spirit: love, joy, peace, patience, kindness, goodness, generosity, gentleness, faithfulness, modesty, self-control and chastity (cf. CCC, no. 1832; Gal 5:22).

FOR DISCUSSION

1 If you have been confirmed, describe what the experience was like. When did it happen? Who confirmed you? How were you prepared?

2. How are the healing and cleansing qualities of anointing with oil symbols of what happens in the Sacraments of Baptism and Confirmation?

3. What are the consequences of the deeper identification with the mission of the Church that comes from Confirmation?

DOCTRINAL STATEMENTS

- Jesus promised the Apostles that he would send the Holy Spirit to them. At Pentecost that promise of Christ was fulfilled (cf. Jn 16:12-15; Acts 2:1-47).

- The effects of Confirmation include a permanent character, a perfection of baptismal grace, an increase in the gifts and fruits of the Holy Spirit, a deepening of our identity as adopted sons and daughters of God, a closer bond to the Church and her mission and helps for bearing witness.

- In the Eastern Churches, Chrismation (Confirmation) is administered immediately after Baptism, followed by participation in the Eucharist. This tradition emphasises the unity of these three Sacraments of Initiation.

- In the Western or Latin Church, Confirmation is administered after the age of reason is attained and is normally conferred by the bishop, signifying one's bond with the Church and its apostolic origins.

- The candidate for Confirmation in the Latin Church should be in the state of grace, be well prepared by prayer and catechesis and be committed to the responsibilities entailed by the Sacrament.

- This is the essential rite of Confirmation in the Western Church: the bishop confers Confirmation through the anointing with Chrism on the recipient's forehead, which is done by the laying on of the hand, while saying the words 'Be sealed with the gift of the Holy Spirit'.

- In the Eastern Churches, after a prayer for the presence and action of the Holy Spirit, the priest anoints the forehead, eyes, nose, ears, lips, chest, back, hands and feet of the candidate with *Myron* (holy oil). With each anointing, he says, 'The seal of the gift of the Holy Spirit'.

- The spiritual, indelible marks (or characters) received in the Sacraments of Baptism, Confirmation and Holy Orders affirm a permanent relationship with God and indicate that these Sacraments may be received only once.

- 'When Confirmation is celebrated separately from Baptism, its connection with Baptism is expressed, among other ways, by the renewal of baptismal promises. The celebration of Confirmation during the Eucharist helps underline the unity of the Sacraments of Christian Initiation' (CCC, no. 1321).

MEDITATION

There are those who have said that courage in witnessing our faith is one of the best proofs for the existence of God. Confirmation is the Sacrament that makes possible courageous witness. The never-ending stories of martyrs and other Christian heroes and heroines throughout the centuries to the present provide ample evidence of the Holy Spirit's gift of courage. Today, there are plenty of opportunities to act courageously on behalf of the teachings of Christ and the Church, to promote the stability of marriage, to support the ideals of family life, to be brave in defending human life from conception to death, to be steadfast in seeking justice for the oppressed and to be determined that the light of Christ's compassion and peace will shine everywhere on earth.

PRAYER

Come, Holy Ghost (A Hymn to the Holy Spirit)

Come, Holy Ghost, Creator blest,
and in our hearts take up thy rest.
Come with thy grace, and heavenly aid
to fill the hearts which thou hast made.

Breathe on me breath of God, my soul with grace refine,
Until this earthly part of me, glows with your fire divine.

— Edwin Hatch

Confirmation is the sacrament of growth in the Holy Spirit.

— SGN, 54

17 THE EUCHARIST: SOURCE AND SUMMIT OF THE CHRISTIAN LIFE

THE HOLY EUCHARIST COMPLETES CHRISTIAN INITIATION
– CCC, NOS. 1322–1419

THE STORY OF L'ARCHE

L'Arche is a worldwide organisation that tries to create true homes where people with intellectual disabilities, and those who assist them, live together in mutual respect, genuine sharing and real affection. L'Arche means 'ark', referring to the Bible story of Noah and the flood. We can imagine what life on board must have been like during the forty-day rainstorm and its aftermath, as the different animals of the world and Noah's extended family lived together in the confined space on the deck and hold of the Ark. In close proximity to each other, they created a community of salvation. The Ark must have been full of joy, in that each and every one on board was aware of being particularly favoured by God.

Community and participation are still the watchwords of L'Arche. The atmosphere of a L'Arche home is quite unlike any other establishment dedicated to the service of people with intellectual disabilities. For a start, there is no official demarcation between those who require care and the caregivers. Those with intellectual disabilities are named 'core members' or residents. Those who give care are the 'assistants'. All the people in the house are part of the community. Some require more help than others, but all need help of some kind and all render help as their assistance is called for. Another intriguing characteristic of L'Arche is the way each and every individual is treasured for his or her special being, not for talent or skill, or even for service and support of others, but for simply being oneself.

For those in L'Arche, the effort to live in community is more important than the particular services or assistance that each gives to others in the house. As the organisation itself claims:

> L'Arche is a place where each person is welcomed as she or he is, with his or her own history, gifts, culture, traditions and religion. In spite of our differences and the challenges these carry, the search for unity is at the heart of what we do and how we live our life together in community.

This quality of L'Arche life came about not just because of deep ideals and personal commitments, though those surely existed; it came about because each individual house, and L'Arche as an organisation, began from the experience of unique human beings.

This was certainly true of the first L'Arche community in Ireland which was founded in the village of Kilmoganny, Co. Kilkenny, in 1978. There had previously been a very high level of community endeavour and involvement in this small country village. Ten separate projects, including a community centre, a local sewage scheme and voluntary housing had already been successfully set up.

One of the team of village volunteers was Nicky. He and his wife, Mary, had a child called Helen, who had a disability. As they got older, Nicky and Mary grew quite concerned about what might happen to Helen when they would no longer be in a position to continue her care. They brought the problem to the community, enquiries were made, and the question landed on the desk of Dr Peter Birch, the Bishop of Ossory.

Bishop Birch was already famous for his social concern. It was less well known that he had a brother with Down's Syndrome. He took special interest in the care of people with disabilities, and had already made the acquaintance of Jean Vanier and his L'Arche foundation in Trosly in France. He suggested that a L'Arche house might be the solution. Moira Moore donated an old house with some land to the Ossory Diocesan Trust and, after renovation, this became the base for the new foundation. And so, Moorefield House, the first L'Arche Community in Ireland, was established.

Bishop Birch then invited Jean Vanier himself to give a retreat in Kilkenny. Jean Vanier, the son of a Canadian military diplomat, was born in Switzerland in 1928. He was educated in England and joined the Royal Navy just after the start of the Second World War in 1945. Five years later he resigned from the service and embarked on the study of philosophy and theology in Paris. After earning his doctorate, and a short career in university teaching, he moved to France to be with his Dominican mentor, Fr Thomas Phillipe, and to share his life with people with intellectual disabilities.

Through his experience and reflection upon it, Jean came to realise that we are all broken, that those who are vulnerable and weak have much to teach those of us who think ourselves capable and self-reliant. If we keep people with disabilities away from us, we miss a valuable opportunity to give of ourselves and grow spiritually.

By 1964, he had decided to live with two men with intellectual disabilities in a permanent community, bought a house in Trosly and named it L'Arche. While working with the residents in L'Arche, he began to give conferences and retreats in different countries. In 1969, after a conference in Toronto, the first L'Arche community was founded in Canada. In 1970, after another Vanier visit, the first Indian house was established. L'Arche was set up in the United Kingdom in 1974, and as we have seen, in 1978 it reached County Kilkenny.

Jean Vanier came to Ireland on the Bishop's invitation. A very tall and charismatic figure, Jean proved impressive in large meetings and persuasive in small groups. An inspiring teacher and an incisive writer, he challenged those who met him to embrace his ideas and follow his example. He approved wholeheartedly of the venture in Kilkenny, and Moorefield House opened its doors to great excitement and justifiable pride. One who was there at the time recalled later:

> Everybody helped … all the locals, two student work camps of three weeks each, with students from fourteen different countries. It really was a wonderful time. We had flamenco guitar playing in Moira Moore's pub at night and much dancing. One of my first jobs was to find a prayer mat for a young Muslim student from Morocco! I met a French student called Michael Patrick Crowley from Paris, who today is still one of my closest friends.

Alva Fitzgerald, a young Irish occupational therapist, arrived shortly afterwards from France. She was our first director of L'Arche Kilkenny. She had spent one year in Trosly, France, in a L'Arche foyer. Then Helen and Paddy arrived and L'Arche was delivered as a practical working reality. We were all delighted.

L'Arche's motto is still Jean Vanier's 'Changing the world, one heart at a time!' The organisation has four communities in Ireland, with houses in Kilkenny, Dublin, Cork and Belfast. There are over 5,000 members worldwide, living in 135 houses in thirty-six countries.

We tell the story of L'Arche and its foundation in Ireland because this ministry to people with intellectual disabilities mirrors very closely the sacrifice of giving – for some people to a heroic degree – that Christian living invites from each of us. L'Arche is an interreligious reality – people of many faiths and none live together in the communities of L'Arche, where a further dimension of its vocation is to celebrate their differences. The story of L'Arche truly models the participation and community that is the fruit of God's saving grace, the powerful presence of Jesus Christ among us and the inspiration and love of the Holy Spirit. These themes find their fullest representation and real energy in the Holy Eucharist, the Mass and the Supper of the Lord.

THE REVELATION OF THE EUCHARIST

The holy Eucharist completes Christian initiation ...
The Eucharist is the efficacious sign and sublime cause
of that communion in the divine life and that unity of the
People of God by which the Church is kept in being.

– CCC, nos. 1322 and 1325, citing Sacred Congregation of Rites,
Instruction on the Worship of the Eucharistic Mystery
(Eucharisticum Mysterium), no. 6

The origins of the Eucharist are found in the Last Supper that Jesus shared with his Apostles. 'In order to leave them a pledge of this love, in order never to depart from his own and to make them sharers in his Passover, he instituted the Eucharist as the memorial of his death and Resurrection and commanded his Apostles to celebrate it until his return; "thereby he constituted them priests of the New Testament"' (CCC, no. 1337, citing Council of Trent: DS 1740).

So rich is this mystery that we have a number of terms to illumine its saving grace: the Breaking of the Bread; the Lord's Supper; the Eucharistic Assembly; the Memorial of Christ's Passion, Death and Resurrection; the Holy Sacrifice of the Mass, the Holy and Divine Liturgy; the Eucharistic Liturgy; Holy Communion and Holy Mass (cf. CCC, nos. 1328–1332).

The use of bread and wine in worship is already found in the early history of God's people. In the Old Testament, bread and wine are seen as gifts from God, to whom praise and thanks are given in return for these blessings and for other manifestations of his care and grace. The story of the priest Melchizedek's offering a sacrifice of bread and wine for Abraham's victory is an example of this (cf. Gn 14:18). The harvest of new lambs was also a time for the sacrifice of a lamb to show gratitude to God for the new flock and its contribution to the well-being of the family and tribe.

These ancient rituals were given historical meaning at the Exodus of God's people. They were united into the Passover Meal as a sign of God's delivering the Israelites from slavery in Egypt, a pledge of his fidelity to his promises and eventually a sign of the coming of the Messiah and messianic times. Each family shared the lamb that had been sacrificed and the bread over which a blessing had been proclaimed. They also drank from a cup of wine over which a similar blessing had been proclaimed.

When Jesus instituted the Eucharist he gave a final meaning to the blessing of the bread and the wine and the sacrifice of the lamb. The Gospels narrate events that anticipated the Eucharist. The miracle of the loaves and fish, reported in all four Gospels, prefigured the unique abundance of the Eucharist. The miracle of changing water into wine at the wedding feast in Cana manifested the divine glory of Jesus and the heavenly wedding feast in which we share at every Eucharist.

In his dialogue with the people at Capernaum, Christ used his miracle of multiplying the loaves of bread as the occasion to describe himself as the

Bread of Life: 'I am the living bread which has come down from heaven ... if you do not eat the flesh of the Son of man and drink his blood, you have no life in you' (Jn 6:51, 53).

THE LAST SUPPER

The account of the institution of the Eucharist may be found in the Gospels of Matthew, Mark and Luke, as well as in Paul's First Letter to the Corinthians (see Mt 26:17-29; Mk 14:12-25; Lk 22:7-20; 1 Cor 11:23-26). Jesus chose the Passover feast as the time in which he would institute the Eucharist and would undergo his dying and rising (cf. CCC, nos. 1339–1340). With the institution of the Eucharist, Jesus gave the Passover its new and definitive meaning. He showed himself to be the High Priest of the New Covenant, offering himself as a perfect sacrifice to the Father. Jesus changed the bread and wine into his Body and Blood, given now as an offering for the salvation of all people.

> For the tradition I received from the Lord and also handed on to you is that on the night he was betrayed, the Lord Jesus took some bread, and after he had given thanks, he broke it, and he said, 'This is my body, which is for you; do this in remembrance of me.' And in the same way, with the cup after supper, saying, 'This cup is the new covenant in my blood. Whenever you drink it, do this as a memorial of me.' Whenever you eat this bread, then, and drink this cup, you are proclaiming the Lord's death until he comes. (1 Cor 11:23-26)

By the words 'Do this in memory of me', Jesus commanded the Apostles and their successors to repeat his actions and words 'until he comes again'. From earliest times, the Church has remained faithful to this command. Particularly on Sunday, the day of Christ's Resurrection, the faithful has gathered for the Breaking of the Bread. This practice has continued unbroken for two thousand years, right up to the present day.

In the Gospel of John, instead of an account of the institution of the Eucharist, there is the narrative of the foot washing (cf. Jn 13:1-20) at the beginning of the Last Supper, which sets the tone of humble service, exemplified by Christ and fulfilled in his death on the Cross. The Church has selected this Gospel for the Holy Thursday liturgy, highlighting Christ's teaching: 'If I, then, the Lord and Master, have washed your feet, you must wash each other's feet. I have given you an example so that you may copy what I have done to you' (Jn 13:14-15).

Christ's Last Supper Discourse (Jn 14:1–17:26) reflects Eucharistic themes of divine love, a union with Christ as intimate as a branch is to a vine, and a priestly prayer for the Apostles and those who would believe through them.

THE MASS FOR THE ROMAN RITE

Since the second century, the Mass (or the Eucharistic Liturgy) has had a structure that is common to all Catholics. While there can be different emphases during the celebration of Mass in Eastern Churches, they maintain the fundamental twofold structure with which members of the Latin Church are familiar. Thus, the Mass unfolds in two major parts that form a single act of worship. First, there is the Liturgy of the Word, with Scripture readings, homily, Profession of Faith and General Intercessions. Second, there is the Liturgy of the Eucharist, with the presentation of the bread and wine, the Eucharistic Prayer and the reception of Holy Communion. The essential elements of Eucharistic celebrations may be summarised in the following four points.

1. The Introductory Rites

The Christian community, united by the Holy Spirit, gathers for worship in response to God's call. Jesus, our High Priest, is the principal agent of our celebration. The bishop or priest acts in the person of Christ, the Head of the Church. All the worshippers participate actively with interior devout attention and with external reverence shown by singing the hymns and giving the responses and, when appropriate, observing silence. There are also the deacon, the lectors, those who present the offerings, the extraordinary ministers of Holy Communion, the altar servers, the musicians and other ministers. This first movement contains the

Introductory Rites, which begin the celebration of the Mass. These include the Penitential Rite, the *Gloria* and the Opening Prayer.

> Mother Church earnestly desires that all the faithful should be led to that full, conscious and active participation in liturgical celebrations which is demanded by the very nature of the liturgy, and to which the Christian people, 'a chosen race, a kingdom of priests, a holy nation, a people to be a personal possession' (1 Pt 2:9, 4-5) have a right and obligation by reason of their baptism. (SC, no. 14)

2. Liturgy of the Word

Over the course of the liturgical year, readings from Scripture, especially the Gospels, provide the heart of this part of the celebration. The proclamation of God's Word and its explanation are meant to arouse our faith and prepare us for an ever-deeper participation in the mystery of the Eucharist. The readings are followed by a homily from a bishop, priest or deacon; the Profession of Faith in the recitation of the Creed and intercessory prayers.

3. Liturgy of the Eucharist

a. *The Preparation of the Gifts* (Jesus took bread and wine). The offerings of bread and wine are received by the priest, who may be assisted by a deacon. 'They will be offered by the priest in the name of Christ in the Eucharistic sacrifice in which they will become his Body and Blood' (CCC, no. 1350). From the earliest days of the Church, there was also an offering of gifts for the poor and needy. This has become the customary place and time for the parish collection.

b. *The Eucharistic Prayer* (Jesus blessed and gave thanks). This is the heart of the Eucharistic Liturgy, which unfolds in the following manner.

- *Thanksgiving* (expressed especially in the Preface): In this prayer, we thank God the Father, through Christ in the Spirit, for the gifts of creation, salvation and sanctification.
- *Acclamation:* The whole congregation joins with the angels and saints in singing or saying the *Sanctus* (Holy, Holy).

THE CHURCH AND THE EUCHARIST

The Church draws her life from the Eucharist. This truth does not simply express a daily experience of faith, but recapitulates the heart of the mystery of the Church. In a variety of ways, she joyfully experiences the constant fulfilment of the promise, 'Look, I am with you always; yes, to the end of time' (Mt 28:20), but in the Holy Eucharist, through the changing of the bread and wine into the Body and Blood of the Lord, she rejoices in this presence with unique intensity. Ever since Pentecost, when the Church, the People of the New Covenant, began her pilgrim journey towards her heavenly homeland, the Divine Sacrament has continued to mark the passing of her days, filling them with confident hope. (St John Paul II, *On the Eucharist* [*Ecclesia de Eucharistia*; EE], no. 1)

- *Epiclesis* (Invocation): The Church implores the power of the Holy Spirit to change the bread and wine offered by human hands into Christ's Body and Blood.

- *Institution Narrative and Consecration:* The priest proclaims Jesus' words at the Last Supper over the bread and wine. 'The power of the words and the action of Christ, and the power of the Holy Spirit, make sacramentally present, under the species of bread and wine, Christ's Body and Blood, his sacrifice offered on the cross for all' (CCC, no. 1353).

- *Anamnesis* (The Remembrance): We recall the death and Resurrection of Christ and look forward to his glorious return.

- *Second Epiclesis*: The Holy Spirit is invoked upon the gathered community, to bring unity to the worshippers who will receive Holy Communion.

- *Intercessions:* With the whole Communion of Saints and all God's people on earth, we pray for the needs of all the members of the Church, living and dead.

- *Doxology and Great Amen:* We conclude the Eucharistic Prayer with praise of God the Father, through his Son Jesus Christ, in the Holy Spirit. This glorification is confirmed and concluded by the people's acclamation 'Amen'.

c. *Communion Rite* (Jesus broke the bread and gave his Body and Blood). After the Lord's Prayer, the Lamb of God is sung or said during the breaking of the Body of Christ, or fraction, then we receive the Body and Blood of Christ in Holy Communion. The Communion Rite concludes with a closing prayer.

4. Concluding Rite

Following the prayer after Holy Communion, the priest blesses the people and dismisses the assembly.

Centuries of reflection on the Eucharist have left us a spiritual heritage that continues to deepen and grow. Three key truths about the Eucharist draw our attention: it is a Sacrifice, a Holy Meal and the Real Presence of Christ.

THE MASS IS A SACRIFICE

The Mass is a sacrifice in the sense that when it takes place, Jesus Christ, through the bishop or priest celebrating the Mass, makes present sacramentally his saving, sacrificial death on the Cross by which he redeemed us from our sins. This Eucharistic sacrifice is the memorial of Christ's redeeming death. The term *memorial* in this context is not simply a remembrance of past events; it is a making present in a sacramental manner the sacrifice of the Cross of Christ and his victory. 'When the Church celebrates the Eucharist, the memorial of her Lord's death and resurrection, this central event of salvation becomes really present and "the work of our redemption is carried out"' (EE, no. 11). The Eucharistic sacrifice is offered to adore and thank God, to pray for all our needs and to gain pardon for our sins.

In this divine sacrifice which is made present in the Mass, especially in the Eucharistic Prayer, the same Christ who offered himself once in a bloody manner on the altar of the Cross offers himself in an unbloody manner. Present and effective, Christ's sacrifice is applied to our lives. 'The blood of goats ... sprinkled on those who have incurred defilement ... How much more will the blood of Christ ... purify our conscience from dead actions so that we can worship the living God' (Heb 9:13-14).

The Mass is also the sacrifice of the Church. The ordained priest in the Mass links the Eucharistic consecration to the sacrifice of the Cross and to the Last Supper (cf. EE, no. 29), thus making it possible that the sacrifice of Christ becomes the sacrifice of all the members of the Church. 'The lives of the faithful, their praise, sufferings, prayer and work, are united with those of Christ and with his total offering, and so acquire a new value' (CCC, no. 1368). This also reminds us of the importance of sacrifice in each individual's life. In a self-centred culture where people are taught to extend themselves only for something in return, the sacrifices each of us make, following the example of Jesus, who freely sacrificed his life in love for all, point to the reality and power of God's love for us.

The offering of Christ unites the members here on earth and those in heaven. The pope, as chief shepherd of the People of God, is named at every Mass for the sake of the unity of the whole Church. The bishop of a diocese is named because he is the shepherd of the local Church and the instrument of its unity. The text of the Eucharistic Prayer also recalls the presence of the Blessed Virgin Mary and all the saints as they join us in this act of worship. Drawing from the benefits of Christ's sacrifice, the Mass is also offered for the faithful departed – who have died in Christ but may not yet be totally purified – so they may enter the glory of heaven.

THE MASS IS A HOLY MEAL

'If you do not eat the flesh of the Son of man and drink his blood, you have no life in you' (Jn 6:53). Jesus Christ shares with us his Body and Blood under the form of bread and wine. Thus the Mass is a sacred banquet that culminates in the reception of Holy Communion. The Church urges us to prepare conscientiously for this moment. We should be in the state of grace, and if we are conscious of a grave or serious sin, we must receive the Sacrament of Penance before receiving Holy Communion. We are also expected to fast from food or drink for at least one hour prior to the reception of Holy Communion. 'Like every Catholic generation before us, we must be guided by the words of St Paul, "Therefore anyone who eats the bread or drinks the cup of the Lord unworthily is answerable for the body and blood of the Lord" (1 Cor 11:27). That means that all must examine their consciences as to their worthiness to receive the Body and Blood of our Lord. This examination includes fidelity to the moral teaching of the Church in personal and public life' (United States Conference of Catholic Bishops, *Catholics in Political Life*, 2004). The Church gives us the humble words of a Roman centurion to say as we prepare to receive Communion: 'Lord, I am not worthy to receive you, but only say the word and I shall be healed' (cf. Mt 8:8).

Although the Church urges us to receive Communion at each Mass, there is an obligation for everyone to receive Communion at least once a year some time during the interval between the First Sunday of Lent and Trinity Sunday. Since Christ is fully present under each form of the Eucharist (that is, both the consecrated bread and wine), it is sufficient to receive him under the species (form) of bread or wine alone. However, the 'sign of communion is more complete when given under both kinds, since in that form the sign of the Eucharistic meal appears more clearly' (CCC, no. 1390).

Holy Communion increases our union with Christ. Just as bodily food sustains our physical life, so Holy Communion nourishes our spiritual life. This Communion moves us away from sin, strengthening our moral resolve to avoid evil and turn ever more powerfully toward God. 'The more we share the life of Christ and progress in his friendship, the more difficult it is to break away from him by mortal sin' (CCC, no. 1395).

THE REAL PRESENCE OF CHRIST

By the power of the Holy Spirit, Christ is present in the proclamation of God's Word, in the Eucharistic assembly, in the person of the priest but above all – and in a wholly unique manner – in the Eucharist. 'This presence is called "real" – by which is not intended to exclude the other types of presence as if they could not be "real" too, but because it is presence in the fullest sense: that is to say, it is a *substantial* presence by which Christ, God and man, makes himself wholly and entirely present' (CCC, no. 1374, citing Pope Paul VI, *Mystery of Faith*, no. 39).

Since the Middle Ages, the change of bread and wine into the Body and Blood of Christ has been called 'transubstantiation'. This means that the substance of the bread and wine is changed into the substance of the Body and Blood of Christ. The appearances of bread and wine remain (colour, shape, weight, chemical composition), but the underlying reality – that is, the substance – is now the Body and Blood of Christ.

The Real Presence of Jesus Christ endures in the consecrated elements even after the Mass is ended. Once Communion has been distributed, any remaining hosts are placed in the tabernacle. If any of the Precious Blood remains, it is reverently consumed. The hosts are reserved to provide Communion for the sick, *Viaticum* (Communion for the dying), and to allow the faithful to worship Christ in the reserved Sacrament and to pray in his presence. As a sign of adoration, Latin Catholics genuflect to the Real Presence of Jesus Christ in the tabernacle or genuflect or kneel when the Blessed Sacrament is exposed for prayer. Eastern Catholics show their reverence by a profound bow rather than a genuflection: 'It is for this reason the tabernacle should be located in an especially worthy place in the Church and should be constructed in such a way that it emphasises and manifests the truth of the real presence of Christ in the Blessed Sacrament' (CCC, no. 1379).

With the passage of time, reverent reflection led the Church to enrich its Eucharistic devotion. Faith that Jesus is truly present in the Sacrament led believers to worship Christ dwelling with us permanently in the Sacrament. Wherever the Sacrament is, there is Christ, who is our Lord and our God. Such worship is expressed in many ways: in genuflection, in adoration of the Eucharist, and the many forms of Eucharistic devotion that faith has nourished.

The Eucharistic Liturgy contains the entire treasure of the Church since it makes present the Paschal Mystery, the central event of salvation. Eucharistic adoration and devotion flow from and lead to the Eucharistic Liturgy, the Mass.

WAYS OF PARTICIPATING IN
THE PASCHAL MYSTERY

Through participation in the Eucharist, we also participate in the Paschal Mystery of Christ, that is, in his dying and rising, which is made present for us in the Eucharistic sacrifice. This participation in the Paschal Mystery of Christ reaches its consummation when we receive his Body and Blood in Holy Communion. Christ's victory and triumph over death is then made present in the lives of those who participate in the Eucharist.

Holy Communion increases our union with Christ. 'Whoever eats my flesh and drinks my blood lives in me and I live in that person' (Jn 6:56). Communion with the Body of Christ preserves, increases and renews the life of grace received at Baptism.

Holy Communion separates us from sin. We receive the Body of Christ 'given up for us' to save us from sin. We receive the Blood of Christ 'shed for many for the forgiveness of sins'. Our love of God is intensified and therefore our disordered attachments are weakened and even broken. Divine love wipes away venial sins.

Holy Communion offers us strength, called grace, to preserve us from mortal sin. By deepening our friendship with Christ, this Sacrament makes it more difficult for us to break our union with him by mortal sin.

Holy Communion expands the life of the Church. The Church as a communion is bound ever more closely together through the celebration of the Eucharist. As an ancient axiom states, the Church makes the Eucharist, and the Eucharist makes the Church. In receiving Communion, we are more fully united to the Church.

Holy Communion commits us to care for the poor. Saint Paul reminded the Corinthians that in sharing the Body of Christ in the Eucharist, they were also called to care for the poorer members of the community (cf. 1 Cor 11:17-34).

Participation in the celebration of the Eucharistic sacrifice is a source and means of grace even apart from the actual reception of Holy Communion. It has also been long understood that when circumstances prevent one from receiving Holy Communion during Mass, it is possible to make a spiritual communion that is also a source of grace. Spiritual communion means uniting one's self in prayer with Christ's sacrifice and worshipping him present in his Body and Blood.

FROM THE CATECHISM

1. What happens at the consecration in the Mass?

By the consecration, the transubstantiation of the bread and wine into the Body and Blood of Christ is brought about. Under the consecrated species of bread and wine, Christ himself, living and glorious, is present in a true, real and substantial manner: His Body and Blood, with his soul and divinity. (CCC, no. 1413; Council of Trent: DS 1640, 1651)

2. What are the effects of Holy Communion?

Communion with the Body and Blood of Christ increases the communicant's union with the Lord, forgives his venial sins and preserves him from grave sins. Since receiving this sacrament strengthens the bonds of charity between the communicant and Christ, it also reinforces the unity of the Church as the Mystical Body of Christ. (CCC, no. 1416)

3. Why is it valuable to visit the Blessed Sacrament?

Because Christ himself is present in the sacrament of the altar, he is to be honoured with the worship of adoration. 'To visit the Blessed Sacrament is ... a proof of gratitude, an expression of love and a duty of adoration toward Christ our Lord.' (CCC, no. 1418; Pope Paul VI, *Mystery of Faith*, no. 66)

THE EUCHARIST TRANSFORMS THE RECIPIENT

To participate actively in the Mass, we need to resist a tendency to passivity when gathered in an audience-like setting. At Mass, we are an assembly of believers called to be a community joined in the praise and worship of God. We do this in the singing of hymns, psalms, recitation of prayers and responses, especially in our 'Yes' to God in the Great Amen. Active participation also requires an interior attention and a profound inner offering, as St Paul urges in Romans 12:1: 'I urge you, then, brothers, remembering the mercies of God, to offer your bodies as a living sacrifice, dedicated and acceptable to God; that is the kind of worship for you.'

When the assembly of the faithful, from the hands of the priest, offers the sacrifice of Christ to the Father, the members of the assembly are called to offer their bodies as a living sacrifice, holy and pleasing to God. In using the word *body*, St Paul does not mean simply our flesh and bones, but rather our very selves. This, then, is a spiritual sacrifice. How can we do this?

In the Eucharistic Prayer, we hear that Jesus took the bread, blessed it, broke it, made it his Body and gave it for our salvation. One way of identifying with this is to pray, 'Lord, take me. Bless me. Break me. Make me a part of your saving, sacrificial gift for the world's bodily and spiritual needs.' Having offered ourselves to the Father in union with Christ, we practise active participation in the Mass in its highest form.

This inner drama at each Mass contributes to the process of our spiritual transformation into Christ. It all takes time. When we receive Communion, we need to remember that we are not changing Christ into ourselves. Jesus is transforming us into himself. This requires a proper understanding of the Real Presence of Jesus under the appearance of bread and wine. It is not simply a symbol that merely points to Jesus. Nor is Christ's presence just a projection on our part in the sense that we make him present when we receive him. As Pope Benedict XVI told the young people gathered for the Twentieth World Youth Day:

> The Body and Blood of Christ are given to us so that we ourselves will be transformed in our turn. We are to become the Body of Christ, his own Flesh and Blood.
>
> We all eat the one bread, and this means that we ourselves become one. In this way, adoration, as we said earlier, becomes union. God no longer simply stands before us as the One who is totally Other. He is within us, and we are in him. His dynamic enters into us and then seeks to spread outwards to others until it fills the world, so that his love can truly become the dominant measure of the world. (Benedict XVI, Homily at Marienfeld, Twentieth World Youth Day [21 August 2005])

The consecrated bread has become Christ's Body. The consecrated wine has become Christ's Blood. Jesus Christ is substantially present in a way that is entirely unique. This happens by the power of the Holy Spirit through the ministry of the priest's or bishop's acting in the person of Christ during the Eucharistic Prayer. At Mass, when we are offered the Host and hear the statement 'The Body of Christ', we answer, 'Amen', that is, 'Yes, I believe'.

Only Jesus can transform us into himself. Our inner receptivity is critical. To receive love, we need to be open to it. The sacrificial gift of self at every Mass is the best way to be continuously transformed into Christ. Then in Christ we become bread for the world's bodily and spiritual hungers.

FOR DISCUSSION

1. What has been your experience of Mass at various times in your life? What has helped you to become a more active participant in the celebration of the Eucharist?
2. Who are the people who have influenced your appreciation of the Eucharist? What do we mean when we speak of the Real Presence of Jesus? What can draw you to visit the Blessed Sacrament more frequently and spend time there in the adoration of Christ?
3. The *Catechism* reminds us that the Eucharist commits us to care for the poor (see CCC, no. 1397). How do you live this commitment during the week? How are you the 'Body of Christ' at work, at home, at school?

DOCTRINAL STATEMENTS

- Jesus instituted the Eucharistic sacrifice, the banquet of divine life, at the Last Supper.
- We need to remember that the Eucharist is the summit and source of our Christian life. Why? Because in the Eucharist is found the entire treasure of the Church – Jesus Christ.
- The Eucharistic celebration begins with the Introductory Rites and the Liturgy of the Word, followed by the Liturgy of the Eucharist – the preparation of the gifts, the Eucharistic Prayer (the prayer of thanksgiving and praise, including the consecration of the bread and wine) and the reception of Holy Communion. The celebration concludes with the sending forth to serve the Lord.

- The Eucharist is the memorial of Christ's saving life, death and Resurrection, made present for our salvation by the action of the liturgy.
- Christ, acting through the ministry of his priests, is both the priest offering the sacrifice and the victim being sacrificed.
- 'Only validly ordained priests can preside at the Eucharist and consecrate the bread and wine so that they become the Body and Blood of the Lord' (CCC, no. 1411).
- The essential signs of the Eucharist for the Latin Church are unleavened wheat bread and grape wine.
- At Mass, the consecrated bread is Christ's Body. The consecrated wine is Christ's Blood. Jesus Christ, whole and entire, is fully present under each form of the Eucharist. He is substantially present in a way that is entirely unique. This happens by the power of the Holy Spirit through the ministry of the priest's acting in the person of Christ during the Eucharistic Prayer.
- 'As sacrifice, the Eucharist is also offered in reparation for the sins of the living and the dead and to obtain spiritual and temporal benefits from God' (CCC, no. 1414).
- To receive Communion, one should be in the state of grace. A person conscious of mortal sin may not receive Communion until absolved from the sin in the Sacrament of Penance (cf. 1 Cor 11:27-29).
- A person who is conscious of grave sin but has no opportunity for sacramental confession may receive Communion for a serious reason; in such a case, the person must first make an act of perfect contrition and have the intention of confessing as soon as possible (cf. CIC, can. 916).
- The fruits of Holy Communion include a deeper union with Christ, a closer identity with all the faithful, a commitment to the poor and a pledge of future glory.
- The faithful are urged to receive Communion at Mass. The Church obliges them to do so at least once a year during the Easter season.
- Once Communion has been distributed, the remaining hosts are placed in the tabernacle to provide Communion for the sick and *Viaticum* for the dying and also to provide opportunity for prayer and worship before Christ in his Real Presence.

MEDITATION

O Jesus, joy of loving hearts,
the fount of life and my true light,
We seek the peace your love imparts
and stand rejoicing in your sight.

We taste in you my living bread
and long to feast upon you still.
We drink of you my fountain head,
my thirsting soul to quench and fill.

For you my thirsting spirit yearns,
where'er our changing lot is cast;
Glad when your presence we discern,
blest when our faith can hold you fast.

O Jesus ever with us stay;
make all our moments calm and bright.
O chase the night of sin away;
shed o'er the world your holy light.

– Attributed to St Bernard of Clairvaux,
Jesu Dulcedo Cordium
(Jesus Joy of Loving Hearts),
Ray Palmer, trans., *Worship Hymnal,* Third Edition, 605

PRAYER

Anima Christi

Soul of Christ, be my sanctification.
Body of Christ, be my salvation.
Blood of Christ, fill all my veins.
Water of Christ's side, wash out my stains.
Passion of Christ, my comfort be.
O good Jesu, listen to me.
In Thy wounds I fain would hide,
N'er to be parted from Thy side,
Guard me, should the foe assail me.
Call me when my life shall fail me.
Bid me come to Thee above,
With Thy saints to sing Thy love,
World without end. Amen.

Ag Críost an Síol

Ag Críost an síol, ag Críost an fómhar,
In iothlainn Dé go dtugtar sinn.
Ag Críost an mhuir, ag Críost an t-iasc,
I líonta Dé go gcastar sinn.
Ó fhás go haois, is ó aois go bás,
Do dhá láimh, a Chríost, anall tharainn.
Ó bhás go críoch, ní críoch ach athfhás,
I bParthas na nGrást go rabhaimid.

SUGGESTIONS AND PROPOSALS
FOR THE YEAR OF THE EUCHARIST 2004
FROM THE CONGREGATION OF DIVINE WORSHIP

COMMUNION

The sign of the Cross at the beginning of the Mass manifests that the
Church is the people gathered together in the name of the Trinity.

They gather together, in the same place, to celebrate the sacred mysteries and to respond to the Heavenly Father who calls his children to himself in Christ, in the love of the Holy Spirit.

The Eucharist is not a private action, but the action of Christ who always associates the Church to himself with an indissoluble marital bond. In the Liturgy of the Word, we hear the same Divine Word, source of communion for all those who put it into practice. In the Eucharistic liturgy we offer up our lives – which we offer together with the whole Church who, in its sacred mysteries, disposes us to enter into communion with Christ in our presentation of bread and wine.

By the power of the Holy Spirit, Christ's sacrifice is made present in the offering of the Church: a spiritual offering, pleasing to the Father, through Christ, with Christ and in Christ. The fruit of this association with the 'living and holy sacrifice' is represented in sacramental communion: 'Grant that we, who are nourished by the body and blood of your Son and filled with his Holy Spirit, may become one body, one spirit in Christ' (Eucharistic Prayer III).

This is the perennial source of ecclesial communion illustrated by St John with the analogy of the vine and the branches, and by St Paul with the image of the body. The Eucharist makes the Church ... filling it with God's charity and spurring it on to live this same charity. That is why the offering of other goods or money for the poor, along with the gifts of bread and wine, serves as a reminder that the Eucharist is also a pledge of solidarity and a commitment to share our goods with others ...

Liturgical prayer, while involving individual participants, is always formulated in the first person plural form 'we'. It is the voice of the Bride which praises and pleads, *una voce dicentes* (speaking with one voice).

The same attitudes taken up by the participants express the communion between members of a single organism ... The sign of peace before Communion ... is expressive of the 'ecclesial communion' needed to enter into sacramental communion with Christ. This Communion builds up the Church as the visible reflection of the communion enjoyed by the Holy Trinity.

Thus is grounded the spirituality of communion sought for by the Eucharist, and brought about by the Eucharistic celebration.

The communion between spouses is modelled after, purified and nourished by participation in the Eucharist.

The ministry of the Church's pastors and the docility of the faithful to the magisterium are coloured by the Eucharist. The union of the sick and infirms' sufferings with those of Christ is sealed by their participation in the Eucharist.

Our sacramental reconciliation after having 'lost our way' is crowned by Eucharistic communion. The harmonious communion amongst multiple charisms, functions, services, groups and movements within the Church is assured by the sacred mystery of the Eucharist.

Communion among the different activities, services and associations within a parish is manifested by their participation in the same Eucharist. The social fabric, woven together by the threads of peace, mutual understanding and concord in the earthly city are sustained by the sacrament of 'God with us and for us'.

GUIDELINES FOR THE CELEBRATION OF FIRST COMMUNION IN IRELAND

The following is a series of guidelines offered to those who are involved in the organisation of the First Communion celebration. They are offered in order to facilitate cooperation between home, school and parish in preparing for the celebration and in order to emphasise the liturgical and sacramental aspects of the occasion. These guidelines may need to be adapted in order to facilitate local practice.

- Organise a meeting with parents/guardians, sponsors, teachers, parish personnel in order to plan for the celebration.
- You might consider holding an 'Enrolment Ceremony' in the Church for those children who will be celebrating First Communion and First Penance. This ceremony is usually celebrated during the first term of Second Class/Primary Four.
- Ensure that the children who intend receiving First Communion are baptised.
- It is a matter of pastoral and ecumenical sensitivity when children of parents of another Christian denomination wish to receive First Communion in the Catholic Church. Prior to proceeding with

admission to First Communion it must be ascertained that the children are to become members of the Catholic Church. The decision to become a member of the Catholic Church must be recorded together with their Baptism in the parish register.

- Encourage parents/guardians, sponsors, teachers and parish personnel to engage with a parish-based communion programme as part of the preparation for the celebration.
- Encourage the school chaplain to visit the First Holy Communion class/es regularly. The preparation for First Communion begins in Junior Infants/Primary One.
- Ideally have the First Communion celebration at one of the Sunday Masses. If children have been participating in a parish-based communion programme that is focused on the Sunday liturgy it would be more appropriate to have the First Communion celebration on Sunday rather than on Saturday.
- Allow the possibility of exploring if some or several of the Sunday Masses (including vigil Masses) during the month of May might be the occasion when First Communion is celebrated. In particular, families might be encouraged to choose the Mass at which they normally worship.
- Remember that if a number of First Communion Masses are to be celebrated during the month of May then the liturgies will require extra organisation.
- Involve in the First Communion celebration members of the parish community who already exercise ministries, e.g. readers, the many forms of music ministry, ministry of welcome, ushers, etc.
- Involve first communicants in the parish liturgical celebration – reciting the prayer of the faithful, preparing the altar, presenting the gifts of bread and wine, singing one of the songs from the school programme after communion etc.
- Involve elements of the school catechetical programme in the parish celebration – using the learned gestures while reciting the Our Father, having the parish choir sing some of the hymns/songs learned in school, etc.
- Become familiar with the liturgical directions for the celebration of First Communion which may be available in either the school or parish preparation programme.

- Pay special attention to the presentation of the gifts by firstly having the altar prepared, then the gifts of bread and wine brought forward and presented. Other gifts and symbols of school life and class activity should not be included here but are better presented at the beginning of Mass.
- Pay special attention to the reception of Holy Communion. Children should approach the altar in silence. To receive the host, the child places one hand under the other and slowly extends both cupped hands towards the priest. When the priest says 'The Body of Christ', the child replies 'Amen'. The priest places the host in the extended hand. The host is then slowly placed in the mouth. It is important that the children be instructed to wait until the host is in the mouth before returning to their seats.

Alternatively, the host can be received directly on the tongue. In this case, ask the children to stand before the priest with their hands joined in prayer. When the priest says 'The Body of Christ', the child replies 'Amen', and then extends his/her tongue, onto which the priest places the host.

In situations where reception under both species is practised, children too may be invited to receive from the chalice. In this case, instruct the children to wait for the priest to offer the chalice with the words 'The Blood of Christ', to which they reply 'Amen'. Then, using both hands, they take the chalice, drink from it, and return it to the priest. When they are ready, they return to their seats. Request that cameras should not be used at this moment in the faith life of the children.

CONDITIONS FOR THE RECEPTION OF HOLY COMMUNION

- Be a baptised member of the Catholic Church.
- Be in a state of grace.
- Believe in the Real Presence.
- Be fasting for one hour.
- Be free from an ecclesiastical censure.

GUIDELINES FOR THE RECEPTION OF COMMUNION DURING THE EXTRAORDINARY FORM OF THE MASS

Children who attend the extraordinary form of the Mass will receive Communion in a different manner from their classmates who attend the ordinary form of the Mass. At Mass in the extraordinary form, Holy Communion is received kneeling and on the tongue. Reception in the hand or while standing is not normally permitted. Communion is received under one kind only, to emphasise the Church's teaching that Christ is received whole and entire under the appearance of bread or wine.

Normally the child will approach the altar with joined hands and will kneel at the Communion rails (although children making their First Communion may use a prie-dieu). The priest recites the formula: *'Corpus Domini nostri Jesu Christi custodiat animam tuam in vitam aeternam. Amen.'* ('May the Body of our Lord Jesus Christ preserve your soul to everlasting life. Amen.') Note that the priest says 'Amen'. The child should make no response.

The sacrament of Confession (or Reconciliation) is often available before and during Mass in churches celebrating Mass in the extraordinary form. Almost exclusively, confession will be in the traditional form, using a confessional box, rather than face-to-face with a priest.

The extraordinary form of the Mass is celebrated with the approval of the Holy Father and permission of the local Bishop, using the rubrics (directions for worshipping priest and people) and Latin text of the Mass as it was before the reform of the Second Vatican Council.

EXPLANATORY STATEMENT ON MASS OFFERINGS FROM THE IRISH BISHOPS 2010

Various misunderstandings about the tradition of Mass offerings and clear dangers of exploitation of the Mass can easily emerge. For this reason, the Irish Bishops wish to make clear the Church's position on Mass Offerings. The following is a brief summary of the Church's teaching and regulation regarding Mass Offerings.

1. The Eucharist, the 'source and summit of the Christian life', is at the heart of our belief, for it preserves the great mystery of our redemption in Jesus Christ. Therefore anything that might weaken or undermine our respect for the Eucharist must be avoided.

2. The practice of giving an offering dates back to the early Church when the faithful brought bread and wine for the Mass and other gifts for the support of the priest and for the poor. Nowadays, a Mass offering is a way for the donor to join him/herself to the sacrifice of the Mass; it unites the donor closely with the life and apostolic activity of the Church, the Body of Christ, as the offering becomes a form of material support for the Church's ministers and pastoral life. The Mass must never be an occasion for 'buying and selling' or 'making money', nor should there be even the slightest appearance of making a profit from Mass offerings.

3. Normally a separate Mass is celebrated for each individual offering, however small. The donor specifies the individual intention and it is up to the donor to decide what amount to give. Because donors may sometimes ask how much is appropriate to give, a current recommended diocesan offering is specified (this amount is agreed by the Bishops at provincial level). A priest may accept less than the recommended offering – and many priests on occasion do.

4. The priest who receives the offering has an obligation to apply Mass for the specific intention of the person who has made the offering. He is to celebrate a Mass within a reasonable time. Irrespective of how many Masses he celebrates in a day, a priest may only keep an offering for one Mass per day. If a priest receives too many Mass intentions he must transfer any surplus Mass offerings, in total, to another priest (normally these offerings will be sent to priests working in needy areas).

5. The Church does not encourage 'collective' or 'multi-intentional' Masses but sees these as an exception. In these exceptional cases, the following must apply: a) It must be made explicitly clear to the donor beforehand that the offering is being combined into a single Mass offering and the donor must give free consent to this; b) The place, date and time for this Mass should be indicated publicly and such Masses may not be celebrated any more than

two days weekly in any church; c) The priest who celebrates Mass for a collective intention must not keep any more than the specified diocesan offering, and must transfer any additional amount, in accordance with canon law, for the purposes prescribed by the Bishop/Provincial.

6. Having signed or stamped Mass cards for sale to the public in shops and other commercial outlets is a practice that is not approved by the Irish Episcopal Conference, the Major Religious Superiors or the Superiors of Missionary Societies. It undermines a correct Eucharistic Theology and is unacceptable. We ask that this practice, wherever it exists, be discontinued.

7. We strongly encourage the donor, where possible, to participate in the Mass. We recommend that the intention for which the Mass is being especially offered is mentioned in the Prayer of the Faithful. Of course the Mass is not exclusively for this intention – every Mass is offered for all people, especially those in need.

The Church's norms and regulations about Mass offerings are clearly set out in the 1983 Code of Canon Law and in the 1991 Decree *Mos Iugiter*.

All my other senses, cannot now perceive,
But my hearing, taught by faith, always will believe:
I accept whatever God the Son has said:
Those who hear the Word of God, by the truth are fed.
– St Thomas Aquinas, *Adoro Te Devote*
(God with Hidden Majesty),
Anthony G. Petti, trans.

The Eucharist, the Sacrament of sacraments, is the source and summit of Christian life. It is the sacrament of our innermost union with God.
– SGN, 54

18 SACRAMENT OF PENANCE AND RECONCILIATION: GOD IS RICH IN MERCY

IN THIS SACRAMENT OF HEALING WE ARE RECONCILED TO GOD AND THE CHURCH – CCC, NOS. 1420–1498

AUGUSTINE: THE SINNER WHO BECAME A SAINT

Very few men have had such an impact on Christianity as St Augustine. He was born in AD 354 in North Africa, at that time a strong and dynamic Christian region. His father was a prominent pagan, but his mother, Monica, was a devout Christian. She intended that Augustine be baptised, but in his adolescence he distanced himself from the Church and did not want to be baptised. He studied Latin literature and became a follower of an esoteric philosophy known as Manichaeism.

He had a mistress with whom he lived for fifteen years. She bore him a son, but he later broke up with her while living in Milan, where he had been given a teaching position. He found himself gradually more attracted to Christianity as he listened to the preaching of St Ambrose, the Bishop of Milan. But he resisted conversion, though his mother prayed persistently for him.

In a book entitled *The Confessions*, written in his later years as a spiritual and theological reflection on his life, Augustine describes the final steps to his conversion. He had felt the tension between attachment to his sinful ways and attraction to Christ and the Gospel. One day in the year 386, he went crying into the garden of the house where he was staying with friends. He was weeping because of his inability to make a decision for conversion. But then he heard the voice of a child from a neighbouring house singing the refrain, 'Take it and read, take it and read.' He picked up the Letters of St Paul and read the first passage his eyes fell upon: 'Let us live decently, as in the light of day; with no orgies or drunkenness, no promiscuity or licentiousness, and no wrangling or jealousy. Let your armour be the Lord Jesus Christ, and stop worrying about how your disordered natural inclinations may be fulfilled' (Rm 13:13-14). Augustine recognised the grace of God in this reading and embraced conversion.

He was baptised by St Ambrose in 387 and returned to North Africa in 388. In 391, while visiting the town of Hippo, he was urged by the Christian population to become a priest; he accepted, though reluctantly. In 395 he became Bishop of Hippo. As a Christian, priest and bishop, he wrote numerous books to explain and defend Christian doctrine. His homilies and sermons were written down, and they witness to the depth and power of his preaching. He died in 430.

Augustine knew the damaging effects of sin. In *The Confessions*, he admits his own sinfulness even as a boy: 'Many and many a time I lied to my tutor, my masters, and my parents, because I wanted to play games or watch some futile show or was impatient to imitate what I saw on the stage.' But he also experienced the greater power of grace, of God's enabling us to overcome sin and accept the Gospel of his Son. Saint Augustine knew God's mercy in the forgiveness of sins gained for us by Jesus Christ. Today Catholics encounter this same mercy and forgiveness in the Sacrament of Penance.

THE FORGIVENESS OF SINS

The Lord Jesus Christ, physician of our souls and our bodies ... has willed that his Church continue, in the power of the Holy Spirit, his work of healing and salvation.

— CCC, no. 1421

Because of human weakness, the new life in Christ, which we receive in the Sacraments of Initiation, is often threatened by sin. Moreover, we all face sickness and death. God constantly reaches out to us to reconcile ourselves to him. Through the gifts of the Church, Jesus, our divine physician, has given us the Sacraments of Healing – Penance and Reconciliation and Anointing of the Sick – for the forgiveness of sins and the ministry to the sick and the dying.

Sins committed after Baptism are forgiven in the Sacrament of Penance and Reconciliation, also called the Sacrament of Forgiveness, Confession and Conversion. We will refer to the Sacrament both as Penance and as Reconciliation, using the terms interchangeably.

Divine mercy and conversion from sin are constant themes in Scripture. God's mercy makes possible the repentance of the sinner and the forgiveness of sin. Time and again in the Old Testament, the sins of the people are met with God's outreach of mercy and the invitation to be healed and return to a covenant relationship. Even when the beloved King David lied, committed adultery and caused the death of an innocent man, he was not beyond God's mercy, to which he had a humble recourse. Psalm 51 gives us words to express the kind of contrition and to trust in God's forgiveness that David felt after committing these sins.

JESUS FORGAVE SINS

The Gospels provide numerous examples of Christ's mission to forgive sins. When a paralytic was lowered through the roof of a house and placed at his feet, Christ first forgave the man's sins and then cured his affliction (cf. Lk 5:17-26). When a sinful woman knelt at his feet in the house of Simon the Pharisee, Jesus forgave her sins because she had 'loved much', unlike the Pharisee, who had little insight into his own sinfulness (cf. Lk 7:36-50). Christ's parable of the prodigal son illustrates the sublime meaning of his earthly ministry, which is to forgive sins, reconcile people to God and lead us to true happiness (cf. Lk 15:11-32).

Jesus died on the Cross and rose from the dead to reconcile sinful people with God through the forgiveness of sins and the gift of new life with the Triune God. Even on the Cross, he forgave those who were killing him and had mercy on the repentant thief.

Only God can forgive our sins. But Jesus willed that the Church should be his instrument of forgiveness on earth. On Easter night the Risen Christ imparted to his Apostles his own power to forgive sins. He breathed on them, imparting the promised Holy Spirit and said, 'Peace be with you'. Jesus was actually filling them with peace that is rooted in friendship with God. But he did more. He shared with them his own merciful mission. He breathed on them a second time and said:

> As the Father sent me, so am I sending you ... Receive the Holy Spirit. If you forgive anyone's sins, they are forgiven; if you retain anyone's sins, they are retained. (Jn 20:21-23)

That night, Jesus gave the Church the ministry of the forgiveness of sins through the Apostles (cf. CCC, no. 1461). By the Sacrament of Holy Orders, bishops and priests continue this ministry to forgive sins 'in the name of the Father, and of the Son and of the Holy Spirit'. In this Sacrament, the priest acts in the person of Christ, the Head of the Church, to reconcile the sinner to both God and the Church. 'When he celebrates the Sacrament of Penance, the priest is fulfilling the ministry of the Good Shepherd who seeks the lost sheep ... The priest is the sign and instrument of God's merciful love for the sinner' (CCC, no. 1465).

The Sacrament of Penance involves a conversion of our hearts to God, a confession of sins to a priest, the forgiveness of our sins, a penance to make some amends for sin and reconciliation with God and the Church. For those who commit mortal sin after Baptism, this Sacrament is necessary for being reconciled to God and the Church.

CONVERSION, CONFESSION, FORGIVENESS

The Sacrament of Penance must be seen within the context of conversion from sin and a turn to God. Peter wept bitterly over his triple denial of Christ but received the grace of conversion and expressed it with a threefold confession of love for Jesus (cf. Lk 22:54-62; Jn 21:15-19). Paul was converted from persecuting Christians to becoming one of the greatest disciples of Christ who ever lived (cf. Acts 9:1-31). These moments of conversion were only the beginning of their lifelong commitment to living in fidelity to the Gospel of Jesus Christ.

Sin harms our relationship with God and damages our communion with the Church. Conversion of heart is the beginning of our journey back to God. Liturgically this happens in the Sacrament of Penance. In the history of the Church, this Sacrament has been celebrated in different ways. Beneath the changes, there have always been two essentials: the acts of the penitent and the acts of Christ through the ministry of the Church. Both go hand in hand. Conversion must involve a change of heart as well as a change of actions. Neither is possible without God's grace.

THE LITURGY OF THE SACRAMENT OF PENANCE

In the Liturgy of Penance, the elements are ordinarily these: a greeting and blessing from the priest, a reading from Scripture, the confession of sins, the giving and accepting of a penance, an act of contrition, the priest's absolution, a proclamation of praise of God and a dismissal. We offer here a description of the acts of the penitent and that of the priest.

Contrition

In order to be forgiven, we need to have sorrow for our sins. This means turning away from evil and turning to God. It includes the determination to avoid such sins in the future. Such sins may either be mortal or venial.

> Sins are rightly evaluated according to their gravity. The distinction between mortal and venial sin, already evident in Scripture (cf. 1 Jn 5:16-17), became part of the tradition of the Church. It is corroborated by human experience. (CCC, no. 1854)

> *Mortal sin* destroys charity in the heart of man by a grave violation of God's law; it turns man away from God, who is his ultimate end and beatitude, by preferring an inferior good to him. *Venial sin* allows charity to subsist, even though it offends and wounds it. (CCC, no. 1855)

Contrition that arises from the love of God above all else is called 'perfect contrition'. This loving sorrow remits venial sins and even mortal sins so long as we resolve to confess them as soon as possible. When other motives, such as the ugliness of sin or fear of damnation, bring us to confession, this is called 'imperfect contrition', which is sufficient for forgiveness in the Sacrament. The Holy Spirit moves us in either case and initiates the conversion.

Confession

Confession liberates us from sins that trouble our hearts and makes it possible to be reconciled to God and others. We are asked to look into our souls and, with an honest and unblinking gaze, identify our sins. This opens our minds and hearts to God, moves us toward communion with the Church and offers us a new future.

In confession, by naming our sins before the priest, who represents Christ, we face our failings more honestly and accept responsibility for our sins. It is also in confession that a priest and penitent can work together to find the direction needed for the penitent to grow spiritually and to avoid sin in the future (cf. CCC, nos. 1455, 1456).

When we have examined our consciences and have taken responsibility for our sins, we then confess them to the priest. We must confess all our mortal sins in kind and number. The Church strongly recommends confessing venial sins, though this is not strictly necessary. In the Latin Church, children must go to confession before making their First Communion.

There are three rites of Reconciliation: the rite for the Reconciliation of individual penitents; the rite for the Reconciliation of several penitents with individual confession and absolution; and the rite of Reconciliation of penitents with general confession and absolution.

In the first rite, which is the most familiar, the penitent goes to a reconciliation room or a traditional confessional and either confesses face to face with the priest or kneels behind a screen to confess the sins. In the second rite, which usually happens in Advent or Lent, there is a communal service during which the Scripture is read and a homily is given. This is followed by individual confession and individual absolution.

WHAT IS THIS SACRAMENT CALLED?

It is called the Sacrament of Conversion because it makes sacramentally present Jesus' call to conversion, the first step in returning to the Father from whom one has strayed by sin. It is called the Sacrament of Penance, since it consecrates the Christian sinner's personal and ecclesial steps of conversion, penance and satisfaction. It is called the Sacrament of Confession since the disclosure or confession of sins is an essential element of this Sacrament. In a profound sense, it is also a 'confession' – acknowledgement and praise – of the holiness of God and of his mercy toward sinful man. It is called the Sacrament of Forgiveness, since by the priest's sacramental absolution, God grants the penitent 'pardon and peace'. It is called the Sacrament of Reconciliation because it imparts to the sinner the love of God who reconciles: 'Be reconciled to God' (2 Cor 5:20). He who lives by God's merciful love is ready to respond to the Lord's call: 'Go, first be reconciled to your brother.' (CCC, nos. 1423–1424, citing Mt 5:24)

General confession and absolution is the third rite and is used only in extraordinary situations, danger of death, or an insufficient number of confessors so that 'penitents would be deprived of sacramental grace or holy communion for a long period of time through no fault of their own' (cf. CIC, can. 961). General absolution involves one priest's giving absolution to a group of people, who do not make individual confessions to a priest. Those penitents guilty of serious or grave sin are expected to make an individual confession as soon as possible but certainly within a year of receiving general absolution. Judgement as to whether the conditions for general absolution are present is a matter not for the confessor, but for the diocesan bishop to determine under the guidance of norms established by the Holy See.

Absolution from the Priest

After we confess our sins to the priest, we are given some encouragement from the priest for our moral and spiritual growth. The priest then gives us a penance and asks us to say an Act of Contrition. Then the priest grants absolution, that is, he sets us free from our sins, using the power that Christ entrusted to the Church and by which he pardons the sins of the penitent (cf. CCC, no. 1424). In the Latin Church, the priest, representing Christ and bringing us his forgiveness, absolves us from our sins with these words:

> God the Father of mercies, through the death and resurrection of his Son, has reconciled the world to himself, and sent the Holy Spirit among us for the forgiveness of sins; through the ministry of the Church may God give you pardon and peace, and I absolve you from your sins in the name of the Father and of the Son and of the Holy Spirit.

Satisfaction

'Absolution takes away sin, but does not remedy all the disorders sin has caused' (CCC, no. 1459). It is obvious that we need to repair certain damages that our sins have caused, such as restoring the reputation of someone we have injured, returning money that we have stolen or rectifying an injustice. Sin also weakens the relationship we have with God and others. Our inner life is harmed by sin and needs restoration.

This is the reason for acts of penance and satisfaction for sins. The penance given by the priest helps us to begin making satisfaction for our sins. Just as when we get physically out of shape, we need to take up some exercise, so also when the soul is morally out of shape, there is the challenge to adopt spiritual exercises that will restore it. Obviously, this is always done in cooperation with God's graces, which are essential for the healing.

> Absolution takes away sin, but it does not remedy all the disorders that sin has caused. Raised up from sin, the sinner must still recover his full spiritual health by doing something more to make amends for sin: he must 'make satisfaction for' or 'expiate' his sins. This satisfaction is called 'penance'. (CCC, no. 1459)

FROM THE CATECHISM

1. How can we prepare for the Sacrament of Penance?
The reception of this sacrament ought to be prepared for by an examination of conscience made in the light of the Word of God. The passages best suited to this can be found in the Ten Commandments, the moral catechesis of the Gospels and the apostolic Letters, such as the Sermon on the Mount and apostolic teaching. (CCC, no. 1454)

2. What is the seal of Confession?
The Church declares that every priest who hears confessions is bound under very severe penalties to keep absolute secrecy regarding the sins that his penitents have confessed to him. He can make no use of knowledge that confession gives him about penitents' lives. This secret, which admits of no exceptions, is called the 'sacramental seal', because what the penitent has made known to the priest remains 'sealed' by the sacrament. (CCC, no. 1467)

3. How does reception of the Sacrament of Reconciliation anticipate a person's judgement before God?
In this sacrament, the sinner, placing himself before the merciful judgement of God, anticipates in a certain way the judgement to which he will be subjected at the end of his earthly life. For it is now, in this life, that we are offered the choice between life and death, and it is only by the road of conversion that we can enter the Kingdom, from which one is excluded by grave sin. In converting to Christ through penance and faith, the sinner passes from death to life and 'does not come into judgement'. (CCC, no. 1470, citing Jn 5:24)

EFFECTS OF THE SACRAMENT

The Sacrament of Penance reconciles us with God. 'The whole power of the Sacrament of Penance consists in restoring us to God's grace and joining us with him in an intimate friendship' (CCC, no. 1468).

This Sacrament also reconciles us with the Church. Sin should never be understood as a private or personal matter, because it harms our relationship with others and may even break our loving communion with the Church. The Sacrament of Penance repairs this break and has a renewing effect on the vitality of the Church itself.

In this Sacrament, the penitent receives the merciful judgement of God and is engaged on the journey of conversion that leads to future life with God. The Church also recommends that a person go regularly to confession, even if only for venial sins. This is because 'the regular confession of our venial sins helps us form our consciences, fight against evil tendencies, let ourselves be healed by Christ and progress in the life of the Spirit' (CCC, no. 1458).

RECOGNISE SIN – PRAISE GOD'S MERCY

The Sacrament of Penance is an experience of the gift of God's boundless mercy. Not only does it free us from our sins but it also challenges us to have the same kind of compassion and forgiveness for those who sin against us. We are liberated to be forgivers. We obtain new insight into the words of the Prayer of St Francis: 'It is in pardoning that we are pardoned.'

By the help of God's grace, our call to holiness will be clearer when we recover an awareness of the reality of sin and evil in the world and in our own souls. Scripture will be enormously helpful in this since it reveals sin and evil clearly and fearlessly. Scriptural realism does not hesitate to pronounce judgement on the good and evil that affects our lives. The New Testament is filled with calls to conversion and repentance, which need to be heard in our culture today.

> If we say, 'We have no sin', we are deceiving ourselves, and truth has no place in us; if we acknowledge our sins, he is trustworthy and upright, so that he will forgive our sins and will cleanse us from all evil. (1 Jn 1:8-9)

In our churches, we behold Jesus nailed to the Cross, an image that reminds us of his painful sacrifice to bring about the forgiveness of all our sins and guilt. If there were no sin, Jesus would not have suffered for our redemption.

Each time we see the crucifix, we can reflect on the infinite mercy of God, who saves us through the reconciling act of Jesus. Despite society's efforts to downplay the reality of sin, there is an instinctive recognition of its existence. Children generally know, even when not told, when they have done something morally wrong. Adults readily admit the evil of terrorism, unjust war, lies, unfair treatment of people and similar matters. Society as a whole must also learn to admit the evil of abortion, physician-assisted suicide and obtaining stem cells from embryos, which results in the death of embryonic human life. Denying evil corrupts us spiritually and psychologically. Rationalising our own evil is even more destructive.

Jesus laid the foundation for the Sacrament of Penance during his ministry and confirmed it after his Resurrection. When Peter asked the number of times a person should forgive, Jesus told him that there should be no limit to forgiving. Jesus forgave Peter his triple denial, showed mercy to the woman taken in adultery, forgave the thief on the Cross and continually witnessed the mercy of God.

Jesus entrusted the ministry of reconciliation to the Church. The Sacrament of Penance is God's gift to us so that any sin committed after Baptism can be forgiven. In confession we have the opportunity to repent and recover the grace of friendship with God. It is a holy moment in which we place ourselves in his presence and honestly acknowledge our sins, especially mortal sins. With absolution, we are reconciled to God and the Church. The Sacrament helps us stay close to the truth that we cannot live without God. 'In him that we live, and move, and exist' (Acts 17:28). While all the Sacraments bring us an experience of the mercy that comes from Christ's dying and rising, it is the Sacrament of Reconciliation that is the unique Sacrament of mercy.

INDULGENCES

Every sin has consequences. It disrupts our communion with God and the Church, weakens our ability to resist temptation and hurts others. The necessity of healing these consequences, once the sin itself has been forgiven, is called temporal punishment. Prayer, fasting, almsgiving and other works of charity can take away entirely or diminish this temporal punishment. Because of the fullness of redemption obtained for us by Christ, the Church attaches to certain prayers and actions an *indulgence* or pardon, that is, the full or partial remission of temporal punishment due to sin. Christ, acting through the Church, brings about the healing of the consequences of sin when an individual uses such a prayer or engages in such an action.

■ FOR DISCUSSION ■

1 What is your attitude to confession today? How would you explain the Sacrament of Reconciliation to people of other faiths?
2. How can Scripture help you discern the reality of sin in the world? Why do we confess our sins to a priest? Why is it necessary to be reconciled to the Church as well as to God?
3. Why do you think that people need to have the burden of sin and guilt lifted from their hearts? Why is it essential to understand the mission of Jesus Christ as the Saviour? How can you commit yourself to a lifelong process of moral and spiritual conversion?

■ DOCTRINAL STATEMENTS ■

• On Easter night, Jesus appeared to the Apostles, greeted them with peace and breathed on them, saying, 'Receive the Holy Spirit. If you forgive anyone's sins, they are forgiven; if you retain anyone's sins, they are retained' (Jn 20:22-23).
• 'The Creed links "the forgiveness of sins" with its profession of faith in the Holy Spirit, for the risen Christ entrusted to the Apostles the power to forgive sins when he gave them the Holy Spirit' (CCC, no. 984).
• Sins committed before Baptism are forgiven by Baptism. Sins committed after Baptism are forgiven in the Sacrament of Penance and Reconciliation, also called the Sacrament of Forgiveness, Confession and Conversion.
• Sin wounds our relationship with God and others and our human dignity. Faith reveals to us the destructive force of sin in our lives and the world.

- The path back to God after sin is a process of conversion initiated by his grace. The return to God includes sorrow for sin and the resolve to sin no more.
- In the Sacrament of Penance and Reconciliation, the acts of the penitent are contrition, confession and satisfaction. The act of the priest is absolution for the sins of the penitent.
- Perfect contrition arises from love for God; imperfect contrition results from other motives.
- The penitent, after an examination of conscience, needs to confess all mortal sins. While it is not necessary to confess venial sins, the Church strongly recommends this practice.
- The priest proposes a penance to the penitent to repair the harm due to sin and to restore the penitent's commitment to be a disciple of Christ.
- Individual confession of grave sins according to kind and number is the only ordinary way of receiving absolution and reconciliation with God and the Church.
- The effects of the Sacrament of Penance and Reconciliation include reconciliation with God and the Church, peace of conscience and spiritual consolation, the remission of eternal punishment due to mortal sin as well as some degree of temporal punishments and a greater power to face spiritual challenges (cf. CCC, no. 1496).
- 'Through indulgences the faithful can obtain the remission of temporal punishment resulting from sin, for themselves and also for the souls in Purgatory' (CCC, no. 1498).

MEDITATION

Extract from the Pastoral Letter of Pope Benedict XVI to the Catholics of Ireland, March 2010

For my part, considering the gravity of these offences, and the often inadequate response to them on the part of the ecclesiastical authorities in your country, I have decided to write this Pastoral Letter to express my closeness to you and to propose a path of healing, renewal and reparation.

It is true, as many in your country have pointed out, that the problem of child abuse is peculiar neither to Ireland nor to the Church. Nevertheless, the task you now face is to address the problem of abuse that has occurred within the Irish Catholic community and to do so with courage and determination. No one imagines that this painful situation will be resolved swiftly. Real progress has been made, yet much more remains to be done. Perseverance and prayer are needed, with great trust in the healing power of God's grace.

At the same time, I must also express my conviction that, in order to recover from this grievous wound, the Church in Ireland must first acknowledge before the Lord and before others the serious sins committed against defenceless children. Such an acknowledgement, accompanied by sincere sorrow for the damage caused to these victims and their families, must lead to a concerted effort to ensure the protection of children from similar crimes in the future.

As you take up the challenges of this hour, I ask you to remember 'the rock from which you were hewn' (Is 51:1). Reflect upon the generous, often heroic, contributions made by past generations of Irish men and women to the Church and to humanity as a whole, and let this provide the impetus for honest self-examination and a committed programme of ecclesial and individual renewal. It is my prayer that, assisted by the intercession of her many saints and purified through penance, the Church in Ireland will overcome the present crisis and become once more a convincing witness to the truth and the goodness of Almighty God, made manifest in his Son Jesus Christ.

Historically, the Catholics of Ireland have proved an enormous force for good at home and abroad. Celtic monks like St Columbanus spread the Gospel in Western Europe and laid the foundations of medieval monastic culture. The ideals of holiness, charity and transcendent wisdom born of the Christian faith found expression in the building of churches and monasteries and the establishment of schools, libraries and hospitals, all of which helped to consolidate the spiritual identity of Europe. Those Irish missionaries drew their strength and inspiration from the firm faith, strong leadership and upright morals of the Church in their native land.

From the sixteenth century on, Catholics in Ireland endured a long period of persecution, during which they struggled to keep the flame of faith alive in dangerous and difficult circumstances. Saint Oliver Plunkett, the martyred Archbishop of Armagh, is the most famous example of a host of courageous sons and daughters of Ireland who were willing to lay down their lives out of fidelity to the Gospel. After Catholic Emancipation, the Church was free to grow once more. Families and countless individuals who had preserved the faith in times of trial became the catalyst for the great resurgence of Irish Catholicism in the nineteenth century. The Church provided education, especially for the poor, and this was to make a major contribution to Irish society. Among the fruits of the new Catholic schools was a rise in vocations: generations of missionary priests, sisters and brothers left their homeland to serve in every continent, especially in the English-speaking world. They were remarkable not only for their great numbers, but for the strength of their faith and the steadfastness of their pastoral commitment. Many dioceses, especially in Africa, America and Australia, benefitted from the presence of Irish clergy and religious who preached the Gospel and established parishes, schools and universities, clinics and hospitals that served both Catholics and the community at large, with particular attention to the needs of the poor.

In almost every family in Ireland, there has been someone – a son or a daughter, an aunt or an uncle – who has given his or her life to the Church. Irish families rightly esteem and cherish their loved ones who have dedicated their lives to Christ, sharing the gift of faith with others and putting that faith into action in loving service of God and neighbour.

In recent decades, however, the Church in your country has had to confront new and serious challenges to the faith arising from the rapid transformation and seculariation of Irish society. Fast-paced social change has occurred, often adversely affecting people's traditional adherence to Catholic teaching and values. All too often, the sacramental and devotional practices that sustain faith and enable it to grow, such as frequent confession, daily prayer and annual retreats, were neglected. Significant too was the tendency during this period, also on the part of priests and religious, to adopt ways of thinking and assessing secular realities without sufficient reference to the Gospel. The programme of renewal proposed by the Second Vatican Council was sometimes misinterpreted and indeed, in the light of the profound social changes that were taking place, it was far from easy to know how best to implement it. In particular, there was a well-intentioned but misguided tendency to avoid penal approaches to canonically irregular situations. It is in this overall context that we must try to understand the disturbing problem of child sexual abuse, which has contributed in no small measure to the weakening of faith and the loss of respect for the Church and her teachings.

Only by examining carefully the many elements that gave rise to the present crisis can a clear-sighted diagnosis of its causes be undertaken and effective remedies be found. Certainly, among the contributing factors we can include: inadequate procedures for determining the suitability of candidates for the priesthood and the religious life; insufficient human, moral, intellectual and spiritual formation in seminaries and novitiates; a tendency in society to favour the clergy and other authority figures; and a misplaced concern for the reputation of the Church and the avoidance of scandal, resulting in failure to apply existing canonical penalties and to safeguard the dignity of every person. Urgent action is needed to address these factors, which have had such tragic consequences in the lives of victims and their families, and have obscured the light of the Gospel to a degree that not even centuries of persecution succeeded in doing.

PRAYER

An Act of Contrition (a traditional version)

O my God, I am heartily sorry for having offended thee
and I detest all my sins, because of thy just punishments,
but most of all because they offend thee, my God,
who are all good and worthy of all my love.
I firmly resolve, with the help of thy grace,
to sin no more and to avoid the near occasions of sin. Amen.

Prayer of the Penitent (Rite of Penance)

Lord Jesus, Son of God
Have mercy on me, a sinner.

Pope Benedict XVI's Prayer for the Church in Ireland

God of our fathers,
renew us in the faith which is our life and salvation,
the hope which promises forgiveness and interior renewal,
the charity which purifies and opens our hearts
to love you, and in you, each of our brothers and sisters.

Lord Jesus Christ,
may the Church in Ireland renew her age-old commitment
to the education of our young people in the way of truth and
goodness, holiness and generous service to society.

Holy Spirit, comforter, advocate and guide,
inspire a new springtime of holiness and apostolic zeal
for the Church in Ireland.

May our sorrow and our tears,
our sincere effort to redress past wrongs,
and our firm purpose of amendment
bear an abundant harvest of grace
for the deepening of the faith
in our families, parishes, schools and communities,
for the spiritual progress of Irish society,
and the growth of charity, justice, joy and peace
within the whole human family.

To you, Triune God,
confident in the loving protection of Mary,
Queen of Ireland, our Mother,
and of Saint Patrick, Saint Brigid and all the saints,
do we entrust ourselves, our children,
and the needs of the Church in Ireland.

Amen.

A Short Act of Contrition (a traditional version)

O my God! I am heartily sorry for all my sins, because they offend Thee, who art infinitely good, and I firmly resolve, with the help of thy grace, never to offend Thee again.

(*A Catechism of Catholic Doctrine*, Dublin: M.H. Gill and Sons Ltd, 1951)

A Short Act of Contrition (a modern version)

O my God, I thank you for loving me. I am sorry for all my sins, for not loving others and not loving you. Help me to live like Jesus and not sin again. Amen.

(The *Alive-O* Programme, Dublin: Veritas Publications, 1996–2004)

An Gníomh Dóláis

A Dhia, gabhaim buíochas leat as ucht do ghrá dom. Tá brón orm faoi mo pheacaí uile: Nach raibh grá agam duitse ná do dhaoine eile. Cabhraigh liom mo shaol a chaitheamh ar nós Íosa agus gan peaca a dhéanamh arís. Áiméan.

Create a pure heart for me, O God.

– Ps 51:12

The sacrament of Penance and Reconciliation celebrates Christ's forgiveness of us and his healing of our hearts and minds.

– SGN, 55

19 ANOINTING THE SICK AND THE DYING

THE SACRAMENT OF ANOINTING OF THE SICK IS THE SECOND OF THE SACRAMENTS OF HEALING – CCC, NOS. 1499–1532

SAINT JOHN PAUL II: STRENGTH IN WEAKNESS

The last quarter of the twentieth century was witness to the most active and most travelled pope in history. John Paul II, Karol Wojtyła, crisscrossed the world, visiting countries on state visits and pastoral journeys, hosting youth days, presiding at Eucharistic Congresses, undertaking pilgrimages and going to places of symbolic significance, like the United Nations in New York, the World Council of Churches in Geneva and the Western Wall in Jerusalem. In all this activity and many appearances through the twenty-six years of his pontificate, he showed a vigour and energy of extraordinary dimensions.

Certainly, John Paul's personality was made for television. He had photogenic features, and was vibrant looking. His reading of a crowd was uncanny, relating with great multitudes in a deeply personal style. His body language communicated his mood and reflected the emotion of the crowd. The airwaves carried his picture to the corners of the earth. Christians in the most remote places saw for themselves the pope's gestures and demeanour. They heard, through the courtesy of television, the urgency and power of John Paul's words. They saw in vivid detail and rich colour the impact and effect of the pope's presence.

Karol Wojtyła's life had been a drama in itself. He was born in a small village of Wadowice in the southern part of Poland on 18 May 1920. He grew up at a precarious time in his country's history, with Europe recovering from one devastating conflict and holding its breath in fear of the next. As a boy, Karol suffered a number of personal losses. His mother died when he was nine years old. His brother Edmund, a young doctor, caught scarlet fever and died when Karol was twelve. Later in his life, he mentioned that a sister had died six years before his birth.

Karol Wojtyła was well aware of death and loss before he became an adult. In 1939, Germany invaded Poland and killing became commonplace. Auschwitz – the German name for the Polish Oswiecim – was just down the road from his home. The Nazi occupation instilled a reign of terror, with round-ups of professors and intellectuals, priests and writers, members of military and civilians, indeed all leadership for the Polish people.

In 1942, Karol's father died suddenly. 'By twenty, I had already lost all the people I loved,' he would later say.

Karol had been fascinated by the theatre since childhood and embarked on university study for a degree in literature and drama. But his father's death was a watershed. After that, he found himself drawn towards the Church, and in the autumn of 1942 he entered the underground course of training for the priesthood in Krakow.

He was ordained on 1 November 1946 in Krakow and duly became a postgraduate student in Rome's Angelicum University. He studied St John of the Cross – the Spanish mystic – for his dissertation. He read John in Spanish, discussed John's ideas in Italian, chatted casually in French at the residence in the Belgian College, and wrote his thesis in Latin. He also spoke Polish and German, of course. Obviously, he was well prepared for the world stage.

More immediately, graduate work fitted him for academic life in Krakow. After a short period in a parish, he began lecturing at the Jagellonian University, his own alma mater. Father Wojtyła spent the next decade or so in the exhilarating company of youth, keeping up with them intellectually and physically, in debates, discussions, hiking and canoe trips to the mountains, as well as retreats, counselling and advising. Graduate study also fitted him to be a bishop. In 1958 he was consecrated Bishop of Krakow, Archbishop in 1964, and he attended the Second Vatican Council.

In the year of the three popes, Karol Wojtyła was elected to the See of Peter as John Paul II on 16 October 1978. At his first blessing, *Urbi et Orbi*, he spoke to the Italian crowd, many of whom resented the fact that the new pope was not an Italian as usual. So he spoke in Italian to them: 'Even if I cannot express myself well in your – our – language, if I make mistakes, correct me.' The crowd came over to his side immediately and began to cheer.

After his election, John Paul II began to kick against the traces of the bureaucracy in the papal routine. He spoke at length spontaneously, without a prepared script. He followed his human instincts and chance encounters. Once, at a press conference, he spent longer than was scheduled, and as he walked to the exit, someone reminded him that he had omitted to bless the news reporters. So he turned on his heel, shouted an apology back, and blessed them then and there. His experience in the theatre stood to him.

The effect on the world was incalculable. Some credit him with a part in the break-up of Communism. Others cite his contributions to Catholic teaching in the realm of the person and sexuality, his strong opposition to war and violence, his respect for other Christians and other religions, his willingness to admit error and so on. Still more point to his admiration of youth, his sense of the global Church, his impact on politics, his critique of economic systems on right and left, and his uncompromising stance on Gospel values.

In 1981, he was shot in St Peter's Square, an assassination attempt he barely survived. Sharp observers began to notice signs of Parkinson's disease in the mid-1990s. By the new millennium, the decline in John Paul's health was obvious. In March 2005, it became known that the Pope was very sick indeed. A sober crowd gathered quietly in St Peter's Square. It was announced that he had been administered the Sacrament of Anointing. The crowd stayed until he finally passed away, with the world at his bedside, on 2 April 2005. The huge funeral congregation in St Peter's Square called for his speedy canonisation: '*Santo Subito*' ('Saint immediately') they chanted. His successor, Benedict XVI, declared him Blessed on 1 May 2011. On 27 April 2014, Pope Francis declared him Saint.

CHRIST'S COMPASSION FOR THE SICK

Christ's compassion toward the sick and his healings of almost every kind of infirmity are a resplendent sign that 'God has visited his people'.

— CCC, no. 1503, citing Lk 7:16

Jesus came to heal the whole person, body and soul. Mark's Gospel, chapter 2:1-12, relates the following event that illustrates this teaching. Jesus was in a house in Capernaum teaching an overflow crowd. The house was probably a stone dwelling whose walls were coated with plaster. The rooms surrounded an inner courtyard. A roof of reeds and sticks packed with thick clay would have kept out the rain. Opening a hole in the roof would have been relatively easy. Since they could not enter by the door because of the crowd, four men, carrying a paralytic, climbed the stairway that led to the roof. They opened a hole in it and lowered their friend into the area where Jesus was preaching.

Jesus said to the paralysed man, 'Your sins are forgiven' (Mk 2:5). Scripture makes no comment on the man's reaction. But into that spiritual moment a discordant note emerged. Some religious scholars in the group complained inwardly that Jesus was blasphemous because, according to them, only God could forgive sins. Jesus, knowing their thoughts, challenged them: 'Which of these is easier: to say to the paralytic, "Your sins are forgiven" or to say, "Get up, pick up your stretcher and walk"? But to prove to you that the Son of man has authority to forgive sins on earth' – he said to the paralytic – 'I order you: get up, pick up your stretcher, and go off home' (Mk 2:9-11). The man rose and went home. The people glorified God for Christ's healing of soul and body.

The Gospels narrate many other occasions when Jesus healed the sick. While Jesus sometimes simply spoke some words to accomplish a healing, he often touched the afflicted person to bring about the cure. In the Church's Sacrament of the Anointing of the Sick, through the ministry of the priest, it is Jesus who touches the sick to heal them from sin – and sometimes even from physical ailment. His cures were signs of the arrival of the Kingdom of God. The core message of his healings tells us of his plan to conquer sin and death by his dying and rising.

On the Cross, Jesus bore the full weight of evil and removed its power over us. He provided a new meaning for suffering by giving it redemptive power. By his grace we are able to unite our pain to his redemptive passion. Saint Paul witnessed this when he wrote, 'It makes me happy to be suffering for you now, and in my own body to make up all the hardships that still have to be undergone by Christ for the sake of his body, the Church' (Col 1:24).

THE CHURCH CONTINUES CHRIST'S MINISTRY OF HEALING

The Church carries forward Christ's healing ministry in a variety of approaches. Catholic families in countless ways care for family members who are ill. There are numerous inspiring stories of an ageing person who personally ministers to an ailing spouse in cases of Alzheimer's and other illnesses. Caregivers find that faith and prayer mean a great deal to them in these situations.

A multitude of religious orders and congregations have established Catholic hospitals to take care of the physical and spiritual needs of the sick. Church-sponsored hospice care is another form of this ministry of healing. Besides the doctors, nurses and chaplains, there are occasional instances of individuals with the charism (gift) of healing. 'The Holy Spirit gives to some a special charism of healing, so as to make manifest the power of grace of the risen Lord' (CCC, no. 1508).

Millions of believers journey to shrines like the one at Lourdes, often in search of physical cures but always to experience a deepening of faith. The Church requires healing miracles as part of the canonisation process, the procedure for declaring the sainthood of a given person.

Above all, the Church continues Christ's healing ministry in the Sacrament of Anointing of the Sick. Saint James describes its celebration in apostolic times: 'Any one of you who is ill should send for the elders of the church, and they must anoint the sick person with oil in the name of the Lord and pray over him. The prayer of faith will save the sick person and the Lord will raise him up again; and if he has committed any sins, he will be forgiven' (Jas 5:14-15).

A SACRAMENT OF HEALING

The Anointing of the Sick 'is not a sacrament for those only who are at the point of death. Hence, as soon as anyone of the faithful begins to be in danger of death from sickness or old age, the fitting time to receive this sacrament has certainly already arrived.'

– CCC, no. 1514, citing SC, no. 73

The Rite of Anointing tells us there is no need to wait until a person is at the point of death to receive the Sacrament. A careful judgement about the serious nature of the illness is sufficient. The Sacrament may be repeated if the sick person recovers after the anointing but becomes ill once again, or if, during the same illness, the person's condition becomes more serious. A person should be anointed before surgery when a dangerous illness is the reason for the intervention (cf. Rite of Anointing, Introduction, nos. 8–10).

Moreover, 'old people may be anointed if they are in weak condition even though no dangerous illness is present. Sick children may be anointed if they have sufficient use of reason to be comforted by this sacrament ... [The faithful] should be encouraged to ask for the anointing, and, as soon as the time for the anointing comes, to receive it with faith and devotion, not misusing the sacrament by putting it off' (Rite of Anointing, nos. 11, 12, 13).

Only bishops and priests may be ministers of the Sacrament of the Anointing of the Sick. A penitential rite followed by the Liturgy of the Word opens the celebration. Scripture awakens the faith of the sick and family members and friends to pray to Christ for the strength of his Holy Spirit. The priest lays his hands on the head of the sick person. He then proceeds to anoint, with the blessed Oil of the Sick, the forehead and hands of the sick person (in the Roman Rite). He accompanies these acts with the words 'Through this holy anointing may the Lord in his love and mercy help you with the grace of the Holy Spirit. May the Lord who frees you from sin save you and raise you up' (CCC, no. 1513).

For those who are about to depart from this life, the Church offers the person Penance, Anointing of the Sick and the Eucharist as *Viaticum* (food for the journey) given at the end of life. These are 'the sacraments that prepare for our heavenly homeland' (cf. CCC, no. 1525). These rites are highly valued by Catholics as powerful aids to a good death. Since Holy Communion is the effective sign of Christ's Paschal Mystery, it becomes for the recipient the opportunity to unite one's own suffering and dying to that of Christ with the hope of life eternal with him. The special words proper to *Viaticum* are added: 'May the Lord Jesus protect you and lead you to everlasting life. Amen.'

EFFECTS OF THE SACRAMENT

When the Sacrament of Anointing of the Sick is given, the hoped-for effect is that, if it be God's will, the person be physically healed of illness. But even if there is no physical healing, the primary effect of the Sacrament is a spiritual healing by which the sick person receives the Holy Spirit's gift of peace and courage to deal with the difficulties that accompany serious illness or the frailty of old age. The Holy Spirit renews our faith in God and helps us withstand the temptations of the Evil One to be discouraged and despairing in the face of suffering and death. Also, a sick person's sins are forgiven if he or she was not able to go to Confession prior to the celebration of the Sacrament of the Anointing of the Sick.

Another effect of this Sacrament is union with the Passion of Christ. By uniting ourselves more closely with the sufferings of Our Lord, we receive the grace of sharing in the saving work of Christ. In this way, our suffering, joined to the Cross of Christ, contributes to building up the People of God.

This Sacrament also prepares us for our final journey when we depart from this life. The Anointing of the Sick completes our identification with Jesus Christ that was begun at our Baptism. Its grace and power fortify us in our final struggles before we go to the Father's house.

THE IMPORTANCE OF THE SACRAMENT FOR THE COMMUNITY

For some, there is nothing more frustrating than being sick. Sickness runs from annoying inconvenience – like a headache or a common cold – to grave, life-threatening cases involving major surgery or incurable disease. In each case, sickness reminds us of our limitations.

FROM THE CATECHISM

1. When should we receive the Sacrament of the Anointing of the Sick?

The proper time for receiving this holy anointing has certainly arrived when the believer begins to be in danger of death because of illness or old age. Each time a Christian falls seriously ill, he may receive the Anointing of the Sick, and also when, after he has received it, the illness worsens. (CCC, nos. 1528, 1529)

2. Who are the ministers of the Sacrament of the Anointing of the Sick?

Only priests ... and bishops can give the Sacrament of the Anointing of the Sick, using oil blessed by the bishop, or if necessary by the celebrating presbyter [priest or celebrant] himself. (CCC, no. 1530)

3. What are the effects of the Sacrament of the Anointing of the Sick?

The special grace of the Sacrament of the Anointing of the Sick has as its effects:

- the uniting of the sick person to the Passion of Christ, for his own good and that of the whole Church;
- [giving the sick person the strength], peace, and courage to endure in a Christian manner the sufferings of illness or old age;
- [imparting] the forgiveness of sins, if the sick person was not able to obtain it through the sacrament of Penance;
- [providing for] the restoration of health, if it is conducive to the salvation of his soul;
- [helping the sick person in] the preparation for passing over to eternal life. (CCC, no. 1532)

Our reaction to infirmity is to seek alleviation. With a perfect understanding of the human person, Christ has provided the Church from its beginning with a spiritual as well as a corporeal remedy for our illness. We are not just flesh and bone. We are spirit, mind and body.

In a very real sense, the Sacrament of the Anointing of the Sick has a very important community dimension. In any illness, particularly one as we near the end of our lives, we should never have to stand alone. We should not have to face infirmity without the consolation of others. In the New Testament's Letter of St James, the sick person is instructed to call for the presbyters (priests) of the Church for an anointing and prayers.

These presbyters represented the Christian community and its concern for the sick person. Such concern is further highlighted in the 'prayer of faith' that St James said will reclaim the one who is ill – the prayer arising from the community of faith, the Church, gathered around the sick person precisely to invoke the 'name of the Lord'.

The *Catechism of the Catholic Church* reminds us that 'the Anointing of the Sick is a liturgical and communal celebration, whether it takes place in a family home, a hospital or church, for a single sick person or a whole group of sick persons' (CCC, no. 1517).

Increasingly today, there is an effort to bring people together for a communal celebration of this Sacrament, usually in a parish church. Since infirmity and old age constitute legitimate reasons for receiving this Sacrament, a parish can easily provide a setting for a number of parishioners to receive the Sacrament of the Anointing of the Sick regularly. It can serve the purpose of the Sacrament and, at the same time, build up the faith of the community itself.

FOR DISCUSSION

1. How would you describe your reaction to illnesses you have had? What do you expect of caregivers? How have you been moved to pray and seek the spiritual resources of the Church?

2. If you have been present at the Sacrament of Anointing of the Sick, what were your impressions? Why is it important to be aware of the proper time to call the priest?

3. From a faith perspective, what value does an experience of illness have for an individual and for the parish community to which he or she belongs? Why is it important to acknowledge and incorporate those who are sick and dying into the faith community?

DOCTRINAL STATEMENTS

- 'Any one of you who is ill should send for the elders of the church, and they must anoint the sick person with oil in the name of the Lord and pray over him. The prayer of faith will save the sick person and the Lord will raise him up again; and if he has committed any sins, he will be forgiven' (Jas 5:14-15).
- The Sacrament of the Anointing of the Sick is for those who are seriously ill or in danger of death or suffering the difficulties of old age. The Sacrament may be received each time the believer falls seriously ill or an illness worsens (cf. CCC, no. 1529).
- Only priests and bishops may administer the Sacrament of the Anointing of the Sick. This is because one effect of this Sacrament can be the forgiveness of sin. They use Oil of the Sick blessed by the bishop or, in necessity, an oil blessed by the priest.
- The rite of the Anointing of the Sick includes the anointing of the forehead and hands of the sick or other parts of the body accompanied by the liturgical prayer that asks for the grace of the Sacrament.
- The gifts of this Sacrament include uniting the sick person with Christ's Passion, for the person's well-being and that of the Church; strength to endure patiently the sufferings of illness and old age; the forgiveness of sins if the person was unable to receive the Sacrament of Penance; and preparation for the passage to eternal life.

MEDITATION

Good Shepherd Psalm

The sick and the dying of every age have been consoled by the verses of the Shepherd Psalm (Ps 23). They are further inspired by Christ's words, 'I am the good shepherd; I know my own and my own know me … I have come so that they may have life and have it to the full' (Jn 10:14, 10). It is not hard for them to see Jesus as the shepherd of the twenty-third Psalm. The Psalm expresses trust in the divine shepherd so needed when one is ill. 'The Lord is my shepherd; / there is nothing I shall want' (v. 1).

'Fresh and green are the pastures / where he gives me repose' (v. 2). A shepherd leads his sheep to the rough herbage, then to the smoother grass, and then to the sweet grass of the green pastures where they rest. Jesus abides with the sick throughout their rough moments and guides them to peaceful acceptance and an experience of a soul at rest.

'Near restful waters he leads me (v. 2). Sheep are nervous about drinking from running streams. The shepherd often constructs pools of still waters to ease their thirst. Illness breaks the running pace of life, but there is still the need of calming down. Jesus brings the patients an inner stillness that permits the believers to drink of the renewing fountains of his love.

'Though I should walk in the valley of the shadow of death, / no evil would I fear, for you are with me. / Your crook and your staff will give me comfort' (v. 4). In search of better pastures, the shepherd sometimes leads the sheep through dangerous valleys. The sheep may fall into a hole. The shepherd uses the curved part at the top of his staff to gently pull the sheep to safety. Wild dogs and wolves may come to threaten the flock. The shepherd uses the pointed end of his staff to kill them or drive them away. Jesus knows that suffering people are in their own dark valley. Jesus is with them to remove their fears and awaken their hope. There are times that Jesus drives away life-threatening ills through his ministers in the Sacrament of the Anointing of the Sick.

'You have prepared a table before me / … My head you have anointed with oil; my cup is overflowing' (v. 5). In some pastures there is so much rough herbage that the shepherd must harvest the edible grasses and place these on table-like stones from which the sheep may dine. Jesus himself is the Bread of Life who comes to his friends in pain. Communion for the sick is one of Christ's most consoling gifts. When the sheep have wounds caused by thorns, the shepherd anoints them with oil. When they have a fever, the shepherd bathes their heads in cool water. With holy oil Jesus anoints the sick.

'In the Lord's own house shall I dwell / for length of days unending' (v. 6). The shepherd knows the sheep need him to guard their home. Jesus says he is the gate of the sheepfold (the enclosure where they live). In biblical times the shepherd served as the gate to the sheepfold. He was the living gate, guarding them with his body. To enter the community of Christ the beloved, both the sick and the healthy must enter through his body that will guard them. People in suffering and pain are disposed to the faith that sees these truths. Christ is their guardian.

PRAYER

Lord Jesus Christ, you chose to share our human nature,
to redeem all people, and to heal the sick.
Look with compassion upon your servants whom we have
  anointed in your name with this holy oil for the healing of
  their body and spirit.
Support them with your power, comfort them with
  your protection,
and give them the strength to fight against evil.
Since you have given them a share in your own passion,
help them to find hope in suffering,
for you are Lord for ever and ever. Amen.

— From Pastoral Care of the Sick

[I was] sick and you visited me.

— Mt 25:36

Through this holy anointing
may the Lord in his love and mercy help you
with the grace of the Holy Spirit.
Amen.

May the Lord who frees you from sin
save you and raise you up.
Amen.

— From the Rite of Anointing of the Sick

From the beginning, Christians have put care for the sick high on
their agenda, knowing that in this they are serving Christ himself.

— SGN, 55

20 HOLY ORDERS

THE SACRAMENT OF HOLY ORDERS IS AT THE SERVICE OF THE COMMUNION OF THE CHURCH – CCC, NOS. 1533–1600

FATHER JOHN SULLIVAN SJ: A SIMPLE PRIEST

One of John Sullivan's biographers once complained that there was very little material for him to work from. Indeed, Sullivan wrote next to nothing, only a couple of prefaces for biographies. Even his personal letters were factual, brief and perfunctory. His sermons and retreat talks were largely taken from the spiritual writers he read. When he delivered his homilies and conferences though, they carried so much of his own personal sincerity that they were intensely persuasive. This detail is reminiscent of the life of an earlier saintly priest from another country and century. Saint John Vianney, the Curé of Ars, used to write out his Sunday sermons patiently on the vesting bench in his sacristy, word for word from the sermons of St Alphonsus Liguori. But when John Vianney preached, these words were invested with so much of his own holiness that whole congregations would repent.

John Sullivan was born in Dublin, of Cork parents, on 8 May 1861. His father, Edward Sullivan, was a Protestant, a highly successful barrister who was appointed Lord Chancellor. His mother, Elizabeth Baily, was from a distinguished Catholic family, with a sister married to the founder of the *Cork Examiner*. As a mixed marriage, the couple had come to an arrangement, common enough in the circumstances, that the female children would be brought up Catholic and the boys raised as Protestants. The Sullivans had five children, Anne, Edward, Robert, William and John, the youngest.

John was educated in Portora Royal School in Enniskillen for six years and then studied Classics at Trinity College for four more, graduating in 1883. He was a talented scholar at Classics, but did not pursue an academic career, opting for Law instead. He entered Trinity Law School, but interrupted his Dublin studies in 1885. That was the same year his father died suddenly of a heart attack. Subsequently, John moved to London, studied for the English Bar in Lincoln's Inns, and became a barrister in 1888.

As a young man he travelled widely, often on foot, touring a number of countries. The Orthodox Monastery at Mount Athos in Greece was one of his destinations, as were many of the sites of classical antiquity with which he was familiar from his studies. Many of these places featured in the reminiscences told to friends and colleagues in later years. He was an avid cyclist and engaging companion, and a frequent guest at fashionable tables.

Thus it was quite a surprise when, in 1896, he was received into the Catholic Church at the Farm Street London Jesuit Church, and another surprise when he joined the Jesuits as a novice on 7 September 1900. His friends and family had noticed signs during his four years of Catholic lay life, but it was in hindsight that they could see their meaning. For one thing, he had been extraordinarily recollected and prayerful, and he had involved himself in charitable activities and discarded his fashionable clothes.

During his two years of Jesuit novitiate and five years of studies, the forty-year-old Sullivan must have found it hard to fit in with the young men who had come straight from school, but he never complained of this difficulty. His companions saw him as genial, kind and humble, certainly pious, deep and thoughtful. He had a gentle sense of humour and a genuine empathy for those in difficulty. It was later that the realisation slowly dawned that they were dealing with a holy man.

Father John Sullivan was ordained on Sunday, 28 July 1907, and appointed to the teaching staff of Clongowes Wood College in County Kildare to teach Greek, Latin and religion. He appears to have lacked the ability, or perhaps the will, to exercise the necessary discipline to direct a class of energetic youths. One of his Jesuit companions remarked: 'It would appear to me as if his vocation was not to put boys through examinations, but by making a divine and lasting impression on them to help them on towards their entrance examination for the next world.'

The boys respected Fr Sullivan for his honesty, his hard work and care for them. They also liked his sense of humour. He was appointed spiritual director for the students, and in that role he was valued and indeed venerated by the boys. The students looked for his advice and consolation, his counselling and even his conversation. More than anything, they crowded to him for the sacrament of penance, or Confession. Through the years, he made a deep impression upon the students, probably summed up in the words of one: 'He was, and is for me, the embodiment of an ideal of Christ-like kindliness and other worldliness, the like of which I do not expect to meet again.'

Personally, Fr Sullivan was an abstemious eater, often satisfying himself with only a dish of rice for lunch and bread and tea for the other meals. He characteristically dressed shabbily, and in all respects lived frugally. His room was bare and hardly heated, his bedding thin. Luggage for any journey was carried in his pockets. He spent much time in prayer, sometimes clearly audible in his room, other times in the chapel.

While at Clongowes, Fr Sullivan ministered at the people's church at the College, which served the inhabitants of the district around Clane. People told of his power of healing, and stories of cures spread far and wide. He was indefatigable in his attendance to the sick, his attention to the poor, his devotion to the sacraments and his fidelity to prayer.

Father Sullivan was much in demand for religious retreats, yet he was by no means an engaging speaker. His demeanour was tense and nervous, his voice sombre, with no variation of pitch. He did not elaborate on the Scripture, and for an educated barrister, his narrative style was, by all accounts, awkward. He was, however, listened to with rapt attention, and, what is more, heeded, for his words seemed to come with authority.

Except for a five-year interlude (1919–24) as Rector in Rathfarnham in the foothills of the Dublin Mountains, Fr Sullivan spent all of his priestly life in Clongowes. After his Rathfarnham appointment, he returned to the college for the remaining years of his life. Early in 1933, he became seriously ill with severe intestinal pain, was removed to hospital and operated upon. He died two days later on 19 February 1933.

SACRAMENTS AT THE SERVICE
OF COMMUNION

Holy Orders and Matrimony belong to the Sacraments at the Service of
Communion. This means they are primarily directed toward the salvation
of others. The recipients of these Sacraments grow in holiness through their
service to others. We reflect on Holy Orders in this chapter and Matrimony
in the next one.

LOOK AT CHRIST, OUR HIGH PRIEST

All eyes ... were fixed on him.

– Lk 4:20

Luke's Gospel reports the appearance of Jesus at a synagogue service in
Nazareth early in his public ministry, his first visit since the beginning of
his public ministry. The synagogue was a simple, unadorned meeting space
for prayer and religious instruction. After a prayer, Jesus was handed a scroll
on which was written Chapter 61 of Isaiah the prophet. He read these
words: The spirit of the Lord is on me, / for he has anointed me / to bring
the good news to the afflicted. / He has sent me to proclaim liberty to
captives, / sight to the blind, / to let the oppressed go free, / to proclaim a
year of favour from the Lord' (Lk 4:18-19).

He rolled up the scroll and sat down. There was a quiet pause as the eyes
of all looked intently at Jesus. He said, 'This text is being fulfilled today
even while you are listening' (Lk 4:21). Jesus presented himself to them as
filled with the Spirit, consecrated and anointed to bring the Good News to
the poor. From the moment of Jesus' conception in the womb of Mary until
his Resurrection, he was filled with the Holy Spirit. In biblical language, he
was anointed by the Holy Spirit and thus established by God the Father as
our high priest.

As Risen Lord, he remains our high priest. 'His power to save those who come to God through him is absolute, since he lives for ever to intercede for them. Such is the high priest that met our need, holy, innocent and uncontaminated, set apart from sinners' (Heb 7:25-26). While all the baptised share in Christ's priesthood, the ministerial priesthood shares this through the Sacrament of Holy Orders in a special way.

HOLY ORDERS: BISHOP, PRIEST, DEACON

The Church adopted the term *order* from its use in the Roman Empire, where it referred to a governing group. In the Sacrament of Holy Orders, there are three degrees or 'orders': bishop, priest and deacon. The rite of ordination is the sacramental act that makes this possible. Ordination 'confers a gift of the Holy Spirit that permits the exercise of a "sacred power" … which can come only from Christ himself through the Church' (CCC, no. 1538).

The first priest figure to appear in the Old Testament is Melchizedek, who offered a sacrifice of bread and wine on behalf of the patriarch Abraham (cf. Gn 14:18-20). He symbolised the permanence of priesthood: 'You are a priest forever, in the line of Melchizedek.' (Ps 110:4). God also chose Aaron and his sons to be priests (cf. Ex 28:1ff.) and designated the tribe of Levi for liturgical service. They acted on behalf of the people and offered gifts and sacrifices for sins. They proclaimed God's Word and led people to communion with him through sacrifices and prayers.

But these priests were unable to provide the fullness of salvation or definitive sanctification for the people. Only the sacrifice of Jesus Christ could bring this about. The priesthood of Melchizedek, Aaron and the Levites prefigured the priesthood of Christ, as is seen in consecration prayers for the ordination of bishops, priests and deacons.

The priesthood of the Old Testament found its perfect fulfilment in the priesthood of Jesus Christ, who is the one mediator between God and us. Jesus' sacrifice of himself on the Cross was a priestly act of perfect self-offering accepted by the Father and culminating in his Resurrection from the dead so that, as Risen Lord and High Priest, he continues to offer salvation to all.

By Baptism, all the members of the Church share in Christ's holy priesthood. It is called 'the common priesthood of the faithful' because the entire Church shares in it. To build up this priesthood, Christ gives to his Church the ordained ministries of bishops, priests and deacons through the Sacrament of Holy Orders. Only the ordained bishop and priest may be ministers of Confirmation (or Chrismation), the Eucharist, the Sacrament of Penance and Reconciliation and the Sacrament of the Anointing of the Sick. Only bishops may ordain deacons, priests and other bishops. 'The ministerial priesthood differs in essence from the common priesthood of the faithful because it confers a sacred power for the service of the faithful. The ordained ministers exercise their service for the People of God by teaching (*munus docendi*), divine worship (*munus liturgicum*) and pastoral governance (*munus regendi*)' (CCC, no. 1592). Deacons in the Latin Church can baptise and witness the Sacrament of Marriage, as do priests and bishops.

The ordained bishop and priest serve the Church in the person of Christ as head of the Body. 'Through the ordained ministry, especially that of bishops and priests, the presence of Christ as head of the Church is made visible in the midst of the community of believers' (CCC, no. 1549). The Sacrament does not preserve the ordained from weakness and sin, but the Holy Spirit guarantees that the minister's sin does not impede the effectiveness of the Sacrament and its graces. The ordained are called to a holiness of life and an attitude of humility that conforms them to Christ whose priesthood they share. The priest acts not only in the person of Christ, the Head of the Church, but also in the name of the Church when presenting to God the prayer of the Church, especially in the Eucharist.

ORDINATION

Let everyone revere the deacons as Jesus Christ, the
bishop as image of the Father, and the presbyters as
the senate of God and the assembly of the apostles. For
without them, one cannot speak of the Church.

– CCC, no. 1554, citing St Ignatius of Antioch, Ad. Trall. 3, 1

Bishops

By ordination to the episcopacy, bishops receive the fullness of the Sacrament of Holy Orders and become successors of the Apostles. Through this Sacrament, a bishop belongs to the college of bishops and serves as the visible head or parish priest of the local church entrusted to his care. As a college, the bishops have care and concern for the apostolic mission of all the churches in union with and under the authority of the pope – the head of the college of bishops, the Bishop of Rome and the successor of St Peter.

Priests

By ordination, 'priests are united with the bishops in [priestly] dignity and at the same time depend on them in the exercise of their pastoral functions; they are called to be the bishops' prudent co-workers' (CCC, no. 1595). With the bishop, priests form a *presbyteral* (priestly) community and assume with him the pastoral mission for a particular parish. The bishop appoints priests to the pastoral care of parishes and to other diocesan ministries. The priest promises obedience to the bishop in service to God's people.

Deacons

The title *deacon* comes from the Greek word *diakonia* meaning 'servant'. A deacon has a special attachment to the bishop in the tasks of service and is configured to Christ, the Deacon – or Servant – of all (cf. CCC, nos. 1569–1570).

'There are two degrees of ministerial participation in the priesthood of Christ: the episcopacy and the presbyterate. The diaconate is intended to help and serve them' (CCC, no. 1554). The three degrees of the Sacrament of Holy Orders – bishop, priest and deacon – are all conferred by ordination.

Deacons receive the Sacrament of Holy Orders from a bishop and are ordained not to the ministerial priesthood but to the ministry of service. Through ordination the deacon is conformed to Christ, who came to serve, not to be served. In the Latin Church, deacons may baptise, proclaim the Gospel, preach the homily, assist the bishop or priest in the celebration of the Eucharist, assist at and bless marriages and preside at funerals. They dedicate themselves to charitable endeavours, which was their ministerial role in New Testament times.

Whether they are involved in the Church's liturgical or pastoral life or in her social and charitable endeavours, deacons are 'strengthened by the imposition of hands that has come down from the Apostles. They would be more closely bound to the altar and their ministry would be made more fruitful through the sacramental grace of the diaconate' (AG, 16, no. 6).

Since the Second Vatican Council, the Latin Church has restored the diaconate as a permanent rank of the hierarchy. Now, diaconate as a permanent office may also be conferred on both married and unmarried men. The Eastern Churches have always retained it. Seminarians preparing for priesthood have always been ordained to the diaconate before ordination to priesthood.

It was left up to National Conferences of Bishops to decide whether or not to restore the diaconate in their region. The Irish Bishops petitioned the Holy See for permission, and accordingly they drew up norms for the formation of permanent deacons:

EXTRACT FROM
THE PERMANENT DIACONATE: NATIONAL DIRECTORY AND NORMS FOR IRELAND 2006

In the course of the past thirty years, large numbers of lay faithful have become actively involved in the apostolate in Ireland, not only in those ministries which were specifically renewed by Pope Paul VI in his apostolic letter *Ministeria quaedam*, but in a wide range of other apostolic activities, including catechetics, baptismal preparation, bereavement counselling, marriage preparation and school management. The intention to restore the permanent diaconate, while it refers to an ordained ministry, will be more correctly understood and more enriching for the life of the Church in Ireland if it is seen as being in partnership with this great diversity of charisms and services, as well as being in communion with the other orders of the hierarchy just as it was in the Christian communities of the Apostolic period.

Permanent deacons are not 'substitute priests', nor are they intended to take the place of religious, or of lay ministers … The diaconate, like the sacred orders of the episcopate and the presbyterate, has very clear theological roots in the person and the ministry of Jesus.

Jesus reminds the disciples that, although he is Lord and Master (Jn 13:13), he is among them as 'the one who serves' (Lk 22:27). His service is first and foremost to his Father, and to the truth. This is reflected in his ministry of preaching. His service is also directed particularly towards those who are oppressed or excluded. He incorporates in his own person the characteristics of the faithful servant of the Lord, who 'bring[s] fair justice', who serves 'the cause of right', and who does not 'break the crushed reed', nor 'snuff the faltering wick' (cf. Is 42:1-7).

There is no dichotomy or conflict between Jesus' service of the truth and his compassion for the poor and the oppressed. As he explained to the Jews, it is the truth that liberates (cf. Jn 8:32). At the core of that truth is the love of God, revealed in the person of Jesus who, as St Paul tells us, 'being in the form of God, did not count equality with God something to be grasped. But he emptied himself, taking the form of a slave' (Phil 2:6-7).

Jesus insisted that service would be a distinguishing characteristic of his disciples (cf. Lk 22:16). Just as he instructed the twelve to celebrate the Eucharist in memory of him, so also he clearly explained to them that his washing of their feet was an example to them of how they should act (cf. Jn 13:12-15). It is not purely a coincidence that the priestly ministry of offering sacrifice and the diaconal ministry of washing feet both have an important resonance, and indeed their model and perfection in the Lord's Supper which itself is inseparably linked with the Cross of Jesus.

THE ESSENTIAL RITE OF HOLY ORDERS

The essential rite of the sacrament of Holy Orders for all three degrees consists in the bishop's imposition of hands on the head of the ordinand and in the bishop's specific consecratory prayer asking God for the outpouring of the Holy Spirit and his gifts proper to the ministry to which the candidate is being ordained.

– CCC, no. 1573

The additional rites surrounding this core ordination rite vary greatly among differing liturgical traditions, but all have in common the expression of aspects of sacramental grace. The only valid minister of ordination is a bishop. Now ascended to the Father, Christ continues to guide the Church through the bishops, who confer this Sacrament of apostolic ministry and hand on the gift of the Holy Spirit.

WHO MAY BE ORDAINED?

Only a baptised man may be ordained in the Sacrament of Holy Orders. Jesus Christ chose men to become part of the Twelve. Throughout his ministry, his attitude toward women was different from the culture, and he courageously broke with it. For example, he did not hesitate to speak with the Samaritan woman even though custom forbade it (cf. Jn 4:4-42). But it was only men whom he chose to be the Twelve Apostles and the foundation of the ministerial priesthood.

Although after the Ascension, Mary occupied a privileged place in the little circle gathered in the Upper Room, she was not called to enter the college of the Twelve at the time of the election of Matthias. The Apostles continued Christ's practice and so, too, did their successors through the centuries.

The Church has the power to determine the way in which the Sacraments are to be celebrated, but she has no ability to change the essential aspects established by the Lord Jesus. Sacramental signs are natural, but they also carry a divine meaning. Just as the Eucharist is not only a communal meal, but also makes present the saving sacrifice of the Lord Jesus, so too ministerial priesthood is more than pastoral service: it ensures the continuity of the ministry Christ entrusted to the Apostles.

The priesthood has a sacramental nature. The priest is a sign of what is happening. Sacramental signs represent what they signify by a natural resemblance. This resemblance is as true for persons as for things. When the priest acts in the person of Christ, he takes on the role of Christ, to the point of being his representative. He is a sign of what is happening and must be a sign that is recognisable, which the faithful can see with ease.

An image used to explain this reality talks of a priest as an 'icon' of Christ. An icon is a religious painting that is considered to make present the mystery of salvation or the saint it depicts. To say a priest is an icon of Christ means, then, that a priest is not just a reminder or image of Christ but is also a real means by which a person can be touched by Christ. Because Christ is a man, it is fitting that a priest as the icon of Christ should also be a man.

Another reason why the Church understands that ordination is reserved to men is the recognition of the priest's responsibility to reflect Christ as the Bridegroom of the Church. This image and understanding can be reflected most truly only when the priest is a man.

The teaching that priestly ordination is to be reserved to men alone has been preserved by the constant and universal Tradition of the Church (cf. Sacred Congregation for the Doctrine of the Faith, *Declaration on the Admission of Women to the Ministerial Priesthood* [*Inter Insigniores*], nos. 9–10, 13, 20–21, 26–27). Saint John Paul II reaffirmed this teaching in these words: 'In order that all doubt may be removed, I declare that the Church has no authority whatsoever to confer priestly ordination on women and that this judgement is to be definitively held by all the Church's faithful' (*On Reserving Priestly Ordination to Men Alone* [*Ordinatio Sacerdotalis*], no. 4). In that same document, the pope underlined the incomparable achievements of women for the benefit of the People of God:

> The New Testament and the whole history of the Church give ample evidence of the presence in the Church of women, true disciples, witnesses to Christ in the family and in society, as well as in total consecration to the service of God and of the Gospel. 'By defending the dignity of women and their vocation, the Church has shown honour and gratitude for those women who, faithful to the Gospel, have shared in every age in the apostolic mission of the whole People of God. They are the holy martyrs, virgins and mothers of families, who bravely bore witness to their faith and passed on the Church's faith and tradition by bringing up their children in the spirit of the Gospel.' (*On Reserving Priestly Ordination to Men Alone*, no. 3, citing *On the Dignity and Vocation of Women* [*Mulieris Dignitatem*], no. 27)

Ordination to the priesthood is always a call and a gift from God. Christ reminded his Apostles that they needed to ask the Lord of the harvest to send labourers into the harvest. Those who seek priesthood respond generously to God's call using the words of the prophet, 'Here am I, send

FROM THE CATECHISM

1. What does the prayer from the Byzantine Rite say about the spiritual gift a priest receives at ordination?

The prayer reads: Lord, fill with the gift of the Holy Spirit, him whom you have deigned to raise to the rank of the priesthood, that he may be worthy to stand without reproach before your altar, to proclaim the Gospel of your kingdom, to fulfil the ministry of your word of truth, to offer you spiritual gifts and sacrifices, to renew your people by the bath of rebirth. (CCC, no. 1587)

2. What is the essential rite of ordination?

The sacrament of Holy Orders is conferred by the laying on of hands by the bishop followed by a solemn prayer of consecration asking God to grant the man being ordained the graces of the Holy Spirit required for his ministry. (CCC, no. 1597)

3. What does it mean to say that the priest acts 'in the person of Christ'?

In the ecclesial service of the ordained minister, it is Christ himself who is present to his Church as Head of the Body, Shepherd of his flock, high priest of the redemptive sacrifice, Teacher of Truth. This is what the Church means by saying that the priest, by virtue of the sacrament of Holy Orders, acts *in persona Christi capitis* (in the person of Christ the head). (CCC, no. 1548)

me' (Is 6:8). This call from God can be recognised and understood from the daily signs that disclose his will to those in charge of discerning the vocation of the candidate.

When God chooses men to share in the ordained priesthood of Christ, he moves and helps them by his grace. At the same time, he entrusts the bishop with the task of calling suitable and approved candidates and of consecrating them by a special seal of the Holy Spirit to the ministry of God and of the Church (*Admission to Candidacy for Priesthood*, 5).

All candidates for ordination in the Latin Church – with the exception of permanent deacons, who can be married at the time of their ordination – are chosen from among those who intend to remain celibate 'for the sake of the kingdom of Heaven' (Mt 19:12). Their celibacy is a sign of their intention to imitate Christ's own celibacy and to serve God in the Church's ministry with an undivided heart. In some cases, married clergy of other Christian churches who convert to Catholicism have been admitted to Holy Orders. In the Eastern Churches, only the bishops must be celibate. Priests and deacons may be married.

EFFECTS OF THE SACRAMENT

This Sacrament configures the bishop and priest to Christ as the Head of the Church in Christ's threefold office of priest, prophet and king. This Sacrament configures the deacon to Christ as servant.

The Sacrament of Holy Orders, like that of Baptism and Confirmation, confers an indelible or permanent character on the recipient. This means that this Sacrament cannot be received again. The indelible character is a reminder to the bishop, priest or deacon that the vocation and mission he received on the day of his ordination marks him permanently. Like Baptism and Confirmation, which also confer a permanent character, Holy Orders is never repeated.

A bishop is given the grace to teach in the name of Christ, to sanctify the Church through the celebration of the Sacraments, to guide, govern, and defend the Church and to be a sign of the unity of the Church.

A priest is given the grace to proclaim the Gospel and preach, to celebrate the Sacraments (except Holy Orders) and to shepherd the people entrusted to him.

A deacon in the Latin Church is ordained to proclaim the Gospel and preach, to baptise, to assist the bishop or priest in the celebration of the Eucharist, to assist at and bless marriages, to preside at funerals and to serve the community through works of charity.

THE SPIRITUALITY OF THE PRIEST

[Priests] should be taught to seek Christ. This along with the *quaerere Deum* [the search for God] is a classical theme of Christian spirituality. It has a specific application in the context of the calling of the Apostles. When John tells the story of the way the first two disciples followed Christ, he highlights this 'search'. It is Jesus himself who asks the question: 'What do you want?' And the two reply, 'Rabbi, where do you live?' Jesus replies, 'Come and see'. '[S]o they went and saw where he lived, and stayed with him that day' (Jn 1:38-39). In a certain sense, the spiritual life of the person who is preparing for priesthood is dominated by this search; by it and by the 'finding' of the Master, to follow him, to be in communion with him. So inexhaustible is the mystery of the imitation of Christ and the sharing in his life that this 'seeking' will have to continue throughout the priest's life and ministry. Likewise this 'finding' the Master will have to continue in order to bring him to others, or rather in order to excite in others the desire to seek out the Master. But all this becomes possible if it is proposed to others as a living 'experience', an experience that is worthwhile sharing. This was the path followed by Andrew to lead his brother Simon to Jesus. The evangelist John writes that Andrew first found his brother Simon, and said to him, '"We have found the Messiah" – which means the Christ' and brought him to Jesus (Jn 1:41-42). And so Simon too will be called, as an Apostle, to follow the Messiah: 'Jesus looked at him and said, "So you are Simon son of John; you shall be called Cephas" – which means Rock' (Jn 1:42) ... An essential element of spiritual formation is the prayerful and meditated reading of the Word of God, a humble and loving listening to him who speaks ... Familiarity with the Word of God will make conversion easy, not only in the sense of detaching us from evil, so as to adhere to the good, but also in the sense of nourishing our heart with the thoughts of God, so that faith (as a response to the word) becomes our new basis for judging and evaluating persons and things, events and problems. (St John Paul II, *I Will Give You Shepherds* [*Pastores Dabo Vobis*], nos. 46–47)

FOR DISCUSSION

1. What qualities of a priest serve to draw people to them? What are a number of ways that the lay faithful and priests support each other for the good of families and the mission of the Church?
2. How can faith be strengthened by the effective preaching of priests and deacons? How can faith be strengthened through the ministry of priests as confessors?
3. What could you do to foster vocations to the priesthood? How could you also foster vocations to the permanent diaconate?

DOCTRINAL STATEMENTS

- Through Baptism all the members of the Church share in the priesthood of Christ. This is known as the 'common priesthood of the faithful'.
- Through Holy Orders there is another participation in Christ's priesthood, the ministerial priesthood of bishop and priest. This differs in essence from the common priesthood because it confers a sacred power for the service of the faithful.
- The ordained ministry occurs in three degrees or orders: bishop, priest and deacon. These ministries are essential for the life of the Church.
- Bishops receive the fullness of the Sacrament of Holy Orders. They are the chief teachers, sanctifiers and shepherds in their dioceses.
- 'Priests are united with the bishops in priestly dignity and at the same time depend on them in the exercise of their pastoral functions; they are called to be the bishops' prudent co-workers' (CCC, no. 1595). With the bishop, priests form a presbyteral (priestly) community and assume with him the pastoral mission for a particular parish.
- Deacons receive the Sacrament of Holy Orders, but not the ministerial priesthood. Through ordination, the deacon is conformed to Christ, who came to serve, not to be served. Deacons in the Latin Church may baptise, read the Gospel, preach the homily, assist the bishop or priest in the celebration of the Eucharist, assist at and bless marriages and preside at funerals. They dedicate themselves to charitable endeavours, which was their ministerial role in New Testament times.

- 'The essential rite of the Sacrament of Holy Orders for all three degrees consists in the bishop's imposition of hands on the head of the ordinand [man to be ordained] and in the bishop's specific consecratory prayer' (CCC, no. 1573). Ordination confers a permanent sacramental character.
- Only men may be ordained.
- Normally in the Western Church, ordination to priesthood is conferred only on those men who freely promise lifelong celibacy.
- Only bishops may confer the Sacrament of Holy Orders in the three degrees.

MEDITATION

Priests should, therefore, occupy their position of leadership as men who do not seek the things that are their own but the things that are Jesus Christ's (cf. 1 Jn 4:1). They should unite their efforts with those of the lay faithful and conduct themselves among them after the example of the Master, who came ... 'not to be served but to serve, and to give his life as a ransom for many' (Mt 20:28). Priests are to be sincere in their appreciation and promotion of lay people's dignity and of the special role the laity have to play in the Church's mission. They should also have an unfailing respect for the just liberty which belongs to everyone in civil society. They should be willing to listen to lay people, give brotherly consideration to their wishes, and recognise their experience and competence in the different fields of human activity. In this way they will be able to recognise along with them the signs of the times. (PO, no. 9)

The ministerial priesthood of bishops and priests and the common priesthood of all the faithful participate in the one priesthood of Christ, each in its own proper way. The two priesthoods complement each other and are ordered to each other while differing essentially. In what sense? The common priesthood of the faithful is exercised by the unfolding of baptismal grace through a life of faith, hope and charity, a life according to the Holy Spirit. The ministerial priesthood is at the service of the common priesthood by unfolding the baptismal grace of all Christians (cf. CCC, no. 1547).

The members of the common priesthood, among other things, are encouraged 'to share their priests' anxieties and help them as far as possible by prayer and active work so that they may be better able to overcome difficulties and carry out their duties with greater success' (PO, no. 9).

PRAYER

May the tribute of my humble ministry be pleasing to you,
   Holy Trinity.
Grant that the sacrifice which I – unworthy as I am –
have offered in the presence of your majesty may be acceptable
   to you.
Through your mercy may it bring forgiveness to me
and to all for whom I have offered it, through Christ our Lord
Amen.

                     – *Placeat* – from Priests' Prayers After Mass,
                                  Amiens sacramentary
                                      (ninth century)

You are a priest forever, in the line of Melchizedek.

                                         – Ps 110:4

Holy Orders is the sacrament through which the mission entrusted by Jesus to his apostles is continued in the Church until the end of time. It is the sacrament of apostolic ministry.

                                         – SGN, 56

21 THE SACRAMENT OF MARRIAGE

MARRIAGE IS A SACRAMENT AT THE SERVICE OF COMMUNION – CCC, NOS. 1601–1666

A MARRIED MAN: GOD'S SERVANT ABOVE ALL

Saint Thomas More was born in London on 7 February 1478, to a middle-class family. His father, John More, was a knight and local judge. As a young boy, Thomas was placed in the service of the Archbishop of Canterbury, John Morton – who was also Chancellor of England. More went on to study at Oxford University and then to study Law in London. He mastered Greek and enjoyed the company of important figures of the Renaissance culture such as Desiderius Erasmus.

His attraction to a deeper spirituality led him to a close relationship with the Franciscans at Greenwich and with the London Carthusians, another religious community with whom he lived for a time. Called to marriage, More wed Jane Colt in 1505. They had four children before Jane died in 1511. After her death, Thomas married Alice Middleton, a widow. Their home was open to their entire family, friends and many acquaintances. More continued his quest for virtue and union with Christ while fostering the faith of his family.

He was elected to Parliament in 1504. This began a political career that saw him knighted in 1521, elected Speaker of the House of Commons in 1523, and finally made Lord Chancellor of England on 25 October 1529, the first layman to hold the position. King Henry VIII, reigning at that time, was desperate to bear a male heir to the throne. Blaming his wife, Queen Catherine of Aragon, for their lack of a son, Henry VIII sought an annulment so that he might marry Anne Boleyn instead, whom he had had his eye on for quite some time. Unable to receive the declaration from Pope Clement VII, the king formally broke from the Catholic Church and declared himself the Supreme Head of the Church of England. If Rome would not grant him an annulment, his own church would. On 15 May 1532, all the English bishops (save St John Fisher) submitted to the king as their new head. The following day, St Thomas More resigned as Chancellor.

In 1534, the English Parliament passed the Act of Succession, which acknowledged the offspring of King Henry VIII and Anne Boleyn, rather than the daughter born to Queen Catherine, as the true heir to the English throne. The nobility and clergy were called to ascribe to an oath upholding the act, and as one of the most respected laymen in the country, so was More. However, More chose to uphold the indissolubility of marriage and refused to take the oath. Even faced with death, St Thomas More would not act against his conscience. As a result, on 1 July 1535, St Thomas More was tried in Westminster Hall and convicted of high treason. On 6 July he was led to execution outside the Tower of London. In his final words before being beheaded, he referred to himself as 'the king's good servant, and God's first'. As a martyr who died for his faith, St Thomas More was beatified by Pope Leo XIII in 1886. He was later canonised by Pope Pius XI in 1935.

In this text we cite the stories of other married people – such as John Boyle O'Reilly, Frederic Ozanam, Maria and Luigi Quattrochi, Edmund Rice, Margaret Ball and Francis Taylor – from the viewpoint of various teachings witnessed in their lives. God's grace blessed them with the faith and virtues that flourished in the marital state. In turn, married people have enriched the life of the Church by their faith and love and by the children whom they have raised and formed in the Christian tradition. Marriage is a Sacrament at the Service of Communion.

GOD IS THE AUTHOR OF MARRIAGE

*The vocation to marriage is written in the very nature
of man and woman as they came from the hand of the
Creator. Marriage is not a purely human institution
despite the many variations it may have undergone
through the centuries in different cultures, social structures
and spiritual attitudes.*

– CCC, no. 1603

Sacred Scripture begins with the creation and union of man and woman and ends with 'the marriage of the Lamb' (Rv 19:7, 9). Scripture often refers to marriage, its origin and purpose, the meaning God gave to it and its renewal in the covenant made by Jesus with his Church.

God created man and woman out of love and commanded them to imitate his love in their relations with each other. Man and woman were created for each other. 'It is not right that the man should be alone. I shall make him a helper ... and they become one flesh' (Gn 2:18; 24). Woman and man are equal in human dignity, and in marriage both are united in an unbreakable bond.

But fidelity to God's plan for the unity and indissolubility of marriage developed gradually among the people of ancient Israel under God's providential guidance. The patriarchs and kings practised polygamy, and Moses permitted divorce. Jesus later cited this case as a toleration of human hardness of heart and taught God's plan for marriage from the beginning (cf. Mt 19:8). It was the prophets of ancient Israel who prepared for Jesus' renewal of God's plan for marriage in their insistence that the permanent and exclusive fidelity of marriage illustrates the unending fidelity of God to his covenant with Israel and his will that Israel be faithful to him alone (cf., e.g., Hos 3 and Ez 16:59-63).

The books of Ruth and Tobit witness the ideals of marriage. They describe the fidelity and tenderness that should exist between the spouses. The Song of Solomon pictures a human love that mirrors God's love, which 'no flood can quench' (cf. Song 8:6-7).

THE UNDERSTANDING OF MARRIAGE IN CONTEMPORARY SOCIETY

There are attempts by some in contemporary society to change the definition or understanding of what exactly constitutes marriage. Efforts to gain approval for and acceptance of same-sex unions as marriages are examples. While the Church clearly teaches that discrimination against any group of people is wrong, efforts to make cohabitation, domestic partnerships, same-sex unions and polygamous unions equal to marriage are misguided and also wrong. The Church and her members need to continue to be a strong and clear voice in protecting an understanding of marriage, which is rooted in natural law and revealed in God's law.

STATEMENT OF THE IRISH EPISCOPAL CONFERENCE
WHY MARRIAGE MATTERS, 2010

We rejoice that so many couples today are living their marital commitment with fidelity. In their daily lives they bear witness to the beauty, goodness and truth of marriage. We also recognise that couples today face many challenges to building and sustaining a strong marriage. Many couples struggle to balance home and work responsibilities; others struggle with serious economic and social burdens. Some feel isolated from wider family support or overwhelmed by the challenges of parenting.

Other challenges arise from developments in our society which undermine the very meaning and purpose of marriage. Lack of confidence in our ability to make long-term commitments and a more casual approach to sexual relationships can make commitment to marriage and the family a more challenging prospect for couples today.

There is also a disturbing tendency today to see marriage as a purely private matter, something which is about the personal satisfaction of the individual rather than the mutual enrichment of the couple and of society.

Changes in the law can also impact on our attitude to marriage. Today, advocacy for the legal recognition of same-sex relationships presents a new challenge to our understanding of marriage and its unique role in society … This is not compatible with seeing the family based on marriage as the necessary basis of the social order and as indispensable to the welfare of the Nation and the State. Nor does it 'guard with special care the institution of Marriage, on which the Family is founded' (Art. 41.3.1, The Irish Constitution) …

The Church upholds the human dignity of homosexual persons and the duty to treat all persons with respect, compassion and sensitivity. All members of the Christian community, including people of homosexual orientation, are called to holiness of life which includes the virtue of chastity. The Church encourages all persons to have chaste friendships. Whether it develops between persons of the same or opposite sex, friendship represents a great good for all. For everyone in the Christian community, the mercy and love of God in the Sacraments and prayer are constantly available. Even when we fall short of our Christian ideals for sexual love in marriage, they help to renew and strengthen us on the path of life and joy to which the Lord invites us in every moment …

Often those who call for legal recognition of same-sex partnerships present it as a matter of fairness, equality and civil rights. The Church holds that basic human rights must be afforded to all people. This can and should be done without sacrificing the bedrock of society that is marriage and the family and without violating the religious freedom of individuals and institutions. To promote and protect the unique nature of marriage as the union of one man and one woman is itself a matter of justice.

CHRIST'S TEACHING ON MARRIAGE

Jesus brought to full awareness the divine plan for marriage. In John's Gospel, Christ's first miracle occurs at the wedding in Cana. 'The Church attaches great importance to Jesus' presence at the wedding at Cana. She sees in it the confirmation of the goodness of marriage and the proclamation that thenceforth marriage will be an efficacious sign of Christ's presence' (CCC, no. 1613).

Jesus unequivocally taught the indissolubility of marriage:

> Some Pharisees approached him, and to put him to the test they said, 'Is it against the Law for a man to divorce his wife on any pretext whatever?' He answered, 'Have you not read that the Creator from the beginning made them male and female and that he said: This is why a man leaves his father and mother and becomes attached to his wife, and the two become one flesh? They are no longer two, therefore, but one flesh. So then, what God has united, human beings must not divide.' (Mt 19:3-6)

Saint Paul reinforces Christ's teaching on marriage: 'a wife must not be separated from her husband ... and a husband must not divorce his wife' (1 Cor 7:10-11). In the Letter to the Ephesians, we read, 'This is why a man leaves his father and mother and becomes attached to his wife, and the two become one flesh. This mystery has great significance, but I am applying it to Christ and the Church' (Eph 5:31-32). Thus the love of husband and wife reflects the love between Christ and the Church. By Christ's will, Marriage is one of the Seven Sacraments.

COVENANT AND LITURGICAL ACT

By their marriage, the couple witnesses Christ's spousal love for the Church. One of the Nuptial Blessings in the liturgical celebration of marriage refers to this in saying, 'Father, you have made the union of man and wife so holy a mystery that it symbolises the marriage of Christ and his Church.' Through the liturgical celebration of marriage, husband and wife enter into a covenant which is also a Sacrament:

The matrimonial covenant by which a man and a woman establish between themselves a partnership of the whole of life, is by its nature ordered toward the good of the spouses and the procreation and education of offspring; this covenant between baptised persons has been raised by Christ the Lord to the dignity of a sacrament. (CCC, no. 1601, citing CIC, can. 1055, and *Code of Canons of the Eastern Churches* [CCEO], can. 776)

The Sacrament of Marriage is a covenant, which is more than a contract. Covenant always expresses a relationship between persons. The marriage covenant refers to the relationship between the husband and wife, a permanent union of persons capable of knowing and loving each other and God. The celebration of marriage is also a liturgical act, appropriately held in a public liturgy at church. Catholics are urged to celebrate their marriage within the Eucharistic Liturgy.

THE CELEBRATION OF MARRIAGE

According to the Latin tradition, the spouses as ministers of Christ's grace mutually confer upon each other the sacrament of Matrimony by expressing their consent before the Church. In the traditions of the Eastern Churches, the priest (bishops or presbyters) are witnesses to the mutual consent given by the spouses, but for the validity of the sacrament their blessing is also necessary.

– CCC, no. 1623

In the Latin Church, the free consent of the couple is at the heart of the marriage celebration. By Church law, when two Catholics marry they must exchange this consent in the presence of the Church's minister, two witnesses and the congregation. The priest or deacon calls forth this consent, but the marriage itself takes place through the public consent of the couple. The priest invites the couple to do so in these words: 'Since it is your intention to enter into marriage, join your right hands and declare your consent before God and his Church.' There are various formulas for this consent. One that may be used is as follows: 'I, [Name], take you, [Name], to be my [wife/husband]. I promise to be true to you in good times and in bad, in sickness and in health. I will love you and honour you all the days of my life.' In the Eastern Churches, the Sacrament is conferred by the blessing of the priest after receiving the couple's consent.

The consent is further symbolised in the Latin Church by the blessing and exchange of rings with the words: 'Take this ring as a sign of my love and fidelity, in the name of the Father, and of the Son, and of the Holy Spirit.'

THE PURPOSES OF MARRIAGE

The marriage covenant, by which a man and woman form with each other an intimate communion of life and love, has been founded and endowed with its own special laws by the Creator. By its very nature it is ordered to the good of the couple, as well as to the generation and education of children. Christ the Lord raised marriage between the baptised to the dignity of a sacrament.

– CCC, no. 1660

The *Catechism* teaches that Christ's grace in the Sacrament of Marriage protects the essential purposes of marriage: the good of the couple and the generation and education of children. These purposes are protected and fostered by the permanence of the marriage bond and the mutual fidelity of the spouses.

'What God has united, human beings must not divide' (Mk 10:9). We have already noted that God's plan for marriage involves a permanent covenant embraced by the couple. The Church declares every valid sacramental consummated marriage to be indissoluble, that is, no one can dissolve the marriage bond.

The Sacrament obliges marital fidelity between the spouses. Love has a definitive quality about it. It is more than a practical arrangement or a temporary contract. Marital intimacy and the good of the children require

FROM THE CATECHISM

1. Why is the family called 'the domestic church'?
The Christian home is the place where the children receive the first proclamation of the faith. For this reason the family is rightly called 'the domestic church', a community of grace and prayer, a school of human virtues and of Christian charity. (CCC, no. 1666)

2. What is essential in the consent of those to be married?
The parties to a marriage covenant are a baptised man and woman, free to contract marriage, who freely express their consent; 'to be free' means:
* not being under constraint;
* not impeded by any natural or ecclesiastical law. (CCC, no. 1625)

3. Why should the couples be prepared for marriage?
So that the 'I do' of the spouses may be a free and responsible act, and so that the marriage covenant may have solid and lasting human and Christian foundations, preparation is of prime importance ... It is imperative to give suitable and timely instruction to young people, above all in the heart of their own families, about the dignity of married love, its role and exercise, so that, having learned the value of chastity, they will be able at a suitable age to engage in honourable courtship and enter upon a marriage of their own. (CCC, no. 1632)

total fidelity to conjugal love. This flows from Christ's own fidelity to the Church, which he loved so much that he died for her. By their mutual fidelity, the spouses continue to make present to each other the love of Christ and lead each other to greater holiness through the grace they receive from the Sacrament.

Married love is ordered to the good of the spouses and to the procreation and education of children. These are the unitive and procreative purposes of marriage. 'By its very nature the institution of marriage and married love is ordered to the procreation and education of the offspring and it is in them that it finds its crowning glory' (CCC, no. 1652; GS, no. 48). The fruitfulness of married love includes the moral, spiritual and faith life the parents hand on to their children. Parents, as principal educators of their children, are at the service of life.

Together with their children, parents form what the Second Vatican Council called the domestic church. The Church lives in the daily life of families, in their faith and love, in their prayers and mutual care. The *Catechism* notes that 'All the members of the family exercise the priesthood of the baptised in a privileged way' (CCC, no. 1657).

Not all married couples are able to have children. 'Spouses to whom God has not granted children can nevertheless have a conjugal life full of meaning ... [and] can radiate a fruitfulness of charity, of hospitality and of sacrifice' (CCC, no. 1654).

EFFECTS OF THE SACRAMENT

The first effect of the Sacrament of Matrimony is the gift of the bond between the spouses. 'The consent by which the spouses mutually give and receive one another is sealed by God himself' (CCC, no. 1639). 'The marriage bond has been established by God himself in such a way that a marriage concluded and consummated between baptised persons can never be dissolved' (CCC, no. 1640).

The grace of this Sacrament perfects the love of husband and wife, binds them together in fidelity and helps them welcome and care for children. Christ is the source of this grace and he dwells with the spouses to strengthen their covenant promises, to bear each other's burdens with forgiveness and kindness and to experience ahead of time the 'wedding feast of the Lamb' (Rv 19:9).

DO ALL YOU CAN TO STRENGTHEN MARRIAGE

The pastoral care of the Church for the support of marriage is shown by a variety of programmes to help men and women to know God's plan for marriage and the Church's teaching. Remote preparation, which can begin in the family, takes on a more organised character in the form of courses in second-level school and college years. As engaged couples draw closer to the celebration of marriage, there are more intense programmes of preparation.

These programmes are all the more necessary because cultural changes in recent times have undermined God's will for marriage. The so-called sexual revolution, aided by artificial contraception, has made it more culturally acceptable for men and women to have sexual relations without having to marry each other. The availability of abortion has reduced the pressure on men and women to worry about the consequences of unwanted pregnancies. The casual acceptance of unmarried cohabitation – and of couples' entering marriage without a permanent commitment – contradicts the very nature of marriage. The political pressure for the legalisation of same-sex unions is yet another step in the erosion of God's plan for marriage and the understanding of marriage in the natural moral order of creation.

In her teaching, the Church gives us a picture of family life that begins with the total gift of love between the spouses evidenced in their resolve to remain exclusively faithful until death. This promise, made before God in the midst of family and friends before an authorised priest or deacon, is supported by the continuing presence of Christ in the life of the spouses as he pours into their hearts the gift of love through the Holy Spirit. The couple does not walk alone and possesses the graced freedom to respond to all natural and supernatural help.

The couple's joyful acceptance of children includes the responsibility to serve as models of Christian commitment for their children and helps them grow in wisdom and grace. In this way, their family becomes a 'domestic church'. The family honours the home as a place of prayer that conveys a sense of the sacred where so much of Christian life occurs.

The couple needs to remember they have entered a relationship between persons. They come to one another with two loves, the one commanded by Jesus and the one caused by their attraction to each other. They are challenged to unite their personal love with Christ's love. Their human love will survive more effectively the cultural challenges they face, as well as the psychological and economic ones, when it is merged with the powerful love of Christ, who wants them to succeed and whose divine grace is ever at their service.

The New Testament shows that Christ's command to love is the door to the whole supernatural order. At the same time, it encourages the couple to know that Jesus affirms the human good of each person. Together the couple must seek the same goals of mutual love united to Christ's love, the raising of a family and the continued growth of their own relationship.

> It can seem difficult, or even impossible, to bind oneself for life to another human being. This makes it all the more important to proclaim the Good News that God loves us with a definitive and irrevocable love, that married couple share in this love, that it supports and sustains them and that by their own faithfulness they can be witnesses to God's faithful love. Spouses who with God's grace give this witness, often in very difficult conditions, deserve the gratitude and support of the ecclesial community. (CCC, no. 1648)

DIVORCE AND PASTORAL CARE

Married couples have always experienced problems that threaten their union: jealousy, infidelity, conflicts and quarrels. Lust and arbitrary domination can ruin a marriage. These issues arise from the impact of sin, both Original and actual. The first sin disrupted the original communion of man and woman. Despite this, God's plan for marriage persisted. He never failed to provide mercy and healing grace to help couples sustain their marriages. Sadly, some spouses fail to benefit from the Lord's help and from the many professional resources and support offered to them.

The Church's fidelity to Christ's teaching on marriage and against divorce does not imply insensitivity to the pain of the persons facing these unhappy situations. When divorce is the only possible recourse, the Church offers her support to those involved and encourages them to remain close to the Lord through frequent reception of the Sacraments, especially the Holy Eucharist. In the case of those who have divorced civilly and remarried, even though the Church considers the second marriage invalid, she does not want these Catholics to be alienated from her.

DECLARATION OF NULLITY OF A MARRIAGE

The consent of the spouses must be an act of the will, free of coercion or external threats. If this freedom is absent, the marriage is invalid. For this reason (or other reasons that render the marriage null and void), the Church, after an examination of the situation by a competent Church court, can declare the nullity of a marriage, that is, that the sacramental marriage never existed. In this case, the contracting parties are free to marry, provided the natural obligations of the previous union are discharged (cf. CCC, nos. 1628–1629; CIC, can. 1095–1107).

Toward Christians who live in this situation, and who often keep the faith and desire to bring up their children in a Christian manner, priests and the whole community must manifest an attentive solicitude, so that they do not consider themselves separated from the Church, in whose life they can and must participate as baptised persons. (CCC, no. 1651)

Thus, they are encouraged to participate in the life of their parish communities and to attend the Sunday Eucharist, even though they cannot receive Holy Communion.

A DECLARATION OF NULLITY (ANNULMENT)

The marriage of two baptised persons celebrated according to the norms of Church law is always presumed to be valid. When a marriage has broken down, this presumption remains in effect until the contrary is proven. The examination of the validity of a marriage is undertaken by a Church tribunal or court. When a Church court issues a declaration of nullity, it does not mean there was no civil, sexual or emotional marital relationship, nor does it mean that the children of the union are illegitimate. The declaration means that no sacramental bond – or, in the case of one party's being unbaptised, no natural bond – took place because at the time of the wedding, the standards for a valid marriage were not met. Grounds for a declaration of nullity (annulment) include flaws in the rite itself, in the legal capacity of the parties to marry (i.e., an 'impediment'), or in the consent they gave – whether they were lacking in discretion or maturity of judgement or were marrying due to force or fear or with an intent to exclude fidelity or the commitment to a life-long union or were placing unacceptable conditions on the marriage (cf. CCC, nos. 1628–1629). Once a declaration of nullity has been granted, if there are no other restrictions, one or both of the parties are free to enter a sacramental marriage in the Catholic Church.

MIXED AND INTERFAITH MARRIAGES

The term *mixed marriage* refers to a union between a Catholic and a baptised non-Catholic. With appropriate permission, a Catholic can marry a baptised non-Catholic either in the Catholic Church or a non-Catholic church. In the first case, a non-Catholic minister can be present for the ceremony just as the Catholic priest can be present in the non-Catholic church with the permission of the bishop.

It is clear that there are differences because of diverse religious traditions, but these differences can be lessened when the spouses share what they have received from their respective traditions and learn from each other how they fulfil their fidelity to Christ. 'But the difficulties of mixed marriages must not be underestimated. They arise from the fact that the separation of Christians has not yet been overcome. The spouses risk experiencing the tragedy of Christian disunity even in the heart of their own home' (CCC, no. 1634).

A marriage between a Catholic and a non-baptised person, which is an *interfaith* marriage and is not a sacramental marriage, can present even greater problems for a marriage. Nevertheless, the very differences regarding faith can be enriching for both spouses and, through God's grace, can lead them closer to him.

FOR DISCUSSION

1. How does the modern, secular view of marriage and the family affect your own family relationships? How do you resist forces that can weaken marriage?

2. What support for your family are you receiving from relatives, friends and your local parish? In what ways is your family a 'domestic church'? How and when do you pray with your spouse? How and when do you pray as a family? What is your practice concerning participation in Sunday Mass?

3. What help can you or your parish provide for other couples, especially those with troubled marriages in your neighbourhood and parish? What do you think will turn the tide back to a society that does everything it can to sustain the ideal of a monogamous, permanent marriage?

DOCTRINAL STATEMENTS

- God is the author of marriage.
- 'The matrimonial covenant by which a man and a woman establish between themselves a partnership of the whole of life, is by its nature ordered toward the good of the spouses and the procreation and education of offspring; this covenant between baptised persons has been raised by Christ the Lord to the dignity of a sacrament' (CCC, no. 1601; see CIC, can. 1055; CCEO, can. 776).
- Marriage is a liturgical act, appropriately held in a public liturgy at church. By their marriage, the couple witnesses Christ's spousal love for the Church.
- In the Latin Church, the spouses, as ministers of Christ's grace, mutually confer upon each other the Sacrament of Matrimony by expressing their consent before the Church. The free consent of the couple is at the heart of the marriage celebration.
- Unity, permanent lifelong commitment and openness to having and caring for children are essential to marriage.
- The remarriage of persons divorced from a living, lawful spouse is not permitted by God's law as taught by Christ. They remain members of the Church but cannot receive Holy Communion. They are called and

encouraged to lead Christian lives by attending Sunday Mass and participating as far as possible in the life of the parish and to bring up their children in the faith.

- 'The Christian home is the place where the children receive the first proclamation of the faith. For this reason the family is rightly called "the domestic church", a community of grace and prayer, a school of human virtues and of Christian charity' (CCC, no. 1666).

━━━ MEDITATION ━━━

Exhortation by the Celebrating Priest from the Liturgy of Marriage in Ireland

Dear children of God,
You have come today to pledge your love before God and before the Church here present in the person of the priest, your families and friends.

In becoming husband and wife you give yourselves to each other for life.

You promise to be true and faithful, to support and cherish each other until death, so that your years together will be the living out in love of the pledge you now make.

May your love for each other reflect the enduring love of Christ for his Church.

As you face the future together, keep in mind that the Sacrament of marriage unites you with Christ, and brings you, through the years, the grace and blessing of God our Father. Marriage is from God: he alone can give you the happiness which goes beyond human expectation, and which grows deeper through the difficulties and struggles of life.

Put your trust in God as you set out together in life.

Make your home a centre of Christian family life.

The Christian home makes Christ and his Church present in the world of everyday things.

May all who enter your home find there the presence of the Lord; for he has said: 'Where two or three are gathered together in my name, there am I in the midst of them.'

PRAYER

Almighty and eternal God,
your fatherly tenderness never ceases to provide for our needs.
We ask you to bestow on this family and this home
the riches of your blessing.
With the gift of grace, sanctify those who live here,
so that, faithful to your commandments,
they will care for each other, ennoble this world by their lives,
and reach the home you have prepared for them in heaven.
We ask this through Christ our Lord. Amen.

– Blessing of Families, *Book of Blessings*

I shall betroth you to myself for ever.

– Hos 2:21

In the Bible, there is no stronger image for the covenant between God and God's people than married love.

– SGN, 56

22 SACRAMENTALS AND POPULAR DEVOTIONS

FORMS OF POPULAR PIETY
– CCC, NOS. 1667–1679

PATRICK PEYTON: THE ROSARY PRIEST

For a half century, from 1940 to 1990, Fr Patrick Peyton CSC was 'the Rosary Priest' to millions of people around the world. To Catholics and other believers in the United States, in Ireland and in many other countries, he was the force behind the familiar slogan, 'The family that prays together, stays together.'

He was born on 9 January 1909 in Carracastle, Attymass, near Ballina, County Mayo, one of nine children. In 1928, Patrick and his brother Tom left home to join their sister Nellie in Scranton, Pennsylvania and seek work. Patrick became a sacristan and caretaker at St Peter's Cathedral. Eventually, he and Tom finished high school. The brothers then entered the seminary at the University of Notre Dame, staffed by the Holy Cross Fathers. He had always wanted to study for the priesthood, but his family could never afford the cost of the education.

Before he finished his theological studies, Patrick contracted tuberculosis, which was regarded as incurable at that time. He wrote of this as his 'darkest hour'.

> God made my worst and darkest hour the start of a new life full of meaning. In the middle of the night, my right lung began to haemorrhage. A doctor came and told me he thought I would die that night. I had been strong, vigorous, independent. Now ambulance attendants placed me on a stretcher, manoeuvred me down a narrow, winding stairway and raced me to the hospital.

I deteriorated until the doctors said, 'Try prayer. Our remedies are useless.'

One of my teachers hurried to visit me. He saw me at my worst – discouraged, depressed, hopeless. 'Mary is alive,' he said, 'She will be as good to you as you think she can be. It all depends on you and your faith.' He activated my dormant faith. I asked Mary with all my heart and soul to pray to her Son for my cure. 'If I survive, I will serve you and Christ for the rest of my life.'

Shortly thereafter, Patrick asked the doctors to examine him again. They took X-rays and made tests. Amazingly, they found no trace of disease in his lungs. In reporting his healing, he wrote, 'I am not describing a miracle. I'm giving witness to the power of Mary's intercession and the quiet unsensational way she works. When I heard the good news I said, "Mary, I hope I will never disgrace you."'

He went on to be ordained a priest in 1941, along with his brother Tom. Wondering how he could pay back his spiritual debts to Christ, Mary and the prayers of his family, seven months later, during a retreat, God gave him the answer: the Family Rosary Crusade. During his illness, he had learned three lessons: solidarity with people and dependence upon others; appreciation of the gift of Christ's mother; and total dependence upon God. He recalled the practice of the nightly family rosary beside the turf fire, and reflected how 'because of the family rosary, my home was a cradle, a school, a university, a library and, most of all, a little church'. At a time when outbreak of war was breaking up the home and juvenile delinquency was rising in the streets, Fr Peyton realised that the Christian family badly needed support.

Father Peyton began with a quarter-hour local radio programme simply praying the Rosary. In 1945, the largest radio network in the United States, Mutual Broadcasting, offered Fr Peyton a half-hour to broadcast the Rosary as part of his campaign. The network owner set conditions for the broadcast: a well-known respected family should pray the Rosary, with the most famous Hollywood stars joining them, the most prominent American Catholic should speak and it would go out on the best day and at the most appropriate time, to attract a large audience.

On Sunday, 13 May, Mother's Day in America, and on the anniversary of the apparition at Fatima, the Rosary was first broadcast nationally with the famous Sullivan family of Iowa, whose five sons were killed in World War II, praying the Rosary, joined by Bing Crosby from Hollywood, with a blessing by Francis Cardinal Spellman of New York. This initiative meant that Fr Peyton, along with Fulton Sheen, was one of the first clergymen to realise the potential of the mass media for evangelisation.

Father Peyton's 'Family Crusade' progressed to establishing the 'Family Theater of the Air', to produce family-value drama for radio and later, for television, with the participation of many well-known Hollywood stars. In the course of its existence, Family Theater made 600 shows.

Father Peyton himself spoke at over forty Rosary rallies in a score of countries attended by an estimated twenty-eight million people. The attendance at two of his rallies, one in Brazil and the other in the Philippines, topped the two million mark. Peyton himself was a tall man, with an open face and a strong Irish accent. He preached simply, humbly and straightforwardly, with power and sincerity, of the importance of family, of prayer and of the Blessed Virgin Mary. People around the world who heard him speak were deeply moved by his witness and faith.

Father Peyton died on 3 June 1992. He is buried on the grounds of the Congregation of Holy Cross at Stonehill College, Massachusetts. Since his death, Holy Cross Family Ministries, a ministry founded by Fr Peyton and sponsored by the Congregation of Holy Cross, has built the Fr Patrick Peyton Center in Easton and the Fr Peyton Memorial Centre in Mayo to honour his memory and continue his mission. In 2000, the cause for the canonisation of the Servant of God, Fr Patrick Peyton, was introduced.

At the end of his life, Fr Peyton mused about his past and his ministry:

> In the summer-times of my childhood, the Ox mountains in Ireland were a blanket of purple flowers. From the other

direction, I heard the moaning of the gigantic waves of the Atlantic coming to their death on the shores. No matter how mighty and powerful, all things, even mountains and oceans come to an end. I gave my life to extol the beauty of the Family Rosary. (Quoted by Holy Cross Family Ministries, http://www. familyrosary.org/main/about-father-priesthood.php)

Father Peyton's fervour in promoting the praying of the Rosary to strengthen family life remains an inspiring context for considering popular devotion and sacramentals. This dimension of Church life has proven to be a perennial source for discovering and relating God's active presence and for applying it to the details of daily Christian life.

SACRAMENTALS

Sacramentals are sacred signs instituted by the Church. They are sacred signs that bear a resemblance to the sacraments.

– CCC, no. 1667

Sacramentals dispose believers to receive the chief effects of the Sacraments. They are sacred signs that resemble the Sacraments in the sense that they signify spiritual effects that are obtained through the intercession of the Church. Sacramentals include blessings, actions such as processions, prayers such as the Rosary and objects such as holy water, palms, ashes, candles and medals.

The Church instituted sacramentals to sanctify certain ministries, states of life and the variety of situations in which Christians are involved. Their use has been guided by bishops' pastoral decisions in responding to specific needs that are particular to a given period of history or locality. They include a prayer, usually with a gesture such as the Sign of the Cross or the sprinkling of holy water.

BLESSINGS

Among the sacramentals, blessings hold a major place. There are blessings for persons, meals, objects, places and special occasions. All blessings praise God for his gifts. Most blessings invoke the Holy Trinity as expressed in the Sign of the Cross – sometimes accompanied by the sprinkling of holy water.

There are blessings that consecrate persons to God: leaders of religious orders or congregations, religious men and women, virgins and widows, and others such as readers, acolytes and catechists. There are blessings for vessels such as chalices or ciboria, bells, medals, rosaries and similar objects for religious use. The text for these and other blessings may be found in *The Veritas Book of Blessing Prayers*. Making the Sign of the Cross at the beginning and the end of each day, saying morning and evening prayers and offering a prayer before and after meals are among the most common ways to invoke God's blessing on our lives.

EXORCISMS

The Gospels report that Jesus performed exorcisms that removed a person from the power of evil as personified in the fallen angels – Satan and the devils. For example, when a man with an unclean spirit entered the synagogue where Jesus was preaching, and the unclean spirit challenged him, Jesus said to the demon, 'Be quiet! Come out of him' (Mk 1:25). The unclean spirit convulsed the man and left him. Christ's exorcisms were both a compassionate act of healing as well as a sign of his power over evil.

From Christ, the Church has received the power and office of exorcism. At each Baptism, there is a simple form of exorcism, accompanied by the renunciation of Satan and sin. Within the Rite of Christian Initiation of Adults, minor exorcisms are celebrated as we are freed from sin and its effects. The elect receive new strength in the midst of their spiritual journey, and they open their hearts to receive the gifts of the Saviour (cf. *Rite of Christian Initiation of Adults*, no. 144). A major exorcism can only be performed by a priest with a bishop's permission. The priest is to act prudently and follow the Church's rules for exorcism strictly. 'Exorcism is directed at the expulsion of demons or to the liberation from demonic possession through the spiritual authority which Jesus entrusted to his

Church' (CCC, no. 1673). One needs to distinguish psychological illness from demonic possession. Illness is the domain of psychological and medical care, whereas demonic possession requires the pastoral care of the Church through exorcism.

POPULAR DEVOTIONS

The faith of the Christian people has developed numerous forms of popular piety and devotions. The religious instincts of the Christian people have always found ways to surround sacramental life with helps to benefit more effectively from them. Popular devotions have proven to be powerful forms of prayer and to be of spiritual benefit to many.

These forms of piety include praying at the Stations of the Cross; making pilgrimages to the Holy Land, Rome, Marian shrines and shrines of other saints; lighting candles in church; having throats blessed on the feast of St Blaise; joining in Corpus Christi processions; wearing medals of the Blessed Virgin and the saints; and honouring sacred relics. Some materials that form part of the Church's liturgical rites, such as the ashes received on Ash Wednesday and the palms distributed on Palm Sunday, are also sacramentals.

Ireland too has its own popular devotions and sacred sites, among them Croagh Patrick and Lough Derg. On the last Sunday in July every year, known as Reek Sunday, as many as 20,000 pilgrims from all over the world climb Ireland's Holy Mountain, Croagh Patrick, in County Mayo, many completing the climb barefoot. The climb commemorates the forty days St Patrick is said to have spent fasting on the mountain. Lough Derg, or St Patrick's Purgatory, also recalls the national saint who is said to have spent time in retreat in a cave on Lough Derg in County Donegal. During his time there, he was subjected to fierce temptation and given a vision of Hell, thus the title 'St Patrick's Purgatory'. To this day, tens of thousands flock to the island to take part in the annual retreats, keeping alive the ancient Irish tradition of prayer, fasting and pilgrimage

Devotions to the Sacred Heart of Jesus, the Divine Mercy of Jesus and the Blessed Mother are frequently part of parish life and often include a *novena*, nine days of prayer associated with the devotion. Prayer groups such as those sponsored by Charismatic Renewal, Cursillo, Marriage Encounter and Taizé have both a strong liturgical foundation as well as a vibrant devotional component.

The praying of litanies (a series of invocations of the Blessed Mother or the saints) and the use of icons, holy pictures and statues as supports for prayer are also forms of popular devotion. The faithful do not worship pictures and statues; they venerate or honour the Virgin Mary and the saints and worship and adore only God. The veneration of Mary and the saints ultimately leads to God. Among the forms of popular devotion, the Rosary holds a unique position because of its relationship to the mysteries of Christ and the faith of the Blessed Virgin Mary.

THE ROSARY

The Rosary takes its inspiration from the Gospel to suggest the attitude with which the faithful should recite it.

– Pope Paul VI, *For the Right Ordering and Development of Devotion to the Blessed Virgin Mary* (*Marialis Cultus*), no. 44

Many of the appearances of Mary, especially at Lourdes and Fatima, have been associated with the praying of the Rosary. Numerous popes and saints have urged the faithful to pray the Rosary. Opening the Marian Year in 1987, the Rosary was a global prayer for peace offered by large groups at Marian shrines such as those in Washington DC, Lourdes, Frankfurt, Manila, Bombay, Rio de Janeiro and Dakar.

The popularity of the Rosary has been attributed to St Dominic and the Dominican Order. It grew out of the laity's desire to have 150 prayers to match the 150 psalms chanted by the monks in monasteries. In 1569, St Pius V officially recommended the praying 'of 150 angelic salutations ... with the Lord's prayer at each decade ... while meditating on the mysteries which recall the entire life of our Lord Jesus Christ'.

The Rosary is a Scripture-based prayer. It begins with the Apostles' Creed, which is itself a summary of the great mysteries of Catholic faith, based on Scripture, from creation through redemption and up to the Resurrection of the body and everlasting life. The Our Father, which

FROM THE CATECHISM

1. What are sacramentals?

Sacramentals are sacred signs instituted by the Church. These are sacred signs that bear a resemblance to the sacraments. They signify effects, especially of a spiritual nature, which are obtained through the intercession of the Church. (CCC, no. 1667)

2. What is the first among the sacramentals?

Among sacramentals, blessings (of persons, meals, objects and places) come first. Every blessing praises God and prays for his gifts. In Christ, Christians are blessed by God the Father 'with every spiritual blessing' (Eph 1:3). This is why the Church imparts blessings by invoking the name of Jesus, usually while making the holy sign of the cross of Christ. (CCC, no. 1671)

3. What is the relationship of popular piety to the liturgy?

These expressions of piety extend the liturgical life of the Church but do not replace it. They 'should be so drawn up that they harmonise with the liturgical seasons, accord with the sacred liturgy, are in some way derived from it and lead the people to it, since in fact the liturgy by its very nature is superior to any of them.' (CCC, no. 1675, citing SC, no. 13, §3)

introduces each mystery, is taken from the Gospels. The first part of the Hail Mary is composed from verses from the Gospel of Luke (1:29 and 1:42), the angel's words announcing Christ's birth and Elizabeth's greeting to Mary. Saint Pius V officially added the second part to the Hail Mary.

The Mysteries of the Rosary centre on the events of Christ's life. The Joyful Mysteries, which recall aspects of the Incarnation, are the Annunciation, the Visitation, the Nativity, the Presentation of Jesus in the Temple and the Finding of the Child Jesus after Three Days in the Temple. The Sorrowful Mysteries, which focus on Christ's suffering and death, are the Agony in the Garden, the Scourging at the Pillar, the Crowning with

Thorns, the Carrying of the Cross and the Crucifixion and Death of Jesus. The Glorious Mysteries are the Resurrection, the Ascension into Heaven, the Sending of the Holy Spirit upon the Apostles at Pentecost, the Assumption of Mary and the Crowning of Mary as the Queen of Heaven and Earth. In October 2002, St John Paul II issued the apostolic letter *On the Most Holy Rosary* (*Rosarium Virginis Mariae*; RVM). In the letter, the Holy Father added the five additional mysteries that he called the Luminous Mysteries: the Baptism of the Lord, the Miracle at Cana, the Proclamation of the Kingdom of God, the Transfiguration and the Institution of the Eucharist.

The repetition of the ten Hail Marys with each Mystery is meant to lead us to restful and contemplative prayer related to the Mystery. Many who say the Rosary think of the words as background music that leads them to rest in the divine presence. The gentle repetition of the words helps us to enter the silence of our hearts, where Christ's Spirit dwells.

FOR DISCUSSION

1. What kind of popular devotions have you experienced? If you have made a pilgrimage, what was the impact on your faith life?
2. Have you witnessed the blessings of homes, persons or special objects used for liturgy? How might praying as a family, such as saying Grace Before Meals or Grace After Meals, strengthen family life as well as faith in God?
3. What are some benefits of praying the Rosary? Why do some people have sacred art such as crucifixes, statues and holy images in prominent places in their homes?

DOCTRINAL STATEMENTS

• Sacramentals are sacred signs instituted by the Church. 'These are sacred signs which bear resemblance to the sacraments. They signify effects, particularly of a spiritual nature, which are obtained through the intercession of the Church' (CCC, no. 1667, citing SC, no. 60).

- Among the sacramentals, blessings hold a major place. There are blessings for persons, meals, objects, places and ceremonial occasions such as graduations, testimonial honours, welcomes and farewells. All blessings praise God for his gifts. Most blessings invoke the Holy Trinity as expressed in the Sign of the Cross, sometimes accompanied by the sprinkling of holy water.
- 'Exorcism is directed at the expulsion of demons or to the liberation from demonic possession through the spiritual authority which Jesus entrusted to his Church' (CCC, no. 1673).
- 'Expressions of piety extend the liturgical life of the Church, but do not replace it. They "should be so drawn up that they harmonise with the liturgical seasons, accord with the sacred liturgy, are in some way derived from it and lead the people to it, since in fact the liturgy by its very nature is far superior to any of them"' (CCC, no. 1675, citing SC, no. 13 §3).

MEDITATION

A number of historical circumstances also make a revival of the Rosary quite timely. First of all, the need to implore from God the gift of peace. The Rosary has many times been proposed by my predecessors and myself as a prayer for peace. At the start of a millennium which began with the terrifying attacks of 11 September 2001, a millennium which witnesses every day in numerous parts of the world fresh scenes of bloodshed and violence, to rediscover the Rosary means to immerse oneself in contemplation of the mystery of Christ who 'is the peace between us', since he made 'the two into one entity and broken down the barrier' (Eph 2:14). Consequently, one cannot recite the Rosary without feeling caught up in a clear commitment to advancing peace, especially in the land of Jesus, still so sorely afflicted and so close to the heart of every Christian.

– RVM, no. 6

PRAYER

Grace Before Meals

Bless us, O God, as we sit together.
Bless the food we eat today.
Bless the hands that made the food.
Bless us, O God. Amen.

Grace After Meals

Thank you, God, for the food we have eaten.
Thank you, God, for all our friends.
Thank you, God, for everything.
Thank you, God. Amen.

Miraculous Medal Prayer

O, Mary, conceived without sin, pray for us who have
recourse to you.

PART III

CHRISTIAN MORALITY:
THE FAITH LIVED

23 LIFE IN CHRIST – PART ONE

THE FOUNDATIONS OF THE CHRISTIAN MORAL LIFE
– CCC, NOS. 1691–2082

JESUS THE TEACHER

Jesus was frequently called a teacher (in Hebrew, *Rabbi*). Jesus taught about God as his Father and the Father of all human beings. He taught about his Father's mercy and forgiveness of sin. He taught about the Kingdom that his Father was establishing, a Kingdom where justice and love conquer injustice and hatred. He taught about himself as the Servant of God, sent by the Father to bring about conversion, even by the sacrifice of his own life.

Jesus also taught his disciples how they were to live in order to achieve the fullness of life and happiness that is God's will for all people. He did this by his own way of life and by his words. His teaching flowed from the tradition of ancient Israel but he also deepened that teaching and perfected it. A good illustration of this is his dialogue with a young man narrated in the Gospel of St Matthew:

> Now a man came to him and asked, 'Master, what good deed must I do to possess eternal life?' Jesus said to him, 'Why do you ask me about what is good? There is one alone who is good. But if you wish to enter into life, keep the commandments.' He said, 'Which ones?' Jesus replied, 'These: You shall not kill. You shall not commit adultery. You shall not steal. You shall not give false witness. Honour your father and your mother. You shall love your neighbour as yourself.' The young man said to him, 'I have kept all these. What more do I need to do?' Jesus said, 'If you wish to be perfect, go and sell your possessions and give the money to

the poor, and you will have treasure in heaven; then come, follow me.' But when the young man heard these words he went away sad, for he was a man of great wealth. (Mt 19:16-22)

In this dialogue, Jesus reiterates the fundamental importance of the Ten Commandments for a moral life. He also goes beyond them and calls for a radical detachment from material goods and their distribution to the poor. Jesus himself lived as a poor man. The attainment of fullness of life and happiness requires fundamental attitudes and virtues such as the one that Jesus recommends to the young man and others that Jesus teaches throughout his public ministry as underlying the keeping of the Commandments.

These attitudes and virtues were proclaimed by Jesus in his Sermon on the Mount.

> How blessed are the poor in spirit:
> the kingdom of Heaven is theirs.
> Blessed are the gentle:
> they shall have the earth as inheritance.
> Blessed are those who mourn:
> they shall be comforted.
> Blessed are those who hunger and thirst for uprightness:
> they shall have their fill.
> Blessed are the merciful:
> they shall have mercy shown them.
> Blessed are the pure in heart:
> they shall see God.
> Blessed are the peacemakers:
> they shall be recognised as children of God.
> Blessed are those who are persecuted in the cause of uprightness:
> the kingdom of Heaven is theirs.
> Blessed are you when people abuse you and persecute you and speak all kinds of calumny against you falsely on my account. Rejoice and be glad, for your reward will be great in heaven. (Mt 5:3-12)

These are called Beatitudes. The word *Beatitude* refers to a state of deep happiness or joy. These Beatitudes are taught by Jesus as the foundations for a life of authentic Christian discipleship and the attainment of ultimate happiness. They give spirit to the Law of the Ten Commandments and bring perfection to moral life. That spirit is ultimately the spirit of love. In response to a question from the leader of the people, Jesus taught that love is at the heart of all law.

> You must love the Lord your God with all your heart, with all your soul, and with all your mind. This is the greatest and the first commandment. The second resembles it: You must love your neighbour as yourself. (Mt 22:37-39)

Jesus is the teacher sent by the Father to bring us to perfect happiness in God. Jesus teaches us the way to the Father.

LIFE IN CHRIST – PART ONE:
THE FOUNDATIONS OF CHRISTIAN MORALITY

Part One of the *Catechism of the Catholic Church* presents the Creed – the revealed truths of the divine plan of salvation and the invitation to faith in this Revelation.

Part Two presents the Seven Sacraments by which the saving grace of God is made available to us. We receive this gift of divine love by our participation in the Christian mysteries.

Part Three explores our life in Christ and the Holy Spirit, which we have received through Revelation and the Sacraments. It unfolds the various ways we respond to divine love through our personal and social moral behaviour.

In Section One of Part Three, the *Catechism* explores the various elements, principles and foundations of Christian morality by addressing the dignity of the human person, the human community and God's salvation through God's law and grace. In Section Two, it applies these principles to each of the Ten Commandments.

We will follow this order, beginning in this chapter with who we are as human beings called to live a moral life.

WE ARE MORAL BEINGS: FUNDAMENTAL ELEMENTS OF CHRISTIAN MORALITY

Made in the Image of God

The most basic principle of the Christian moral life is the awareness that every person bears the dignity of being made in the image of God. He has given us an immortal soul and through the gifts of intelligence and reason enables us to understand the order of things established in his creation. God has also given us a free will to seek and love what is true, good and beautiful. Sadly, because of the Fall, we also suffer the impact of Original Sin, which darkens our minds, weakens our wills and inclines us to sin. Baptism delivers us from Original Sin but not from its effects – especially the inclination to sin, concupiscence. Within us, then, is both the powerful surge toward the good because we are made in the image of God, and the darker impulses toward evil because of the effects of Original Sin.

But we should always remember that Christ's dying and rising offers us new life in the Spirit, whose saving grace delivers us from sin and heals sin's damage within us. Thus we speak of the value, dignity and goal of human life, even with its imperfections and struggles. Human life, as a profound unity of physical and spiritual dimensions, is sacred. It is distinct from all other forms of life, since it alone is imprinted with the very image of its Creator.

The Responsible Practice of Freedom

The second element of life in Christ is the responsible practice of freedom. Without freedom, we cannot speak meaningfully about morality or moral responsibility. Human freedom is more than a capacity to choose between this and that. It is the God-given power to become who he created us to be and so to share eternal union with him. This happens when we consistently choose ways that are in harmony with God's plan. Christian morality and God's law are not arbitrary, but are specifically given to us for our happiness. God gave us intelligence and the capacity to act freely. Ultimately, human freedom lies in our free decision to say 'yes' to God. In contrast, many people today understand human freedom merely as the ability to make a choice, with no objective norm or good as the goal.

An opposite tendency to one that makes the act of choosing the core of human freedom is one that denies that we are free at all. Some believe that due to outside forces, inner compulsions, social pressures, childhood experiences or genetic makeup, our behaviour is already determined and we are not truly free. Though we do recognise that 'the imputability or responsibility for an action can be diminished or nullified by ignorance, duress, fear, and other psychological or social factors' (CCC, no. 1746), normally we are still free and responsible for our actions. Our freedom may be limited but it is real nonetheless.

The best way to grow in freedom is to perform good acts. Good deeds help to make us free and develop good habits. The road to loss of freedom is through evil acts. Sin makes us slaves of evil and reduces our capacity to be free. Freedom comes from being moral. Slavery to sin arises from being immoral.

The Understanding of Moral Acts

Another important foundation of Christian morality is the understanding of moral acts. Every moral act consists of three elements: the objective act (what we do), the subjective goal or intention (why we do the act), and the concrete situation or circumstances in which we perform the act (where, when, how, with whom, the consequences, etc.).

For an individual act to be morally good, the object, or what we are doing, must be objectively good. Some acts, apart from the intention or reason for doing them, are always wrong because they go against a fundamental or basic human good that ought never to be compromised. Direct killing of the innocent, torture and rape are examples of acts that are always wrong. Such acts are referred to as intrinsically evil acts, meaning that they are wrong in themselves, apart from the reason they are done or the circumstances surrounding them.

The goal, end or intention is the part of the moral act that lies within the person. For this reason, we say that the intention is the subjective element of the moral act. For an act to be morally good, one's intention must be good. If we are motivated to do something by a bad intention –

even something that is objectively good – our action is morally evil. It must also be recognised that a good intention cannot make a bad action (something intrinsically evil) good. We can never do something wrong or evil in order to bring about a good. This is the meaning of the saying, 'the end does not justify the means' (cf. CCC, nos. 1749–1761).

The circumstances and the consequences of the act make up the third element of moral action. These are secondary to the evaluation of a moral act in that they contribute to increasing or decreasing the goodness or badness of the act. In addition, the circumstances may affect one's personal moral responsibility for the act. All three aspects must be good – the objective act, the subjective intention and the circumstances – in order to have a morally good act.

This teaching, which recognises both the objective and subjective dimension of morality, is often at odds with a perspective that views morality as a completely personal or merely subjective reality. In such a view, held by some in our culture, there are no objective norms capable of demanding our moral compliance. Such a denial of an objective and unchanging moral order established by God results in a vision of morality and moral norms as being a matter of personal opinion or as established only through the consent of the individual members of society.

The Reality of Sin and Trust in God's Mercy

We cannot speak about life in Christ or the moral life without acknowledging the reality of sin, our own sinfulness and our need for God's mercy. When the existence of sin is denied it can result in spiritual and psychological damage because it is ultimately a denial of the truth about ourselves. Admitting the reality of sin helps us to be truthful and opens us to the healing that comes from Christ's redemptive act.

> Sin is an offence against reason, truth and right conscience; it is failure in genuine love for God and neighbour caused by a perverse attachment to certain goods. It wounds the nature of man and injures human solidarity. It has been defined as 'an utterance, a deed or a desire contrary to the eternal law'. (CCC, no. 1849, citing St Augustine, *Contra Faustum*, no. 22)

Thus, by its very definition, sin is understood as an offence against God as well as neighbour and therefore wrong. Sins are evaluated according to their gravity or seriousness. We commit mortal sin when we consciously and freely choose to do something grave against the divine law and contrary to our final destiny.

There are three conditions for a sin to be a mortal sin: grave matter, full knowledge and deliberate consent (freedom). Mortal sin destroys the loving relationship with God that we need for eternal happiness. If not repented, it results in a loss of love and God's grace and merits eternal punishment in hell, that is, exclusion from the Kingdom of God and thus eternal death.

A venial sin is a departure from the moral order in a less serious matter. 'Every kind of wickedness is sin, but not all sin leads to death' (1 Jn 5:17). Though venial sin does not completely destroy the love we need for eternal happiness, it weakens that love and impedes our progress in the practice of virtue and the moral good. Thus, over time, it can have serious consequences. 'Deliberate and unrepented venial sin disposes us little by little to commit mortal sin' (CCC, no. 1863).

In considering sin we must always remember that God is rich in mercy. 'However much sin increased, grace was always greater' (Rm 5:20). God's mercy is greater than sin. The very heart of the Gospel is the revelation of the mercy of God in Jesus Christ. 'For God sent his Son into the world not to judge the world, but so that through him the world might be saved' (Jn 3:17).

To receive this mercy, we must be willing to admit our sinfulness. Sorrow for sin and confession of sin are signs of conversion of heart that open us to God's mercy. Though we can judge a given offence to be the occasion for mortal sin, and thus an act of objective wrongdoing, we must always entrust the judgement of the person to the mercy and justice of God. This is because one person cannot know the extent of another individual's knowledge and freedom, which are integral factors determining when an occasion for mortal sin becomes an actual sin for which we are morally responsible.

The Formation of Conscience

The formation of a good conscience is another fundamental element of Christian moral teaching. 'Conscience is a judgement of reason by which the human person recognises the moral quality of a concrete act' (CCC, no.

1796). 'Man has in his heart a law inscribed by God ... His conscience is man's most secret core, and his sanctuary' (GS, no. 16).

Conscience represents both the more general ability we have as human beings to know what is good and right and the concrete judgements we make in particular situations concerning what we should do or about what we have already done. Moral choices confront us with the decision to follow or depart from reason and the divine law. A good conscience makes judgements that conform to reason and the good that is willed by the Wisdom of God. A good conscience requires lifelong formation. Each baptised follower of Christ is obliged to form his or her conscience according to objective moral standards. The Word of God is a principal tool in the formation of conscience when it is assimilated by study, prayer and practice. The prudent advice and good example of others support and enlighten our conscience. The authoritative teaching of the Church is an essential element in our conscience formation. Finally, the gifts of the Holy Spirit, combined with regular examination of our conscience, will help us develop a morally sensitive conscience.

Because our conscience is that inner sanctuary in which we listen to the voice of God, we must remember to distinguish between our subjective self and what is objectively true outside ourselves. We can be subjectively in error about something that is objectively true. On the objective level, if our conscience is 'correct', then there is no error between what is internally perceived to be true and truth itself. If there is an incorrect conscience, that means that the conscience is erroneous in its view of truth.

On the subjective level we can have a 'certain' conscience, which means we believe that our conscience is in conformity with what is objectively true. A person can have a 'certain' conscience on the subjective level but an 'incorrect' one on the objective level. For example, a person thinks that Ash Wednesday is a Holy Day of Obligation and chooses to miss Mass anyway. The person thinks it is a Holy Day (certain subjectively but incorrect objectively) and acts on it. This person has a certain but incorrect conscience. But because the conscience acted against what it perceived to be objectively the good, the conscience chooses to sin.

There are some rules to follow in obeying one's conscience. First, always follow a certain conscience. Second, an incorrect conscience must be changed if possible. Third, do not act with a doubtful conscience. We must always obey the certain judgements of our conscience, realising that our conscience can be incorrect, that it can make a mistake about what is truly the good or the right thing to do. This can be due to ignorance in which, through no fault of our own, we did not have all we needed to make a correct judgement.

However, we must also recognise that ignorance and errors are not always free from guilt, for example, when we did not earnestly seek what we needed in order to form our conscience correctly. Since we have the obligation to obey our conscience, we also have the great responsibility to see that it is formed in a way that reflects the true moral good.

> Through loyalty to conscience Christians are joined to other men in the search for truth and the right solution to many moral problems which arise both in the life of individuals and from social relationships. Hence, the more a correct conscience prevails, the more do persons and groups turn aside from blind choice and try to be guided by the objective standards of moral conduct. (GS, no. 16)

The Excellence of Virtues

The Christian moral life is one that seeks to cultivate and practise virtue. 'A virtue is an habitual and firm disposition to do the good. It allows the person not only to perform good acts, but to give the best of himself' (CCC, no. 1803). An effective moral life demands the practice of both human and theological virtues.

Human virtues form the soul with the habits of mind and will that support moral behaviour, control passions and avoid sin. Virtues guide our conduct according to the dictates of faith and reason, leading us toward freedom based on self-control and toward joy in living a good moral life. Compassion, responsibility, a sense of duty, self-discipline and restraint, honesty, loyalty, friendship, courage and persistence are examples of desirable virtues for sustaining a moral life. Historically, we group the human virtues around what are called the Cardinal Virtues. This term comes from the Latin word *cardo* meaning 'hinge'. All the virtues are related to or hinged to one of the Cardinal Virtues. The four Cardinal Virtues are prudence, justice, fortitude and temperance.

FROM THE CATECHISM

1. How are we created in the image of God?

It is in Christ, 'the image of the unseen God' (Col 1:15) that man has been created 'in the image and likeness' of the Creator ... By virtue of his soul and his spiritual powers of intellect and will, man is endowed with freedom, an 'outstanding manifestation of the divine image' (GS, no. 17). (CCC, nos. 1701, 1705)

2. What is freedom?

Freedom is the power to act or not to act, and so to perform deliberate acts of one's own. Freedom attains perfection in its acts when directed toward God, the sovereign Good ... The right to the exercise of freedom, especially in religious and moral matters, is an inalienable requirement of the dignity of man. But the exercise of freedom does not entail the putative right to say or do anything. (CCC, nos. 1744, 1747)

3. What are virtues?

Virtue is a habitual and firm disposition to do good ... The human virtues are stable dispositions of the intellect and will that govern our acts, order our passions and guide our conduct in accordance with reason and faith. They can be grouped around the four cardinal virtues: prudence, justice, fortitude and temperance ... There are three theological virtues: faith, hope and charity. They inform all the moral virtues and give life to them. (CCC, nos. 1833, 1834, 1841)

There are a number of ways in which we acquire human virtues. They are acquired by frequent repetition of virtuous acts that establish a pattern of virtuous behaviour. There is a reciprocal relationship between virtue and acts because virtue, as an internal reality, disposes us to act externally in morally good ways. Yet it is through doing good acts in the concrete that the virtue within us is strengthened and grows.

The human virtues are also acquired through seeing them in the good example of others and through education in their value and methods to acquire them. Stories that inspire us to want such virtues help contribute to their growth within us. They are gained by a strong will to achieve such ideals. In addition, God's grace is offered to us to purify and strengthen our human virtues, for our growth in virtue can be hampered by the reality of sin. Especially through prayer and the Sacraments, we open ourselves to the gifts of the Holy Spirit and God's grace as another way in which we grow in virtue.

The Theological Virtues of faith, hope and charity (love) are those virtues that relate directly to God. These are not acquired through human effort but, beginning with Baptism, they are infused within us as gifts from God. They dispose us to live in relationship with the Holy Trinity. Faith, hope and charity influence human virtues by increasing their stability and strength for our lives.

Each of the Ten Commandments forbids certain sins, but each also points to virtues that will help us avoid such sins. Virtues such as generosity, poverty of spirit, gentleness, purity of heart, temperance and fortitude assist us in overcoming and avoiding what are called the seven deadly or Capital Sins – pride, avarice or greed, envy, anger, lust, gluttony and sloth or laziness – which are those sins that engender other sins and vices.

Growth in virtue is an important goal for every Christian, for the virtues play a valuable role in living a Christian moral life.

LOVE, RULES AND GRACE

Our culture frequently exalts individual autonomy against community and tradition. This can lead to a suspicion of rules and norms that come from a tradition. This can also be a cause of a healthy criticism of a legalism that can arise from concentrating on rules and norms.

Advocates of Christian morality can sometimes lapse into a legalism that leads to an unproductive moralising. There is no doubt that love has to be the essential foundation of the moral life. But just as essential in this earthly realm are rules and laws that show how love may be applied in real life. In heaven, love alone will suffice. In this world, we need moral guidance from the Commandments, the Sermon on the Mount, the Precepts of the Church and other rules to see how love works.

Love alone, set adrift from moral direction, can easily descend into sentimentality that puts us at the mercy of our feelings. Popular entertainment romanticises love and tends to omit the difficult demands of the moral order.

In our permissive culture, love is sometimes so romanticised that it is separated from sacrifice. Because of this, tough moral choices cannot be faced. The absence of sacrificial love dooms the possibility of an authentic moral life.

Scripturally and theologically, the Christian moral life begins with a loving relationship with God, a covenant love made possible by the sacrifice of Christ. The Commandments and other moral rules are given to us as ways of protecting the values that foster love of God and others. They provide us with ways to express love, sometimes by forbidding whatever contradicts love.

The moral life requires grace. The *Catechism* speaks of this in terms of life in Christ and the inner presence of the Holy Spirit, actively enlightening our moral compass and supplying the spiritual strength to do the right thing. The grace that comes to us from Christ in the Spirit is as essential as love and rules and, in fact, makes love and keeping the rules possible.

FOR DISCUSSION

1. What is the source of the love needed for moral life? Some current understandings of the word *love* refer to behaviour that is actually contrary to the true meaning of love. What are some examples of this?

2. Why are the Ten Commandments, the Beatitudes, and other rules needed for us to be moral? What happens when we rely on the Ten Commandments and other rules without love? Can you name someone who models living the Ten Commandments, the Beatitudes, and other rules in real life in a loving way?

3. What are ways or means by which a person forms his or her conscience? What is the role of the Church in conscience formation?

DOCTRINAL STATEMENTS

- Every person bears the dignity of being made in the image of God. The Creator has given us an immortal soul and enables us to understand the order of things established by him. God has given us a free will to seek and love what is true, good and beautiful.

- Because of the Fall, we also suffer the impact of Original Sin, which darkens our minds, weakens our wills and inclines us to sin. Baptism delivers us from Original Sin, but not from its effects – especially the inclination to sin, concupiscence.

- Jesus calls us to be happy and shows us how to attain this. The desire for happiness is a principal motivation for the moral life. Our sinful inclinations, attitudes and actions prevent us from being totally happy on earth. In heaven, we will have perfect joy.

- God gives us intelligence and the capacity to act freely. We can initiate and control our acts. Social pressures and inner drives may affect our acts and limit our freedom. Normally we are free in our actions.

- 'The imputability or responsibility for an action can be diminished or nullified by ignorance, duress, fear and other psychological and social factors' (CCC, no. 1746).

- The best way to have more freedom is to perform good acts. Good deeds make us free. The road to loss of freedom is through evil acts. Sin makes us slaves of evil and reduces our capacity to be free.

- Every moral act consists of three elements: the objective act (what we do), the subjective goal or intention (why we do the act) and the concrete situation or circumstances in which we perform the act (where, when, how, with whom, the consequences, etc.). All three elements must be good for the act to be morally acceptable.

- Moral laws assist us in determining what is good or bad. Some acts are always wrong – that is, intrinsically evil – and may never be done, no matter what the intention or the circumstances.

- 'Conscience is a judgement of reason by which the human person recognises the moral quality of a concrete act' (CCC, no. 1796).

- A good conscience requires lifelong formation. The Word of God is a principal shaper of conscience when assimilated by study, prayer and practice. The prudent advice and good example of others support and enlighten our consciences. The authoritative teaching of the Church is an essential element in our conscience formation.

- A good conscience makes judgements that conform to reason and the good that is willed by the wisdom of God.
- We 'must always obey the certain judgement of [our] conscience. Conscience can remain in ignorance or make erroneous judgements. Such ignorance and errors are not always free of guilt' (CCC, nos. 1800, 1801).
- An effective moral life demands the practice of human and Theological Virtues. Such virtues train the soul with the habits of mind and will that support moral behaviour, control passions and avoid sin.
- Virtues guide our conduct according to the dictates of faith and reason. We group these virtues around the Cardinal Virtues of prudence, justice, fortitude and temperance.
- We will benefit greatly from practising the Theological Virtues of faith, hope and charity. We receive these virtues from God. They are called theological because they dispose us to live in relationship with the Holy Trinity. Faith, hope and love influence our human virtues by increasing their stability and strength for our lives.

MEDITATION

Jesus Christ is the ultimate Teacher of morality. He indeed ratified the Ten Commandments, and he also pointed out that every Commandment in the Law and the Prophets is rooted in the two fundamental precepts of love of God and love of neighbour. Though the Old Testament also taught love of God and neighbour, the Lord's precepts were new because he taught us the right measure of love, which includes the love of enemies. We are to love one another 'as I have loved you', that is, with a measure of love never seen before on earth. He taught by words and by his life that love essentially involves self-giving and self-sacrifice. We are never deliberately to do evil to anyone to achieve any objective whatsoever.

PRAYER

I pray that the God of peace,
who brought back from the dead our Lord Jesus,
the great Shepherd of the sheep,
by the blood that sealed an eternal covenant,
may prepare you to do his will in every kind of good action;
effecting in us all whatever is acceptable to himself through
Jesus Christ, to whom be glory for ever and ever. Amen

– Heb 13:20-21

Return to me – [the Lord] declares – and I will return to you.

– Zec 1:3

The freedom we have is not so that we can choose indiscriminately
between good and evil, but so that we can of our own accord choose
what is good and what corresponds to the truth.

– SGN, 57

24 LIFE IN CHRIST – PART TWO

THE PRINCIPLES OF THE CHRISTIAN MORAL LIFE
– CCC, NOS. 1691–2082

FRANK DUFF: AN ORDINARY IRISHMAN

Some people symbolise their period in history and their country to an extraordinary degree. Vincent de Paul, for example, has been called 'the greatest saint of the greatest era', a reference to pre-revolutionary France. John Henry Newman was the quintessential Englishman of the Victorian Age. In a similar way, Francis Michael Duff can represent the ordinary Irishman of his time. At his funeral in 1980, Cardinal Ó Fiaich remarked that Duff may in time be recognised by the Catholic Church as 'the Irishman of the century'.

Frank Duff was born in Phibsboro, Dublin, on 7 June 1889 of civil servant parents, the eldest of seven children. The family moved to Kingstown (now Dún Laoghaire) after a promotion for Mr Duff and a fortunate inheritance for his wife. The parents could now send the children to good schools, and Frank went to the Jesuit College at Belvedere as a child and to Blackrock College with the Holy Ghost Fathers (Spiritans) as a young teenager.

His parents hoped for Frank to go to university and then to the civil service at a higher grade than they enjoyed, but his father's ill-health and early retirement (he died in 1918) meant that his eldest son had to secure a permanent pensionable position to become the principal family bread winner.

So Frank Duff sat the civil service examination in 1907, finished first in Ireland, and entered the profession. His career was one of devotion to duty with much accomplishment and achievement. He served in the

Land Commission and the Department of Finance and seemed to be working his way up the promotional ladder satisfactorily when he took early retirement to dedicate himself full-time to Catholic apostolic work. He had served the public for twenty-six years.

The road to that decision was circuitous and providential. It looked like a series of chance encounters. The first was in October 1913, when a colleague invited him to join the St Vincent de Paul Society (VDP). Frank Duff confessed that he was not, at that time, very religious, but the invitation proved to be life-changing. He joined because he liked the man, so his motives were quite mixed. He reflected later that God often works that way, using 'normal, natural motives'.

The VDP led him into the Pioneer Total Abstinence Association and that, in turn, led to the first meeting of a group undertaking the visitation of the sick poor in the Dublin Union Hospital under the care of the Sisters of Mercy. The inaugural meeting of what was then called the Association of Our Lady of Mercy took place on Wednesday, 7 September 1922 in Myra House, Francis Street, with fifteen participants, including Frank Duff and a curate from the parish. Later, that event was recognised as the foundation of the Legion of Mary.

During this period of his life, Frank Duff learned two things: the first was from Louis de Montfort's book *The True Devotion of Mary*, where he discovered the central role of the Blessed Virgin Mary in God's plan of salvation as the Mediatrix of all graces. The second happened when, through a simple Catholic bootmaker and a reformed alcoholic called Joe Gabbett, Duff's eyes were opened to the importance of the apostolic work of laymen and women in the life of the Church.

Joe Gabbett was energetic, direct and simple in his approach to faith, in his concern for the poor and in his encouragement of others in the apostolate. It led Frank Duff to comment: 'I was truly a disciple at his feet and he certainly fired me with the whole business … I was incredibly captivated by Gabbett because I had never met anybody like him … I hadn't seen Catholicism of Gabbett's type before.'

These two insights – the central role of the Mother of God in the dispensation of grace and the impact on faith of personal witness – were the basis for his extraordinary contribution to the beginning and development and phenomenal growth of the Legion of Mary. Of course, his civil service training and organisational ability were attributes that also played a considerable part in its success.

For years Frank Duff denied being the 'founder' of the Legion, and it is true that others took the lead in the early days. But he was certainly unique as he placed the new association on a sure footing with his theological and spiritual inspiration, both in person and through his writing of the Legion Handbook. His prophetic vision that the Legion would spread beyond Irish shores, and his careful foresight in crafting the rules with terminology drawn from the ancient Roman Army (independent of modern culture), ensured members were ready for the international challenge.

The ideas embodied in the Legion of Mary were well ahead of their time. Some priests and bishops were understandably wary of engaging with it for two reasons. They doubted the theological competence of lay people, who were not well-educated even in secular terms. And they feared the dangers of undue enthusiasm and excessive zeal for the good order of parish and diocese.

This was particularly the case at home in Ireland. 'A prophet is despised only in his own country and in his own house' (Mt 13:57). Duff encountered opposition where he might have reasonably expected support and collaboration. Though personally saddened and often frustrated by such hostility, he never failed to obey and sought accommodation with the lawful authorities of the Church. His loyalty and support for his bishop was never in doubt.

In the end, Gamaliel's Law prevailed. 'But if it does in fact come from God you will be unable to destroy them …' (Acts 5:39). The Legion was set up throughout Ireland and abroad, especially in mission lands, aided by the approval of popes and nuncios. Today it has four million active members, ten million auxiliary members, and exists in at least 170 countries. Duff died on 7 November 1980, and Dublin came to a standstill for his funeral. In 1998, the process of beatification for the Servant of God, Francis Michael Duff, was inaugurated at the instigation of the Archbishop of Dublin.

Frank Duff enjoyed the natural human satisfaction of world recognition when he was invited as a lay observer to the Second Vatican Council. He had, after all, in many ways anticipated the Council's vision. Bishop Heenan was speaking when he spotted Duff entering the gallery. The bishop immediately announced his arrival to the Council Fathers, and the assembled 2,500 bishops rose spontaneously, in a standing ovation, to an ordinary Irishman and extraordinary apostle.

LIFE IN CHRIST – PART TWO

'So always treat others as you would like them to treat you; that is the Law and the Prophets' (Mt 7:12). This 'Golden Rule' taught by Jesus in his Sermon on the Mount is a golden thread that weaves its way through the moral life of the Christian. It is a behaviour that flows from life in Christ and in the Holy Spirit. Our journey in the moral life begins by looking at the person of Jesus, listening to his voice and responding to the strong yet gentle movement of the Holy Spirit.

The *Catechism of the Catholic Church* presents to us the elements, foundations and principles that serve as a sturdy point of departure for reflecting on Christian morality. This guidance from Christ brought to us through the Church is designed to help us answer his invitation to be holy, to be moral, to be fulfilled exactly in the way that God intended. The previous chapter focused on the individual human being as called to act morally. This chapter discusses morality as it pertains to the individual as situated within a community.

HUMAN COMMUNITY AND DIVINE ASSISTANCE: FURTHER FUNDAMENTAL ELEMENTS OF CHRISTIAN MORALITY

Consciousness of Solidarity and Social Justice

An awareness of the social dimension of human life is an important principle in understanding Christian morality, especially in light of the great emphasis on individualism in our society. The social aspect of what it means to be human is revealed in the natural inclination we have to seek social interaction and establish community. This awareness serves as a moral foundation for an attitude of solidarity with each other and leads to a dedication to social justice for everyone. Our Gospel commitment to Christ's Kingdom of love, justice and mercy always includes advocating and supporting fairness for all. God calls us to form community and to correct both the symptoms and causes of injustice that rip apart the solidarity of a community.

Before God gave the Commandments at Sinai, he entered into a covenant of love with the community of Israel (cf. Ex 19:3-6). Once the covenant was established, God gave the people the Ten Commandments in order to teach them the way to live the covenant of love.

In Christ we have been called to a New Covenant and a New Law that fulfills and perfects the Old Law. We also are invited to experience God's love for us and to return that love to God and to our neighbour. Our love of neighbour includes our solidarity with the human community and a commitment to social justice for all.

We need to respect the human dignity of every person. Governments and all other social institutions should serve and enhance the dignity of people. Society has the responsibility to create the conditions that favour the growth of virtues and of authentic spiritual and material values.

People need to live in a human community where the authority is based on human nature and recognised and understood as having its origin in God (cf. CCC, nos. 1898, 1899). Political authority should be used for the common good. 'The common good comprises "the sum total of social conditions which allow people, either as groups or as individuals, to reach their fulfilment more fully and easily"' (CCC, no. 1924, citing GS, no. 26 §1). Governments ought to use morally acceptable means to foster the common good of all and establish the conditions that assure citizens of the proper exercise of their freedom. In fostering this common good excessive intervention by the government in the lives of individuals is to be avoided. The principle of subsidiarity teaches that governments should help and support individuals and groups for whom they are responsible without controlling their freedom and initiative (cf. CCC, no. 1883).

Just as governments and social institutions need to respect the unique human dignity of every individual, it is also the responsibility of every individual to do the same. Attitudes of prejudice and bias against any individual for any reason, as well as actions or judgements based on prejudiced or biased views, violate God's will and law.

Social justice is both an attitude and a practical response based on the principle that everyone should look at another person as another self. It is also a virtue that directs all the other virtues of individuals toward the common good. Civil laws can partially help to eliminate fears, prejudices and attitudes of pride and selfishness that cause injustice, but an inner spiritual conversion is also needed.

Solidarity with others at every level is a way of accomplishing this. Solidarity takes many forms: 'solidarity of the poor among themselves, between rich and poor, of workers among themselves, between employers and employees in a business, solidarity among nations and peoples' (CCC, no. 1941).

Examples of offences against human solidarity are slavery and racism. Slavery reduces a human being to an object to be bought and sold. It is a failure to recognise the God-given dignity and rights of a human being. Racism is an attitude that rejects the fundamental equality of all human beings. It shows itself in discrimination and unjust actions against people of other races. Both slavery and racism are gravely immoral.

God's Law as Our Guide

We are assisted to know God's plan for our salvation through his law written in our human nature and revealed to us in his word. All things come to be and find their purpose and goal in God's plan. Thus we can speak of the eternal law as the wisdom of God ordering all things rightly.

It is God who brings creation into being; thus the physical world acts according to his plan found in the physical laws of nature. He also made man and woman in his own image and likeness. Human beings, then, are also directed according to God's created plan, written in their hearts and implanted in their human nature. 'Man participates in the wisdom and goodness of the Creator who gives him mastery over his acts and the ability to govern himself with a view to the true and the good. The natural law expresses the original moral sense which enables man to discern by reason the good and the evil, the truth and the lie' (CCC, no. 1954). We come to know it through our human reason and through its confirmation in Divine Revelation.

Through our human reason, we can come to understand the true purpose of the created order. The natural law is thus our rational apprehension of the divine plan. It expresses our human dignity and is the foundation of our basic human rights and duties. This law within us leads us to choose the good that it reveals. Its most pronounced expression is found in the Ten Commandments, described as 'the privileged expression of the natural law' (CCC, no. 2070).

Because the natural law is rooted in God's plan found in human nature, it applies to all people in all places and at all times. While situations may vary greatly, the natural law is unchangeable. It abides at the core of what makes us human and thus is not affected by the flow and currents from cultural ideas and customs. While a given person, region, culture, or era of time may attempt to suppress it, the fundamental principles of the natural law never die and soon reappear, even where they were once rejected.

We come to know God's plan for us not only through an understanding of our human nature and his created order but also because he speaks directly to us. In the Old Testament, God communicated to Moses the Ten Commandments. This Law prepared the world for the Gospel. Christian tradition reveres this Law as holy but in need of God's grace for its fulfilment. It is like a teacher who can tell us what to do but is not able to give us the strength to perform it. Nonetheless, we honour this Law as an aid to God's people on the way to the Kingdom. It prepared people to receive Christ.

In Jesus, Revelation comes to us in its fullness. His words shed light on the human condition in a way that transcends and fulfils the law written in our heart and God's plan revealed in the Old Testament.

In the Sermon on the Mount, Jesus revealed the full meaning of the Old Testament Law. 'Do not imagine that I have come to abolish the Law or the Prophets. I have come not to abolish but to complete them' (Mt 5:17). Christ's teaching releases the hidden meaning of the Old Law and reveals its Divine Truth and human truth. Jesus established the law of love because love is poured into our hearts by the Holy Spirit. It is a law of grace, as we note in the next section.

Grace and Justification

God also directly assists us in living our moral life through the divine gift of grace and justification, first bestowed upon us in Baptism when we become members of the Church. We are justified – cleansed from our sins and reconciled to God – through the power of the Holy Spirit. Justification is both the Spirit's work in bringing us forgiveness of sins and our acceptance or reception of the holiness of God, which we call sanctification through participation in divine life. Christ's Passion merited justification for us. We receive justification in Baptism and become friends of God. We are thus conformed to the righteousness of God who justifies us. Justification's goal is God's glory and the glory of Christ and the gift of eternal life. It is a work of God's mercy (cf. CCC, no. 2020).

Grace is the free and undeserved assistance God offers us so that we might respond to his call to share in his divine life and attain eternal life. God's grace, as divinely offered gift, does not take away or restrict our freedom; rather, it perfects our freedom by helping us overcome the restricting power of sin, the true obstacle to our freedom. We call the grace of the Holy Spirit that we receive through faith in Jesus Christ the New Law. Significant expressions of this Law are found in Christ's Sermon on the Mount and his Last Supper discourse, where he emphasises union with him in love as the substance and motivation for his law of grace.

> Grace is the help God gives us to respond to our vocation of becoming his adopted sons. It introduces us into the intimacy of the Trinitarian life. The divine initiative in the work of grace precedes, prepares and elicits the free response of man. Grace responds to the deepest yearnings of human freedom, calls freedom to cooperate with it and perfects freedom. Sanctifying grace is the gratuitous gift of his life that God makes to us; it is infused by the Holy Spirit into the soul to heal it of sin and to sanctify it. (CCC, nos. 2021–2023)

In addition to speaking about sanctifying grace, we also speak of actual graces. These refer to the particular interventions God offers us to aid us in the course of the work of sanctification. We recognise that many times and in many ways God's special love is such that he offers us help to live in a way that leads to sharing his life. Finally, there are sacramental graces, which are proper to the celebration of the Seven Sacraments, and special graces or charisms, which, while given to individuals, are meant for the common good of the Church (cf. CCC, no. 2003).

In this recognition of the reality and important role of grace in the Christian moral life, we face a struggle prompted by our culture's understanding that everything is within our human power. 'My power is sufficient.' Compare this with our understanding that we are indeed blessed and gifted, but much of what we fight to achieve – while written in our hearts – still needs God's grace because of the presence of sin and our inherent human weakness. The New Law is truly Good News, for not only does God give us the moral law that leads us to salvation, but through grace we receive divine assistance to follow it. We should always take heart from the words Our Lord spoke to St Paul: 'My grace is enough for you: for power is at full stretch in weakness' (2 Cor 12:9).

The Church as Mother and Teacher

God assists us in living the moral life through the Church, who is our mother and teacher. The faith of the Church is found in its Creed and in its ordinary teaching, as articulated by its shepherds, the pope and the bishops in communion with him.

Jesus said to the Apostles, 'Anyone who listens to you listens to me' (Lk 10:16). In the Church, when we deal with matters of faith and morals, the authoritative voice of Christ is exercised by the pope and bishops, successors of Peter and the Apostles who form the Magisterium. They are guided by the Holy Spirit, who abides with the Church to lead us into all truth.

The Church hears the perennial questions that each person asks at some point: 'How shall I live?' 'What values or principles shall I accept?' 'What norms shall I make my own?' 'What gives meaning to my life?' To answer questions such as these, we turn to a wise teacher. Christ is the ultimate teacher, and he continues to be heard in and through the Church today. The *Catechism* notes that 'the *Magisterium of the Pastors of the Church* in moral matters is ordinarily exercised in catechesis and preaching, with the help of the works of theologians and spiritual authors' (CCC, no. 2033). In the task of teaching and applying the vision and practice of Christian morality, the Church relies on the dedication of pastors and the studies of theologians, as well as the contributions of all people of goodwill (cf. CCC, no. 2038).

FROM THE CATECHISM

1. Why is happiness a motivation to be moral?

The Beatitudes respond to the natural desire for happiness. This desire is of divine origin: God has placed it in the human heart in order to draw man to the One who alone can fulfil it. (CCC, no. 1718)

2. What is social sin?

Sin makes men accomplices of one another and causes concupiscence, violence and injustice to reign among them. Sins give rise to social situations and institutions that are contrary to the divine goodness. 'Structures of sin' are the expression and effect of personal sins. They lead their victims to do evil in their turn. In an analogous sense, they constitute a 'social sin'. (CCC, no. 1869)

3. What is the New Law?

The New Law or the Law of the Gospel is the perfection here on earth of the divine law, natural and revealed. It is the work of Christ and is expressed particularly in the Sermon on the Mount. It is also the work of the Holy Spirit, and through him it becomes the interior law of charity: 'I will establish a New Covenant with the house of Israel ... I will put my laws into their minds, and write them on their hearts, and I will be their God, and they shall be my people.' (CCC, no. 1965, citing Heb 8:8, 10)

The response based on faith that Catholics must give to the Church's teaching authority – the Magisterium – extends also to moral principles:

> The Church, the 'pillar and bulwark of the truth', 'has received this solemn command of Christ from the apostles to announce the saving truth'. 'To the Church belongs the right always and everywhere to announce moral principles, including those pertaining to the social order, and to make judgements on any human affairs to the extent

that they are required by the fundamental rights of the human person or the salvation of souls.' (CCC, no. 2032, citing 1 Tm 3:15; LG, no. 17; CIC, can. 747 §2)

CAN WE BE SAINTS?

Frank Duff wrote a twenty-page pamphlet with this title in 1916, as he was embarking on the work of his lifetime. It has been reprinted many times in the last near-hundred years since that date. Simple, sensible and straightforward, the words lift the veil on his attitude to his own efforts in the apostolate, and the way he approached them. Here are some extracts:

The Call to Good Works

In times of retreat, or at your prayers, or by the invitation of a friend, a call to some good work will come. It may be from on high, so do not lightly refuse. You may miss your life's vocation. Saint Augustine speaks solemn words: 'Fear Jesus passing by … He may not again pass your way.'

How We Can Do Big Things

With industry, self-sacrifice, and some knowledge of human nature, we can all produce results: (a) by organising – by making things ready for people who will not make them ready for themselves; (b) by bringing to people, who would never get them for themselves, things which will benefit them; (c) by appealing individually to people who would never respond to a general appeal.

In other words, we are to be the bridge that covers the chasm between what people will do of themselves and what God wants them to do.

For example:
1. A pilgrimage is organised. Everything is cut-and-dried. All that one has to do is to buy the ticket and take one's place. One thousand persons go. Would any have gone had the pilgrimage and its details never been arranged?

2. An appeal is made from a pulpit to support a certain religious publication. Only a handful of people respond. A house-to-house canvass later on, bringing the paper directly under the people's notice, produces hundreds of fresh readers.

3. Everybody in a town knows the needs of a local charity. Yet few subscribe, until a door-to-door call is organised. Then all give.

'Thou Shalt Love Thy Neighbour As Thyself'

The foregoing are only indications of what might be done. Your own tastes, surroundings, conscience, will suggest many powerful means of benefitting your own soul by benefitting the souls of other people. 'Love thy neighbour as thyself' is a hard saying. But keep in mind who said it, and neglect no way of helping others on towards good. Ask St Vincent de Paul, who is the patron of all such works, to inspire you with knowledge of what will suit you best. Perhaps you might make a beginning by joining the society which bears his name.

Breaking New Ground

Perhaps you could band together others in association to do good, and give the first impulse to what St Vincent calls the sacred contagion of charity. Start a little organisation. Gather a few around you for some good work. Hold a regular meeting – weekly, if possible – and discuss your little efforts under the auspices of prayer. You have it on His own word that He, Who can make your efforts fruitful, is there in the midst of you.

Do not soar too high. Do not be over-anxious. Look above all to the routine duties and the small details of the meeting. A punctual start, carefully written minutes, attendance-roll regularly marked up, discussion of business and business only, affection among the members, these – far more than organising ability or exceptional workers – will ensure a lasting success.

It cannot be over-emphasised that the progress and the permanence of the organisation depend upon the meetings, and that the meetings in turn depend upon the system, the prayerfulness and the fraternity which are found in them. Act mindfully of this: face calmly the inevitable ups and downs and your work may be multiplied exceedingly. All the great movements have had just such simple origins.

THE PRECEPTS OF THE CHURCH
(SEE CCC, NOS. 2041–2043)

In addition to presenting the foundations for Christian morality, the *Catechism of the Catholic Church* includes a section on the Precepts of the Church. These are rules set in the context of a moral life, bound to and nourished by liturgical life. The obligatory character of these positive laws decreed by the pastoral authorities is meant to encourage on the part of the faithful the indispensable foundations for their lives as Catholics. The precepts are as follows:

- You shall attend Mass on Sundays and Holy Days of Obligation. Sunday, the day of the Resurrection, should be treated differently from the other days of the week. We do that in making the day holy by attending Mass and refraining from doing unnecessary work. Holy Days of Obligation, when we celebrate special feasts of Jesus, the Blessed Mother and the saints, should be marked in the same way.

- You shall confess your sins at least once a year. This obliges in particular those who are conscious of serious sin. Regular reception of the Sacrament of Penance and Reconciliation helps to prepare us not only to receive the Eucharist but also to continue the process of conversion begun in Baptism.

- You shall receive the Sacrament of the Eucharist at least during the Easter season. This extends from the First Sunday of Lent to Trinity Sunday. Because the Holy Eucharist is both the source and summit of life for all in the Church, the Church teaches that every member for his or her own good must receive Communion at least once a year.

- You shall observe the prescribed days of fasting and abstinence. *Fasting* is refraining from food or drink to some degree. *Abstinence* is refraining from eating meat. The Church identifies specific days and times of fasting and abstinence to prepare the faithful for certain special feasts; such actions of sacrifice can also help us to grow in self-discipline and in holiness.

- You shall help to provide for the needs of the Church. This means contributing to the support of the activities of the Church with time, talent and financial resources, each according to their ability.

Some Homely Ways of Doing Great Work

The following are some of the many ways in which a multitude of men and women are spending their free time serving God. Judgement Day alone will show the joy they have given Him, and the good they have effected.

The few examples given will make it clear that such work is within the capacity of anyone with perseverance.

The Catechism Teacher. The saintly Pius X was once asked by a lady who was desirous of doing some really good work for God, what he would suggest to her. He surprised her by answering: 'Teach children the Catechism.' Take a class and put your heart into it. Acquire a large stock of anecdotes by which you can both train and interest these little ones who are, as has been beautifully said, wax to receive, marble to retain. Many of them will some day do great things for God. And it will be through you ...

Visiting the Sick. The first concern of St Ignatius of Loyola and his companions on coming to each new town was to visit the sick in the hospitals, knowing that in doing this, they did it to Christ Himself. Pick some hospital, by preference a workhouse hospital, and find one or more of the very many patients who are without friends or visitors. Be you both friend and visitor to them. Visit them regularly. Your smiling face and cheerful words will make your visits longed for. And what wonderful prayers will ring up to high Heaven for you from these poor suffering ones of Christ, whom you have succoured.

– From Frank Duff, *Can We Be Saints?* (Dublin: Catholic Truth Society, 1958)

▬ FOR DISCUSSION ▬

1. As you review fundamental elements of Christian moral living, which ones gave you a new perspective on Christian moral life? How can all of them become a regular part of the growth of your life in Christ and the Spirit?
2. Moral life based on the teaching of Scripture flows from God's loving plan for us. How does this correspond to your view of what the moral life is about? How would you live out such a plan?
3. You are called to faithful assent to the Church's teachings on faith and morals. What challenges do you experience? How do you handle them? What motivates you to be a morally good person?

▬ DOCTRINAL STATEMENTS ▬

- God's divine law establishes our final destiny and the path to reach it. God has planted within each of us the natural law that is a reflection of his divine law.
- The natural law is our rational apprehension of the created moral order, an ability we have because we are made in God's image. It expresses our human dignity and forms the basis of our basic rights and duties.
- Divine wisdom leads us through various types of law (divine law, natural law, civil law, ecclesiastical [Church] law) designed to guide us to the very goals that will answer our deepest human aspirations.
- Revealed law is seen in the Old Testament when God communicated the Ten Commandments to Moses. The Commandments, along with the teaching of the Prophets and other revealed law, prepared the world for the Gospel.
- Christ's teachings release the hidden meaning of the Old Law and reveal its Divine Truth and human truth. The Gospel is a law of love because of the love poured into our hearts by the Holy Spirit.

- 'Justification is the most excellent work of God's love made manifest in Christ Jesus and granted by the Holy Spirit' (CCC, no. 1994). Justification is both the Spirit's work in bringing us forgiveness of sins and our acceptance or reception of the holiness of God, which we call sanctification through participation in divine life.
- 'Sanctifying grace is a habitual gift, a stable and supernatural disposition that perfects the soul itself to enable it to live with God, to act by his love. Habitual grace, the permanent disposition to live and act in keeping with God's call, is distinguished from actual graces, which refer to God's interventions, whether at the beginning of conversion or in the course of the work of sanctification' (CCC, no. 2000).
- 'Sanctifying grace is the gratuitous gift of his life that God makes to us; it is infused by the Holy Spirit into the soul to heal it of sin and to sanctify it' (CCC, no. 2023).
- Christ's Passion merited justification for us. We receive justification in Baptism and become friends of God. We are thus conformed to the righteousness of God who justifies us.
- God called Israel to be holy. 'You must therefore be holy because I am holy' (Lev 11:45). Saint Peter extended this invitation from God to Christians. 'As obedient children, be yourselves holy in all your activity, after the model of the Holy One who calls us, since scripture says, "Be holy, for I am holy"' (1 Pt 1:15-16).
- Jesus said to the Apostles, 'Anyone who listens to you listens to me (Lk 10:16). In the Church, when we deal with matters of faith and morals, the authoritative voice of Christ is exercised by the pope and bishops who, as the successors of Peter and the Apostles, form the Magisterium. They are guided by the Holy Spirit, who abides with the Church to lead us into all truth.
- 'The Magisterium of the Pastors of the Church in moral matters is ordinarily exercised in catechesis and preaching, with the help of the works of theologians and spiritual authors' (CCC, no. 2033).
- 'Society ensures social justice by providing the conditions that allow associations and individuals to obtain their due' (CCC, no. 1943). Social justice deals with the essential needs of people who are called to live together in community with respect for each other's dignity. These needs include food, clothing, shelter and an income that supports the family.

- 'The principle of solidarity, also articulated in terms of "friendship" or "social charity", is a direct demand of human and Christian brotherhood' (CCC, no. 1939). This involves a love for all peoples that transcends national, racial, ethnic, economic and ideological differences. It respects the needs of others and the common good in an interdependent world.

MEDITATION

The Secret of Influencing Others

There is an art in the moving of others, and those that work for their neighbour must study it.

Do not say 'I cannot', or 'I am not fitted', or 'Nobody heeds me'. For there is one thing that can clothe you with power in your dealings with others: affection for them. This is the great secret of all real influence. To possess it, follow this simple rule – Look only for good qualities in anyone you meet; you will find them. Never look for faults, for you would find them. Act thus, and you will easily develop the habit of love. Convince those around you, by deeds, not phrases, that you truly have this feeling for them, and you can lead them where you like.

– From Frank Duff, *Can We Be Saints?* (Dublin: Catholic Truth Society, 1958)

PRAYER

Act of Hope

O my God,
Relying on your infinite goodness and promises,
I hope to obtain pardon of my sins,
The help of your grace, and life everlasting,
through the merits of Jesus Christ, my Lord and Redeemer.

Now you are set free from sin and bound
to the service of God, your gain will be
sanctification and the end will be eternal life.

— Rm 6:22

The Decalogue ('the ten words'), revealed by God to Moses, proclaims God's law. It confirms the implications of belonging to God.

— SGN, 60

25 THE FIRST COMMANDMENT: BELIEVE IN THE TRUE GOD

'I, THE LORD, AM YOUR GOD ... YOU SHALL NOT HAVE
OTHER GODS BESIDES ME' (EX 20:2-3)
– CCC, NOS. 2083–2141

EVIE HONE: HALLOWED FIRE

 During the Second World War, the large east window of Eton College Chapel near London was destroyed by a German bomb. The artist chosen to replace this significant religious symbol was Evie Hone, probably the most radical stained-glass artist in Ireland. This was a large window and Hone planned it in a number of panels, including a Crucifixion, a Resurrection, a Last Supper and several Old Testament figures. While she worked on the final process of installation, the Cultural Relations Committee of Ireland commissioned a short film about her art entitled *Hallowed Fire*.

The title was surely evocative, quoting the final phrase of John Milton's 'Ode on the Morning of Christ's Nativity'. The words remind the reader of the prophet Isaiah's lips touched by a glowing ember from the holy altar to purify him to speak the word of the Lord. Similarly, the poet imagines his own words hot and glowing from the coming of Christ into his life. This is an image for the religious artist. Gazing at an expanse of bright colour, refracting the rays of the rising sun throughout the chapel, Milton's image was never so apt, both visually and spiritually. Evie Hone's east window in Eton Chapel was to seal her reputation as one of the greatest stained-glass artists of the era.

Evie Hone was born in 1894 in Mount Merrion, Dublin, to a family with a long history in the arts; Nathaniel Hone, the eighteenth-century painter, was a forebear. She suffered early tragedy when she contracted poliomyelitis at the age of twelve, and spent much time in her teens under the care of doctors at home and abroad. This condition left her with a discernible limp and in a vulnerable state of health in her adult years.

With her lifelong friend, Mainie Jellett, she embarked on the study of art in London and demonstrated a natural talent. In 1921, both women moved to Paris to study contemporary art and Cubism in particular. They were the first Irish artists to adopt this style and bring it back home. Their exhibitions in Dublin and elsewhere, especially during the 1920s, influenced other Irish artists, ensuring that Ireland was brought into the European mainstream of art. The Cubist style abandoned representation, offered a variety of views of the same experience, reduced natural shapes to fundamental forms, and rejoiced in the contrast and combination of colour and shade. It has been commented that the discipline Hone acquired studying a very strict form of Cubism for ten years gave her the ability to handle shape and colour unobtrusively and apparently effortlessly in her best stained glass.

Evie Hone was also moving in the European mainstream in another dimension. A visit to Italy, and Assisi in particular, opened her up to a vibrant and visual religious tradition. She was so deeply moved that in 1925 she decided to try her own vocation to the religious life. As the Hone family was Church of Ireland, she thought about entering an Anglican convent of contemplative nuns in Truro, Cornwall, in the picturesque south of England. The postulancy did not work out. The nuns stipulated that the young aspirant refrain from painting until she should discern her future.

Evie returned to Ireland but she was still heavily influenced by religion. The art of Georges Rouault, with his powerful, brooding sincerity, broad colour and deep emotion, along with the stained glass of Chartres Cathedral and early Irish Celtic art, made an impact on her imagination. There was already a stained-glass movement in Ireland, spearheaded by Sarah Purser and promoted by Edward Martyn. Evie Hone became a member and embarked on mastering the craft of glass.

The Christian Churches were eager patrons for stained glass, and a number of Irish artists met the demand, including Harry Clarke and his studio, Michael Healy, and others. Evie Hone joined them. Her style was quite distinctive, being expressionist and abstract with an energy of colour derived from the medieval Irish and Italian Catholic tradition. In 1937, Evie Hone converted to Catholicism, being received into the Church by Archbishop John Charles McQuaid.

In 1939, she completed a commission in stained glass for the Irish Pavilion at the New York World Fair called 'My Four Green Fields'. It earned great acclaim and is now displayed in Government Buildings, Merrion Square, Dublin. Over the next fifteen years, Evie Hone designed stained-glass windows for churches and chapels in many places in Ireland, England and the United States. Notable examples of her windows in Ireland are the Church of Ireland in Dundrum, Co. Dublin; various chapels at Clongowes and Blackrock College; at the Church in Kingscourt, Co. Cavan; in Tullabeg, Co. Offaly; in the Jesuit Church at Gardiner Street, Dublin; and in the Manresa Retreat House in Clontarf. One of her last works is the rose window in All Hallows College chapel in Drumcondra.

Evie Hone's stained glass bypasses elaborate detail to concentrate on meaning and emotion. It is dynamic rather than static, strong rather than delicate, spiritual rather than sensual. Stained glass as an artistic medium strives to reveal to the viewer a world beyond. As well as any other worker in stained glass, Evie Hone succeeds in doing that.

Personally, Evie Hone struck people as friendly and approachable, with a lightness of touch and an air of self-deprecation. She was devout and earnest. Evie Hone died suddenly, at the start of Mass in her parish church in Rathfarnham, on 13 March 1955.

The artist can be self-centred and inner-directed, communicating an individual grasp of the reality captured in art. The creative imagination is, of course, the goal of all artists, writers, musicians, painters and sculptors. The Eastern Christian Church, however, regards the icon painter as more than an artist, indeed, as one called to be a saint. This is because, aware of the spiritual realm, the religious artist has a further task to convey the gleam of heaven's glory as well as the earthly vision. Evie Hone was surely touched with 'hallowed fire'. She made that fire glow in glass in the walls of many of our Irish churches.

>⟩ >⟩ >⟩ >⟩ >⟩

THE ROLE OF THE COMMANDMENTS

God helps us in many different ways to live a moral life. He gives us grace, which awakens in us the desire to say no to temptation and sin and to choose only that which is good. He gives us the Theological and Cardinal Virtues and the grace to practise human virtues so that we can grow stronger in them. God gives us help and grace through the Church and through our reception of the Sacraments. He also teaches us how we should live. One way he does this is by giving us laws to guide our actions. The Ten Commandments are laws that God has revealed to us. Heeding the guidance God gives us in the Commandments will help us know how to serve God and how we should live with each other. It also helps us to be open to the grace of the Holy Spirit and what God can accomplish in us and through us by that grace.

THE FIRST COMMANDMENT

The first three Commandments treat our relationship to God. The last seven concern our relationship with each other. The First Commandment calls us to have faith in the true God, to hope in him and to love him fully with mind, heart and will. We respond to God, who has created and redeemed us and extends his providential care to us every minute of each day. The First Commandment fosters the virtue of religion that moves us to adore God alone because he alone is holy and worthy of our praise.

> Adoring God, praying to him, offering him the worship that belongs to him, fulfilling the promises and vows made to him are acts of the virtue of religion which fall under obedience to the first commandment. (CCC, no. 2135)

All the Commandments call us to practise certain virtues and forbid a number of immoral behaviours. The positive invitation of the First

Commandment calls us to practise the Theological Virtues of faith, hope and charity by believing in the three Persons of the Holy Trinity, placing all our hope in them and loving them with our whole heart and mind.

Faith

God has given us the virtue of faith, which is a personal response to the Lord's Revelation of his holiness, love, beauty and transcendence. We experience hints of his majesty in creation, traces of his love in the human love we receive and impulses of his concern for us in our inner life, especially in the movements of conscience. Our faith is also communal, coming to us from our families and parish community. Above all, our faith in God is a gift of grace and is constantly nourished by the Holy Spirit from the moment of our Baptism, through our prayer life, our participation in the Eucharist and the Sacraments and our Christian witness.

While it is the duty of all to worship and serve God, regrettably, there are some who do not believe in him and others who seriously doubt his existence. Some hesitate to believe because they cannot overcome their objections to faith, or are puzzled by the mystery of God. Some of the baptised later lapse into heresy. '*Heresy* is the obstinate post-baptismal denial of some truth which must be believed with divine and catholic faith, or it is likewise an obstinate doubt concerning the same' (CCC, no. 2089).

Apostasy is a total repudiation of the faith (cf. CCC, no. 2089). *Schism* is the refusal to submit to the pope's authority as head of the Church. Christ calls us to have a prayerful, reconciling attitude toward people with difficulties in their faith, to help them toward assent to the truth of faith.

Hope

God has given us the virtue of hope. Hope fills us with the confidence that God accompanies us on our journey through life and guides us to eternal life with him. If we refuse this gift of hope, we stray into presumption or its opposite, despair. In the sin of presumption, we think we will be saved without any personal commitment to the moral life. In the sin of despair, we lose hope in God's mercy and believe we cannot be saved.

Love

Finally, God has given us the virtue of love, the very love that he has for us. Our Lord asks us to accept this love and respond to him with it. Jesus made the love of God the first of the two greatest Commandments: 'You must love the Lord your God with all your heart, with all your soul, and with all your mind' (Mt 22:37). We sin against this call to love by indifference, ingratitude, lukewarmness, spiritual sloth and hatred of God (cf. CCC, no. 2094).

ISSUES RELATED TO THE FIRST COMMANDMENT

Idolatry

The First Commandment prohibits idolatry, the worship of false gods. In ancient times, people worshipped created things such as the sun, moon, stars, trees, bulls, eagles and serpents. In some cases, emperors and kings were considered divine, and worship of them was expected.

Israel was forbidden to make images of God: 'Do not corrupt yourselves by making an image in the shape of anything whatever' (Deut 4:16). This injunction against 'graven images' was based on the conviction that God is greater and more mysterious than any artistic representation of him. It also restrained Israel from carving idols like the pagans and lapsing into idolatry. But the people of Israel could make images that symbolically pointed toward salvation by the Messiah, such as the bronze serpent, the Ark of the Covenant and the cherubim (cf. CCC, no. 2130).

Christians, however, have been permitted to fashion religious art. The veneration of icons – religious images of Christ, Mary, the angels and the saints – was upheld by the seventh Ecumenical Council at Nicea (AD 787), in opposition to the iconoclasts – those who rejected the use of religious images such as statues, paintings and mosaics. The fact that, in the Incarnation, Christ took on human nature provided the foundation for the Church's tradition that artistic images such as icons can portray mysteries of salvation. Whoever venerates a holy image venerates the person portrayed. This veneration of Mary and the saints – and images of them – differs from the adoration that belongs to God alone.

Today idolatry has emerged in new forms, whenever something created is given absolute value. Examples of where this happens include power, money, materialism and sports. Also, those who resort to astrology, palm reading and interpretation of omens by mediums, clairvoyants and others who claim to control time and history weaken their faith in God, lapse into superstition and sometimes fall into sin. Those who get involved with cults or the occult (e.g. magic, witchcraft, Satanism) open themselves to evil influence, undermine their faith in the true God and commit sin.

Some contemporary individuals turn to a New Age spirituality. This spirituality does not have a doctrinal basis but reflects many religious strands from the non-Christian East, various occult practices like astrology and some insights from psychology. Practitioners tend to abandon doctrinal teaching on the Trinity, Jesus Christ, the Church and the sacraments. They also ignore the moral teaching of God and the Church.

Atheism

In the context of our culture, atheism often wears the face of secularism in its extreme form. Atheists or radical secularists deny God's existence. Some are strict materialists, believing that ultimately there is nothing spiritual whatsoever. Some are secular humanists, who claim that humans should control history and the world with no reference to God. Christians must always examine their own behaviour because lack of consistency with the Gospel in their lives can encourage others in atheism.

> Believers ... have more than a little to do with the rise of atheism. To the extent that they are careless about their instruction in the faith, or present its teaching falsely or even fail in their religious, moral or social life, they must be said to conceal rather than reveal the true nature of God and of religion. (GS, no. 19)

Agnosticism

This is another way to evade the call of the First Commandment. The term *agnostic* means 'I don't know'. It comes in different forms. Some agnostics admit God's existence but claim nothing can be known about him. Others say it is impossible to know whether there is a God. Some agnostics are searching for God; others do not try. Many are practical atheists, who may not consciously deny God's existence, but live as if he does not exist.

FROM THE CATECHISM

1. Why should we adore the true God alone?
We adore God because he is God and deserving of our adoration. Human life finds its unity in the adoration of the one God. 'Idolatry is a perversion of man's innate religious sense' (CCC, no. 2114). The Commandment to worship God alone integrates man and saves him from an endless disintegration.

2. What is the link between God's love and the Commandments?
God has loved us first. The love of the One God is recalled in the first of the 'ten words'. The commandments then make explicit the response of love that man is called to give to his God. (CCC, no. 2083)

3. How is it possible to obey God's commands?
What God commands he makes possible by his grace. (CCC, no. 2082)

THE HOLINESS OF GOD IN DAILY LIFE

When God appeared to Moses on Mount Horeb, he said, 'The place where you are standing is holy ground' (Ex 3:5). The sixth chapter of Isaiah describes the prophet's vision of God and hearing the angels sing, 'Holy, holy, holy is [the Lord]' (Is 6:3). Moses reacts to God's holiness with awe, a deep reverence for the all-embracing majesty of God. Isaiah responds to God's holiness with an awareness of the profound and infinite purity of God. Both men undergo a spiritual transformation that they attribute to their experience of God's holiness.

The First Commandment is more than a reference to an abstract idea of God. It is an announcement of the presence of the most holy God, both in outward creation and within the human soul. His existence does call for our faith.

Our surrounding culture is filled with many distractions that shut out the majestic voice of our holy and glorious God. Saint Augustine, commenting on his troubled youth, speaks of this experience with these words, 'You were with me, but I was not with you. Created things kept me from you; yet if they had not been in you they would not have been at all.' But God was not simply a passive presence to Augustine, a diffident lover wondering what to do. Augustine tells us that God spoke with a vigorous voice. 'You called, you shouted and you broke through my deafness. You breathed your fragrance on me ... I have tasted you, now I hunger and thirst for more' (*The Confessions*, bk. 10, no. 27).

This is the best context for appreciating the importance of the First Commandment. As God did with Augustine, he does for us again – calling, shouting, trying to break through our deafness, breathing his fragrance upon us.

Many, indeed, are listening. Numerous Catholics are seeking a deeper relationship with God through daily Mass, frequent reception of the Sacraments, the prayerful reading of Scripture, retreats, spiritual direction, diverse forms of prayer and devotional practices. With Augustine, they can say, 'You touched me, and I burned for your peace.'

FOR DISCUSSION

1. Many people in Ireland would say that they believe in the existence of God. What causes the disconnection, where it is to be seen, between that belief and their behaviour?
2. How do you find that acts of faith, hope and love bring you closer to God and make your behaviour an act of praise to the Lord?
3. How can we discover the presence of God in our lives? How can we share an awareness of this reality with others?

DOCTRINAL STATEMENTS

- 'I am [the Lord] your God ... You shall have no other gods to rival me ... You must love [the Lord] your God with all your heart, with all your soul, with all your strength' (Ex 20:2-3; Deut 6:5).

- The positive invitation of the First Commandment calls us to practise the Theological Virtues of faith, hope and charity by believing in, hoping in and loving God, and by our willingness to adore the Holy Trinity. The Theological Virtues relate directly to the living God.
- 'Adoring God, praying to him, offering him the worship that belongs to him, fulfilling the promises and vows made to him are acts of the virtue of religion which fall under obedience to the first commandment' (CCC, no. 2135).
- Based on our faith in the Incarnation of Christ, we venerate images of Christ, Mary, the angels and the saints. We do not worship the images themselves, but in venerating the image, we venerate whoever is portrayed – Jesus Christ, Mary, a saint or an angel. This in turn can lead us to a deeper contemplation of God himself.
- The First Commandment forbids idolatry, which is the worship of a creature or an object.
- Other sins against the First Commandment include tempting God, which means that we put his power to the test as Satan did with Jesus in the temptations in the desert; sacrilege, which means treating with disrespect persons, places or things consecrated to God – above all the Eucharist; and simony, which is the buying or selling of spiritual things.
- 'Since it rejects or denies the existence of God, atheism is a sin against the first commandment' (CCC, no. 2140).
- At the heart of our faith is our assent of mind and will to all that God reveals, all that the Church defines and all that is presented by the Church in her ordinary and universal Magisterium as Christ's way to salvation.

MEDITATION

Prayer of the Heart

Prayer and converse with God is a supreme good: it is a partnership and union with God. As the eyes of the body are enlightened when they see light, so our spirit, when it is intent on God, is illumined by his infinite light. I do not mean the prayer of outward observance but prayer from the heart, not confined to fixed times or periods but continuous throughout the day and night.

Our spirit should be quick to reach out toward God, not only when it is engaged in meditation; at other times also, when it is carrying out its duties, caring for the needy, performing works of charity, giving generously in the service of others, our spirit should long for God and call him to mind, so that these works may be seasoned with the salt of God's love and so make a palatable offering to the Lord of the universe.

– St John Chrysostom, Homily 6, 'On Procreation',
the *Liturgy of the Hours*, vol. II, 68–69

PRAYER

Act of Love

O my God, I love you above all things,
with my whole heart and soul,
because you are all good and worthy of all my love.
I love my neighbour as myself for the love of you.
I forgive all who have injured me,
and ask pardon of all whom I have injured.

Your way, O God, is in the holy place.
What god is as great as our God?
Grant us, that without fear we might worship you
in holiness all our days.

– Ps 77:14; cf. Lk 1:73

26 THE SECOND COMMANDMENT: REVERENCE GOD'S NAME

'YOU SHALL NOT TAKE THE NAME OF THE LORD
YOUR GOD IN VAIN' (EX 20:7)
– CCC, NOS. 2142–2167

JOB: THE POOR MAN PRAISES GOD

Why do the innocent suffer? This has been an age-old question that is addressed in Scripture as well, perhaps most extensively in the Book of Job. Written probably in the sixth century BC, it tells the story of a prosperous and prestigious man named Job, father of a large family and deeply devoted to God. In a series of calamities provoked by Satan, Job loses everything – family, wealth and even his own health. In the midst of all this loss, he cries out:

> Naked I came from my mother's womb,
>   naked I shall return again.
> [The Lord] gave, [the Lord] has taken back.
>   Blessed be the name of [the Lord]! (Job 1:21)

Nothing could shake his faith in God. His wife, seeing his pitiable state, tells him, 'Curse God and die' (2:9). He responds, 'If we take happiness from God's hand, must we not take sorrow too?' (2:10). Three friends come to see Job and argue with him, telling him that he must have sinned against God and so is being punished. But Job insists that he has done nothing to offend God and is not deserving of such punishment. No matter how deep his anguish, he maintains his confidence in God:

> I know that I have a living Defender
>   and that he will rise up last, on the dust of the earth.
> After my awakening, he will set me close to him,
>   and from my flesh I shall look on God.
> He whom I shall see will take my part:
> my eyes will be gazing on no stranger.
> My heart sinks within me. (19:25-27)

Job does question why God has afflicted him in this way, and he wants to plead his cause before God. He narrates all the good things he has done and wants God to respond to his questioning. A young man joins the conversation between Job and his friends. He is severe in his condemnation of Job's questioning of God. But then God suddenly appears to Job and says to him:

> Who is this, obscuring my intentions
>   with his ignorant words?
> Brace yourself like a fighter;
>   I am going to ask the questions, and you are to inform me!
> Where were you when I laid the earth's foundations?
>   Tell me, since you are so well-informed!
> Who decided its dimensions, do you know? (38:2-5)

God then discloses to Job the majesty and order of creation, revealing himself as the Creator of all and as always mysterious in his workings. Job, the innocent man who has suffered, is privileged with an extraordinary revelation of God's wisdom and hiddenness. He is awed and overwhelmed by God's coming to him. He repents of his questioning and responds to God by acknowledging his greatness:

> I know that you are all-powerful:
>   what you conceive, you can perform.
> … You have told me about great works that I cannot understand,
>   about marvels which are beyond me, of which I know nothing.

... Before, I knew you only by hearsay
    but now, having seen you with my own eyes,
I retract what I have said,
    and repent in dust and ashes. (42:2-5)

God then corrects the three friends 'for not having spoken about me correctly, as my servant Job has done' (42:8). God then restores Job to health, grants him a family and makes him prosperous once again. Even in the midst of great suffering, Job praised God and, because of his fidelity, experienced the awesomeness, majesty and holiness of God. In every circumstance of his life, he kept holy God's name.

THE NAME OF GOD IS HOLY

The second commandment [requires] respect for the Lord's name. Like the first commandment, it belongs to the virtue of religion and more particularly it governs our use of speech in sacred matters.

– CCC, no. 2142

At the burning bush, Moses asked God for his name. God replied, 'I am he who is ... This is what you are to say to the Israelites, "I am has sent me to you"' (Ex 3:14). The Hebrews treated this name for God with such respect that they did not speak it. It was honoured in silence. Only the high priest, once a year at the feast of atonement, pronounced this name at the incense offering in the Holy of Holies in the temple. Out of reverence for the revealed holy name, the people substituted the name *Adonai*, which means 'Lord'. Modern Jews adapt this custom by writing *'G-d'* instead of the customary spelling.

The Second Commandment calls us to the virtue of reverence for God, which trains us to know and to preserve the difference between the Creator and the creature. Respect for God's name keeps us from reducing him to a mere fact, or even a thing that we can control or manipulate. At the same time, a gracious God desires to be intimate with us, even becoming incarnate in Jesus Christ and dwelling in us through the Holy Spirit. In John's Gospel, Jesus applies to himself the expression 'I am' (cf. Jn 8:58), thus identifying himself with God. He distinguishes himself from his Father and from the Holy Spirit, whom he will send to the world after his Resurrection. This was one way Jesus opened us to understanding God as Trinity.

A name in some way conveys the reality of a person – the origin, the history, the very being of the person. That is why people are protective about their names and expect them to be treated with honour. The name of God obviously deserves the highest honour and respect. The Lord gives us a Commandment that asks us to reverence his name and not to use it in a disrespectful or manipulative way. When Jesus taught the Our Father, his first petition was 'Hallowed be thy name'. We also praise God's holy name in every Mass at the beginning of the Eucharistic Prayer when we recite or sing the Holy, Holy, Holy.

We also draw strength from recalling our Baptism, which initiated us into the Church 'in the name of the Father and of the Son and of the Holy Spirit'. To be baptised in the name of the Trinity means to be immersed into the very life of the Father, Son and Spirit. God's name sanctifies us. In Baptism, we also commonly receive the name of a saint, a disciple of Christ who has led an exemplary life, to remind us of our call to holiness. Patron saints – that is, the saint or saints whose name we have been given – serve as examples of the way to holiness by their witness to faith, hope and love. They also intercede with God for our benefit. God calls us by name. Our name is sacred. We need to honour God's name and the names of others to make our world a centre of dignity and respect.

THE WRONG USE OF GOD'S NAME

The Second Commandment forbids the wrong use or misuse of God's name. There are a number of ways in which this happens. Blasphemy uses the name of God and of Jesus Christ as well as those of the Blessed Mother and the saints in an offensive manner. The *Catechism* teaches that blasphemy

FROM THE CATECHISM

1. What does the Second Commandment ask of us?
The Second Commandment *prescribes respect for the Lord's name*. Like the First Commandment, it belongs to the virtue of religion and more particularly it governs our use of speech in sacred matters. (CCC, no. 2142)

2. Name one act forbidden by the Second Commandment.
The Second Commandment forbids every improper use of God's name. Blasphemy is the use of the name of God, of Jesus Christ, of the Virgin Mary and of the saints in an offensive way. (CCC, no. 2162)

3. Why is our baptismal name important?
In Baptism, the Christian receives his name in the Church. Parents, godparents and the [parish priest] are to see that he be given a Christian name. The patron saint provides a model of charity and the assurance of his prayer. (CCC, no. 2165)

consists 'in uttering against God – inwardly or outwardly – words of hatred, reproach or defiance' (CCC, no. 2148). This is gravely sinful. Habitual disrespect for God, displayed in cursing and even in the use of vulgar language, can create an attitude that erodes our relationship with the Lord.

At the same time, we recognise diminished culpability when the name of God is used because of an outburst of undisciplined speech due to passion or unexpected incitement to anger. We need to cultivate a persistent reverence for sacred names; if we do not, we can end up giving bad example and also fall into the sin of blasphemy. It should also be noted that in Scripture, the sometimes passionate language of the Prophets, in which they lament the troubles of their times and utter loud complaints to God, is not blasphemy or the taking of God's name in vain. It is actually prayer addressed to God.

We are forbidden to use God's name to witness a perjury or false oath, thereby using him to approve our lie.

God's name has been invoked to justify unjust wars and terrorism, slaughter enemies and impose unwarranted power over others. Many have used the God of love to promote hatred, the God of trust to facilitate betrayal and the God of mercy to validate acts of cruelty. Critics of religion cite the suffering and cruelty caused by the excesses by some of those who participated in the Crusades, the wars of religion during the Reformation and the Troubles in Northern Ireland as examples of using God's name to justify such acts. The sins of Christians do indeed undermine the credibility of faith. The name of God must never be used to support immoral acts.

O LORD, HOW GLORIOUS IS YOUR NAME OVER ALL THE EARTH (CF. PS 8:2)

When we bring to our culture this experience of the holiness of God's name, we arrive with a gift for society that can be all the better when the sacred is accepted as beneficial for the culture. It is no secret that irreverence for God and sacred matters is present in certain sectors of our society. For believers this is embarrassing, painful and inappropriate. Public discourse at times routinely displays little sensitivity to the revered values of people of faith. Of course, this is not universally true. There are many people who show respect for religious matters. People of goodwill can be as dismayed as men and women of faith at the departures from decency in speech and the disregard for the holiness of God's name.

Everyone's name is important. We honour the dignity of persons by using their names with respect. Surely we will honour each other's names if we acquire a habitual reverence for God's name. Reverencing the name of God honours him. This is the beginning of treating each other with the respect for a dignity that is based on our being created as an image of God.

Scripture highlights numerous ways in which God's name is vital for our faith life. When Job was in the midst of his worst sufferings, he said, '[The Lord] gave, [the Lord] has taken back. / Blessed be the name of [the Lord]!' (Job 1:21). God's name sustained him in his suffering. When the psalmist wanted to express exultant praise of God and thanksgiving for favours received, the holy name was invoked, 'Bless the Lord, O my soul, / and all within me, his holy name' (Ps 103:1).

Jesus taught that he would be present to those who come together in his name. 'For where two or three meet in my name, I am there among them' (Mt 18:20). Saint Peter staked his entire ministry on the utter uniqueness of Jesus, the only Saviour, by employing the power of his name: 'Only in him is there salvation; for of all the names in the world given to men, this is the only one by which we can be saved' (Acts 4:12). Saint Paul proclaimed that the name of Christ is an occasion for the adoration of the Son of God:

> God raised him high,
> and gave him the name
> which is above all other names;
> so that all beings
> in the heavens, on earth
> and in the underworld,
> should bend the knee at the name of Jesus. (Phil 2:9-10)

When the Blessed Virgin Mary praised God for calling her to be the Mother of his Son, she chanted, 'Holy is his name' (Lk 1:49). All of these sublime tributes to God's name enliven our faith and love for God. They provide us with the context to understand the meaning of the Second Commandment.

This is a good time for people of faith to witness their love for God's name by appealing to those who err in this regard to reconsider what they say and appreciate how it affects others. Those who are involved in preaching and catechising should always remember to model and encourage adoration. In order to be examples to society, believers themselves need to be temperate in the use of their tongues.

■ FOR DISCUSSION ■

1. In your family or workplace, what means do you take to eliminate the wrong use of God's name? What have you found to be the most effective approaches?
2. How do you help young people to address the use of coarse language in films, TV and music? What has proven to be the most successful method?
3. Why is it correct to say that blasphemous talk and similar types of language corrupt the user? What are some new ways to elevate public taste and the moral quality of public entertainment?

▬▬ DOCTRINAL STATEMENTS ▬▬

- The Second Commandment requires *respect for the Lord's name*. Like the First Commandment, it belongs to the virtue of religion, and more particularly it governs our use of speech in sacred matters (cf. CCC, no. 2142).
- The Second Commandment forbids the wrong use of God's name. There are a number of ways in which it happens. Blasphemy uses the name of God and of Jesus Christ and the names of the Blessed Virgin and the saints in an offensive manner.
- In Baptism, the Christian receives a name in the Church. Parents, godparents and the parish priest are to see that he or she be given a Christian name. The patron saint provides a model of charity and the assurance of prayer (cf. CCC, no. 2165).
- We are forbidden to use God's name to witness a perjury or false oath, thereby using him to approve our lie.

▬▬ MEDITATION ▬▬

The Letter of James in the New Testament contains a reminder of the power of human speech:

> For we all trip up in many ways. Someone who does not trip up in speech has reached perfection and is able to keep the whole body on a tight rein. Once we put a bit in the horse's mouth, to make it do what we want, we have the whole animal under our control. Or think of ships: no matter how big they are, even if a gale is driving them, they are directed by a tiny rudder wherever the whim of the helmsman decides. So the tongue is only a tiny part of the body, but its boasts are great. Think how small a flame can set fire to a huge forest; The tongue is a flame too. Among all the parts of the body, the tongue is a whole wicked world: it infects the whole body; catching fire itself from hell, it sets fire to the whole wheel of creation. Wild animals and birds, reptiles and fish of every kind can all be tamed, and have been tamed, by humans; but nobody can tame the tongue – it is a pest that will not keep still, full of deadly poison. We

use it to bless the Lord and Father, but we also use it to curse people who are made in God's image: the blessing and curse come out of the same mouth. My brothers, this must be wrong – does any water supply give a flow of fresh water and salt water out of the same pipe? Can a fig tree yield olives, my brothers, or a vine yield figs? No more can sea water yield fresh water.

– Jas 3:2-12

PRAYER

The Divine Praises
Blessed be God.
Blessed be his holy Name.
Blessed be Jesus Christ, true God and true Man.
Blessed be the name of Jesus.
Blessed be his most Sacred Heart.
Blessed be his most Precious Blood.
Blessed be Jesus in the most holy Sacrament of the altar.
Blessed be the Holy Spirit, the Paraclete.
Blessed be the great Mother of God, Mary most holy.
Blessed be her holy and Immaculate Conception.
Blessed be her glorious Assumption.
Blessed be the name of Mary, Virgin and Mother.
Blessed be Saint Joseph, her most chaste spouse.
Blessed be God in his angels and in his saints.

Bless the Lord, O my soul,
and all within me, his holy name.

– Ps 103:1

27 THE THIRD COMMANDMENT: LOVE THE LORD'S DAY

REMEMBER TO KEEP HOLY THE LORD'S DAY
– CCC, NOS. 2168–2195

MARGARET BALL AND FRANCIS TAYLOR: IRISH LAY MARTYRS

It is a curious fact that nobody seems to have been martyred when the Irish people were first converted to Christianity by Patrick and the early missionaries. So far as we know, the Irish changed to the new Christian religion with extraordinary ease. This is often attributed to the original Celtic spirituality, through which people had a deep sense of creation as a reflection of the Creator, appreciation of nature as creation and a belief in a life after death. Whatever the reason, unlike that of Rome, for example, early Irish Christian history is devoid of stories of persecution and religious discrimination.

That certainly changed in the sixteenth century. The wars of religion between Protestants and Catholics did not spare Ireland. As often happens, religion becomes confused with political power and marks out those who believe in a different form of worship as enemies of the state. Even inside families, political and religious differences bring venomous divisions and personal hatred. As Jesus predicted, parents can turn against children and children against parents, brother and sister against brother and sister. It is a mystery how this can happen, but it is unfortunately no mystery why political powers want to make sure that all religious beliefs are compatible with national ambitions, and that all visions provide support and motivation for the current power structure. It is inconvenient for the government to have determined good men and women refusing to bow the knee.

The word 'martyr' means 'witness'. Martyrs are witnesses in two senses. First, a martyr knows that a better world is possible and is able to live confidently in the knowledge of what is to come. Second, the martyr who has glimpsed the glory of God's promise gives testimony to the power of that vision by fidelity 'in spite of dungeon, fire and sword' ('Faith of our Fathers'). Hence, martyrs are powerful evidence of faith. As the old saying has it, 'The blood of martyrs is the seed of the Church.'

This was certainly the case for the Irish martyrs of the 1500s and 1600s. Through the religious and political conflicts of the era, their extraordinary commitment to the Mass, the priesthood, and loyalty to the pope as head of the Church over the claims of the English monarch, and their extreme sacrifice on behalf of the faith, inspired the loyalty of the Irish people to Catholicism for the next three centuries.

There were seventeen martyrs in the sixteenth and seventeenth centuries whose stories were particularly inspiring, and whose lives were sufficiently well-documented that they could be selected and proposed for beatification by the Church. Eleven of them were bishops, priests and religious: Bishop Patrick O'Healy, Fr Conn O'Rourke, Bishop Cornelius O'Devany, Fr Patrick O'Loughran, Fr John Kearney (Franciscans), Fr Patrick Higgins and Bishop Terence Albert O'Brien (Dominicans), Fr William Tirry (Augustinian), Br Dominic Collins (Jesuit), Bishop Dermot O'Hurley (Cashel) and Fr Maurice MacKenraghty (Clonmel). There were four laymen from Wexford: Matthew Lambert, Robert Tyler, Edward Cheevers and Patrick Cavanagh. (Two more Wexford men were executed but their names have been lost.) Finally there were two from prominent Dublin families: Margaret Ball (nee Bermingham) and Francis Taylor. All seventeen were beatified by St John Paul II in 1992.

Margaret Bermingham was born in County Meath in 1515. Her name tells us that she came from English stock. It is said indeed that on her mother's side, she was a distant relative of Edward I. Margaret married Bartholomew Ball, a Dublin merchant, and they settled in Hillcrest House. She gave birth to twenty children but only five survived to adulthood: Walter, Nicholas, Thomas, Katherine and Eleanor.

Bartholomew was successful politically and became Mayor of Dublin in 1553. He died in 1568, leaving his wife very well off. Margaret Ball then became active in Catholic circles in the city. The Reformation had come to Ireland and the religious climate in Dublin was ever-changing. There had even been a public burning of relics, including the crozier of St Patrick. In between times of tension, however, Catholics could continue to have Mass and other devotions, provided they were discreet and did not draw undue attention to themselves.

Margaret Ball's prestige and family position afforded her and her house a measure of protection. Margaret sponsored a number of Catholic priests, provided a meeting place for the celebration of Mass and even organised religious classes for the youth. On one occasion, her house was raided during Mass, resulting in the arrest of her and the priest and the confiscation of sacred vessels and vestments. Political influence, however, ensured that she was soon released and the religious property returned.

She could not continue her charmed existence for long. Her son, Walter, converted to Protestantism, and in 1580 he was elected Mayor of Dublin, like his father some years before. The political climate had changed again. The outbreak of rebellion in County Wicklow meant that suspicion of Catholic underground activities was high, and Walter had to move against his mother. Margaret was arrested, hauled through the streets of Dublin on a hurdle and thrown into a damp, dark cell in Dublin Castle.

Walter Ball allowed the law to take its course, and as often happens, events moved slowly. Margaret, now in her late sixties, languished in jail for three years in dreadful conditions, suffering from arthritis and deprivation of all kinds. In the end, there was no need for a trial. She died in 1584 without a formal condemnation.

Thirty years later, history repeated itself. Francis Taylor, in 1613, was elected an alderman of Dublin. He was a devout Catholic and his appointment was opposed by the mayor who was a devout Protestant. This happened even though Francis Taylor was a prominent and successful businessman, and had himself been elected mayor in 1594. The upshot was that Taylor was arrested and sent to prison.

We do not know where Francis Taylor was imprisoned, but it is certain that he spent the rest of his life in jail. Eight years later, he died in his prison cell, on 30 January 1621. By coincidence, that only providence can explain, he was married to a granddaughter of Margaret Ball, but it is almost certain that the two never met. Their martyrdom is remembered today in the form of statues beside St Mary's Pro-Cathedral in Dublin's Marlborough Street.

In their own time, and during the canonical investigation of their lives of holiness and heroic virtue afterwards, no one was in any doubt about the reason for their deaths. Both Margaret Ball and Francis Taylor were persecuted because they refused to obey human rulers rather than God, and continued to be faithful to their Church. In this they typified the traditional Irish loyalty to Sunday Mass.

THE SABBATH DAY

The *Catechism* starts its reflection on the Third Commandment with the scriptural meaning of the Sabbath. Exodus 20:8-11 states that the Sabbath was the seventh day on which the Lord rested after the work of the previous six days. Deuteronomy 5:12 adds that the Sabbath is a day of our renewing the covenant with God. The Sabbath is connected to creation and covenant.

God's 'rest' on the seventh day was his contemplative gaze enjoying the good of creation, especially its crown in man and woman. It was not a matter of divine inactivity, but rather the deeper 'work' of contemplation and the restful act of loving us (cf. CCC, nos. 2184–2185). This is true also of ourselves. If we never stop working, when would we ever have time to contemplate and worship God and nourish a love relationship with him or with anyone else? Every human person, having been created by God, owes him worship and thanksgiving for what the Lord has done and continues to do.

The scriptural history of the Sabbath demonstrates that it was a day of worship of God and relaxation with one's family: 'Then [on the Sabbath] you will find true happiness in [the Lord], and I shall lead you in triumph over the heights of the land' (Is 58:14). At their liturgies, the people of ancient Israel remembered the great works God performed on their behalf. They looked back on their history and family roots in the light of God's plans for them. They sang praises to God for his love and mercy. They recalled, 'Everything belongs to God!' The Christian Sunday carries forward Sabbath themes of contemplative rest and worship.

THIS IS THE DAY THE LORD HAS MADE

Jesus rose from the dead 'on the first day of the week'.
... For Christians it has become the first of all days, the
first of all feasts, the Lord's Day.

– CCC, no. 2174

The Third Commandment calls us to keep holy the Sabbath day. For Christians, the observance of the Sabbath is transferred to Sunday, the day that Jesus rose from the dead. God, through the Church, obliges us to make Sunday holy by participation in the Eucharist and by our being prayerfully reflective as far as possible. Sunday observance fulfils the interior law inscribed in the human heart to render to God visible and public worship as a sign of radical dependence upon God and as gratitude for all the blessings we have received.

Every seven days, the Church celebrates the Easter mystery. This tradition goes back to the time of the Apostles. It takes its origin from the actual day of Christ's Resurrection. Sunday extends the celebration of Easter throughout the year. It is meant to be illumined by the glory of the Risen Christ. It makes present the new creation brought about by Christ.

Sunday also recalls the creation of the world. The Genesis account of creation, expressed in poetic style, is a hymn of awe and adoration of God in the presence of the immensity of creation.

The Fathers of the Second Vatican Council explained how we should celebrate the Eucharist on Sunday, or its vigil on Saturday evening:

> The Church, therefore, earnestly desires that Christ's faithful, when present at this mystery of faith, should not be there as strangers or silent spectators. On the contrary, through a good understanding of

the rites and prayers they should take part in the sacred action, conscious of what they are doing, with devotion and full collaboration. They should be instructed by God's word and be nourished at the table of the Lord's Body. They should give thanks to God. Offering the immaculate victim, not only through the hands of the priest, but also together with him, they should learn to offer themselves. Through Christ, the Mediator, they should be drawn day by day into ever more perfect union with God and with each other, so that finally God may be all in all. (SC, no. 48)

Our presence at Eucharist must be more than a passive experience of the work of the priest and the music from the choir. We should join actively in the worship, where everyone present pours out adoration of and love for God. The more we meditate upon what we are doing, the more we will worship in spirit and truth and benefit from the grace that flows from the Eucharist. We will grow in our love and worship of God as well as in respect and love for one another.

WHY GO TO CHURCH ON SUNDAY?

The intimate bond between Sunday and resurrection of the Lord is strongly emphasised by all the churches of East and West. In the tradition of the Eastern churches in particular, every Sunday is the anastaseos hemera, the day of resurrection, and this is why it stands at the heart of all worship.

– St John Paul II, *Day of the Lord*
(*Dies Domini*; DD), no. 19

While it is the first day of the week, Sunday is also called the 'eighth day' – a day signifying eternity. Sunday fulfils and completes the Sabbath because it anticipates our eternal rest in God. The Sabbath remembered the first creation. Sunday recalls the new creation in Christ and the Spirit.

The heart of Sunday is the celebration of the Holy Eucharist. The practice of celebrating the Eucharist on Sunday dates from the earliest times. For example, St Justin Martyr (AD 100–165) wrote as follows: 'We all gather on the day of the sun, for it is the first day [after the Jewish sabbath, but also the first day] when God, separating matter from darkness, made the world; and on this same day Jesus Christ our Saviour rose from the dead' (I *Apol.* 67: cf. PG, 6, 429 and 432; cf. CCC, no. 2174). By their Sunday celebration of the Eucharist, the Catholic faithful fulfil both the Third Commandment to 'keep holy the Lord's day' and the words of Jesus to his disciples at the Last Supper: 'Do this in remembrance of me' (Lk 22:19).

The Third Commandment has been concretised for Catholics by one of the Precepts of the Church.

> Because the faithful are obliged to attend Mass unless there is a grave impediment, pastors have the corresponding duty to offer everyone the real possibility of fulfilling the precept … Yet more than a precept, the observance should be seen as a need rising from the depths of Christian life. It is crucially important that all the faithful should be convinced that they cannot live their faith or share fully in the life of the Christian community unless they take part regularly in the Sunday Eucharistic assembly. (DD, nos. 49, 81)

For a Catholic, the Sunday Eucharist must be the most important religious exercise of the week. In it, we offer our lives in sacrifice with Jesus to the Father, thereby participating directly in the great mysteries of our faith.

The Catholic parish, shepherded by the priest under the authority of the diocesan bishop, is the ordinary setting for Sunday worship and is central to the preparation for and celebration of all the Sacraments.

While Sunday is the time for worship, it is also an occasion for rest and relaxation. We should make time to be with one another in meals, conversation and activities that deepen family life. 'Every Christian should avoid making unnecessary demands on others that would hinder them from observing the Lord's Day. Traditional activities (sports, restaurants, etc.), and social necessities (public services, etc.), require some people to work on Sundays, but everyone should still take care to set aside sufficient time for leisure' (CCC, no. 2187; cf. no. 2186). The Eucharistic celebration does not stop at the church door. Those who participate at Mass carry their joy, faith and concern for others from the Mass into the rest of the day, and indeed into the week that follows.

FROM THE CATECHISM

1. What is our Sunday obligation?

Sunday 'is to be observed as the foremost holy day of obligation in the universal Church. On Sundays and other holy days of obligation the faithful are bound to participate in the Mass.' (CCC, no. 2192, citing CIC, cann. 1246 and 1247; see Glossary in this book for list of Holy Days of Obligation)

2. May we work on Sunday?

On Sundays and other holy days of obligation the faithful are bound ... to abstain from those labours and business concerns which impede the worship to be rendered to God, the joy which is proper to the Lord's Day or the proper relaxation of mind and body. (CCC, no. 2193)

3. What Sabbath principle governs rest and relaxation?

The Sabbath brings everyday work to a halt and provides a respite. It is a day of protest against the servitude of work and the worship of money. (CCC, no. 2172)

RESTORE SUNDAY

After the Christian religion obtained its freedom under the Roman emperor Constantine in the fourth century, civil laws were passed to limit unnecessary work on Sunday. The greatest beneficiaries were the poor who otherwise worked long hours every day of the week. Centuries later, at the height of the Industrial Revolution, many men, women and children worked fifteen hours a day, often on Sundays.

Today in some places, seven-day work has returned. This is both an injustice to the poor and also an abuse of Sunday rest, and we need to find ways to correct this. 'God's action is a model for human action. If God "rested and was refreshed" on the seventh day, man too ought to "rest" and should let others, especially the poor, "be refreshed"' (CCC, no. 2172).

Many people today deny themselves a day of rest. Incessant activity, so characteristic of a consumer society, means that Sunday is rarely a day of rest. Exceptions are made for those who must work for the public good, but this is not the problem. Too many people are just as busy and exhausted on Sundays as they are on weekdays. For many, Sunday is neither a day of rest nor a time for worship.

God built into human nature the rhythm between work and rest. We should treat this rest as sacred because it is our way of withdrawing from the demands of our work so that we have time to realise God's providential care of creation. Our remarkable progress in gaining control over the world can cause us to forget that God is the Creator upon whom everything depends. Science and technology are admirable gifts, but they must not be allowed to obscure the real author of all that is. Keeping the Lord's Day holy can also serve as a helpful corrective for a 'consumer' society that tends to place value on people for their productivity and material possessions.

Sunday rest puts our whole life into perspective. It helps us stand back from material concerns and reflect on spiritual values. Taking a rest from the pressures of the workplace, we are freed to open our souls to matters that have eternal significance. Sunday rest allows us to look again at the wonders of nature and experience the harmony and peace placed there by God. It is a precious time for rediscovering the fundamental goodness of creation as it comes from God's providential hand.

Sunday also provides the opportunity for families to be together and to engage in common activities. Weekday schedules often require members of the family to spend much time away from each other. Participation in the Eucharist and other activities can renew the bonds of love and unity.

Sporting events for young people have sometimes interfered with the Sunday Mass observance of Catholic youth. Until recently, Sunday morning was a sacred time in most communities and neighbourhoods, set aside for church attendance. Before this is abandoned on behalf of sports activities or other unexpected intrusions, it is hoped that Catholic priests and other Christian religious leaders, with the support of their congregations, may prevail on sponsors of sporting events to adapt their programmes to the religious needs of youth. We must preserve the opportunity to go to Mass on Sundays without competition from sporting events, work or other temptations.

On Sunday, we can also seek out forms of culture and entertainment that enhance the message of the Gospel and foster spiritual growth. A proper observance of Sunday can thus be a prophetic stance in our culture, offering a witness that is both wholesome and healing for the great number of people who need to be less frantic and more willing to let go and settle down to what best corresponds to their spiritual nature and yearnings.

FOR DISCUSSION

1. What is your Sunday like? How can it become a balance of worship, restful reflection and personal spiritual renewal? What pressures make this a challenge for you, and what can you do about them? How does Sunday Mass enrich your life, your relationships and the rest of your week?
2. What can be done to free up poor people from unfair working practice that deprive them of the gift of the Christian Sunday? How can families reverse the trend sponsored by those who schedule sporting events for children and young people on Sunday morning?
3. How does consumerism eat away at the Christian ideals of Sunday? What are ways that family gatherings could again become a regular feature of Sunday life?

DOCTRINAL STATEMENTS

• 'Observe the Sabbath day and keep it holy, as [the Lord] your God has commanded you. Labour for six days, doing all your work, but the seventh day is a Sabbath for [the Lord] your God' (Deut 5:12-14).
• For Christians, the observance of the Sabbath has been transferred to Sunday, the day that Jesus rose from the dead. On Sundays and other holy days of obligation, the Catholic faithful are bound to participate in the Mass. A Catholic who deliberately fails to participate in Mass on Sundays and Holy Days of Obligation commits a serious sin.
• Sunday extends the celebration of Easter throughout the year. It is meant to be illumined by the glory of the Risen Christ. It makes present the new creation brought about by Christ.

- Sunday also recalls the first creation as well as the new creation. The Genesis account of creation, expressed in poetic style, is a hymn of awe and adoration of God in the presence of the immensity of creation. On Sunday, we remember the wonder of what the risen Son of God has done for us in his new creation.
- While Sunday is a time for worship, it is also an occasion for rest and relaxation. We should make time to be with one another in meals, conversation, cultural and social growth and the deepening of family life.

MEDITATION

Church attendance and participation in worship has declined in modern societies, including Ireland. There is, however, still some reason for hope. There are more worshippers at Mass in Ireland on a single weekend than the attendance at all the football games in the country. About 1,700,000 people attend Mass each Sunday.

Nevertheless, Catholics cannot afford to be self-righteous or smug. We are called to recognise that we all have a role in sharing the joy and hope of our faith with others. It is true that we should thank God for what we have, but that is not a reason for complacency but rather for seeing the need for new evangelisation, and, in particular, for a richer celebration of the liturgy.

This certainly means involvement in readings and prayers and singing. More fundamentally, however, it is about bringing our lives and every part of our lives as individuals and as a community to be offered to the Father as part of the Body of Christ together with Christ's giving of his Body and pouring out of his Blood. The only function of the more obvious kinds of liturgical enrichment is to increase that participation in the sacrifice of Christ.

Here are ways to help us prepare better for Sunday Mass:

- Go to Mass prepared to worship God.
- Approach the Mass with the intention of participating fully and actively in the celebration, singing the hymns and psalms and reciting the prayers with conviction and faith.

- Enter into the mystery of faith in the Mass. The sacrificial self-gift of Christ to the Father is made present through the Holy Spirit. If we unite ourselves with him in his self-gift, we truly fulfil what is at the heart of being a priestly people.
- Read and pray over the Scripture texts for the Sunday liturgy in order to prepare for the Mass. Pray for light from God's Word on your needs.
- Spend time learning about the Mass: its structure, intentions and the meanings within the prayers and its rituals.
- Come to Mass with a community-minded attitude. Keep in mind that we are called by God into the Church. The word 'Church' means 'called', and so the priest, acting in the name of Christ, calls us as Christ's body in the making present of Christ's death and resurrection.
- Also keep in mind that our faith is strengthened by contact with other believers in a context where the Holy Spirit is forming the worshippers into the unity of the Church, the Body of Christ.
- Always remember the sacrifice of the Mass is the Church's greatest prayer of praise and thanksgiving to God the Father in which the Lord Jesus is truly present as Saviour of the world and is received in the Sacrament of the Eucharist as food for eternal life.

PRAYER

Come, let us ring out our joy to the Lord;
　　hail the rock who saves us.
Let us come into his presence, giving thanks;
　　let us hail him with a song of praise.
A mighty God is the Lord,
　　a great king above all gods.
In his hands are the depths of the earth;
　　the heights of the mountains are his.
O come; let us bow and bend low.
　　Let us kneel before the God who made us.

– Ps 95:1-4, 6

Give the Lord the glory of his name.
Bring an offering and enter his courts.

– Ps 96: 8

28 THE FOURTH COMMANDMENT: STRENGTHEN YOUR FAMILY

HONOUR YOUR FATHER AND YOUR MOTHER
– CCC, NOS. 2196–2257

THE MARRIED AMONG THE BLESSED

On 21 October 2001, Rome witnessed an unprecedented event when three siblings attended the beatification of their parents, the first husband and wife raised together to the rank of the Blessed.

Maria Corsini was born in Florence on 24 June 1884. Luigi Beltrame Quattrocchi was born in Catania on 12 January 1880. They met in Rome as teenagers and were married in the basilica of St Mary Major on 25 November 1905.

Maria was the daughter of an army captain. A lover of music, she became a professor of education and wrote widely on the subject. A member of Women's Catholic Action, she spoke frequently to women's lay groups. She worked in relief efforts in Ethiopia during World War II.

Luigi was a talented lawyer whose career brought him into the Italian government as an assistant attorney general. He was close to many leaders of the government and worked with them in the reconstruction of Italy after the end of World War II.

Maria and Luigi had four children, two boys and two girls. The boys became priests. Filipo, now Fr Tarcisio, is a diocesan priest in Rome. Cesare, now Fr Paolino, is a Trappist. Enrichetta is a consecrated lay woman. Stefania, who became Sr Maria Cecilia, a cloistered Benedictine nun, died in 1963.

The Quattrocchis were a middle-class family whose home was a welcoming place and even became a shelter for refugees during World War II.

The couple went through a crisis in 1913 when Maria became pregnant. Doctors told her that she would not survive the pregnancy and that the child also would die. They said that an abortion could save her life. Maria and Luigi knew that if they followed the doctors' advice, they would be guilty of a grave sin. They simply put their trust in God's protection. Maria ultimately delivered Enrichetta safely. The whole experience brought the family to a new level of living their faith and trust in God.

In his homily at the beatification of this couple, St John Paul II cited this question of Jesus, 'When the Son of man comes, will he find faith on earth?' (Lk 18:8). The pope said that Luigi and Maria were an example of a positive reply to Christ's question. The husband and wife lived in the first half of the twentieth century, a time when faith was severely challenged. In this setting, they always said 'yes' to Christ.

Throughout those difficult years, Luigi and Maria kept the lamp of faith burning and passed it on to their four children. Acknowledging the presence of three of them at the beatification, the pope quoted a line their mother had written about them: 'We brought them up in the faith, so that they might know and love God.'

The beatification was held on the twentieth anniversary of the publication of *On the Role of the Christian Family in the Modern World* (*Familiaris Consortio*; FC), a document from St John Paul II. *Familiaris Consortio* asks couples to follow the path of holiness by virtue of the sacramental grace 'which is not exhausted in the actual celebration of the sacrament, but rather accompanies the married couple throughout their lives' (FC, no. 56).

Blessed Luigi and Blessed Maria walked that journey of holiness in the light of the Gospel and in a deeply human way. Their son Fr Tarcisio remembered that 'the aspect that characterised our family life was the atmosphere of normality that our parents created in the constant seeking of spiritual values'.

No family is without its steady dose of disappointments and trials. Many are tempted to discouragement. There are those who face illness and those who endure the death of a child or a spouse. Luigi and

Maria had their share of troubles and handled them with courage and faith.

Addressing the married couples at the beatification, the Holy Father asked them to learn from the example of Maria and Luigi, 'as you face difficulties and trials in being faithful to your vocation, in cultivating conjugal and family harmony, in carrying out the mission of parents and participating in the life of society'. Luigi died in 1951, Maria in 1965.

Luigi and Maria lived their ordinary life in an extraordinary way. They centred their life on the daily Eucharist. They also had a strong devotion to the Virgin Mary, to whom they prayed every evening. They met regularly with their spiritual director. Their fidelity to the Gospel and their heroic virtues were verified in their lives as spouses and parents. Their prayers and example can guide us in our reflection on the Fourth Commandment.

THE CHRISTIAN FAMILY

Marriage and family are ordered to the good of the spouses, to the procreation and education of children … Children owe their parents respect, gratitude, just obedience and assistance.

– CCC, nos. 2249, 2251

The first three Commandments help us to understand how to love God with our whole selves. The next seven Commandments teach us how to love each other as we love ourselves.

The Fourth Commandment deals with all aspects of family life – parental and filial duties and responsibilities, that is, those of love from child to parent. This includes the duties of children toward their parents, the duties of brothers and sisters toward each other and the responsibilities of adult children toward their older parents. This Commandment also addresses the duties of government and the duties of citizens (cf. CCC, nos. 2234–2246), including the responsibility of the state and society to foster family values and to strengthen the family in every possible way.

THE DOMESTIC CHURCH – THE CHURCH OF THE HOME

The Catholic family as a domestic church is the fundamental community or cell of the parish, the diocese and the universal Church. Christ has called all family members to union with God through Baptism and the other Sacraments and to share in the mission of the whole Church. Family members carry out the Church's mission by fostering mutual love in the home and, through that love, by building up the community of the Church and society.

> The Christian home is the place where children receive the first proclamation of the faith. For this reason the family home is rightly called 'the domestic church', a community of grace and prayer, a school of human virtues and of Christian charity. (CCC, no. 1666)

The Christian family forms an environment within which faith is professed and witnessed. When family members pray together, engage in lifelong learning, forgive one another, serve each other, welcome others, affirm and celebrate life and bring justice and mercy to the community, they help each other live the faith and grow in faith. Some families may not understand themselves as a domestic church. Perhaps they consider their family too broken to be used for the Lord's purposes. They need to remember that a family is holy not because it is perfect, but because God's grace is at work in it.

What is a family? 'A man and a woman united in marriage, together with their children, form a family' (CCC, no. 2202). A family as defined in the *Catechism* may be found in a considerable portion of the households in our nation. Other familial arrangements have developed, such as single-parent families, blended families, and families in which adult children care for their parents as well as their own children. All families are beset with many challenges. They deserve compassion and the hope that they can be faithful to Christ's way of love.

The Christian family is called to be a community of faith, hope and love in an environment of prayer. Aided by a number of other virtues, such as prudence, justice, fortitude and temperance, the family that practises them begins to actualise its spiritual calling as a domestic church. When a family becomes a school of virtue and a community of love, it is an image of the loving communion of the Father, Son and Holy Spirit. It is then an icon of the Trinity.

CHILDREN'S LOVE FOR THEIR PARENTS

Respect for parents derives from a grateful heart toward those who gave us the gift of life and nourished, loved and supported us throughout all our stages of growth. Filial love is shown by genuine obedience from children to their parents while living in their parents' home and by responsible concern of grown children toward their elderly parents.

> With all your heart honour your father, / never forget the birthpangs of your mother. / Remember that you owe your birth to them; / how can you repay them for what they have done for you? (Eccles [Sir] 7:27-28)

God offers each member of the family the grace for creating family solidarity so that it may grow as a domestic church. Parents utilise the energies of their love, their education and their experience for their children. In this way, they make a positive and essential contribution toward building a truly human and Christian family. Children respond in love and should work to reduce rivalries, angers, hurts and hostilities among brothers and sisters.

Adult children of elderly parents are asked to care for them with a generous heart: 'Listen to your father from whom you are sprung, do not despise your mother in her old age' (Prov 23:22). The family remains a major source of support for the elderly. The elderly who have no adult children should be helped by the considerate care of others.

While adult children may sometimes experience a strain between raising their own children and caring for their parents, they must do what they can to help their parents. Still, not only do adult children help their parents, but many of the elderly parents also help their adult children by their continuing love, their example and the benefit of their lifetime experience. While it is right for society to help care for the elderly, the family remains the rightful source of support.

PARENTS' LOVE FOR THEIR CHILDREN

Parents exercise their love for their children by caring for their physical, spiritual, intellectual, emotional and moral needs. Concern for these needs takes much time and commitment on the part of both mother and father. Giving proper example to children is the most powerful form of childrearing. Helping children to grow in virtue contributes to their character formation. Inspirational stories, good parental example and repetition of acts of virtue are basic ways of forming the young.

Parents should teach their children to pray by praying with them from their earliest years. Parents, as the first and primary educators, must also ensure their children's Catholic religious education and regular participation in Mass and other aspects of parish life. Sharing with them the lives of the saints, bringing them to church, helping them to participate in the Mass and encouraging them to go to Confession are necessary ways to help children grow in faith. Catholic schools and parish religious education programmes can help parents fulfil their responsibility to educate their children in the Catholic faith. Parents are encouraged to use Catholic schools and parish programmes whenever possible.

Parental example in all these areas is essential, for the young need to see a living faith in those they love. Emphasis on fundamental elements of the faith – such as fostering a relationship with Christ and devotion to Mary, the angels and saints, along with love and concern for everyone they meet – gradually forms the religious life of the young in a productive and creative way.

When children become adults, they assume the responsibility of how they will live and work. Parents should not exert undue pressure on their children when the children are faced with these decisions (cf. CCC, no. 2230). However, since parents often know their children well, they can direct their children to make decisions in harmony with their gifts and education. Since the family is the domestic church, it is fitting that parents always encourage their children to make life decisions with serious consideration about the best ways to live out their faith. Parents, by their own faith and commitment to the Church, create an environment in their homes that is conducive to helping children begin to think about a religious vocation. They should not hesitate to invite a son or daughter to consider becoming a priest or a vowed religious. In particular, parents should always encourage and support a child who is discerning such a call.

THE FAMILY AND SOCIETY

Authority, stability and a life of relationships within the family constitute the foundations for freedom, security and fraternity within society. The family is the community in which, from childhood, one can learn moral values, begin to honour God and make good use of freedom. Family life is an initiation into life in society.

– CCC, no. 2207

The family and society need to work together to defend the good of each human being. The state should encourage responsible initiatives for families and should provide them with all the economic, educational, political and cultural assistance they need to exercise their responsibilities.

Civic authorities should defend and protect the family as created by God and based on the permanent and exclusive union of a man and woman in marriage. The first obligation of civil authorities is to establish laws that reflect and protect proper moral order. If the governing authority attempts to impose a law contrary to the moral order, then the citizens have a moral obligation to seek to try to change the law. If that fails, they should refuse to obey such a law.

The Church, too, has the mission and obligation to critique and challenge any civil laws, societal organisations or political structures that infringe upon or deny the fundamental rights of human persons and communities. Jesus spoke of the difference between serving God and the state when he said, 'Pay Caesar what belongs to Caesar – and God what

FROM THE CATECHISM

1. What is a family?

A man and a woman united in marriage, together with their children, form a family. This institution is prior to any recognition by public authority, which has an obligation to recognise it. It should be considered the normal reference point by which the different forms of family relationship are to be evaluated. (CCC, no. 2202)

2. What are the basic elements of filial love?

Children owe their parents respect, gratitude, just obedience and assistance. Filial respect fosters harmony in all of family life. (CCC, no. 2251)

3. What is expected of parental love?

Parents have the first responsibility for the education of their children in the faith, prayer and all the virtues. They have the duty to provide as far as possible for the physical and spiritual needs of their children. (CCC, no. 2252)

belongs to God' (Mt 22:21). Catholics have the duty to vote, to participate in the political arena and to help shape society in light of Catholic teaching.

THE CHARTER OF FAMILY RIGHTS

In his apostolic exhortation *On the Role of the Christian Family in the Modern World* (*Familiaris Consortio;* FC), St John Paul II cites a list of rights of the family. Among those rights, we note the following:

- the right to exist and progress as a family, that is to say, the right of every human being, even if he or she is poor, to found a family and to have adequate means to support it;
- the right to exercise its responsibility regarding the transmission of life and to educate children;

- the right to the intimacy of conjugal and family life;
- the right to the stability of the bond and institution of marriage;
- the right to believe in and profess one's faith and to propagate it;
- the right, especially of the poor and the sick, to obtain physical, social, political and economic security;
- the right to housing suitable for living family life in a proper way;
- the right to form associations with other families and institutions, in order to fulfil the family's role suitably and expeditiously;
- the right to protect minors by adequate institutions and legislation from harmful drugs, pornography, alcoholism, etc.;
- the right of the elderly to a worthy life and a worthy death;
- the right to emigrate as a family in search of a better life;
- the right to bring up children in accordance with the family's own traditions and religious and cultural values, with the necessary instruments, means and institutions. (FC, no. 46)

WITNESS FIDELITY IN MARRIAGE

God commands all couples to witness fidelity in their marriages. An enduring marriage is more than simply endurance. It is a process of growth into an intimate friendship and a deepening peace. Couples need to renew their commitment to each other regularly, to seek enrichment often and to ask for pastoral and professional help when necessary. They need to welcome children lovingly from God, whether through birth or adoption.

There needs to be mutuality in the relationships, roles and responsibilities of all members of the family. Each and every family member must work at giving love, respect, commitment and support to and for each other.

Finally, family members need to take time to be with each other. Prayer and worship together is important, especially Sunday Mass and family prayers such as the Rosary. Shared meals should be a priority. A family can establish certain traditions and rituals that enrich and strengthen family life. They can also take part together in retreats or family education programmes. They can watch television together and discuss the values being promoted.

Family members can also benefit from taking some time to be in solitude, to reflect on and to hear God's Word.

FOR DISCUSSION

1. Reflect on your family life. When have you felt God's presence in your midst? Why was this? What was happening?
2. What pressures have caused pain for your family? How did you deal with them? Did this bring you closer or drive you farther apart as a family?
3. What is it about your family that matters most to you? How well do your family members share themselves with each other? How are you balancing time and commitment to family, work and community? What choices can be made to improve your family as a faith community?

DOCTRINAL STATEMENTS

- 'A man and a woman united in marriage, together with their children, form a family. This institution is prior to any recognition by public authority, which has an obligation to recognise it. It should be considered the normal reference point by which the different forms of family relationships are to be evaluated' (CCC, no. 2202).
- 'The Christian home is the place where children receive the first proclamation of the faith. For this reason the family home is rightly called 'the domestic church', a community of grace and prayer, a school of human virtues and of Christian charity' (CCC, no. 1666).
- Children call forth the gifts of their parents who – through their love – use their education and experience to benefit their children. In this way, children make a positive and essential contribution toward building a truly human and Christian family.
- Adult children of elderly parents are asked to care for them with a generous heart. 'Listen to your father from whom you are sprung, / do not despise your mother in her old age' (Prov 23:22).
- Parents exercise their love for their children by caring for their physical, spiritual, intellectual, emotional and moral needs. Responding to these needs requires time and commitment by both mother and father. Parents have the first responsibility for the education of their children.
- The family is the basic unit of society. A healthy family is the prerequisite of a healthy society. The authority, stability and loving relationships that

are found in families are essential for a society that wants to sustain freedom, security and community responsibility.

• Presidents, legislators, judges and other civil leaders are given their authority in order to serve people. Their decisions ought to reflect God's plan for humanity, the natural law and the dignity of each person.

■ MEDITATION ■

Excerpt: Reflections at Nazareth by Pope Paul VI

Nazareth is the school in which we begin to understand the life of Jesus. It is the school of the Gospel. Here we learn to observe, to listen, to meditate and to penetrate the profound and mysterious meaning of that simple, humble and lovely manifestation of the Son of God. And perhaps we learn almost imperceptibly to imitate Him. Here we learn the method by which we can come to understand Christ. Here we discover the need to observe the milieu of His sojourn among us – places, period of time, customs, language, religious practices, all of which Jesus used to reveal Himself to the world. Here everything speaks to us; everything has meaning. Everything possesses twofold significance.

We cannot depart without recalling briefly and fleetingly some fragments of the lesson of Nazareth.

The lesson of silence: may there return to us an appreciation of this stupendous and indispensable spiritual condition, deafened as we are by so much tumult, so much noise, so many voices of our chaotic and frenzied modern life. O silence of Nazareth, teach us recollection, reflection and eagerness to heed the good inspirations and words of true teachers; teach us the need and value of preparation, of study, of meditation, of interior life, of secret prayer seen by God alone.

The lesson of domestic life: may Nazareth teach us the meaning of family life, its harmony of love, its simplicity and austere beauty, its sacred and inviolable character; may it teach us how sweet and irreplaceable is its training, how fundamental and incomparable its role on the social plane.

The lesson of work: O Nazareth, home of 'the carpenter's son'. We want here to understand and to praise the austere and redeeming law of human labour, here to restore the consciousness of the dignity of labour, here to recall that work cannot be an end in itself, and that it is free and ennobling in proportion to the values – beyond the economic ones – which motivate it. We would like here to salute all the workers of the world, and to point out to them their great Model, their Divine Brother, the Champion of all their rights, Christ the Lord!

– Pope Paul VI, *The Pope Speaks* 9:3 (1964)

PRAYER

A Blessing by Parents for Their Children

Father,
inexhaustible source of life and author of all good,
We bless and we thank you
for brightening our communion of love by your gift
   of children.
Grant that our children will find in the life of this family
   such inspiration
that they will strive always for what is right and good
and one day, by your grace,
reach their home in heaven … Amen.

– *Book of Blessings*, no. 190

[Jesus] went down with [Mary and Joseph] then and came to Nazareth and lived under their authority.
His mother stored up all these things in her heart.

– Lk 2:51

The primary place of encounter with God for most adults, and children, is family life. For Christians, the family is the first experience of Church.

– SGN, 82

29 THE FIFTH COMMANDMENT: PROMOTE THE CULTURE OF LIFE

YOU SHALL NOT KILL
– CCC, NOS. 2258–2330

CATHERINE McAULEY: WOMAN FOR LIFE

One of the hallmarks of Christianity is concern for the poor, the sick and the suffering – wherever human life is under threat. This concern is at the heart of the Gospel. Jesus shows his compassion at every turn: the lepers, the blind, the grieving, the lost and directionless multitudes, all arouse his empathy and desire to respond to their need. It is easy for us to insulate ourselves from the sorrows and difficulties faced by others. God tells Moses that he has heard the cry of the poor. Christians in every age have attuned their ears to the pleas of those who need help desperately. Every life is worth living; every person is worth saving; every voice is worth hearing. The Church in Ireland today has benefitted from those in the past who learned to hear what God hears, and acted with determination to bring hope and help and healing to anybody who called on them.

Catherine McAuley was born on 29 September 1778 in Drumcondra, Dublin. She was descended from an old Westmeath family who had fallen on hard times after Cromwell, but had managed to survive and do well. The eighteenth century was a period of severe oppression and social exclusion for all Irish Catholics. Business was the only career option open to them, and some enterprising Catholics took up commerce and prospered despite the restrictions, provided they kept their heads down.

Catherine's father, James, was just such an ambitious and energetic merchant. He started out as a carpenter and craftsman and progressed to an elegant residence on twenty-one acres in north Dublin city. A devout Catholic, tried in the fire of discrimination and prejudice, he extended help to poor Catholic parents and taught *Catechism* weekly to their children. Unfortunately, he died when Catherine was five years old.

This led directly to what must have been a sad childhood. Her mother, in poor health, died before Catherine was twenty years old. Catherine, as a result, spent most of her youth in the houses of others: relatives on her mother's side, some poor, and unfortunately none providing the security and support that might be needed by a young adult. Her upbringing was very unsettled. She sought refuge in studying the Bible and praying. Eventually the Callaghans, who were a Church of Ireland and Quaker family, adopted her, giving her a home in Coolock.

Catherine was acutely aware by now, through her observation and experience, of the importance of taking care of people, and indeed of what caring really means. For Catherine, care was more than material relief; it included a very human quality of compassion and understanding founded on the love of God and Jesus Christ. It meant a respect for the dignity of each person. It involved a sense of urgency, as the changing circumstances of life always call for a loving response in the moment. 'The poor need help now, not next week,' Catherine would say later. Every person and every human life is sacred in every moment. This conviction would frame her apostolate in the future.

The first focus of her apostolate was the village of Coolock and Mrs Callaghan herself. The woman of the house, a Quaker, was seriously ill, and Catherine nursed her through her last days. At the end, the lady asked to be baptised into the Catholic faith, provided her husband was not told. Mrs Callaghan died in 1819.

Catherine's next mission was the care of six orphans from the village. William Callaghan, the widower, took a direct interest in Catherine's good works and decided to make her his heir. He appreciated her energy and ambition to do good, and wished to enable her to continue after his death. When he died in 1822, he too received the sacraments of the Catholic Church, and was greatly consoled to be told, at that late date, that his wife had anticipated him.

Catherine began to teach in a school in the city, and this gave her a new focus. With the money from the Callaghan bequest, she bought and staffed a house for young women and girls, to teach them, train them and form them in the virtues and talents they needed to achieve success in this life and salvation in the next. In 1827, she opened the House of Mercy on Baggot Street, a fashionable south Dublin thoroughfare. Two hundred girls enrolled on the first day of school and thirty girls were accommodated in residence.

During the fifteen years left to her, under Catherine's direction the Mercy community in Baggot Street began to look more and more like a convent. The ladies who ran the house kept to a rule of life, simple dress and daily timetable, with common prayer, work and living. There was some doubt, indeed, about the status of the Sisters of Mercy, as they began to be generally called, on the part of the public, the clergy, and even the Archbishop of Dublin. Catherine herself was surprised, but she resolved the dilemma by immediately arranging that the Sisterhood should become an official diocesan congregation. The Archbishop approved and Catherine applied to Rome for official recognition which was readily granted. The Sisters of Mercy adopted the purposes of 'the visitation of the sick poor and the charitable instruction of poor females'.

The Sisters soon recruited over a hundred new members, and new foundations at home and abroad were added every year. By Catherine's death, there were twelve houses in Ireland and England. She had established a very successful formula: the exercise of charity and mercy, the practice of home visitation and educational work on three levels – primary, secondary, and vocational training and teacher formation. To these, Catherine added her own lightness of touch, depth of prayer and grounded practicality. The years had taken their toll, though, and the founder died of tuberculosis at the House of Mercy on 11 November 1841.

The Sisters of Mercy went from strength to strength. One of Mother McAuley's ambitions was to open a hospital where the poor would always have access to treatment. This came to fruition when the Sisters of Mercy purchased a site on Eccles Street on Dublin's northside, and opened the Mater Misericordiae Hospital (Mother of Mercy) in 1861, now known familiarly as the Mater. The Irish Republic honoured her achievement by commemorating it on the front of the five punt note (and depicted a Mercy schoolroom on the reverse). A sister hospital was founded in Belfast in the 1880s, the Mater Infirmorum Hospital (Mother of the Sick) on the Crumlin Road. It too is known to all as the Mater.

Through the decades, the Mercy Sisters journeyed from Ireland around the world, bringing the vision of mercy to new places. Today the Sisters of Mercy are found in many countries, in hospitals, schools, care centres, in the streets of cities and in the homes of the poor. In Ireland they number over three thousand members. Saint John Paul II bestowed the title 'Venerable' on Mother Catherine McAuley, Sister of Mercy, in 1990.

RESPECT HUMAN LIFE

Human life is sacred because from its beginning it involves the creative action of God and it remains for ever in a special relationship with the Creator, who is its sole end. God alone is the Lord of life from its beginning until its end: no one can under any circumstance claim for himself the right directly to destroy an innocent human being.

– CCC, no. 2258; citing *The Gift of Life*
(*Donum Vitae*), no. 5

God's creative action is present to every human life and is thus the source of its sacred value. Each human life remains in a relationship with God, who is the final goal of every man and woman.

The Fifth Commandment calls us to foster the physical, spiritual, emotional and social well-being of self and others. For that reason, it forbids murder, abortion, euthanasia and any life-threatening acts. We are called to create the culture of life and work against the culture of death. This presents us with three challenges.

1. We need to counter the relativism that imperils human life, by recognising that human freedom needs to be consistent with God's intentions and the laws that govern moral life.

2. We must witness God's providential presence to all creation and particularly to each human being. 'Where God is denied, and people live as though he did not exist, or his commandments are not taken into account, the dignity of the human person and the inviolability of human life also end up being rejected or compromised' (St John Paul II, *The Gospel of Life* [*Evangelium Vitae*; EV], no. 96).

3. We need to confront the weakening of conscience in modern society. Too many people fail to distinguish between good and evil when dealing with the value of human life. Moral confusion leads many to support choices and policies that desecrate life. Choices that were once considered criminal and immoral have become socially acceptable. Many consciences that were once formed by the Ten Commandments, Christ's moral teachings and the Holy Spirit's grace-filled guidance are now swayed by the moral confusion of the spirit of the times. We should deal with the weakening of conscience by helping people to understand the Church's teaching on conscience as the capacity to make judgements in agreement with God's law, to protect human dignity and reject anything that degrades it.

LIFE ISSUES THAT CONFRONT US

Murder

> *The deliberate murder of an innocent person is gravely contrary to the dignity of the human being, to the golden rule and to the holiness of the Creator.*
>
> – CCC, no. 2261

God forbids murder. 'Do not cause the death of the innocent or upright' (Ex 23:7). The intentional murder of any person is strictly forbidden by this commandment (cf. CCC, nos. 2268–2269). Such actions are gravely sinful.

Self-defence against an unjust aggressor is morally permitted. There is also a moral duty for the defence of others by those who are responsible for their lives. Self-defence or the defence of others has the goal of protecting the person or persons threatened. Once the threat is eliminated, no further action is required. In such situations, the deliberate killing of the aggressor can be permitted only when no other solution is possible (cf. CCC, no. 2265). Any response to aggression must be proportionate to the nature of the threat or the act of aggression.

Abortion

Legalised abortion has a destructive effect on societies. Few other actions when legalised by public policy so profoundly undermine a country's values or upset the moral compass of a people. The Church has always condemned abortion. In the *Didache* (*The Teaching of the Apostles*), 2, 2, written toward the end of the first century and revered as an honoured guide for Christian life, we read, 'You shall not kill the embryo by abortion.' This teaching has never changed and it will not change.

> From its conception, the child has the right to life. Direct abortion, that is, abortion willed as an end or as a means, is a 'criminal' practice (GS, no. 27 §3), gravely contrary to the moral law. The Church imposes the canonical penalty of excommunication for this crime against human life. Because it should be treated as a person from conception, the embryo must be defended in its integrity, cared for and healed like every other human being. (CCC, nos. 2322–2323)

Modern technology has enabled us to appreciate how quickly the growing child in the womb takes on human features. This has made many more people aware of the fact that human life begins at conception, the moment that the egg is fertilised. Many common forms of artificial birth control cause abortions by not allowing the newly conceived human child to implant in the mother's womb.

The pro-life commitment of the Church is reflected in her compassion for those who so often regret having had an abortion, her understanding for those who are facing difficult decisions and her assistance for all who choose life. People who have been involved with an abortion are encouraged to seek the mercy of God in the Sacrament of Penance and Reconciliation and to obtain the necessary counselling. Pro-life ministries work with expectant mothers who are considering abortion by encouraging them to choose life for their children. They also provide alternatives to abortion through prenatal care, assistance in raising children and adoption placement services.

In Vitro Fertilisation

While *in vitro* fertilisation is more appropriately treated in relation to the integrity of the link between fertility and love, it deserves brief mention here. This is because very often in the process, eggs that have been fertilised and are beginning to grow as a human person are discarded or destroyed. This action is the taking of human life and is gravely sinful.

Stem-Cell Research and Cloning

Every human body contains stem cells, undifferentiated cells that have the potential to mature into a wide variety of body cells. They develop early in the human embryo after fertilisation or conception. They are also found in the placenta, the umbilical cord, as well as in the adult brain, bone marrow, blood, skeletal muscle and skin. Scientists theorise that these stem cells may be used for therapeutic purposes for curing diseases such as Parkinson's or Alzheimer's.

Some scientists, however, maintain that the best source for stem cells is the human embryo. The moral problem is that in order to retrieve the stem cells, the growing child must be killed. But every embryo from the moment of conception has the entire genetic makeup of a unique human life. The growing child must be recognised and treated as completely and fully human. He or she needs only time to grow and develop. To destroy an embryo is to take a human life, an act contrary to God's law and Church teaching.

Some argue that the good obtained by healing serious diseases justifies the destruction of some human embryos. But this reduces a human being to a mere object for use. It assumes there are no moral absolutes that must be held in all circumstances. It violates the moral principle that the end does not justify the means. Embryonic stem-cell research is an immoral means to a good end. It is morally unacceptable.

Similarly, cloning, whether for reproductive or therapeutic uses, is immoral on many levels, not the least of which is because it too involves the destruction of human embryos.

> No objective, even though noble in itself, such as a foreseeable advantage to science, to other human beings or to society, can in any way justify experimentation on living human embryos or fetuses, whether viable or not, either inside or outside the mother's body. (Congregation for the Doctrine of the Faith, *Instruction on Respect for Human Life in its Origin and on the Dignity of Procreation* [Vatican City: Libreria Editrice Vaticana, 1987])

On the other hand, stem cells can be obtained from adults with their informed consent. Stem cells from placenta, bone marrow and the umbilical cord are being used to treat leukemia. This is a promising field of research and does not involve the moral implications of embryonic stem-cell research.

Euthanasia and Doctor-Assisted Suicide

Intentional euthanasia, sometimes called mercy killing, is murder. Regardless of the motives or means, euthanasia consists of putting to death those who are sick, are disabled, or are dying. It is morally unacceptable. The emergence of doctor-assisted suicide, popularised by the right-to-die movement, seeks to legalise what is an immoral act.

Suicide is gravely sinful whether committed alone or aided by a doctor. Serious psychological disturbances, anxiety, fear of suffering or torture can diminish the responsibility of the one committing suicide. The question is often asked whether persons who have committed suicide receive eternal salvation. Although suicide is always objectively sinful, one 'should not despair of the eternal salvation of persons who have taken their own lives. By ways known to him alone, God can provide the opportunity for salutary repentance. The Church prays for persons who have taken their own lives' (CCC, no. 2283). The pastoral care of family and friends of those who have taken their own lives is an important focus for the Church's healing and compassionate ministry.

Catholic moral tradition has always taught that we can discontinue medical procedures that are burdensome, extraordinary and disproportionate to the outcome. However, respect for every human being demands the ordinary treatment of the dying by the provision of food, water, warmth and hygiene. Ordinary treatment is always a moral requirement.

There is also extraordinary treatment. The Church recognises that some medical treatment may not provide benefits commensurate with the risks of certain medical procedures. Extraordinary medical treatment may not be morally required and can even cease in certain cases, depending on the benefits to the sick person and the burdens it will or may impose. For example, in instances when a person has been declared brain-dead, the patient can be disconnected from mechanical devices that sustain breathing and the heart since there is little hope of the person's recovery.

The Death Penalty

Following the lead of St John Paul II's *The Gospel of Life*, the *Catechism* teaches that governmental authority has the right and duty to assure the safety of society, and to punish criminals by means of suitable penalties. This includes imposition of the death penalty if there is no other way to protect society (cf. CCC, no. 2267). But this principle has a very restrictive application:

> If, however, non-lethal means are sufficient to defend and protect people's safety from the aggressor, authority will limit itself to such means, as these are more in keeping with the concrete conditions of the common good and more in conformity with the dignity of the human person. Today, in fact, as a consequence of the possibilities which the state has for effectively preventing crime, by rendering one who has committed an offence incapable of doing harm – without definitively taking away from him the possibility of redeeming himself – the cases in which the execution of the offender is an absolute necessity 'are very rare, if not practically non-existent'. (CCC, no. 2267, citing EV, no. 56)

When dwelling on legal and moral arguments concerning the death penalty, we should do so not with vengeance and anger in our hearts, but with the compassion and mercy of our Lord in mind. It is also important to remember that penalties imposed on criminals always need to allow for the possibility of the criminal to show regret for the evil committed and to change his or her life for the better.

War

Saint John XXIII wrote that peace is a gift from God:

> So magnificent is this aim [for peace] that human resources alone, even though inspired by the most praiseworthy good will, cannot hope to achieve it. God himself must come to man's aid with his heavenly assistance, if human society is to bear the closest possible resemblance to the Kingdom of God. (*Peace on Earth* [*Pacem in Terris*], no. 168)

The best way to avoid war is to safeguard peace by letting go of the anger and hatred that breed war and by eliminating the poverty, injustice and deprivation of human rights that lead to war. Disarmament needs to be encouraged. 'The arms race is one of the greatest curses on the human race and the harm it inflicts on the poor is more than can be endured' (CCC, no. 2329, citing GS, no. 81 §3).

While every possible means must be taken to avoid war, there are times when a use of force by competent authority may be justified to correct a manifest injustice, especially to defend against a threat to one's homeland. The tradition of the Church going back to St Augustine (AD 354–430) has developed the conditions for war to be moral. These are known as the just-war conditions. They are listed as follows in the *Catechism*:

> The strict conditions for *legitimate defence by military force* require rigorous consideration. The gravity of such a decision makes it subject to rigorous standards of moral legitimacy. At one and the same time:
>
> - the damage inflicted by the aggressor on the nation or community of nations must be lasting, grave and certain;
> - all other means of putting an end to it must have been shown to be impractical or ineffective;
> - there must be serious prospects of success;

- the use of arms must not produce evils graver than the evil to be eliminated. The power of modern means of destruction weighs very heavily in evaluating this condition.

These are the traditional elements enumerated in what is called the 'just war' doctrine. The evaluation of these conditions for moral legitimacy belongs to the prudential judgement of those who have responsibility for the common good. (CCC, no. 2309)

War may never be undertaken from a spirit of vengeance, but rather from motives of self-defence and of establishing justice and right order. The government has the right and duty to enlist citizens in defence of the nation. Special provision should be made for those who refuse to bear arms for reasons of conscience. These men and women should serve their country in some other way.

The Church and human reason assert the permanent validity of the moral law during armed conflict. Civilians, wounded soldiers and prisoners should be treated humanely. Exterminating people by ethnic cleansing is an intrinsic and grave moral evil.

Terrorism

Terrorist attacks throughout the world have killed thousands of people. We are aware, along with all people of good will, of the unmitigated evil of such acts. These deeds have raised our awareness of similar acts of terror around the world.

There can be no religious or moral justification for such acts. Such claims by terrorists can be countered by the teachings of the world's religions and by the constructive actions of religious believers. At the same time, we are called to mitigate problems such as violations of human rights and poverty, which cause widespread frustration and anger. While never excusing acts of terrorism, we still need to address issues associated with poverty and injustice that are exploited by terrorists.

FROM THE CATECHISM

1. Why is suicide morally wrong?
Suicide contradicts the natural inclination of the human being to preserve and perpetuate his life. It is gravely contrary to the just love of self. It likewise offends the love of neighbour because it unjustly breaks the ties of solidarity with family, nation and other human societies to which we continue to have obligations. Suicide is contrary to love for the living God. (CCC, no. 2281)

2. What are the roots of war?
Injustice, excessive economic or social inequalities, envy, distrust and pride raging among men and nations constantly threaten peace and cause wars … Insofar as men are sinners, the threat of war hangs over them and will so continue until Christ comes again; but insofar as they can vanquish sin by coming together in charity, violence itself will be vanquished. (CCC, no. 2317)

3. What are some reasons for punishing criminals?
Punishment, then, in addition to defending public order and protecting people's safety, has a medicinal purpose: as far as possible, it must contribute to the correction of the guilty party. (CCC, no. 2266)

Scandal

In its focus on the preservation of life, the Fifth Commandment also is concerned with the care we show for each other's moral life. A person whose words or actions lead others to believe that evil or sinful behaviour is acceptable and not morally wrong is guilty of the sin of scandal.

Scandal can also be caused by laws or institutions that legitimise sinful actions. An example from history can be seen in laws that allowed slavery. A modern example is seen in those laws that allow abortion.

The Right of the Dying to Live

Some argue that a person has a right to die and therefore can legitimately ask a doctor or medical professional to help in the hastening of a painless death. These are some of the arguments against this claim of a 'right to die', which really means 'the legal right to choose when one will die':

- Many doctors take the Hippocratic Oath, by which they commit themselves to do no harm. The relationship between a doctor and a patient should be marked by compassion. Doctors should not be the killers of their patients. It would perversely affect their self-understanding and would reduce their desire to look for cures for disease, if killing instead of curing were to become the option;
- We should not allow the elderly and infirm to be pressured to consent to their own deaths by assisted suicide or euthanasia;
- We should protect the poor and minorities from exploitation. Pain is a significant factor in the desire for physician-assisted suicide. The poor and the minorities often do not have the resources for the alleviation of pain;
- We should protect all people with disabilities from societal indifference, antipathy and any bias against them;
- We should never present suicide as a socially acceptable solution to life's difficulties.

The Pontifical Academy for Life on 8 March 1999, issued a statement that included the following comments about euthanasia and the alleviation of the pain of the dying:

> With absolute conviction we vigorously reject any kind of euthanasia, understood as recourse to those actions or omissions which are intended to cause a person's death in order to prevent suffering and pain. At the same time, we want to express our human and Christian closeness to all the sick, especially to those who know they are approaching the end of their earthly life and are preparing to meet God, our beatitude. We ask that these brothers and sisters of ours be spared the 'therapeutic neglect' which consists in denying them the treatment and care that alleviate suffering. Nor should this treatment and care be lacking for financial reasons.

Greater efforts are being made today to provide patients whose medical conditions cause great pain with medications or treatments that relieve their suffering. People are being encouraged to use advanced directives to make sure that medical treatment and end-of-life care is both humane and in conformity to the moral teachings of Christ and the Church. The personal presence, prayer and love of relatives and friends, supporting their loved one through the final stages of life's journey, are also essential parts of the process of Christian dying. The Church, through her ministers, also accompanies the dying person through the Sacrament of the Anointing of the Sick, *Viaticum*, and Prayers for the Dying.

FOR DISCUSSION

1. How can individuals and families promote respect for life and the value of life in the world today?
2. How can Catholics promote peace and understanding in the face of terrorism and violence in the world today?
3. What are root causes of the culture of death? How can we promote the value of human life in all its stages in contrast to abortion, euthanasia and capital punishment?

DOCTRINAL STATEMENTS

- God's creative action is present to every human life and is thus the source of its sacred value. Each human life remains in a relationship with God, who is the final goal of every man and woman. God alone is the Lord of human life from its beginning to its end.
- 'The deliberate murder of an innocent person is gravely contrary to the dignity of the human being, to the golden rule and to the holiness of the Creator' (CCC, no. 2261).
- 'The prohibition of murder does not abrogate the right to render an unjust aggressor unable to inflict harm' (CCC, no. 2321).
- Direct abortion is the intended destruction of an unborn child and is an act gravely contrary to the moral law and the holiness of the Creator.

- Euthanasia consists in putting to death the sick, the disabled, or the dying. Regardless of the motives or means, it is never morally permissible.
- Doctor-assisted suicide is suicide performed with the aid of a doctor. The emergence of doctor-assisted suicide, popularised by the right-to-die movement, seeks to legalise what is an immoral act. Suicide is wrong whether committed alone or aided by a doctor.
- The human embryo from the moment of conception has the entire genetic makeup of a unique human life. The growing child must be treated as completely and fully human. He or she needs only time to grow and develop. Killing the embryo is killing human life, an act contrary to God's law and Church teaching.
- 'Today, in fact, as a consequence of the possibilities which the state has for effectively preventing crime by rendering the one who has committed the offence incapable of doing harm … the cases in which the execution of the offender is an absolute necessity "are very rare, if not practically non-existent"' (CCC, no. 2267, citing EV, no. 56).
- While every possible means must be taken to avoid war, there are times when legitimate defence of one's homeland by military force may be taken under the strictest conditions.
- In addition to the respect for bodily life, there must also be reverence for the souls of others. One must always avoid scandal, which is a grave offence when, by deed or omission, one leads another to sin gravely (cf. CCC, nos. 2284–2287).
- The Fifth Commandment also forbids other sins: bigotry and hatred, physical or emotional abuse, violence of any kind against another person, inattention to one's health, or the abuse of alcohol or drugs (cf. CCC, nos. 2288–2291).

MEDITATION

Christ's blood reveals to man that his greatness, and therefore his vocation, consists in the sincere gift of self. Precisely because it is poured out as the gift of life, the blood of Christ is no longer a sign of death, of definitive separation from the brethren, but the instrument of a communion which is richness of life for all. Whoever in the Sacrament of the Eucharist drinks this blood and abides in Jesus (cf. Jn 6:56) is drawn into the dynamism of his love and gift of life, in order to bring to its fullness the original vocation to love which belongs to everyone (cf. Gn 1:27; 2:18-24).

It is from the blood of Christ that all draw the strength to commit themselves to promoting life. It is precisely this blood that is the most powerful source of hope, indeed it is the foundation of the absolute certitude that in God's plan life will be victorious. 'There will be no more death', exclaims the powerful voice which comes from the throne of God in the Heavenly Jerusalem (Rv 21:4). And St Paul assures us that the present victory over sin is a sign and anticipation of the definitive victory over death, when there 'shall come to pass the saying that is written: "Death is swallowed up in victory. Death, where is your victory? Death, where is your sting?"' (1 Cor 15:54-55).

– St John Paul II, *The Gospel of Life*
(*Evangelium Vitae*), no. 25

Mercy

Mercy is a woman of indeterminate age
and unremarkable appearance.
She is not fussy about the company she keeps
And tends to be full of excuses for her friends
Having seen life from their angle.

Her heart, like her pockets, is capacious.
She has a voice rich in tender understanding.
But is at her best in silence
When she sits alongside
The grief-stricken and the guilty
And their sorrow seeps into her soul

Curiously, she sees herself reflected
In the eyes of both murderer and victim
So sits not in judgement but companionably.
She is a subtle teacher.

She makes strong cups of tea, cup after cup.
Her hands are worn by work
But eagerly sought by the dying.
Her feet are calloused from long roads
Trudged with refugee and beggar.
She is an endurer of all horrors.

Mercy has a face wrinkled by kindness
And worn by the cost of living,
But even in hovels she has been given to laughter
and awareness of simple pleasures.
She has a store of lore and wisdom
But is never heard to complain
That she's heard the story before,
Believing each teller to be
Entitled to a hearing as if to the one and only.

Mercy is a lady comfortable to be with
the safest and soundest
blessed in her being
with the indisputable reality
that she is true daughter,
in manner and mind
of the maker of the universe.

– Mary Wickham RSM

PRAYER

Lord, make me an instrument of your peace.
Where there is hatred, let me sow love; where there is
    injury, pardon;
where there is doubt, faith, where there is despair, hope;
where there is darkness, light; and where there is sadness, joy.
Grant that I may not so much seek to be consoled as
    to console,
to be understood as to understand, to be loved as to love;
for it is in giving that we receive, it is in pardoning that we
    are pardoned,
and it is in dying that we are born to eternal life.

                                        – St Francis of Assisi

I am offering you life or death …
Choose life, then, so that you and your descendants may live.

                                        – Deut 30:19

30 THE SIXTH COMMANDMENT: MARITAL FIDELITY

YOU SHALL NOT COMMIT ADULTERY
– CCC, NOS. 2331–2400

POPE PAUL VI: A SHEPHERD FOR THE RENEWAL OF THE CHURCH

The Second Vatican Council was a major event in the life of the Catholic Church in the twentieth century. From 1962 until 1965, it brought together approximately 2,500 bishops from all over the world for four sessions in Rome – each session lasting about three months – to discuss and make decisions about the life of the Church in the modern world. Saint John XXIII had convoked the Council and presided over its first session. When he died in June of 1963, the College of Cardinals elected as his successor Cardinal Giovanni Battista Montini, who took the name Paul VI. Pope Paul VI presided over the next three sessions of the Council and guided the Church through the time of change and renewal that followed the Council.

Giovanni Battista Montini was born in northern Italy in 1897. He was ordained a priest in 1920 and two years later began service in the Vatican's Secretariat of State. He worked very closely with Pope Pius XII until 1954, when he was named Archbishop of Milan. In 1958 St John XXIII named him to the College of Cardinals.

His knowledge of the universal Church through his service in the Holy See, his intellectual abilities and wide reading in theology, and his pastoral experience in Milan all served him well when he was elected pope. His constant concern was to maintain the unity of the

Catholic Church even in times of considerable controversy. He guided the Church through a series of reforms and the renewal of the liturgy. In 1970, he authorised the publication of a new *Roman Missal*. He fostered dialogue with other churches and ecclesial communities. He worked diligently for peace, even visiting the headquarters of the United Nations in New York in 1964 to deliver an urgent appeal against war.

Throughout his pontificate, Paul VI emphasised the importance of the family for the Church and society. In his apostolic exhortation *On Evangelisation in the Modern World* (*Evangelii Nuntiandi*) of 1975, he wrote, 'The family, just like the Church, must always be regarded as a centre to which the Gospel must be brought and from which it must be proclaimed. Therefore in a family which is conscious of this role all the members of the family are evangelisers and are themselves evangelised' (no. 71).

Because of controversy in the Church surrounding the morality of artificial contraception, he issued his encyclical *On the Regulation of Birth* (*Humanae Vitae*; HV) in July of 1968. He reaffirmed the teaching of the Church that artificial contraception is gravely immoral because it contravenes God's will for the conjugal act, which unites the spouses in their love and must also be open to the creation of new life. He warned of the consequences for the moral tenor of society that would come from ignoring God's plan. He recognised the difficulties that married couples might have in following this teaching, but he encouraged them to have constant recourse to God's grace through the Sacrament of Penance and Reconciliation and the Sacrament of the Eucharist.

Pope Paul VI was a courageous shepherd for the renewal of the Church and the defence of her teaching. The cause for his beatification was initiated in 1993. Pope Paul VI's clear teaching on family, marriage and moral issues such as artificial contraception shows him to be a most important figure in fostering the values and virtues embodied in the Sixth Commandment. His beatification will take place on 19 October 2014.

PRACTISE MARITAL FIDELITY

God created human beings as male and female. In so doing, he gave equal dignity to both man and woman. In his plan, men and women should respect and accept their sexual identity. God created both the body and sex as good. Hence, we do not approach sexuality with fear or with hostility to the flesh. It is a gift of God by which men and women participate in his saving plan and respond to his call to grow in holiness.

The *Catechism* states that sexuality involves the whole person. '*Sexuality* affects all aspects of the human person in the unity of his body and soul. It especially concerns affectivity, the capacity to love and to procreate, and in a more general way the aptitude for forming bonds of communion with others' (CCC, no. 2332).

The Sixth Commandment summons spouses to practise permanent and exclusive fidelity to one another. Emotional and sexual fidelity are essential to the commitment made in the marriage covenant. God established marriage as a reflection of his fidelity to us. The vows made by the spouses at their wedding to be faithful to one another forever should witness the very covenant God has made with us.

CHASTITY

All people – married, single, religious and ordained – need to acquire the virtue of chastity. 'Chastity means the successful integration of sexuality within the person and thus the inner unity of man in his bodily and spiritual being' (CCC, no. 2337). Chastity unites our sexuality with our entire human nature. It approaches sexuality as related to our spiritual natures so that sex is seen as more than a physical act. Sexuality affects the whole person because of the unity of body and soul. Jesus is the model of chastity. 'Chastity includes *an apprenticeship in self-mastery* which is a training in human freedom' (CCC, no. 2339). The acquisition of chastity depends on self-discipline and leads to an internal freedom, which enables human beings to temper sexual desires according to God's plan for the appropriate expression of love in the marital relationship of a man and a woman.

The *Catechism* describes the acquisition of chastity in the following way:

> Self-mastery is a *long and exacting work*. One can never consider it acquired once and for all. It presupposes renewed effort at all stages of life. The effort required can be more intense in certain periods, such as when the personality is being formed during childhood and adolescence. (CCC, no. 2342; cf. Ti 2:1-6)

> Chastity has *laws of growth* which progress through stages marked by imperfection and too often by sin. (CCC, no. 2343) Chastity presupposes respect for the rights of the person, in particular the right to receive information and an education that respect the moral and spiritual dimensions of human life. (CCC, no. 2344)

> Chastity is a moral virtue. It is also a gift from God, a *grace*, a fruit of spiritual effort. The Holy Spirit enables one whom the water of Baptism has regenerated to imitate the purity of Christ. (CCC, no. 2345; cf. Gal 5:22, 1 Jn 3:3)

> The virtue of chastity blossoms in friendship … Chastity is expressed notably in *friendship with one's neighbour*. Whether it develops between persons of the same or opposite sex, friendship represents a great good for all. It leads to spiritual communion. (CCC, no. 2347)

There are a number of acts that are sins against chastity:

- *Lust* is a 'disordered desire for or an inordinate enjoyment of sexual pleasure', especially when sought for itself (CCC, no. 2351).
- *Masturbation* is sinful because it misuses the gift of sexuality in an inherently selfish act, devoid of love. It is a problem for which a counsellor, spiritual director, or a confessor can be of considerable help. A person often needs assistance to understand the causes of this behaviour, which are often habitual or in response to emotional stress or unexamined underlying attitudes.
- *Fornication* (sexual intercourse between unmarried persons) is sinful because it violates the dignity of persons and the nuptial meaning and

purpose of sexuality, which is ordered only to the unitive and procreative goals of married people.

- *Incest* (sexual relationships between close relatives) is always wrong, harming both the individuals involved as well as the family itself.
- *Sexual abuse* of any kind harms the victim on many more levels than only the physical. Forcing sexual intimacy of any type on a child or minor is an even graver evil (cf. CCC, no. 2356), which often scars the victim for life (cf. CCC, no. 2389).
- *Pornography* (sexually explicit material) has become even more available through the internet. This presents real difficulties for both individuals and society, as viewing pornography is not only sinful in itself but can also become an addiction and lead to dangerous sexual behaviours. It has also led to a greater exploitation of children as sexual objects.
- *Prostitution* reduces the person 'to an instrument of sexual pleasure', an object to be used. It increases the spread of sexually transmitted diseases. To protect innocent members of society, prostitution can legitimately be forbidden by civil authority. It is more prevalent where a culture exploits the physical and social vulnerability of women (CCC, no. 2355).
- *Rape* is an act of violence in which a person forces a sexual act on an unwilling partner. 'Rape deeply wounds the respect, freedom and physical and moral integrity to which every person has a right … It is always an intrinsically evil act' (CCC, no. 2356).
- '*Homosexual acts* are intrinsically disordered' and immoral. 'They are contrary to the natural law. They close the sexual act to the gift of life. They do not proceed from a genuine affective and sexual complementarity' (CCC, no. 2357). Having homosexual inclinations is not immoral. It is homosexual acts that are immoral.

'The number of men and women who have deep-seated homosexual tendencies is not negligible. This inclination, which is objectively disordered, constitutes for most of them a trial. They must be accepted with respect, compassion and sensitivity. Every sign of unjust discrimination in their regard should be avoided. These persons are called to fulfil God's will in their lives and, if they are Christians, to unite to the sacrifice of the Lord's Cross the difficulties they may encounter from their condition' (CCC, no. 2358).

THE LOVE OF HUSBAND AND WIFE

The spouses' union achieves the twofold end of marriage:
the good of the spouses themselves and the transmission of life.

– CCC, no. 2363

The bond between husband and wife is both conjugal and procreative. Conjugal mutual love and fidelity is the *unitive* aspect of marriage. The *procreative* aspect of marriage concerns the conception, birth and education of children. The bond between the unitive and procreative may not be broken.

Unitive Faithful Love

The unitive aspect of marriage involves the full personhood of the spouses, a love that encompasses the minds, hearts, emotions, bodies, souls and aspirations of husband and wife. They are called to grow continually in unitive love and fidelity so that they are no longer two but one flesh. Their mutual self-giving is strengthened and blessed by Jesus Christ in the Sacrament of Matrimony. God seals the consent that the bride and groom give to each other in this Sacrament.

> The acts in marriage by which the intimate and chaste union of the spouses takes place are noble and honourable; the truly human performance of these acts fosters the self-giving they signify and enriches the spouses in joy and gratitude. (CCC, no. 2362, citing GS, no. 49)

Acceptance of a spouse's faults and failures as well as of one's own is a recognition that the call to holiness in marriage is a lifelong process of conversion and growth.

Procreative Love

God calls the married couple to be open to children, remembering always that having a child is not a right, but rather a gift from God (cf. CCC, no. 2378). In this way, they share the creative power and fatherhood of God. In giving birth to children and educating and forming them, they cooperate with the love of God as Creator. Marital love by its nature is fruitful. The marriage act, while deepening spousal love, is meant to overflow into new life. Families are images of the ever-creative power and life of the Holy Trinity and the fruitfulness of the relationship between Christ and his Church.

Respecting the Link of Fertility and Love

'A child does not come from outside as something added on to the mutual love of the spouses, but springs from the very heart of that mutual giving, as its fruit and fulfilment. So the Church, which is "on the side of life" teaches that "it is necessary that each and every marriage act remain ordered *per se* to the procreation of human life"' (CCC, no. 2366, citing FC, no. 30, and HV, no. 11, respectively).

This passage underlines the Church's teaching that God established an inseparable bond between the unitive and procreative aspects of marriage. Each and every sexual act in a marriage needs to be open to the possibility of conceiving a child. Thus, artificial contraception is contrary to God's will for marriage because it separates the act of conception from sexual union. Efforts to achieve pregnancy outside of the act of sexual intercourse (e.g. *in vitro* fertilisation) are morally wrong for the same reason – they separate conception from sexual intercourse.

Contemporary methods of natural family planning are making it possible for couples, in cases of legitimate need, to space the births of their children while remaining faithful to God's plan for marriage. These methods allow a couple to have a more precise knowledge of the time of ovulation to enable them to either avoid or achieve a pregnancy. 'The regulation of births represents one of the aspects of responsible fatherhood and motherhood. Legitimate intentions on the part of the spouses do not justify recourse to morally unacceptable means (for example, direct sterilisation or contraception)' (CCC, no. 2399).

In the course of their marriage, couples may, for serious reasons, decide to avoid a new birth for the time being or even for an indeterminate period, but they must not use immoral means to prevent conception. Couples should also be mindful of the fact that their love is expressed in more ways than just the conjugal act. Abstaining from intercourse at certain times can be an act of sacrifice which gives rise to a deeper relationship.

In relation to physical, economic, psychological and social conditions, responsible parenthood is exercised either by the thoughtfully made and generous decision to raise a large family, or by the decision, made for grave motives and with respect for the moral law, to avoid a new birth for the time being or even for an indeterminate period. (HV, no. 10)

THREATS TO MARRIAGE

The *Catechism* lists the following behaviours as acts that undermine the purpose and dignity of marriage.

Adultery is gravely sinful because it violates God's call to a loving covenant of fidelity between a married man and woman. The act of adultery is an injustice to the wounded spouse. It weakens the institution of marriage and the stability of the family.

Divorce is contrary to the natural law for it breaks the promise 'to which the spouses freely consented to live with each other till death' (CCC, no. 2384). Jesus clearly taught that God's original plan for marriage excluded divorce (cf. Mt 5:31-32, 9:3-9; Mk 10:9; Lk 16:18; 1 Cor 7:10-11). Marriage is an indissoluble union. Jesus removed the accommodations for divorce that had been tolerated under the Old Law.

The couple may be allowed a separation in certain cases, such as when adultery is occurring or some type of abuse is present. A separation can be, at times, a prudent action to take. 'If civil divorce remains the only possible way of ensuring certain legal rights, the care of the children, or the protection of inheritance, it can be tolerated and does not constitute a moral offence' (CCC, no. 2383). In such cases, a Catholic can still receive the Sacraments.

Cohabitation (an unmarried couple living together) involves the serious sin of fornication. It does not conform to God's plan for marriage and is always wrong and objectively sinful. Cohabitation does not guarantee successful married life, as has been revealed in the painful experience of many, and is detrimental to future commitment.

Polygamy (having more than one spouse at a time) violates the understanding of the equal dignity that a man and woman bring to marriage and contradicts the unitive purpose of marriage.

FROM THE CATECHISM

1. What is the divine plan for marriage?
Each of the two sexes is an image of the power and tenderness of God, with equal dignity though in a different way. The *union of man and woman* in marriage is a way of imitating in the flesh the Creator's generosity and fecundity. (CCC, no. 2335)

2. What is the link between charity and chastity?
Charity is the *form* of all the virtues. Under its influence, chastity appears as a school of the gift of the person. Self-mastery is ordered to the gift of self. Chastity leads him who practises it to become a witness to his neighbour of God's fidelity and loving kindness. (CCC, no. 2346)

3. What is the marital covenant?
The covenant which spouses have freely entered into entails faithful love. It imposes on them the obligation to keep their marriage indissoluble. (CCC, no. 2397)

Attempts to justify same-sex unions or relationships or to give them matrimonial status also contradict God's plan – as revealed from the beginning both in nature and in Revelation – for marriage to be a lifelong union of a man and a woman.

THE THEOLOGY OF THE BODY

The many ways in which one can depart from God's call to chastity and marital fidelity are more than evident in contemporary culture. The exploitation of sexuality for commercial gain is manifested in countless ads and other means of engaging our attention through television and allied media. The cult of the body, not just for health reasons but for hedonistic attraction, is a prime example of the effect of an exaggerated focus on sex and sexuality.

What is needed is a healing vision of sexuality, the body and the human person. Saint John Paul II offers us this perspective in his theology of the body. He begins with the idea that God willed each human being for his or her own sake. This means that none of us is merely a part of something else, or a means of gaining some result. God created us as free and unique human persons. We are not things to be used, but persons to be respected.

God created human beings to love one another. Since God is a communion of persons, it makes sense that we, being made in his image, would reach out to love others, forming our own communion of persons. Marital love witnesses the total self-giving of man and woman. The miracle is that in the act of self-giving, each spouse gains a greater sense of self while enriching the other spouse.

The Nuptial Meaning of the Body

We experience our selfhood through our bodies. We are embodied as man and woman. Genesis teaches that it is not good for man to be alone. We are rescued from our solitude by a complementary existence as man and woman. Saint John Paul II calls the capacity of the male body and the female body to serve mutual self-giving the nuptial meaning of the body.

Sin, particularly lust, obscures the nuptial meaning of the body and its capacity to witness the divine image. In this case, the woman's body ceases to reveal her as a person to be loved, but rather as an object to be used. Conversely, a man's body would not disclose him as a person to be loved, but rather as an instrument to be exploited. Sin erodes spousal love.

Shame may enter the relationship. Saint John Paul II notes there is an instinctive shame that can ward off utilitarian sex. Shame leads the woman to protect herself from the aggressive, lustful sexuality of the man. In the opposite case, shame causes the man to resist a sexual advance from the woman that is merely lustful. God calls for spousal love as the remedy for moving beyond the sex appeal of the body alone to its nuptial meaning, revealing the person as made in his image.

The Redemption of the Body

Saint John Paul II retrieves the nuptial meaning of the body by taking us back to life before the Fall, to a time of original innocence and original nakedness. The first man and woman did not experience any shame in their nakedness because the attraction of male and female served love alone. This was more than virtuous self-control. The man and woman dwelt so intimately in their bodies that each body expressed to the other the beauty of the human person and the image of God. Bodily sexuality was integrated into the energy of spousal love.

Original Sin caused a rupture in the unity of body and soul. The body now could *obscure* as well as reveal the person. Christ's saving act included the redemption of the body by which he restored the lost unity of soul and body. This is a *process of restoration*, partly completed here and fully restored in the next life. While there will not be marriage in the future life, masculinity and femininity will endure. Saint John Paul II relates this to consecrated celibacy and virginity in which the nuptial meaning of the body is not denied. The body's nuptial meaning serves love in ways other than marriage.

We seldom do justice to the ways in which our bodies share in and reveal our interior personal lives. We have drawn attention here to St John Paul II's meditation on the nuptial meaning of the body because we believe it is a vision of sex, marriage and the person best suited to rebuilding a wholesome, faith-filled and loving approach to these most precious gifts.[6]

FOR DISCUSSION

1. How can we best show respect for human sexuality in the light of a culture that demeans it? What are the ways of reversing the degradation of sexuality?

2. Why is marital fidelity so important for the stability of the family and society? What spiritual means does the Church offer to strengthen marriages or rebuild troubled marriages?

3. How does St John Paul II's theology of the body help you to appreciate the beauty of the gift of sexuality and its integration into your life?

---

[6] See St John Paul II, *Love and Responsibility* (New York: Farrar, Straus, Giroux, 1981); and his *Original Unity of Man and Woman: Catechesis on the Book of Genesis* (Boston: St Paul Editions, 1981).

▬▬▬▬ DOCTRINAL STATEMENTS ▬▬▬▬

- God is the author of marriage and the family. The Sacrament of Marriage, along with the Fourth, Sixth and Ninth Commandments, illustrate the principal ways in which God's plan for marriage and the family is to be lived.
- The Sixth Commandment summons the spouses to practise permanent and exclusive fidelity to one another. God established marriage as a reflection of his fidelity to us.
- The Sixth Commandment forbids adultery, which is sexual relations between a married person and someone other than one's spouse.
- Chastity integrates bodily sexuality within the broader human reality. It approaches sexuality as related to our spiritual natures so that sexuality is seen as more than a physical act. Sexuality affects the whole person because of the unity of body and soul. Jesus is the model of chastity. Every person is called to chastity according to one's state in life.
- 'Among the sins gravely contrary to chastity are masturbation, fornication, pornography and homosexual practices' (CCC, no. 2396).
- God calls married couples to grow continually in unitive love and fidelity so that they are no longer two but one flesh. Their mutual self-giving is strengthened and blessed by Jesus Christ in the Sacrament of Matrimony. God seals the consent that the bride and groom give to each other in this Sacrament.
- 'The acts in marriage by which the intimate and chaste union of the spouses takes place are noble and honourable; the truly human performance of these acts fosters the self-giving they signify and enriches the spouses in joy and gratitude' (CCC, no. 2362, citing GS, no. 49).
- God calls the married couple to be open to children. In this way, they share the creative power and fatherhood of God. In giving birth to children and educating and forming them, they cooperate with the love of God as Creator (cf. CCC, no. 2367).
- 'In relation to physical, economic, psychological and social conditions, responsible parenthood is exercised either by the thoughtfully made and generous decision to raise a large family, or by the decision, made for grave motives and with respect for the moral law, to avoid a new birth for the time being or even for an indeterminate period' (HV, no. 10).

MEDITATION

At a time in history like the present, special attention must also be given to the *pastoral care of the family*, particularly when this fundamental institution is experiencing a radical and widespread crisis. In the Christian view of marriage, the relationship between a man and a woman – a mutual and total bond, unique and indissoluble – is part of God's original plan, obscured throughout history by our 'hardness of heart', but which Christ came to restore to its pristine splendour, disclosing what had been God's will 'from the beginning' (Mt 19:8). Raised to the dignity of a Sacrament, marriage expresses the 'great mystery' of Christ's nuptial love for his Church (cf. Eph 5:32).

On this point the Church cannot yield to cultural pressures, no matter how widespread and even militant they may be. Instead, it is necessary to ensure that through an ever more complete Gospel formation Christian families show convincingly that it is possible to live marriage fully in keeping with God's plan and with the true good of the human person – of the spouses, and of the children who are more fragile. Families themselves must become increasingly conscious of the care due to children, and play an active role in the Church and in society in safeguarding their rights.

– NMI, no. 47

PRAYER

O God, who, to reveal the great design you formed in your love,
willed that the love of spouses for each other
should foreshadow the covenant you graciously made with your people,
so that, by fulfilment of the sacramental sign,
the mystical marriage of Christ with his Church
might become manifest
in the union of husband and wife among your faithful

– From the Nuptial Blessing (B)
Roman Missal, 3rd typical edition

Set me like a seal on your heart, / like a seal on your arm.

– Song 8:6

31 THE SEVENTH COMMANDMENT: DO NOT STEAL – ACT JUSTLY

YOU SHALL NOT STEAL
– CCC, NOS. 2401–2463

FREDERIC OZANAM: THE POOR IN OUR MIDST

Frederic Ozanam was born in Milan, Italy, on 23 April 1813. He was not a Milanese, nor even an Italian. At that time, the Age of Napoleon, Milan was in the control of France. His father, Antoine, was from Lyon in France. As a young man, Antoine had been bankrupted by a defaulted loan and he moved with his young wife to Italy to forge his path in the world. Landing on his feet, he found an opening as a tutor, and then embarked on the study of medicine. Antoine soon qualified, and settled into a doctor's practice, resolving to start a family. Frederic was the fifth child. Then fate intervened again. Napoleon was toppled and Austria moved into Northern Italy and Milan. Antoine had to pull up roots, move back to his native city of Lyon and start all over again.

So Frederic, born in Italy, grew up in France in difficult circumstances. His mother lost eleven of her fourteen children in childhood. The young boy Frederic was, as he confessed, headstrong, disobedient and, at times, lazy. At the age of fifteen, he was assailed with intellectual doubts about God and the Church, which threatened to upset his faith before it had been fully fledged. A patient and insightful priest gave him books, challenged his thinking and afforded

455

a kindly ear to the troubled teenager. After more than a year, his doubt was calmed and Frederic looked ahead with confidence.

At the age of sixteen, Frederic was apprenticed to a prominent Lyon lawyer. He was a reticent understudy, seeming shy and retiring, until he felt moved to speak. Then his speech was impressive and totally persuasive. The following example illustrates his approach. During one discussion, he remarked to a friend: 'I watch and wait and at the end of ten years, I shall say what I think!' Where matters of faith were concerned, he was more forward, involving himself in defending Catholicism against contemporary attacks, even in print. This was quite unusual for one not yet out of his teens. Aged eighteen, in 1831 Frederic travelled to Paris to study law.

There, Frederic was befriended by the great scientist, André Ampère, who offered him accommodation. He met many of the influential Catholic intellectuals and thinkers of the generation, a wonderful opportunity for the young and intelligent student. This company gave the young man confidence and poise. With other believing Catholic students, he began to engage in arguments with lecturers who offended or attacked people of faith. On occasion they managed to extract an apology, and a pledge to avoid future offence, from a professor.

Among other campaigns, the Catholic students approached the Archbishop of Paris to establish a Chair of Preaching in the college. The idea was to improve the standard of sermons and homilies given by priests from the altar. Their request induced the archbishop to invite Henri Lacordaire – a noted preacher – to deliver a series of sermons during Lent at the Cathedral of Notre Dame. These sermons have been recognised as a historic step in the practice of homiletics.

In the midst of the study and debate, Ozanam and his companions made a discovery and embarked on a path that was truly historic for the Church. During their debates, they were often confronted by the taunt of unbelievers: 'Religion is dead. Everything you profess is an idle dream. Show us religion in action. Where is the power of God today?' This was not a challenge that could be passed on to the hierarchy or clergy to respond to. Nor was it one that could be answered by theory or thought alone.

Ozanam and the others saw that they were being called upon to act. With their mentor and friend, Emmanuel Bailly, they convened a group of six like-minded young men, all of them around the age of twenty, with the purpose of helping the poor. Ozanam had observed how his own parents engaged in charity. Their success, even in circumstances of limited resources, was through visitation of the poor in their own homes. 'We must do what Our Lord Jesus Christ did when preaching the Gospel,' he said, 'Let us go to the poor.' In May 1833, the small group met in what was recognised afterwards to be the first meeting of the St Vincent de Paul Society.

Bailly, with his wise experience and spiritual insight, laid down a few principles for the members of the Conference of Charity, as it was then called. No member was to use the conference for personal advancement or credit. Funds were to be contributed by members at each meeting in a secret bag (in fact a hat!). Each meeting of the conference, placed under the patronage of St Vincent de Paul, should include a spiritual reading. Finally he sent the young men to a Daughter of Charity experienced in working with the poor. Sister Rosalie Rendu (beatified by John Paul II in 2003) gave them guidance and advice in the task of visitation.

With this foundation, the conferences spread rapidly to other French cities, to locations in Europe and then around the world. Frederic Ozanam continued to engage with the expanding work of the Society throughout his life. But he was pursuing the life of an academic scholar as well. Law was his father's suggested direction for a career, but Frederic himself preferred the study of literature. So he ended up studying the two subjects, emerging from university with doctorates in both law and letters.

Ozanam was to spend twelve years lecturing on literature in the prestigious Sorbonne, a respected researcher on Dante, specialising in the Catholic religious influence on European civilisation.

Ozanam briefly considered a religious life, being particularly attracted to the Dominican Order, following the preacher Lacordaire. He decided against it in the end. He fell in love with Amelie Soulacroix, from Lyon, and the couple were married. He suffered poor health, however, and was forced to take time out from teaching to recuperate in Italy. He wrote powerfully about the problem of poverty and seized the chance to extend the Society wherever he visited. But the illness took its toll, and he died in September 1853 at the age of forty.

By the time of his death, there were two thousand members of the St Vincent de Paul Society in Paris alone and five hundred conferences in France, as well as conferences in England, Ireland, Spain, America and even in Jerusalem. Today the membership of the society is given as over 900,000 working in over 130 countries.

The work of the St Vincent de Paul Society has made an immense contribution to the Church and to the world in forming consciences about the plight of the poor. For this reason, the founder, Frederic Ozanam, was beatified by St John Paul II in Notre Dame Cathedral, Paris, during the papal visit to France in 1997.

RESPECT PEOPLE AND THEIR POSSESSIONS

The seventh Commandment forbids theft. Theft is the usurpation of another's goods against the reasonable will of the owner ... Every manner of taking and using another's property unjustly is contrary to the seventh commandment. The injustice committed requires reparation. Commutative justice requires the restitution of stolen goods.

– CCC, nos. 2453–2454

The Seventh Commandment forbids stealing or theft, which involves taking someone's money or property 'against the reasonable will of the owner'. Theft includes not only robbery but also actions such as embezzlement, computer theft, counterfeit money, fraud, identity theft, copyright violations (including pirating things such as music or computer software) and mail scams.

To keep this Commandment, we need to acquire the virtues of moderation in our possessions, justice in our treatment of others, respect for their human dignity and solidarity with all peoples. Moderation curbs our attachment to worldly goods and restrains our appetite for consumerism. Justice helps us respect our neighbour's rights and be interested in their human well-being. Solidarity opens our hearts to identifying with the whole human family, reminding us of our common humanity.

THE RIGHT TO RELIGIOUS FREEDOM

A basic duty every human person owes to God is regular worship. Because of this, and because of the basic longing each person has for God, a fundamental human right is the right to worship freely. No one should be prohibited from a free exercise of their faith, either in public or in private, and no one should ever be forced to worship in a manner that violates their beliefs and convictions. Because freedom of religion and worship is such an important and fundamental right, governments need to enact and enforce laws that respect and protect this right (cf. CCC, nos. 2105–2109).

We should not steal from each other, pay unfair salaries, cheat in business or exploit people's weaknesses to make money. Promises should be kept and contracts honoured to the extent that the issues are morally just (cf. CCC, no. 2410). We need to safeguard property rights, pay our debts and fulfil obligations freely incurred. The government has the right and duty to safeguard legitimate ownership of money and property and to protect people from robbery and injury.

PRACTISE THE CHURCH'S SOCIAL TEACHINGS

Man is himself the author, centre and goal of all economic and social life. The decisive point of the social question is that goods created by God for everyone should in fact reach everyone in accordance with justice and with the help of charity.

– CCC, no. 2459

For over a century, the Church, especially through the teaching of the popes, has given special attention to the development of her social doctrine. The Church's social doctrine is related to the understanding of what it means to be a human being, to the origin of human dignity, to the problem of the Fall and to the promise of Redemption. We are seriously weakened by Original Sin and actual sin but are redeemed by Christ's saving death and Resurrection with its gift of divine life, a source of moral strength (cf. CCC, nos. 355–431).

The Church's social doctrine also relates to an understanding of participation in social life, the role of authority, the importance of the common good, natural law, social justice and human solidarity (cf. CCC, nos. 1897–1948). Finally, there is the Seventh Commandment, which includes consideration of the relationship between the economy and social justice, the importance of solidarity among nations and a preferential love for the poor (cf. CCC, nos. 2401–2463).

Catholic social teaching embraces both the Church's perennial concern for people's social needs since New Testament times as well as an explicit social doctrine.

> The Church makes a judgement about economic and social matters when the fundamental rights of the person or the salvation of souls requires it. She is concerned with the temporal common good of men because they are ordered to the sovereign Good, their ultimate end. (CCC, no. 2458)

The central focus of the Church's social teaching is justice for all, especially for the helpless and the poor. It involves the removal of the symptoms and causes of poverty and injustice.

The Church's social doctrine addresses a wide range of issues that include the dignity of work, the need of workers to receive a salary that will enable them to care for their families, a safe working environment and the responsibility of the state for areas such as a stable currency, public services and protecting personal freedom and private property. Church teaching also speaks to the need of business enterprises to consider the good of the employees, not just the profit motive. Wage earners should be able to represent their needs and grievances when necessary.

The major themes of Catholic social doctrine build on each other and complement each other. All of the Church's social teaching is rooted in the fundamental principle of the sacredness of human life and the fundamental dignity of every single individual. Out of these truths flows the rest.

FROM THE CATECHISM

1. What should be the attitude of business toward the environment?

Those *responsible for business enterprises* are responsible to society for the economic and ecological effects of their operations. They have an obligation to consider the good of persons and not only the increase of *profits*. (CCC, no. 2432)

2. Who should have access to employment and professions?

Access to employment and to professions must be open to all without unjust discrimination: men and women, healthy and disabled, natives and immigrants. For its part society should, according to circumstances, help citizens find work and employment. (CCC, no. 2433)

3. When is a strike permissible?

Recourse to a *strike* is morally legitimate when it cannot be avoided, or at least when it is necessary to obtain a proportionate benefit. It becomes morally unacceptable when accompanied by violence, or when objectives are included that are not directly linked to working conditions or are contrary to the common good. (CCC, no. 2435)

EXCERPTS FROM THE LAUNCH OF THE IRISH BISHOPS' STATEMENT *FROM CRISIS TO HOPE: WORKING TO ACHIEVE THE COMMON GOOD* FEBRUARY 2011

Our objective is to hold up a vision of society which is working to achieve the common good, to remind those seeking political office of their special responsibility to seek the common good, and voters to exercise their franchise in the light of their judgement as to which party or individual best promotes this ideal.

... There is nothing abstract or opaque about proposing a vision that is grounded in the concept of the common good, which is the only real alternative set of values to the rugged individualism, survival of the fittest ethos that shapes our consumerist/capitalist culture today – one that despite the many benefits that it has brought to society, shows little awareness of the fact that not everything is earned and not everything is motivated by self-interest ...

The concept of the common good gives a clear definition of the purpose of politics, the centrality of justice and equity in any form of governance and the need for those in power to pay special attention to the more vulnerable members of society, i.e. those who are at a disadvantage in terms of defending their rights and advocating their legitimate interests.

In today's Ireland, the common good will only be served to the extent that a major effort is made to restore trust in our institutional framework, i) through attention to the place of ethics in governance, and ii) by acknowledging that the common good is damaged by economic policies that target the most vulnerable in our society ... (Fr Eoin Cassidy)

Human dignity ... represents the foundation on which all human rights rest. So what are the implications of our Christian obligation to defend human dignity in Ireland today? Defence of human dignity means:

- Protecting human life, from the moment of conception to its natural end;
- Protecting our children from poverty and ensuring that they have access to all the services they require for health and education, as well as the opportunity to develop their talents through those cultural and sporting activities that are so important for personal growth;
- Ensuring that our young people are not forced to leave their home country as a result of a lack of opportunities;
- Strengthening and protecting family life. Families are the cornerstone of strong communities, and, ultimately, a strong society;
- Ensuring that every person in this country can access the healthcare they require on the basis of need;
- Providing support and assistance to people with disabilities;
- Enabling older people to live dignified and independent lives.

This is by no means an exhaustive list, but it serves to highlight key issues that should not be overlooked at a time of difficult political and economic choices. Closely linked to human dignity is the question of participation – if we recognise the value and worth of every human being, then we support their right to participate in society and make their contribution. This belief obliges us to work to eliminate the obstacles that can prevent people availing of that right. (Bishop Raymond Field)

'For the wisdom of the world is folly to God. As scripture says: *He traps the crafty in the snare of their own cunning ...*' (from St Paul's First Epistle to the Corinthians 3:19).

These words of St Paul to the young Church at Corinth almost 2,000 years ago are still relevant today. Perhaps it is a little touch of serendipity that they occur in the context of today's world. It is the so-called wisdom of this world leading to greed that has given rise to the crisis in our country and all over the globe. The wisdom of this world suggested 'light touch regulation' and 'bonus culture' and we now know where these have got us.

People neglected the principles of solidarity and placed private sectional interests ahead of the good of the community as a whole. Greed became dominant, trust was betrayed and the result was the recession in which we now find ourselves.

At national level the failure of so many institutions, including sadly the Church itself, led to a betrayal of trust by ignoring or trivialising the importance of ethics in business. Those in authority failed to act in the interest of the common good and in some cases showed a flagrant disregard to anything associated with it. Pope Benedict XVI's ... encyclical letter *Charity in Truth* comments on the global situation and states, 'today it is this trust which has ceased to exist and the loss of trust is a grave loss'.

One of the key features of Catholic Social Teaching is the promotion of the common good. This is the sum total of all the social conditions which allow the human dignity of all persons, as groups or individuals, to be respected and their basic needs to be met to reach their fulfilment more easily (CCC, no. 1906). Every person and group must take account of other persons and groups not only in Ireland but overseas as well. Thus we have a responsibility in this globalised world for people struggling with poverty, environmental degradation and conflict in other parts of the planet. (Bishop John Kirby)

THE POOR IN OUR MIDST

We do not have to look beyond Ireland to find the ravages of poverty. There are homeless people in the streets of our cities, families in economic and social difficulties, and neglected children. The causes of poverty are many, but they all call forth the compassion of the Church – through her members and through her various structures, such as Catholic charities and the St Vincent de Paul Society.

On his death bed, St Vincent de Paul (1580–1660) was asked by a novice what was the best way to serve the poor. He responded by telling the novice that the most important thing is to love them because loving them makes it possible for the needy to forgive those who give food to them. Saint John Chrysostom said this about ministry to the poor: 'Not to enable the poor to share in our goods is to steal from them and deprive them of life. The goods we possess are theirs, not ours' (Homily on the Parable of Lazarus and the Rich Man).

Jesus teaches us, 'Anyone who has two tunics must share with the one who has none, and anyone with something to eat must do the same' (Lk 3:11). Saint James reinforces this truth. 'If one of the brothers or one of the sisters is in need of clothes and has not enough food to live on, and one of you says to them, "I wish you well; keep yourself warm and eat plenty," without giving them these bare necessities of life, then what good is that?' (Jas 2:15-16).

Acts of charity for the poor are a good way to start living the Church's social teaching. Personal contact with those who need our help fulfils Christ's command to love the poor most effectively. But we are called to heal not only the symptoms of poverty and injustice but also their causes. This requires participation in political and social processes to correct unjust laws and structures of injustice.

━━━━━━━━━━━━ FOR DISCUSSION ━━━━━━━━━━━━

1. How does the Seventh Commandment guide us to respect and care for property that is not our own, that belongs to others, or that is public property?
2. Why is it important to realise that you are more than an individual, that you are a social being meant to be in solidarity with others? What social

justice issues have caught your attention recently? What did you do about them?

3. What insights have you gained from reflecting on the statement of themes related to Catholic social teaching? What are some stories you could share about people you admire who have helped you to acquire a social conscience?

DOCTRINAL STATEMENTS

- 'The Seventh Commandment forbids theft. Theft is the [taking] of another's goods against the reasonable will of the owner. Every manner of taking and using another's property unjustly is contrary to the Seventh Commandment. The injustice committed requires reparation. Commutative justice requires the restitution of stolen goods' (CCC, nos. 2453–2454).

- In creating the universe, God entrusted the resources of the earth to the stewardship of all people. The Church, applying this truth, upholds the principle that the universal destination of the goods of the earth is meant for the common good of all people. At the same time, the Church stands by the right of private property.

- The Church teaches that human dignity can be protected and a healthy community can be achieved only if human rights are protected and responsibilities are met. Therefore, every person has a fundamental right to life and a right to those things required for human decency. Corresponding to these rights are duties and responsibilities – to one another, to our families and to the larger society.

- We show our respect for the Creator by our stewardship of creation. Care for the earth is a requirement of our faith. We are called to protect people and the planet, living our faith in relationship with all of God's creation. This environmental challenge has fundamental moral and ethical dimensions that cannot be ignored.

- The Church's social doctrine addresses a wide range of issues that include the ability to freely practise one's faith, the freedom to participate in cultural life, the dignity of work, the need of workers to receive a salary that will enable them to care for their families, the need for a safe working environment, and the responsibility of the state for areas such as a stable currency, public services and the protection of personal freedom and private property.

- Church teaching also speaks to the need of business enterprises to consider the good of the employees, not just the profit motive. Wage earners should be able to represent their needs and grievances when necessary.
- It can never be stated often enough that love and care for the poor is a major priority for every Christian. 'Giving alms to the poor is a witness to fraternal charity: it is also a work of justice pleasing to God' (CCC, no. 2462).
- The central interest of the Church's social teaching is justice for all, but especially for the helpless and the poor. It involves the removal of the symptoms and causes of poverty and injustice.
- 'The moral law forbids acts which, for commercial or totalitarian purposes, lead to the enslavement of human beings, or to their being bought, sold or exchanged like merchandise' (CCC, no. 2455).
- True social and economic development is concerned with the whole person and with increasing each person's ability to respond to God's call.

MEDITATION

Certainly we need to remember that no one can be excluded from our love, since 'through his Incarnation the Son of God has united himself in some fashion with every person'.

Yet, as the unequivocal words of the Gospel remind us, there is a special presence of Christ in the poor, and this requires the Church to make a preferential option for them. This option is a testimony to the nature of God's love, to his providence and mercy; and in some way history is still filled with the seeds of the Kingdom of God which Jesus himself sowed during his earthly life whenever he responded to those who came to him with their spiritual and material needs.

In our own time, there are so many needs which demand a compassionate response from Christians. Our world is entering the new millennium burdened by the contradictions of an economic, cultural and technological progress which offers immense possibilities to a fortunate few, while leaving millions of others not only on the margins of progress but in living conditions far below the minimum demanded by human dignity. How can it be that even today there are still people dying of hunger? Condemned to illiteracy? Lacking the most basic medical care? Without a roof over their heads?

... We must therefore ensure that in every Christian community the poor feel at home. Would not this approach be the greatest and most effective presentation of the good news of the Kingdom? Without this form of evangelisation through charity and without the witness of Christian poverty the proclamation of the Gospel, which is itself the prime form of charity, risks being misunderstood or submerged by the ocean of words which daily engulfs us in today's society of mass communications. The charity of works ensures an unmistakable efficacy to the charity of words.

– NMI, nos. 49–50

PRAYER

O God, who in the Heart of your Son,
wounded by our sins,
bestow on us in mercy
the boundless treasures of your love,
grant, we pray,
that, in paying him the homage of our devotion,
we may also offer worthy reparation.
Through our Lord Jesus Christ, your Son,
who lives and reigns with you in the unity of the Holy Spirit,
one God, for ever and ever.

– Alternative Collect, Solemnity of the Most Sacred Heart of Jesus
(Roman Missal, 2011)

Let justice flow like water,
and uprightness like a never-failing stream!

– Am 5:24

32 THE EIGHTH COMMANDMENT: TELL THE TRUTH

YOU SHALL NOT BEAR FALSE WITNESS
AGAINST YOUR NEIGHBOUR
– CCC, NOS. 2464–2513

SAINT COLUMCILLE

Saint Columcille is also known as Columba. Columba means 'dove' in Latin. We may conjecture that those who bestowed it on the newly baptised baby (or the young monk taking vows) expressed a vision for his future. It was an appropriate name: the dove symbolises the inspiration of Holy Spirit. The dove is reputed to be gentle and kind. The dove is the homeless traveller, like the dove that Noah sent out from the ark on Mount Ararat. Columba lived up to these expectations, being a celebrated scholar, a man of peace and then, in penance, embarking on permanent pilgrimage from his native land.

Columcille (or 'the dove of the Church') was a title earned by a long career of missionary work. The central date in Columba's life is 563, when he set out with twelve companions to establish a monastery on a remote island off the western coast of Scotland. That monastery, on the island of Iona, became the centre of evangelisation for the western Scottish isles and highlands, where Columba's memory is still kept green. It is even said that Columba's mission reached as far as the Picts in the north. Iona is still receiving pilgrims and seekers today, fifteen centuries later, affording rest and retreat to travellers, being a sign of reconciliation, especially for divided Christians.

It is not clear what events sent Columba on his missionary pilgrimage. An ancient tradition says that he studied as a young monk at the monastery of Clonard under St Finian. Finian had just come back from Rome with a copy of the Psalter, the Biblical Psalms translated by St Jerome in the Latin version known as the Vulgate. The young scholar was gripped by the study of Finian's Psalter.

As Columba wanted to continue studying it when he left Clonard, he sat up secretly in the library by night and copied out the book by hand. When Finian found out what Columba had done, he erupted in anger and demanded that Columba hand over his copy. Columba refused and the matter went for judgment to the High King of Ireland himself. The High King handed down the verdict: 'To every cow, its calf; to every book, its copy.' This ancient example of copyright was a bitter defeat for Columba and he was forced to surrender his copy to Finian.

That was not the end, however. The upshot, by all accounts, was a pitched battle between the High King's army and Columba's native clan in the North, in which 3,000 soldiers died. The northerners prevailed but Columba still did not emerge victorious. A Church synod held Columba responsible for the slaughter. He himself had been appalled by what had happened and knew himself to be guilty. So Columba proposed that he undertake the penance of exile from Ireland until he had converted the same number of pagans to Christianity who had died in the battle. Whatever the historical truth of the tradition, and the reason for the journey, Columba certainly set off with his companions from Derry to the island of Iona in 563.

Columba was born in Gartan, County Donegal, around 520. His family had links to Irish royalty, being connected to Niall of the Nine Hostages. Therefore Columba was intimately familiar with Gaelic social and political life and culture, and could mix easily with those of high standing in Church and society. He was charismatic and eloquent, persuasive and influential – in short, a natural leader.

These human qualities were augmented by a deep spirituality and evident sanctity. Despite early signs of temper and stubbornness (as evinced in the matter of the Psalter), his temperament was redeemed by a strong determination and humble flexibility in his later years. He seems to have learned by his mistakes and developed into a compassionate and humane elder statesman, to whom king and abbot, bishop and faithful, turned for sage advice.

This was the Columba who landed on Iona and established the church and abbey that was to change Scotland's religious and secular history. He made contact with the Scot chiefs in Argyle and up the west coast. Historians relate that he travelled to the north and east of Scotland converting the nation of Picts. Later generations looked back to Columba as the great missionary of Scotland.

It is recorded that Columba consecrated Aidan as King of the Dalriada. Ancient chroniclers wrote that he attended the meeting of kings at Drumceatt, near Limavady, County Derry. Columba facilitated King Aidan from Scotland and Aedh of Ireland to negotiate a treaty, and he secured from the assembly the retention of the poets who had been threatened with suppression in Ireland. Then, as now, those who speak the truth freely like the ancient poets disturb those in power.

He established Christian communities with monasteries to support them. He is regarded as the founder of the monasteries of Derry, Durrow and Kells, and many in Scotland and the Isles. His influence, however, exceeded his own direct ministry. Abbots consulted with him, and even after his death on 8 June 597, missionaries under his inspiration ventured throughout England and across Europe.

Columba's first biographer, Adamnan, said that he set out to Iona wishing to travel for Christ (*'pro Christo perigrinari volens enavigavit'*). Irish missionaries – religious and lay – through the centuries since have done the same in the open spirit of Columba – Colum of the Churches. They travelled in the 'Protection of Columcille', an ancient Irish poem, attributed to Columba himself:

> The path I walk, Christ walks it.
> May the land in which I am, be without sorrow.
> May the Trinity protect me wherever I stay,
> Father, Son and Holy Spirit.

Columba, or Columcille, had discovered the hard way that Christians must speak and do the truth. Deceit has no part in the Christian life. Columba is recognised as one who eventually came to acknowledge his own deceit, admit it honestly, and, with true humility, seek to repair the harm and hold on to truth and honesty. This had the effect that many trusted him, heard his message and accepted his advice. May Columba, Colum of the Church, honoured by all in Ireland, pray to God for Christians here that we may overcome the divisions, recognise the truth and live in peace together. Amen.

SPEAK THE TRUTH AND LIVE THE TRUTH

Truth or truthfulness is the virtue which consists in showing oneself true in deeds and truthful in words, and guarding against duplicity, dissimulation and hypocrisy. ... Respect for the reputation and honour of persons forbids all detraction and calumny in word or attitude.

— CCC, nos. 2505 and 2507

You shall not give false evidence against your neighbour..

— Ex 20:16

The Bible teaches that God is the source of truth. Jesus not only taught the truth; he also said, 'I am the truth' (cf. Jn 14:6). The Hebrew word for truth, *emeth*, refers both to truth in words and truthfulness in deeds. Jesus both personalised truth and spoke nothing but the truth. When Christ stood before Pilate, Pilate asked Jesus if he were a king. In his reply, Jesus declared that his Kingdom was not political but spiritual; he had come to bear witness to truth. A spiritual kingdom is based on truth. Pilate could not understand Christ's reply. Jesus reached out to him and offered him the possibility of change. Pilate could only say, 'Truth? ... What is that?' (Jn 18:38).

In our culture, relativism challenges our ability to tell the truth because it claims there is no objective truth. This attitude undermines the distinction between truth and lies; it leads to an environment of deceit. In such an atmosphere, even Christ's teachings, based on divine truth, fail to persuade those whose trust in the possibility of objective truth has disappeared. This is the climate in which the Church needs to call people back to the reality of objective truth and to the link between doctrinal truth and everyday life.

INTEGRITY AND TRUTH

John Paul II named St Thomas More the Patron Saint of Statesmen, Politicians and Lawyers. This saint's willingness to die rather than compromise the truth serves as an example to all. Often, society tries to convince us that faith is personal and should not influence political or legal positions and decisions. Saint Thomas More is someone who reminds us that this is a false understanding. His example reminds men and women who serve in public office or who practise law of the importance of personal integrity, which is, after all, a form of truth. Integrity requires that we allow our faith to shape every aspect of life, public as well as private.

SINS AGAINST TRUTH

'Lying is the most direct offence against the truth … By injuring man's relation to truth and to his neighbour, a lie offends against the fundamental relation of man and of his word to the Lord' (CCC, no. 2483). People sin against the truth when they are guilty of ruining the reputation of another by telling lies, when they practise rash judgement, or when they engage in detraction (the unjust telling of someone's faults), perjury (lying under oath) or calumny (telling lies about another).

Scripture is clear about the evil of lying. In the Sermon on the Mount, Jesus said, 'All you need say is "Yes" if you mean yes, "No" if you mean no; anything more than this comes from the Evil One' (Mt 5:37). This reminds us not only that we need to be truthful, but also that hypocrisy – saying one thing while doing the opposite – is a sin against truth.

In the Gospel of John, Jesus describes the devil as father of lies (cf. Jn 8:44). Saint Paul discouraged lying: 'Do not lie to each other' (Col 3:9); 'Speak the truth to one another, since we are all parts of one another' (Eph 4:25).

FROM THE CATECHISM

1. What principle guides us in revealing the truth to another?

The golden rule ['Do unto others as you would have them do unto you'] helps one discern, in concrete situations, whether or not it would be appropriate to reveal the truth to someone who asks for it. (CCC, no. 2510)

2. What is the responsibility of the media regarding truth?

Society has a right to information based on truth, freedom and justice. One should practise moderation and discipline in the use of the social communications media. (CCC, no. 2512)

3. How do art and beauty help us with truth?

Arising from talent given by the Creator and from man's own effort, art is a form of practical wisdom, uniting knowledge and skill, to give form to the truth of reality in a language accessible to sight or hearing. To the extent that it is inspired by truth and love of beings, art bears a certain likeness to God's activity in what he has created. (CCC, no. 2501)

Happily, history is filled with stories of people who valued the truth so highly that they were willing to die for it. Saint John Fisher (1469–1535) and St Thomas More (1478–1535) surrendered their lives rather than approve of the divorce of King Henry VIII or deny the truth that the pope is Christ's appointed head of the Church. During the French Revolution, a convent of Carmelite nuns chose to ignore laws that disbanded their monastery and continued to live together as a community. They courageously went to the guillotine rather than abandon the truth for which their vows stood. During World War II, Franz Jagerstatter, an Austrian farmer, refused to accept the lies of the Nazis, and he was martyred for his commitment to Christ's truth.

We can testify to the truths of our faith in our everyday living, especially when we come in contact with those who do not hold the fullness of faith taught by the Catholic Church. This is done by living out the responsibilities and implications of our faith, as well as by being prepared to dialogue with others on issues of doctrine and morality where differences occur. 'Always have your answer ready for people who ask you the reason for the hope that you have. But give it with courtesy and respect and with a clear conscience' (1 Pt 3:15-16).

THE RIGHT TO KNOW THE TRUTH

'No one is bound to reveal the truth to someone who does not have the right to know it' (CCC, no. 2489). The security of others, their right to privacy and a respect for the common good are reasons for keeping silent or being discreet in our language concerning matters that should not be disclosed. It is also for these reasons that gossiping is a sinful violation of the privacy of others.

Professionals such as politicians, doctors, lawyers, psychologists and others in positions where confidences are entrusted should preserve confidentiality, unless there is a grave and proportionate reason for divulging the information. The same is true about ordinary personal relationships in which confidences are shared.

THE MEDIA

In our culture, the communications media hold an influential place in disseminating information, forming attitudes and motivating behaviour. Technological advances are increasing the role of the media and its capacity to shape public opinion. 'The information provided by the media is at the service of the common good. Society has a right to information based on truth, freedom, justice and solidarity' (CCC, no. 2494). In the assembling and publishing of news, the moral law and the lawful rights and human dignity of men and women should be followed.

LIES HAVE DEVASTATING EFFECTS

Lying is linked to the tragedy of sin and its perverse consequences, which have had, and continue to have, devastating effects on the lives of individuals and nations. We need but think of the events of the past century, when aberrant ideological and political systems willfully twisted the truth and brought about the exploitation and murder of an appalling number of men and women, wiping out entire families and communities. After experiences like these, how can we fail to be seriously concerned about lies in our own time, lies which are the framework for menacing scenarios of death in many parts of the world. Any authentic search for peace must begin with the realisation that the problem of truth and untruth is the concern of every man and woman; it is decisive for the peaceful future of our planet. (Benedict XVI, 'Message for World Day of Peace', 1 January 2006)

The requirements of justice and charity must guide communications just as much as other public institutions. Those who undertake to form public opinion need to be governed by these principles. Human solidarity is one of the positive effects of media communications when a commitment to a right-minded policy is followed – one that supports a free circulation of ideas that advances knowledge and people's respect for each other. Mutually respectful dialogue also aids the quest for truth.

TRUTH AND OPINIONS

The more our culture has moved away from acceptance of objective truth, the more it has moved toward the culture of opinions. Each day, newspapers give us a diet of opinions on their editorial pages. Talk shows on television have turned the sharing of opinions into a national pastime. Editors and talk show hosts strive to give us a range of opinions that stretch from one end of the spectrum to another. At the high end of these presentations, experts and scholars are recruited to offer us their best current research. At another level, people are simply enlisted to share their thoughts and feelings publicly on any number of social, moral and political matters. Sometimes debate degenerates into expressions of hatred.

Though the intuition remains that there is really such a thing as objective truth, it tends to be lost in a marathon of inconclusive discussions. As a result, some spend valuable time sharing only feelings or uninformed opinions. Much of what passes for truth is the effort to justify individual behaviour. In its unsettling form, this generates an attitude of scepticism and even suspicion about any truth claims. Thus objective truth is considered unattainable.

In this kind of cultural environment, how can we speak of the invitation of the Eighth Commandment to tell the truth and avoid lying? Speaking the truth is the opposite of lying. The distinction between lying and truth-telling presupposes that there is a truth that can be told. Although a real problem is that some people lie, there is also the related issue of scepticism about the possibility of knowing truth.

The best way to step outside the constriction of these biases is through study, love and practice grounded in faith. The Church never ceases to urge, 'Know the truth. Love the truth. Live the truth.' And the truth is Jesus Christ.

■ FOR DISCUSSION ■

1. Why do we believe what people say? What happens when we discover that someone has lied? What is the relationship between trust and truth?

2. When you encounter people who cause you to be sceptical about the truth of the Church's doctrinal and moral teachings, how should you react?

3. What steps can be taken to restore conviction about objective truth and concrete moral standards in our society? What are some inspiring stories about truth in word and deed that you can share?

DOCTRINAL STATEMENTS

- 'You shall not give false evidence against your neighbour' (Ex 20:16). Scripture teaches that God is the source of truth. Jesus not only taught the truth; he also said, 'I am the truth' (cf. Jn 14:16). At the Last Supper, Jesus identified himself with truth. Jesus both personalised truth and spoke nothing but the truth.
- The natural law requires all people to speak and live by the truth in words and deeds.
- 'The golden rule ["Do unto others as you would have them do unto you"] helps one discern, in concrete situations, whether or not it would be appropriate to reveal the truth to someone who asks for it' (CCC, no. 2510).
- The right to know the truth is not absolute. Charity and justice govern what may be communicated. People's safety, respect for privacy and the common good are reasons for being silent or using discreet language about what should not be known.
- 'No one is bound to reveal the truth to someone who does not have the right to know it' (CCC, no. 2489).
- Members of the media have the responsibility to always be at the service of the common good.
- In the assembling and publishing of the news, the moral law and the lawful rights and human dignity of men and women should be upheld.
- 'Arising from talent given by the Creator and from man's own effort, art is a form of practical wisdom, uniting knowledge and skill, to give form to the truth of reality in a language accessible to sight or hearing. To the extent that it is inspired by truth and love of beings, art bears a certain likeness to God's activity in what he has created' (CCC, no. 2501).
- 'An offence committed against the truth requires reparation' (CCC, no. 2509).

■■■ MEDITATION ■■■

Truth is more than an idea. It reveals goodness and beauty. This is what moved Pope Paul VI to speak of the 'inherent attractiveness of Gospel truth'. Love beholds truth as a revelation of beauty. Once it is known and loved, truth is meant to be practised. Saint Ignatius offered this wise advice regarding the need to foster truth:

> Every good Christian ought to be more ready to give a favourable interpretation to another's statement than to condemn it. But if he cannot do so, let him ask how the other understands it. And if the latter understands it badly, let the former correct him with love. If that does not suffice, let the Christian try all suitable ways to bring the other to a correct interpretation so that he may be saved. (Saint Ignatius of Loyola, *Spiritual Exercises*, 22)

■■■ PRAYER ■■■

Blessing of Centres of Social Communication

Lord God Almighty,
We humbly praise you,
for you enlighten and inspire
those who by probing the powers implanted in creation
develop the work of your hands in wonderful ways.
Look with favour on your servants
who use the technology discovered by long research.
Enable them to communicate truth,
to foster love, to uphold justice and right,
and to provide enjoyment.
Let them promote and support
that peace between peoples
which Christ the Lord brought from heaven,
for he lives and reigns for ever and ever.
Amen.

— *Book of Blessings* (1990), no. 830

I never take my seat with liars
and with hypocrites I shall not go.

–Ps 26:4

33 THE NINTH COMMANDMENT: PRACTISE PURITY OF HEART

YOU SHALL NOT COVET YOUR NEIGHBOUR'S WIFE – CCC, NOS. 2514–2533

MARIA GORETTI: A MODEL OF PURITY

Maria Goretti was born in Corinaldo, Italy, on 16 October 1890. She was one of six children born to Luigi Goretti and Assunta Carlini. In 1896, the family moved to Ferriere di Conca, where the Gorettis became sharecroppers for Count Mazzolini. The Goretti family lived in an old cheese factory building on the estate, where Assunta worked hard to make a home for her family.

Due to the hard labour of draining the flooded estate, Luigi soon contracted malaria and was unable to adequately manage the land for which he was responsible. On account of this, Count Mazzolini sent Giovanni Serenelli and his son Alessandro to share half the work, half the profits and half of the building which the Goretti family had made into a home.

The Goretti parents soon became aware that the Serenellis were not people of high moral character. As Luigi's malaria became more severe, Luigi and Assunta regretted their leaving Corinaldo.

The position of the Goretti family took a tragic turn upon Luigi's death in 1902. Since Assunta was now forced to work in the fields to provide for the family, she put Maria in charge of the duties at home. Maria had grown in virtue and grace throughout her childhood. She also had a great devotion to the Blessed Sacrament, which she received for the first time in May of that same year.

Alessandro began stalking Maria and making suggestive advances towards her, advances that she always unhesitatingly refused. Ultimately, her refusal sparked him to take matters into his own hands.

On 5 July 1902, Maria – who was not yet twelve years old – was peacefully stitching and caring for her little sister, Theresa. Alessandro, who was eighteen years old, grabbed Maria's arm, dragged her into the kitchen and attempted to rape her. She fought him and pleaded with him to stop, exclaiming that what he was attempting was a sin forbidden by God. Her resistance infuriated Alessandro who, after failing to choke her into submission, stabbed her fourteen times.

Maria was taken to a hospital, where she suffered for an entire day. Upon gaining consciousness, she fixed her gaze on a statue of the Blessed Mother that was at the foot of her bed. Before receiving *Viaticum*, she forgave Alessandro for what he had done and expressed the desire that he might join her in heaven. She died of her wounds on 6 July 1902.

Alessandro Serenelli was soon apprehended, convicted and sentenced to thirty years in prison for his crime. Eight years into his sentence, Maria appeared to him in a dream. In that dream, Maria gathered lilies, which she then handed to him. The lilies took on a radiance that assured him of her forgiveness. This vision led to a conversion, which brought him into reconciliation with God, the Church and the Goretti family.

Pope Pius XII canonised Maria Goretti on 24 June 1950. Her mother Assunta and her murderer Alessandro Serenelli were both present. Saint Maria Goretti has been named the Patroness of Modern Youth. Her love for her attacker – shown in her forgiveness of him – and her spiritual and physical purity of heart serve as a model for all Christians. Her purity exemplifies the Ninth Commandment.

THE MORALITY OF THE HEART

The heart is the seat of moral personality: 'Out of the heart come evil thoughts, murder, adultery, fornication' (Mt 15:19). The struggle against carnal covetousness entails purifying the heart and practising temperance.

– CCC, no. 2517

We experience tensions between spiritual and physical desires. This struggle belongs to the heritage of sin. This does not mean that we are to despise the body and emotions that, with the soul, constitute our nature. It does make us realise that we will face a daily spiritual struggle to acquire virtues that help us obey the saving action of the Holy Spirit and overcome vices that cause us to resist him.

The grace of Baptism purifies us from sins, but a certain tendency to sin remains. We must struggle against disordered desires by practising purity of mind, heart and body with daily vigilance. To do this, we need to examine our motives as well as our deeds, so that we always seek God's will. This will cause us to discipline our feelings and imagination. Finally, since purity is a gift of God, we need to pray for it, as St Augustine did:

> I thought that continence arose from one's own powers, which I did not recognise in myself. I was foolish enough not to know ... that no one can be continent unless you grant it. For you surely would have granted it if my inner groaning had reached your ears and I with firm faith had cast my cares on you. (*The Confessions*, bk. 6, chap. 11, no. 20)

MODESTY

Modesty is a virtue necessary for purity. It flows out of the virtues of temperance, chastity and self-control. A modest person dresses, speaks and acts in a manner that supports and encourages purity and chastity, and not in a manner that would tempt or encourage sinful sexual behaviour. Modesty protects the mystery of the person in order to avoid exploiting the other. This attitude instils in us the patience and reserve we need for avoiding unbecoming behaviour. Modest relationships reflect the connection between the marital state and sexual behaviour. Modest behaviour respects the boundaries of intimacy that are imbedded in our natures by the natural law and the principles of sexual behaviour laid out in Divine Revelation. Modesty ensures and supports purity of heart, a gift that enables us to see God's plan for personal relationships, sexuality and marriage.

RECOVERING MODESTY

Modesty protects the mystery of persons and their love.
It encourages patience and moderation in loving relationships.
… It inspires one's choice of clothing. It keeps silence or reserve
where there is evident risk of unhealthy curiosity. It is discreet.

— CCC, no. 2522

We need to maintain the concern for chaste living prayerfully in our hearts. Faith is the proper foundation in the quest for a clean heart. Growth in modesty requires loving support from family and friends as well as wise counsel and the practise of virtues.

The attitude of modesty is difficult to maintain in a culture that prizes sexual permissiveness. Countless appeals for erotic satisfaction assail us daily from all the major forms of communication. This environment of indecency challenges all men and women of faith to choose and to witness to modesty as a way of life and as a method for healing a culture that has strayed from God's plan for sexuality and marriage.

Those who have accepted the approach of the permissive culture have been persuaded that freedom is the right to do what we want to do, not what we should do. At the beginning of Christianity, the Apostles preached and witnessed Christ's Gospel to the permissive cultures of Greece and Rome, a fact well-illustrated in St Paul's Letters to the Corinthians. Difficult as it was, the first preachers prevailed over the allurements of the culture, won numerous converts and encouraged the virtue of modesty.

FROM THE CATECHISM

1. What is the teaching of the Ninth Commandment?
'If a man looks at a woman lustfully, he has already committed adultery with her in his heart' (Mt 5:28). The Ninth Commandment warns against lust or carnal concupiscence. (CCC, nos. 2528–2529)

2. What is the antidote to lust?
The struggle against carnal lust involves purifying the heart and practising temperance. Purity of heart will enable us to see God: it enables us even now to see things according to God. (CCC, nos. 2530–2531)

3. How do we purify our hearts?
Purification of the heart demands prayer, the practise of chastity, purity of intention and of vision. Purity of heart requires the modesty which is patience, decency and discretion. Modesty protects the intimate centre of the person. (CCC, nos. 2532–2533)

The Church calls us to be signs of contradiction in an overly-eroticised society. All members of the Church should respond to the immodest aspects of society and culture with a deep and conscious spirituality. The Gospel can renew and purify what is decadent in our culture and gradually can displace the attraction of sin. We must assert Christ's Gospel by word and witness to transform the moral tone of our culture. This approach fosters virtue in the human heart and its development through the grace of the Holy Spirit.

As we have mentioned, in New Testament times, the Apostles encountered moral challenges every bit as awesome as ours. Faced with his own struggles, St Paul appeared discouraged when he said, 'What a wretched man I am! Who will rescue me from this body doomed to death? God – thanks be to him – through Jesus Christ our Lord' (Rm 7:24, 25). The gifts of faith and grace enabled Paul to meet the demands of the Gospel of Jesus. They will do the same for us.

FOR DISCUSSION

1. What are modesty and purity of heart? What are ways you have found to help you acquire these virtues? Share stories of people you admire who witness to these values.
2. Why is it important to be as vigilant about our interior attitudes toward sexuality as we are about external acts? What are other examples you can cite about the link between inner attitudes and external behaviour?
3. While it may seem daunting, what are strategies that could be adopted to turn back the cultural influences that undermine modesty and purity of heart? What will help you trust in the power of the Gospel of Jesus to bring this about?

DOCTRINAL STATEMENTS

- You must not set your heart on your neighbour's spouse (Deut 5:21).
- "'If a man looks at a woman lustfully, he has already committed adultery with her in his heart" (Mt 5:28). The Ninth Commandment warns against lust or carnal concupiscence' (CCC, nos. 2528–2529).
- 'Modesty protects the mystery of persons and their love. It encourages patience and moderation in loving relationships … It inspires one's choice of clothing. It keeps silence or reserve where there is evident risk of unhealthy curiosity. It is discreet' (CCC, no. 2522).
- *Concupiscence* refers to our disordered desires and the inclination to sin that is a consequence of Original Sin. The term describes rebellion of our passions and desires against the dictates of right reason.
- 'Purification of the heart demands prayer, the practise of chastity, purity of intention and of vision. Purity of heart requires the modesty which is patience, decency and discretion. Modesty protects the intimate centre of the person' (CCC, nos. 2532–2533).
- The Gospel can renew and purify what is decadent in our culture and gradually displace the attraction of sin. Asserting Christ's Gospel by word and witness helps to transform the moral tone of our culture. This approach fosters virtue in the human heart and its development through the grace of the Holy Spirit.

■■■■■■■■■■■■■ MEDITATION ■■■■■■■■■■■■■

At the conclusion of the Jubilee Year 2000, St John Paul II reflected on his meetings with young people throughout that year:

> And how could we fail to recall especially the joyful and inspiring gathering of young people? If there is an image of the Jubilee of the Year 2000 that more than any other will live on in memory, it is surely the streams of young people with whom I was able to engage in a sort of very special dialogue, filled with mutual affection and deep understanding. It was like this from the moment I welcomed them in the Square of St John Lateran and St Peter's Square. Then I saw them swarming through the city, happy as young people should be, but also thoughtful, eager to pray, seeking 'meaning' and true friendship. Neither for them nor for those who saw them will it be easy to forget that week, during which Rome became 'young with the young' …
>
> Yet again, the young have shown themselves to be for Rome and for the Church a special gift of the Spirit of God. Sometimes when we look at the young, with the problems and weaknesses that characterise them in contemporary society, we tend to be pessimistic. The Jubilee of Young People however changed that, telling us that young people, whatever their possible ambiguities, have a profound longing for those genuine values which find their fullness in Christ. Is not Christ the secret of true freedom and profound joy of heart? Is not Christ the supreme friend and the teacher of all genuine friendship? If Christ is presented to young people as he really is, they experience him as an answer that is convincing and they can accept his message, even when it is demanding and bears the mark of the Cross. For this reason, in response to their enthusiasm, I did not hesitate to ask them to make a radical choice of faith and life and present them with a stupendous task: to become 'morning watchmen' (cf. Is 21:11-12) at the dawn of the new millennium.

– NMI, no. 9

PRAYER

Prayer for Purity of Body and Mind

Lord, set aflame my heart and my entire being
with the fire of the Holy Spirit,
that I may serve you with a chaste body and pure mind.
Through Christ our Lord. Amen.

– Daily Roman Missal

Blessed are the pure in heart:
they shall see God.

– Mt 5:8

34 THE TENTH COMMANDMENT: EMBRACE POVERTY OF SPIRIT

YOU SHALL NOT COVET YOUR NEIGHBOUR'S GOODS – CCC, NOS. 2534–2557

EDMUND RICE: BUSINESSMAN AND EDUCATOR

Edmund Rice was born on 1 June 1762 in Callan, County Kilkenny. His family was comfortable, working a farm of over 150 acres, prosperous in the improving political and economic climate for Catholics. The Penal Laws were being lifted during the last quarter of the eighteenth century, a process which would continue up to and beyond Catholic Emancipation in 1829. Edmund was educated in Callan and in the city of Kilkenny to secondary school level.

When he left school, Edmund joined his uncle, Michael Rice, in Waterford City to learn the victualling business. Waterford was a thriving port town and the Rice business provisioned many of the vessels leaving the harbour. Edmund was ambitious and practical. Eventually he succeeded his uncle as the proprietor of the firm and achieved financial success and a standing in the commercial life of the city. At the age of twenty-three, he married Mary Elliott and had one daughter who, it later emerged, was in need of life-long care. His wife died shortly after the child was born, and Edmund raised the child himself. When she was older, his daughter went to live with her extended family.

Edmund Rice was canny, yet caring and compassionate. He spent much time visiting the poor, helping the sick, and even paying off debts for poor prisoners in jail. But he noticed that those needing the most help were Catholic children. Waterford was a city with a high level of education, but not for Catholics. The only free schools were run by Protestants, and ambitious Catholic parents were tempted to send their children to them for their education. The Bishop of Waterford, and the city's Quakers, had controversially protested loudly and long against this unfair situation because it placed the children's Catholic faith in peril.

The Presentation Nuns (founded by Nano Nagle) had begun to educate Catholic girls in Cork, and a parish priest in Waterford heard of their work. He organised a Presentation foundation for Waterford, and it eventually opened in 1801. The priest had asked Edmund Rice for advice and assistance in procuring property and funding. Now, the nuns were teaching the girls. The boys were still on the street. Edmund Rice saw the problem and had the solution.

He began by teaching a few boys himself. With his own funds and the encouragement, support and financial assistance of two bishops, he established a school for boys in a rented stable in 1802. Having tried out his new vocation, he next retired from his business to take up teaching full time. Soon after, with two companions, he built a two-storey house where he and they might live a simple religious life devoted to teaching poor boys. He then erected a bigger school in Mount Sion, Waterford. It opened on 1 May 1804 and a new chapter in Irish education dawned.

Education in England and Ireland at that time was dependent on private initiative. Ireland had fared better than England in that the colonial power had an interest in teaching the native Irish people true religion (Protestant) and the English language. To accomplish these ends, a wide variety of schools had been established at different times since the Reformation. In addition, many Protestant fee-paying schools flourished, as did a wide variety of technically illegal Catholic ones, but these could educate only those children whose parents could, like the Rice's of Callan, afford the tuition. Now, following the example of Nano Nagle, Edmund Rice had changed that situation. Irish Catholic Education, for Catholic girls and boys, for the poor as well as the rich, was now available.

What manner of man was the one who filled the gap? Edmund Rice was very religiously motivated. This was not a man simply concerned with social improvement, development of talent or material progress. In the words of a friend, 'he wished to see boys Godly'. He wanted to save souls, that is, strengthen religious faith, encourage hope for heaven and fan the flames of Christian love. If the Kingdom were assured, all the rest would follow, as the Saviour had promised.

Edmund Rice had considered entering religious life himself, following the example of his younger brother, John, who had joined the Augustinian order and been ordained a priest. Edmund, however, became convinced through his experience of life that he was called by God to the Catholic education of poor boys. Events were surely to prove him right.

Rice had always been devout and contemplative, studying the Bible at length when it was unusual to do so and adopting an approach to the spiritual life suited to the active life of business. He turned his religious conviction and faith, his zeal and devotion to duty, as well as his business thinking and organisational ability, to the challenge of founding schools and establishing a permanent corps of Catholic religious teachers to run them. By his energy and purpose he persuaded many to join him in a new religious congregation to teach Catholic boys. With his acumen and strategic approach, he gained Church approval for his foundation and a pivotal position in the Irish educational scene for their schools.

The rest of his life becomes the story of his foundations, the Irish Christian Brothers and the Presentation Brothers, and their network of schools in Ireland and overseas. The two congregations Rice founded (together with the Presentation Sisters and Mercy Sisters) were important factors in the salvation of the Irish poor for the Church in the nineteenth century. As a consequence, their schools ensured the preservation of Irish national heritage and the education of a proud and strong Irish Catholic working class. It is ironic, and providential, that a directly religious mission should result in such a successful political and social transformation.

Brother Edmund Rice died in 1844, at which time the Brothers ran thirty-seven schools in Ireland and six in England. Saint John Paul II made Edmund Ignatius Rice one of the Blessed of the Church in 1996. His feast day falls on 5 May.

WHERE YOUR TREASURE IS, THERE ALSO WILL YOUR HEART BE (MT 6:21)

*The tenth commandment unfolds and completes the
ninth, which is concerned with concupiscence of the
flesh. It forbids coveting the goods of another, as the
root of theft, robbery and fraud, which the seventh
commandment forbids ... The tenth commandment
concerns the intentions of the heart.*

– CCC, no. 2534

When Jesus began the Sermon on the Mount, he proclaimed the eight
Beatitudes as the ways to authentic happiness. The first of these stated that
poverty of spirit would enable us to inherit the Kingdom of God. In other
words, the first step on the road to joy begins with a healthy detachment
from material goods. Later on in the same sermon, Jesus taught that building
up wealth for its own sake is foolishness. We should be more interested in
spiritual riches.

> Do not store up treasures for yourselves on earth, where moth and
> woodworm destroy them and thieves can break in and steal. But store
> up treasures for yourselves in heaven, where neither moth nor
> woodworm destroys them and thieves cannot break in and steal. For
> wherever your treasure is, there will your heart be too. (Mt 6:19-21)

The financial scandals that periodically occur in our culture remind us that
greed is a constant threat to moral behaviour. It leads many to conclude that
money is the root of all evils. But in fact, 'the love of money is the root of
all evils' (1 Tm 6:10). In the study of the Seventh Commandment, we dealt
with the visible acts of stealing and injustice. The Tenth Commandment
looks at the interior attitudes of greed and envy that lead us to steal and act
unjustly.

On the positive side, the Tenth Commandment calls us to practise poverty of spirit and generosity of heart. These virtues liberate us from being slaves to money and possessions. They enable us to have a preferential love for the poor and to be witnesses of justice and peace in the world. They also enable us to adopt a simplicity of life that frees us from consumerism and helps us preserve God's creation.

Sinful inclinations move us to envy what others have and lead to an unrestrained drive to acquire all that we can. We do have a reasonable need to acquire the means needed to care for our families. Greed is the distortion of this desire. The greedy person will stop at nothing to get all the money and possessions possible.

We need to remember that envy is the companion of greed; it is an attitude that fills us with sadness at the sight of another's prosperity. Envious people can be consumed with so much desire for what others have that they will even commit crimes to get what they want.

Baptised people should counter envy with humility, thanksgiving to God for his gifts to oneself and to others, goodwill and surrender to the providence of God (cf. CCC, no. 2554). 'Christ's faithful "have crucified self with all its passions and its desires" (Gal 5:24); they are led by the Spirit and follow his desires' (CCC, no. 2555). Poverty of heart is a way to avoid greed and envy. 'Abandonment to the providence of the Father in heaven frees us from anxiety about tomorrow. Trust in God is a preparation for the blessedness of the poor. They shall see God' (CCC, no. 2547, citing Mt 6:25-34).

TO BE A CHRISTIAN STEWARD: A SUMMARY OF THE US BISHOPS' PASTORAL LETTER ON STEWARDSHIP

'Each one of you has received a special grace, so, like good stewards responsible for all these varied graces of God' (1 Pt 4:10).

What identifies a steward? Safeguarding material and human resources and using them responsibly are one answer; so is generous giving of time, talent and treasure. But being a Christian steward means more. As Christian stewards, we receive God's gifts gratefully, cultivate them responsibly, share them lovingly in justice with others and return them with increase to the Lord.

Disciples as Stewards

Let us begin with being a disciple – a follower of our Lord Jesus Christ. As members of the Church, Jesus calls us to be disciples. This has astonishing implications:

- Mature disciples make a conscious decision to follow Jesus, no matter what the cost;
- Christian disciples experience conversion – life-shaping changes of mind and heart – and commit themselves to the Lord;
- Christian stewards respond in a particular way to the call to be a disciple. Stewardship has the power to shape and mould our understanding of our lives and the way in which we live. Jesus' disciples, as Christian stewards, recognise God as the origin of life, the giver of freedom, and the source of all things. We are grateful for the gifts we have received and are eager to use them to show our love for God and for one another. We look to the life and teaching of Jesus for guidance in living as Christian stewards.

Stewards of Creation

The Bible contains a profound message about the stewardship of material creation: God created the world, but entrusts it to human beings. Caring for and cultivating the world involves the following:

- Joyful appreciation for the God-given beauty and wonder of nature;
- Protection and preservation of the environment, which is the stewardship of ecological concern;
- Respect for human life – shielding life from threat and assault and doing everything that can be done to enhance this gift and make life flourish;
- Development of this world through noble human effort – physical labour, the trades and professions, the arts and sciences. We call such effort 'work'.

Work is a fulfilling human vocation. The Second Vatican Council points out that, through work, we build up not only our world but also the Kingdom of God, already present among us. Work is a partnership with God – our share in a divine human collaboration in creation. It occupies a central place in our lives as Christian stewards.

Stewards of Vocation

Jesus calls us as his disciples to a new way of life – the Christian way of life – of which stewardship is a part. But Jesus does not call us as nameless people in a faceless crowd. He calls individually, by name. Each one of us – clergy, religious, layperson, married, single, adult, child – has a personal vocation. God intends each one of us to play a unique role in carrying out the divine plan.

The challenge, then, is to understand our role – our vocation – and to respond generously to this call from God. Christian vocation entails the practice of stewardship. In addition, Christ calls each of us to be stewards of our personal vocations, which we receive from God.

Stewards of the Church

Stewards of God's gifts are not passive beneficiaries. We cooperate with God in our own redemption and in the redemption of others.

We are also obliged to be stewards of the Church, collaborators and cooperators in continuing the redemptive work of Jesus Christ, which is the Church's essential mission. This mission – proclaiming and teaching, serving and sanctifying – is our task. It is the personal responsibility of each one of us as stewards of the Church.

All members have their own roles to play in carrying out this mission.

- Parents who nurture their children in the light of faith.
- Parishioners who work in concrete ways to make their parishes true communities of faith and vibrant sources of service to the larger community.
- All Catholics, who give generous support – time, money, prayers and personal service according to their circumstances – to parish and diocesan programmes and to the universal Church.

FROM THE CATECHISM

1. What two attitudes does the Tenth Commandment forbid?

The tenth commandment forbids *greed* ... It requires that envy be banished from the human heart. (CCC, nos. 2536 and 2538)

2. How can we acquire poverty of spirit?

Abandonment to the providence of the Father in heaven frees us from anxiety about tomorrow. Trust in God is a preparation for the blessedness of the poor. They shall see God. (CCC, no. 2547)

3. How can we be free of exaggerated dependence on material goods?

Desire for true happiness frees man from his immoderate attachment to the goods of this world so that he can find his fulfilment in the vision and beatitude of God. 'The promise [of seeing God] surpasses all beatitude ... In Scripture, to see is to possess ... Whoever sees God has obtained all the goods of which he can conceive.' (CCC, no. 2548, citing St Gregory of Nyssa, *De Beatitudinibus* 6: PG, 44, 1265A)

Obstacles to Stewardship

People who want to live as Christian disciples and Christian stewards face serious obstacles ... A dominant secular culture often contradicts religious convictions about the meaning of life. This culture frequently encourages us to focus on ourselves and our pleasures. At times, we can find it far too easy to ignore spiritual realities and to deny religion a role in shaping human and social values.

As Catholics ... many of us also have been adversely influenced by this secular culture. We know what it is to struggle against selfishness and greed, and we realise that it is harder for many today to accept the challenge of being a Christian steward.

It is essential, therefore, that we make a special effort to understand the true meaning of stewardship and live accordingly.

A Steward's Way

The life of a Christian steward models the life of Jesus. It is challenging and even difficult in many respects, yet intense joy comes to those who take the risk to live as Christian stewards. Women and men who seek to live as stewards learn that 'God works with those who love him' (Rm 8:28).

After Jesus, we look to Mary as the ideal steward. As the Mother of Christ, she lived her ministry in a spirit of fidelity and service; she responded generously to the call.

We must ask ourselves, do we wish to be disciples of Jesus Christ and Christian stewards of our world and our Church?

Central to our human and Christian vocations, as well as to the unique vocation each one of us receives from God, is that we be good stewards of the gifts we possess. God gives us this divine-human workshop, this world and Church of ours. The Spirit shows us the way. Stewardship is part of that journey. (USCCB, 'To Be a Christian Steward', *Stewardship: A Disciple's Response* [Washington, DC: USCCB, 2002], 45ff.)

BLESSED IS THE GENEROUS HEART

Some say that helping the poor involves only making sure that all their physical or material needs are addressed. But is this enough? Should we not also focus on helping people to develop to their utmost potential?

The first step in helping the disadvantaged is to acknowledge the sacred dignity and image of God found in each person. What is also required is a conscience formation from which flow the beliefs, attitudes and actions that will help the poor. Having more is never enough. Being more is paramount.

Christian discipleship means, among other things, working to ensure that all people have access to what makes them fully human and fosters their human dignity: faith, education, healthcare, housing, employment and leisure. Members of the Church are called to build up the resources of the Church herself and of civil society in making possible the sharing of God's blessings and social goods with others. This they do by their own generosity in the use of their time, talents and treasures with others. Such generosity flows from hearts grateful to God for his generosity in creating and saving us.

▬▬▬▬▬▬ FOR DISCUSSION ▬▬▬▬▬▬

1. While it is necessary to acquire earthly goods for the care and well-being of our families, there are forces that motivate us to become overly attached to wealth. How does the media contribute to this? What role does envy play in this drive toward the love of money?
2. What habits have you developed to help you have a healthy detachment from worldly goods? How would generosity counter the tendency to be attached to material things?
3. What do you need to do as a Christian steward?

▬▬▬▬▬▬ DOCTRINAL STATEMENTS ▬▬▬▬▬▬

- 'The tenth commandment unfolds and completes the ninth, which is concerned with concupiscence of the flesh. It forbids coveting the goods of another, as the root of theft, robbery and fraud, which the seventh commandment forbids … The tenth commandment concerns the intentions of the heart' (CCC, no. 2534).
- 'For wherever your treasure is, there will your heart be too' (Mt 6:21).
- Envy is an attitude of sadness at the sight of another's prosperity. It can create a disordered desire to acquire such goods, even by unjust means. Envy tightens the heart and subdues love. For this reason, envy is considered a Capital Sin.
- 'The baptised person combats envy through goodwill, humility and abandonment to the providence of God. Christ's faithful "have crucified self with all its passions and its desires" (Gal 5:24); they are led by the Spirit and follow his desires' (CCC, no. 2555).
- 'The tenth commandment forbids *greed* and … requires that *envy* be banished from the human heart' (CCC, nos. 2536 and 2538).
- The Christian practice of giving and sharing is a powerful alternative to greed and a positive contribution to a peaceful and just society.
- 'Detachment from riches is necessary for entering the Kingdom of heaven. "Blessed are the poor in spirit"' (CCC, no. 2556).
- 'Envy often comes from pride; the baptised person should train himself to live in humility: "Would you like to see God glorified by you? Then rejoice in your brother's progress and you will immediately give glory to

God. Because his servant could conquer envy by rejoicing in the merits of others, God will be praised"' (CCC, no. 2540, citing St John Chrysostom, *Homiliae in ad Romanos*, no. 71, 5).

■ MEDITATION ■

The Church witnesses the fact that human dignity cannot be destroyed, whatever the situation of poverty, scorn, rejection or powerlessness to which a human being has been reduced. [The Church] shows her solidarity with those who do not count in a society by which they are rejected spiritually and sometimes even physically. She is particularly drawn with maternal affection toward those children who, through human wickedness, will never be brought forth from the womb to the light of day, as also for the elderly, alone and abandoned. The special option for the poor ... manifests the universality of the Church's being and mission.

– Congregation for the Doctrine of the Faith,
Instruction on Christian Freedom and Liberation (1986), no. 68

■ PRAYER ■

The Prayer of a Poor Man (The Canticle of the Sun)
Most high, all powerful, all good Lord!
All praise is yours, all glory, all honour, and all blessing.
To you, alone, Most High, do they belong.
No mortal lips are worthy to pronounce your name.
Be praised, my Lord, through all your creatures,
especially through my lord Brother Sun, who brings the day;
and you give light through him.
And he is beautiful and radiant in all his splendour!
Of you, Most High, he bears the likeness.
Be praised, my Lord, through Sister Moon and the stars;
in the heavens you have made them, precious and beautiful.
Be praised, my Lord, through Brothers Wind and Air,
and clouds and storms and all the weather,
through which you give your creatures sustenance.

Be praised, My Lord, through Sister Water;
she is very useful, and humble, and precious and pure.
Be praised, my Lord, through Brother Fire,
through whom you brighten the night.
He is beautiful and cheerful, and powerful and strong.
Be praised, my Lord, through our sister Mother Earth,
who feeds us and rules us, and produces various fruits with
    coloured flowers and herbs.
Be praised, my Lord, through those who forgive
for love of you;
through those who endure sickness and trial.
Happy those who endure in peace, for by you, Most High, they
    will be crowned.
Be praised, my Lord, through our Sister Bodily Death,
from whose embrace no living person can escape.
Woe to those who die in mortal sin!
Happy those she finds doing your most holy will.
The second death can do no harm to them.
Praise and bless my Lord, and give thanks, and serve him with
    great humility.

– St Francis of Assisi

Craving for dishonest gain brings trouble on a house.

– Prov 15:27

The Christian tradition understands all creation as the gift of God. God's ongoing creative activity includes not only the work of origins but that of salvation and consummation as well.

– SGN, 14

PART IV

PRAYER:
THE FAITH PRAYED

35 GOD CALLS US TO PRAY

THE FOUNDATIONS OF PRAYER
– CCC, NOS. 2558–2758

COLUMBA MARMION: THE POWER OF PRAYER

 The question is sometimes asked about monasteries or convents: what use are they? How can those who withdraw from society, who live in communities that separate them from real life, who spend their time in contemplation, prayer and spiritual exercises, ever contribute anything valuable to the world? On occasion, people will commend the services provided to the poor, the sick and the oppressed by religious people, even when they do not share their beliefs; but they often remain unconvinced of the utility and contribution of the monastic life.

One monk had, at the beginning of the twentieth century, a profound influence on Catholic and Christian life far beyond the walls of his monastery. His first vocation was to the diocesan priesthood, and then he thought of trying the foreign missions, but he ended up, by the grace and will of God, in a Belgian abbey. From there, he became one of the great spiritual writers of the Church in the twentieth century. The themes of his talks, retreats and sermons, published in three great books during the First World War, opened up new possibilities for Christian life, not by advocating novelty or innovation, but by restating in a fresh and human way the perennial message of the Good News of Jesus Christ. He was a Dublin man. His name was Joseph Marmion.

Joseph Marmion was born on 1 April 1858, the son of an Irish father and a French mother. He received a solid Catholic upbringing (three of his sisters became nuns, and indeed, Reverend Mothers). Marmion also profited from an excellent education from the Jesuits of Belvedere

503

College. He excelled in his studies, won a scholarship and entered Clonliffe College, the Dublin Diocesan Seminary, at just fifteen years of age in 1874. He settled in well, and progressed admirably, the only setback being the untimely death of his father in 1878. This left his family in some financial difficulty, and Joseph was to assume the financial burden for the education of his younger brothers. In the meantime, his outstanding scholarly ability encouraged the Archbishop of Dublin to send him to Rome to study theology at an advanced level.

In Rome, Marmion resided at the Irish College studying at the Propaganda College from 1879 to 1881. Ordained in 1881, he did not, however, proceed to his doctorate because of weak health. On the way home to Dublin, he visited a companion in Maredsous Abbey in Belgium, and this visit was a turning point. His friend Joseph Moreau was a novice there. He had joined the Benedictines to volunteer to join Dom Salvado at the new Benedictine foundation at New Norcia, just north of the city of Perth in Western Australia.

Marmion had himself visited Monte Cassino, the historic Benedictine Monastery south of Rome, and even considered joining the Benedictines in Western Australia. He wrote two letters to Dom Salvado expressing his hope to do just that. The combination of contemplation with the missionary apostolate clearly appealed to the young priest, but the Archbishop of Dublin advised him to spend some time in a parish first. Besides this, he needed to support his family, at least in the short term, and this persuaded him that the bishop had given sound counsel for the moment.

His first appointment was to the parish of Dundrum. Though he stayed only two years as a curate, he was remembered fondly. Marmion was a happy man, able to relate with people easily, zealous and prayerful, but open and amiable. Illness appeared to convince him finally that the tough life of a missionary was not his vocation. He was then appointed to Clonliffe College to teach philosophy and theology for another four years. At the end of that time, he asked Archbishop Walsh for clearance to join the Benedictine Monastery at Maredsous, and the archbishop agreed.

The life of a monk is regular and stable. Joseph Marmion took a new name, Columba (after the great Irish missionary), and he was to spend the rest of his life at Maredsous, except for an interlude as prior of a new foundation at Louvain. He served the monastery in turn as assistant novice master, prior, and eventually in 1909, as the third abbot.

This, however, does not tell the whole story, for Columba was increasingly in demand as a preacher, retreat master, lecturer and spiritual director. He conducted many conferences and devotional exercises, and kept up a large correspondence with many priests, religious brothers, nuns and personal friends through the forty years of his ministry. He travelled frequently throughout Belgium, England, Ireland and Wales. In this way, his vocation for missionary work came true, but not exactly as he had anticipated.

The reason for his popularity and attraction as a preacher and retreat master was his teaching. Grounded in the theology of St Thomas Aquinas and the insights of St Augustine, steeped in the Bible, with a true pastoral genius and a natural gift for communication, Dom Columba was uniquely capable of explaining to his hearers about the love of God for us and the immense gift of our adoption as children of God, brothers and sisters of Jesus. He could spell out the consequence of this teaching in a way that excited the believer with something new and incredibly consoling, the Good News of Jesus Christ.

Of course, this was not new doctrine at all – it was St Paul's teaching in his epistles and the centre of Christian theology – but Dom Columba made it come alive in a new century with contemporary simplicity so that it burst upon the consciousness with a power and immediacy that convinced utterly. The discovery for the spiritual life of the individual was revolutionary. Beginning from the need of the person for God, prayer became no longer a technique or a duty, but a simple state of remaining in the presence of God, delighting in his love, listening to his word, sharing in his life. Because God became man, we can become divine, adopted by God as his sons and daughters. Christ becomes the source of all life, for, as St Paul says: 'It is no longer I, but Christ living in me' (Gal 2:20).

During the First World War, Columba brought together his notes from retreats in a book published as *Christ, the Life of the Soul*. This proved to be an instant success as spiritual writing and excited a demand for more words from the Abbot of Maredsous. Because he had already written up his material for talks and sermons, the second and third books followed in quick succession: *Christ in His Mysteries* in 1919 and *Christ the Ideal of the Monk* in 1922.

As abbot, administration consumed much of his time and energy, coping as he was with the demands of wartime, as well as with proposed new foundations in the Congo, Jerusalem and a reorganisation of the Belgian Benedictines. Worn out by influenza, he died on 30 January 1923 and was buried in Maredsous. He was beatified by John Paul II on 3 September 2000, on the same day as John XXIII and Pius IX.

GOD'S UNIVERSAL CALL TO PRAYER

'For me, prayer is a surge of the heart; it is a simple look turned toward heaven, it is a cry of recognition and of love, embracing both trial and joy.'

– CCC, no. 2558, citing St Thérèse of Lisieux,
Manuscrits Autobiographiques, C 25r

Descriptions of prayer are abundant throughout Christian history. 'True prayer,' wrote St Augustine, 'is nothing but love.' Prayer should arise from the heart. 'Prayer,' said St John Vianney, 'is the inner bath of love into which the soul plunges itself.' 'Everyone of us needs half an hour of prayer each day,' remarked St Francis de Sales, 'except when we are busy – then we need an hour.' For Marmion, according to Fr Mark Tierney OSB, his biographer, the 'definition of prayer is quite simple – just spending time with God'. Definitions of prayer are important, but insufficient. There is a huge difference between knowing about prayer and praying. On this issue, the Rule of St Benedict is clear: 'If a man wants to pray, let him go and pray.'

Saint John Damascene gave a classic definition of prayer: 'Prayer is the raising of one's mind and heart to God or the requesting of good things from God' (CCC, no. 2559, citing St John Damascene, *De Fide Orth.* 3, 24).

The *Catechism* clearly defines prayer as a 'vital and personal relationship with the living and true God' (CCC, no. 2558). Prayer is Christian 'insofar as it is communion with Christ' (CCC, no. 2565), and a 'covenant relationship between God and man in Christ' (CCC, no. 2564).

It is important to remember that all of Part Two of the *Catechism* also deals with prayer as it is found in the celebration of the Sacraments and in the Liturgy of the Hours. Liturgical prayer, which is the action of the Church, joins us to Christ, interceding with the Father – in the Holy Spirit – on behalf of our salvation.

We should consider Part Four's reflection on the foundations of prayer and the meaning of the Our Father as essentially related to liturgical prayer and a basic complement to it. Because catechetical teaching may never be disconnected from prayer, which is the soul of truth, every chapter in this text includes a meditative section and a liturgical or scriptural prayer.

This chapter on prayer has four sections: Scripture, the sources and manner of praying, guides for prayer and expressions of prayer.

SCRIPTURE

Scripture reveals the relationship between God and his people as a dialogue of prayer. He constantly searches for us. Our restless hearts seek him, though sin often masks and frustrates this desire. God always begins the process. The point where his call and our response intersect is prayer. The event is always grace-filled and a gift.

OLD TESTAMENT PEOPLE AT PRAYER

The Role of Faith in Prayer

Abraham, Isaac and Jacob witnessed the role of faith in prayer. God's call came first. These patriarchs responded in faith, but not without a struggle. Essential to their prayer was trust in God's fidelity to his promises. Centuries later, God called Moses to be his instrument for the salvation of Israel from slavery. Moses dramatised the value of intercessory prayer as he vigorously begged God for mercy and guidance for the people making their journey to the Promised Land.

After the people had settled in the Promised Land, there were many powerful witnesses to the importance of faith in prayer. One example is the holy woman Hannah, who longed for a child. Year after year, she made a pilgrimage to the shrine at Shiloh, where she prayed to the Lord and made him a vow that if he would give her a child, she would dedicate the child to God. The Lord answered her prayer, and she conceived and bore a son, whom she called Samuel. He grew up to be a prophet and a judge, a religious leader of God's people. Her song of joy at the dedication of her son to God is a canticle of praise.

> My heart exults in [the Lord] …
> [The Lord] makes poor and rich,
>   he humbles and also exalts.
> He raises the poor from the dust,
>   he lifts the needy from the dunghill …
> for to [the Lord] belong the pillars of the earth. (1 Sm 2:1, 7-8)

Examples of Prayer

The People of God learned how to pray at the shrine of God's presence, before the Ark of the Covenant in the temple. God raised up priests, kings and prophets to lead the people in prayer. The people assimilated the prayerful attitudes of awe, wonder and adoration of God at the celebration of the various feasts and liturgies. The books of the Prophets in particular show them praising God in prayer, seeking his help and crying out to him in times of opposition and persecution.

The Book of Esther is the story of a woman of faith who was an example for her people of the importance of relying on God in prayer. A prominent official in the Persian Empire conspired to destroy in a single day all the Jews in the empire. At the same time, a Jewish woman, Esther, was the queen. She sought the help of God, praying, 'My Lord, our King, you alone are God. Help me, who am alone and have no help but you' (Est C:14).

With courage, she explained the plot to her husband the king: 'Grant me my life – that is my request; and the lives of my people' (Est 7:3). He heard her plea, cancelled the massacre and executed the official. The people praised God that their sorrow was turned into joy.

Esther's actions are remembered by the annual observance of the Feast of Purim. The feast celebrates God's providential care of his people in response to Queen Esther's prayers.

The Psalms: Prayers of the Assembly

Poets like King David and many other holy authors over a number of years composed the masterpiece of prayer known as the Psalms. These incomparable prayers nourished the people both personally and communally. They embraced every age of history, while being rooted in each moment of time. They were sung at the Temple, in local synagogues, in family settings, on pilgrimages and in the solitude of personal prayer. They formed the basis of the prayer of Jesus and, as such, can be used to draw us into his prayer as well. The Psalms are part of every celebration of Mass. They also form the heart and soul of the Liturgy of the Hours, that public daily prayer of the Church which prolongs the Eucharistic celebration and gives praise to God.

The Canticle of Judith belongs to the genre of psalms and memorialises the vivid story of how God delivered his people through the leadership of the valiant woman Judith. The Book of Judith cites her example as a way to help God's people trust in the divine presence among them. Despite all the troubles the people of ancient Israel faced, they had trusted in him as the Lord of history.

This book describes how the Assyrian army besieged the Jewish people. Judith developed a successful plan to defeat the Assyrians. The emphasis in the narrative is on God's intervention to save his people. Judith led her people in a prayer of praise that has many features of the Psalms and was meant to be a prayer of the whole assembly:

> Break into song for my God,
>   to the tambourine,
> I shall sing a new song to my God.
>   Lord, you are great, you are glorious,
>   wonderfully strong, unconquerable.
> May your whole creation serve you!
>   For you spoke and things came into being. (Jdt 16:1, 13-14)

PRAYER IN THE NEW TESTAMENT

The Prayer of Jesus

As a child, Jesus first learned to pray from Mary and Joseph. As he grew in age, he also joined in prayer at the synagogue and at the Temple. But he also had his heavenly Father as the source of his prayer. It was a filial prayer he revealed when he was twelve: 'I must be in my Father's house' (Lk 2:49). Jesus addressed his Father by the name '*Abba*', which in the language of his day was used by children to speak to their fathers.

The Gospels also describe the numerous times Jesus went away from the crowds and his disciples to pray by himself. In the Garden of Gethsemane, he prayed in agony to the Father knowing the Cross that awaited him, but also praying with acceptance of and obedience to the mission the Father had given him.

Jesus also taught his disciples to pray. In the Gospel of Matthew, for example, he instructed them to pray with simplicity of words and confidence in the Father (cf. Mt 6:5-15; 7:7-11).

Prayer in the New Testament Church

At Pentecost, after nine days of prayer in the Upper Room, the disciples experienced the gift of the Holy Spirit for the manifestation of the Church. The first community of believers in Jerusalem devoted themselves to the Apostles' teaching and fellowship, to the breaking of the bread, and to prayers (cf. Acts 2:42). The infant Church was born in prayer, lived in prayer and thrived in prayer.

The Letters of St Paul show him to be a man of intense prayer. Throughout his Letters, there are prayers of praise to God for blessings the Church and he himself have received. There are also prayers of intercession as he seeks God's grace for the communities he has evangelised. And he describes his own personal prayers to God, especially in times of difficulty.

The Holy Spirit taught the Church the life of prayer and led her to deeper insights into basic ways of praying: adoration, petition, intercession, thanksgiving and praise.

Adoration

This form of prayer flows from an attitude that acknowledges we are creatures in the presence of our Creator. It is an act by which we glorify the God who made us. We adore God from whom all blessings flow.

Petition

This is a prayer that takes many forms: to ask, to implore, to plead, to cry out. In each case, it acknowledges how much we depend on God for our needs, including forgiveness and persistence in seeking him. We need to practise the prayer of petition, remembering Christ's call to ask in order to receive, to seek in order to find and to knock in order that the door may be opened (cf. Mt 7:7).

The first movement of the prayer of petition is asking forgiveness of our sins as did the tax collector in the parable where he was compared to the Pharisee whose prayer lacked humility (cf. CCC, no. 2631). The tax collector begins his prayer with the words, 'God, be merciful to me, a sinner' (Lk 18:13). Humility and repentance characterise a prayer that returns us to communion with Christ.

Intercession

This is the prayer that we make on behalf of the needs of others. Jesus Christ himself, our great High Priest, incessantly intercedes for us. God calls us also to intercede for each other and even for our enemies. Intercessions for others' needs are part of the Mass and the Liturgy of the Hours.

Thanksgiving

This form of prayer flows from the Church's greatest prayer, the celebration of the Eucharist. Every moment or event can become a thanksgiving offering. We are called to thank God for all the gifts we have received, including our joys and sorrows, all of which, through love, work towards our benefit.

Praise

'Praise is the form of prayer which recognises most immediately that God is God … It shares in the blessed happiness of the pure of heart who love God in faith before seeing him in glory' (CCC, no. 2639). Scripture is filled with outpourings of praise for God. When we exult in him with simplicity and an open heart, we obtain a glimpse of the joy of the angels and saints who glory in the ways of God.

THE SOURCES AND MANNER OF PRAYING

We must do more than rely on an impulse for our prayer life. Saint Paul calls us to 'pray constantly' (1 Th 5:17). The will to pray in a daily, sustained and structured manner is essential for becoming a prayerful person. The Holy Spirit guides the Church at prayer through her reading of Scripture, her celebration of the liturgy and the practice of faith, hope and love.

Daily familiarity with Scripture is a rich source of prayer. We need to do more than read or study Scripture; we should also converse with God, whose Spirit lies within the text and who draws us to appreciate 'the supreme advantage of knowing Christ Jesus' (Phil 3:8).

By our active participation in the liturgy, the prayer of the Church, we encounter the Father, and the Son, and the Holy Spirit, who impart to us the gifts of salvation. Spiritual writers tell us our heart can be an altar of adoration and praise. Prayer internalises the liturgy both during and after its celebration (cf. CCC, no. 2655).

Faith puts vitality in prayer because it brings us to a personal relationship with Christ. Hope carries our prayer to our final goal of permanent union with God. Love, poured into our heart by the Holy Spirit, is the source and destiny of prayer.

Saint John Vianney (1786–1859) wrote: 'My God, if my tongue cannot say in every moment that I love you, I want my heart to repeat it to you as often as I draw breath' (CCC, no. 2658, citing *Prayer*).

'Because God blesses the human heart, it can in return bless him who is the source of every blessing' (CCC, no. 2645).

Christian prayer is always Trinitarian. The sweep of our prayer should direct us toward the Father. But access to the Father is through Jesus Christ. Therefore, we also address our prayer to Christ and can do so using titles of Jesus found in the New Testament: Son of God, Word of God, Lamb of God, Son of the Virgin, Lord and Saviour, etc. Christ is the door to God.

We must never tire of praying to Jesus. Yet it is the Holy Spirit who helps us to draw near to Jesus.

'Nobody is able to say, "Jesus is Lord" except in the Holy Spirit' (1 Cor 12:3). The Church invites us to invoke the Holy Spirit as the interior Teacher of Christian prayer. (CCC, no. 2681)

PRAYER IN COMMUNION WITH MARY

'Because of Mary's singular cooperation with the action of the Holy Spirit, the Church loves to pray in communion with the Virgin Mary, to magnify with her the great things the Lord has done for her, and to entrust supplications and praises to her' (CCC, no. 2682). This twofold movement of joining Mary in praising God for his gifts to her and seeking her intercession has found a privileged expression in the Hail Mary.

The Hail Mary

Along with the Lord's Prayer, the Hail Mary is one of the most widely used prayers in the Catholic Church. The first half of the Hail Mary comes from Luke's Gospel accounts of the Angel Gabriel's annunciation to Mary that she was called to be the Mother of God's Son (cf. Lk 1:26-56). The second half is an intercessory prayer developed in the Church's tradition.

- 'Hail Mary, full of grace.' This is the greeting the Angel Gabriel spoke to Mary of Nazareth. Gabriel proclaims that Mary is full of grace, meaning that she is a sinless woman, blessed with a deep union with God, who had come to dwell in her.
- 'The Lord is with thee.' Mary has been chosen by God for this great privilege. He is with her, having already preserved her from sin and filled her with grace. This does not mean that Mary is deprived of her freedom. She lives in graced friendship with God and freely offers him her undivided heart.
- 'Of all women you are the most blessed.' This was the greeting given Mary by her cousin Elizabeth when Mary came to visit and help Elizabeth with the birth of her forthcoming child (Lk 1:42). As Scripture points out, Mary holds a singular place among all God's chosen ones in the history of salvation. Mary is the world's most honoured woman.
- 'Blessed is the fruit of thy womb, Jesus.' This is another beatitude or blessing uttered by Elizabeth, who spoke these words after her child,

John the Baptist, leaped in her womb at the moment she hears the greeting of Mary. Elizabeth is inspired by the Holy Spirit to bless Mary for believing the message of Gabriel. Elizabeth acknowledges the presence of God in Mary's womb: 'Why should I be honoured with a visit from the mother of my Lord?' (Lk 1:43). This is the first time in Scripture that Mary's faith is praised.

- 'Holy Mary, Mother of God.' Sometime in the Middle Ages, the second half of the Hail Mary, which begins by invoking her title of Mother of God, was composed. This title comes from the earliest days of Christian faith. Mary is the Mother of God, because she is the mother of Jesus who is true God and true man, as defined by the Council of Ephesus in AD 431. The Eastern Churches call Mary *Theotokos*, or 'Birth-giver of God' (sometimes translated as 'Godbearer'). Mary's response to God engages her in the plan of human salvation through motherhood of Jesus.

- 'Pray for us sinners.' We have noted that intercessory prayer concerns the needs and hopes of others. Jesus Christ, our High Priest, always intercedes for us before the Father, and he calls us to intercede for others as well. The saints and the Blessed Virgin Mary continue this prayer of intercession in heaven. As Mother of the Church, Mary continues to pray with a mother's care for the Body of her Son on earth. At Cana, Mary interceded with Jesus on behalf of the couple who had run out of wine. Jesus heard her prayer and turned water into wine. Mary's last words in Scripture are spoken to us: 'Do whatever he [Jesus] tells you' (Jn 2:5). Our holy Mother always brings us to Jesus.

- 'Now and at the hour of our death. Amen.' In her life, Mary walked a pilgrimage of faith. Even with all the grace she received from God, she encountered the mysterious ways of God and profound suffering, especially at the death of her Son. She knows what a journey of faith entails, and she accompanies us with prayer as we make our journey to God throughout our lives and at death.

Other Prayers to the Blessed Virgin

In the Latin Church, the Rosary, a venerable and powerful form of prayer, developed out of popular piety. Praying the Rosary involves the recitation of vocal prayers, including the Our Father, the Hail Mary and the Glory Be, while meditating on mysteries in the life of Jesus. In the Eastern

Churches, litanies and hymns to the Mother of God are more commonly prayed.

We do not pray to Mary in the same way we pray to God. In praying to Mary, we invoke her intercession on behalf of our needs, whereas when we pray to God we ask him directly for gifts and favours.

GUIDES FOR PRAYER

Throughout Church history, saints have left a heritage of prayer 'by the example of their lives, the transmission of their writings', and their continued prayers in heaven on our behalf. Numerous schools of spirituality, such as Benedictine, Franciscan, or Ignatian, have come down to us as part of the heritage of the saints. This authentic diversity of spiritualities is united by the Holy Spirit within the living tradition of the Church (CCC, no. 2683).

Parents are the first teachers of prayer. Family prayer, practised on a daily basis, in which the children witness the prayer of adults closest to them, is an excellent school of prayer. Priests and deacons have a public responsibility to lead people in prayer with genuine reverence. They should also teach people how to pray and encourage them by their example.

Men and women religious who embrace the consecrated life profess a commitment to prayer. Their example and willingness to dedicate themselves to Christ encourages us to pray with added fervour and dedication. Lay ministers have a unique opportunity to encourage and inspire the laity to incorporate prayer into their daily lives.

The lifelong religious education of Catholics at every level should always include training in how to pray as well as having time set aside for communal prayer. Prayer groups also have been admirable sources of the contemporary renewal of prayer. Places for prayer include the parish church, retreat centres, shrines, the home and any situation in which people can achieve sufficient concentration of mind and heart.

LECTIO DIVINA

Lectio divina is a reflective reading of Scripture leading to meditation on specific passages. This is a centuries-old practice of prayer which relies on the guidance of the Holy Spirit within the heart as the person praying reads a Scripture passage and pauses to seek out the deeper meaning that God wants to convey through his Word.

'It is especially necessary that listening to the word of God should become a life-giving encounter in the ancient and ever valid tradition of *lectio divina*, which draws from the biblical text the living word, which questions, directs and shapes our lives' (NMI, no. 39).

EXPRESSIONS OF PRAYER

At Mass when the reading of the Gospel begins, we place the sign of the Cross on our foreheads, lips and hearts, and pray, 'May the Lord be in our minds, on our lips, and in our hearts.' Lips, minds and hearts – these symbolise three kinds of prayer: vocal, meditative and contemplative. These modes of prayer include formal and informal paths, personal and communal expressions, popular piety and the liturgical prayer of the Church.

Vocal Prayer

The disciples were drawn to Jesus' own prayer. He taught them a vocal prayer, the Our Father. Jesus prayed aloud in the synagogues and the Temple and 'raised his voice to express' personal prayers such as his surrender to the Father's will in Gethsemane. The seventeenth chapter of John's Gospel records a lengthy vocal prayer of Jesus, revealing the depth of his intimacy with his Father and his loving concern for his disciples (cf. CCC, no. 2701).

Since we are body as well as spirit, we need to express ourselves orally. Spoken and sung prayers arise from our souls; they can be complemented by bodily gestures such as the Sign of the Cross, genuflection, kneeling and bowing. When we become inwardly aware of God, to whom we speak, our vocal prayer can become an initial step toward contemplative prayer.

FROM THE CATECHISM

1. What are some erroneous conceptions of prayer?

Some people view prayer as a simple psychological activity, others as an effort of concentration to reach a mental void. Still others reduce prayer to ritual words and postures. Many Christians unconsciously regard prayer as an occupation that is incompatible with all the other things they have to do. (CCC, no. 2726)

We must respond with humility, trust and perseverance to these temptations that cast doubt on the usefulness or even the possibility of prayer. (CCC, no. 2753)

2. How is prayer connected to Christian life?

Prayer and *Christian life are inseparable*, for they concern the same love and the same renunciation, proceeding from love; the same filial and loving conformity with the Father's plan of love; the same transforming union in the Holy Spirit who conforms us more and more to Christ Jesus; the same love for all men, the love with which Jesus has loved us. (CCC, no. 2745)

3. What should we remember when our prayers seem unanswered?

Do not be troubled if you do not receive immediately from God what you ask him; for he desires to do something even greater for you, while you cling to him in prayer. (CCC, no. 2737, citing Evagrius Ponticus, *De Oratione*, 34: PG, 79, 1173)

Filial trust is put to the test when we feel that our prayer is not always heard. The Gospel invites us to ask ourselves about the conformity of our prayer to the desire of the Spirit. (CCC, no. 2756)

Meditative Prayer

'Meditation is above all a quest. The mind seeks to understand the why and how of the Christian life, in order to adhere and respond to what the Lord is asking' (CCC, no. 2705). In meditative prayer, we use our minds to ponder the will of God in his plan for our lives. What does God ask of us? The Church provides many aids for meditation: 'the Sacred Scriptures, particularly the Gospels, holy icons, liturgical texts of the day or season, writings of the spiritual fathers ... the great book of creation and that of history – the page on which the "today" of God is written' (CCC, no. 2705). 'Meditation engages thought, imagination, emotion and desire' (CCC, no. 2708). It is meant to deepen our faith in Christ, to convert our hearts and to strengthen us to do God's will.

'There are as many and varied methods of meditation as there are spiritual masters' (CCC, no. 2707). Most prominent among these are the *Lectio Divina* of St Benedict, the radical simplicity of Franciscan spirituality and the Spiritual Exercises of St Ignatius. These spiritualities also include guidance for contemplation.

Contemplative Prayer

'Contemplative prayer ... is a gaze of faith fixed on Jesus, an attentiveness to the Word of God, a silent love' (CCC, no. 2724). Like all prayer, this form requires a regular time each day. When one gives God time for prayer, he will give time for one's other responsibilities.

Contemplative prayer is a gift to which we dispose ourselves by resting attentively before Christ. It involves hearing and obeying God's Word. It is a time of silent listening and love.

THE WORK OF PRAYER

Prayer requires time, attention and effort. We need to discipline ourselves for what spiritual writers call 'spiritual combat'. They cite problems such as *acedia* (a form of sloth or laziness) that arises from a lax ascetical behaviour, a laxity that needs to be corrected. The Tempter will try to pull us away from prayer. Distraction and dryness will discourage us.

The remedy is faith, fidelity to times for prayer, constant conversion of heart and watchfulness. The *Catechism's* section 'The Battle of Prayer'

(CCC, nos. 2725–2745) answers many questions that beginners are likely to ask. Its advice is practical and experiential. For example, the section addresses the issue of distraction, a major obstacle for most beginners. Distractions interfere with all forms of prayer. The temptation to fight them entraps one; all that is needed is to turn back to the presence of the Lord in our hearts. A distraction reveals our attachments, but a humble awareness of this can move us to offer Christ our hearts for the needed purification.

PRAY CONSTANTLY (1 TH 5:17)

It is often said that we should pray as if everything depended on God and act as if everything depended on us. Many believers, however, substitute self-reliance for prayer. People are not conscious of their need for God.

Despite the general cultural preference for an independent spirit that idealises the achievements of the self in getting things done, studies about religion indicate a significant counter movement. A majority of Irish people claim they believe in God. A high number of people report they pray on occasion.

Within our Church, spirituality movements, including traditional schools of spirituality such as Benedictine, Carmelite, Franciscan and Ignatian, stress the importance of liturgical and meditative prayer. In addition, new immigrants enrich the life of the Church through their traditions of popular piety.

Some people find spiritual strength in the Chaplet of Divine Mercy. There is a growing interest among many people from all walks of life in praying the Liturgy of the Hours. Parish missions, retreats and spiritual movements such as Cursillo and Charismatic Renewal have helped many to begin the journey of prayer and have led people onward to meditation and contemplation. A significant number of people are attracted to the practice of *lectio divina* that weds scriptural reflection with elements of contemplation.

In our noisy and activist culture, prayer has brought Christ's peace and hope to many. Small faith communities, Scripture study groups and charismatic groups make prayer a large component of their gatherings.

Many parishes have instituted hours of adoration of the Blessed Sacrament, a form of prayer that is growing steadily. Popular piety attracts large numbers of the faithful, especially pilgrimages and devotions to Our Lady and the saints. Many recite the Rosary regularly. A growing number of people are seeking spiritual direction. These are some highlights of the increasing turn to spirituality and prayer.

Bishops and priests continue to emphasise the centrality of the liturgy in Catholic prayer life, while strongly supporting the wide-ranging aspects of personal prayer, piety and meditation. They also provide constant reminders about the relationship between liturgy, other forms of prayer and the call to witness Christ's Kingdom of love, justice and mercy in everyday lives. Prayer is the soul of discipleship and can strengthen us for a life of mission.

In the longstanding tradition of the Church, prayer is centred upon God. It is an emptying of oneself not for its own sake, but for the sake of being filled with God and entering into a deeper relationship with him. There are forms of spirituality in contemporary culture that focus more on one's own self and the achievement of a superficial tranquillity. Genuine Christian prayer is attentive to the presence of God and seeks ways to be of greater service to God and others.

▬ FOR DISCUSSION ▬

1. Why do you pray? When do you pray? How do you pray?
2. If you practise some form of meditation regularly, how would you describe it? What means have you taken to persevere in meditation? How have you maintained a bond between prayer and an active Christian mission to others?
3. What are you doing to deepen your prayer life? What are you learning from spiritual reading to help you with your prayer? If you have a spiritual director, how has this been effective for your prayer?

DOCTRINAL STATEMENTS

- Prayer is the raising of one's mind and heart to God and the requesting of good things from him. It is an act by which one enters into awareness of a loving communion with God. 'Prayer is the response of faith to the free promise of salvation and also a response of love to the thirst of the only Son of God' (CCC, no. 2561).

- Scripture reveals the relationship between God and people as a dialogue of prayer. God constantly searches for us. Our restless hearts seek him, though sin often masks and frustrates this desire. God always begins the process. The point where his call and our response intersect is prayer. The event is always a grace and a gift.

- Jesus taught his disciples 'to pray with a purified heart, with lively and persevering faith, with filial boldness'. He called them to vigilance and invited them 'to present their petitions to God in his name' (CCC, no. 2621).

- The infant Church was born in prayer, lived in prayer, thrived in prayer. The Holy Spirit taught the community the life of prayer and led them to deeper insights into basic ways of praying: adoration, petition, repentance, intercession, thanksgiving and praise.

- 'The Word of God, the liturgy of the Church, and the virtues of faith, hope and charity are the sources of prayer' (CCC, no. 2662).

- Christian prayer is always Trinitarian. The sweep of our prayer moves us toward the Father. But access to the Father is through Jesus Christ. Therefore we also address our prayer to Christ. Yet it is the Holy Spirit who helps us to draw near to Jesus. The Church invites us to invoke the Holy Spirit as the interior teacher of Christian prayer.

- 'Because of Mary's singular cooperation with the action of the Holy Spirit, the Church loves to pray in communion with the Virgin Mary, to magnify with her the great things the Lord has done for her, and to entrust supplications and praises to her' (CCC, no. 2682).

- The first teachers of prayer are parents or other members of the family, the domestic church.

- Our guides for prayer within the Church include ordained ministers, those in consecrated life, catechists and spiritual directors.

- Places for prayer include the parish church, retreat centres and shrines, the home, and many other circumstances that afford the opportunity to pray.
- 'The Church invites the faithful to regular prayer: daily prayers, the Liturgy of the Hours, Sunday Eucharist, the feasts of the liturgical year' (CCC, no. 2720).
- There are three kinds of prayer: vocal, meditative and contemplative.
- Prayer requires humility, trust and perseverance in order to battle temptations that cast doubt on the usefulness or even the possibility of prayer (see CCC, nos. 2726–2753).
- 'Pray constantly' (1 Th 5:17).

MEDITATION

'I Shall Keep the Silence of My Heart'

I don't think there is anyone who needs God's help and grace as much as I do. Sometimes I feel so helpless and so weak. I think this is why God uses me. Because I cannot depend on my own strength, I rely on him twenty-four hours a day. All of us must cling to God through prayer. My secret is simple: I pray. Through prayer I become one in love with Christ. I realise that praying to him is loving him.

We cannot find God in noise or agitation. Nature: trees, flowers and grass grow in silence. The stars, the moon and the sun move in silence. What is essential is not what we say but what God tells others through us. In silence he listens to us; in silence he speaks to our souls. In silence we are granted the privilege of listening to his voice.

Silence of our eyes.
Silence of our ears.
Silence of our minds.
… In the silence of the heart God will speak.

– Blessed Teresa, cited in *The Power of Prayer*
(New York: MJF Books, 1998), 3, 7–8

PRAYER

I lift up my eyes to the mountains;
   from where shall come my help?
My help shall come from the Lord
   who made heaven and earth.
He will keep your foot from stumbling.
   Your guard will never slumber.
No, he sleeps not nor slumbers,
   Israel's guard.
The Lord your guard, the Lord your shade
   at your right hand.
By day the sun shall not smite you,
   nor the moon in the night.
The Lord will guard you from evil;
   he will guard your soul.
The Lord will guard your going and coming,
   both now and forever.

– Ps 121

Like the deer that yearns for running streams,
   so my soul is yearning for you, my God.
My soul is thirsting for God, the living God;
   when can I enter and appear before the face of God?

– Ps 42:2-3

36 JESUS TAUGHT US TO PRAY

THE LORD'S PRAYER: OUR FATHER
– CCC, NOS. 2759–2865

'SO YOU SHOULD PRAY LIKE THIS' (MT 6:9)

Jesus prayed always. Saint Luke, for example, tells us in his Gospel: 'While Jesus after his own baptism was at prayer, heaven opened' (Lk 3:21).

Jesus prayed before his choice of the Twelve Apostles and before he asked the Apostles who they thought he was. He prayed regularly in the synagogue and Temple. He prayed before the prediction of his Passion and during the Transfiguration. 'As he was praying, the aspect of his face was changed and his clothing became sparkling white' (Lk 9:29). Jesus prayed at the Last Supper, in Gethsemane, and on the Cross.

He prayed for long periods of time, sometimes for a whole night. 'He went up into the hills by himself to pray' (Mt 14:23). The Gospels rarely describe what his prayer was like, simply noting that he prayed often. One thing is clear, the Apostles were so moved by the constancy and depth of his prayer that they asked him to help them to pray: 'Lord, teach us to pray' (Lk 11:1).

Jesus responded with what is now known as the Lord's Prayer. In St Matthew's Gospel, he precedes his gift of this prayer with teachings about how *not* to pray. In St Luke's Gospel, he adds advice about the need to pray with confidence that our prayer will be answered. The Gospel of Matthew introduces the Lord's Prayer with these words:

> When you pray, do not imitate the hypocrites: they love to say their prayers standing up in the synagogues and at the street corners for people to see them. In truth I tell you, they have had their reward.

But when you pray, *go to your private* room, shut yourself in, and so pray to your Father who is in that secret place, and your Father who sees all that is done in secret will reward you. In your prayers do not babble as the gentiles do, for they think that by using many words they will make themselves heard. Do not be like them; your Father knows what you need before you ask him.

So you should pray like this:

Our Father in heaven, / may your name be held holy, / your kingdom come, your will be done, / on earth as in heaven. / Give us today our daily bread. / And forgive us our debts, / as we have forgiven those who are in debt to us. / And do not put us to the test, / but save us from the Evil One. (Mt 6:5-13)

The Gospel of Luke also offers counsel about prayer:

So I say to you: Ask, and it will be given to you; search, and you will find; knock, and the door will be opened to you. For everyone who asks receives; everyone who searches finds; everyone who knocks will have the door opened. What father among you, if his son asked for a fish, would hand him a snake? Or if he asked for an egg, hand him a scorpion? If you then, evil as you are, know how to give your children what is good, how much more will the heavenly Father give the Holy Spirit to those who ask him! (Lk 11:9-13)

It is clear, therefore, that Jesus framed his gift of the Lord's Prayer with guidance to help us pray more effectively.

Saint Luke records another of Christ's instructions on prayer in the parable of the self-important Pharisee and a humble tax collector:

Two men went up to the Temple to pray, one a Pharisee, the other a tax collector. The Pharisee stood there and said this prayer to himself, 'I thank you, God, that I am not grasping, unjust, adulterous like everyone else, and particularly that I am not like this tax collector here. I fast twice a week; I pay tithes on all I get.' The tax collector stood some distance away, not daring even to raise his eyes to heaven; but he beat his breast and said, 'God, be merciful to me, a sinner.' This man, I tell you, went home again justified; the other did not. For everyone who raises himself up will be humbled, but anyone who humbles himself will be raised up. (Lk 18:10-14)

Jesus gave us not only the gift of the Lord's Prayer, but also the context in which it should be understood and prayed. With this in mind, we offer the following reflection on this, the greatest of prayers.

THE CENTRAL PRAYER OF SCRIPTURE

The Lord's Prayer is the most perfect of prayers ... In it we ask, not only for all the things we can rightly desire, but also in the sequence that they should be desired. This prayer not only teaches us to ask for things, but also in what order we should desire them.

– CCC, no. 2763, citing St Thomas Aquinas,
Summa Theologiae, II–II. 83, 9

The Our Father is called the 'Lord's Prayer' because Jesus, our Lord and model of prayer, is its author. There are two versions of the Lord's Prayer in the Gospels. Saint Luke's account of the event contains five petitions. Saint Matthew's lists seven. The Church's liturgy follows Matthew's version.

Saint Augustine wrote seven commentaries on the Our Father. So moved was he by its depth that he wrote, 'Run through all the words of holy prayers [in Scripture], and I do not think you will find anything in them that is not contained in the Lord's Prayer' (*Letter*, 130, 12, 22). The Our Father is an integral part of sacramental liturgies (Baptism, Confirmation and the Anointing of the Sick) and of the Eucharist itself. At Mass, it comes after the Eucharistic Prayer, summing up the intercessions of that prayer and preparing us for Holy Communion when we receive Jesus Christ, who is the Bread of Life. It is at the heart of every individual and communal prayer (cf. CCC, no. 2776).

WE ADDRESS THE FATHER

Before we make our own this first exclamation of the Lord's Prayer, we must humbly cleanse our hearts of certain false images drawn 'from this world'. Humility makes us recognise that 'no one knows the Son except the Father, and no one knows the Father except the Son'. ... The purification of our hearts has to do with paternal or maternal images, stemming from our personal and cultural history, and influencing our relationship with God. God our Father transcends the categories of the created world ... To pray to the Father is to enter into his mystery as he is and as the Son has revealed him to us.

– CCC, no. 2779, citing Mt 11:27

Our Father

We call God 'Father' only because Jesus, the Son of God made man, revealed him as such. Because of our union with Jesus through Baptism, we are given the grace of an adopted, filial relationship with the Father. This begets in us a new self-understanding due to this extraordinary intimacy with the Father and the Son. A term that our Lord uses for Father is *'Abba!'* This implies that Jesus is saying that a relationship with God should be like that of a child, very close, personal and dependent.

While we recognise that there is no gender in God, we will be inclined to draw upon our experiences with our earthly fathers when thinking of this title for God. The image of a human father is generally a positive one, and this helps us to draw near to God as Father. Yet, sadly, there are cases of fathers who have fallen short of the responsibilities of fatherhood.

An understanding of God as Father is already evident in the Old Testament, where God describes himself as being in a special relationship of providential care for the people of Israel and in particular for their king. Jesus' revelation of God as his Father flows from a profound awareness not only of that same providential care but also of an indescribable intimacy (cf., e.g., Jn 14). 'As you are sons, God has sent into our hearts the Spirit of his Son crying, "Abba, Father"' (Gal 4:6).

When we say 'Our', we recognise that we are a people bound together by the New Covenant that God has made with us through his Son in the Holy Spirit. While we are indeed individual persons, we are also persons in communion with each other because we have been baptised into communion with the Holy Trinity. The Our Father is a prayer of the Church, hence we pray with the Church when we recite these words, together calling God our Father.

Who Art in Heaven

'Who art in heaven' does not refer to a place but to God's majesty and his presence in the hearts of the just. Heaven, the Father's house, is the true homeland toward which we are heading and to which, already, we belong.

– CCC, no. 2802

Heaven is the culmination of our relationship with the Father, Son and Holy Spirit begun in Baptism.

THE SEVEN PETITIONS

In the Our Father, the object of the first three petitions is the glory of the Father: the sanctification of his name, the coming of the kingdom, and the fulfilment of his will. The four others present our wants to him: they ask that our lives be nourished, healed of sin, and made victorious in the struggle of good over evil.

– CCC, no. 2857

Hallowed Be Thy Name

Hallowed means 'to be made holy'. We do not make God's name holy; God is the source of his own holiness that is his perfection and glory. But we give witness to his holiness by doing his will, being people of prayer and establishing the earthly conditions by which his holiness is manifested.

God gradually revealed his name. First of all he revealed it to Moses, through whom he tells us that he is 'I Am', a person who chooses to be close to us yet remains mysterious. As salvation history unfolded, the people of Israel developed other names they used to refer to God, such as Lord, Shepherd of Israel and King.

But God's definitive revelation of who he is was through Jesus Christ, who taught us that God is his Father and he is the Son. Through Christ's salvation and the Sacrament of Baptism, we become adopted children of God by grace. Hence we can legitimately call God 'Father'.

Thy Kingdom Come

In this petition, we pray that the Kingdom promised us by God will come – the Kingdom already present in Christ's Passion, death and Resurrection. In Matthew's Gospel, there is an extensive revelation of the many aspects of what Christ's Kingdom means in moral and spiritual terms as well as its relationship to the Church. It is a Kingdom of love, justice and mercy, where sins are forgiven, the sick are made whole, enemies are reconciled, captives are freed and the needs of the poor are met.

It is all these things and more, for ultimately the Kingdom is Jesus Christ and all he means for us. The Kingdom is already here because of the redemption of Jesus Christ. But in another sense, it is 'not yet' here, since Christ's final transformation of individuals, society and culture has yet to happen in its fullness. This is why we need to pray this petition every day and work for its coming.

Thy Will Be Done on Earth as It Is in Heaven

In the third petition, we ask our Father to unite our will to that of Jesus so as to fulfil the plan of salvation in the world. We need God's help and protection to make this possible (cf. CCC, no. 2860).

Jesus gave us an example of this when he was in Gethsemane on the eve of his Passion and death. He first asked that the cup of suffering might pass from him but also prayed, 'Let your will be done, not mine' (Lk 22:42).

What is God's will? In creating us, God established a plan for how to live in a fully human and spiritual manner. Jesus came to us to show us exactly what that means. The Lord Jesus asks us to be his disciples and shape our lives by faith. The Second Vatican Council reminds us that 'the disciple is bound by a grave obligation toward Christ ... to understand the truth received from him, faithfully to proclaim it and vigorously to defend it' (*Declaration on Religious Liberty* [*Dignitatis Humanae*], no. 14).

Give Us This Day Our Daily Bread

'"Our daily bread" refers to the earthly nourishment necessary to everyone for subsistence, and also to the Bread of Life: the Word of God and the Body of Christ' (CCC, no. 2861). We draw our life from the Eucharist each time we receive Holy Communion.

Just before he left this earth, the Lord Jesus promised to be with us every day. In a remarkable manner, Jesus is present to us in the Divine Sacrament, because he is himself the Bread of Life available to us. The Church's contemplation always centres itself on the Lord in this Sacrament, which contains the whole treasure of the Church, Jesus Christ.

At the same time, we ask for our material needs. While we seek what we need for our own maintenance and development, we must never forget the poor of the world, who so often lack daily bread. We are called to have solidarity with them and work for their physical and spiritual welfare. We pray for our 'daily' bread, implying that we pray for what we need for today and will pray again each day for the needs of that day.

Forgive Us Our Trespasses as We Forgive Those Who Trespass Against Us

> *The fifth petition begs God's mercy for our offences,*
> *mercy which can penetrate our hearts only if we have*
> *learned to forgive our enemies, with the example and*
> *help of Christ.*
>
> – CCC, no. 2862

The best way to obtain mercy is to be merciful. As Jesus taught us, 'Blessed are the merciful: they shall have mercy shown them' (Mt 5:7). Failure to forgive others is a major human problem. Holding grudges is common. Failure to forgive routinely tears apart families, neighbourhoods and even nations. Jesus stressed mercy and forgiveness in numerous ways such as when he asked the Father to forgive those who crucified him (cf. Lk 23:34). We pray to God that we may be able to forgive as much as we are forgiven.

And Lead Us Not into Temptation

God wants to set us free from evil; he tempts no one (cf. CCC, no. 2846).

> When we say 'lead us not into temptation' we are asking God not to allow us to take the path that leads to sin. This petition implores the Spirit of discernment and strength; it requests the grace of vigilance and final perseverance. (CCC, no. 2863)

We know that preventive medicine is desirable so that curative medicine may not be needed. Preventing the possibility of sin is preferable to sinning with its negative impact on our lives. Traditionally we have been taught to avoid the occasions of sin, that is, persons or situations that may lead us to sin. Virtue grows stronger with its practise.

In this petition, we entrust ourselves to the Holy Spirit to keep us alert to the dangers of sin and give us the grace to resist temptation. A meditation on how Christ resisted temptation in the desert is a fruitful and inspiring example of how we should conduct ourselves in the face of temptation (cf. Mt 4:1-11; Lk 4:1-12). 'It is by his prayer that Jesus vanquishes the tempter, both at the outset of his public mission and in the ultimate struggle of his agony' (CCC, no. 2849).

But Deliver Us from Evil

> *In the last petition, 'but deliver us from evil', Christians pray to God with the Church to show forth the victory, already won by Christ, over the 'ruler of this world', Satan, the angel personally opposed to God and to his plan of salvation.*
>
> — CCC, no. 2864

As always throughout this prayer, we are reminded that we pray with the Church. We do not pray alone but in union with the community of believers around the world – all of us bound by our union with Jesus in the Spirit and with an adoptive filial relationship to the Father.

The *Catechism* emphasises that we ask God to deliver us from the Evil One – Satan, the devil (cf. Jn 17:15). The evil we confront is not just an

FROM THE CATECHISM

1. How is the Lord's Prayer related to the Gospel?

The Lord's Prayer is truly the summary of the whole Gospel. (CCC, no. 2774, citing Tertullian, *De Orat.* 1: PL, 1, 1251-1255)

[It is] the quintessential prayer of the Church. (CCC, no. 2776)

2. What is contained in the first three petitions of the Our Father?

The first series of petitions carries us toward [God], for his own sake: *thy* name, *thy* kingdom, *thy* will! (CCC, no. 2804)

3. What is the focus of the last four petitions of the Our Father?

The four others present our wants to him: they ask that our lives be nourished, healed of sin, and made victorious in the struggle of good over evil. (CCC, no. 2857)

abstract idea, but an evil, fallen angel who wants to prevent our salvation. We entrust ourselves to God so that the devil may not lead us into sin.

'One who entrusts himself to God does not dread the devil. "If God is for us, who is against us?"' (CCC, no. 2852, citing St Ambrose, *On the Sacraments*, 5, 4, 30; cf. Rm 8:31). We ask God to deliver us from all evils – past, present and future – of which Satan is the author or instigator.

Doxology

There is a final doxology which was added by the early Church: 'For the kingdom, the power and the glory are yours, now and forever' (cf. *Teaching of the Twelve Apostles* [*Didache*] 8, 2; *Apostolic Constitutions*, 7, 24). It is recited by Latin Catholics after the prayer which follows the recitation of the Our Father during Mass. These words of praise echo the first three petitions, and we use them as words of adoration in union with the liturgy of heaven.

Amen

We conclude with the 'Amen', which means, 'So be it'. We joyfully ratify the words that Jesus has taught us (cf. CCC, no. 2856).

PRAY IN ORDER TO BELIEVE, BELIEVE IN ORDER TO PRAY

A closer look at the *Catechism of the Catholic Church* will reveal its method of weaving prayer into presentations of doctrine. Though certain sections have been designated as dealing specifically with prayer, such as Part Two on the liturgy and this Part Four on prayer, there is a contemplative spirit to the whole presentation. Identifying certain parts with prayer does not imply some kind of false separation between doctrine and prayer.

The *Catechism* reminds us that the Lord Jesus asks us to believe in order to pray and to pray in order to believe. There is a complementarity in which knowing and loving God support each other. Belief in the Father, Son and Spirit should be essentially and immediately connected to a prayerful and loving communion with the Trinity.

Belief in Catholic doctrine draws us to prayer and to a divine reassurance about the validity of these revealed truths of God to which we have responded in faith. We give ourselves to prayer to deepen our personal relationship with God in a loving communion. Experiencing God in prayer shows us the vitality of the truthfulness of doctrine and puts energy into our spiritual and moral witness.

Just as the understanding of doctrine requires study and effort, so also does the practice of prayer. 'Prayer is both a gift of grace and a determined response on our part. It always presupposes effort' (CCC, no. 2725). Since prayer is a loving relationship with God, it places demands upon us. No love exists without sacrifice.

In our busy culture, time has become one of our most precious possessions. Of all the things we can give to the ones we love, among the best is our time. Often something else must be sacrificed to make this possible.

When it comes to prayer, we must choose regular times for prayer each day. We need to step aside from the rush of daily life and compose our souls before God, as Jesus did when he spent time with his Father.

How do we know when we really begin to pray? The different kinds of prayer have already been noted: liturgical and private; vocal, meditative and contemplative prayer. Underneath all these forms should be our hearts actively opening to God.

> Where does prayer come from? ... In naming the source of prayer, Scripture speaks sometimes of the soul or the spirit, but most often of the heart (more than a thousand times). According to Scripture, it is the *heart* that prays. If our heart is far from God, the words of prayer are in vain. (CCC, no. 2562)

In the biblical or Semitic mind, the heart is beyond the grasp of reason and deeper than our psychic drives. It is the very centre of our selves, the mysterious place where we make our fundamental decisions. It is the ground of encounter with God. Unlike the busy-ness of mental life, the heart is a zone of silence.

The heart is the environment where our most serious dedication takes place. As the setting for meeting God, whether at liturgy or in meditation, the heart is the place for enjoying our covenant with him. It can be an awesome moment, as the author of the Book of Revelation tells us: 'I fell at his feet as though dead' (Rv 1:17).

Understanding the heart as the source of prayer should also help us realise how it affects our commitment to Christian teaching. If we treat doctrine simply as an academic study, we will have a tendency to miss its connection with our union with God. Jesus said, 'I am Truth' (Jn 14:6). He also said, 'Anyone who loves me will keep my word' (Jn 14:23). Jesus never divorced his teaching from his person. The two went together.

Likewise, doctrine and prayer go together. The heart is the shrine of the Word and of Love. The heart links these gifts into one satisfying unity.

This focus on our efforts need not distract us from the humble realisation that the prayer of the heart is prompted by the Holy Spirit. It is he who presides over our study of doctrine and our life of prayer. We will always find ourselves weaving between dependence on God and reliance on ourselves. But ultimately we will find ourselves echoing the saints who so often say, 'All is grace'.

FOR DISCUSSION

1. What is the link between belief and prayer? How do the teachings of Christ and his Church enrich our prayer?
2. How do we develop our dependence and reliance upon God in a world that promotes self-reliance?
3. What is the importance of the heart in prayer? How might one balance the intellectual and the intuitive approaches to God in prayer? How could you help others be open to the prayer of the heart?

DOCTRINAL STATEMENTS

- 'The Lord's Prayer is the most perfect of prayers ... In it we ask, not only for all the things we can rightly desire, but also in the sequence that they should be desired. This prayer not only teaches us to ask for things, but also in what order we should desire them' (CCC, no. 2763, citing St Thomas Aquinas, *Summa Theologiae*, II–II, 83, 9).
- The Church includes the Our Father in her liturgies. The communal praying of the Lord's Prayer at Mass gathers up the intercessions that accompany the consecration of the bread and wine into Christ's Body and Blood and prepares the worshippers for Holy Communion.
- The divine mystery is beyond our understanding and imagining. We call God 'Father' only because Jesus, the Son of God made man, revealed him as such.
- Because of our union with Jesus through Baptism, we are given the grace of an adopted, filial relationship with the Father. This begets in us a new self-understanding based on this extraordinary intimacy with the Father and the Son.
- Prayer to the Father inclines us to be like him and to acquire a humble and trusting heart (cf. CCC, no. 2800).
- '"Who art in heaven" does not refer to a place but to God's majesty and his presence in the hearts of the just. Heaven, the Father's house, is the true homeland toward which we are heading and to which, already, we belong' (CCC, no. 2802).
- 'In the Our Father, the object of the first three petitions is the glory of the Father: the sanctification of his name, the coming of the kingdom

and the fulfilment of his will. The four others present our wants to him: they ask that our lives be nourished, healed of sin, and made victorious in the struggle of good over evil' (CCC, no. 2857).

- *Hallowed* means 'to be made holy'. We do not make God's name holy; God is the source of his own holiness that is his perfection and glory. We hallow God's name by showing honour, respect and adoration to God (cf. CCC, no. 2807). We give witness to God's holiness by doing his will, being people of prayer and establishing the earthly conditions by which God's holiness is manifested.

- 'Thy kingdom come' turns our attention to the final coming of Jesus and the ultimate fulfilment of his Kingdom. This was the prayerful cry of the early Christians who had a vivid sense of Christ's final coming – Maranatha! 'Come, Lord Jesus' (Rv 22:20).

- 'In the third petition, we ask our Father to unite our will to that of his Son, so as to fulfil his plan of salvation in the life of the world' (CCC, no. 2860).

- '"Our daily bread" refers to the earthly nourishment necessary to everyone for subsistence, and also to the Bread of Life: the Word of God and the Body of Christ' (CCC, no. 2861).

- 'The fifth petition begs God's mercy for our offences, mercy which can penetrate our hearts only if we have learned to forgive our enemies, with the example and help of Christ' (CCC, no. 2862).

- 'When we say "lead us not into temptation", we are asking God not to allow us to take the path that leads to sin. This petition implores the Spirit of discernment and strength; it requests the grace of vigilance and final perseverance' (CCC, no. 2863).

- 'In the last petition, "but deliver us from evil", Christians pray to God with the Church to show forth the victory, already won by Christ, over the "ruler of this world", Satan, the angel personally opposed to God and to his plan of salvation' (CCC, no. 2864).

- We conclude with the 'Amen', which means, 'So be it'. We joyfully ratify the words that Jesus has taught us (cf. CCC, no. 2856).

MEDITATION

The proper ordering of our external activities can only be achieved once we have re-established conscious contact with the centre of all these activities and concerns. This centre is the aim of our meditation. In St Teresa's words, 'God is the centre of the soul.' When our access to this centre is opened up, the Kingdom of God is established in our hearts. That kingdom is nothing less than the present power and all-pervasive life of God himself permeating all creation. In the words of John Cassian: 'He who is the author of eternity would have men ask of him nothing that is uncertain, petty or temporal.'

This is not because he does not want us to enjoy the good things of life, but because we can fully enjoy them only when we have received his gift of himself who is goodness itself. The proof of his generosity is also what St Paul calls 'The ground of our hope'. It is the love of God flooding our inmost hearts through the Holy Spirit he has given us (cf. Rm 5:5).

This is not an experience reserved for the selected few. It is a gift available to all men and women. To receive it we must return to the centre of our being, where we find the infusion of God's love through the Spirit of Jesus.

– John Main OSB, *Word into Silence*
(Mahwah, NJ: Paulist Press, 1981), 66–67

PRAYER

Our Father, who art in heaven,
hallowed be thy name.
Thy kingdom come.
Thy will be done on earth, as it is in heaven.
Give us this day our daily bread;
and forgive us our trespasses
as we forgive those who trespass against us,
and lead us not into temptation,
but deliver us from evil. Amen.

– cf. Mt 6:9-13

Worthy is the Lamb that was sacrificed
    to receive power, riches, wisdom, strength,
    honour, glory and blessing …
To the One seated on the throne and to the Lamb,
    be all praise, honour, glory and power,
    for ever and ever.

                                  – Rv 5:12-13

The pattern of all Christian prayer and the prayer that unites all
Christians is the Lord's Prayer, the prayer Jesus taught his disciples.
It is a summary of the whole Gospel and holds within it a synopsis of
all that is meant by Christian prayer.

                                  – SGN, 61

CONCLUSION
AND
APPENDICES

CONCLUSION:
A SOURCE OF MEANING
AND HOPE

The Second Vatican Council declared that 'the future of humanity is in the hands of those men who are capable of providing the generations to come with reasons for life and optimism' (GS, no. 31). No one can live without the hope that life has ultimate and lasting meaning beyond the concerns and struggles, the joys and satisfactions of each day. Catholics find that meaning and hope in Jesus Christ, whom God the Father has sent into the world for the salvation of all peoples.

But the world can be a disturbing place. There is war and anxiety because of terrorism. There is the fierceness of competition and the injustices that come from greed. There are continuous distractions that come from the media, the numerous hours given to television, radio and internet. There are the unrelenting demands of work and family life.

Yet in the midst of all this, people are generously loving within their families, with their friends and for their communities. Nevertheless, a nagging question remains: where is all this going? There is a persistent thirst for meaning and hope.

Many people find refuge in various types of spiritual activities and communities that promise serenity in a hectic world and refuge from its pressures. They look to meditation techniques and to well-publicised personalities for ways to find tranquillity and some hope for themselves. In the midst of such a culture, the Catholic Church offers a message that is not its own but comes from God's self-revelation in Jesus Christ two thousand years ago, yet is ever new and renewing as it is received, celebrated, lived and contemplated today. The Church offers to all people the possibility of encountering the living God today and finding in him lasting meaning and hope.

God continues to be present in the Church as the Gospel of his Son, Jesus Christ, is proclaimed and received by her members through the life-giving power of the Holy Spirit. In the first part of this *Irish Catholic Catechism for Adults*, we have studied the summary of faith in the Apostles' Creed and have learned how the Gospel of Jesus Christ is transmitted faithfully from generation to generation, continuing to be heard by countless believers in a way that leads them to an ever-greater understanding of God's love and their destiny.

God continues to be present in his Church as her members are brought together by the Holy Spirit to celebrate the Seven Sacraments, most especially the Eucharist. In Part Two of this *Catechism*, we have learned how Jesus Christ continues to endow his people with his gifts of salvation. Through Baptism, he makes them children of the Father, his disciples and members of the Church. Through Confirmation, he deepens within them the presence of the Holy Spirit. Through the sacrifice of the Eucharist, he nourishes them with his Body and Blood. Through Penance and Reconciliation, he brings them from sin to grace. Through the Anointing of the Sick, he helps them bear – and sometimes lifts from them – the burdens of serious illness. Through Marriage, he reveals the absoluteness of love and its life-giving creativity. Through Holy Orders, he establishes bishops, priests and deacons to ensure his continuous shepherding of the Church.

God continues to be present in the Church as her members strive to live according to the example and teaching of Jesus Christ. In Part Three of this *Catechism*, we have learned how the Beatitudes and the Ten Commandments guide the consciences and lives of the members of the Church so that they make alive, in the midst of humanity, the power of God's love to transform society by the wisdom, compassion, justice and fidelity that flow from God himself. The Holy Spirit is the dynamic presence of God, enabling the members of the Church to live a truly Christian life.

God continues to be present in the Church as her members contemplate the great things God has done through his Son by the power of the Holy Spirit for the salvation of all people. In Part Four of this *Catechism*, we have learned about the significance of prayer and popular piety as ways in which the members of the Church continue to encounter the living God within their own hearts and within their own communities.

The Church is a community of human beings who are still subject to sin, and so it is with humility that she offers herself as the meeting place with the living God. Her existence for two thousand years demonstrates the unceasing mercy and love of God in maintaining her in his grace as a faithful and repentant people. In a world of passing fads and transitory ambitions, she offers the substance of the wisdom of the Gospel and her growing understanding of it through two millennia. She offers the possibility of enriching the present moment with the gifts of a tradition rooted in God's self-revelation and with the hope and meaning for human life that come from God himself. In a world torn by war and injustice, she celebrates the death and Resurrection of Jesus Christ, the gift of himself made eternally present and effective, to make all peoples one with him as head of a reconciled and healed community. In a world of violence against human life, the Church mightily defends life by her works of justice and charity as well as by her advocacy for the protection of all human life.

Of her very nature, the Church is missionary. This means her members are called by God to bring the Gospel by word and deed to all peoples and to every situation of work, education, culture and communal life in which human beings find themselves. The members of the Church seek to transform society not by power but by persuasion and by example. Through participation in political life – either as voters or as holders of public office – they work for increasing conformity of public policy to the law of God as known by human reason and Divine Revelation. This they do especially by showing the coherence of Catholic teaching with the fundamental yearnings and dignity of the human person.

The Constitution of Ireland maintains the freedom of its citizens to worship according to their consciences and has prohibited infringement upon religious freedom by the government. For some, this leads to the conclusion that religion is a purely private matter and should not exercise a public voice in debates about moral issues. That would infringe against religious freedom, by legally permitting only the private practice of religion. Catholics (and all citizens of whatever creed or none) must be able to participate in political life and bring to bear upon it – by their voice and their vote – what they have learned about human nature, human destiny and God's will for human beings from his self-revelation. The Gospel of Jesus Christ is relevant for all times and all places.

This *Catechism* provides Catholics with a knowledge and understanding of the Gospel that enables them to give an account of their faith to all whom they meet with clarity and persuasiveness. They are more effectively enabled to proclaim what God has done for them through his Son in the Holy Spirit, and to explain the rich tradition of belief that is our heritage. This proclamation and catechesis are essential to the new evangelisation to which the Church commits herself today: to bring the Gospel of salvation to those near and far.

APPENDIX A
GLOSSARY

- A -

ABORTION: The intentional destruction of an unborn child; such an act is gravely contrary to the moral law and the will of the Creator.

ABSOLUTION: The act of the priest, using the power Christ entrusted to the Church, in the Sacrament of Penance by which he pardons sin(s) of the penitent.

ADVENT: A period of roughly four weeks prior to Christmas, during which the faithful prepare themselves spiritually for the celebration of the birth of Christ.

AGNOSTIC: One who claims to be unable to know whether or not God exists.

AMEN: A Hebrew word meaning 'so be it' or 'it is so'; its use serves as an affirmation of what was said previously; this term most often is used to conclude prayer.

ANAMNESIS (The Memorial): Prayer after the words of consecration at the Mass in which we recall the death and Resurrection of Christ and look forward to his glorious return.

ANGEL: A spiritual, personal, immortal creature with intelligence and free will, created by God to serve him unceasingly and to act as a messenger to carry out the plan of salvation.

ANGER: When considered as one of the Capital Sins, anger is that passion which leads one to either harm a person or want to harm a person because of a desire for vengeance.

ANNULMENT (DECLARATION OF NULLITY OF A MARRIAGE): The consent of the spouses entering into marriage must be a free act of the will, devoid of external or internal invalidating factors. If this freedom is absent, the marriage is invalid. For this reason, the Church, after an examination of the situation by a competent Church court, can declare the nullity of a marriage, i.e., that the sacramental marriage never existed. In this case, the contracting parties are free to marry, provided the natural obligations of the previous union are discharged (cf. CCC, nos. 1628–1629; CIC, cann. 1095–1107; CCEO, cann. 1431–1449).

ANOINTING OF THE SICK, SACRAMENT OF: This Sacrament of healing is given to a person who is seriously ill or in danger of death due to sickness or old age. Elderly people may be anointed if they are in a weak condition though no dangerous illness is present.

APOSTASY: The term applied to a baptised person who has abandoned the Christian faith.

APOSTLE: The title traditionally given to those specially chosen by Jesus to preach the Gospel and to whom he entrusted responsibility for guiding the early Church. The names of the Twelve are Peter, Andrew, James, John, Thomas, James, Philip, Bartholomew (or Nathaniel), Matthew, Simon, Jude (or Thaddeus), and Matthias (who replaced Judas Iscariot after Judas betrayed Jesus and then took his own life). Saint Paul, though not one of the Twelve, was also called later by the Lord to be an Apostle.

APOSTLES' CREED: A statement of the Christian faith, developed in the early centuries of the Church and used in the Sacrament of Baptism. It expresses the faith passed down to us from the Apostles.

APOSTOLIC SUCCESSION: The passing on of the office of bishop from the Apostles to bishops, and from them to other bishops down each generation, by means of ordination. This office includes the sanctifying, teaching and governing roles within the Church.

APOSTOLIC TRADITION: Jesus entrusted his revelation and teachings to his Apostles. They passed it on by their preaching and witness. Along with others, they began writing the message down in what became the New Testament.

ARIANISM: The heresy in Church history that was widely spread by a man named Arius (AD 250–336), who argued that Jesus was not fully divine, but that God the Son was a kind of lesser God who became the man Jesus. His heresy was refuted by the Councils of Nicea (AD 325) and Chalcedon (AD 451).

ASCENSION: The entry of Jesus' humanity into divine glory to be at the right hand of the Father; traditionally, this occurred forty days after Jesus' Resurrection.

ASSUMPTION: The dogma that when the Blessed Virgin Mary's earthly life was finished, because she was sinless, she was kept from corruption and taken soul and body into heavenly glory.

ATHEIST: One who denies the existence of God.

ATONEMENT: By his suffering and death on the Cross, Jesus freed us from our sins and brought about our reconciliation with God the Father.

AVARICE: See 'Greed'.

- B -

BAPTISM: The first Sacrament of Initiation by which we are freed from all sin and are endowed with the gift of divine life, are made members of the Church and are called to holiness and mission.

BEATIFICATION: The last step before being declared a saint. The main steps in the canonisation process (determining eligibility for sainthood) are as follows: Servant of God (Venerable), Blessed and Saint.

BEATITUDES: The eight Beatitudes form part of the teaching given by Jesus during the Sermon on the Mount, which set forth fundamental attitudes and virtues for living as a faithful disciple.

BIBLE: See 'Sacred Scripture'.

BISHOP: The highest of the three degrees of Holy Orders; a bishop is normally ordained to teach, to sanctify and to govern a diocese or local church; a bishop is a successor of the Apostles.

BLASPHEMY: The use of the name of God, of the Virgin Mary and of the saints in an offensive way.

BLESSINGS: Among the sacramentals, blessings hold a major place. There are blessings for persons, meals, objects, places and ceremonial occasions such as graduations, testimonial honours, welcomes and farewells. All blessings praise God for his gifts. Most blessings invoke the Holy Trinity along with the sign of the Cross, sometimes with the sprinkling of holy water.

BODY OF CHRIST: A name for the Holy Eucharist (see 'Eucharist, Sacrament of'). It is also a title for the Church, with Christ as her head, sometimes referred to as the Mystical Body of Christ. The Holy Spirit provides the members with the gifts needed to live as Christ's Body.

- C -

CANONISATION: The name for the solemn declaration by the pope that a deceased member of the faithful may be proposed as a model and intercessor to the Christian faithful and venerated as a saint, on the basis of the fact that the person lived a life of heroic virtue or remained faithful to God through martyrdom.

CAPITAL SINS: Those seven sins, sometimes called 'deadly', that can lead us into more serious sin. The Capital Sins are lust, avarice (greed), envy, pride, sloth, gluttony and anger.

CATECHESIS: The act of handing on the Word of God intended to inform the faith community and candidates for initiation into the Church about the teachings of Christ, transmitted by the Apostles to the Church. It also involves the lifelong effort of forming people into witnesses to Christ and opening their hearts to the spiritual transformation given by the Holy Spirit.

CATECHISM: The name given to a written work that contains a summary of all the beliefs of the faith and is used for catechetical instruction.

CATECHUMEN: An unbaptised candidate for the Sacraments of Initiation.

CATECHUMENATE: An extended period of preparation for the Sacraments of Initiation incorporating ritual, prayer, instruction and spiritual and moral support by the parish community.

CHARITY (LOVE): The Theological Virtue by which we give love to God for his own sake and love to our neighbour on account of God.

CHASTITY: Connected to purity of heart, this is a virtue that moves us to love others with generous regards for them. It excludes lust and any wish to exploit them sexually. It helps us see and put into practise God's plan for the body, person and sexuality. All people are called to pursue and live the virtue of chastity according to one's state in life.

CHRISM: Perfumed oil consecrated by a bishop at the annual Mass of the Chrism during Holy Week; it is used in those Sacraments which confer a permanent mark or character – Baptism, Confirmation and Holy Orders.

CHRISMATION: The name for Confirmation in the Eastern Churches.

CHRIST: The title given to Jesus meaning 'The Anointed One'; it comes from the Latin word Christus, which in its Greek root is the word for Messiah.

CHRISTMAS: The annual celebration of Jesus' Nativity or birth.

CHURCH: This term refers to the whole Catholic community of believers throughout the world. The term can also be used in the sense of a diocese or a particular parish.

CIVIC RESPONSIBILITY: Citizens should work with civil authority to build a society of truth, justice, solidarity and freedom. In conscience, citizens may not obey civil laws that are contrary to the moral order.

COLLEGE OF BISHOPS (Collegiality): All bishops, with the pope as their head, form a single college, which succeeds in every generation the college of the Twelve Apostles, with Peter at their head. Christ instituted this college as the foundation of the Church. The college of bishops, together with – but never without – the pope, has the supreme and full authority over the universal Church.

COMMON GOOD: By the 'common good is to be understood, "the sum total of social conditions which allow people, either as groups or as individuals, to reach their fulfilment more fully and more easily"' (CCC, no. 1906, citing GS, no. 26, §1).

COMMUNION, HOLY: See 'Eucharist'.

COMMUNION OF THE SAINTS:
This refers to members of the Church through all time – those presently now in the Church and those members who have already gone before us and are either in Purgatory or heaven.

CONCUPISCENCE: The disorder in our human appetites and desires as the result of Original Sin. These effects remain even after Baptism and produce an inclination to sin.

CONFIRMATION, SACRAMENT OF: This is a Sacrament of Initiation in which the bishop or a delegated priest confers Confirmation through the anointing with chrism on the recipient's forehead, which is done by the laying on of the hand, while saying, 'Be sealed with the gift of the Holy Spirit'. Confirmation completes the grace of Baptism by a special outpouring of the gifts of the Holy Spirit, which seals and confirms the baptised in union with Christ and calls them to greater participation in the worship and apostolic life of the Church.

CONSCIENCE: The practical judgement about the moral quality of particular humans acts as well as the inner ability to make such a judgement.

CONTEMPLATION: Wordless prayer in which a person focuses the whole person in loving adoration on God and his very presence.

CONTRITION: Sorrow for sin with a firm purpose of amendment, which is the intention to avoid sin in the future. Contrition is imperfect when a person is motivated by fear of punishment. Contrition is perfect when the motive is a response to God's love for us. Contrition on the part of the penitent, either imperfect or perfect, is a necessary part of the Sacrament of Penance and Reconciliation.

CORPORAL WORKS OF MERCY:
These are charitable actions by which we help our neighbours in their bodily needs. The corporal (bodily) works of mercy are to feed the hungry; to give drink to the thirsty; to clothe the naked; to visit the imprisoned; to shelter the homeless; to visit the sick; and to bury the dead.

COVENANT: A solemn agreement made between people or between God and a person or persons. In the Old Testament, God established covenants with Noah, Abraham and Moses. The Prophets prepared people for the new and eternal covenant established by Jesus Christ. Marriage is a covenant of life and love.

CREATION: God – Father, Son, Holy Spirit – out of love for us made the world out of nothing, wanting to share divine life and love with us. The original creation became a new creation in Jesus Christ.

CREED: This term comes from the Latin word *credo*, meaning 'I believe'. It is used to refer to a statement of belief.

CREMATION: 'The Church permits cremation (the burning of a deceased human body into ashes), provided that it does not demonstrate a denial of faith in the resurrection of the body' (CCC, no. 2301). In cases where cremation is planned, the Church counsels that the body should be present for the funeral. The cremated remains should always be treated with the same respect given to the human body from which they came. After the funeral liturgy, the cremated remains are buried in a grave or placed in a mausoleum or columbarium, not scattered.

- D -

DEACONS: Men ordained by the bishop to serve. They receive the Sacrament of Holy Orders but not the ministerial priesthood. Through ordination, the deacon is conformed to the Christ who said he came to serve, not to be served. Deacons in the Latin Church may baptise, read the Gospel, preach the homily, assist the bishop or priest in the celebration of the Eucharist, assist at and bless marriages, and preside at funerals. They dedicate themselves to charitable endeavours, which was their ministerial role in New Testament times.

DECALOGUE: Another name for the Ten Commandments.

DEISM: A worldview that admits that God created the world but denies that he has any further providential care or concern for it. (See also 'Providence'.)

DEPOSIT OF FAITH: The heritage of faith contained in Sacred Scripture and Tradition, handed on in the Church from the time of the Apostles, from which the Magisterium draws all that it proposes for belief as divinely revealed.

DEVILS: Angels who, in pride, turned away from God and have fallen from grace are named demons or devils, and they tempt human beings to sin.

DEVOTIONAL PRAYER: Devotional prayer refers to the numerous forms of personalised prayer that have grown up outside, but complementary to, the liturgical prayer of the Church. (See Chapter 22 on 'Sacramentals and Popular Devotion.') These devotions include the rosary; the Stations of the Cross; pilgrimages to shrines in the Holy Land and Rome, Marian shrines and those dedicated to saints; novenas; litanies; and similar expressions of faith.

DISCIPLE: Name given in the New Testament to all those men and women who followed Jesus and were taught by him while he was alive, and who, following Jesus' death, Resurrection, and Ascension, formed the Church with the Apostles and helped spread the Good News, or Gospel message. Contemporary members of the Church, as followers of Jesus, can also be referred to as disciples.

DIVINE FILIATION: An effect of Baptism and Confirmation: becoming adopted sons and daughters of God, participating in God's life and love.

DIVINE PERSON: The term used to describe the Father, Son and Holy Spirit in their relation to and distinction from one another within the unity of the Trinity. Each of the three divine Persons is God in one divine nature.

DIVINE PROVIDENCE: God's loving care and concern for all he has made; he continues to watch over creation, sustaining its existence and presiding over its development and destiny.

DOCTOR OF THE CHURCH: A person from any era in Church history whose sanctity and writings have had a profound influence on theological and spiritual thought. A person is declared a Doctor by the pope.

DOCTRINE/DOGMA: The name given to divinely revealed truths proclaimed or taught by the Church's Magisterium; the faithful are obliged to believe these truths.

DOMESTIC CHURCH: 'The Christian home is the place where children receive the first proclamation of the faith. For this reason the family is rightly called "the domestic church", a community of grace and prayer, a school of human virtues and of Christian charity' (CCC, no. 1666).

DOXOLOGY: The name given to a prayer of Trinitarian adoration in which the three Persons of the Trinity are invoked.

- E -

EASTER: The annual celebration of the Resurrection of Jesus.

EASTERN CHURCHES AND WESTERN CHURCHES: The Eastern Churches originated in that region of the world that was at one time part of the Eastern Roman Empire. These churches possess their own distinctive traditions that may be seen in their liturgy, theology and law. The Western Church, focused in Rome, is sometimes called the Latin Church. All individual churches, Eastern or Western, that are in communion with the Apostolic See (Rome) are part of the Catholic Church.

ECUMENICAL COUNCIL: This is a gathering of the world's bishops, exercising their collegial authority over the universal Church in union with the pope.

ECUMENISM: The efforts among all Christians to bring about the fulfilment of Christ's will for the unity of his followers.

ELECT: The name given to those who are already with the Lord Jesus in heaven. It also can refer to catechumens who are in the final stage of formation prior to entering the Church.

ENVY: One of the Capital Sins; it is the inordinate desire for the possessions of another, even to the point of wishing harm on the other or rejoicing in another's misfortunes.

EPICLESIS (INVOCATION): During the celebration of the Eucharist, the priest invokes the Father to send the Holy Spirit to come upon the gifts of bread and wine that they may be changed into Christ's Body and Blood. In every Sacrament, the prayer asking for the sanctifying power of God's Holy Spirit is an *epiclesis*.

EPISCOPACY: The office of bishop.

EUCHARIST, SACRAMENT OF: During the celebration of the Mass, by the power of the Holy Spirit and the proclamation of Jesus' words by the priest, the bread and wine are changed into the Body and Blood of Christ, which is offered in an unbloody manner in sacrifice for us and in praise to the Father. The assembly actively participates by prayers, hymns, psalms, responses and an inner self-offering along with Christ to the Father. All who are properly prepared can receive Holy Communion, by which Jesus gradually transforms the receivers into himself and which leads them to Gospel witness in the world.

EUTHANASIA: An action or an omission which purposely results in the death of sick, disabled or dying persons. Regardless of the motives or means, it is always gravely wrong and morally unacceptable.

EVANGELICAL COUNSELS: Those vows taken by men or women who enter religious life; there are three vows: poverty, chastity and obedience.

EVANGELISATION: This is the ministry and mission of proclaiming and witnessing Christ and his Gospel with the intention of deepening the faith of believers and inviting others to be baptised and initiated into the Church.

EXCOMMUNICATION: A severe penalty imposed or declared by the Church upon a Catholic who has committed a grave crime or offence according to Church law; a person who is excommunicated is barred from celebrating or receiving the Sacraments. This penalty is imposed as a remedy for serious sin, not as a punishment. Remission of the penalty can be granted only by those authorised to do so by the Church.

EXEGESIS: The process used by Scripture scholars to determine the literal and spiritual meanings of the biblical text.

EXORCISM: 'Exorcism is directed at the expulsion of demons or to the liberation from demonic possession through the spiritual authority which Jesus entrusted to his Church' (CCC, no. 1673, citing CIC, can. 1172). One needs to distinguish psychological illness from demonic possession. Illness is the domain of psychological and medical care, whereas the presence of the Evil One needs the attention of an exorcist. In the Rite of Baptism, there is also a Prayer of Exorcism prior to the anointing with the Oil of the Catechumens; in this prayer, the priest or deacon asks that the one about to be baptised be freed from Original Sin.

- F -

FAITH: This is both a gift of God and a human act by which the believer gives personal adherence to God (who invites his or her response) and freely assents to the whole truth that God has revealed.

FALL (THE): A title for the event in which the first man and woman, traditionally called Adam and Eve, disobeyed God with the result that they lost their place in Paradise, passed Original Sin to all their descendants, and made Redemption necessary.

FAMILY: 'A man and a woman, united in marriage, together with their children, form a family. This institution is prior to any recognition by public authority, which has an obligation to recognise it. It should be considered the normal reference point by which the different [authentic] forms of family relationships are to be [recognised]' (CCC, no. 2202).

FATHERS OF THE CHURCH: Church teachers and writers of the early centuries whose teachings are a crucial witness to the Tradition of the Church.

FILIAL LOVE: The love that children owe their parents through respect, gratitude, just obedience and assistance.

FORTITUDE: The Cardinal Virtue by which one courageously and firmly chooses the good despite difficulty and also perseveres in doing what is right despite temptation, fear or persecution.

FRUITS OF THE HOLY SPIRIT: The Tradition of the Church lists twelve fruits of the Holy Spirit: love, joy, peace, patience, kindness, goodness, generosity, gentleness, faithfulness, modesty, self-control and chastity (cf. CCC, no. 1832).

FULL COMMUNION (RECEPTION INTO): This refers to the entrance of baptised Christians of other Christian ecclesial communions into full communion with the Catholic Church, through a profession of faith and the Sacraments of Confirmation and the Eucharist.

- G -

GIFTS OF THE HOLY SPIRIT: These gifts are permanent dispositions that move us to respond to the guidance of the Spirit. The traditional list of these gifts is derived from Isaiah 11:1-3: wisdom, understanding, right judgment, courage, knowledge, reverence and wonder and awe in God's presence.

GLUTTONY: The Capital Sin that describes actions of eating and drinking more than what is necessary.

GNOSTICISM: In the first Christian centuries, this blend of Christianity and paganism denied that Jesus was human and sought salvation through occult 'wisdom'. The earliest Church Fathers, especially St Ignatius of Antioch, rejected the Gnostics and vigorously defended the humanity of Jesus Christ, conceived by the Holy Spirit in the womb of the Virgin Mary, who gave birth to Jesus.

GOD: The eternal unchanging being who created all that is and who continues to oversee and guide all things. Through the centuries, God has revealed himself to us as one being who is a Trinity of Persons – Father, Son and Holy Spirit. Traditionally, *God* has been used to refer to the Father, or the First Person of the Trinity, as well as to the whole Godhead.

GOSPEL: The proclamation of the entire message of faith revealed in and through Jesus Christ, the Son of God and the Second Person of the Trinity. The word *Gospel* also refers to one of the four books of the New Testament – Matthew, Mark, Luke and John – that contain a record of the life, teaching, death and Resurrection of Jesus.

GRACE: The help God gives us to respond to our vocation to become his adopted sons and daughters. The divine initiative of grace precedes, prepares and elicits our free response in faith and commitment. Sanctifying grace is a habitual gift of God's own divine life, a stable and supernatural disposition that enables us to live with God and to act by his love. Actual graces refer to God's interventions in our lives, whether at the beginning of conversion or in the course of the work of sanctification.

GREED (AVARICE): An inordinate attachment to the goods of creation, frequently expressed in the pursuit of money or other symbols of wealth, which leads to sins of injustice and other evils.

- H -

HERESY: A religious teaching that denies or contradicts truths revealed by God.

HOLINESS: A state of goodness in which a person – with the help of God's grace, the action of the Holy Spirit and a life of prayer – is freed from sin and evil. Such a person, when gifted with holiness, must still resist temptation, repent of sins that may be committed and realise that remaining holy is a lifelong pilgrimage with many spiritual and moral challenges. The struggles evident in the lives of the saints are instructive when trying to explain and describe holiness.

HOLY DAYS OF OBLIGATION: In Ireland, the Holy Days of Obligation are: Nativity of the Lord (December 25); The Epiphany of the Lord (January 6); St Patrick (March 17); The Assumption of the Blessed Virgin Mary (August 15); All Saints (November 1); The Immaculate Conception (December 8). On these days there is an obligation to attend Mass and to refrain from servile work as much as possible.

HOLY ORDERS, SACRAMENT OF: The Sacrament in which a bishop ordains a man to be conformed to Jesus Christ by grace, to service and leadership in the Church. A man can be ordained a deacon, priest or bishop. Through this Sacrament, the mission entrusted by Christ to his Apostles continues to be exercised in the Church. This Sacrament confers a permanent mark or character on the one who receives it.

HOLY SPIRIT: The Third Person of the Trinity who builds up, animates and sanctifies the Church and her members.

HOPE: The Theological Virtue through which a person both desires and expects the fulfilment of God's promises of things to come.

- I -

ICONS: A form of sacred art developed in the Eastern Churches. The artists consider their calling a sacred vocation. Their works have a mystical impact meant to draw the one praying beyond the picture into the realm of the divine.

IMAGE OF GOD: God has made us in his image by giving us the capacity for intelligence, love, freedom and conscience. By Baptism, our bodies are made temples of the Holy Spirit.

IMMACULATE CONCEPTION: A dogma of the Church that teaches that Mary was conceived without Original Sin due to the anticipated redemptive graces of her Son, Jesus.

IMMORTALITY: 'The Church teaches that every spiritual soul is created immediately by God – it is not "produced" by the parents – and also that it is immortal: it does not perish when it separates from the body at death and it will be united with the body at the final Resurrection' (CCC, no. 366).

INCARNATION: By the Incarnation, the Second Person of the Holy Trinity assumed our human nature, taking flesh in the womb of the Virgin Mary. There is one Person in Jesus and that is the divine Person of the Son of God. Jesus has two natures, a human one and a divine one.

INDEFECTIBILITY: The Lord Jesus ensures that his Church will remain until the Kingdom is fully achieved.

Indefectibility means that the Church does not and cannot depart from proclaiming the authentic Gospel without error in spite of the defects of her members.

INDISSOLUBILITY OF MARRIAGE: 'What God has united, human beings must not divide' (Mk 10:9). God's plan for marriage is a permanent covenant embraced by the spouses, hence the bond is indissoluble – not able to be dissolved (cf. CIC, can. 1055; CCEO, can. 776).

INDULGENCE: The remission of temporal punishment due to sin, granted to the faithful who recite specified prayers, visit a specified place of pilgrimage or engage in a specified act of charity; punishment is remitted through the power of the Church and in the mutual exchange of spiritual goods, particularly the merits of Christ and the saints.

INERRANCY: Because the authors of Sacred Scripture were inspired by God, the saving meaning or truth found in the Scriptures cannot be wrong. (See also 'Inspiration'.)

INFALLIBILITY: This is the gift of the Holy Spirit to the Church whereby the pastors of the Church – the pope, and bishops in communion with him – can definitively proclaim a doctrine of faith and morals, which is divinely revealed for the belief of the faithful. This gift flows from the grace

of the whole body of the faithful not to err in matters of faith and morals. The pope teaches infallibly when he declares that his teaching is ex cathedra (literally, 'from the throne'); that is, he teaches as supreme pastor of the Church.

INSPIRATION: This is the divine assistance given to the human authors of the books of Sacred Scripture. Guided by the Holy Spirit, the human authors made full use of their talents and abilities while, at the same time, writing the truth that God intended.

- J -

JEALOUSY: An attitude related to envy as well as greed; a jealous person is possessive of what one has or thinks one should have, as well as resentful toward others for what they have.

JESUS: The name given to the Son of God, the Second Person of the Trinity. This name, which means 'God Saves', was revealed to both the Blessed Virgin Mary and to St Joseph (cf. Lk 1:31; Mt 1:21).

JUST WAR: *Just War* is the term used for the proper use of military force to defend against an unjust aggressor. The strict conditions for engaging in a just war are known as the Just War Conditions. These conditions require that at one and the same time:

- The damage inflicted by the aggressor on the nation or

community of nations must be lasting, grave and certain;

- All other means of putting an end to it must have been shown to be impractical or ineffective;

- There must be serious prospects of success;

- The use of arms must not produce evils graver than the evil to be eliminated;

- The power of modern means of destruction weighs very heavily in evaluating this condition. These are the traditional elements in what is called the 'just war' doctrine;

- The evaluation of these conditions for moral legitimacy belongs to the prudential judgement of those who have responsibility for the common good (CCC, no. 2309).

JUSTICE: The Cardinal Virtue by which one is able to give God and neighbour what is due to them.

JUSTIFICATION: The term used to refer to the action of God by which we are freed from our sins and sanctified and renewed by the grace of God.

- K -

KINGDOM OF GOD: The actualisation of God's will for human beings proclaimed by Jesus Christ as a community of justice, peace, mercy and love, the seed of which is the Church on earth, and the fulfilment of which is in eternity.

- L -

LAITY: Members of the Church, distinguished from the clergy and those in consecrated life, who have been incorporated into the People of God through the Sacrament of Baptism.

LAST JUDGEMENT: The moment at the end of time when everyone will appear before Christ and receive an eternal recompense in accord with their earthly life.

LAW: A code of conduct established by a competent authority. Moral and civil law should all be based on divine law, whether it is natural or has been revealed by God.

LECTIO DIVINA: A manner of praying with Scripture; the person praying either reflectively reads a passage from Scripture or listens attentively to its being read, and then meditates on words or phrases that resonate.

LECTIONARY: The official liturgical book of the Church containing Scripture passages for use in the Liturgy of the Word.

LENT: This is an annual period of forty days beginning on Ash Wednesday, which is set aside for penance, fasting and almsgiving in preparation for the coming celebration of Easter. It is modelled in part on the forty days that Jesus spent in the desert prior to beginning his public ministry. The penance, fasting and almsgiving are meant to help lead the believer to ongoing conversion and a deeper faith in the Lord who redeemed us.

LITANY: Literally a list, such as in the list, or litany, of saints. In such a prayer, the name of the saints is spoken or sung and the congregation responds with a repeated invocation, 'Pray for us'. For example, in the Litany of Loreto, the list of qualities of the Virgin Mary are recited or sung, again with the response, 'Pray for us'.

LITURGICAL YEAR: The calendar that guides the liturgies and prayers of the Church. It commences on the First Sunday of Advent and ends with the celebration of Christ the King. It includes Advent, the Christmas Season, Lent, the Easter Season and Ordinary Time, as well as various Feasts of Mary, the Apostles and many other saints.

LITURGY: From the Greek, meaning 'public work'. It refers especially to the public worship of the Church, including the Mass and the Liturgy of the Hours. By their Baptism, all God's people are called to offer a sacrifice of praise to God at liturgy. The ordained priest at liturgy acts in the person of Christ, the Head of the Church, to make Christ's saving grace present by the power of the Holy Spirit.

LITURGY OF THE HOURS: The public daily prayer of the Church, which extends the praise given to God in the Eucharistic celebration.

LORD'S DAY, (THE): A name used synonymously for Sunday, the day of the Lord Jesus' Resurrection.

LORD'S PRAYER, (THE): Another name used for the prayer more commonly known as the Our Father. This prayer is sometimes called the Lord's Prayer because it is a prayer taught by Jesus to his Apostles and disciples.

LOVE: See 'Charity'.

LUST: One of the Capital Sins; it is an inordinate desire for earthly pleasures, particularly sexual pleasures.

- M -

MAGISTERIUM: The teaching office of the pope, and bishops in communion with him, guided by the Holy Spirit. The pope and bishops are the authoritative teachers in the Church.

MARKS OF THE CHURCH: The name given to four singular characteristics of the Church: the Church is one, holy, catholic and apostolic.

MARRIAGE, SACRAMENT OF: 'The matrimonial covenant by which a man and a woman establish between themselves a partnership of the whole of life, is by its nature ordered toward the good of the spouses and the procreation and education of offspring; this covenant between baptised persons has been raised by Christ the Lord to the dignity of a sacrament' (CCC, no. 1601, citing CIC, can. 1055 §1; cf. GS, no. 48 §1, CCEO, can. 776).

MARTYR: One who witnesses to Christ and the truth of the faith, even to the point of suffering.

MASS AS A SACRED MEAL: The Mass is a sacred banquet, like the Last Supper, in which bread and wine become Christ's Body and Blood, received in Holy Communion.

MASS AS A SACRIFICE: Through the ministry of the ordained priest, the Holy Spirit makes present at Mass Christ's Paschal mystery, his dying and rising in which Christ is offered to the Father to give him adoration and praise to save us from our sins and bring us divine life.

MATRIMONY: Another name for the Sacrament of Marriage.

MEDITATION: Prayer in which, in order to respond to the Lord, one tries to understand more fully or deeply God's Revelation of the truths of the faith.

MINISTERIAL PRIESTHOOD: This priesthood, received in the Sacrament of Holy Orders, differs in essence from the priesthood of the faithful. The ministerial priesthood serves the priesthood of the faithful by building up the Church in the name of Christ, who is head of the Body, by

offering prayers and sacrifices to God on behalf of people. A priest is given the power to consecrate the Eucharist, forgive sins and administer the other Sacraments, except Holy Orders.

MODESTY: A modest person dresses, speaks and acts in a manner that supports and encourages purity and chastity and not in a manner that would tempt or encourage sinful sexual behaviour.

MORALITY: In one sense, this is the goodness or evil of particular actions. For a Catholic, it also refers to the manner of life and action formed according to the teaching laid down by Christ Jesus and authoritatively interpreted by the Church.

MORTAL SIN: Mortal sin is when we consciously and freely choose to do something grave against the divine law and contrary to our final destiny. There are three conditions for a sin to be a mortal sin: grave matter, full knowledge and deliberate consent (freedom). Mortal sin destroys the loving relationship with God that we need for eternal happiness. If not repented, it results in a loss of love and God's grace and merits eternal punishment in hell, that is, exclusion from the Kingdom of God and thus eternal death.

MOTHER OF THE CHURCH: '[Mary] is clearly the mother of the members of Christ … since she has by her charity joined in bringing about the birth of believers in the Church, who are members of its head' (LG, no. 53; CCC, no. 963).

MOTHER OF GOD: Mary is truly the Mother of God since she is the mother of the Son of God made man. In the Eastern Churches, Mary is honoured as the *Theotokos*, or 'Birth-giver of God' (sometimes translated as 'God-bearer').

MYSTERY: The term has several complementary meanings. First, it reminds us that we can never exhaust God's divine and infinite meaning. Second, mystery tells us that God is 'wholly other' (not us), and yet so near that in him we live and move and have our being. Third, the union of the divine and human in Christ is so unique that we revere it as holy mystery. Fourth, mystery also applies to the celebration of the Sacraments in which God, Father, Son and Spirit, are present and active for our salvation.

- N -

NATURAL FAMILY PLANNING: A morally permissible system for the regulation of births, which employs the natural fertility patterns and can be used within certain conditions of marriage and family life. (See CCC, nos. 2366–2372.)

NATURAL LAW: The natural law is our rational apprehension of the created moral order, an ability we have due to our being made in God's image.

It expresses the dignity of the human person and forms the basis of our fundamental rights.

NEOPHYTYE: This term designates an adult who has been newly received into the Catholic Church.

NESTORIANISM: A significant heresy affecting early Christianity, founded by Nestorius (who died around AD 451) who believed Mary gave birth to the human Jesus, to whom the Son of God was united in some way. Hence Mary would not be the Mother of God. The Council of Ephesus repudiated Nestorius and proclaimed Mary as *Theotokos* – Birth-giver of God (sometimes translated as 'God-bearer').

NEW LAW: The title given to the manner of living and acting taught by Jesus. When we follow the New Law, we are maintaining our part of the covenant with God.

NEW TESTAMENT: The designation for the second part of the Bible; this part contains the four Gospels, the Acts of the Apostles, various Letters or Epistles and the Book of Revelation.

NICENE CREED: This creed resulted from the deliberations of the bishops at the Councils of Nicea (AD 325) and First Constantinople (AD 381). These Councils clarified and defended the ancient teachings of the Church about the humanity and divinity of Christ and the divinity of the Holy Spirit.

NOVENA: Nine days of prayer, usually invoking the intercession of the Virgin Mary or a saint. The novena traces its development to the scriptural nine days of prayer by Mary, the Apostles and disciples asking for the gift of the Holy Spirit after the Ascension of Jesus Christ into heaven.

- O -

OBEDIENCE OF FAITH: Faith is hearing the Word of God and resolving to obey what God is asking of us. Jesus said, 'Blessed … are those who hear the word of God and keep it' (Lk 11:28).

OIL OF THE CATECHUMENS: Oil blessed by the bishop during Holy Week to be used in preparing a candidate for the Sacrament of Baptism.

OIL OF THE SICK: Oil blessed by the bishop in Holy Week to be used for the Sacrament of Anointing of the Sick. In necessity, a priest may also bless this oil.

OLD LAW: The term refers to the Ten Commandments and the way a faithful Israelite was called to observe them; following this Law was the manner in which a believer held up their part of the old covenant with God.

OLD TESTAMENT: The first part of Sacred Scripture that contains the Pentateuch (the first five books), the Historical Books, Wisdom Literature and Prophetic Books. These come to us from the people of Ancient Israel before the coming of Christ. The books of the Old Testament were inspired by God.

ORDINARY TIME: The designation for the period during the Church's Liturgical Year that falls outside the times of Advent, Christmas, Lent and Easter.

ORIGINAL HOLINESS AND JUSTICE: The 'grace of original holiness was to share in divine life' (CCC, no. 375). 'The inner harmony of the human person, the harmony between man and woman and finally the harmony between the first couple and all creation, comprised the state called "original justice"' (CCC, no. 376).

ORIGINAL SIN: The personal sin of disobedience committed by the first human beings, resulting in the deprivation of original holiness and justice and the experience of suffering and death. It also describes the fallen state of all human beings, including the experience of concupiscence, ignorance of God and suffering and death.

- P -

PARACLETE: A name, given to the Holy Spirit by Jesus, which means adviser or consoler.

PASCHAL MYSTERY: In the Sacraments Jesus Christ enacts his Paschal Mystery. In speaking of the Paschal Mystery we present Christ's death and Resurrection as one, inseparable event. It is *paschal* because it is Christ's passing into death and passing over it into new life. It is a *mystery* because it is a visible sign of an invisible act of God.

PASSOVER: The name of the Jewish feast that celebrates the deliverance of Israel from Egypt and from the Angel of Death who passed over their doors marked by the blood of sacrificed lamb. Jesus Christ inaugurated the new Passover by delivering all people from death and sin through his own blood shed on the Cross. The celebration of the Eucharist is the Passover feast of the New Covenant.

PENANCE, SACRAMENT OF: Also called the Sacrament of Confession, Reconciliation, Conversion and Forgiveness, this is the Sacrament in which sins committed after Baptism are forgiven. It results in reconciliation with God and the Church.

PENTECOST: Celebrated each year fifty days after Easter, Pentecost marks the day when the Holy Spirit came upon the Apostles and disciples. The first Pentecost is sometimes referred to as the birthday of the Church because it was on this day that the Apostles, inspired by the Holy Spirit, first publicly preached the Good News to others.

PEOPLE OF GOD: God calls the Church into existence as his people centred in Christ and sustained by the Holy Spirit. The visible structure of the People of God as the Church is the means intended by Christ to help guarantee the life of grace for the whole.

PERPETUAL VIRGINITY: Mary was a virgin in conceiving Jesus, in giving birth to him, and in remaining always a virgin ever after.

POPE: The successor to St Peter who serves as the Bishop of Rome and as the visible and juridical head of the Catholic Church.

PRAGMATISM: A philosophy that asserts that acts have value only in terms of their usefulness and practicality.

PRAYER: The raising of one's mind and heart to God in thanksgiving and in praise of his glory. It can also include the requesting of good things from God. It is an act by which one enters into awareness of a loving communion with God. 'Prayer is the response of faith to the free promise of salvation and also a response of love to the thirst of the only Son of God' (CCC, no. 2561).

PRECEPTS OF THE CHURCH: Laws made by the Church that indicate basic requirements for her members.

PREJUDICE: Negative preconceived judgement of another; irrational suspicion or hatred of another because the person belongs to a particular race, religion or group.

PRESBYTER: A term referring to an ordained priest.

PRIDE: The Capital Sin that involves excessive self-esteem and a strong desire to be noticed and honoured by others; excessive pride sets one in opposition to God.

PRIEST: A baptised man ordained through the Sacrament of Holy Orders. 'Priests are united with the bishops in priestly dignity and at the same time depend on them in the exercise of their pastoral functions; they are called to be the bishops' prudent co-workers' (CCC, no. 1595). With the bishop, priests form a presbyteral (priestly) community and assume with him the pastoral mission for a particular parish. They serve God's People in the work of sanctification by their preaching, teaching and offering the Sacraments, especially the Eucharist and the forgiving of sins.

PRIESTHOOD OF THE FAITHFUL: Christ gives the faithful a share in his priesthood through the Sacraments of Baptism and Confirmation. This means that all baptised and confirmed members of the Church share in offering prayer and sacrifice to God. The priesthood of the faithful differs in essence from the ministerial priesthood.

PRIVATE REVELATIONS: These are revelations made in the course of history that do not add to or form part of the Deposit of Faith, but rather may help people live their faith more fully.

PROCREATIVE PURPOSE OF MARRIAGE: The aspect of marriage that requires that a married couple be open to the children that God may send them and resolve to raise them as true followers of Jesus Christ. The unitive and procreative aspects of marriage form an unbreakable bond.

PROVIDENCE: See 'Divine Providence'.

PRUDENCE: The Cardinal Virtue by which one knows the true good in every circumstance and chooses the right means to reach that end.

- R -

RCIA: The Rite of Christian Initiation of Adults. This is the title of the process designed to prepare adults for entrance into the Catholic Church by the reception of the Sacraments of Initiation.

REAL PRESENCE: When the bread is consecrated, it is changed into Christ's Body. When the wine is consecrated, it is changed into Christ's Blood. Jesus Christ is substantially present in a way that is entirely unique. This happens through the power of the Holy Spirit and the ministry of the priest or bishop acting in the person of Christ during the Eucharistic prayer.

REDEMPTION: The salvation won for us by Jesus. By his Incarnation, ministry, death and Resurrection, Jesus has freed us from original and actual sin and won eternal life for us.

REINCARNATION: The false belief that a dead person's spirit returns to life in another body either of an animal or another person. This belief is not compatible with the Catholic faith, which teaches that every human person has only one body and one soul, and is unique and unrepeatable.

RELATIVISM: The position that there is no objective truth, only subjective opinions.

RELIGION, VIRTUE OF: The habit of adoring God, praying to him, offering him the worship that belongs to him and fulfilling the promises and vows made to him are acts of the virtue of religion that fall under the obedience of the First Commandment.

RELIGIOUS OR CONSECRATED LIFE: A permanent state in life into which certain men or women freely commit themselves to a life of special service to Christ, marked by the profession of the evangelical counsels: poverty, chastity and obedience.

RESURRECTION: This is the triumph of Jesus over death on the third day after his crucifixion. Christ's risen body is real, but glorified, not restrained by space or time.

REVEALED LAW: There is revealed law as seen in the Old Testament when God communicated to Moses the Ten Commandments. This law prepared the world for the Gospel. Jesus revealed the full meaning of Old Testament law.

REVELATION: God's communication of himself and his loving plan to save us. This is a gift of self-communication, which is realised by deeds and words over time and most fully by his sending us his own divine Son, Jesus Christ. Public Revelation, which must be believed, ended with the death of the last Apostle. There can still be private revelation, which is intended only for the good of the person who receives it and does not need to be believed by others.

- S -

SABBATH: In Scripture, the Sabbath was the seventh day of the week that the people of Ancient Israel were to keep holy by praising God for the creation and the covenant and by resting from their ordinary work. For Christians, the observance of the Sabbath has been transferred to Sunday, the day of the Lord's Resurrection. (See also 'Sunday'.)

SACRAMENT: An efficacious sign of grace, instituted by Christ and entrusted to the Church, by which divine life is dispensed to us by the work of the Holy Spirit (CCC, nos. 1131, 774).

SACRAMENT OF SALVATION: By God's gracious plan, the Church is a sacrament of salvation, that is, a visible community in and through which Jesus Christ offers salvation through the Seven Sacraments, the preaching of the word and the spiritual and moral witness of the members.

SACRAMENTAL CHARACTER: An indelible spiritual mark that is the permanent effect of the Sacraments of Baptism, Confirmation and Holy Orders. It brings a new conformity to Christ and a specific standing in the Church. The reception of these Sacraments is never repeated (cf. CCC, Glossary).

SACRAMENTALS: These are sacred signs instituted by the Church and that bear a resemblance to the Sacraments. They signify effects, especially of a spiritual nature, that are obtained through the intercession of the Church (CCC, no. 1667).

SACRAMENTS OF HEALING: Designation given to the Sacrament of Penance and Reconciliation and the Sacrament of the Anointing of the Sick.

SACRAMENTS OF INITIATION: Designation given to those Sacraments that bring a person into membership in the Church – Baptism, Confirmation and the Holy Eucharist.

SACRAMENTS AT THE SERVICE OF COMMUNION: The term *communion* refers to the Community of the Church. Holy Orders and Matrimony are the Sacraments at the Service of Communion (the community of the Church). This means they are primarily directed toward the salvation of others. If they benefit the personal salvation of the ordained or married person, it is through service to others that this happens.

SACRIFICE: A ritual offering made to God by a priest on behalf of the people as a sign of adoration, gratitude, supplication, penance and/or communion.

SAINT: A person who, after having lived a life of virtue, dies in the state of grace and has been granted the reward of eternal life by God. The saints enjoy the beatific vision and unceasingly intercede for those still in earthly life. They also serve as a model and inspiration to us. (See also 'Canonisation'.)

SANCTIFYING GRACE: See 'Grace'.

SATISFACTION: An act by which a sinner makes amends for sin. The penance received from the priest in Confession is a form of satisfaction. All real satisfaction for sin needs to be a participation in the satisfaction for sin won for us by Christ.

SCRIPTURE (BIBLE): The books that contain the truth of God's revelation and that were composed by human authors, inspired by the Holy Spirit and recognised by the Church.

SCRUTINIES: During three Sundays of Lent, those preparing for entrance into the Church are led through prayerful reflections designed to help them turn from sin and grow in holiness.

SENSES OF SCRIPTURE: Tradition notes that there are two senses or aspects of Scripture – the literal and the spiritual. The literal meaning is that meaning conveyed by the words of Scripture and discovered by exegesis following rules of sound interpretation. The spiritual meaning points to realities beyond the words themselves and is subdivided into three categories. These categories are:

- *Allegorical* – This recognises the significance of the Scriptures in Christ, that is, the way in which images in Scripture serve as a type or foreshadowing of Christ and his actions.

- *Anagogical* – This views realities and events in Scripture in terms of their eternal significance.

- *Moral* – What is read in Scripture inspires or motivates one to live justly (cf. CCC, nos. 115–117).

SIN: Sin is an offence against God as well as against reason, truth and right conscience; it is a failure in genuine love for God and neighbour caused by a perverse attachment to certain goods. It wounds the nature of man and injures human solidarity. It has been defined as 'an utterance, a deed or a desire contrary to the eternal law' (CCC, no. 1849).

SLOTH: One of the Capital Sins; it involves a lack of effort in meeting duties and responsibilities to God, to others and to oneself.

SOCIAL JUSTICE: Society ensures social justice by providing the conditions that allow associations and individuals to obtain their due (CCC, no. 1943). Social justice deals with the essential needs of people if they are to live together in community with respect for each other's dignity. These needs include food, clothing and shelter and an income that supports the family.

SOCIAL SIN: Sins that produce unjust social laws and oppressive institutions. They are social situations and institutions contrary to divine goodness. Sometimes called 'structures of sin' they are the expression and effect of personal sins. They lead the victims to do evil. In a certain sense, they constitute a social sin (CCC, no. 1869).

SOCIAL TEACHINGS OF THE CHURCH: While the Church from New Testament times has always been concerned about the social needs of the orphan, widow, alien and other helpless people, she began to develop an explicit social doctrine to respond to the social problems that have arisen because of the industrial and technological revolutions. These teachings are found in papal encyclicals beginning with Pope Leo XIII's 1891 encyclical *On Capital and Labour* (*Rerum Novarum*) to those of the present. They are also contained in conciliar and episcopal documents.

SOLIDARITY: 'The principle of solidarity, also articulated in terms of "friendship" or "social charity", is a direct demand of human and Christian brotherhood' (CCC, no. 1939). This involves a love for all peoples that transcends national, racial, ethnic, economic and ideological differences. It respects the needs of others and the common good in an interdependent world.

SOUL: The immortal spiritual part of a person; the soul does not die with the body at death, and it is reunited with the body in the final resurrection.

SPIRITUAL WORKS OF MERCY: These are actions that help our neighbour in their spiritual needs. They include counselling the doubtful, instructing the ignorant, admonishing the sinner, comforting the sorrowful, forgiving injuries, bearing wrongs patiently and praying for the living and the dead.

STATE OF GRACE: A condition in which our sins have been forgiven and we are reconciled with God, though purification from sin's effects may still be needed. A person is first in a state of grace, sharing in God's life, following Baptism. If a person falls out of that state, he or she can be subsequently reconciled to God, especially through the Sacrament of Penance.

SUBSIDIARITY: 'A community of a higher order should not interfere in the internal life of a community of a lower order, depriving the latter of its functions, but rather should support it in case of need and help it to coordinate its activity with the activities of the rest of society, always with a view to the common good' (CCC, no. 1883).

SUNDAY: Christians celebrate Sunday because it is the day of the Lord's Resurrection and the beginning of the new creation. Catholics are obliged to participate in the celebration of the Eucharist on Sundays and to devote the remainder of the day to rest, relaxation, spiritual reflection and activities that are consonant with this.

- T -

TABERNACLE: A noble repository located in a prominent place in a Catholic church in which unconsumed hosts that have become the Body of Christ are reserved for later use as well as a focus for adoration and prayer.

TEMPERANCE: The Cardinal Virtue by which one moderates the desire for the attainment of and pleasure in earthly goods.

TEMPLE OF THE HOLY SPIRIT: The Holy Spirit dwells in the Church in each member, providing the gifts and fruits that make the Church's members holy.

TEN COMMANDMENTS: Laws guiding human actions given to Moses by God on Mount Sinai.

THEOLOGICAL VIRTUES: The Theological Virtues are faith, hope and charity. They call us to believe in God, hope in him and love him. The Theological Virtues relate directly to the living God.

THEOLOGY: Theology is the reflective study of Revelation as found in the Scripture, in Apostolic Tradition and in Church teaching.

TRADITION: The living transmission of the message of the Gospel in the Church, flowing from the oral preaching of the Apostles and the written message of salvation under the inspiration of the Holy Spirit (Scripture). Tradition is preserved and handed on as the Deposit of Faith under the guidance of the bishops, successors to the Apostles.

TRANSUBSTANTIATION: A term used to describe the unique change of bread and wine into the Body and Blood of Christ. By the consecration, the substance of bread and wine is changed into the substance of Christ's Body and Blood.

TRIDUUM: In the Church's liturgical calendar, these are the three days that follow the conclusion of Lent. The Triduum begins with the Mass of the Lord's Supper on Holy Thursday and concludes with the celebration of Evening Prayer on Easter Sunday.

TRINITY: One God in three Persons – Father, Son, Holy Spirit.

TRUTH: Reality and authenticity according to God's design. Through God's revelation, truth is found in Apostolic Tradition, in Scripture and in the Magisterium of the Church guided by the Holy Spirit. In the human order, truth is discovered by the light of reason and reinforced by love of truth and truthful behaviour.

- U -

UNITIVE PURPOSE OF MARRIAGE: The aspect of marriage that requires that it be a lifelong union. God willed that husband and wife be united in a permanent communion of love. Their communion reflects and is strengthened by the Trinity's communion of love.

- V -

VENIAL SIN: A venial sin is an offence against God in a less serious matter. Though venial sin does not completely destroy the love we need for eternal happiness, it weakens that love and impedes our progress in the practice of virtue and the moral good. Over time, repeated venial sin can have serious consequences.

VIATICUM: The Holy Eucharist when received by a dying person as the spiritual food for one's passing from this world to the Father.

VICE: Vice is the habitual practise of repeated sin.

VIRTUE: 'Virtue is a habitual and firm disposition to do good ... The human virtues are stable dispositions of the intellect and will that govern our acts, order our passions and guide our conduct in accordance with reason and faith. They can be grouped around the four cardinal virtues: prudence, justice, fortitude and temperance ... There are three theological virtues: faith, hope and charity. They inform all the moral virtues and give them life (CCC, nos. 1833, 1834, 1841).

VOCATION: The term given to the call to each person from God; everyone has been called to holiness and eternal life, especially in Baptism. Each person can also be called more specifically to the priesthood or to religious life, to married life and to single life, as well as to a particular profession or service.

APPENDIX B
TRADITIONAL
CATHOLIC PRAYERS

Sign of the Cross

In the name of the Father
and of the Son
and of the Holy Spirit. Amen.

Comhartha na Croise

In ainm an Athar, agus an Mhic,
agus an Spioraid Naoimh. Áiméan.

Our Father

Our Father who art in heaven,
hallowed be thy name.
Thy kingdom come.
Thy will be done on earth, as it is in
    heaven.
Give us this day our daily bread,
and forgive us our trespasses,
as we forgive those who trespass against
    us,
and lead us not into temptation,
but deliver us from evil. Amen.

An Phaidir

Ár nAthair atá ar neamh,
Go naofar d'ainm,
Go dtaga do ríocht,
Go ndéantar do thoil ar an talamh
Mar a dhéantar ar neamh.
Ár n-arán laethúil tabhair dúinn inniu,
Agus maith dúinn ár bhfiacha,
Mar a mhaithimidne dár bhféichiúna
    féin,
Agus ná lig sinn i gcathú,
Ach saor sinn ó olc. Áiméan.

Hail Mary

Hail Mary, full of grace,
the Lord is with thee.
Blessed art thou among women
and blessed is the fruit of thy womb,
    Jesus.
Holy Mary, Mother of God,
pray for us sinners,
now and at the hour of our death.
    Amen.

'S é do Bheatha, a Mhuire

'S é do bheatha, a Mhuire,
Atá lán de ghrásta,
Tá an Tiarna leat.
Is beannaithe thú idir mhná,
Agus is beannaithe toradh do bhroinne,
    Íosa.
A Naomh Mhuire, a mháthair Dé,
Guigh orainn, na peacaigh,
Anois agus ar uair ár mbáis. Áiméan.

Glory Be (Doxology)

Glory be to the Father
and to the Son
and to the Holy Spirit,
as it was in the beginning
is now, and ever shall be
world without end. Amen.

– Traditional wording

Glóir don Athair

Glóir don Athair,
Agus don Mhac,
Agus don Spiorad Naomh.
Mar a bhí ó thús,
Mar atá anois,
Mar a bheas go brách,
Le saol na saol. Áiméan.

Glory to the Father, and to the Son,
and to the Holy Spirit.
As it was in the beginning, is now,
and will be forever. Amen.

– wording as found in the
Liturgy of the Hours

The Apostles' Creed

I believe in God,
the Father almighty,
Creator of heaven and earth,
and in Jesus Christ, his only Son, our
    Lord,

who was conceived by the Holy Spirit,
born of the Virgin Mary,
suffered under Pontius Pilate,
was crucified, died and was buried;
he descended into hell;
on the third day he rose again from the
    dead;
he ascended into heaven,
and is seated at the right hand of God
    the Father almighty;
from there he will come to judge the
    living and the dead.

I believe in the Holy Spirit,
the holy catholic Church,
the communion of saints,
the forgiveness of sins,
the resurrection of the body,
and life everlasting. Amen.

Cré na nAspal

Creidim i nDia,
an tAthair uilechumhachtach,
    Cruthaitheoir neimhe agus talún,
agus in Íosa Críost, a Aon-Mhacsan,
ár dTiarna,
a gabhadh ón Spiorad Naomh,
a rugadh ó Mhuire Ógh,
a d'fhulaing páis faoi Phointias Píoláit,
a céasadh ar an gcros, a fuair bás agus a
    adhlacadh,
a chuaigh síos go hifreann,
a d'éirigh an treas lá ó mhairbh,
a chuaigh suas ar neamh,
atá ina shuí ar dheis Dé an tAthair
    uilechumhachtach;
as sin tiocfaidh sé chun breithiúnas a
    thabhairt ar bheo agus ar mhairbh.

Creidim sa Spiorad Naomh,
sa Naomh-Eaglais Chaitliceach,
i gcomaoin na naomh,
i maithiúnas na bpeacaí,
in aiséirí na colainne,
agus sa bheatha shíoraí. Áiméan.

The Nicene Creed

I believe in one God,
the Father almighty,
maker of heaven and earth,
of all things visible and invisible.

I believe in one Lord Jesus Christ,
the Only Begotten Son of God,
born of the Father before all ages.
God from God, Light from Light,
true God from true God,
begotten, not made, consubstantial with
    the Father;
through him all things were made.
For us men and for our salvation
he came down from heaven,

and by the Holy Spirit was incarnate of
the Virgin Mary,
and became man.

For our sake he was crucified under
Pontius Pilate,
he suffered death and was buried,
and rose again on the third day
in accordance with the Scriptures.
He ascended into heaven
and is seated at the right hand of the
Father.

He will come again in glory
to judge the living and the dead
and his kingdom will have no end.

I believe in the Holy Spirit, the Lord, the
giver of life,
who proceeds from the Father and the
Son,
who with the Father and the Son is
adored and glorified,
who has spoken through the prophets.

I believe in one, holy, catholic and
apostolic Church.
I confess one Baptism for the forgiveness
of sins
and I look forward to the resurrection of
the dead
and the life of the world to come. Amen.

An Chré Nicea-Constaintínópail

Creidim in aon Dia amháin,
an tAthair uilechumhachtach,
a rinne neamh agus talamh,
agus an uile ní sofheicthe agus
dofheicthe.

Agus in aon Tiarna amháin Íosa Críost,
Mac Aonghine Dé,
an té a rugadh ón Athair
sula raibh aon saol ann,

Dia ó Dhia, solas ó sholas,
Fíor-Dhia ó Fhíor-Dhia;
an té a gineadh agus nach ndearnadh,
agus atá de chomhshubstaint leis an
Athair:
is tríd a rinneadh an uile ní.
Ar ár son-na, an cine daonna, agus ar son
ár slánaithe,
thuirling sé ó neamh.
Ionchollaíodh le cumhacht an Spioraid
Naoimh é
i mbroinn na Maighdine Muire
agus ghlac sé nádúr daonna.

Céasadh ar an gcros é freisin ar ár son
faoi Phointias Píoláit;
d'fhulaing sé páis, agus adhlacadh é.
D'aiséirigh an treas lá de réir mar a
d'fhógair na Scrioptúir;
chuaigh suas ar neamh; tá ina shuí ar
dheis an Athar.

Tiocfaidh sé an athuair faoi ghlóir,
le breithiúnas a thabhairt ar bheo agus ar
mhairbh,
agus ní bheidh deireadh lena ríocht.

Creidim sa Spiorad Naomh,
Tiarna agus bronntóir na beatha,
an té a ghluaiseann ón Athair agus ón
Mac.
Tugtar dó adhradh agus glóir,
mar aon leis an Athair agus leis an Mac:
is é a labhair trí na fáithe.

Creidim san aon Eaglais, naofa,
chaitliceach, aspalda.
Admhaím an t-aon bhaisteadh amháin
chun maithiúnas na bpeacaí.
Agus táim ag súil le haiséirí na marbh,
agus le beatha an tsaoil atá le teacht.
Áiméan.

Morning Offering

O Jesus, through the Immaculate Heart
of Mary,

I offer you my prayers, works, joys and
suffering of this day

for all the intentions of your Sacred
Heart,

in union with the Holy Sacrifice of the
Mass throughout the world,

for the salvation of souls, the reparation
for sins, the reunion of all Christians,

and in particular for the intentions of
the Holy Father this month. Amen.

Act of Faith

O my God,

I believe in you

And in all that your holy Church teaches

Because you have said it

And your Word is true.

You are the Christ, the Son of the living
God.

You are my Lord and my God.

Lord, I believe; increase my faith.

Gníomh Creidimh

A Dhia liom,

Creidim ionat

agus i ngach a mhúineann d'Eaglais
Naofa

mar gur tusa a dúirt

agus go bhfuil do Bhriathar fíor.

Is tusa an Críost, Mac Dé beo.

Is tú mo Thiarna agus mo Dhia.

A Dhia, creidim, méadaigh ar mo
chreideamh.

Act of Hope

O my God,

I put my hope in you

Because I am sure of your promises.

Deliver us, Lord, from every evil

And grant us peace in our day,

As we wait in joyful hope

For the coming of our Saviour, Jesus
Christ.

Gníomh Dóchais

Cuirim mo dhóchas ionat

mar táim cinnte de do ghealltanais

Saor sinn, a Thiarna, ó gach olc.

Tabhair dúinn síocháin lenár linn,

agus sinn ag súil go lúcháireach

le teacht ár slánaitheora, Íosa Críost.

Act of Love

O my God,

I love you with all my heart,

With all my soul, and with all my
strength.

Lord, increase our love.

Help us to love one another.

Gníomh Grá

A Dhia liom,

Gráim thú ó mo chroí go hiomlán,

Ó m'anam go hiomlán, agus le mo neart
iomlán.

A Thiarna, méadaigh ár ngrá.

Cabhraigh linn chun grá a thabhairt dá
chéile.

An Act of Spiritual Communion

My Jesus, I believe that you are present
in the Most Blessed Sacrament.

I love you above all things, and I desire
to receive you into my soul.

Since I cannot at this moment receive
you sacramentally, come at least
spiritually into my heart.

I embrace you as if you were already
there and unite myself wholly to you.

Never permit me to be separated from
you. Amen.

Prayer to the Holy Spirit

V. Come, Holy Spirit, fill the hearts of your faithful.

R. And kindle in them the fire of your love.

V. Send forth your Spirit and they shall be created.

R. And you shall renew the face of the earth.

Let us pray:

O God, who has taught the hearts of the faithful by the light of the Holy Spirit, grant us in the same Spirit to be truly wise, and ever to rejoice in his consolation, through Christ, Our Lord. Amen.

Prayer at Stations of the Cross

We adore you, O Christ, and we praise you,

because by your holy Cross you have redeemed the world.

Hail, Holy Queen

Hail, Holy Queen, Mother of Mercy,
hail our life, our sweetness and our hope.
To thee do we cry,
poor banished children of Eve.
To thee do we send up our sighs,
mourning and weeping in this valley of tears.
Turn then, most gracious advocate,
thine eyes of mercy toward us,
and after this exile
show unto us the blessed fruit of thy womb, Jesus.
O clement, O loving,
O sweet Virgin Mary.
Pray for us, O Holy Mother of God,
that we may be made worthy of the promises of Christ.

Memorare

Remember, O most gracious Virgin Mary, that never was it known that anyone who fled to thy protection, implored thy help, or sought thy intercession, was left unaided. Inspired by this confidence I fly unto thee, O Virgin of virgins, my Mother. To thee do I come, before thee I stand, sinful and sorrowful. O Mother of the Word Incarnate, despise not my petitions, but in thy mercy hear and answer me. Amen.

Angelus

V. The Angel of the Lord declared unto Mary.

R. And she conceived of the Holy Spirit.

Hail, Mary, full of grace,
the Lord is with thee.
Blessed art thou among women
and blessed is the fruit of thy womb, Jesus.
Holy Mary, Mother of God,
pray for us sinners,
now and at the hour of our death.
Amen.

V. Behold the handmaid of the Lord.

R. Be it done unto me according to thy word.

Hail Mary…

V. And the Word was made flesh.

R. And dwelt among us.

Hail Mary…

V. Pray for us, O holy Mother of God.

R. That we may be made worthy of the promises of Christ.

Let us pray:

Pour forth, we beseech thee, O Lord, thy grace into our hearts; that we, to whom the Incarnation of Christ, thy Son, was made known by the message of an angel, may by his Passion and Cross be brought to the glory of his Resurrection. Through the same Christ, our Lord. Amen.

Queen of Heaven *(Regina Caeli)*

Queen of heaven, rejoice, alleluia.
The Son whom you merited to bear,
   alleluia,
has risen as he said, alleluia.
Pray for us to God, alleluia.
Rejoice and be glad, O Virgin Mary,
   alleluia!
For the Lord has truly risen, alleluia.

Let us pray:

O God, who through the resurrection of your Son, our Lord Jesus Christ, did vouchsafe to give joy to the world; grant, we beseech you, that through his Mother, the Virgin Mary, we may obtain the joys of everlasting life. Through the same Christ our Lord. Amen.

Jesus Prayer

Lord Jesus Christ, Son of the living God, have mercy on me, a sinner.

Act of Contrition

O my God, I am heartily sorry for having offended Thee; and I detest all my sins above every other evil, because they displease Thee. O my God, Who for Thine infinite goodness art so deserving of all my love; and I firmly resolve, with the help of thy grace never more to offend Thee, and to amend my life. Amen.

– Traditional version

Act of Contrition (or Prayer of the Penitent)

My God,
I am sorry for my sins with all my heart.
In choosing to do wrong
and failing to do good,
I have sinned against you
whom I should love above all things.
I firmly intend, with your help,
to do penance,
to sin no more,
and to avoid whatever leads me to sin.
Our Saviour Jesus Christ suffered and
   died for us.
In his name, my God, have mercy.

– Alternate version from the Rite of Penance

Act of Contrition (or Prayer of the Penitent)

Lord Jesus, Son of God
have mercy on me, a sinner.

– Alternate version from the Rite of Penance

Act of Contrition

O my God, I thank you for loving me.
I am sorry for all my sins.
For not loving others, and not loving
   you.
Help me to live like Jesus and not sin
   again. Amen.

Grace Before Meals

Bless us, O Lord, and these thy gifts,
which of thy bounty we are about to
receive, through Christ our Lord. Amen.

– Traditional version

Grace Before Meals

Bless us, O God, as we sit together.
Bless the food we eat today.
Bless the hands that made the food.
Bless us, O God. Amen.

– Modern version

Altú roimh Bhia
Beannacht ó Dhia orainne atá ag suí
chun boird le chéile.
Beannacht ar an mbia a ithimid inniu.
Beannacht ar na lámha a d'ullmhaigh
dúinn é.
Beannacht, a Dhia dhílis, orainn féin.
Áiméan.

Grace After Meals
We give thee thanks, Almighty God,
for all thy benefits;
who lives and reigns,
world without end. Amen.

– Traditional version

Grace After Meals
Thank you, God, for the food we have
eaten.
Thank you, God, for all our friends.
Thank you, God for everything.
Thank you, God. Amen.

– Modern version

Altú tar éis Bhia
Go raibh maith agat, a Dhia, mar is tú a
thug bia dúinn.
Go raibh maith agat, a Dhia, mar is tú a
thug cairde dúinn.
Go raibh maith agat, a Dhia, mar is tú a
thug gach rud dúinn.
Go raibh maith agat, a Dhia. Áiméan.

The Divine Praises
Blessed be God.
Blessed be his holy Name.
Blessed be Jesus Christ, true God and
true Man.
Blessed be the name of Jesus.
Blessed be his most Sacred Heart.
Blessed be his most Precious Blood.
Blessed be Jesus in the most holy
Sacrament of the altar.

Blessed be the Holy Spirit, the Paraclete.
Blessed be the great Mother of God,
Mary most holy.
Blessed be her holy and Immaculate
Conception.
Blessed be her glorious Assumption.
Blessed be the name of Mary, Virgin and
Mother.
Blessed be Saint Joseph, her most chaste
spouse.
Blessed be God in his angels and in his
saints.

Anima Christi
Soul of Christ, be my sanctification.
Body of Christ, be my salvation.
Blood of Christ, fill all my veins.
Water of Christ's side, wash out my stains.
Passion of Christ, my comfort be.
O good Jesu, listen to me.
In Thy wounds I fain would hide,
N'er to be parted from Thy side,
Guard me, should the foe assail me.
Call me when my life shall fail me.
Bid me come to Thee above,
With Thy saints to sing Thy love,
World without end. Amen.

– Blessed John Henry Newman

Anima Christi
Soul of Christ, sanctify me.
Body of Christ, save me.
Blood of Christ, inebriate me.
Water from the side of Christ, wash me.
Passion of Christ, strengthen me.
O good Jesus, hear me.
Permit me not to be separated from thee.
From my malignant enemy, defend me.
In the hour of my death, call me.
And bid me come to Thee.
That with thy saints
I will praise thee for ever and ever. Amen.

– Traditional poetic translation

Prayer for Peace

Lord, make me an instrument of your
    peace.
Where there is hatred, let me sow love;
    where there is injury, pardon;
where there is doubt, faith; where there
    is despair, hope;
where there is darkness, light; and where
    there is sadness, joy.
Grant that I may not so much seek to be
    consoled as to console,
to be understood as to understand, to be
    loved as to love;
for it is in giving that we receive, it is in
    pardoning that we are pardoned,
And it is in dying that we are born to
    eternal life.

– St Francis of Assisi

Prayer for the Souls in Purgatory

Eternal rest grant unto them, O Lord,
    and let perpetual light shine upon
    them.
May the souls of all the faithful
    departed, through the mercy of God,
    rest in peace. Amen.

Prayer to St Michael the Archangel

St Michael the Archangel, defend us in
    battle,
be our protection against the wickedness
    and snares of the Devil.
May God rebuke him, we humbly pray.
And do thou, O Prince of the Heavenly
    Host, by the Power of God,
thrust into hell Satan and all evil spirits
    who wander the earth seeking the
    ruin of souls. Amen.

Prayer to One's Guardian Angel

Angel of God, my guardian dear,
to whom God's love commits me here,
ever this day be at my side,
to light and guard, to rule and guide.
    Amen.

How to Pray the Rosary

Make the Sign of the Cross. Holding the Crucifix, say the Apostles' Creed.

On the first bead, say an Our Father.

Say three Hail Marys on each of the next three beads. Say the Glory Be.

Go to the main part of the rosary. For each of the five decades, announce the Mystery, then say the Our Father. While fingering each of the ten beads of the decade, next say ten Hail Marys while meditating on the Mystery. Then say a Glory Be.

(After finishing each decade, some say the following prayer requested by the Blessed Virgin Mary at Fatima: 'O my Jesus, forgive us our sins, save us from the fires of hell, lead all souls to Heaven, especially those who have most need of your mercy.')

After saying the five decades, say the Hail, Holy Queen, followed by this dialogue and prayer:

V. Pray for us, O holy Mother of God.

R. That we may be made worthy of the promises of Christ.

Let us pray:

O God, whose only-begotten Son, by his life, death and resurrection, has purchased for us the rewards of eternal life, grant, we beseech thee, that meditating on these mysteries of the most holy Rosary of the Blessed Virgin Mary, we may imitate what they contain and obtain what they promise, through the same Christ our Lord. Amen.

Mysteries of the Rosary

Joyful Mysteries

1. The Annunciation
2. The Visitation
3. The Nativity
4. The Presentation in the Temple
5. The Finding of the Child Jesus after Three Days in the Temple

Luminous Mysteries

1 The Baptism at the Jordan
2. The Miracle at Cana
3. The Proclamation of the Kingdom and the Call to Conversion
4. The Transfiguration
5. The Institution of the Eucharist

Sorrowful Mysteries

1. The Agony in the Garden
2. The Scourging at the Pillar
3. The Crowning with Thorns
4. The Carrying of the Cross
5. The Crucifixion and Death

Glorious Mysteries

1. The Resurrection
2. The Ascension
3. The Descent of the Holy Spirit at Pentecost
4. The Assumption of Mary
5. The Crowning of the Blessed Virgin as Queen of Heaven and Earth

APPENDIX C
FOR FURTHER READING

The Irish Catholic Catechism for Adults *draws from these resources:*

Reference/Foundational Texts

Catechism of the Catholic Church © 1994, Libreria Editrice Vaticana (Dublin: Veritas, 1994).

Code of Canon Law (Codex Iuris Canonici): New English Translation. Washington, DC: Canon Law Society of America, 1998.

Code of Canons of the Eastern Churches (Codex Canonum Ecclesiarum Orientalium): New English Translation. Washington, DC: Canon Law Society of America, 2001.

Papal Documents

Unless otherwise noted, these and other papal documents may be found on the website of the Vatican in multiple languages: *www.vatican.va.*

Saint John XXIII

Encyclical *Peace on Earth* (*Pacem in Terris*). 11 April 1963.

Pope Paul VI

Apostolic Exhortation *On Evangelization in the Modern World* (*Evangelii Nuntiandi*). 8 December 1975.

Encyclical *On the Holy Eucharist* (*Mysterium Fidei*). 3 September 1965.

Encyclical *On the Regulation of Birth* (*Humanae Vitae*). 25 July 1968.

Saint John Paul II

Apostolic Letter *At the Close of the Great Jubilee of the Year 2000* (*Novo Millennio Ineunte*). 6 January 2001.

Apostolic Exhortation *The Church in America* (*Ecclesia in America*). 22 January 1999.

Encyclical *The Gospel of Life* (*Evangelium Vitae*). 25 March 1995.

Apostolic Exhortation *I Will Give You Shepherds* (*Pastores Dabo Vobis*). 25 March 1992.

Apostolic Letter *On the Coming of the Third Millennium* (*Tertio Millennio Adveniente*). 10 November 1994.

Encyclical *On Commitment to Ecumenism* (*Ut Unum Sint*). May 1995.

Apostolic Letter *On the Dignity and Vocation of Women* (*Mulieris Dignitatem*). 15 August 1988.

Encyclical *On the Eucharist* (*Ecclesia de Eucharistia*). 17 April 2003.

Apostolic Letter *On Keeping the Lord's Day Holy* (*Dies Domini*). 31 May 1998.

Apostolic Letter *On the Most Holy Rosary* (*Rosarium Virginis Mariae*). 16 October 2002.

Apostolic Letter *On Reserving Priestly Ordination to Men Alone* (*Ordinatio Sacerdotalis*). 22 May 1994.

Apostolic Exhortation *On the Role of the Christian Family in the Modern World* (*Familiaris Consortio*). 22 November 1981.

Second Vatican Council Documents

A number of translations are available for documents from the Second Vatican Council. Unless otherwise noted, this book has consulted the translation of Austin Flannery OP, *Vatican Council II: Volume 1: The Conciliar and Post Conciliar Documents*, new rev. ed. (Northport, NY: Costello Publishing, 1996).

Constitution on the Sacred Liturgy (*Sacrosanctum Concilium*). 4 December 1963.

Declaration on the Relation of the Church to Non-Christian Religions (*Nostra Aetate*). 28 October 1965.

Declaration on Religious Liberty (*Dignitatis Humanae*). 7 December 1965.

Decree on the Church's Missionary Activity (*Ad Gentes Divinitus*). 7 December 1965.

Decree on Ecumenism (*Unitatis Redintegratio*). 21 November 1964.

Decree on Priestly Life and Ministry (*Presbyterorum Ordinis*). 7 December 1965.

Dogmatic Constitution on the Church (*Lumen Gentium*). 21 November 1964.

Dogmatic Constitution on Divine Revelation (*Dei Verbum*). 18 November 1965.

Pastoral Constitution on the Church in the Modern World (*Gaudium et Spes*). 7 December 1965.

Holy See Documents

Unless otherwise noted, these and other documents of the Holy See may be found on the website of the Vatican in multiple languages: *www.vatican.va*.

Declaration on the Admission of Women to the Ministerial Priesthood (*Inter Insigniores*). 1976. From the Sacred Congregation for the Doctrine of the Faith.

Instruction on Christian Freedom and Liberation. 1986. From the Congregation for the Doctrine of the Faith.

Instruction on Respect for Human Life in its Origin and on the Dignity of Procreation. 1987. From the Congregation for the Doctrine of the Faith.

Irish Episcopal Conference Documents, Statements and Letters

Share the Good News: National Directory for Catechesis in Ireland. 2010. From the Irish Episcopal Conference.

Letters and statements of the Irish Episcopal Conference can be found on the conference website: *www.catholicbishops.ie*.

ACKNOWLEDGEMENTS

Images used with permission.

Monks at work, p. 3, © Photos.com.
Moses, p. 13, drawings by Gustave Doré © shutterstock.com.
St John XXIII, p. 23, © Solodov Alexey/shutterstock.com.
John Henry Newman, p. 37, © thinkstock.com.
Photo of Nicholas Callan, p. 55, © the Maynooth College Collection.
St Vincent de Paul, p. 73, © shutterstock.com.
Mother Mary Martin, p. 85, © MMM Image Library.
Hospice image, p. 165, © shutterstock.com.
St Patrick, p. 183, © istockphoto.com.
Holy Faith Sisters logo, p. 221 © Holy Faith Sisters.
L'Arche logo, p. 233, © L'Arche community
St Augustine, p. 261, © shutterstock.com.
St John Paul II, p. 279, © Knock Shrine Publications.
Fr Patrick Peyton, p. 327, © Holy Cross Family Ministries.
Evie Hone, p. 375, © The Irish Times.
Job, p. 387, engraving by Gustave Doré © istockphoto.com.
Blessed Luigi and Maria Quattrocchi, p. 411; courtesy of Catholic News Service.
Pope Paul VI, p. 441 © istockphoto.com.
St Columba with cloak and shepherd's crook in a stained glass window in St Margaret's Chapel, Edinburgh Castle, p. 469 © shutterstock.com.
St Maria Goretti, p. 481 © Zvonimir Atletic/shutterstock.com.
Praying hands, p. 525 © Jesus Cervantes/shutterstock.com.

Scripture texts used in this work are taken from the *New Jerusalem Bible*, copyright © 1985 and 1990, Darton Longman & Todd Ltd, and are used by permission of the copyright owner. All rights reserved.

The following texts are acknowledged as source material for a number of the biographies in this work:

Various: James McGuire and James Quinn (eds), *Dictionary of Irish Biography*, 9 Volumes (Cambridge: Cambridge University Press, 2009).

John Henry Newman: L. MacRedmond, *Thrown Among Strangers: John Henry Newman in Ireland* (Dublin: Veritas, 1990).

Nicholas Callan: P. J. McLaughlin, *Nicholas Callan: Priest-Scientist (1799–1864)* (Dublin: Clonmore & Reynolds, 1965); W. Reville, 'Nicholas Callan', *The Irish Times*, 21 February 2002.

Bishop Joseph Shanahan/Mother Mary Martin: M. Kearney, *They Brought the Good News* (Dublin: Veritas, 1980).

Matt Talbot: T. J. Craughwell, *Saints Behaving Badly* (NY: Doubleday, 2006); M. Purcell, *Matt Talbot and His Times* (Dublin: Gill, 1955).

Nano Nagle: T. J. Walsh, *Nano Nagle and the Presentation Sisters* (Presentation Sisters, Monasterevin, 1959).

Edel Quinn: M. Kearney, *They Brought the Good News* (Dublin: Veritas, 1980).

Knock: Knock Shrine website, http://www.knock-shrine.ie/ (accessed 31 October 2012); Catholic Encyclopedia, www.newadvent.org/cathen (accessed 15 August 2011); T. Lane, *Reflecting on Knock: Before Our Merciful Lamb* (Dublin: Columba, 2007).

Christian Hospice Story: Irish Hospice Foundation website, http://hospicefoundation.ie/ (accessed 31 October 2012); Our Lady's Hospice Harold's Cross website, http://www.olh.ie/ (accessed 31 October 2012). Obituary of Cecily Saunders by Caroline Richardson in the *British Medical Journal*, http://www.bmj.com/content (accessed 1 August 2011); G. B. Risse, 'Shifting Hospice-Hospital Boundaries: Historical Perspectives on the Institutional Care of the Dying', http://www.gbrisse.com/hospicepaper.html (accessed 31 October 2012); G. B. Risse, *Mending Bodies, Saving Souls: A History of Hospitals* (Oxford: Oxford University Press, 1999); Catholic Encyclopedia, www.newadvent.org/ cathen (accessed 15 August 2011.

Saint Patrick: J. Duffy, *Patrick in His Own Words* (Dublin: Veritas, 1972/2000).

Margaret Aylward: J. Prunty, *Margaret Aylward: Lady of Charity, Sister of Faith* (Dublin: Four Courts Press, 1999).

L'Arche: L'Arche Ireland website, http://www.larche.ie/ (accessed 10 October 2011); Jean Vanier website, http://www.jean-vanier.org/en (accessed 20 August 2011).

John Sullivan SJ: F. McGrath, *Father John Sullivan SJ* (Dublin: Irish Messenger, date unknown).

Frank Duff: T. O'Flynn, *Frank Duff As I Knew Him* (Dublin: Praedicanda, 1981); R. Bradshaw, *Frank Duff: Founder of the Legion of Mary* (Bayshore, NY: Montford, 1985); F. Kennedy, *Frank Duff* (Dublin: Continuum, 2011); *Can We Be Saints?* by Frank Duff, Australian Catholic Truth Society, 1939/Dublin: Catholic Truth Society, 1958: digital copy can be found at http://www.ecatholic2000.com/cts/untitled-69.shtml (accessed 31 October 2012).

Irish Lay Martyrs: D. Forristal, *Seventeen Martyrs* (Dublin: Columba, 1990); P. Corish and B. Millett (eds), *The Irish Martyrs* (Dublin: Four Courts Press, 2005); C. Brady, 'The Beatified Martyrs of Ireland (4): Margaret Ball (nee Birmingham)', *Irish Theological Quarterly* 64 (4), 2000, 353–361.

Catherine McAuley: Sisters of Mercy website, http://www.sistersofmercy.ie/ (accessed 1 October 2013). 'Mercy' by Mary Wickham RSM, taken from *In the Water Was the Fire*, reprinted in *Souvenirs of Spirit* (Melbourne: Spectrum, 1995; 2005), used with the permission of the author.

St Columcille: T. Craughwell, *Saints Behaving Badly* (NY: Doubleday, 2006); L. Whiteside, *In Search of Columba* (Dublin: Columba, 1997).

Columba Marmion: M. Tierney, *Dom Columba Marmion: A Biography* (Dublin: Columba, 1995).

Directly taken or amended from the original US text: Moses; John XXIII; Peter the Rock; John B. O'Reilly; Thomas More; Patrick Peyton; Job; Maria Corsini; Paul VI; Maria Goretti; Jesus Taught Us to Pray.

Excerpts from St Patrick's *Confession*, taken from *Patrick in His Own Words*, by Bishop Joseph Duffy, published by Veritas, 1972/2000.

Excerpts from Fr Patrick Peyton taken from www.familyrosary.org, used with permission of Holy Cross Family Ministries.

Excerpt from Blessed Teresa, cited in *The Power of Prayer*, copyright © 1998 by MJF Books, New York.

Excerpt from Fr Dan Eclid OFM of Edel Quinn's 'Words of Life', published by the Legion of Mary, De Montford House, Morning Star Avenue, Brunswick Street, Dublin 7.

SCRIPTURAL INDEX

The numbers following each citation refer to the text page numbers.
An asterisk indicates that the citation has been paraphrased.

Genesis

1:1	61, 66*
1:27	76, 438*
1:31	61
1-2:4	62*
2:16-17	77
2:18	311
2:18-24	438*
2:24	311
3:4-5	77
3:5	78
3:8	7*
3:15	15*
9:16	20*
14:18	237*
14:18-20	295*
49:24	59

Exodus

3:1-6	17*
3:1-15	14*
3:5	382
4:10-16	14*
11-13	186*
19:3-6	361
20:2-3	375, 383
20:7	387
20:8-11	400*
20:16	472, 478
23:7	427
28:1ff	295*

Leviticus

11:45	153

Deuteronomy

5:12	400*
5:12-14	406
5:21	486*
6:4	59, 69
6:5	383
30:19	440

1 Samuel

2:1	508
2:7-8	508

2 Samuel

7:28	69

Tobit

1:16-18	174*, 178*

Judith

16:1	509
16:13-14	509

Esther

7:3	508
C:14	508

INDEX

Page numbers in italics indicate location of definition in glossary.

OTHER RESOURCES

Irish Catholic Catechism for Adults Study Guide

This companion text follows the layout of the *Irish Catholic Catechism for Adults*, with each chapter providing a summary of the catechetical theme and its application to today's culture; citations of relevant Scripture passages and references to the Universal Catechism and Irish Catechism; discussion questions based on the Irish Catechism; and suggestions for further reading and study.
9781847305527 • €12.99/£11.00

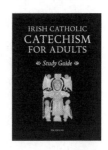

Share the Good News
National Directory for Catechesis in Ireland

Published in 2010 by the Irish Episcopal Conference, the *National Directory for Catechesis in Ireland* seeks to 'address the specific catechetical issues that arise in the Irish context now' and 'make the Good News of Jesus Christ more fully known and available to all'. There is a vital connection between *Share the Good News* and the *Irish Catholic Catechism for Adults* in that both are rich sources for those dealing with religious education or those interested in knowing more about the Catholic faith. Both of these initiatives have the capacity, with the help of the Holy Spirit, to revitalise the faith of the Catholic Church in Ireland.
9781847302588 • €16.99/£14.50

Compendium of the Catechism of the Catholic Church

'The Compendium, which I now present to the Universal Church, is a faithful and sure synthesis of the Catechism of the Catholic Church. It contains, in concise form, all the essential and fundamental elements of the Church's faith … I entrust this Compendium above all to the entire Church and, in particular, to every Christian, in order that it may awaken in the Church … renewed zeal for evangelisation and education in the faith, which ought to characterise every community in the Church and every Christian believer …' *Pope Benedict XVI*
9781853909986 • €10.95/£8.99

To order these resources, visit www.veritas.ie, call 01-878 8177, or drop into any of our stores located around Ireland:
Abbey Street and Blanchardstown, Dublin • Belfast • Cork
Derry • Ennis • Letterkenny • Monaghan • Naas • Newry • Sligo
Veritas also has a store located in Lourdes.

VERITAS
www.veritas.ie